Dedicated to my Grandfather,

Ernest William Lofting

An ordinary family man called up to play his part in these extraordinary times.

Acknowledgements

I have relied to a great extent on the work of Peter Schenk and his excellent work on detailing the German preparations involved in Operation Sea Lion. Without this insight it would have been very difficult to understand how the German's plans would have impacted on the ability of the British armed forces to counter it.

Elsewhere I have utilised various published works and national documents to enhance or corroborate my research. Unfortunately, I have not been able to record in the text exactly where this has taken place in most cases due to the length of time it has taken to produce this work and hope that the authors listed in the bibliography can accept this unintentional oversight.

I would like to express my thanks to the staff of the National Archives and Imperial War Museum for their support in helping me gather all the information I needed.

Cover: Photograph courtesy of the Imperial War Museum (image H1084)

Between pages 103 and 113: Photographs courtesy of the author

Page 234: Map courtesy of the National Archives (*file: Air28/509*)

Page 259: Map courtesy of the National Archives (*file: WO166/4656*)

Rear: Map showing the defensive preparations of Greatstone by 7th Somerset Light Infantry courtesy of the National Archives (file: WO166/4658)

CHAPTERS

	Page
Introduction	1
Chapter 1: Operation Sea Lion, the German plans	4
Chapter 2: British Strategy	27
Chapter 3: The Royal Navy	35
Chapter 4: The Royal Air Force	44
Chapter 5: The British Army	53
Chapter 6: Invasion Day	129
Chapter 7: S Day and Beyond	150
Appendix 1: British Army Order of Battle	185
Appendix 2: Home Guard	262
Appendix 3: Anti Aircraft Command	284
Appendix 4: Coastal Artillery	304
Appendix 5: Special Forces	312
Appendix 6: Army Notes	317
Appendix 7: Miscellaneous Statistics	327
Appendix 8: The GHQ Line	331
Appendix 9: Royal Navy Order of Battle	337
Appendix 10: Royal Air Force Order of Battle	353
Appendix 11: Observer Corps	371
Appendix 12: Civil Defence	373
Maps	377
Bibliography	388
Index	391

INTRODUCTION

The story of the Battle of Britain is well known. With a certain justification it can be claimed that the Royal Air Force's Fighter Command was primarily instrumental in saving the United Kingdom and therefore the cause and existence of western democracy from the threats posed by Adolf Hitler's Nazi regime and, to a lesser extent, its junior partner of Fascist Italy.

Nevertheless, during the summer and autumn of 1940 the British people found themselves in a situation for which they were totally unprepared - an invasion of their country and an end to their traditional way of life. For nearly a century the nation had not needed to seriously consider the prospect of an enemy landing on their coast and fighting through their towns and countryside. Underlying this sense of security was the belief in the ability of the Royal Navy to protect their shores, as they had successfully done for nearly three hundred years. The First World War had seen the introduction of attack from the air and, though this had been largely confined to London and its approaches, it had identified serious concerns for the future security of the country. In the lead up to the Second World War there had been much prophesised about mass air attacks on civilian targets, including the use of poison gas at the outset, with great effort being made by the civilian authorities to prepare for such an eventuality. Fortunately, this never materialised and with the onset of the "Phoney War" in 1939 the nation had once again largely grown complacent to the threat that still loomed over their country.

All this was to change dramatically in the few short weeks during May and June of 1940. The British people had been severely shocked to find their Continental allies overrun with such apparent ease and, as a consequence, its own Army and Air Force hastily ejected from the Continent with little more than what could be carried, having been forced to leave behind almost all the modern heavy weapons, tanks, vehicles and supplies that had represented the best of what the country could provide. Now, coupled with the new concerns that enemy parachute troops could be expected to descend anywhere and anytime while "Fifth Columnists" may already be amongst them, the nation suddenly found that the frontline was now literally on its own doorstep. The British people as a whole now found themselves standing alone in Europe against an apparently invincible Germany, watching the struggles in the skies overhead and waiting daily for the seemingly inevitable invasion with a determined resolution to resist it to the last, if need be, while the rest of the World watched with baited breath.

With the fall of France the German Supreme Command had two crucial facts to deal with: the existence of an unbeaten and unbowed Great Britain and the danger of intervention in the east by the Soviet Union. It was clear to most in the military that the former must be dealt with first. In his book 'Lost Victories', Field Marshal Erich von Manstein, one of Germany's preeminent strategists and a nominated commander of one of the invasion Corps, noted three options to defeat Britain (and his opinion on the effect) – naval and air blockade (not feasible in the short term), destroying British forces and influence in the Mediterranean and Middle East (though grave this would not in itself bring Britain to its knees and would tie down significant German resources) and invasion of the country (quickest way to overpower their enemy but was unlikely to force her out of the War entirely).

An invasion could only be mounted with the involvement of the German Navy - the Kriegsmarine. At the outset of the War this service had began planning an invasion of the

United Kingdom, based loosely on one proposed during the First World War. It had shown little enthusiasm for a project that it saw more as a paper exercise than as a feasible option. However, with the fall of France this planning fast became a reality, more so as the German Army now become the prime mover in the preparations. The proposed landing zone was moved from the coast of East Anglia to the Kent and Sussex coastlines, but there remained a continued general lack of co-ordination between the three services, especially at high command level; in July it was finally recognised that the planning staff in both the German Army and Navy had been working from different perspectives - for strategic reasons the Army looked at landing on as wide a front as possible in order to provide as large an initial lodgement as possible while the Navy believed that it could only secure a narrow crossing, based both on its own resources and a healthy respect for the Royal Navy - with neither force truly appreciating the difficulties the other faced. The Luftwaffe, the German Air Force, had little time for either service as it was embroiled in its own efforts to knock the British out of the war. A meeting on 7 August involving Colonel General Franz Halder, the Army's Chief of General Staff, and Admiral Otto Schniewind, the Chief of Staff of the Naval War Staff, led to the eventual compromise and now allowed preparations to take a more solid and organised form.

This plan identified a number of conditions that had to be met before such an undertaking could be recommended; the most important of these were:

- Neutralisation of the Royal Air Force
- Destruction of Britain's war industry
- Destruction or dispersal of all British naval forces stationed on the south coast
- Securing the flanks of the planned invasion routes by means of minefields and coastal artillery.

These conditions were not impossible to achieve, as the Germans had largely demonstrated during their conquests to date; but they required time to properly prepare, during which more detailed plans would be produced covering all aspects of the invasion and, if required, subsequent occupation of Great Britain.

Unknown to both the British and Germans at the time, Adolf Hitler never really had a desire to destroy the British Empire, an institution that he secretly admired and wished to emulate. He sincerely believed that the British would accept German control of the Continent if their own imperial structure was left intact but was surprised and confused that the British would not accept the seemingly logical decision to accede to his demands. However, as the air campaign failed to break the British will and capacity to resist, he took the final decision to postpone the invasion in October 1940. The Germans were keenly aware that failure of an invasion attempt, whilst not fatal to their armed forces, would be far reaching politically and this was one danger that Hitler could not risk.

Despite this setback, planning and preparations for the invasion carried on with May 1941 being the next target period, though by this time Hitler's attention was firmly focused elsewhere. Nevertheless, had the Luftwaffe been able to achieve air supremacy over south east England, the German Navy been more enthusiastic and, more importantly, Hitler resolved to invade, it is likely that Operation Sea Lion would have been launched.

Although there has previously been much published about Operation Sea Lion, most works are either fictional, gloss over the military details or are set in early summer 1940. Very little has been written about the actual ability of the British armed forces and in particular its Army to confront and defeat the planned invasion. While part of the reason may lie in the fact that many official records kept at the time were fragmentary at best, I believe that the main reason lies in the fact that the aerial Battle of Britain, supposedly a precursor to the actual invasion, took on a life and importance all of its own and as a result of the outcome Operation Sea Lion was consigned to history's backwaters.

This work seeks to address that omission by clarifying the real state of the nation's defences at the planned time and presents its strategy, planning and capability for defeating such an invasion, together with its order of battle available for this purpose. While this work concentrates on the Army it would not be proper to ignore the other armed services as this Operation would have seen the first true combined air-land-sea defence in history, requiring the combination and co-operation of all concerned to be able to repel an invasion, even should it get established ashore. While it is not my purpose to predict the outcome of such an invasion, I feel that it is proper to provide some guidance on how the days and weeks following the invasion may have developed, based on the plans, objectives, expectations and resources plus the recent and immediately future combat experience of both sides.

I hope that the reader will now be better informed to consider what may have been the result of Operation Sea Lion had it been launched. One thing is clear - urged on by Winston Churchill, the British people were generally determined to resist any attempt to destroy their way of life, as shown by the overwhelming response to the formation of the Local Defence Volunteers. As Churchill stated on 14 July 1940 "And now it has come to us to stand alone in the breach and face the worst that the tyrant's might and enmity can do ... We are fighting by ourselves alone; but we are not fighting for ourselves alone." On 20 August Count Ciano, Italy's Foreign Minister, commented that "behind that facade of beautiful words and strong affirmations there is a will and a faith."

With so much riding on the outcome, Operation Sea Lion would almost certainly have seen the most important armed struggle between two of the greatest military powers of the time.

CHAPTER ONE: OPERATION SEA LION, THE GERMAN PLANS

It is not realistic to consider the British preparations without first explaining the German plans. On 16 July 1940 Adolf Hitler issued Directive 16. It began: "As England, in spite of the hopelessness of her military position, has so far shown herself unwilling to come to any compromise, I have decided to begin to prepare for, and if necessary to carry out, an invasion of England. This operation is dictated by the necessity of eliminating Great Britain as a base from which the war against Germany can be fought, and if necessary the island will be occupied". The codename assigned to this undertaking was Operation Sea Lion.

As far back as May 1939, when Hitler informed his military of his intention to invade Poland, he recognised that Britain was to be Germany's principal enemy and outlined the strategy to be used against it: If Holland, Belgium and France were defeated then the fundamental conditions for a successful war aganst Britain will have been secured. Britain can then be blockaded by the Luftwaffe and the submarines of the Kriegsmarine. He acknowledged that much of Britian's strength lay in its geopolitical safety due to its navy and air force. On 18 June 1940 Hitler met Mussolini to discuss the French armistice terms and stated his reservations about demolishing the British Empire, which he considered an important factor in maintaining the world's political equilibrium. As such he was inclined to offer mild terms – the return of Germany's former overseas territories and renunciation of Britain's future influence in Europe.

On 30 June General Alfred Jodl, Chief of Operations in the Supreme Command (OKW), submitted a review on the continuation of the war against England. It offered two courses if Britain refused peace:

1. War against Britain's empire aided by countries interested in its collapse (Italy, Spain, Russia and Japan). This would mainly feature diplomatic pressure and provision of limited military support to its allies
2. Direct action against Britain, focusing on its air force, war industry and blockade. Invasion was only to be used to finish off a country economically paralysed.

The first OKW Directive to begin invasion preparations was issued on 2 July 1940. It required the Army to produce an estimate of the British Army's state of combat effectiveness and how German coastal artillery could be employed to support an invasion, the Navy to identify suitable invasion areas and means of conducting a landing and the Air Force an appreciation of when air superiority could be attained.

Directive 16 stated the conditions that would make invasion possible. These were:

- The Royal Air Force must be neutralised
- British minefields must be cleared from the invasion routes
- The Straits of Dover and the western entrance to the English Channel must be cut off by minefields
- Coastal artillery would be used to provide an artillery screen against the coastal area on the immediate front
- The Royal Navy should be pinned down in the North Sea and Mediterranean.

In October 1940 the British General Headquarters Home Forces produced its own review of the possible scale of invasion, which was similar to the Germans. It stated that a successful enemy invasion demands:

- Sufficient military forces to be able to gain a decision rapidly
- Sufficient military and air supplies
- Sufficient shipping, suitably disposed
- A reasonable chance of local command of the sea
- Some degree of local air superiority
- Sufficiently good morale to be able to face what must be at any time a hazardous undertaking.

It further stated that these main factors were all inter-dependent; inadequacy in one could be compensated by an advantageous position in another. Any attempt at invasion implied a considerable risk - it must depend on the urgency of the need for a quick decision and on the enemy's estimate of the results that might follow failure.

In early July General Jodl reasoned that as Britain commanded the sea any landing must be made on England's south east coast, as the crossing time was short and concerns over command of the sea could best be redressed through air power. His general plan noted that the landing should be effected in the form of a mighty river crossing on a broad front, where the air force takes the role of artillery; he recognised that the first assault wave must be very strong and that the role of bridge building needed to be replaced by creating a sea transport "road", completely secure against attack from sea.

It is amusing to record that an intelligence summary of the British 45th Infantry Division contained a report from two British officers who, while escaping after Dunkirk, posed as refugees in a French café and engaged in a conversation with some German soldiers; those soldiers believed that the English Channel was not more than five kilometres wide and was capable of being crossed by pontoon bridges. They would not believe the truth until the café's owner confirmed the reality! Given that the shortest distance between Great Britain and occupied Europe was more than twenty miles this concept is hard to understand unless it is remembered that Germany is essentially a Central European country and its Army, the senior and most influential of the armed services, only had experience of conducting operations within Continental Europe. Until the Germans reached the English Channel in May 1940 relatively few Germans had seen the sea, let alone crossed it.

It must also be remembered that for the Germans, and indeed for all of the World's military powers, large-scale amphibious operations were still rare events. The German Army had only a limited experience in the Baltic during the First World War and the Norwegian Campaign in April 1940 for reference, the latter relying on warships and transports to seize the main ports by surprise; with all this in mind it is not surprising that they had to initially largely rely on their knowledge of assault river crossings to prepare for such an undertaking and, in doing so, reduced their planning of the invasion to the simplest level possible - that of an opposed river crossing. Nevertheless, they were keenly aware of their limitations; indeed Hitler was later recorded as saying that "even if the way is short, this is not just a river crossing, but the crossing of a sea which is dominated by the enemy. This is not the case of a single crossing operation, as in Norway; operational surprise cannot be expected; a defensively prepared and utterly determined enemy faces us. The most difficult part will be the material reinforcements and stores. We cannot count on supplies of any kind being available to us in England."

The German Navy (Kriegsmarine), who were to be responsible for delivering the Army to England's shores and then keeping it supplied, was more tuned to the problems of such an undertaking; especially the effects of tides and weather and the problems of finding and loading enough suitable shipping (they calculated that the second wave would require two million tons of shipping alone). However, the Commander in Chief of the Kriegsmarine was quoted as saying that `the course of the War so far had shown that operations and landings which had previously seemed impossible were now feasible, thanks to the superior leadership and to the exceptional moral and offensive power of the armed forces`.

In planning terms it is interesting to note that the Directive was announced only six weeks after the Dunkirk evacuation, four weeks since France had capitulated and a mere two weeks since Hitler ordered preparations to start - thus allowing only ten weeks before the operation was to take place. This was in contrast with the issuing, five months in advance, of orders for the Polish Campaign and seven months for the French and Low Countries operations; of course, the speed of success of the recent campaigns had equally caught the German military by surprise and this had led to a frantic re-examination of their options. It was felt by many German generals after the war that if initial planning had started whilst the battle for France and the Low Countries was still raging then it could have been feasible to launch an invasion by the middle of August. Von Manstein went further with his criticism – He stated that since Hitler had accepted the risks of a war against France and the United Kingdom in September 1939 it was his duty to consider beforehand how he should cope with these powers in various contingencies.

It was clear that this Operation was to be the most hazardous and unfamiliar than any that had gone before it; before the War little thought had been given to amphibious operations and few actual exercises were conducted, certainly none to war standards as there was neither the time nor resources made available. In his document produced in 1947 for the British Admiralty, Admiral Kurt Assman addressed the question of why the Germans did not attempt the invasion in early summer, when the potential for a quick success was best. He believed it was down to the naval situation at that time, stating that it was not possible to "swim over" to England. All the disparate shipping had to be found, equipped, crews trained and moved to the assembly ports, many of which had been damaged in the recent fighting; British minefields had to be swept and protective minefields had to be laid. This document did not consider the position of the other armed forces.

True to normal German practice during the Second World War there was no unified command structure, with the three armed services carrying out their own preparations with a minimum of liaison between them. Hitler preferred this method as it suited his personality as well as ensuring that no one service could dominate and so profit from its success. Unlike Churchill, Hitler allowed the various commanders in chief practically no influence on grand strategy, with Hitler making the decisions on the basis of his own deliberations. The German Supreme Command was thus relegated to a secretarial role. The overall plan went through several changes in both scope and timing, due mainly to the Army and Navy holding largely opposite views, before eventually recommending an invasion for 15 September. The Navy preferred a landing two hours after high tide to aid unloading but the Army preferred a dawn landing. This would mean a night crossing, so moonlit nights were preferred. It was accepted that the order for the actual invasion would have to be given no later than ten days before that date to allow for final preparations to be completed. The period of 19 to 26 September was identified, with 24 to 27 September being the optimum time. This period was also the last viable date in the year due to the expected onset of rough autumnal weather that would hamper the landing and subsequent buildup.

The Army's High Command (OKH) issued its preparatory operational instruction on 30 August, setting out its operational plan. It entrusted the land operation to Army Group A, consisting of Ninth and Sixteenth Armies. The Army Group commander was Colonel General Gerd von Rundstedt, one of Germany's most respected senior commanders and whose headquarters had already been responsible for the main German breakthroughs in France; as a result its staff was a highly regarded and very capable organisation. Most of the Army planning for the invasion was conducted by Headquarters Sixteenth Army, with Colonel General Ernst Busch being a strong believer in the potential success of the operation.

After much debate, the Army Group eventually agreed to prepare for an assault on the English coast between Hythe and Brighton. The invasion (S Day) would feature a first wave of four infantry corps, comprising seven infantry, two mountain and one airborne divisions, supported by 260 amphibious tanks and a host of specialist vehicles, equipment and weapons, to secure the initial beachhead; this part of the Operation was to involve about 140,000 troops, 67,000 of whom would take part in the initial landings. A further four panzer, three motorised and seven infantry divisions in two panzer and four infantry corps were expected to land in the second and third waves to provide the breakout forces, involving up to another 162,000 men. Most of these troops had recent combat experience and all had a high morale to draw upon.

As with the Normandy Landings four years later it was considered essential to capture a working port as soon as possible - Dover being the primary target, with Newhaven, Folkestone and, to a much lesser degree, Rye being the only other viable alternatives within the landing zone. The first wave was expected to seize and secure a beachhead in Kent and East Sussex about 65 miles long and averaging a depth of twenty miles; this was to be defended against counter attacks and within which the mechanised forces of the second wave could then be landed and organised for the breakout.

The Germans also planned to use both Pevensey and St Mary's Bays, the latter near Hythe, as safe anchorages to supplement the landing of the follow up forces and supplies; all of these were to be protected by both coastal artillery and anti aircraft guns expected to be landed as quickly as possible after the initial assault. Although Deal had been considered as a landing zone in the initial plan and subsequently dropped due to the lack of shipping resources, planning still required a speedy capture of the area to allow for future unloading within an anchorage safer than the other two, protected as it is by the Goodwin Sands. The Army had to accept the vulnerability of its left wing landing west of Beachy Head, leaving it outside of the Navy's mine barriers running south of that Head. It had plans in place to land follow on forces in Pevensey Bay for those assault units. It is clear from the German plans that they were determined to avoid assaulting the coastal towns directly (as the British and Canadians were to try unsuccessfully at Dieppe in 1942), preferring to land in the more open sectors in between and clear the seaside towns from the rear.

Plans called for the bulk of the assault divisions to be landed by the third day (S+3), with rear elements of the first wave completed landing by S+10. The second wave, comprising the breakout forces, was to start landing on the returning transports from S+4, with this process to be completed by S+33 (Ninth Army's schedule was slightly longer due to the extended crossing time and shipping plans involved). This means that the Germans expected that it would take up to a month before they had enough troops to undertake the breakout. Although only Sixteenth Army's landing schedule remains, it provides a useful guide. VII and XIII Corps were to complete their landing by S+9 (S+3 for the assault units). In the second wave, 8th Panzer and 30th Infantry Divisions were to land between S+4 and S+15, 10th Panzer and 12th Infantry Divisions were to land between S+16 and S+27, 29th Motorised Division between S+22 and S+33 and the independent infantry regiments between S+28 and S+33.

When the Army Group considered itself ready it was then to break out of the beachhead with the aim of achieving the First Operational Objective, which involved the neutralisation of enemy forces in southern England up to a line stretching from the Thames Estuary near Dartford, skirting around the south of London and then on to Fareham, near Portsmouth. Ninth Army was expected to act as the pivot in this phase, due to the slower build up of its forces. The boundary between the two Armies running inland from St Leonards (near Hastings) to Reigate via Mayfield and East Grinstead; of these towns Ninth Army was to be responsible for securing East Grinstead and Sixteenth Army the others. The Supreme Command planned that at least 23 divisions would have landed within the first six weeks.

As soon as it was able, the Army Group was then expected to move on to the Second Operational Objective. This involved Sixteenth Army forcing its way around the west of London to the Essex coast, thus isolating the capital. Ninth Army was to advance north and west to extend the front line that was to run from Maldon in Essex to Gloucester, via St Albans and Oxford. The boundary between the two Armies was to extend from Reigate to Banbury via Windsor. Of these towns, Sixteenth Army was to be responsible for Windsor and Ninth Army for Banbury. Due to the uncertainties of the campaign no timescales were recorded for these Objectives to be achieved.

A further Army (Field Marshal Walther von Reichenau's Sixth Army in Army Group B) was available for operations. It was originally planned to land in Dorset's Lyme Bay, if circumstances permitted. It was initially assigned one infantry corps, with a panzer corps available as a second wave and another infantry corps making up the third wave – a total of two panzer, five infantry and one SS motorised divisions. Sixth Army had the role of securing south west England, including Bristol. Should its original plan not be feasible, there was a proposal for this force to be landed within the existing beachhead in Kent and Sussex so it could still carry out its role in line with the Second Operational Objective. However, this would depend on having sufficient shipping capacity and forming up locations without detracting from the needs of the other two Armies.

Future operations would then depend on the political situation but would have had to feature neutralising the remaining British armed forces, pacification of the civilian population and possible occupation of key industrial centres and major ports not already taken. This was expected to feature mobile formations making rapid thrusts with infantry divisions undertaking occupation duties in ther rear. Any future operations, such as the occupation of Scotland and Northern Ireland, would be carried out as special operations from forces readily available. The Nazi apparatus was separately planning its activities once combat operations had ceased in each area. It was planned that all British males aged between 17 and 45 would be "arrested" and shipped to the Continent with prisoners of war as far as was practical during the invasion phase.

Sixteenth Army was responsible for the eastern sector of the beachhead and was commanded by the ardent Nazi, General Busch; his chief staff officer was Lieutenant General Walter Model, destined to be one of Germany's best Field Marshal's and regarded as an excellent tactician. General Busch planned to use two Infantry Corps in the assault:

- XIII Corps, commanded by General Heinrich von Vietinghoff, was to land between Hythe and Dungeness with 17th and 35th Infantry Divisions. The Corps had secured the southern flank of the blitzkrieg through the Ardennes but neither division had served with it.
    - 17th Infantry Division was a pre war Bavarian formation commanded by Major General Herbert Loch that had fought well in both Poland and France;
    - 35th Infantry Division was a pre war Wurttemberg and Baden formation commanded by Lieutenant General Hans Reinhard that had already fought against the British in Belgium.

- VII Corps, under Colonel General Eugen von Schobert, was to land in Rye Bay with 7th Infantry and 1st Mountain Divisions. The Corps had also helped secure the southern flank of the blitzkrieg through the Ardennes but again neither division had served with it.
    - 7th Infantry Division was also a pre war Bavarian formation commanded by Lieutenant General Eccard von Gablenz that had fought well in both Poland and against the BEF;
    - 1st Mountain Division was a joint pre war Bavarian and Austrian formation commanded by Major General Ludwig Kubler that had fought in Poland but had played only a minor role against the French.

The initial boundary between the two Corps was to run along the line Greatstone-Isle of Oxney-Rolvenden-Sissinghurst-Paddock Wood.

Sixteenth Army's second wave consisted of XLI Panzer Corps and V Corps.
- V Corps, under General Richard Ruoff, had two infantry divisions - 12th and 30th. The Corps had been a part of the blitzkrieg through Belgium and then through central France.
    - 12th Infantry Division was a Pomeranian unit that had distinguished itself in both the Polish and French/Belgian campaigns under Major General Walter von Seydlitz-Kurzbach;

- 30th Infantry Division was from Schleswig Holstein and fought in Poland (where its commander, General Kurt von Briessen, received the first Knight's Cross presented to a divisional commander) and in Belgium.

- XLI Panzer Corps, under General Georg-Hans Reinhardt, had formed part of Panzer Group Guderian during the French Campaign and comprised:
    - 8th Panzer Division, equipped with Czech built tanks it had fought in Poland and France and was commanded by Lieutenant General Adolf Kuntzen;
    - 10th Panzer Division had operated in Poland before fighting well in France. It was commanded by Major General Ferdinand Schaal;
    - 29th Motorised Division, commanded by Major General Walter von Boltenstern, had also fought hard in the Polish and French campaigns;
    - Grossdeutschland Motorised Infantry Regiment, an elite Army formation that had fought well in France under Oberst Gerhard Count von Schwerin;
    - Waffen SS Leibstandarte Motorised Infantry Regiment, commanded by the formidable SS Colonel "Sepp" Dietrich. This had served as an independent formation in both Poland and France.

It was planned that V Corps was to sail from Rotterdam and XLI Panzer Corps from Antwerp, with the former taking over responsibility for clearing North Kent from 17th Division. Once the second wave had landed the inter-corps boundaries were expected to run as follows: V/XIII Corps - Dymchurch-Ashford-Maidstone, with V Corps responsible for Maidstone; XIII/VII Corps - Dungeness-Rolvenden-Lamberhurst-Tunbridge Wells, with VII Corps responsible for the last two towns.

Sixteenth Army's third wave was to consist of XLII Corps and IV Corps, both with two infantry divisions.

- IV Corps was commanded by General Viktor von Schwedler and its headquarters had fought against the BEF. It now comprised:
    - 24th Infantry Division, a pre war formation that had fought well in Poland and France under Lieutenant General Hans von Tettau;
    - 58th Infantry Division, a pre war Saxon formation that had played a minor role in France under Lieutenant General Iwan Heunert.

- XLII Corps was commanded by General Walter Kuntze was part of the General Reserve during the French campaign. It now comprised:
    - 45th Infantry Division, a pre war Austrian formation that had fought in Poland and France under Lieutenant General Friedrich Materna;
    - 164th Infantry Division, formed in January 1940 as a training formation and commanded by Major General Josef Folttmann.

In addition to these forces the 22nd Infantry Division was made available, but not assigned, to Sixteenth Army by 20 September due to its air landing capabilities. Part of the Division had undertaken this role in support of the 7th Air Division operations in Holland and was equipped on a lighter scale of heavy weapons and equipment than a normal infantry division. The commander of this Division was Lieutenant General Hans Count von Sponeck, who had been seriously wounded in Holland.

Ninth Army was responsible for the western sector and was commanded by Colonel General Adolf Strauss. He planned to use three infantry corps in the assault:

- XXXVIII Corps, under the impressive General Erich von Manstein, was to land between Bexhill and Eastbourne with:
    - 26th Infantry Division, a pre war Rhineland formation commanded by Lieutenant General Sigismund von Forster. It had played minor parts in both the Polish and French campaigns;
    - 34th Infantry Division, a Rhineland and Hesse formation that had fought in France under Lieutenant General Werner Sanne.

  The Corps had operated against the British and French in Normandy and Brittany, though neither division had served with it.

- VIII Corps, under General Walter Heitz, was to land between Rottingdean and Seaford with:
    - 8th Infantry Division, commanded by Lieutenant General Rudolf Koch-Erpach;
    - 28th Infantry Division, commanded by Major General Johann Sinnhuber.

  Both were Silesian formations that had fought well with this Corps in both Poland and France.

- General Christian Hansen's X Corps assigned 6th Mountain Division to land at Cuckmere Haven; The Corps headquarters had fought against the BEF, while this Division was only formed during the winter of 1939 and, under the command of Major General Ferdinand Schorner, had played a minor role in France. The Corps Headquarters was to land with the first wave in the XXXVIII Corps sector.

The second wave consisted of XV Panzer Corps and the other division of X Corps.

- XV Panzer Corps had led the charge across France and was led by another experienced panzer leader in Colonel General Hermann Hoth. It comprised:
    - 4th Panzer Division, commanded by General Willibald von Langermann und Erlenkamp, had distinguished itself in Poland, Holland, France and against the BEF;
    - 7th Panzer Division was commanded by the already famous Major General Erwin Rommel and equipped mainly with former Czech tanks. It had fought with distinction in Poland, Belgium and France;
    - 20th Motorised Division was commanded by Lieutenant General Mauritz Wiktorin zu Hainburg and had fought well in Poland and France and against the BEF.

The other X Corps formation was 121st Infantry Division, which had only just been mobilised in September. It was commanded by General Curt Jahn.

The third wave comprised XXIV Corps, under General Leo von Schweppenburg, a former military attaché to England. Although designated as a Panzer Corps it was only allocated two infantry divisions for this operation, namely:

- 15th Infantry Division, a Rhineland formation commanded by Lieutenant General Ernst-Eberhard Hell from August 1940. It had guarded the Saar during the French campaign;
- 78th Infantry Division, a Wurttemberg formation commanded by Lieutenant General Curt Gallenkamp. It had played a minor role during the French campaign.

In Sixth Army, II Corps was the first wave. It was commanded by General Walter von Brockdorff-Ahlefeldt and had fought in Poland, Belgium and France. It had been reorganised in early September and contained three infantry divisions:

- 6th Infantry Division, a Westphalian formation, was commanded by Lieutenant General Arnold von Biegeleben and had fought through Luxembourg and France. The General died of a heart attack on 11 October 1940;
- 216th Infantry Division, a Hanoverian formation, was commanded by Lieutenant General Kurt Himer from 8 September and also fought through Luxembourg and France;
- 256th Infantry Division, a largely Saxon formation, was commanded by Lieutenant General Gerhard Kauffmann and had fought in Holland, Belgium and France.

XXII Panzer Corps, forming the second wave, had formerly been Panzer Group von Kleist, a headquarters that had controlled two panzer corps in the breakout through France.

- 1st Panzer Division was commanded by Lieutenant General Friedrich Kirchner and had fought in Poland and led the breakout through the Ardennes;
- 3rd Panzer Division, commanded by Lieutenant General Friedrich Kühn it had fought in Poland and France;
- Waffen SS Totenkopf Motorised Division, commanded by SS General Theodor Eicke, one of the toughest and most ruthless Nazis. It had fought in Belgium.

A fourth wave of divisions from the Supreme Command reserve was to be designated on S-10, if required.

Several of the commanders mentioned above were already famous and respected - notably von Rundstedt, Guderian and Rommel - while many more were to rise through the command chain and gain more fame during the War; all were thoroughly schooled in the German Army's art of war. For the first couple of days the success of land operations would depend on the abilities of the regimental and divisional commanders.

In line with its blitzkrieg doctrine, German Army offensive operations were characterised by combining speed and firepower at the point of maximum effort. German assault units were assigned general objectives, with their commanders being allowed some freedom in implementing the general operational order. In normal operational circumstances the advance reconnaissance units were to mount a series of probing attacks to find weak points or gaps once contact was made with the enemy. Once found these gaps would be attacked in detail until a break was created and enlarged, allowing armour and other supporting troops to pass through into the enemy's rear or flanks. If a gap or weak point was not readily identified a concentration of firepower, including air support, would be put down on the defenders until the attackers could break into the enemy's positions. The Luftwaffe's ability to deliver close air support within 45 minutes of it being requested both impressed and demoralised the allied troops during the early 1940 campaigns.

To provide this close air support the Luftwaffe planned to move ground attack and fighter units to England as soon as captured airfields were made operational again or new landing fields prepared. To prevent the RAF from providing effective close air support the Germans had invested heavily in providing powerful yet mobile light anti aircraft weapons, something the RAF's light bombers had found to their cost during the Low Countries campaign.

This blitzkrieg doctrine would have to be slightly adapted to fit in with the invasion plans, notably at the initial stages. The advance detachments would become the initial contact units and, due to the inevitable confusion of transporting the invading troops in a multifarious collection of craft over a long distance, coupled with a likely violent and dogged reaction by the defenders, it would be up to individual leaders to find or create the necessary gaps with whatever troops they had at hand. As indicated above, the organisation and training of the German Army allowed and even promoted this type of combat as a short-term measure. To limit the chaos the German Army decided to restructure its assault divisions to better tailor them to their specific missions, while taking into consideration the lack of a normal logistical support and having to fit in with the Navy's transport plans.

The assault divisions were therefore divided into two echelons: the first generally contained two reinforced infantry regiments (each equivalent to British brigades) that were to carry out the initial assault, whilst the second comprised the remaining infantry regiment, headquarters and divisional support units that were to be landed from the late afternoon on S Day onwards. These assault forces were brought up to strength and provided with extra, more modern and more mobile resources, making them the best equipped formations the German Army had yet produced.

The infantry and mountain divisions were traditionally organised as follows:

- Three infantry regiments, each of three infantry battalions (with three infantry and one heavy weapons companies) an anti tank company and light infantry gun company (6th Mountain Division only had two mountain infantry regiments)
- An artillery regiment of three or four battalions (each assault division had two batteries re-equipped with lighter, more mobile, mountain guns)
- An anti tank battalion (mostly towed)
- An engineer battalion
- A reconnaissance battalion (mostly cycle mounted, as was one infantry company per first echelon infantry regiment)
- A light anti aircraft gun company, several of these weapons being mechanised

The mountain divisions had lighter equipment, especially artillery, due to their traditional role. Typically the infantry divisions had about 19,000 men, 12 medium and 36 field artillery guns, 75 anti tank guns, 126 mortars plus 1,200 vehicles, 1,000 motorcycles and 1,200 bicycles.

Many of the motor vehicles and bicycles were provided from captured stocks for the Operation and replaced, where possible, many of the horses that each division normally relied on, while the anti tank guns were largely replaced with towed or mechanised French or Czech 47mm guns, the German 37mm gun having proved rather inadequate. One problem that does not seem to have been taken into account was that the additional vehicles needed petrol, lubricants and shipping space, which in turn increased the already heavy demands of securing sufficient stocks and resources.

A panzer division had:

- A brigade of two tank regiments of two battalions each (a total of 230 tanks)
- A brigade of two motorised infantry regiments also with two battalions each
- An artillery regiment of three battalions (toalling 24 field and 12 medium guns)
- A reconnaissance battalion
- An anti tank battalion
- An engineer battalion.

Generally speaking the first echelon of each assault division comprised 6,700 men in two reinforced regiments, 14 light field guns, 8 mountain guns, 72 heavy mortars, 27 anti tank guns, 1900 bicycles, 180 motorcycles, 127 vehicles and 340 horses.

Each assaulting division formed one or more advance detachments, mostly based on an infantry battalion, with additional light artillery and engineer support attached. These were formed from the first echelon forces and were to spearhead the assault with the express aim of disrupting and overcoming the enemy's coastal defences, then moving as far inland as possible, before the main landings took place. This role was considered vital due to the slow rate of disembarkation expected from the customised landing barges and other craft bringing the rest of the assault troops, especially those carrying the important amphibious tanks. Depending on the tides the landings were to start shortly after six o'clock in the morning and around high tide, with the detachments allowed about an hour to complete their operations before the main landings were to begin. The detachments were to be mainly carried in the minesweepers and auxiliary patrol ships (themselves already tasked with protecting the invasion fleets during the crossing; each was to carry up to sixty troops, two assault boats and up to six dinghies) and barge tows (each consisting of a tug or trawler towing two barges and a smaller "pusher" boat, averaging about seventy troops and four vehicles per barge) - an average of six escort ships, ten trawlers and two tows being required for each detachment. Of these ships only one barge per tow had "armoured" protection, consisting of concrete filled sides.

Most assault barges had either a field gun, anti tank gun or light anti aircraft gun set up on a makeshift platform to provide both artillery support during the landings and a measure of self defence during the crossing; these weapons were to be landed after the initial landings were complete, increasing the artillery support available to the assault divisions as most of the divisional artillery was to be landed with the second echelon. In Sixteenth Army 140 75mm artillery guns and 35 47mm anti tank guns were assigned to this task.

The German Army considered it vital that tanks support its assault infantry during the initial landing and trialled three types of vehicles for this purpose. The first was the amphibious tank. These were to be carried in a total of five adapted vehicle ferries and thirty-four barges (each barge carrying three or four tanks) and which were expected to be unloaded in no more than four metres of water. Generally the lighter mark II tank had floats attached to their sides, enabling them to "swim" at a top speed of nearly six km/h from the barges, while the heavier mark III and IV tanks were made "submersible", using floating hoses to both provide air and expel fumes while being guided by telephone from the landing craft. These tanks were either to be lowered by crane or deployed by ramp once the landing craft had deployed both bow and stern anchors to steady themselves. This would be when they were most vulnerable. Once landed these tanks would have a combat radius of up to 200km, some retaining their amphibious equipment for crossing water obstacles later.

A total of four battalions were organised from the 2nd Panzer Regiment, providing a total of 42 mark IV, 168 mark III and 52 mark II tanks, giving it the combat power equal to that of a panzer division. Each battalion was organised into three companies of four platoons, one with four mark II light, two with five mark III medium and one with four mark IV heavy tanks. There would be two tanks per barge, with more on the larger adapted ferries. Two battalions were assigned to XIII Corps, one to VII Corps and one to XXXVIII Corps and all were expected to land immediately after the advance detachments.

The second innovation was the flame-thrower tank. These were converted mark II light tanks, each with two flamethrowers in place of a main tank gun. The tanks were formed as Tank Detachment 100 and organised into three companies of flame-thrower tanks, each with three platoons of one gun armed mark III and four mark II flame-thrower tanks - a total of 36 mark II and 17 mark III tanks. Each company required twenty support vehicles, as each flame-thrower tank would be emptied after only fifteen minutes firing. Twenty of these flame-thrower tanks were assigned to the advance detachments within Sixteenth Army, the rest to cross with VII Corps` first echelon, carried by barges and landed directly onto the beaches.

The third new innovation was the self-propelled assault gun. These were based on the mark III medium panzer chassis with thickened frontal armour and armed with a fixed 75mm gun. Although they had yet to see combat they were destined to prove very effective in support of the infantry later in the war. They were organised into eight batteries of six assault guns each (four batteries per Army) and were assigned either to the advance detachments or first echelon of the assault divisions.

The Army also planned to use the 800th Special Purposes Construction Training Battalion "Brandenburg". This unit was in reality the German Army's own special forces unit trained by the Abwehr, the Army's intelligence organisation. Despite its cover title it was in actual fact a regiment of three battalions, each with four companies, most of its personnel being ethnic Germans from other countries. Its personnel had already gained a mix of combat and covert intelligence gathering experience during the War. Elements of I and III Battalions were now assigned roles for the invasion, with Sixteenth Army and Ninth Army respectively:

- 1st Company (I Bn) was to land with the 35th Division's advance detachment near New Romney, capture the coastal and railway artillery batteries there and neutralise defences along the Royal Military Canal before joining the forces assigned to the capture of Dover.
- The bulk of 4th Company (I Bn) was given the unenviable task of raiding Dover harbour and its coastal artillery batteries using twenty five fast motorboats.
- 11th Company (III Bn) was to land at Pevensey Bay and attack coastal defences, radar stations and command posts in the Pevensey and Beachy Head areas.

For mobility both 1st and 11th Companies were to use motorcycles. One problem they all faced was the lack of English speakers, most companies having fewer than twenty percent fluent within their ranks.

Additional combat support troops were allocated to each Army and Corps, notably artillery and engineers. Each Army had an anti aircraft Corps, each comprising four regiments of three 88mm and two 20mm batteries each. In addition to supporting the assaulting forces and protecting the beachhead, they were also tasked with protecting the Continental invasion harbours, reinforced by other anti aircraft units put under their command. For the landings some of the heavy anti aircraft guns were to be carried on barges and special catamaran ferries during the assault phase, the ferries also being assigned to protect the flanks during the landings, before being landed as soon as possible to supplement the divisional anti aircraft units. The Germans had recognised the vulnerability of the embarkation ports; Rotterdam was to have nine heavy and seven light anti aircraft batteries, Antwerp had eight heavy and five light anti aircraft batteries, Zeebrugge had two heavy anti aircraft batteries, Ostend had five heavy and four light anti aircraft batteries and Calais had six heavy and four light anti aircraft batteries.

Sixteenth Army also had the newly formed and secret 51st Rocket Regiment, with seventy-two sextuple 150mm launchers organised in nine batteries. It was due to be shipped in the second and third waves to enhance the heavy artillery support. 16th and 9th Armies were also each given command of Artillery Command 106 and 109 respectively. These were newly established groups of coastal artillery, each with twelve 150mm and twelve 100mm guns. They were to be shipped over in three stages (Command 106 planned to be shipped over S+4 to 9, S+22 to 27 and S+34 to 39) and installed to complete the heavy coastal artillery support on both sides of the Channel, especially in defending the captured ports and landing zones. In addition to this heavy coastal artillery the German Army and Navy had established by August five heavy artillery batteries, totalling thirteen guns, and another five batteries, totalling twenty three rail mounted guns, with calibres of between 21cm and 30.5cm in the Pas de Calais area to help protect the eastern barrier. On S Day Dover was to be shelled by the Siegfried (two 38cm), Friederich August (three 30.5cm) and Grosserkurfast (four 28cm) Batteries, while the Siegfried Battery was also to be available to in support of the landings as far west as Dungeness.

Additional engineer support included units responsible for putting captured ports back into operation as soon as possible and constructing or clearing airfields. Other engineer units were responsible for constructing fixed wooden landing bridges on the beaches to provide a more efficient method of unloading barges and transports until harbours were made available; the downside being the eight days estimated for construction. Each assault division was allocated 80 metres of wooden bridging for a sixteen ton structure, 120 metres for an eight ton structure, 340 metres of trackway and 400 metres for trestle bridges. These structures were to be built at Hythe, Rye, Hastings and Eastbourne. Sixteenth Army expected to set up two landing commands at Hastings and Dover, each with seven officers, and assigned military police and transport units; these commands were expected to co-ordinate their activities with the Navy. Ninth Army must have had similar plans, though their records are missing. Each Army also arranged for a non-operational divisional headquarters to be responsible for co-ordinating the logistics chain through the embarking ports in France, Belgium and Holland.

Of the three services the Luftwaffe was the least involved in invasion planning due to its own politically inspired agenda of bringing the United Kingdom to its knees. Hitler issued his Directive 17 on 1 August, which moved planning and operations from a siege based outlook to that of assault. Six tasks were identified, almost all directed at the Luftwaffe and which extended their normal range of operations. The tasks were:

- First to overcome the RAF with all forces available by attacking firstly air units, ground organisation, communications, aircraft industry and anti aircraft deployments;
- Second, after air supremacy was achieved, shift the attack to ports, especially those handling food imports but sparing southern ports as practicable;
- Third, attacks on naval and merchant shipping was to be reduced unless it contributed to the second task;
- Fourth, to remain ready to support naval operations and Operation Sea Lion;
- Fifth, to reserve terror attacks in reprisal;
- Sixth, to intensify the air war at the discretion of the Luftwaffe, while the Navy were granted freedom to begin projected intensified naval warfare.

The Luftwaffe planned to use the three Air Fleets (Luftflotte) already in action, with Air Fleet 3 (Field Marshal Sperrle) supporting Ninth Army from western France and Air Fleet 2 (Field Marshall Kesselring) supporting Sixteenth Army from the Low Countries and Northern France. Air Fleet 5 (Colonel General Stumpf) in Norway would support diversionary and anti shipping operations in the North Sea. The largest tactical formation was the Geschwader, or air wing with up to 120 aircraft; each wing comprised an average of four Groups, which could operate independently, and these had three or four squadrons each.

The two main Air Fleets were organised as follows:

Air Fleet 2
- I Air Corps had four bomber Geschwaders (KG1, 30, 76 and 77) to provide close support to the Army;
- II Bomber Corps had three bomber and one Stuka Geschwaders (KG2, 3, 53 and StG 26) to attack communications to the north of London within a boundary formed by Banbury, Kings Lynn and Colchester;
- XI Air Division had two bomber Geschwaders (KG4 and KGr 126) to carry out mostly mine laying operations;
- Fighter Force 2 had five fighter Geschwaders (JG3, 26, 51, 52 and 54) to protect the bomber force.

- A long range reconnaissance Group (Aufkl. 122) and a coastal reconnaissance Group (Auf Gr. 106)

Air Fleet 3
- IV Bomber Corps had one Stuka (StG 3) and five bomber Geschwaders (LG1, KG27, Kgr100, KGr606 and Kgr806) to attack communications and army camps to the west and south west of London;
- V Bomber Corps had two bomber Geschwaders (KG51 and KG54) to attack communications and army camps to the west and south west of London;
- VIII Air Corps had three Stuka Geschwaders (StG 1, 2 and 77) and one bomber Group (II/LG2) to provide close support to the Army within a line running from Faversham to Mayfield via Lenham and Goudhurst;
- Fighter Force 3 had four fighter Geschwaders - JG2, 27, 53 and ZG76) to protect these Corps
- A long range reconnaissance Group (Aufkl 123) and nine other squadrons and a coastal reconnaissance Group (Auf Gr 506)

For the landings VIII Air Corps was to assign two Stuka wings to attack coastal defences at Dover and Folkestone, one Stuka squadron to the coastal battery at Dungeness and most of two Stuka groups to support VII Corps landing, leaving one Stuka group in reserve. The bomber units were also to hit the RAF's bomber airfields and supply depots. In addition 11th Air Division (KG4 and KGR126) was to carry out mine laying operations around the Thames Estuary, east coast and south coast naval ports. To counter the Royal Navy it would have to largely rely on the experienced Ju88 bombers, especially as the Luftwaffe's air launched torpedoes were only really effective at night due to the low altitude and slow speed at which they had to be dropped.

The Luftwaffe organised two groups of ground crew that were to land with the first two invasion waves in order to prepare advance landing grounds and support air operations from them. JG26, StG77 and part of LG2 (a "training" ground attack Geschwader) were to be based in England as soon as possible while JG3, JG27, JG53 and StG1 would cross later. It had been noted that fighter and dive bomber units would move once a line running from Tunbridge Wells to Chichester had been secured, while bomber units would only move after the Second Operational Objective was achieved.

Each assault division was also allocated a flight of ten HS126 light aircraft to lay protective smokescreens at the invasion beaches to complement the smoke generators aboard the minesweepers. Additional aircraft were available to strengthen the screen or put down smoke over British rear positions, especially artillery positions and observation posts.

It is clear that the Luftwaffe had been asked to do a lot and, whilst effective support of the Army was feasible, achieving and maintaining air superiority over southern England at the same time was a massive demand. The Luftwaffe could not hope to carry out all their tasks simultaneously and so they were planned in phases. As only the records for Air Fleet 2 remain it makes sense to show them as a guide.

- From about S Day-8 VIII Air Corps was to attack the coastal batteries, while II Air Corps, VIII Air Corps, 9th and Italian Air Divisions were to attack naval ports and any warships found at sea, with 9th Air Division also carrying out mine laying north of Dover
- On S Day-1 further attacks on ports and mine laying operations would be undertaken
- During S Day VIII Air Corps would have provided close support for the landings, while II and rest of VIII Air Corps` were to attack British defences further inland. 9th and Italian Air Divisions were to reinforce II Air Corps's efforts in supporting the advance on Folkestone and Dover.

For the airborne forces about 750 operational transport aircraft, organised in one Geschwader of nine groups, were available; these were not enough to lift its parachute force - 7th Air Division - in one go (a full parachute regiment required one group of 220 aircraft, or 53 aircraft to carry one battalion). 7th Air Division was formed just before the war and remained under the command of the Luftwaffe, but was to come under the command of XIII Corps once it had landed. Its three main roles were to secure crossings over the Royal Military Canal around Hythe for the seaborne forces, safeguard its landing zones by advancing from them to the north and north west, in doing so blocking the main Canterbury to Folkestone road and, thirdly, assisting in the capture of Dover. The Army had previously requested that the Division be landed northwest of Dover but the Luftwaffe had rejected this due to an active British anti aircraft defence, the ability to re-supply it and difficulty in finding sufficient landing zones.

Although it had not been expected to operate as a complete division many of its units had already seen combat and earned an elite reputation out of all proportion to its numbers. The success of these troops led to the force's rapid expansion throughout the summer of 1940 from an under strength division (in May it had only two parachute infantry regiments with a total of five infantry battalions) to a Corps (XI Fliegerkorps, which was to include 22nd Airlanding Infantry Division). 7th Air Division was now commanded by General Putziger (General Student having been severely wounded in Holland) and comprised:

- Three parachute infantry regiments (each with three infantry battalions, an infantry gun company and anti tank company),
- One assault regiment of two infantry and one engineer battalions, an infantry gun company and anti tank company,
- An artillery battalion with two field gun batteries (8x75mm guns each),
- A newly formed machine gun battalion with three companies,
- One engineer battalion,
- One anti tank battalion with three anti tank companies (a total of 36x37mm guns),
- One anti aircraft battalion (36x20mm)

In all it had about 11,000 men, 7000 of whom were parachute trained. However, only the stripped down artillery pieces were able to be dropped by parachute; these were adapted mountain guns, each broken down into about eight parachute loads; the other heavy weapons, including those of the infantry gun and anti tank units, had to be either brought in by transport aircraft or landed from the invasion fleet. The parachute infantry battalions were smaller than the usual infantry ones (about 750 men) but included a mortar section with each company that was expected to provide most of the initial artillery support. The parachute elements relied on the respected Ju52 transport plane, able to carry twelve paratroopers and four containers, while the others used the DFS 230 glider, 150 of which were available and each capable of carrying up to ten troops. The Storm Assault Regiment was a Corps asset, which had also been enlarged from the battalion that had famously overcome the defences on the River Albert in Belgium.

The Germans had never practised night assaults and had only conducted company level training to date. Their parachutes were not steerable and a full stick of twelve men jumping quickly would expect to land in a line about 200 metres long, with daylight allowing quicker re-organisation on landing. General Student commented on the recent operations that the parachute troops had been lucky, due mainly to achieving surprise and acting aggressively; the weather had been kind, allowing the aircraft to find their objectives. However, he was concerned that the troops would be unable to sustain their operations due to the lack of an organic logistics organisation and heavy weapons landing with them. Most of the Division was to be landed on S Day in two waves, though without its heavy weapons or equipment; remaining support units expecting to land at either Lympne or Hawkinge airfields from S+5.

The Army had deployed its 22nd Infantry Division in an airmobile role in support of the paratroops during the campaign in the Low Countries. This required landing zones to be secured so units could be flown in by Ju52 transport aircraft. There are no documents available to show its involvement in Sea Lion, though it remained available in the west throughout this period and elements could have been flown in as reinforcements if required.

The Luftwaffe also provided two anti aircraft corps - I Corps to co-operate with Ninth Army and II Corps with Sixteenth Army, each comprising four regiments. Both Corps were tasked with providing air defence during loading and unloading of the invasion fleets, supporting the assault troops and convoy protection. Of the units assigned to protect the beachheads only a third were able to be carried with the first wave, each Army only having three 88mm and two 20mm batteries at their disposal as a result. Each panzer and motorised division had their own integral light anti aircraft regiment.

The German Navy had made major changes to its command structure to accommodate the Operation. Two new posts created were Naval Commander West, filled by Vice Admiral Lutjens (destined to go down with the Bismarck in 1941), responsible for the tactical command of warships and transports, and Chief of Sea Transportation, held by Captain Heinz Degenhardt, responsible for the requisitioning and movement of ships in France. He was also designated Special Commander of the Naval High Command in England. Grand Admiral Saalwachter, Commander in Chief of Naval Group West, was responsible for the planning and implementation of the naval part of the Operation; he had been the tactical commander for the invasion of Norway. In addition to its own resource plannng the Navy was only too aware that it had to curtail the power of the Royal Navy and so secure local command of the invasion sectors. The British had already accepted that the sea covered too large an area for them to guarantee that the Germans could not attain such local command, particularly in the southern part of the North Sea and English Channel.

With relatively few warships available the Navy had to rely heavily on captured warships and coastal vessels deemed suitable to carry heavy weapons. In the end they allocated five auxiliary heavy and twenty-seven auxiliary light gunboats (coasters armed with one or two heavy guns depending on their size), supported by ten auxiliary minesweeper, eight auxiliary patrol and four "R" boat flotillas (the first two being a mix of adapted and armed coasters or trawlers mostly armed with 105mm guns and the last being lightly armed motor launches), to protect the invasion fleet.

Six submarines and twenty-two "S" Boats (motor torpedo boats) were allocated to the Eastern Barrier covering the North Sea. 1st S Boat Flotilla was based at Rotterdam, the 2nd Flotilla at Boulogne and the 3rd Flotilla at Vlissingen. This Barrier formed two lines - one from Kent's North Foreland to Zeebrugge and the other from Dover to Calais involving a total of 1,300 mines. The Western Barrier, which ran from Beachy Head to Dieppe and consisting of 4,250 mines, was to be supported by twenty-five submarines (nine covering the Barrier with the others covering the Western Approaches), eight destroyers (5th & 6th Flotillas) and nineteen "T" boats (these were armed with up to three 105mm guns). Most of the minefields were laid from early September without any interference from the British, who were concentrating on the enemy side of the Channel.

The Battle Fleet, with two battle cruisers, two light cruisers and three "T" boats, supported by seven submarines (five patrolling the Royal Navy's main fleet base at Scapa Flow in the Orkneys and two off the Tyne Estuary) were allocated with four large transports to diversionary operations in the North and Norwegian Seas. In addition, the pocket battleship `Admiral Scheer` was at the same time to sortie into the Atlantic to attack the shipping routes.

An additional 23,500 sailors were found to man the invasion craft, mostly taken from the non-operational ships of the Battle Fleet but also including anyone with maritime or engineering experience. The invasion fleets eventually totalled 160 transports, 2500 barges, 580 trawlers and 130 tugs located at Rotterdam, Antwerp, Ostend, Nieuport, Dunkirk, Gravelines, Calais, Boulogne and Le Havre. A third of these craft were found from the occupied territories. An assessment of shipping on 19 September found that 80% could be assembled on time.

In all there would be four landing zones, the Navy organising a transport fleet for each:

- Zone B was the stretch of coast between Hythe and Dungeness with the Fleet consisting of 57 transports, 314 barges and 100 trawlers, protected by 9 light gunboats and 9 AA ferries sailing from Rotterdam, Ostend and Dunkirk;
- Zone C was Rye Bay with the Fleet consisting of 57 transports and over 300 barges, protected by 6 minesweepers, 9 light gunboats, 7 R boats and 9 AA ferries sailing from Calais and Antwerp;
- Zone D was Pevensey Bay with the Fleet consisting 330 barges protected by 10 light gunboats, 30 patrol boats, 9 AA ferries and 3 minesweepers sailing from Boulogne;
- Zone E was the stretch of coast between Beachy Head and Brighton with the Fleet consisting of 50 transports, 100 coasters, 223 trawlers and 4 tugs with 5 barges (these were for the tank company), protected by 5 heavy gunboats, 8 R boats and 8 AA ferries sailing from Le Havre, with smaller groups sailing from Dieppe, Caen and Fecamp.

These Fleets were to leave port in enough time to reach their assigned assembly areas. These assembly areas were to be reached between S-8½ hours to S-18 hours depending on the convoy, meaning that the slowest had to sail in the morning before S Day. This mission stretched the Navy to its limits in terms of both material and personnel, leaving it to the Luftwaffe to largely protect the shipping. In addition to the invasion fleet there was a whole host of support craft including tankers, hospital ships, salvage ships and 49 tugs fitted with hoses to counter oil fires on the sea. A special unit was formed to start re-laying communications cables between Calais and St Margaret's Bay, just north of Dover, from S+5 or S+7 using two cable laying ships.

The main assault forces in the first echelon were to be shipped mainly in barges or lighters, towed by tugs or other suitable craft; the second echelon was mainly to be carried in transports. Although some of the barges and lighters were self-powered it was decided that they should be towed across the Channel in order to ensure their engines were conserved for the landing and so that a decent convoy speed could be maintained. The tactical formation agreed was a "tow" consisting of two barges a pusher boat and a tug, with six tows forming a group with a command boat. During the crossing these groups would be deployed in four columns, with escort and gun support craft on the flanks. In addition to the Army artillery units assigned to protect the invasion craft the Navy also formed a light anti aircraft detachment (Marine Flak Abteilung 200). It was considered essential that all the barges used could operate up to sea state 2, though trials found most could withstand up to state 8 (though those on board would likely feel differently!). Convoy speed was set at five knots for barges and eight knots for the transports, though there was great variation in the actual speed of the vessels employed.

As mentioned above, the advance detachments were to be largely carried in the escort vessels, supplemented by some barge tows. The exception was for those detachments due to land at Cuckmere Haven, Seaford and Rottingdean, who would be carried in fishing craft and coasters. In all cases the landing procedure was to be the same: the escorts would stop offshore (between 300 to 1000 metres from the shore) and launch their assault boats and dinghies; these craft were expected to return to take the next group, if required. During this phase the barge tows would approach the beach, supported by the artillery of the invasion fleet and the Luftwaffe and also hopefully protected by smokescreens laid by both aircraft and escort ships.

A standard procedure was to be adopted for barge landings. The tow was to approach the beach bow on and just before the tugs grounded they were to turn into the current to anchor, while at the same time the motorised barge aft cast off to beach on its own power. The attached pusher boat was also to cast off and tie up aft of the un-powered barge before pushing it towards the beach, letting go just before grounding. The barges were to drop their stern anchor about twenty metres from the beach and their bow anchor at ten metres to ensure they beached bow on. Most of the barges had been provided with ramps that had to be positioned after grounding to allow vehicles to be disembarked, while lighter ramps were provided for rapid landing of troops. The vehicle ramps required up to twenty men and about four minutes to properly position, though cables would need to be laid if there was a rising tide. To support the beaching process a large number of mostly ex French Army lightly armoured tracked vehicles were assigned. The Navy organised beach parties, each comprising two officers and forty men (each Army had seven parties assigned), which were to supervise the beach landings, advising the Army engineers who would be responsible for unloading the invasion craft. The beach parties were later to form the basis of harbour administration for captured ports.

A major problem the Germans faced was the inability to undertake significant naval manoeuvres to practice these towing and beaching skills. Only one significant exercise took place with fifty barges sailing from Boulogne in good weather and visibility. Despite the favourable conditions less than half of these barges managed to land on schedule.

It was planned that the crossing, unloading, return and reload of a transport was to be achieved within six days and four days for a barge. Each transport would require about twenty barges to unload it onto the beaches and to ensure this, half of the barges and tugs were to remain at the beaches to assist with the unloading of further waves. Empty barges were to be escorted back across the Channel in groups of ten tows (four transports to an escorted group). The biggest concern to both the Navy and Army was the slow turnaround of the transports and barges, due to the schedules being tied to the state of the tides. The barges used to land the first echelon could not be re-used until the second high tide, leaving only the barges attached to the transports to begin their unloading; as it required several barge loads to unload a transport this process would take up to three days to achieve, leaving these ships and their cargos vulnerable to attack. In some cases the escort vessels were also to aid unloading of the transports, if not needed elsewhere. An example of the landing schedule for VII Corps in Rye Bay showed:

- 05:32 - First high tide
- 07:00 - Advance detachments due to land
- 07:30 - First echelon barge tows to begin landing
- 09:30 - First echelon transports due to arrive
- 10:30 - Barges to start unloading from the transports
- 12:09 - Low tide
- 16:00 - The first barges were to be towed free to return to the transports
- 17:00 - Second unloading from the transports to start
- 19:20 - Barges to land after second high tide.
- 05:00 S+1 - Barges to be towed free to allow more offloading from transports
- 06:00 - Unloading from transports to recommence
- 07:00 - High tide at 07.00.
- 08:00 - Barges to begin landing and unloading
- 18:00 - Barges to return to transports after low tide
- 21:00 - Barges to begin landing and unloading

This process would continue until 22.15 on S+2 when the last barges were to have landed and the transports made ready to sail back to the Continent. In all Sixteenth Army was allocated 115 transports and 630 barges to ship the assault divisions, while Ninth Army was allocated 50 transports, 300 coasters or trawlers and 500 barges. It was envisaged that convoys returning to the Continent for reloading should consist of at least four transports or ten tows, with appropriate escorts. The Navy estimated that 30% of the First Wave shipping would be lost (50% for those in the extreme west sector), 15% of the Second Wave and 5% of the remaining waves.

On 14 September Army Group A produced its forecast of the progress of the initial assault. It expected that the leading assault troops landing at dawn would face stiff enemy defence. When local beach heads were won energetic junior commanders must co-ordinate the mixed units and gain important features inland. Gradually weak but coherent fronts will form. These would gradually be extended by the continual arrival of reinforcements. Heavy counter attacks by the enemy, equipped with heavy weapons, were to be expected very soon and stiff fighting would develop. Everything was to depend on courageous and determined leaders who must not yield a foot of ground. Corps and Army staff must do their utmost to supply these troops. Senior commanders with small staffs will cross only when the fighting power of the assault forces landed had been sufficiently reinforced. Extensive Corps and Army staffs may only be sent over once forces required for the fighting have crossed and progress has been made inland. After daylight on S Day, but not before, the Luftwaffe will support the main effort of the landing forces. Small but complete units of the armoured divisions will be incorporated at an early stage in the first wave, in order to support the infantry. The landing of complete armoured divisions will take place only when a sufficient area of the island has been won. The gradual development of operations, landing, penetration inland and establishment of the beach head is the probable picture of events. If favourable circumstances allow, the operation is to be speeded up as our very mobile and flexible command will be able to adapt itself to to this favourable situation as quickly as in former operations.'

General Busch estimated that the initial operations to establish the beachhead would take a week and that the assault forces would have to rely on their own resources for about eight days before substantial reinforcements could be readied. He believed that at the outset small unit combat would be the rule of the day, with tanks and heavy weapons pushed forward at speed no matter where they landed or to whom they belonged. Organisational confusion and mixed units during the landing phase was conceded and, with this in mind, divisional commanders were authorised to command all units that came within their area of responsibility. He urged flexibility of organisation and independent responsibility of the commander on the ground to hold and push on. He is reported as saying "the first requisite is to join battle. Each ship or barge is to be loaded so that the men, weapons, equipment and supplies together make up a self contained combat unit."

The Army High Command recorded that 'Heavy battles with strong British forces were expected to develop by the time the first major objective was reached. Local crises would have to be anticipated as there was no possibility of envelopment on a large scale and the actions against troops fighting with tenacity and determination would be mainly frontal. However, once local breakthroughs had been achieved, the British operational command, possessing little flexibility, will not be in a position to master the difficult situations arising. The success of the German attacker then is unquestionable. Air superiority and air support would be of decisive importance at this time. Thereafter, when the fighting elements of the British Army have been defeated in southern England, only local and incoherent enemy resistance is still to be expected in the further course of operations. These battles therefore will probably be easier and quicker.'

While confident in their ability to mount another successful campaign, with senior German leaders publicly claiming at the end of July that their forces need only to reckon with a poorly equipped British Army that had not had time to apply the lessons learnt in Flanders, they privately retained a strong and healthy respect for the British Army. They recognised that the longer it took to mount the Operation the stronger their opponents would be. It was therefore vital to the German Army that they should know their opponent's defensive plans, its order of battle and state of its equipment. Faced with an almost complete absence of covert intelligence gathering methods available within the United Kingdom the Germans had to rely mostly on wireless interception and air reconnaissance to build up a picture of Britain's defences. Attempts by German intelligence services to infiltrate spies into the United Kingdom were completely unsuccessful and demonstrated an embarrassingly amateurish approach.

In early July the Supreme Command estimated that the British Army had between 15-20 divisions of fighting value (including the remnants of 14 former BEF divisions); coastal forces and the home guard were rated has having slight combat value.

The Army submitted a memorandum to the Supreme Command on 10 August on the expected opposition to their landing between Folkestone and Eastbourne. It stated 'In this sector we must already reckon with a fully prepared coastal defence, consisting of about four divisions, apart from the personnel of the coastal fortifications. Between Margate and Folkestone there are presumed to be two further divisions and between Eastbourne and Portsmouth two more; if both the latter sectors are not attacked they could come to the assistance of the first sector. Behind these forces the British command is sure to have available between London and Salisbury at least five operational divisions, one of which is armoured; in case of necessity there will be available one further division at Chatham and one in London'. It further noted that 'the British defence would be conducted on an offensive basis, with their forces dispersed. If they conducted a strictly defensive response then the formation of an English defence front on the line Chatham-Brighton would be rendered impossible from the start; pressure on the British could lead to the rapid abandonment by them of the whole area south and south east of London'. In fact the British had only the equivalent of seven divisions in London and the south east!

On 15 August they reported that the British had thirty nine divisions at home, of which twenty were regarded as completely operational, though with only half their normal artillery strength. On 5 September they reported that the region Tonbridge to Beachy Head was characterised by a large and excellently camouflaged labyrinth of fortifications. Hastings was a strongly established centre of defence, while the Isle of Wight was the most fortified part of the English south coast. On 17 September they re-estimated that the British had thirty four field divisions available nationwide, eighteen of which were fully operational and with nearly two thirds of them allocated to beach defence (the British Army actually only had twenty nine active divisions at that time). Worse still was that they were only able to correctly identify less than half of these formations in or near their actual locations. For example, they had identified 45th Division but placed it in 1st London Division's sector, covering the coast between Dover and Dungeness, and they believed the 55th Division was deployed between Dungeness and Brighton (this Territorial Division was actually in Norfolk). On 9 October they reported that the coastal sector of Brighton-Dover was defended as follows:

    i)   The first defence line actually on the coastline
    ii)   300 yards inland were machine gun nests
    iii)   1000 yards inland were heavy long-range guns at intervals of about 800 yards
    iv)   3000 yards inland was a line of light artillery and machine guns
    iv)   2½ miles inland was a line that included armoured cars and 230 tanks. Total strength in this line was about 75,000 men

vi) Behind these lines, in reserve, were about 50,000 men in a zone about 12½ miles deep, distributed on the same principle as the first lines of defence.

This was a significant overestimation of the real defensive situation they would face. For example in the whole of Kent and Sussex there were less than thirty operational tanks available.

On 20 September, the Kriegsmarine estimated available British naval forces to be 3 battleships, 2 battlecruisers, 2 aircraft carriers, 8 heavy and 20 light cruisers, 76 destroyers and about 550 patrol vessels. They also estimated that four light cruisers and two destroyer flotillas could intervene immediately on either flank of the invasion while heavy forces could arrive from Scapa Flow within two days. Whilst their assessment of the Royal Navy's dispositions was slightly more accurate, the Luftwaffe's estimation of the Royal Air Force, including its repair and production capacity, was even worse.

As part of the diversionary operations the Luftwaffe was to send individual aircraft on the eve of the landings along the east, south west and Irish coasts with naval and signals intelligence personnel aboard to transmit false radio sightings at appropriate times, aided by having cracked both the RAF's code and part of those used by the Royal Navy's auxiliary patrol.

German intelligence expected that it would take the British four days and nights to move their strategic reserves into action, this timing mainly being influenced by Luftwaffe claims to be able to effectively cut road and rail links to the invasion area, so allowing the invasion forces time to establish a strong beachhead capable of defeating the expected counterattacks. Although the invasion forces could expect to obtain some supplies from the areas captured, they would be dependent on their own logistics organisation to be able to supply the vital fuel, spares and replacement equipment. Although some of this could be flown in the bulk would need to be shipped across a vulnerable Channel.

Nevertheless, Colonel General von Rundstedt wrote on 23 August "Once we gain a foothold on the enemy coast with strong forces and are advancing inland our superiority in this form of operation will show itself clearly". The unknown element in this statement was whether the British armed forces and in particular its Army would allow them?

CHAPTER TWO: BRITISH STRATEGY

It is generally considered that the main goal of modern warfare is to break the enemy's will to resist and as such wars tend to be fought on two levels - the physical and the moral.

This was never to be better demonstrated than at this time. Winston Churchill replaced the dejected and spent Neville Chamberlain as Prime Minister on 10 May 1940, the day the Germans began their blitzkrieg against Western Europe, and immediately set about the vital task of changing the moral outlook of the British people. His first speech to the House of Commons on 13 May was short and to the point, sweeping any illusions away by stating that "we have before us many long months of struggle and of suffering". He then laid out his policy of "waging war by sea, land and air with all our might" and confirmed the chief aim being victory - "victory at all costs, victory in spite of all terror, victory however long and hard the road may be; for withou victory there is no survival. Let it be realised; no survival for the British Empire." Although this statement might now seem somewhat overblown it did confirm the new Government's will to fight and prevail and as a result served to raise the morale of both the British people, its Empire and Comonwealth and their combined armed forces, something desperately needed at this critical time.

On 28 May came one of Churchill's most famous speeches in which he stated that "we shall go on to the end, we shall fight in France, we shall fight on the seas and oceans, we shall fight with growing confidence and growing strength in the air, we shall defend our island, whatever the cost may be, we shall fight on the beaches, we shall fight on the landing grounds, we shall fight on the fields and in the streets, we shall fight on the hills; we shall never surrender, and even if, which I do not for a moment believe, this island or a large part of it were subjugated and starving, then our Empire beyond the seas, armed and guarded by the British fleet, would carry on the struggle, until in God's good time, the New World with all its power and might, steps forth to the rescue and liberation of the old". This affirmation of a new, stronger, policy was to define the way the British armed forces were expected to approach the defence of their homeland.

It also recognised the vital support of the Empire and Commonwealth countries, not only in terms of military forces but also in facilities, industrial potential and provision of vital raw materials. Indeed, Britain had to rely on its imperial resources until America's entry into the war some eighteen months after the fall of its key pre-war ally, France. However, this support could not be always guaranteed. Even before the First World War the Dominions were becoming increasingly preoccupied with their own regional security and Britain's increasingly inability to provide it. At the Dominions Conference in 1937 South Africa favoured neutrality and Canada isolation in case of a European war and in May 1939 the Committee of Imperial Defence submitted plans for war based on the assumption that at least one Dominion would remain neutral. Indeed, the Germans had devoted significant political capital in South Africa to achieve this. However, by the time war was declared the Dominions had all agreed to fully support Britain's imperial stance. Every colonial government was obliged to produce its own war plan, with the Overseas Defence Committee coordinating them. From June 1940 Whitehall established regional control organisations across the Empire to coordinate efforts should Britain fall. In August 1940 the US guaranteed the security of Canada through the Ogdensburg Declaration, creating a joint structure for the defence of the region.

In addition to being Prime Minister, Churchill was also the Minister for Defence and as such it was accepted that he assume responsibility for the general direction of the war, subject to the support of the War Cabinet and House of Commons. In his book "The Second World War" Churchill noted that the key change on his taking over was the supervision and direction of the Chiefs of Staff Committee as the Minister of Defence with undefined powers. In this position he had the wide powers of selection and removal of all political and professional persons.

This situation was actually to benefit the armed services, as it now provided the Chiefs of Staff Committee with direct daily contact with the head of the Government for the first time and permitted them full control, with Churchill, over the strategic conduct of the war and the armed forces. This move by Churchill helped to simplify the higher chain of command. The First Lord of the Admiralty and Secretaries of State for War and Air were not members of the War Cabinet and did not attend meetings of the Chiefs of Staff Committee, but did remain responsible for the development and administration of their respective armed services and were kept fully apprised of the Committee's deliberations. General Hastings Ismay was the Deputy Secretary (Military) to the War Cabinet and, as such, was Churchill's representative on the Chiefs of Staff Committee. General Ismay had spent most of his career in a range of staff appointments and was regarded by both Churchill and the armed forces as an efficient administrator. At this stage of the war the Committee met daily and was responsible for advising the Prime Minister on the strategic development of the war; but it was not designed to play an active role in conducting the actual defence of the United Kingdom. The three heads of the armed forces which made up the Committee at this time were Air Marshall Sir Cyril Newall for the RAF (until replaced by Air Marshal Charles Portal on 24 October), General Sir John Dill and Admiral of the Fleet Sir Dudley Pound. General Dill was also Chief of the Imperial General Staff. He had been the BEF's I Corps commander until promotion to Vice Chief of the Imperial General Staff in April 1940 and subsequent promotion in June. Air Marshal Sir Cyril Newall was regarded as the prime architect of the wartime airforce. Despite the conflicting priorities, traditional inter-service rivalries and differing personalities involved it was generally agreed that this Committee was to remain an effective body that served both Churchill and the armed forces with equal vigour.

When he took command of the Army's Home Forces in mid July, General Alan Brooke noted that one point above all constituted a grave danger in the defensive organisation of the country - the lack of a combined operational command over the three services. Each of the services had their own command and reporting structure linked either directly to the Prime Minister or through the Chiefs of Staff Committee. This dual structure could be bureaucratic and cumbersome, as for example senior meetings often included representatives from up to nine sub commands (five Navy, three RAF and one Army), leading to un-needed duplication. In the event of an invasion there would have been no single military command level able to co-ordinate the necessary actions between all three services which, with traditional inter service rivalry, could have spelt disaster. General Alan Brooke was also concerned that if an invasion occurred Churchill, acting as both Prime Minister and Defence Minister, would have attempted to co-ordinate or interfere with the actions of the various commands and so dominate operations, especially given the strength of his personality and convictions. He felt this would have been wrong and highly dangerous, especially with Churchill's impulsive nature and tendency to arrive at decisions by intuition. He further noted that the only problem with the location of the Army's Battle Headquarters in Whitehall was its proximity to the Prime Minister!

On his part, Churchill accepted that he as Defence Minister should not act in any purely military matter contrary to the corporate opinion of the Chiefs of Staff Committee. At a meeting of the War Cabinet on 5 July 1940 Churchill noted how the planning for home defence had progressed following the start of the German offensives. He confirmed that 'now a complete machinery existed for advising the War Cabinet on general policy at home and abroad. The Chiefs of Staff were constantly at work on all aspects of the War. For the conduct of the operations we had the Commander in Chief, Home Forces (General Alan Brooke), whose position was the same as that of the Commander in Chief for the BEF. He received his general instructions from the War Office, who assisted him in every way and placed such forces as might be necessary under his command. He then made the plan for the operations. It was clearly impossible that any one man could command all three services, so it had been arranged for him to have a Rear Admiral and Air Vice Marshal placed on his staff to ensure the fullest co-operation.'

In a speech during the winter of 1941 he stated that "I do not think there has ever been a system in which the professional heads of the fighting services have had a freer hand or a greater of more direct influence or have received more constant and harmonious support from the Prime Minister and the Cabinet under whom they serve." While he may persuade them by his delivery or persistence it would still be their military judgement that should count. Whether this position would have remained so, following an invasion, is one of the great unknowns of Churchill's (and Brooke's) character.

At a lower strategic level there was an improvement in the means of concerting military and civil plans. As an executive body, the Home Defence Executive set up in May proved unwieldy. In June it became a co-ordinating body lead by an experienced civil servant who was also the Chief Civil Staff Officer to General Alan Brooke. Regional Commissioners were to ensure effective co-ordination happened between local civilian and military authorities in the affected areas, with arrangements made to avoid the problems with the movement of refugees inadvertantly aiding the invading forces, as had been widely experienced across the Continent. By the middle of July over 200,000 civilians had been evacuated from the most threatened coastal towns and the rest warned that they were expected to stay where they were in the event of invasion, unless ordered to evacuate by local commanders. In many cases the populations of coastal towns fell by up to half. Even the civilians who remained were expected to play their part by, for example, reporting enemy movements, hiding or denying anything likely to be of value to the enemy and remaining calm; in this they were guided by material supplied by the Ministry of Information. Local authorities were to assist in ensuring that lines of communication and public utilities continued to function and arrangements for the denial to the invader of important commodities, notably petrol supplies, were also made in conjunction with local Army units, though it was made clear that authorisation had to be granted by the senior local commander before such activities could be undertaken so as not to hamper Army operations. Defence plans for key towns and villages often included detailed instructions for the civilians remaining, including medical, feeding and safety arrangements. Further information on the role of civilian authorities following invasion can be found in Appendix 17 at the end of this book.

In late May 1940 the Chiefs of Staff responded to a review requested by Churchill, the terms of reference being "In the event of France being unable to continue in the war and becoming neutral, with the Germans holding their present position and the Belgian Army being forced to capitulate after assisting the British Expeditionary Force to reach the coast; in the event of terms being offered to Britain which would place her entirely at the mercy of Germany through disarmament, cession of naval bases, etc; what are the prospects of our continuing the war alone against Germany and probably Italy? Can the Navy and Air Force hold out reasonable hopes of preventing serious invasion, and could the forces gathered in this island cope with raids from the air involving detachments not greater than 10,000 men; it being observed that a prolongation of British resistance might be very dangerous for Germany, engaged in holding down the greater part of Europe?" The conclusions of the review were as follows:

1. Whilst our Air Force is in being, our Navy and Air Force together should be able to prevent Germany carrying out a serious sea-borne invasion of this country
2. Supposing Germany gained complete air superiority, we consider that the Navy could hold up an invasion for a time, but not for an indefinite period
3. If, with our Navy unable to prevent it, and our Air Force gone, Germany attempted an invasion, our coast and beach defences could not prevent German tanks and infantry getting a firm footing on our shores. In the circumstances envisaged above our land forces would be insufficient to deal with a serious invasion
4. The crux of the matter is air supremacy. Once Germany had attained this she might attempt to subjugate this country by air attack alone
5. Germany could not gain complete air superiority unless she could knock out our Air Force and the aircraft industries
6. Air attacks on those aircraft factories would be made by day or by night. We consider that we should be able to inflict such casualties on the enemy by day as to prevent serious damage. Whatever we do however by way of defensive measures - and we are pressing on with these with all dispatch - we cannot be sure of protecting the large industrial centres, upon which our aircraft industries depend, from serious material damage by night attack. The enemy would not have to employ precision bombing to achieve this effect
7. Whether the attacks succeed in eliminating the aircraft industry depends not only on the material damage by bombs but also on the moral effect on the workpeople and their determination to carry on in the face of wholesale havoc and destruction
8. If therefore the enemy presses home night attacks on our aircraft industry, he is likely to achieve such material and moral damage within the industrial area concerned as to bring all work to a standstill
9. It must be remembered that numerically the Germans have a superiority of four to one in aircraft. Moreover, the German aircraft factories are well dispersed and relatively inaccessible
10. On the other hand, so long as we had a counter offensive bomber force we can carry out similar attacks on German industrial centres and by moral and material effect bring a proportion of them to a standstill
11. To sum up, our conclusion is that *prima facie* Germany has most of the cards; but the real test is whether the morale of our fighting personnel and civil population

will counterbalance the numerical and material advantages that Germany enjoys. We believe it will.

On 25 May 1940 the Chiefs of Staff Committee stated that there were three ways Germany could break the resistance of the United Kingdom - unrestricted air attack aimed at breaking public morale, starvation of the country by attacks on shipping and ports and, lastly, occupation by invasion. It noted that these factors could not be assessed with certainty, though it believed that the British people would endure the greatest strain if they realised, as they were beginning to do so, that the existence of the Empire is at stake. In terms of the second factor, they felt that if 60% of present imports could be maintained there would be enough food for the population and raw materials for essential armament production. Ministry of Supply data throughout the rest of 1940 showed that, despite increasing merchant shipping losses, this import level was often surpassed.

At the meeting of the War Cabinet on 5 July 1940 it was reported that a number of government ministers had expressed a feeling of remoteness from the planning of Home Defence, which impinged upon their daily responsibilities. Much of this related to re-assuring industry and the populace on what was being done to protect them. Mr Churchill noted that there was much understandable anxiety but it was essential that people have confidence in those responsible for planning the defence. He said that 'no guarantee could be given that a particular part of the country was safe; people should not be allowed to suppose that landings could be entirely prevented; indeed, a landing would be the beginning of the action, not the end of it. Although there would certainly be much destruction, and terrible events of a kind never before known in this island, people should be confident that the enemy would be thrown back`.

The British Civil Service was happy to play its part – by clarifying just what an invasion meant to them. A memo to the Cabinet Office from the Dominions Office asked the Joint Planning Sub Committee to say whether or not, in their considered opinion, the invasion of the United Kingdom had actually commenced. The response dated 13 August stated "From the information at our disposal, we understand that the word "invade" is derived from the Latin "in", meaning "in", and "vadere" meaning "to go". Hence we may deduce invade means to go in. The invasion must date from the moment enemy forces "go in". 'Forces' must presume armed forces since if unarmed they cannot be considered as threatening the country unless they enter for purposes of espionage. Spies alone cannot invade a country and, in any event, they, like the poor, are always with us. An airman landing by parachute cannot be considered an invader even if he makes some effort to evade capture. This, however, cannot include parachutists pushed out of aircraft, with the intent on the part of the pusher, to land them in the country. In the light of the above considerations, which I am sure will be as clear to you as they are to me, the Sub Committee hold that invasion has not as yet started." Presumably this statement would have re-assured everyone.

The last time the British authorities had seriously considered the land defence of their country was in the 1860's, when they believed France was once more intent on expanding its imperial desires and, in doing so, would again interfere with Britain's own imperial development. This concern had led to a major construction project along Britain's southern and eastern coasts that produced major defensive fortifications, especially around the most important seaports, to supplement the Martello Tower chain that had been constructed in the earlier Napoleonic

Wars. These distinctive towers were mainly constructed in a way that allowed them to provide supporting fire; each tower was circular, with walls between six to eight feet thick and over twenty seven feet high, constructed with about half a million bricks and covered with a concrete outer shell. There was an open firing platform on the top with living quarters and storerooms below; entry was usually by a ladder at the rear. The towers were usually grouped to cover certain possible landing beaches, notably covering the Folkestone to Hythe and Pevensey to Eastbourne sectors. On the south coast the largest examples of the new Victorian fortifications were to be found at Dover, Newhaven and Portsmouth; at Dover and Newhaven new forts and redoubts overlooked the harbours, while the Naval base at Portsmouth was protected both by forts guarding the land approaches and others built in the sea off the Isle of Wight. Both the Napoleonic and later Victorian "Palmerston" fortifications (named after the British Prime Minister of the time) would be reactivated and upgraded during the two World Wars.

The First World War showed the potential vulnerability of the country to attack by modern weapons, something clearly demonstrated by the shock felt following both the German naval bombardments of Lowestoft, Scarborough and Hartlepool in 1914 and air attacks over the southern and midland counties of England between 1915 and 1918. While the air attacks led to the British Army developing an anti aircraft organisation, in co-operation with the defending allied air forces on both sides of the Channel, the naval bombardments more importantly led to an upgrading of the coast artillery organisation and the retaining of large numbers of soldiers along the east coast to counter a potential invasion there, even until late in the War.

In early 1916 the British Army estimated that a force of 160,000 German troops could be landed on the east coast in one wave and proposed that 460,000 men was the minimum force required to destroy such an invasion, based on three mounted and nine Territorial infantry divisions, five mounted and ten infantry brigades and over twenty cyclist battalions; of these just over half could be considered mobile. These formations were grouped into three parts - East Anglia, Yorkshire and Scotland, though the actual strength of the field force in the country at that time was just over 124,000 men. At the same time a forerunner of the Home Guard was being organised around the country, often without official support. Unknown to the British at the time, Germany had developed some plans to invade, landing in East Anglia and then moving on London, though this was not seriously pursued. Despite the new threat there was little serious planning to counter an invasion, though a number of the pillboxes and trenches constructed at the time along the east coast and around London were to be re-occupied in 1940. After the First World War the British authorities returned to their customary position of assumed safety, leading largely to the dismantling of the defensive structure at home and a shelving of the knowledge gained.

Defence of the United Kingdom must also be considered by appreciating the strategic situation around the World. In its report on 25 May 1940 the Chiefs of Staff Committee noted that in a long-term approach Germany, in concert with Italy, would strive to overthrow Britain's position in Egypt and the Middle East. With the collapse of France, Italy would be able to concentrate her strength against Malta, Gibraltar and Egypt. It believed that Malta could probably withstand one serious assault as it had six months of food reserves, while Gibraltar could remain in use as a naval base, unless Spain became hostile; even then it should be able to hold out for two months without re-supply. It agreed that a capital ship fleet should be based on Alexandria to forestall any Italian moves on Egypt but if a successful attack was made from Libya then the fleet could be withdrawn to Aden and the Suez Canal blocked. It felt that the Army in Egypt was strong enough to withstand Italian attacks as it had 90 days of military supplies for full operational activity. It felt that with German and Italian control over the Balkans internal security problems in the Middle East would increase; for example it was proposed that should the situation in Iraq deteriorate British forces should withdraw to protect Basra and its oilfields. Whilst it did not believe there was a direct military threat to India they did not feel they could rely on withdrawing any British troops based there. Retention of Singapore was considered very important for economic and political reasons. To forestall any Japanese aggression, and in the absence of naval reinforcements, the United States should be asked to safeguard British interests in the Far East and Australia asked to reinforce its Singapore garrison. In summary, they felt that 'we should endeavour to maintain our position in all our overseas possessions. In view of the necessity for concentration of all British resources at vital points, consideration should be given whether responsibility for isolated garrisons could not be taken over by the Dominions, e.g. that Canada take over defence of the West Indies and Iceland.

It might be forgiven to assume that the British authorities were solely focused on the defence of the country during 1940. This is not so. The Chiefs of Staff Committee submitted a paper to the War Cabinet on 4 September about future strategy, examining how the current situation affected Britain's ability to defeat Germany and making military recommendaitons on the governance of the war effort. It was a very detailed document that looked globally and at exisiting and potential enemy threats. It conceded that the strategy should be primarily defensive whilst building up their strength and that security in the Middle East was highly important. It largely negated Italy's potential influence on the course of the War. It stated that it should not be the policy to raise and land on the Continent an Army comparable in size with that of Germany, but should aim that as soon as the naval blockade and air offensive had secured conditions when numerically inferior forces could be employed with a good chance of success, to re-establish a striking force on the Continent with which to enter Germany and impose Britain's terms. It felt that the earliest this could be achieved was mid 1942. It looked at Russia and concluded that 'neither we nor the Germans trust Russia, but neither side wish to quarrel with her openly at present. Russia, on her part, is evidently anxious to avoid hostilities with a Great Power. Consequently, Russia hopes at best to see both sides exhausted in the struggle, and in the meantime look to improve her strategic position and raise her prestige by regaining her previous frontiers.' Regarding its former ally, France, it noted that 'as time goes on and France feels the pinch of our blockade, a deeper hatred of war and those who are prolonging it will be felt. Whether this hatred will be vented on ourselves or on Germany remains to be seen. However, it is unlikely that Germany will succeed in forcing France into active hostilities against us, particularly as there will always be elements that remain true to their old alliance and these may be expected to rally to our side as soon as the defeat of Germany seems probable. In the French colonial possessions the situation is unclear. There are those colonies which from their strategic situation we cannot at present hope to control, and those over which we can expect to be able to exercise some form of control. In general, it seems unlikely that our earlier hopes of inducing the French colonies to continue to fight on our side spontaneously will be realised.' On Japan it noted 'Japan's attitude will continue to be menacing, and that her sympathies will be with our enemies.' For the United States it felt that 'There is no doubt that the sympathies of the vast majority of the American people are with us, and that they would view a German victory with the very gravest concern. American opinion is, however, somewhat divided at present as to the scale of assistance which should be given to us. Most seek to avoid actual intervention in the war, while doing everything possible short of this to hinder our enemies. To what extent we can count upon economic and financial support is still uncertain; on the one hand there is a genuine and wide-spread desire to do everything practicable to help us, although not necessarily gratis; on the other the fear that even with this help we may be defeated, and that America's own defences must have the first claim on all American resources. The full extent of American co-operation is likely to remain obscure until after the forthcoming Presidential election; all we can say at present is that it would be wrong to count upon the actual intervention of the United States at any stage, but that we are justified in expecting a large measure of financial and economic co-operation, provided America remains convinced of our ability to avoid defeat and to defeat Germany with such co-operation.'

Churchill's desire to go on the offensive whenever and wherever possible had already been demonstrated throughout the summer and early autumn. British forces had occupied a neutral Iceland and the Faroes, attacked the French fleet in north Africa as well as securing French ships in British controlled harbours, attempted to capture the vital port of Dakar which threatened Britain's Atlantic trade routes (although as a consequence the Free French forces were able to continue on and secure Vichy colonies in Equitorial Africa and then deploy for the Eritrean campaign in 1941), used political pressure to influence neutral countries and conducted initial commando operations on the Continent.

In his book "The Second World War", Winston Churchill noted in mid September 1940 `All the evidence of impending invasion multiplied. It was impossible to watch these growing preparations, week after week, in the photographs and reports without a sense of awe. A thing like this gets hold of you bit by bit. The enemy would not come unless he had solid assurance of victory and plans made with German thoroughness. Might there also not be surprises? All our night bombing was concentrated on the invasion ports, but the results of this bombing had disappointed me several times. The Chiefs of Staff were, on the whole, of the opinion that invasion was imminent, while I was sceptical. Nevertheless, it was impossible to quell that inward excitement which comes from the prolonged balancing of terrible things. Certainly we strained every nerve to be ready. Nothing was neglected that could be achieved by the care and ingenuity of our commanders, the vigilance of our now large and formidable armies, and the unquenchable and fearless spirit of our whole people`.

CHAPTER THREE: THE ROYAL NAVY

The Royal Navy had long been regarded as the guardian of the country's security. It was greatly feared and respected by its enemies, but now faced a dilemma in how to oppose another invasion attempt. Even before the start of the War the Admiralty had decided to adopt a defensive strategy in protecting the sea-lanes and preventing the enemy's surface fleet from breaking out, whilst establishing a blockade of the Continent. The maritime strategy adopted in 1939 mirrored that of 1914. In terms of priority the objectives were to:

- Defend the integrity of the United Kingdom,
- Cut off the enemy from the rest of the world and weaken its economy by blockade,
- To hold key points and areas overseas through zones of control and
- Bring supplies to the United Kingdom that is essential to its survival.

Its tactical doctrine, as formulated in the Fighting Instructions of 1939, was now made more flexible than ever before and stressed improvisation and initiative, stressing that offensive tactics were to be employed wherever possible. Even before 1939 there were indications that the old concept of how the strategy would be implemented now was not valid, but the extent of the changes, especially the impact of the air threat, were not fully realised until mid 1940.

The Admiralty's war plans were approved in January 1939 and issued to all naval commanders to enact when war was declared. They were framed to deal with a war against both Germany and Italy, with account taken of the unfriendly attitude of Japan. Paramount importance was given first to the home theatre and then the Mediterranean theatre, which secured the vital oil shipping routes from the Middle East (As in the First World War, France was to be the primary strength in this theatre). Third in importance was the Far East.

The Board of the Admiralty was tasked with being the strategic operations centre of the Navy, with its Navy Staff meeting daily to review reports and decide matters on which immediate action was required and its Plans Division tasked with planning of any future operations; the Director of Plans met with his Army and Air Force counterparts as the Joint Planning Committee to advise the Joint Chiefs of Staff. The Operations Division was responsible for the distribution of the Royal Navy's operational strength, its Trade Division controlled the merchant shipping (the Ministry of Shipping was responsible for the procurement and manning of these merchant ships) and organised its armament (by the end of 1940 some 3400 of 5500 ships had been armed), the Minesweeping Division was only formed in October 1939 and its Local Defence Division was formed in May 1939 for the defence of ports and bases.

Up until 1938 Rosyth, near Edinburgh, was to be the main base for the Home Fleet, as it had been at the end of the First World War. The main reasons for this choice were its location making it suitable for intercepting German warships trying to break out of the North Sea into the Atlantic, its existing port facilities and that its air defence could be easily integrated within existing arrangements for Edinburgh. However, this plan was soon re-examined and Scapa Flow, in the Orkneys, was adopted as the primary base, with Pentland Firth being a secondary choice, as these were considered to be better positioned and more able to counter the mine threat more effectively. The development of Scapa Flow as the main fleet base had been held up due to the decision in the mid 1930's to upgrade the fleet bases at Singapore and

Alexandria; this lack of resources was to continue well into 1941 (its vulnerability was demonstrated by the sinking of the battleship HMS Royal Oak in October 1939). In the first few months of the Second World War Loch Ewe and the Clyde estuary were also used as temporary anchorages for the Home Fleet, though these were poorly protected and badly located for operational requirements.

The Royal Navy was one of the largest navies in the World, having 15 battleships, 3 battle cruisers, 9 aircraft carriers, 11 heavy and 57 light cruisers, some 212 destroyers, 45 sloops, 58 corvettes and 73 submarines. Although there had been a building programme (2 battleships, 2 aircraft carriers, 12 light cruisers, some 62 destroyers, 14 sloops, all 58 corvettes and 22 submarines were built in 1939 and 1940) a substantial number of operational warships were from the First World War era (11 battleships, 3 battle cruisers, 2 aircraft carriers, 17 light cruisers, 69 destroyers, 1 sloop and 9 submarines); all of those however had been modernised. Not all of these ships would be operational at the same time and some would require significant time to be repaired or refitted. To date the Navy had not experienced a high loss rate (1 battleship, 2 aircraft carriers, 3 cruisers, 34 destroyers, 3 sloops, 1 corvette and 19 submarines), with new ships exceeding those lost.

From the outset of the War the Navy had managed to integrate its manpower reserves into the fleet, especially in bringing the reserve fleet up to operational levels, but its training programme had been hindered by changes in strategy, new equipment and new branches that were needed to address the growing needs of a modern warfare at sea. Those conscripted were usually only trained for the type of ship they were expected to be posted to. Drafting pools were soon established to provide the trained manpower necessary to keep the ships operational, while a scheme to call up those not covered by the National Defence Act (i.e. those under 18 or partially fit) for local defence of shore establishments was quite successful. The lack of a central training regime hampered efficiency but personnel selection generally worked well. Given the vulnerability of the main naval bases (Portsmouth, Plymouth and Chatham Divisions) to air attack it was decided early on to move as much of the training away (gunnery and engineering remained in place) with the main Divisions being used to accommodate the drafts for their ships. A number of holiday camps were taken over to accommodate the new recruits and basic training. In July anti-submarine training was relocated to Scotland and a sea training base established where every ship tasked with this role had to undergo a month's extensive training.

Appointed before the War, due mainly to his seniority, the First Sea Lord, Sir Dudley Pound, had previously been the Commander in Chief Mediterranean Fleet. It was felt within the Service that he brought to Whitehall a great deal of experience not only of high naval command at sea but also of the working of every side of the Admiralty. He had previously been the Director of Naval Plans, Chief of Staff in the Mediterranean Fleet, commander the Atlantic based battle cruiser squadron and in the early 1930's had been the Second Sea Lord, mainly responsible for administration. He was not, however, regarded as a great strategist or tactician, and was prone to try interfering with ongoing naval operations instead of allowing his subordinates to command unimpeded (a trait he shared with Churchill); he often came into conflict with Admiral Forbes who, as Commander in Chief of the Home Fleet, was the senior Navy officer tasked with the actual naval defence of the country. This Admiral had been appointed in 1938 and was regarded as being technically able, outspoken and forthright. Admiral Tovey was Admiral Forbes` second in command and was to succeed him in December, later to be responsible for most of the operations that brought the Kriegsmarine to its knees. Rear Admiral Curteis in Sheerness was regarded high enough to become second in command of the Home Fleet in 1941. The Flag Officers of Nore, Portsmouth and Western Approaches Commands were in place from the outset. It was on these officers, together with the squadron and flotilla commanders, that the duty of destroying the invasion fleets and follow up shipping would fall.

It was vital that the anti-invasion operations be co-ordinated to ensure maximum effectiveness. In theory the Admiralty, while having the right to issue orders directly to any ship or command unit, limits its instructions to the strategic movements and dispositions of its own forces, supplying commanders in chief and subordinate flag officers the plans it wants executed and intelligence on enemy intentions. The tactical conduct of operations is normally left to the flag officers concerned. In practice, however, conditions of modern warfare would make constant and uniform adherence to these principles difficult. In November 1939 Admiral Pound reiterated his determination that commanders in chief should normally be left free to conduct their own operations without constant intervention from Whitehall. On 30 June the Admiralty noted the need for better liaison with the other armed forces, especially the Army.

When the allies commanded the English Channel it was accepted that enemy invasion could only have realistically been made across the North Sea. Now, with the loss of France and the Low Countries, the task of protecting Britain's extensive coastline was made even harder by the German occupation of the continental coastline from Norway to Spain, in the process turning the Channel into a potential trap for the Royal Navy. The English Channel, however, was not to be dominated by the Germans as the Royal Navy continued to undertake operations throughout its length.

On 28 May 1940 the Admiralty issued its principles in countering the invasion threat. It correctly expected that the enemy would attempt a landing by choosing the shortest route, with diversionary operations mounted at other points. They expected the Germans would make the greatest possible effort in these operations and be prepared to accept catastrophic losses to achieve their object. To defeat such an undertaking the Admiralty stressed the importance of attacking before the invasion craft left their ports. The gathering of intelligence and reconnaissance on such craft and dispositions was vital, while air attack, mining and shore bombardment were to be employed on the ports. In case "attack before departure" was impossible or unsuccessful it was essential to "attack at the point of arrival". As this latter point was not known the Navy was forced to dispose the Navy's resources to cover the wide area from the Wash to Newhaven. The Admiralty expected that the major ships of the German surface fleet would be used in diversionary operations (another correct assumption) and that these should also be engaged.

To deal with an invasion fleet at sea the Admiralty decided that a striking force of four destroyer flotillas (36 ships at full strength), with the support of light cruisers, would be required. They also stated that the maximum number of escort ships that could be spared from normal duties should be allotted to this role; additionally, a number of small craft (the Auxiliary Patrol) should be collected immediately to provide close inshore observation. As early as 15 May new anti invasion striking forces were established at the Humber, Harwich, Sheerness and Dover and based on the destroyer flotillas. At the end of May the Admiralty stated that the best way to defeat an invasion was to hit as hard as possible, as soon as possible. To achieve this aim the Royal Navy was to undertake offensive patrols, bombardments and minelaying, with most of these activities to be done at night due to the air threat. The Admiralty ordered destroyer sweeps to support the Auxiliary Patrol Service in the English Channel; anti submarine trawlers were to use their underwater detection system to hear for the engines of invasion craft from patrol stations four miles off the English shore, while inshore the Auxiliary Patrol were to report and attack any enemy craft encountered. The Auxiliary Patrol generally consisted of local sea going craft manned by volunteers and were lightly armed. A system of flares, rockets and wireless was established to ensure rapid transmission of reports ashore.

Flag Officer Dover, in common with other operational commands, observed three levels of readiness:

- Third level encompassed normal naval operations
- Second level had destroyers and cruisers at sea, torpedo boats at instant readiness between 21.30 and 06.00 and at one hour's notice for the rest, with all commanding officers to be available at short notice
- First level had all destroyers and cruisers at sea, all torpedo boats at instant readiness, all Auxiliary Patrol craft on inshore patrol and all minelayers not on operations to be at thirty minutes notice.

That Flag Officer instituted two destroyer patrol routes covering the area to the north east and south west of Dungeness respectively; supporting these patrols the Auxiliary Patrol had five inshore and two offshore patrol craft covering Rye Bay, nine and four craft respectively covering Dungeness to Folkestone and six and eight craft respectively deployed to cover Deal to North Foreland.

In June Flag Officer Portsmouth instituted "Operation JB". When the first indications of a landing taking place were transmitted to him, a signal would go to all operational warships under his command to raise steam and move to standby positions at anchor off Spithead and in the Solent (the body of water between Portsmouth and the Isle of Wight). When ordered to they were to sail to the invasion area in the best possible tactical formation, not too large to be unwieldy but not too small as to be ineffective, with speed of attack to be essential. Naval forces from Portland were to co-operate if possible, but Portsmouth based units were not to wait for them. At the end of June that Flag Officer also instituted "Operation JC", nightly sweeps of the enemy coast by Portsmouth based destroyers, along a line running from both Cherbourg to Le Havre and between Le Havre and Dieppe. The Auxiliary Patrol within this Command's area operated from Newhaven and Littlehampton.

Not to be outdone Flag officer Western Approaches, in Plymouth, had "Operation GL", an eastward sweep by destroyers from a line running from the Lizard to Ushant. For example, on 23 September six British and Polish destroyers sailed at 20.30 hours, returning at dawn.

The Admiralty expected that even with as little as twenty four hours notice of invasion, forces could be moved from the northern bases to the threatened point in good time. The Royal Navy had already demonstrated its ability to do this during the Dunkirk operations, with destroyers detached from the Home Fleet in Scotland reaching Dover in a day. Atlantic convoy escorts could also be detached and reach the invasion area in less than two days as they only went as far as a line 300 miles west of Ireland; the regular east coast convoy shuttle, sailing between Southend in Essex and Methil in Fife, Scotland, could also lose its small escort. On 25 September there were seven convoys at sea in home waters – three Atlantic outward bound from Liverpool and four along the east coast with a total of eighteen escorts (in early July trans Atlantic convoys were re-routed from the south western approaches to the north west approaches due to the threats posed by German control of the French coast).

In terms of its main striking force, the Admiralty wanted a number of battleships to be based either at Plymouth or in the Clyde, in order to counter possible actions against the Irish Republic; Admiral Forbes considered that a strong Northern Patrol and a powerful covering force based on Scapa Flow provided the best defensive option in protecting the trans-Atlantic routes (a weaker Western Patrol was established on 2 August). If the enemy showed signs of moving an invasion fleet across the North Sea the Home Fleet was to move to Rosyth. By July the Admiralty had come to an agreement with Admiral Forbes that allowed for the heavy ships of the Home Fleet to go into either the English Channel or southern North Sea only if the German Navy's own heavy ships were present there. This would not have happened as those ships were assigned diversionary operations off Scotland, something the Royal Navy was not aware of or indeed of the serious losses suffered by the German Navy during the Norwegian campaign and which now significantly restricted their combat potential. The two aircraft carriers available to the Royal Navy would have been of limited value as their primary roles were still reconnaissance and attacking enemy capital ships in order that the Navy's own heavy forces could reach and engage them.

By mid September the Royal Navy had available for initial operations against the invasion the following ships (see appendix 9 for location details):
- To attack from the north - 5 light cruisers, 24 destroyers, 3 submarines and 20 light attack craft
- To attack from the west - 3 light cruisers, 19 destroyers, 6 submarines and 27 light attack craft.

The possible deployment of these forces can be ascertained by looking at the night of 8 September, when two strike groups from both Sheerness and Harwich, each of a light cruiser and three destroyers, conducted sweeps of the Channel looking for invasion craft seen moving south during the day. These groups had their navigation assisted by lighting certain lighthouses and lightships, while tugs and rescue craft were held ready. In addition a destroyer flotilla sailed from Portsmouth and motor torpedo boats from Harwich operated closer to the enemy coast. Their effectiveness in destroying the invasion fleets in daylight could have been severely hampered by the Luftwaffe, who had already more or less closed the Channel to daylight shipping, and German naval plans for extensive mine and submarine barriers to protect the landing zones. However, catching the fleets during the night would have casued much confusion, possibly to both sides. The naval forces to the north of the invasion area would have to operate from Sheerness and Harwich as other ports were too far away to provide a quick response or too small to support such operations. Of these two bases Sheerness was particularly handicapped by the shallow waters of the Thames and Medway Estuaries, which soon became vulnerable to mines laid by aircraft. The main forces to the west would have operated from Portsmouth, Plymouth and Portland; though the latter was handicapped by the lack of proper base facilities to keep ships operational, the other two were also susceptible to aircraft laid mines in their narrow approaches and submarines lurking offshore. Another important concern was the air defence of these naval bases - Sheerness and Portland, in particular, were poorly protected by anti aircraft defences, having only light guns deployed to supplement the ships' own weapons.

The effectiveness of the Royal Navy largely depended on the quality of its ships. As already mentioned, most of its capital warships dated from the First World War era and generally suffered from slow speed, but were still to be feared for their firepower; newer battleships had been ordered in 1934 but would not be ready in time; the cruisers were generally more modern in design and were expected to provide the strength in both the firepower and speed necessary to operate in the invasion area. In an effort to counter the lack of cruisers the Royal Navy had decided to fall back on the armoured merchant cruiser, large merchant and cruise ships fitted with a number of six inch guns, which had been first used in the First World War. These were far from ideal but fitted the premise that "something is better than nothing" and were deployed on convoy escort, far away from the invasion area. Although many destroyers had been damaged during the Dunkirk evacuation they had performed well enough to lift a large proportion of the Army. The main strength of these ships was their speed which, coupled with daring leadership, would also play an important role in defeating the invasion and preventing the landing of follow up forces. The motor torpedo boats available at the time were smaller than their German counterparts and suffered from temperamental engines, vulnerable as petrol not diesel driven and were more lightly armed than their counterparts.

The Navy's effectiveness also suffered in two important areas - its ship borne anti aircraft fire control and its signals intelligence operations were both considered largely ineffective, the former would improve but the latter was more of a problem due to a pre war organisation that was stll reluctant to modernise and adapt. All these problems would have severely tested the Navy's ability to either destroy the invasion fleets or disrupt the following flow of supplies and reinforcements, while also accepting the commitment of enduring heavy losses that such operations would no doubt result in.

Unlike the other services the Navy had to accept a long repair time for its damaged ships in bases and port facilities that were also harder to duplicate in areas protected from attack (for example, the light cruiser HMS Galatea was in dry dock for about a month after striking a mine). The Navy`s main repair and refit bases were Chatham, Plymouth, Liverpool and in the Tyne, with London, Southampton and Swansea undertaking minor work. It was also making use of the wider civilian shipbuilding and ship repair industry.

The Navy had an established system of depots serving the fleet. Fuel depots were located at Invergordon, Greenock (Torpedo Factory), Mountblow (Clyde), Llanreath (Pembroke), Swanpool (Falmouth), Rosyth, Portsdown (Portsmouth), Dover and Lyness. Its armaments depots were at Belfast, Kilnappy (Derry), Bandeath (Stirling), Beith (Ayrshire), Coulport (Clyde), Crombie (Clyde), Dalbeattie (South Scotland), Broughton Moor (Cumbria), Charlesfield (Scotland), Wrabness (Harwich), Chatham (Torpedo Depot), Chattenden (Chatham), Upnor (Chatham), Grain (Sheerness), Woolwich, Gosport, Marchwood (Southampton), Weymouth

(Torpedo Depot), Bull Point (Plymouth), Ernesettle (Plymouth), Trecwn (Fishguard) (mines), Milford Haven (Mine Depot).

Nevertheless, as already mentioned, by mid September the Navy had already started to take the offensive by raiding some of the invasion ports with their cruisers, destroyers and light forces, these elements expecting to be supplemented by the monitor HMS Erebus and the gunboat HMS Locust, both of which had been moved to Sheerness specifically for this role. The deployment of HMS Erebus is an example of Churchill's involvement in operational matters. On 25 August he demanded that she be used to attack the German heavy coastal guns, her armoured deck being protection against bombing. His Naval staff had to remind him that it took time to work up the crew in order to achieve the degree of gunnery accuracy that would make such an operation worthwhile, also that she was very slow and rather un-manoeuvrable so that even an armoured deck may not be enough to protect her. Her first attempt was the night of 28 September, escorted by two destroyers and two tugs, but was defeated by heavy weather. A second attempt two nights later resulted in seventeen 15 inch shells being fired at Calais, though results were not reported as the assigned spotter aircraft could not communicate with the ships! However, the outcome was completely different when the battleship HMS Revenge, supported by a destroyer flotilla and a diversion force of two cruisers, shelled Cherbourg on the night of 10 October. The success of this operation was put down to thorough planning, the manoeuvrability of the ships and an air raid laid on by the RAF to mask the bombardment. These operations demonstrated that the Royal Navy remained a potent threat to any invading force.

Another type of operation planned was Operation Lucid. This involved two groups of destroyers escorting an old tanker each from Sheerness and Portsmouth to attack Boulogne and Calais respectively. The plan was to send the tankers into the harbours where they would be turned into fireships to destroy the collected invasion craft there. This was planned for 25 September, though failed as both tankers broke down, causing the Operation to be abandoned. This further demonstrated the desire to consider any type of offensive action.

Unlike the other two services the Royal Navy would have to rely mostly on its own resources as there were only a handful of ships from the Royal Canadian Navy present in the United Kingdom as Atlantic convoy escorts, while many of the allied naval ships that had escaped from occupied Europe were of little immediate operational value due either to crew or equipment shortages. The Royal Canadian Navy had only 6 British built destroyers and 4 minesweepers in September 1939, although 64 corvettes were ordered in February 1940 and were being built in Canada. It undertook its own training but its wartime expansion was not very efficient and its initial performance was poor. Both the British and Canadian authorities felt that the Royal Canadian Navy should be allowed to expand at a moderate pace, but the outcome of the continental campaigns upset this timescale. In early 1940 the Canadian Government ordered 64 corvettes and 28 minesweepers, while 7 of the old American Lend Lease destroyers were allocated to the Canadians in the autumn. By this time new naval bases were also being developed along its eastern seaboard.

The allied ships, on paper, provided 11% of the operational destroyers, 35% of the escort ships and 26% of the submarines. A significant number of the destroyers and escorts were assembled at Portsmouth and would have been invaluable against the invasion fleets. Many of these crews were experienced and, like their air force compatriots, shared the desire to destroy the enemy who had taken their homelands. A large number of these allied ships required refitting and re-training to once again make them operational, not least in understanding how they were to fit in with the Royal Navy's operational doctrine. The Royal Australian Navy had deployed significant resources to the Middle East. Canada, Australia and New Zealand were, as with the other armed forces, dependent on the United Kingdom for much of their training, ships and equipment. However, they were, together with other colonial naval forces, able to take over responsibility for their own local defence, releasing units of the Royal Navy for operations elsewhere.

The Navy's own air force - the Fleet Air Arm - was mainly shore based and equipped with a small number of reconnaissance and attack aircraft of varying quality, which would be nevertheless be pressed into action alongside the RAF, though the Admiralty reserved the right of how and when it would deploy. The Arm had operated within its means during the Norwegian and Dunkirk campaigns and had proved quite effective, sinking a light cruiser in one of the first successful air attacks on a significant warship in the war. Despite its service in the First World War, the Fleet Air Arm was only reborn in 1937, although the Navy had provided personnel and ships up to then the Royal Air Force had been in command and provided maintenance personnel afloat. Until the early 1930's the conventional view prevailed that naval aircraft would only be able to assist in bringing about a decision at sea and could not strike decisive blows by themselves or defend the fleet alone. In 1931 the first Rear Admiral, Aircraft Carriers, was appointed and the role for such aircraft re-appraised, though the availability of modern aircraft was relegated in priority. The doctrine of 1939 summarised the duties of naval aircraft to provide fleet reconnaissance, attack enemy warships with a view of reducing their speed and manoeuvrability, to help protect the fleet from air and submarine attack and provide spotting for naval or shore bombardments. In 1938 the Navy increased its training of aircrew and maintenance personnel, though their availability was still inadequate as shown by the fact that in December 1940 some 2000 RAF personnel were still assigned to the Fleet Air Arm; however, it was strong enough to provide three naval air squadrons to the RAF for aerial minelaying. Pilot training was undertaken by the RAF at Luton, Elmdon (Essex), Sydenham (Oxfordshire) and Netheravon (Wiltshire).

From the outset of the War the Royal Navy had established a number of defensive minefields in the North Sea and English Channel, the most important being those running along the east coast from the Orkneys to Dungeness - over 3600 mines were laid in the Dover Straits and between Folkestone and Cap Gris Nez (on 3 September two new lines were laid across the direct Calais to Dover route), while more smaller minefields were established to protect harbours and major estuaries. In August the 1st Minelaying Squadron, consisting of four converted merchant ships, completed both the east coast and southern Irish Sea barriers (over 8900 mines), while a new northern barrier was laid in September. To keep their own ports and sea lanes open from enemy mines the Navy had recognised its lack of minesweepers and adapted a large number of trawlers and drifters, still largely manned by volunteer civilian crews, to undertake the bulk of the minesweeper tasks. It was these vessels that would be needed for the critical tasks of keeping the base ports open and breaking through the German minefields that were protecting their landings, so allowing the Navy's warships better chances of getting closer to the vulnerable enemy shipping, as well as allowing them a greater freedom of action.

The Navy's submarine service was hampered by extensive enemy air and surface patrolling in coastal waters, the availability of an airborne depth charge and the enemy's ability to locate many of our submarines through their own wireless interception service. Between June and August 1940 six submarines were lost and as a result the Admiralty abandoned inshore patrols and redeployed them to intercept enemy submarines in the Bay of Biscay and North Sea. Initial training continued at HMS Dolphin (Portsmouth), then Blyth for practical experience and the Clyde for operational experience. Allied submarines made up almost a quarter of those available at this time.

The enemy's superiority in intelligence at this time was put down to the regular and efficient air reconnaissance of our naval bases and the skilful work of their wireless interception service. That the latter should have continued for so long was mainly attributed to misplaced confidence in the security of the Admiralty's ciphers. It was only in mid 1940 that it was realised that the Germans were reading these messages and as a result these were changed in August, proving to be a substantial setback for German naval strategy.

The Royal Navy had learned some hard lessons in the Norwegian campaign, not least due to the Navy being caught unprepared and German retention of the initiative. The first lesson concerned the effect of air power. It was undeniable that if effective air cover was lacking then warships could not operate for a long period without sustaining crippling losses; the second lesson was that if a secure base could not be established in an overseas theatre of war a land campaign cannot prosper; thirdly the need for careful planning and preparation before launching a combined operation. The most fundamental lesson was that the command structure must be clear and workable. Although the campaign had been a failure it did confirm that the Royal Navy had conducted most of its operations successfully and had generally out fought the enemy, crippling their surface fleet in the process. Its successful evacuation of British and allied forces, royalty, key economic and war materials from the continent had shown its flexibility, courage and determination and, as such, maintained its reputation as a force to be respected.

CHAPTER FOUR: THE ROYAL AIR FORCE

Of the three armed services available to protect the United Kingdom in the summer of 1940, the Royal Air Force (RAF) was the one that most were looking at to be this country's first line of defence; indeed, it was the main one already actively engaging the enemy on a daily basis.

In 1940 the RAF was organised into five main Commands - Bomber, Fighter, Coastal, Training and Barrage Balloon. In July 1936 Fighter and Bomber Commands had been set up by splitting up the Air Defence of Great Britain (ADGB), an organisation that would be set up again later in the War.

Although the RAF had one of the few assets left, in Bomber Command, that was available to truly take the offensive in the summer of 1940, such strategic designs were expected to be put aside to assist wholeheartedly in repelling the actual invasion when it came. Unfortunately, this vital task was still resisted by the RAF's senior commanders, even in these darkest of days, as they saw it as a diversion from their main purpose. Nevertheless, Bomber Command had been playing a major supporting role during this period, devoting a major effort to attacking the Luftwaffe's airfields and infrastructure as well as the assembling invasion fleet (ten per cent of the latter was destroyed or badly damaged by air attack up to the middle of September). Despite this effort bombing accuracy was still generally poor and numbers of aircraft despatched relatively small; all this would have to change when invasion occurred, especially as all available aircraft would be required to attack both sea and land targets around the clock from its air bases along the east coast. The Command had initially favoured daylight formation based operations but the devastating losses early in the War, due mainly to the aircrafts' poor defensive armament and air speed, had forced their hand into switching to night operations for their heavy bombers, while the lighter bombers continued "hit and run" operations during the day.

On 19 September the Air Ministry re-confirmed the RAF's main roles in the event of invasion. These involved the reconnaissance of enemy ports, attacking invading troops and shipping and the defence of vital areas against attack. The Air Officer Commanding Bomber Command was to retain operational control of his forces, with the exception of those in Northern Ireland and those assigned to the Army in Scotland. If there was a surprise landing the General in charge of that Army Command could appeal directly to 2 Group (or 1 Group if in the north) for use of a squadron, once a suitable target was known. The Air Officers' Commanding were to ensure that communications with the nearest Army Command Headquarters were kept open to facilitate this, backed up by undertaking air reconnaissance. It would be up to the Air Officer Commanding to judge whether he had sufficient information and aircraft to attack specific targets effectively.

In the case of a full invasion the Commander in Chief Home Forces was to approach the Air Officer Commanding Bomber Command directly with a list of targets he wanted attacked and he was to ensure that a prompt and adequate response was provided to the Army. All bomber operations at sea were to be co-ordinated with the Air Ministry and the Admiralty, while the Air Ministry was to decide when and how to implement Operation Banquet (see Appendix 10 for further details). 49 Bomber Squadron's diary noted the actions to be taken after receiving an invasion alert: all aircraft in operational squadrons not already detailed for operations during the next twelve hours were to be bombed up and brought to standby, while the aircrews were to remain on the station; the stations were to inform Group headquarters of the numbers of aircraft they were prepared to receive from the Flying Training Command and 22 Group under the Banquet Scheme; station defence personnel, both ground and anti aircraft, were kept ready for immediate action by day and night.

At the start of the War RAF tactical support doctrine emphasised attacks on the enemy's air power and its infrastructure, whilst support for the Army emphasised interdiction of an enemy's reserves and supplies and disruption of its command and control systems; close air support over the battlefield was viewed as a temporary measure. All this related back to the RAF's doctrine at the end of the last War and as such ignored the reality that it no longer had the capability to implement it effectively.

Fighter Command was, of course, to be found in the forefront of the country's defence and was the most effective and modern fighting force the RAF had available. The expansion scheme had enabled the Command to modernise both its aircraft and command and control organisation, bringing together all elements of national air defence. It had probably the best command and control organisation in the world, with a centre at Command Headquarters filtering the reports to provide accurate and timely passing of information down to the Groups (having tactical command of their area) and Sectors (having command of their assigned squadrons).

With the success of the German offensives it was necessary to expand the Command's responsibilities to the north and west of the country. Losses sustained during the Continental campaigns coupled with almost continuous combat throughout the following summer months and the need to cover the country's long coastline had already stretched the capability of the Command near to breaking point, especially with regard to aircrew. Fortunately, the Command was able to rest and re-vitalise its squadrons in quieter sectors to the north and west of Britain, as the Luftwaffe was unable to reach these sectors in sufficient force. Nevertheless Air Chief Marshal Sir Hugh Dowding contemplated in private during this summer that if his losses became unsustainable, and if invasion was considered imminent, then he was determined to withdraw his Command northwards to re-group in order that his forces could be in a better position to oppose the Luftwaffe and fulfil its primary role of home defence.

On 14 September Headquarters Fighter Command produced a memorandum on the tasks of the Command in repelling an invasion. It correctly noted that the main feature of the preliminary struggle for air supremacy was that heavy bomber and fighter attacks would be directed against airfields, aircraft factories and other important objectives, with the object of destroying the fighter squadrons either in the air or on the ground. It confirmed that these attacks were to be met in accordance with the general principles on which the Command had been organised and trained, but noted the important responsibility of also protecting the Royal Navy and its bases from enemy attack. During the period of assembling, embarking and sailing of the invasion forces the Command was to cover the operations of the other Commands and Royal Navy as best as possible, noting the limitations that range and aircraft availability would have. The memorandum noted that the approach and landing of the invasion forces would become, temporarily, the focus of the air battle, with the enemy probably seeking to land troops by air as well as by sea, covered by intensive bomber attacks against the defences and with strong fighter support. The primary aim of the Command was to destroy enemy troop carrying aircraft, subject to the continued protection of the Royal Navy. Further tasks the Command must also be prepared to undertake, in order of importance, were:

- Providing fighter cover to bomber and "Banquet" aircraft attacking the enemy's invasion craft
- Attacking those invasion craft containing tanks or artillery with cannon armed fighters
- Attacking enemy tanks that have landed with cannon armed fighters
- Provide fighter protection to own troops being attacked by enemy dive bombers.

In his book "The Second World War", Winston Churchill noted that 'September, like June, was a month of extreme opposing stresses for those who bore the responsibility for British war direction. The air battle raged with its greatest ferocity and rose steadily to its climax. We could not tell whether even heavier air attacks were to be expected or how long they would go on. The fine weather facilitated daylight fighting on the largest scale. Hitherto we had welcomed this but by the second week in September a slight but definite change in outlook was noticed. I now had the distinct feeling that a break in the weather would no longer be regarded as a misfortune. In my talks with Air Chief Marshal Dowding, the sense of Fighter Command being at its utmost strain was evident. The weekly aircraft figures showed we had adequate numbers, provided the weight of the hostile attack did not increase. But the physical and mental stresses upon the pilots were not reflected on the paper charts. For all their sublime devotion, often facing odds of five or six to one, there are limits to human endurance'.

In 1936 Coastal Command was formed when the Royal Navy's Fleet Air Arm was split away. The Air Ministry directed that the new Command's primary roles would be trade protection, reconnaissance and co-operation with the Royal Navy. Unfortunately it was low down in the list of priorities in getting resources and as a result was not really ready for extensive operations in 1939. The aircraft were generally not suitable for their tasks, the Anson being unable to reach Norway for example. One important concern was the provision of a viable command organisation, with the Group headquarters structure only being completed after War was declared. Despite these problems it co-operated closely with the Royal Navy and maintained continuous air patrols over coastal convoys and off enemy coastlines, these tasks remaining unglamorous though vital. The shortage of aircraft meant that Fighter Command was often called upon to provide air defence of convoys and naval bases, while Bomber Command attacked enemy warships. The Norwegian Campaign had posed a hitherto unconsidered quandary for the Command - it was not trained, equipped or prepared for offensive action. In May the Command was made primarily responsible for reconnaissance over the enemy's coasts to check on the build up of invasion forces, while also supporting Bomber Command's coastal mine laying and bombing operations of the invasion ports. Although not properly designed or prepared for the role, the available aircraft were now expected to attack any enemy vessels encountered (between June and September 1940 the RAF flew nearly 2600 sorties to attack shipping, losing 45 aircraft but sinking only two ships). Indeed Coastal Command should be in the best position to first sight either the invasion fleet or the main German battle fleet as they sailed and would, in any case, be brought directly into offensive operations with the other Commands to counter the invasion regardless of the risks involved. The Command had instituted a number of patrol routes over the North Sea and English Channel, with four of these routes mounted between Cherbourg and Dunkirk, mostly conducted at dusk.

Whilst it was vitally important that the Training Command and the RAF's equipment support organisations remained capable of the quick and efficient repair or provision of new aircraft and aircrew to replace the heavy losses expected, Training Command was also allocated an anti invasion role (Operation Banquet), which could include the use of chemical weapons. With this latter issue in mind the RAF had developed plans before the War to respond to gas attacks and had undertaken training with converted water tanks attached to certain aircraft. In the summer of 1940 sixteen squadrons (two Wellington, five Blenheim, four Battle and five Lysander) had been earmarked to deploy mustard gas using a mixture of spray tanks and bombs, if ordered to do so. On 20 June there were 200 spray tanks available for the Lysanders and 800 for the Battles and Blenheims, each aircraft having two tanks each. At this time there were about 30,000 30-pound bombs and 9,000 250-pound filled bombs available, with a monthly production of 8,000 and 2,000 bombs respectively.

The last operational Command - Barrage Balloon - had continued to expand throughout this period but was still able to replace the large number of balloons lost from all causes and so remained an important part of the air defence network, co-ordinating closely with Fighter Command and the Army's Anti Aircraft Command. The personnel were also allocated ground defence roles but had not received much in the way of equipment or training to meet this contingency. The same could be said of the ground personnel on the various RAF bases and at the supply depots, from which quick reaction forces were organised and equipped as best as possible.

Initially the RAF had to rely on its own resources. The Royal Canadian Air Force (RCAF) was heavily committed to the development and administration of the British Commonwealth Air Training Plan, which allowed for the uninterrupted training of British and Commonwealth aircrew in Canada from April 1940. In addition to its responsibility for air defence, this made it necessary to retain the greater part of the RCAF at home. Only three operational squadrons could be spared for overseas service in the early months of the war. The first of these units was 110 Army Co-operation (Auxiliary) Squadron RCAF, arriving in Britain in February 1940, and began training with the intention of accompanying the Canadian divisions to France. Four months later, when the war situation was extremely critical, 112 Army Co-operation (Auxiliary) Squadron RCAF and 1 Fighter Squadron RCAF, reinforced by personnel from 115 (Auxiliary) Squadron RCAF, also came to Britain. The fall of France relegated the two Army Co-operation squadrons to a long period of waiting, but 1 Fighter Squadron was to be fully involved in the Battle of Britain.

A large number of the foreign forces evacuated to the United Kingdom were aircrew, some with their aircraft. Many of these were sent on to Canada to improve their capabilities but the more competent and aggressive, notably the Poles and Czechs, were brought into first line service with four fighter and three bomber squadrons as soon as they could be made operational. Initially, the Air Ministry and Royal Air Force were opposed to using these foreign assets, based mainly on ill formed judgements and reports on the behaviour and operations of these forces in the recent campaigns. The pace and importance of modern air combat meant that the Royal Air Force had little room to make mistakes and so the decision to re-equip, train and deploy these additional resources was resisted for as long as possible. On 14 July Sir Hugh Dowding, commanding Fighter Command, expressed strong reservations about the infiltration of foreign pilots into British squadrons. He claimed that pilot morale was the greatest asset he possessed and, unless he could be assured of their fighting spirit, he would rather do without their services. The subsequent service provided by these foreign pilots would soon quash these fears.

The RAF had sent two air groups to France with the British Expeditionary Force (BEF) - the Advanced Air Striking Force and the Air Component of the Field Force. The former contained light bombers whilst the latter was subordinate to the BEF and provided reconnaissance and fighter squadrons. This format was a direct descendent of how the RAF had operated on the Western Front in the First World War. Despite some successes, especially the fighters, these forces were unable to operate as proposed. The ground support aircraft had been largely overwhelmed and were only able to cause delays to the German columns, while the reconnaissance aircraft were useful but vulnerable.

A report completed after Dunkirk noted with concern that there was a quick breakdown in the communications network, allowing the initiative to pass from the RAF, not helped by some requests for assistance having to go through the Air Ministry in London. There was also a problem in the turn around of aircraft between operations - ten to fifteen minutes for fighters and twenty minutes for bombers, depending on the numbers involved and availability of personnel - so that the situation on the ground would almost certainly have changed and opportunities passed. It also noted with concern the large amount of vehicles needed when squadrons were forced to move. Despite the intended mobile operations of the two air groups very little thought had been given to the actual requirements during their relocation and the amount of co-ordination required to ensure they remained operationally effective. The logistics organisation had also failed to deliver once the panzers broke through, though as their vehicles were often commandeered for other tasks during the campaign this was not all their fault. The speed of the German advance had also made ineffective the network of navigational beacons used for night operations, while the recovery and repair of damaged aircraft was often impossible for the same reason, leading to the inopportune loss of much needed aircraft. The report recommended self-sealing petrol tanks and better armour protection for light bombers given the unexpectedly fierce German anti aircraft defences encountered. One problem not noted by the RAF, but by the Army, was the lack of co-ordination between the two services at airfields with the situation often arising that when the airfields were abandoned due to the enemy's advance the Army personnel assigned to its defence were not informed. This situation was less likely to occur now as station and sector commanders had integrated ground defence and local counter attack forces into their command and control organisation. Despite its losses, Fighter Command had come out of the campaign with credit - its leaders had proved themselves; it had gained much needed combat experience and as a result retained a high morale.

The War Office and Air Ministry interpreted the Luftwaffe's employment of air power over the battlefield differently. The former requested dive bombers and even went as far as calling for an Army Air Arm as the RAF was unable or unwilling to provide the resources, while the latter argued that attaining air superiority and degrading the enemy's command and control infrastructure enabled effective close air support. In a sense both were right.

To better co-ordinate operations with the Army, and given the lessons learnt from recent operations, a RAF Operations Room had been established at the Rear Headquarters Home Forces in London. Its main role was to reduce the time taken to supply air support by maintaining an up to date record of enemy movements on the ground, allotting tasks and objectives to bombers, arrange and co-ordinate reconnaissance missions, submit requests for additional support and arrange with Fighter Command for fighter cover. It was also to ensure that it kept the RAF's High Command and Air Ministry apprised of developments. Each Army Command and Corps headquarters had smaller organisations. A staff exercise in July found that this arrangement worked well. In December the RAF established the Army Co-operation Command as a result of this work.

A vital component to the efficiency of the air defence was the Radio Detection Finding (RDF) organisation (later to be known as Radar). Tests in the mid 1930s found it possible to detect aircraft at a distance using radio waves. From June 1936 a chain of detection stations were constructed around the eastern and southern coasts of England and made the responsibility of the RAF in 1938. There were two types of station: Chain Home High, providing cover at high altitude with a range of one hundred and twenty miles, and Chain Home Low, providing low level cover with a range of fifty miles. In addition mobile units were available with a range of ninty miles, some serving with the Anti Aircraft Command. Tests in the summer of 1939 found the system worked well. The Battle of Britain was to show how hard it was to knock out these stations by bombing.

The "Phoney War" and subsequent campaign had allowed the RAF time to revise, modify and adopt tactics and equipment to better meet the needs of a modern air war; a process that had began with its own expansion scheme in 1936. The most important aspects of that scheme were:

- A preference for modern all metal monoplanes,
- An improved engine design,
- Production of duplicate factory facilities (largely based on the car industry),
- Better use of modern technology (especially in the development of a Radio Detection Finding (RDF) system)
- An accelerated programme of building new airfields, particularly in East Anglia for its bomber force, training and storage sites and
- The formation of the RAF Volunteer Reserve to bolster the regular and Auxiliary Air Forces

On 14 May 1940 a Ministry of Aircraft Production was formed from the Air Ministry's research and production departments. Under the leadership of the dynamic Lord Beaverbrook the new organisation brought together all possible production resources and maximised the output of aircraft. It was agreed to concentrate production on five main types - the Wellington, Whitley and Blenheim bombers, and Spitfire and Hurricane fighters. Between February and May 1940 4,638 aircraft were planned (866 fighters) and 3,939 produced (899 fighters); between June and August 1940 the figures were 4,111 (903) planned and 4,857 (1,418) produced. These figures show just how well the new organisation worked in so short a space of time.

Although still strong as a force, and respected by its enemies, the RAF would require all its resources to cope with the great number and variety of tasks that would be demanded of it. The most important of these were:

- Maintaining air superiority over the threatened areas
- Co-ordinating bomber and fighter missions
- Co-operating with the Army in their operations, and
- Protecting important installations (notably ports, war industry factories, airfields and communication centres).

This would have been made even more difficult with the probable loss of airfields and, more importantly, radar stations in the south of England coupled with the probable dislocation of the Observer Corps, upon which it would have had to rely more on as gaps appeared in the vital radar network (Rye, Fairlight, Beachy Head and Pevensey stations were immediately vulnerable to invasion). The RAF had used twenty three mobile radar units in France, half taken from anti aircraft units, and had these plus others in reserve to help cover any gaps in the coverage, though the quality and range of these sets were not as high as the established stations, especially over land. The commanders of the static radar stations were issued instructions on what to do if attacked following an invasion. It was important that sufficient RAF personnel to work the equipment and the complete Army guard were to remain at their posts until either the station was overrun or was unable to continue functioning. It was also important that the secret equipment be destroyed so that the enemy would not learn its full range of abilities. Station commanders had the authorisation to evacuate important specialists if the situation dictated it, with them moving on foot to the nearest nodal point, where they were to be transported to a suitable rendezvous for subsequent collection by their own Group headquarters.

The RAF also had a signals intercept service, set up in March 1940 at Hawkinge and obtained its first intercepts from German pilots in May 1940. The unit initially had problems as no German speakers were assigned, but soon began to provide to the Air Ministry excellent intelligence. In June it briefly moved to Fairlight, near Hastings, before settling in August at West Kingsdown, near Sevenoaks. By October further stations had been established at Street in Devon (for 10 Group), Gorleston in Norfolk (for 12 Group), Scarborough in Yorkshire (for 13 Group) and at Beachy Head.

In 1938 a committee was formed to consider the problem of maintaining airfields in wartime. It quickly concluded that it would be necessary to establish pools of labour, materials and plant machinery needed for repair work. The result was that twenty-five works repair depots were formed on a geographical basis to cover all RAF stations in their area and be able to reach them within two hours of being required. Between June and September 1940 an additional fourteen depots were established. Each depot had an establishment of forty eight tradesmen and between eighty and a hundred and twenty men from the Ministry of Transport. In the southeast depots were established at Ashford (Kent), Addington (Surrey), Harlow (Essex), Eastcote (Middlesex), Havant and Weyhill (both Hampshire). In addition an establishment of fifteen tradesmen was allotted to each operational station. All of these personnel were civilians. In order to ensure repairs were undertaken efficiently stocks of materials were dumped at operational stations and a priority list of necessary repairs was compiled.

Experience on the Continent had shown the need for greater speed and more facilities if the bombing of airfields was not to result in the grounding of the air force. The result was an increase in personnel and materials at the depots. The need for a force of men available at operational stations to actually undertake vital repairs was met by the Army, who allocated a number of General Construction Companies of the Royal Engineers. Units of up to one hundred men each were posted to one hundred and ten important airfields, a total of some 7,000 soldiers. From the end of 1940 most of these were re-assigned, but the ability of the RAF to keep their airfields operational despite long periods of attack throughout the Battle of Britain is a testament to the effectiveness of the repairs organisation.

Before the 1930's expansion scheme the RAF's aviation petrol storage installations consisted of 12,000 gallon tanks kept in open pits. In addition, oil companies were required to provide a supply and distribution role, while their reserve amounted to about 8,000 tons, representing about ten days war consumption (based on 1937 estimates). In 1935 the RAF adopted mobile road tankers to improve operational readiness, while operational airfields should have enough petrol stored for six weeks intensive operations, not exceeding 72,000 gallons. In 1936 the Air Council, with the approval of the Oil Board, decided to constitute a reserve of aviation fuel equivalent to three months war consumption (90,000 tons), which would be maintained by the oil companies. At the same time the Committee of Imperial Defence advised that reserves of aviation fuels should be built up to meet requirements for the first six months of war, increasing the Air Ministry's storage requirement to 290,000 tons, increased to 800,000 tons in 1938 in view of probable strict American neutrality. In mid 1940, with the continued expansion of the RAF, an additional 15,000 tons of storage was required. By mid 1938 the RAF had available the 16,000 tons stored at both Ardrossan (Ayrshire) and Llandarcy, 14,440 tons stored at Brixham (south Devon) and 12,000 tons each at Avonmouth (Avon), Stanlow and Stourport (both in Worcestershire). These and other reserve depots were constructed west of the Edinburgh-Southampton "safe" line, in accordance with Chiefs of Staff policy. In addition to traditional storage tank farm sites a growing number of artificial underground sites were constructed, using disused cuttings and quarries. The first three were at Micheldever (Hampshire), Buxton (Derbyshire) and Much Wenlock (Shropshire). During the War only seven fuel depots were attacked but damage was slight, due mainly to the construction methods employed. In 1937, to meet overseas and temporary deployments, the RAF decided to supplement its bulk fuel operations with petrol tins. A joint Army scheme was developed with filling factories established at Ardrossan and Stanlow, located next to refineries and capable of producing 30,000 tons a day. Forty-six dumps of packed or tinned petrol were established around the country, totalling 120,000 tons. A central stores depot was built at Milton (near Bournemouth) to accommodate the increasing numbers and diversity in an expanding air force.

In terms of bomb stores it was agreed during the 1930's expansion programme to store six months anticipated war demand of 82,000 tons of high explosive and 16,000 tons of incendiary bombs, 48,000 tons of which would be filled. However, only two small ammunition depots and station storage existed at that time. The storage and distribution scheme envisaged main holdings being located in three sections of the country - northern, midland and southern. In each section distribution would be by rail from the filling factories to underground storage depots. The bombs would be moved when required by rail to advanced air ammunition parks, located centrally to bomber bases and served by rail and road services. The holdings of these parks was intended to be seven days war consumption for all stations served in addition to the four days holding of each station. The main reserve depot was expected to have a capacity of 10,000 tons of filled bombs, while incendiary bombs were to be located above ground in separate depots close to the main reserve depots.

In 1936 The RAF began to construct aircraft storage units, with the intention that they would share airfields with flying training schools. Tern Hill (Shropshire), Kemble (Gloucestershire), Aston Down, Hullavington (Wiltshire) and Shawbury (Shropshire) were chosen for this vital role to ensure that replacement aircraft could be delivered quickly. At the same time aircraft repair and engine repair depots were expanded at Sealand (Cheshire) and St Athan (Glamorganshire), while similar facilities were constructed at Digby (Lincolnshire), Castle Bromwich (Warwickshire), Catfoss (East Yorkshire), Duxford (Cambridgeshire) and Hawkinge (Kent).

CHAPTER FIVE: THE BRITISH ARMY

The end of the First World War had found the British Army the strongest it had ever been, in terms of manpower, equipment and tactics; it had gained a wealth of hard won experience during that War in conducting a wide range of operations in a relatively short period of time. The War, and its aftermath, had seen the Army take the lead in new military theory and the development of new weapons, methods and tactics which would be copied by many of the World's armies.

However, during the inter war years the Army had severely contracted, returning to its primary role of policing the Empire and accordingly was allocated the lowest priority in defence spending. The Government confirmed this by stating in the mid 1930's that "The Army's task is to defend the United Kingdom, police the Empire, guard our overseas possessions and deal with a second class power in the Middle East. It is only to be equipped and trained for these tasks". This statement was an extension of the almost universal desire across Western Europe during the two decades following the Great War to avoid another catastrophic war, preferring a policy of appeasement rather than adopting the precept that the best way of ensuring peace is to prepare for war. Appeasement, coupled with the economic depression of the time, not only served to starve the Army of financial support but also a disincentive to modernise; this situation was not helped by the civil emergencies in Egypt and Palestine during 1935 and 1936 which further stripped the home forces of equipment and men and severely disrupted its training schedules.

The Defence Requirements Committee's first report in February 1934 signalled a fundamental change in Government policy. Having previously ruled out the likelihood of a European based war for the previous decade it was now forced to assume one was probable within five years, due to the political developments across Europe. It didn't recommend full re-armament. The Government finally recognised the inevitable confrontation and belatedly announced a five-year re-armament programme in 1937; but it still failed to address many of the real issues and underlying problems the Army faced. In the same year, the post of Master General of the Ordnance was abolished, its responsibilities being taken over by the Adjutant General's staff in the War Office. This was to prove a major impediment to the re-armament process as, due to the failure to determine the nature of the Army's future role, no definite conclusions had been reached as to the types of weapons and equipment required and, as such, production orders were delayed and disorganised, quality control was non existent and, most importantly, no provision had been made to build up reserve stocks. This last concern had led to shortages of equipment and spares in all areas, leaving field units under equipped and a training establishment unable to function effectively.

When the Second World War began it soon become rather obvious to many of those involved that the Army's General Staff had failed to develop an appropriate doctrine on how to fight a modern war, and in particular counter the blitzkrieg, elements of which had been successfully trialled by the Germans in the Spanish Civil War and was being honed in its Polish Campaign. The British were not unaware of the blitzkrieg doctrine, especially as many of its principles had first been proposed by leading strategic thinkers in the British Army following the First World War, but the senior Army commanders had failed to appreciate its real operational potential in the hands of a properly trained enemy. This oversight is even more difficult to accept as British officers had observed German Army field exercises in the late 1930's and produced detailed reports on their return. They began by stating that the basis of all blitzkrieg tactics was speed; the Germans believed that if carried out quickly and with determination then the operation was bound to succeed. Other impressions were that:

- Headquarters and command teams were always found well forward in the attack and there was generally good intercommunication with all units, except with those on the flanks
- Command orders from regimental level down were always verbal and repeated
- However, it was felt that there was a shortage of efficient junior officers
- There was a general reticence to conduct night attacks
- Fitness and endurance of all combat troops was high (more so due to an inefficient supply system)
- Training was realistic, with ammunition, vehicles and equipment provided up to war scale; the choice of training ground changed as often as possible to ensure that troops trained on unfamiliar ground (the officers commented that the German Army was never refused anything it asked for, with resources and facilities appropriated from their civilian owners)
- Traffic control was generally poor
- Little training or awareness of gas warfare
- Post exercise conferences occurred immediately, irrespective of the time.

The British Army was then forewarned of how the German blitzkrieg operated in reality by Major General Sir Carton de Wiart, commander of the British Military Mission in Poland. His reports pointed out that the German success could be put down to three factors:

1. The Luftwaffe had destroyed the Polish Air Force, disrupted the Polish command and control system, prevented large scale troop movements and provided close air support to its own troops
2. The Germans had concentrated their tanks and used them boldly
3. The Polish armed forces had been unable to operate at the same tempo as the Germans and, as a result, were always trying to react to out of date developments.

Despite this warning the general consensus among the British and French hierarchy before May 1940 was that the Germans would not be able achieve this level of success against them. Among the reasons they gave themselves were that Poland had prepared itself for war against its traditional enemy of Russia, which had a different strategic approach to operations; the Poles had been taken by surprise and could not fully mobilise, whereas the western allies had already deployed; the weather had been kind to the Germans, allowing their tanks to operate over normally restrictive terrain and the Germans had operated boldly as they knew the Poles had few if any mobile forces available for counter attacks. British military intelligence was of the opinion that these conditions would rarely present themselves in other theatres of war.

A War Office memorandum produced in August 1940, having now experienced blitzkrieg itself, reinforced the main tactical characteristics of the German Army to be speed and determination, co-operation between all combat arms and simplicity and flexibility of the plan. It believed that the main role of the panzer division was to seize and disrupt the enemy's communication and logistics centres without consolidating gains; the mechanised forces were to be responsible for protecting the panzers' flanks and consolidate their gains. It was felt that the mobility of the panzer forces was due to their speed, good supply and maintenance organisation, good training, the availability of spare crews and quality of its tanks.

The Army's own strategy, developed by the British General Staff during the inter war years, was determined by the government's requirement to have a small, professional and well equipped mechanised Army that was expected to win quickly and cheaply by substituting technology for manpower - a crucial factor created by the need to avoid the crippling human losses suffered during the First World War and which remained a bedrock of the British military psyche. The Army was able to develop a combined arms doctrine before the Second World War, but it contained many flaws that were to be painfully exploited during the German blitzkrieg. Most notable of these flaws were:

- The desire to put the need for mobility over the requirement for and control of firepower,
- An autocratic and inefficient command, communication and intelligence system and
- The insistence of consolidating gains before exploiting success - essential for conventional fighting but contrary to the German blitzkrieg concept.

The issue of consolidating ground was a product of the First World War battles, where success was too often undone by failing to adequately prepare against counter attacks and quickly reinforce success.

In preparing for the War the Army's General Staff identified eight principles as the basis for its operational doctrine:
1. Maintenance of the objective, notably destruction of the enemy on the battlefield
2. Offensive action
3. Surprise. A most effective force multiplier, with the need for night operations and troop movement to be accorded a higher priority
4. Concentration of effort at the decisive point
5. Economy of effort, especially the efficient use of resources
6. Security, especially protection of your own forces
7. Mobility, essential to the success of offensive action and in achieving surprise.
8. Co-operation, in order to exert maximum effort.

It was believed that the application of these principles would reduce the natural chaos of the battlefield to a manageable level.

The British Army's doctrine of employing machinery rather than manpower was expressed in its organisation and equipment. The need to produce operational formations that were highly mobile, capable of producing superior firepower while being economical with manpower was paramount. Such formations must also be flexible enough to cope with the demands of modern warfare. The main combat formation for the Army remained the division. This formation had evolved greatly during the First World War to have greater firepower that commanders at all levels could control but at the expense of mobility, given the nature of operations they faced then. Post War trials and the need to resolve competing demands of economy, flexibility, fire power and mobility dictated that a division's combat units should only be equipped with those supporting weapons that they had constant need of, while tanks and heavy weapons should be allocated to the control of higher command. 1934 saw the start of the most intensive programme of modernisation, mechanisation and reorganisation undertaken by the Army between the wars. The outcome was the model 1938 infantry and mobile divisions, the latter being the forerunner of the armoured division. However both these types of divisions still had fewer support weapons, mortars and heavy machine guns than their German counterparts.

In early September 1939 the War Cabinet's Land Forces Committee recommended that operational planning should be based on the assumption that the War would last for at least three years. It agreed that Britain should raise a field force of fifty five fully equipped divisions (including fourteen Commonwealth, four Indian and five allied). At that time the Army could field thirty three divisions (two armoured, seven regular infantry, twelve first line Territorial and twelve second line Territorial infantry divisions) and five independent tank brigades around the world; all were short of equipment and spares and the second line divisions exisited only on paper. Nevertheless, it believed that twenty divisions could be equipped by September 1940, as long as the expansion of factory space began at once, the Ministry of Labour was given priority of labour and raw materials resources and that the protection of skilled labour was rigorously enforced. However, by February 1940 it was clear that the goal of raising and equipping fifty five divisions would have to be a longer term one due to the limited production capacity of Britain's industrial base; the War Office revised its estimate to equip thirty six divisions by September 1941. The eight months of the "Phoney War" in 1939-40 had seen little improvement in war production as senior military and political leaders felt that Germany was unlikely to mount a serious offensive in 1940. The Army was able to despatch to the Continent before the blitzkrieg five regular and eight territorial infantry divisions, though three of the latter were classed as labour formations as they lacked equipment and training.

After the withdrawal from the Continent in June 1940 there was considerable argument about whether the division was too big and cumbersome an organisation for modern war. As a result more emphasis was placed on brigade sized operations, particularly for counter attacks. Opponents to this change, in particular those arms of the Army tasked with providing fire and logistical support, recognised that it would mean a decentralised supply and support effort, preventing the crucial ability to concentrate artillery fire and denying their own commanders the ability to exercise effective control over their own units. Large scale operations in 1941 and 1942 were subsequently to show the limitations of brigade sized forces acting independently.

The pre war Army was organised into the Regular Force and Territorial Army. The former was mainly deployed in combat formations and overseas garrisons (by 1937 there were 196,700 Regulars with over 90,000 of these serving overseas), with the British controlled Indian Army being regarded as a separate entity. The Territorial Army was reformed in 1920 and was to be responsible for home defence, with a second line combat role in the Field Army, with the expectation of being combat ready within six months of mobilisation. Many of its infantry units were re-roled in the mid 1930's into anti aircraft and coastal artillery units so that by March 1939 more than 40% of the Territorial Army was assigned these roles (75,000 men to the former and 8,000 to the latter).

Formed in 1936, and affiliated to the Territorial Army, the National Defence Corps was one of several reserve formations assigned to home defence, using men aged between 45 and 55 with previous military experience, but of a lower fitness category, to supply guard detachments. The Regular Army was supported by both the Regular Reserve, men who had completed at least six years service with the Regulars, and the Supplementary Reserve, supplying specialist personnel. When war was declared over 546,000 men were mobilised from these organisations. Therefore, by late September 1940 the Army had over 1.7 million men and 36,000 women deployed around the country, while about another 173,000 men were based overseas.

In 1938 the Auxiliary Territorial Service (ATS) was formed, allowing women over 18 to enlist for local or general service in vital support roles, many of which would no doubt involve frontline contact during an invasion, despite legal advice to the contrary (In 1941 field headquarters were told that in the event of combat operations all woman drivers had to be replaced due to their status of being non operational). The Royal Navy and Royal Air Force also had many women serving in similar roles, including operating the radar stations around the coast.

The combat capability of the British Army depended equally on the quality and quantity of its personnel. It was generally recognised that both the pre war Regular Army and Territorial Army had failed to attract enough men of suitable quality and then failed to develop them adequately enough for them to provide the core of an expanded civilian wartime Army (in 1937 the manpower deficit was recorded as being five per cent of Regulars and twenty five per cent of Territorials). These failings were not seriously addressed until the late 1930's when the Government sought to make the Army a more attractive career option, encouraging promotion by merit and lowering the retirement age for all officers, although this last issue was resisted by the Army's hierarchy.

Even with conscription, through the National Service Act 1939, the Army still failed to make optimum use of the personnel it got as it lacked an appropriate selection system for identifying possible leaders or specialists. The result was that conscripts were often allowed to choose their preference, the infantry inevitably losing out to the more fashionable "trade" corps, reflecting the Army's doctrinal commitment to conducting a war of material over manpower. Basil Liddell Hart, a leading military theorist of the time, commented in 1937 "If the Army is to attract men of intelligence it must be able to convince them that their effort will not be wasted. They want a clear idea of the Army's purpose and a reasonable assurance that its organisation and training are fitted to that purpose". Field Marshal Harold Alexander supported this view, when he wrote in his memoirs after the Second World War, that "I affirm that there are no better soldiers than those of the British race, provided they have a cause worth fighting for - and dying for, if necessary. They object to being pushed around - they are intelligent enough to want to know what it is all about and they will become unhappy and disgruntled if they feel that unfairness exists. Yet, if their leaders are worthy of them, they will follow them anywhere. They are very patient and tough in defence. Yet though the British will go into the attack with great bravery and tenacity, as a whole they are not quick to exploit a success or to react to a sudden emergency." It was generally accepted in the 1930's that modern warfare demanded an ever rising degree of intelligence and initiative and that the soldier must be fit, psychologically as well as physically. Lieutenant Colonel Brian Horrocks, one of the promising field commanders in 1940, stated "The modern soldier is more highly educated, more imaginative and more intelligent than his father who fought in 1914-18. He is capable of rising to great heights, but he can also sink to greater depths. He will give of his best only if he understands the reason for what he is doing. As a rule the front line soldier has no idea at all about what is going on elsewhere, even on the front of another company in his own battalion. His view of the war is restricted to the field and hedgerow in his immediate foreground. To pierce this fog of ignorance requires forethought and much hard work, but it is well worth the effort." The 1934 Training Regulations Manual noted that "modern warfare needed considerable decentralisation of responsibility to junior leaders and individuals. The soldier must therefore be intelligent, adaptable and capable of acting on their own initiative. These qualities are to be developed by education, itself an integral part of military training."

The characteristics of modern operations were correctly recognised as far back as the 1924 Field Service Regulations, the Army's operational manual that was to form the bedrock of British offensive doctrine during the coming war. It stated that "troops engaged in close fighting are soon affected by physical and moral exhaustion; recovery from the former is ensured by rest but recovery from the latter is a longer process. If troops, as is probable, are to be engaged with the enemy for long periods of time, it is important that their moral qualities should not be reduced to a point at which comparatively speedy recovery is impossible. The individual soldier should not therefore be engaged to the point of exhaustion and he should be made aware of the task that lies before him. Apart from providing every available means of support to those in attack, the allotment of a definite objective to units ensures that the demands likely to be made on their physical and moral powers receives due consideration."

The 1936 Field Service Regulations emphasised that high command in war required "the broadest possible outlook and knowledge, of social as well as of military questions. War is now more than ever a social problem: a major war affects the whole of the national life and every class of citizen, and there is a corresponding civil influence on the conduct of military operations". In 1937 Liddell Hart noted that in the British Army soldiering was, unlike civilian life, a sheltered occupation except in war, with the soldier gaining little or no psychological experience as a fighter during peace, while his training and discipline would come to the fore quicker in combat. At the time, he believed that the civilian turned soldier would be unable to take on the more professional functions of the Army without needing years of military experience, commenting that "without knowledge of military technique the ablest man would be handicapped, especially in dealing with forces which have a well established system of operation. The principles of fighting are based on common sense, but something more is needed to apply them effectively in the handling of armies. The better a man's mental equipment the less time he will take to acquire an adequate knowledge of such a technique. It is difficult for an older soldier to have a sure grasp of weapons (and machinery) he has never handled and of methods he has never carried out. Moreover, if his technical experience lies several steps back, it becomes more difficult for him to gauge the next step forward".

The Territorial Army was also to benefit from Government support in the late 1930's, with better training opportunities improving interest and standards, a greater thoroughness of pre annual camp instruction, development of instructors by allowing them wider access to training courses, better organised annual camps and the appointment of Regular staff officers with keenness and knowledge for their new roles. To promote the Territorial Army within the War Office the decision was taken in 1938 to appoint a senior Territorial officer to the post of

Deputy Director General of the Territorial Army, with the rank of Major General. The lack of modern equipment was a serious check on training, the Territorial Army having no access to tanks, mortars, little mechanised transport and even few gas masks in the mid 1930's.

A 1932 Army committee looking at whether lessons gained during the last War had been adequately applied to training reported that the methods of training were too stereotyped. It was not until 1937 that the time recruits devoted to formal parade drill was reduced, the freed hours given to elementary fieldcraft. However, such developments were few and far between. As Liddell Hart put it, "the object of a soldier's training is threefold: to make him skilled in handling his weapons under battle conditions; to make him an interlocking and frictionless cog in the military machine and, lastly, to make him conquer his own sense of fear". He believed that the basis of achieving this was through discipline and drill.

After receiving basic training at their depot the recruits were posted to their units where the main training was to be undertaken; however, the main problem with unit training was that there was little if any co-ordination of effort and doctrine as each junior officer was responsible for training their own troops. They often received little guidance from both training regulations that allowed personal interpretation and their own senior officers. Many units emphasised physical fitness, weapons training and sports in their training programmes rather than battle fitness; in armoured units, for example, mornings were typically assigned to work on the tanks, though this more often meant cleaning them, with afternoons spent at sport. While sport is useful for building fitness, competitiveness and team spirit it is far from the best training to prepare to combat a competent and tactically astute foe.

Liddell Hart commented in 1937, after observing many field exercises, that "Conformity to the manuals, the confusion due to constant changes of detail and the excessive emphasis on meticulous order writing has produced a slow motion habit which is inimical to the exploitation of opportunities. Instead of building tactical art on a basis of battle drill, thus quickening its application, we have turned tactics into a slow time drill. Today we are the masters of the obvious instead of being masters of surprise. Instead of developing ingenuity, the main effort had too often been towards simplifying the enemy's problem to defending himself." He also noted that "nothing had been more disappointing in recent years` exercises than the way that mechanization has been wasted by moving units and formations at the pace of their slowest portion, owing to the desire to move complete." He did, however, add that "some skills were being developed which showed promise, notably the skill and subtlety shown by many troops in concealing themselves from air observation, the cultivation of night sense and increased use of attacks in the dark" (many in the BEF were to comment later that the German Army rarely rarely carried out operations during the night, preferring to use this time to rest and reorganise). Training for the Territorial Army was further complicated due to their voluntary nature, having to rely on four training weekends and a two week training camp a year to provide even basic unit training. This activity was made more difficult by the Government's decision to double the size of the Territorial Army in the spring of 1939, a controversial act not supported by the Army's Chiefs of Staff as there was not enough material, accommodation or trainers available to cope with such a sudden increase. It was noted in more than one Territiorial regiment that proper training was impossible for several months due to the need to re-organise and provide the many new recruits with even just the basic skills. Even after mobilisation these units rarely received any tactical training due to the constant demands of preparing defensive positions – 5th Green Howards noted in its war history that between February 1940 and the start of the German offensive that May the battalion only managed one weekend on the rifle ranges after deploying with the BEF.

Some senior officers recognised that the training system failed to instil in junior leaders a common understanding of the Army's tactical doctrine. Although junior officers in the "trade" corps (artillery, engineers, logistics, signals and armour) went to their own corps schools to learn the technical aspects of their chosen trade, those in the infantry suffered from not having a tactics school. General Andrew Thorne noted that "entrusting a young man with responsibility early in his career could only test his powers of leadership". He proposed that potential officers undertake the normal initial training course for recruits followed by a period spent as an assistant instructor before going to Sandhurst, then spend six months with a home service unit before attending a new Staff School. He hoped that by this time the individual would have been thoroughly tested and kept abreast of developments in tactics, weapons and organisation through frequent courses. As expected, this revolutionary idea received little support from the establishment. Similarly, a proposal in 1937 to create a "College of Tactics" was rejected because, as Field Marshal Sir Cyril Deverell, then Chief of the Imperial General Staff, noted "if a young officer cannot learn his job in his own unit, there is something wrong with the unit. Schools are to produce instructors, not teach the elements". It was not until March 1939 that it was agreed to establish a tactics school, requiring all officers to pass before gaining promotion to major, but this came too late to have any real effect on the Army before it went to war and promotion continued to be largely based more on seniority rather than merit until 1940. A Senior Officers' School was established in 1920, aimed at preparing majors for unit command and, in doing so, spread a common understanding of tactical doctrine throughout the Army. This met with limited success, placed too much emphasis on strategy than operational techniques and failed to detect those who were most likely to break down under the stresses imposed by a modern battlefield.

The training of Territorial Army regimental officers was even more haphazard, with relatively few junior officers able to spare the time to attend external courses and potential senior officers were not required to attend the Senior Officers' School. Much commander training devolved on to TEWTS (training without troops), a series of table top exercises. The overall result was that there were too many officers who, through no fault of their own, had no tactical experience of actually commanding men in the field. Wartime commissioned officers required considerable training after they joined their unit but this was even harder to achieve due to the dilution of the Regular officer corps after the expansion of the Army. Nevertheless, a growing number of senior officers realised the type of war that was approaching and sought to modernise their approach to officer training. As a brigade commander in 1937, Montgomery insisted that his unit commanders train their junior officers to take command of larger units as "the junior officer of today is the commanding officer of tomorrow" while encouraging senior officers to be detached as umpires or in liaison roles in an effort to widen their outlook.

The 1924 Field Service Regulations asserted that commanders had to be clear about their own objectives and impress the determination to succeed upon their subordinates by issuing clear orders. However, junior commanders were not generally encouraged to interpret these orders, often leading to inflexibility. The General Staff hoped that scientific and technological developments would provide field commanders with rapid and flexible means of communications with their units. Field exercises and experiments highlighted the need for mobile units to rely on wireless radio; however, to ensure that communications were not susceptible to collapse above battalion level a mixed system of wireless, cable, despatch riders and liaison officers was adopted.

Although the Army's General Staff accepted as early as 1934 that it should prepare for another European war it did little to provide senior commanders with experience of actually commanding troops in the field. Indeed, when the BEF formed in September 1939 it had no one in it with war experience at high command; General Ironside, the other choice as Commander in Chief, was the only senior officer still on active service who had previously held a high command position during war, that of commanding the Expeditionary Force in northern Russia after the Bolshevik Revolution. Corps sized exercises lasted only a couple of days and occurred only twice between the wars. Two major reasons for this were problems the British Army had always faced - the lack of a suitably sized training area in the country and lack of sufficient modern military equipment, with flags and dummy vehicles often replacing artillery fire and armoured vehicles. The situation was not helped when, for example in 1936, 1st Infantry Division was sent to Palestine during the emergency after having only carried out the first of its exercises, 4th Infantry Division's exercise was curtailed by an outbreak of foot and mouth disease across its exercise area, while 5th Infantry Division's programme was hampered by being largely retained in Egypt due to internal disturbances there.

Other command and co-operation exercises of the time also lacked the reality of battlefield conditions, many keeping to office hours. Liddell Hart commented that "if the Army exercises of 1935 and 1936 left one outstanding impression it was the futility of seeking a solution on the old lines. The attacks which had the least effect, and looked the least deserving of it, were those in which the resemblance to 1918 was the most marked." He also made an interesting observation that there was doubt whether sufficient senior officers could be found or trained to be capable of directing and handling high mobility forces until a new generation, born in the motor age, had grown up. Too many senior commanders were still averse to interfere with training their units, even during the so called "Phoney War" period of 1939-1940, preferring to offer advice or provide general directions rather than ensure that a decent training regime was identified and implemented.

The newly promoted Brigadier Montgomery commented in 1937 "We have to develop new methods and learn new techniques, the main plank laying in the command posts at brigade and divisional level. It was vital in modern warfare that the commander must make a plan and begin early to force his will on the enemy. Success in the initial encounters will go to the commander who knows what he wants, has a plan to achieve it, does not allow his command to drift aimlessly into battle but puts it into battle on a proper plan from the outset." He emphasised that the commander must have his headquarters well forward in order to gain the earliest possible information, see the ground and be able to plan ahead and issue orders to subordinates before their units arrive. Thereafter the headquarters should be pulled back so as never to become embroiled in the actual fighting while the commander remains mobile, together with his artillery and engineer commanders, and supported by adequate mobile communications." During the "Phoney War" period of 1939-1940 Montgomery further considered that in a frontline division it was necessary to have commanders who "have the character and personality that will inspire confidence and enthusiasm in others; they must be mentally robust, possessed of initiative, energy and drive."

The upshot of this diversity in applying training methods within the British Expeditionary Force (BEF) was that on the eve of the German offensive in May 1940 Lord Gort VC, its Commander in Chief, believed that his Regular troops were not as well trained as their 1914 predecessors while the Territorials were still fit only for static operations - neither complimentary to the men or reflecting well on many of the senior commanders (including himself) who had had an additional seven months grace to prepare their men for modern war.

Although good training was vital, it wasn't the only serious concern facing the commanders and men of the BEF. Lieutenant General Alan Brooke noted in his diary in April 1940 "Though there was now no doubt about the fighting quality and efficiency of the men the tools their country had given them were not enough. The gravest defects of all were the lack of armoured vehicles and poor air co-operation; the only armoured division was still at home awaiting its long promised equipment, including artillery and specialist engineering equipment; there was also an acute shortage of spare parts and anti aircraft guns." Montgomery later claimed the BEF was totally unfit to fight a modern war on the continent of Europe and further felt that the Regular Army was unfit to even take part in a realistic exercise.

The Army's "trade" corps represented the pre war investment and comprised both "teeth" arms and support arms. Given the Army's doctrine, the Royal Armoured Corps (RAC) and the Royal Tank Regiment were key to its offensive strategy. Unfortunately, the tanks available were the product of doctrine, finance and bureaucracy during the inter war years. The Army decided that it needed three types:

- A medium tank capable of destroying the enemy,
- A close support tank to provide close fire support for the mediums
- A light tank to perform the roles of reconnaissance and flank protection.

The RAC, formed from the traditional cavalry regiments, were equipped with the light and cruiser tanks, while the Royal Tank Regiment had the heavier infantry tanks.

Due to financial constraints development work on the first two types was halted until rearmament began in 1936, by which time the Army had revised its needs and decided to produce only infantry support and cruiser tanks. The upshot of this change was that while the Army had an effective light tank it lacked the necessary design, engine and main gun armament to produce a satisfactory medium tank. Such was the speed necessary to get these from the drawing board to production that almost every type suffered from poor design and development, leading to underpowered engines, mechanical unreliability and a main gun armament that soon lacked real killing power; most of the tanks lost in France were due to technical problems. It was due to their mechanical fragility that the War Office had decided at the outset that long distance movements were to be made by railway, as suitable road transporters were not available at that time in sufficient numbers. To conform to the gauges used by the railways tanks had a size and weight restriction, which in turn limited the size of main gun that could be fitted into its turret. The 2-pounder gun was accepted as the standard but planners forgot to include a high explosive (H.E.) shell capability, severely limiting the tank's ability to engage anti tank weapons.

Experiments in the 1920's had already shown that tanks could not expect to operate successfully alone. Army doctrine believed that armoured units should be used either to pierce the enemy's front or penetrate the enemy's flanks and rear by means of rapid movement. If they were to attempt the first they would require artillery and infantry support to neutralise the enemy's artillery and anti tank support. The Field Service Regulations (1935), the Army's main doctrinal manual, noted that infantry divisions supported by infantry tanks were to be responsible for breaking through prepared positions, while the Mobile Division (the forerunner of the 1st Armoured Division) would exploit the breakthrough with its cruiser and light tanks in a typical cavalry fashion. By 1939 the Mobile Division had also been tasked with countering penetrations by the enemy's own armour. A major concern illustrated by experiences in France was the lack of a proper field recovery and repair organisation; each tank was a vital asset and needed to be recovered from the battlefield quickly but this was almost impossible, due mainly to the lack of tank transporters (the Army had two types in 1939, though one was only suitable for light tanks. Trials involving the RAC and RASC began in the late autumn to redress this deficiency).

By 1939 the Army had three types of tanks available:

- The light mark VI tank was already regarded as being obsolete for anything other than its primary role of reconnaissance. The lack of enough cruiser and infantry tanks in the summer of 1940 meant that this light type had to make up most of the tanks in the 2nd Armoured Division, one of the two main counter attack formations in September 1940!
- The cruiser tanks only started entering service in 1939 and, though only slightly heavier armoured, were fast and armed with the standard 2-pounder main gun; several variants existed including one with a mortar for close infantry support. They were generally proven to be effective in combat but suffered from mechanical reliability and an underpowered engine.
- The heavy infantry tanks were also effective in combat not least due to the heavy armour protection, a fact that shocked the Germans during the Arras counter attack in May. However, they were slow, also mechanically unreliable and had a short operational radius, managing only 40 miles before needing refuelling. The mark I infantry tank had only one heavy machine gun as its armament. The mark III Valentine infantry tank was being developed, the first production model only coming off the lines in May 1940, and only started reaching operational units by mid September. It would, nevertheless, also prove to be rather effective in combat, with good armour protection and being more mechanically reliable but still relying on the 2-pounder gun.
- The only other tank available was the already obsolete Vickers Medium, which had long been relegated to training units.

The RAC also had several versions of armoured tracked carriers, used for mainly reconnaissance and command roles, and light armoured or scout cars. The tracked carriers had proven very useful in a multitude of tasks, the Universal (Bren gun) Carrier especially gaining a reputation for robustness and versatility among the infantry. The Corps did not begin to develop heavy modern armoured cars until late 1940, having seen how effective the German ones had been, but was still forced to equip one of its key armoured brigades with them; as such these would be suitable for flank protection and general reconnaissance roles only.

During the First World War the Royal Regiment of Artillery had grown from providing infantry support to dominating the battlefield, having developed many new techniques to increase its power and effectiveness. These developments continued during the inter war years. In 1929 it was accepted that the best way to gain fire superiority was by centralising control at divisional level. Inter war trials sought to resolve the problem of balancing mobility and producing accuracy and shell power, while the choice of firepower deployed would depend on the accuracy of information on the enemy and the time available. Accurate fire could only be achieved by accurate weather prediction, survey, gun calibration, time to properly register on the target and issuing fire control orders. The ability to predict fire and engage targets without prior registration had been perfected by 1918 and was based on surveying, using several methods to ensure accuracy. The survey work was organised within the Corps level Survey Regiment, containing a flash spotting and sound ranging capability.

Although supporting combat units was a vital role, the main role of the artillery was counter battery (engaging the enemy's own artillery), with overall control exercised at Corps level headquarters. Ideally, counter battery action was built up from battery level until all artillery units to be involved, up to Corps level, were registered on a grid system. With the introduction of decent scale maps in 1936, accurate fire of an entire divisional artillery could be brought to bear within thirty minutes.

In May 1939 field regiments were reorganised into two double batteries in an effort to increase mobility and firepower, with three field regiments to an infantry division. Extra field regiments were also assigned to Army or Corps command with the medium and heavy regiments. This arrangement meant that while field commanders nominally had more artillery weapons on call than their opponents the concern of whether and when it was supplied depended on how well their communications with the gunners worked. If this organisation was not flexible enough the construction of effective fire plans could take longer and significantly affect the tempo of operations. German infantry divisions had countered this flaw by providing each infantry regiment with a battery of eight infantry guns to provide instant local fire support and under their own command. Nevertheless, it was found that artillery support during the BEF operations had worked well.

The mainstay of the field regiments was the 25-pounder gun/howitzer, adopted in 1937. This superb weapon also proved a capable anti tank weapon. However, there were never enough of these weapons so a large number of old 18-pounder guns were adapted (known as 18/25-pounders). While improving the range and mobility of existing First World War medium guns by fitting new barrels and pneumatic tyres, it was only in August 1939 that the War Office approved production of a modern 5.5-inch howitzer and the design of the 4.5-inch howitzer. This lack of both a modern medium gun and a truly mobile heavy gun was a major handicap to the Corps, the main reasons again being the financial constraints and the pre war Army's doctrine of mobility over firepower. The Regiment had lost all of its medium and heavy artillery on the Continent but was fortunate in having reserve stocks to call upon. These were deployed to the most vulnerable areas but were vulnerable to attack by having very limited mobility; for example, the 9.2-inch heavy howitzer would need to be broken down into three loads to be moved, a process that could take several hours.

Up to 1940 dedicated anti tank weapons were still a novelty. The Army conducted many experiments during the inter war years to counter the threat posed by enemy tanks until, in 1934, the General Staff agreed to adopt the 2-pounder high velocity gun for both tanks and anti tank units. The infantry wanted all anti tank guns under their direct control but this was vetoed and remained the responsibility of the Royal Artillery, each infantry division being allocated a regiment of forty eight guns. Despite this setback the infantry experimented by forming an additional anti-tank company in each infantry brigade, manned by personnel from the infantry battalions within it. When the BEF deployed these companies were equipped with the French 25mm Hotchkiss guns, as there was still not sufficient 2-pounder guns available. Generally speaking, the anti tank gunners performed well in action; during the invasion period many of the brigade companies were made more mobile but equipped with what ad hoc weapons could be provided. Shortly after, these companies were disbanded. The General Staff agreed to a 6-pounder anti tank version in April 1940, using re-conditioned naval guns, but production was not given a high priority due to the manufacturing and tooling capability required. In addition to these weapons the infantry also had the 0.55-inch Boys anti tank rifle, which entered service in 1937, and while initially effective despite the vicious recoil it quickly became dated as frontal armour protection increased on enemy tanks. However, this weapon was to be widely distributed during the invasion period on the same principle that 'something is better than nothing'.

Since the Victorian era the establishment of coast artillery was based on the principle that there was no place on the British coast where an invasion fleet could operate without a superior British fleet intervening within a relatively short space of time. From this followed the conclusion that coast artillery should only be permanently established in peacetime to defend naval bases and major commercial ports, while a list of other less important ports was drawn up for defences to be provided on the outbreak of hostilities. The German naval bombardments of some east coast ports in the First World War had shown the ineffectiveness of the exisiting coastal artillery organisation, which led to improvements and more resources being allocated in the inter war years, notably the re-roling of a significant part of the Territorial Army to provide the majority of the coastal artillery units. The effectiveness of the improved organisation was shown by the coastal artillery units being among the first to fully mobilise in the last week of August 1939. There were three levels of coastal artillery: the heavy 9.2-inch guns of First World War vintage; the medium 6-inch guns which formed the backbone of the organisation, many of which had been upgraded before the War; and the lighter guns of mostly 6 and 12-pounder calibre, used to protect entrances at close range. In addition there were a small number of shore-based torpedo launching sites.

While each coastal battery had its own command and observation posts, all fire positions were controlled by a central fire command headquarters, normally organised from the coastal regiment's headquarters, to co-ordinate the defence of ports and anchorages with searchlights and naval forces. In September 1939 the Royal Marines established coastal guns at Blyth, Sunderland and Yarmouth, as the Navy intended to establish minor operational bases at these ports, while the War Office decided to provide further guns at Dundee, Aberdeen and Lowestoft in March 1940, where defence works already existed. In April lighter calibre guns were also placed at Sunderland, Hartlepool, Yarmouth, Lowestoft, Newhaven and Ramsgate in an anti motor torpedo boat role. From May, with the growing number of emergency batteries placed to cover vulnerable places, it was decided to establish small group headquarters to administer several batteries, where the nearest coast artillery regimental headquarters was unable to provide cover. There were also a number of radar stations dedicated to coastal artillery, developed before the War and able to identify ships of over 2000 tonnes up to twenty four miles away. These stations were also linked to the nearest co-ordinating headquarters.

The Royal Regiment of Artillery was also responsible for the Anti Aircraft Command. This formation was unique in that it was operationally under the command of the RAF's Fighter Command (the Royal Engineers was responsible for the searchlight units until mid 1940). When Neville Chamberlain became Prime Minister in 1937 he ruled that the provision of anti aircraft defences was to have absolute priority over all other forms of war material. Nevertheless, when war broke out the Command was still inferior in terms of weapons, equipment, personnel and organisation; it was fortunate that the "Phoney War" period gave them more time to improve their capabilities, tempered as it was by having to cope with continually increasing demands placed upon them. When deployed with the BEF it quickly became clear that, again, demand outpaced availability; it was soon decided that the bulk of the guns would be deployed to protect the lines of communication, headquarters and airfields, with the combat forces largely having to rely on their own resources for their protection. The 1930`s did, however, see important technical advances involving radar, rockets and modern heavy guns. Gun laying radar, based on two trailer mounted cabins, was able to provide reasonably accurate data from a distance of seventeen miles and was in service by the outbreak of War. Although the Command had a small number of modern heavy 4.5-inch guns the bulk of the heavy anti aircraft guns were First World War vintage 3-inch guns; these were mobile but lacked the range and accuracy needed to tackle modern bombers. The need for a modern heavy and mobile gun was addressed by the introduction of the 3.7-inch weapon, with a towing road speed of 25mph, a "time into action" of just fifteen minutes and a rate of fire of ten rounds per minute. The Command was woefully lacking in terms of light anti aircraft weapons; the Swedish Bofors 40mm gun was already highly regarded and increasing numbers were built under licence in Great Britain, though demand constantly outpaced availability, especially after many were lost with the BEF. Although some 3-inch guns were impressed and a small number of 20mm Hispano canons were produced, the Command had to rely from the outset on machine guns, mostly the First World War Lewis gun.

Of the main support and service corps, the Royal Army Service Corps (RASC) was in the forefront of the army's pre war mechanisation process, despite the usual financial, technical and bureaucratic constraints. As a result of its efforts the British Army was to be the only truly mechanised Army at the outbreak of the War. The Corps underwent some further important changes in the 1930's to its organisation, notably the creation of divisional supply companies as an integral part of the formation they served and separate petrol companies, which led to the development of a complete petrol supply system. Another development was the introduction of a double echelon supply system, an integral part of the maintenance structure for mechanised and mobile forces. Troop carrying companies were created, each having the capacity to move an infantry brigade in coaches or lorries.

The Army's peacetime complement of vehicles was only about 2,000 vehicles, which were only purchased in small numbers until the re-armament process began (85,000 vehicles were available by the start of the War). To cope with the expected demand on mobilisation the Corps enlarged the Inspectorate of Supplementary Transport, responsible for identifying civilian vehicles suitable for military use, especially those required for complex engineering tasks, and allocated collection centres for them. By the start of the War the War Office had standardised on 8-cwt, 15-cwt, 30-cwt and 3-ton load capacity vehicles, the lighter ones generally assigned to field units as transport for signals, support weapons and unit stores while the heavier ones were used to move supplies and men into forward combat areas as well as allowing for conversion to specialist roles. One of the notable successes of mechanisation was the development of a range of gun towing tractors, the first into service (in 1938) being the Guy "Quad-Ant", a robust all wheel drive vehicle that could accommodate the gun crew and a hundred rounds of ammunition. All of the Army's vehicles had to be mechanically reliable, easy to maintain and suitable for rapid mass production in wartime, the latter meaning that suitable vehicles had largely to be based upon existing proven civilian designs. Although the Army experimented with tracked and half tracked vehicles this aspect was not pursued at the time for cost and production reasons. Due to their civilian design, many of the Army's vehicles only had two wheel drive, so limiting their off road capabilities, and suffered from reduced load carrying and speed. A theme common to all parts of the Army was the lack of sufficient spare parts for their vehicles and key equipment.

The RASC had agreed in 1937 that the Army's main fuel reserves would be held in the United Kingdom and that distribution would, where possible, be handled in bulk. Arrangements were handled in close co-operation with the civil industry, but were hampered by the lack of a military POL (Petroleum, Oil, Lubricants) organisation, as civilian contractors had previously carried out this role as required. The main problem with a POL organisation, such as that developed for the BEF, was that it was not mobile and so vulnerable to attack. During the invasion period the POL arrangements were strengthened and made more robust but its storage and transportation still remained vulnerable.

With rare Treasury support the Corps also sought to build up reserves of supplies, material and accommodation during the mid 1930's, the latter by increasing the number of depots at home, though this process was still ongoing when war broke out. By early 1940 the Army's total food reserves had risen to 100,000 tons, excluding the daily requirements of its home establishment as the Ministry of Food supplied this. To help cope with the Army's massive expansion the Corps instituted a stock control and forecast system.

As part of its apparent obsession with dismantling the successful apparatus of the British Army at the end of the First World War, the Army's Intelligence Corps was disbanded by 1922, its skills and experiences lost except in paper records. Although a Manual of Military Intelligence was produced that year, providing in great detail the intelligence organisation at various levels of command and listing the duties of the intelligence staff, it did not explain how these duties were to be performed. Fortunately the Military Intelligence Directorate in the War Office did survive, though on a severely reduced basis, and staffed for once by senior officers of ability and intellect. However, this Directorate was starved by the lack of finances and support from politicians and high command respectively. In May 1937 General Sir Edmund Ironside wrote "if we didn't have so many constant changes in the Intelligence Branch we should have better results ... in the armies on the Continent the intelligence officers make a profession of their branch and remain in it for years. They do not aspire to go out and command but remain as specialists." For the British, intelligence work was always destined to be the preserve of the amateur, as it was believed, with some justification, that they would have a more diverse background and non-conformist attitude essential for such a role. It didn't help that intelligence appointments did not count towards a recommendation for command or that there was no mention of field intelligence in the syllabuses at any of the officer training establishments.

While the Field Service Regulations stressed the importance of collecting accurate intelligence on the enemy's order of battle and capabilities it ignored the importance of analysing their enemy's organisational and doctrinal framework. As already mentioned, the Army failed to understand that the German's operational doctrine was essentially different from their own, this dogma reinforced by inter war training that assumed that their enemy would be organised, trained and equipped in the same way as they were! It was not until 1936 that officers attending the Staff College were required to study foreign armies and make them the basis for producing training schemes. Reliance on the notion that when it came to a crisis the British Army would always be able to improvise successfully seemed to be a mainstay of the General Staff's doctrinal thinking, preferring to state general principles rather than concrete examples. In 1940 General Wavell, who had played a major role in establishing the Intelligence Corps on the outbreak of the First World War, remarked "British military authorities have seldom realised that an intelligence system cannot be improvised but has to be built up over a period of years."

An intelligence section was authorised for each field headquarters, manned by personnel selected within that command to varying standards. In its 1937 plans for the BEF the intelligence structure provided for an Intelligence Corps headquarters, a General Headquarters section and individual sections for the divisions, lines of communications and RAF liaison - a total of one hundred and seventy five officers and men (in reality over four hundred served with the BEF). The main problem, not considered until the Munich Crisis, was that there was no one trained or earmarked to fill these appointments; there were only about thirty officers in the Reserve who had experience from the First World War. Of the initial intelligence officers dispatched with the BEF in 1939 few were considered fluent in French, let alone German! In addition, very few soldiers had been trained in field security, which had been the responsibility of the Corps of Military Police since 1937.

The man credited with ensuring that the Intelligence Corps even existed on the outbreak of war was Major (later Field Marshal) Templer in the War Office, who had barely months to repair decades of neglect. The War Office's Directorate of Military Intelligence handled the selection of intelligence officers; training courses were held in each home Command to train intelligence officers and to identify much needed instructors to improve the quality of training. Recruitment was also helped by adverts ran in national newspapers and through the BBC! At the start of the war a School of Military Intelligence was established in Derbyshire for instructors while basic Corps training occurred at both Oxford and Mytchett. At the same time both the Intelligence Corps and Field Security Police wing were activated, the latter moving from Mytchett to Sheerness then Winchester in mid 1940, when it was renamed the Field Security Centre and Depot.

The Royal Corps of Signals was another support arm that tried to embrace the modern age. Of the communications available to commanders - wireless, cable and despatch rider - wireless was in theory the primary signals method forward of divisional headquarters but the technology was still new, the first viable tactical radio set with a range of ten miles only being issued in 1938; many commanders were reluctant to rely on radio, especially as there were too few sets available outside the tank and artillery units and too few personnel trained to operate them. Cable was preferred as it could carry a greater volume of traffic, was quite secure and was better understood, though this placed a great strain on the Royal Signals personnel in laying, repairing and recovering the cables, especially during mobile operations. In addition, the differing availability of wireless equipment within the various elements also hampered attempts at combined arms operations, with the three main arms - tanks, artillery and infantry - all relying on different preferences of communication.

The British Expeditionary Force (BEF) was the Army's first opportunity to put its developments in doctrine, organisation and equipment into operation on a modern battlefield. The result showed that whilst the Germans did not outfight the British Army they did manage to generally out-think and outmanoeuvre it. The Army's General Staff believed that the defeat owed much to the outdated and inflexible strategic allied plan that the BEF was tied to: notably the expectation that the campaign would commence with a short period of mobile warfare before the front stabilised so allowing full mobilisation, while at the same time degrading the German war effort, before finally mounting a decisive counter offensive. The Commander in Chief, General The Viscount Gort VC, was considered a brave leader in battle (his Victoria Cross was proof of this) but was not considered a strategist. Lieutenant Colonel Horrocks recorded that "Even when Commander in Chief he remained essentially a frontline regimental officer who was always more interested in the details of battle than in the strategic picture. Yet, where a more brilliant soldier might have lost his nerve, Gort remained staunch to the end, and thus showed the one essential quality required in times of adversity by all commanders - mental toughness."

The actual campaigns, including Norway, showed that the British Army was unable to successfully mount either a prolonged static defence or serious mobile counteroffensive on the Continent; it was also clear that the Army failed to properly consider how their enemy's own doctrine and organisation was likely to interact with their own. Although the BEF had the best equipment and weapons that were available to it, this was still not enough from an industrial base that was still gearing up for war; of the thirteen infantry divisions in the BEF only ten were equipped for combat but these were still largely engaged in training and construction work when the blitzkrieg burst upon them, while the only armoured division available arrived incomplete and after the blitzkrieg had began so negating the possibilities of having a proper work up period. It was a disgrace that after the BEF was evacuated from Dunkirk those units left in France, mostly in Brittany and Normandy, could find in the huge base depots a mere twelve field guns (in for reconditioning), a single howitzer with no recoil mechanism, forty anti tank guns and twenty six infantry tanks. The 1st Armoured Division had left its 40mm Bofors anti aircraft guns in the UK as it expected to get replacements on arrival in France. In fact, there were no spare Bofors guns on the Continent at all. Churchill told Parliament that "the best of all we had to give has gone with the B.E.F. and although they had not the number of tanks they were a very well and finely equipped army. They had all the first fruits of all our industry had to give, and that is gone. An effort the like of which has never been seen in our records is now being made. Work is proceeding everywhere night and day, Sundays and weekdays. Capital and labour have cast aside their interests, rights and customs, and put them into the common stock. Already the flow of munitions has leapt forward. There is no reason why we should not, in a few months overtake the sudden and serious loss that has come upon us without retarding development of our general programme." Whether he truly believed this statement or used the occasion to provide disinformation or a morale boost at a critical time is not known.

In late June the Home Army found itself large in manpower but mostly operationally static and weakly equipped. Former BEF units were struggling to reorganise after Dunkirk while the home units had much of their equipment and weapons removed or replaced with older ones, in order to rearm the field army. In the country at that time there were only 844 light tanks, 236 medium cruiser tanks, 137 heavy infantry tanks and 52 armoured cars, 810 field guns (126 18-pounder, 269 18/25-pounder, 90 25-pounder and 325 4.5-inch howitzers), 153 medium or heavy guns (94 6-inch howitzer, 20 6-inch and 39 9.2-inch howitzers), 378 anti tank guns and 15,545 anti tank rifles, 2073 anti aircraft guns (369 4.5-inch, 932 3.7-inch, 379 3-inch, 296 40mm and 97 2-pounder), 6713 3-inch mortars and 3578 2-inch mortars. These included what the BEF had managed to bring back: 13 tanks (7 cruiser and 6 light) 322 artillery guns, 4739 vehicles, 533 motor cycles, 32,300 tons of ammunition, 33,000 tons of stores, 1000 tons of petrol and most of its stocks of chemical weapons; almost all of these came from the Lines of Communication left after the BEF had evacuated plus the reinforcements and supplies sent out to reform the BEF but not landed. These figures compare badly to the equipment lost on the Continent: 600 tanks, 1016 field, 273 medium and 58 heavy artillery guns, 607 anti tank guns, 264 anti aircraft guns, nearly 64,000 vehicles, 20,500 motorcycles, 76,100 tons of ammunition, nearly 417,000 tons of stores and 165,000 tons of petrol. It was estimated by the War Office that it would take about three months to replace these losses from the existing industrial base.

Despite the impending invasion Britain's war industry was still at this stage far from reaching the high levels of production necessary, many firms still working to peacetime levels of timekeeping and labour. An example was delivery of the impressive 25-pounder field gun howitzer. By May the monthly production had increased to thirty five but each infantry division had an establishment of seventy two and there were twenty seven of these divisions who needed those guns urgently. Between January and the end of April 1940 industry had produced 97 light, 123 cruiser and 57 infantry tanks, 845 armoured carriers, 397 2-pounder guns (both tank and anti tank versions), 107 25-pounder and 123 18/25-pounder field guns, 245 3.7-inch and 77 4.5-inch anti aircraft guns, 157 40mm light anti aircraft guns, 10,606 3-ton lorries, 5200 30-cwt, 2920 15-cwt and 2982 8-cwt trucks plus 806 gun towing tractors. In addition, during this time, the Royal Army Service Corps (RASC) was responsible for repairing 600 vehicles received from its overseas forces. However from June, industry, galvanised by the catastrophe facing the country, worked to increase production, though the totals of vital equipment still were short of what the Army needed.

Since the early 1930's a lot of consideration had been given to moving the industry supporting the armed forces to areas of the country that had not recovered from the economic depression, while the Government also ensured that a significant proportion of production orders also went to these areas. As there was a significant under capacity in many of the traditional industries it was decided to utilise their expertise and tooling to produce war materials; for example the cotton industry was used to manufacture artillery shells. The increasing proportion of war capable industry around London concerned the military authorities, due to their vulnerability to air attack. In 1934 the Chiefs of Staff looked at locating the war industry in safer areas of the country, generally west of a line running from Weston Super Mare to Linlithgow via Stow on the Wold, Stafford, Stockport and Haltwhistle. They also believed that vital war production should not be closer than twenty miles from the coast. The use of existing industrial premises was also recommended, as this would be less obvious to enemy reconnaissance. The availability of skilled labour was also to dominate the location of industrial capacity, though wholesale redeployment of industry leading up to the war was not pursued, as this would involve dislocating production at this critical period. Between 1936 and 1938 the War Office pursued a vigorous policy of strategically spreading its important explosives and weapons factories about the country, west of the safe boundary and mainly in Scotland, the northwest and south Wales. This foresight would have proved its worth with an invasion occurring in the south east.

Many of the War Office related factories were placed under government control and managed by the chemicals conglomerate ICI, with new producers grouped together to ease the administrative burden. This war industry continued to grow after the outbreak of hostilities, with its important production facilities largely duplicated to ensure that production was not dislocated by enemy action. The Government never succeeded in establishing a single supply organisation, each of the armed services continued to have a different Government ministry assigned - The Ministry of Supply provided the Army with its needs, the Ministry of Aircraft Production supplied the RAF and the Admiralty Controller supplied the Royal Navy - while the War Ministry's Defence Committee was the supreme co-ordinating agency in respect of war production. Inevitably, there was some overlap in production schedules and output. While the Royal Ordnance factories provided the expertise in war production and handled ammunition production, the War Office ensured that production orders were also passed to private industry. With this in mind the London Munitions Assignment Board was formed to control production, importation and allocation of munitions and related materials.

The traditional set up of Britain's industrial base had made the rapid improvisation and growth of a war industry possible. Early in the war an interdepartmental Building Committee was set up under the Ministry of Labour to co-ordinate future construction work for all of the armed forces; although much needed it suffered from two main defects - no precise knowledge of the civil engineering labour force available and no system to allocate the meagre resources available on a priority basis. In addition, there was the also lack of heavy plant construction equipment.

It was clear that the resulting continental campaigns had revealed major weaknesses in the Army's preparations, deployment and command. As a result the General Staff set up a Committee in June under General Sir William Bartholomew, a former Commander in Chief of Northern Command, to consider the operational lessons of the recent campaign and, if necessary, suggest changes to the Army's organisation and training; the Royal Artillery and Royal Armoured Corps formed their own committees, the recommendations of which were fed into this one. The Bartholomew Committee sought the opinions of all the senior officers involved in the campaign and was able to produce its main report by 2 July. It is important to consider this Committee in some depth as it demonstrates the thinking of the many senior commanders who had recently fought the Germans and provides guidance on how they thought best to adapt and improve all facets of the British Army in order that it could defeat the enemy when it next met.

The Committee opened its Report by remarking that the BEF operations had "consisted of a series of withdrawals compelled by a need to conform to the movements of allied forces on its flanks. On no account was it forced to relinquish its main position by a frontal attack, despite being outnumbered and having to hold long fronts". It confirmed that "the German was a first class soldier who fought with great determination, pressing through any weak spot without regard to any dangers posed by having exposed flanks; if checked, their organisation is such that rapid support from air and artillery is soon available. With great ingenuity the enemy concentrated his means of attack on the opposition's morale through application of noise from air attack and artillery, fire and movement and ruses. To counter them we must be physically and mentally active". The Report was split into various sections:

Lessons
The Committee believed that the most important of these were as follows -
- The need to have an Army headquarters structure below GHQ to command in the field, leaving the latter to provide liaison and strategic overview
- The GHQ signals organisation was not suitable for mobile operations and quickly fell apart
- While the division should remain the essential combat organisation its brigades were the best organisation to undertake the fighting and, as such brigade and battalion commanders must work more on their own initiative than before
- Divisions should have their own armoured reconnaissance unit, better light anti aircraft, medium machine gun and anti tank resources
- Independent reconnaissance groups were required to replace the divisional cavalry. Attached engineers and artillery observers should support it
- It believed that the motor division should be abolished, as it was an uneconomic use of available motor transport.

Tactics
- It recognised that river defences were good but were likely to be overlooked due to the terrain and that offensive action would be limited for the same reasons
- It was essential that the forward line be covered by obstacles, themselves covered by observation and fire support and with a stop line constructed in the rear, while the main defensive position must be provided in depth. In taking up these defensive positions it was essential that reconnaissance and organisation of forces occur quickly but soundly, while observation should be strengthened by having more snipers (it suggested raising the number of snipers in an infantry battalion)
- Concealment of positions needed to be greatly improved (too often German reconnaissance teams were able to find positions by seeing our own soldiers walking around them without due care)
- Defensive positions must be constructed for all round defence and troops should not become overly concerned by enemy penetrations behind them, but make use of alternative positions. In all cases defence must be aggressive

- It was felt that enemy attacks would be best countered by effective reconnaissance of the ground and artillery fire, with any enemy penetrations subject to immediate counter attacks. In this, the carrier platoons provided immense value due to their mobility, weapons and potential for providing diversions; mortars were insufficient for their role, with the numbers needing to be increased and their crews provided with better communications; artillery support plans needed to be flexible and speedy.

Artillery
- The Report recommended that the experimental organisation of field regiments be reversed so that they now had three batteries of two troops, each with four guns
- It noted that the 6-inch howitzer's range was insufficient for its counter battery role
- It suggested using the 4.5-inch howitzer in an infantry gun role in an attempt to emulate the German's successful use of theirs. However, this was found to be impractical as additional resources could only be made at the expense of 25-pounder gun production
- It recognised the general effectiveness of its own anti tank weapons, but expressed the importance of the new 6-pounder gun to cope with added armour protection that the German's would undoubtedly produce
- It noted that its own anti aircraft protection was poor and that more mobile light weapons should be available in forward areas. The 3-inch gun was considered better suited for mobile operations than the 3.7-inch, while the 40mm was found to be very effective at ranges up to a thousand yards; in all cases it was believed that these weapons should not engage single aircraft unless necessary. With this in mind, passive air defence was regarded as being extremely important and something that required great discipline
- It noted with concern the lack of reserves so that any guns lost could not be replaced. There was a shortage of ammunition, with stocks unable to meet the high rates of expenditure experienced
- The Report noted the good German air co-operation, with ground forces having to wait less than 25 minutes for air support (it was also noted that local air supremacy was a very important aspect in this issue)
- The Report noted a lack of appreciation of RAF operations within the Army - it suggested that in future the RAF at least fly "morale" flights over the front line so that the soldiers would see them. It was important that unless local air supremacy was achieved fighter support for army co-operation aircraft was vital.

Royal Engineers
- It found the basic field company to be adequate in action, but suggested that its equipment load be reduced for mobile operations, the remainder to be held by the field park or stores units
- It found the bridging policy was too complicated and that the units involved be split into smaller groups
- The shortage of weatherproof explosives was noted as a concern.

Command
- It was believed that only in exceptional circumstances should ad-hoc formations be formed as these rarely had the necessary command or administrative structure to make it effective
- Headquarters in all formations should be organised into a command post and rear headquarters. It noted that the staffs at brigade level and above were mostly improvised around a couple of trained officers, a system which diluted the commander's ability to effectively command
- In the BEF it was noted that orders issued by the higher level formations often took the form of conferences and verbal, but not confirmed
- The role of motorised "contact" or liaison officers was considered invaluable, especially in mobile operations. It believed that in most field units the commander should have a mobile ability to make them truly effective.

Signals
- One of the first problems the BEF faced at the start of the German offensive was the collapse of its communications system at high level, many of its cable lines being cut by bombing while also having to deal with an unco-operative local French or Belgium telephone system
- Wireless transmission was hindered by a lack of sets, trained personnel, lack of an efficient cipher procedure (suggested relying on simple code words), fear of interception by the enemy and an ingrained habit of wireless silence imposed during the "Phoney War"
- Handicapped by this collapse senior commanders had to improvise, utilising the GHQ "Phantom" signals and intelligence service, an overworked liaison officer system or issuing verbal orders personally, confirmed later in brief written form and supplemented by map tracings where possible
- Little thought was given to signals counter measures
- The use of wireless below Corps level needed to be simplified
- The Number 3 wireless set was found to be too cumbersome
- The lack of proper cross country vehicles for cable laying was highlighted as the BEF had been forced to lay them by roads and found these more often cut by enemy action or accident.

Administration
- It found that the BEF's plans were too complicated to cope with the modern warfare encountered and, instead thought that instructions should be issued in the form of directives
- It did, however, note that the supply system and movement control organisation did generally work well
- It noted great concern over the lack of reserve equipment and spares, notably weapons and armoured vehicles
- It recommended that dumping of supplies should be reduced to a minimum
- The units in the lines of communications needed to be more mobile, with the administrative "tail" of all units be reduced to a more flexible level
- Troop carrying units must have wireless communications to be truly efficient.

The Royal Armoured Corps' own report concluded that it found the organisation of the Armoured Division to be generally satisfactory, but felt that its independent brigades were not best suited to combat in its present organisation. It made the following observations:

- The brigade headquarters was too small to be truly effective in action
- RAF liaison officers should be directly attached to Divisional Headquarters, in order to better co-ordinate air support
- Cruiser and infantry tanks should be organised in separate units due to their different roles and capabilities
- The A10 Cruiser tank was found to be unsatisfactory as it was underpowered, slow and lacked good cross country performance. However, the other cruiser tanks were considered satisfactory and the 2-pounder tank gun quite effective
- The amount of infantry allocated to the armoured division was inadequate, these often being used to protect assembly and rear areas rather than assist in combat (1st Armoured Division had theirs sent to defend Calais)
- Reconnaissance, artillery and engineer resources allocated needed to be improved in both quantity and quality of equipment
- Armoured units should follow German doctrine by laagering up at the end of the day or period of operations to allow its supply services to come up to it rather than withdraw to them
- Armoured cars were invaluable but noted these must have four-wheel drive in order to improve cross-country capabilities.

The Royal Artillery review confirmed that the new field artillery organisation had largely failed to live up to its potential. Its main points were:

- The three troop field battery, designed for attack, was found not to be suitable for defensive operations as it proved too awkward to handle and too slow in providing a regimental fire concentration
- Common with other combat arms the lack of wireless sets was felt
- It recommended the field regiment be re-organised to its pre war set up
- The re-introduction of a regimental survey party would enable the artillery to predict fire and engage targets without prior fire registration
- Provision of armoured Observation Post (OP) vehicles
- The speeding up of fire control and planning to cope with fast moving tactics used by the Germans.

The review also thought it necessary to properly instruct armoured and infantry commanders in how to use artillery as a major combat asset. Another aspect that needed to be looked at again was counter battery fire - the engagement of the enemy's artillery. Although this had been successfully applied during static defence operations it quickly fell apart during the mobile phases, notably due to lack of wireless sets with observation units and lack of both mobility and range of the heavier artillery pieces that was required. The essence of the review was the need for more and heavier guns with longer range, more mobility, faster procedures and better methods of communication.

The campaign found that while both types of anti tank guns used were quite effective there were concerns that improvements in the enemy's armour protection would soon reduce their potency. The campaign had also not changed the Royal Artillery's views on the infantry controlling their own anti tank guns and a growing opposition to the brigade companies was to lead to their dissolution.

The 2nd Irish Guards, following its defence of Boulogne in May 1940, produced a 'lessons learnt' report. It noted:

- The (Bren gun) carriers were invaluable given their mobility
- The anti tank guns were too cumbersome and slow and relied on towing vehicles; many guns were lost as a result. Guns must be properly sited, dug in and protected; anti tank rifles proved worthless
- The 2 and 3-inch mortars were very effective, but their effect was reduced by numbers and ammunition (many only had smoke shells)
- The provision of anti tank mines would have greatly aided defence
- The need to dig in troops at every opportunity to mitigate air attack
- The lack of proper transport reduced the efficiency of the battalion by half
- Wireless sets should be issued to each brigade and battalion headquarters as telephone cable, despatch riders and civilian telephone lines were too easily disrupted. Constant moves exasperated this problem
- The battalion's light anti aircraft machine guns should be sited in cover rather than in the open, as otherwise they were too exposed. Having said that, their ammunition lacked armour penetration and so was rarely effective.

Despite these comments, it finished upbeat, saying that had the battalion enjoyed artillery, air and engineer support its operations could have turned out differently. It also noted that despite its many shortcomings it took a well equipped, fully supported and highly mobile force a full day to force the battalion back a mere mile and a half.

The Anti Aircraft Command was also included in the Royal Artillery review. The problem of countering dive-bombers raised a lot of discussion, although the only immediate solution was to provide more light anti aircraft (LAA) guns, the Bofors 40mm being particularly effective but in poor supply. To provide a more effective base, especially against low flying aircraft, the need for advance warning was especially required. With the technology and resources lacking, the immediate solution was to provide advance observation posts with the combat units at the front. Although the review recommended that each division be provided with its own light anti-aircraft (LAA) regiment, this could not be acted upon at the time due mainly to the prior need to provide LAA defences to the many vulnerable points around the country with the weapons currently available (many of these places having to rely on old light machine guns rather than 20mm or 40mm cannons). Although by mid July there was a feeling that the AA defences were performing reasonably well in daylight, the review noted the need to improve the performance of heavy anti aircraft artillery (HAA), particularly at night. Performance would improve with experience, especially as this Command was the Army's most operationally active element during this period.

Major G Chapman RA, who had been part of the BEF's General Headquarters, produced his personal note on anti aircraft action by the BEF soon after his return from Dunkirk. He noted that improved fire discipline by the HAA gun crews was needed as the tendancy had been to open fire at extreme range and at differing rates of fire. Success in action was down to careful preparation, accurate use of instruments and holding fire until the target was well within range. He noted that once an aircraft began taking avoiding action fire should be withheld. The need for sturdy firing platforms and good fields of fire was also noted. A major problem lay with the LAA detachments. Too often they opened fire on single reconnaissance aircraft or were dug in so giving their positions away in both cases; they also tended to open fire too early. He felt that change of position should be frequent and that dive bombers should be left to the LAA guns as they were best suited to this role. He felt that the searchlights performed well.

In June 1940 it was decided to concentrate the HAA guns into sites of four guns in order to produce a more effective and better equipped unit. To counter ground attacks the Bofors guns were provided with anti tank ammunition, while the 3.7-inch gun had already proven itself capable of engaging tanks. The expected invasion also prompted a lot of work to prepare each static gun and searchlight site as a defended place, including constructing trenches and pillboxes, deploying barbed wire and improving camouflage. The Command also looked at the value of dummy sites, both to divert attacks from genuine sites and to exaggerate the density of AA cover, though little was actually done at this time. The urgency of this work was clear but, as a report on 19 June stated, "Still more remains to be done. We have not yet shaken ourselves out of a rut. In some places officers of experience, imagination and drive have achieved excellent results. In others there is an air of complacence, of orthodoxy and of failure to realise that tomorrow may be too late". General Pile ordered that "Regimental commanders go out continually and see for themselves what is happening, advise the inexperienced and drive the contented."

It was accepted that following an invasion some sites would find themselves being overrun; if possible the units would remove their guns and equipment to new sites, otherwise the troops were expected to adopt an infantry role after destroying their valuable guns and equipment. The Command did allocate a significant proportion of both heavy and light anti aircraft guns (120 and 84 guns respectively, averaging about 16% of those available) to support field forces in event of invasion, these mainly tasked with protecting their lines of communications and assembly areas, but these guns were still less than the number judged necessary to provide a truly effective cover. Although many of the guns not assigned to supporting the field forces were nominally mobile, the reality was that it would take a lot of time and resources to re-deploy when necessary.

The Light Anti-Aircraft gun situation was still far from satisfactory. On 21 August there were 430 40mm, 135 3-inch, 158 2-pounder and 40 20mm Hispano guns, backed by 7364 Lewis light machine guns (4473 deployed to protect HAA and searchlight sites, the rest deployed to the growing list of vulnerable places). The greatest concentration of LAA weapons was in east Kent, including 25% of the important 40mm guns. Attacks on the radar stations in August showed the ineffectiveness of the LAA defences assigned to their protection (each site had a troop of three 40mm guns), notably that their deployment was too remote to provide proper protection and the site layout often had arcs that were not covered. As a result the guns were quickly moved closer and sites better prepared.

In addition to the main Royal Artillery Report the Anti Aircraft Committee produced its own report on 16 August on air defence requirements following the fall of France. It had three main considerations - the increased risk to western and northern Britain, concerns over the use of the Irish Republic by the Germans and anticipated increases in the enemy air strength. The Report basically required more of everything - six new balloon barrages were proposed for the southwest, south Wales and Belfast, coupled by denser searchlight belts supported by a mobile reserve. More guns were planned to thicken existing Gun Defended Areas (GDA) and establish new ones, not only to deter attacks but also to bolster civilian morale. 1512 additional HAA guns were requested - 672 to the new GDA, 496 to bolster existing GDA, 272 to defend airfields and 72 for a mobile reserve; it was further intended that half of all these would be mobile. 2550 additional LAA guns were requested to cover 425 new vulnerable points. In reality, these requests were fantasy, given the production facilities and resources available at the time. The reality was that the Command held only about a third of the HAA and a tenth of modern LAA guns that was required, much of which was statically deployed. One area that could be fulfilled was the provision of unguided rockets from August - 8000 3 inch single or double launchers and 160 24 barrel projectors.

By early September the Command was able to assess its strengths and weaknesses as a result of action during the "Battle of Britain". It found its control and warning organisation had stood the test with amazing resilience and adaptability; although the 40mm Bofors guns had also performed well, LAA performance was weaker than expected, due partly to the poor standard of training and partly because there were insufficient weapons to go around. Fortunately, the summer of 1940 also provided a much needed opportunity for most anti aircraft units to visit established gunnery camps, to improve their performance and test their command structure.

The coastal artillery organisation was also reviewed, given the impending fall of France and Belgium. On 19 May the Royal Navy made available some one hundred and fifty 6-inch guns to strengthen the coastal artillery defences. These guns had been earmarked for the arming of merchant ships but were now to be deployed on the east and south coasts in the newly authorised emergency batteries; these batteries were mostly initially manned with temporary Royal Navy or Royal Marine personnel until such time as the Royal Artillery could provide the necessary manpower. The guns were eventually deployed in forty seven two-gun batteries, the first eight being operational only fifteen days after the proposal had been agreed. On 16 June the Navy provided fourteen 4.7-inch guns for seven new batteries, with another sixteen guns in eight batteries added on 16 July. By the end of August a total of sixty five emergency batteries were operational, defending ports and vulnerable landing places around the entire country. Each battery was expected to be responsible for its own defence and camouflage, while dummy installations were also constructed to help distract the enemy. Although mostly sited by the Royal Artillery these batteries were mainly located on or close to the shoreline and, as such, would have had a short operational life before being overrun or knocked out by an invading force. For command and control purposes these were either administered by the existing coast regiments or newly formed small ad hoc group headquarters, but were rarely included in a general fire plan due to their isolation from both each other and existing coastal artillery units.

The main Bartholomew Report concluded by stating that against an enemy like the Germans it was difficult, indeed almost impossible, for a unit to recover if put into battle badly in the first instance. All commanders of whatever rank must possess initiative and courage and in the end it would be the initiative and fighting spirit of the junior commander and individual soldier that would win battles. Although the main Report was completed in early July it was to be many months before its contents would be generally accepted, as it was passed to anyone with a major interest in it for their comments and feasibility of implementation. The Army hierarchy did not seek to make a more radical reappraisal of its doctrine at the time because it felt that due to the imminent invasion it would be impractical to contemplate it to the depth required. They believed that the most that could be done was to adapt existing structures and doctrine to meet the immediate problem of how to counter an invading force that was itself better equipped and able to operate at a higher tempo. Contemplating the main Committee's Report in July the Assistant Chief of the Imperial General Staff, Lieutenant General Carr, noted concern about "circulating the recommendations too widely as they may create a feeling that the Army's organisation and some of its methods are faulty. It might cause more harm than good if we tried any considerable reorganisation at this stage". In December 1940 the Army's Director of Staff Duties referred to the Dunkirk campaign as a special set of circumstances that were unlikely to arise again. Nevertheless, the Army was to adopt in the next few years most of the proposals put forward at this time and which eventually made the British Army better prepared and organised to defeat their enemy.

Despite all of the problems identified above there were positive aspects to the BEF's performance. The BEF escaped from the Continent relatively intact, in part due to the steadfastness of its troops in defence, the ability to improvise at all levels, the aggressive use of its local counter attack forces, an efficient movement control system (as demonstrated by the quick and effective redeployment of II Corps from south of Dunkirk during 26-28 May), the physical fitness of its soldiers, the mental toughness of many of its field commanders, the effectiveness of the Royal Artillery and other supporting arms and, on top of all this, an innate self confidence by the British in ultimate victory (something that annoyed and confused enemy and ally alike during the war). Immediately after Dunkirk, Anthony Eden, the Secretary of State for War, visited a number of Army camps around the country in which the returned troops of the BEF had been hurriedly quartered. He noted, "I had half expected some questioning or complaint, for there was enough to criticize. Our infantry had had no armour to support them; even its equipment had revealed some woeful shortages. But the mood of the officers and men showed none of this. On the contrary, their temper was that of victors, with no sign that they had had to retreat during days of continuous fighting before an overwhelmingly stronger enemy. I felt that having measured their opponent in these conditions, they were convinced that, given the weapons, they could match and outfight him. Even those brigades that had suffered the heaviest casualties were as confident and resolute as their more fortunate comrades. For me the hours I could spend among these men were a tonic, for there was in them the temper of those who knew they could not be beaten, whereas in Whitehall I had only too much reason to reckon how heavy must soon be the odds." It was these qualities that would be once again tested to the full when the Germans landed on Britain's shores, as they were now expected to do so.

A major problem facing General Headquarters Home Forces was that of the sixteen operational divisions in the UK at the beginning of June (one armoured and three infantry divisions were still in France with the newly reconstituted BEF under General Alan Brooke) only nine had reached a fair standard of combat training. Although the British leadership had to wait until 4

September before the Chiefs of Staff were able to present a full scale review of British strategy, once more giving priority to the RAF's Bomber Command and Royal Navy as the only elements capable of offensive action at the time, the Army had already been given a secondary role and accordingly a lower priority in production of equipment and weapons, though not in manpower. In any case, the army's training organisation was still facing major problems with almost everything being in short supply - equipment, accommodation, ammunition, training land and quality training personnel - priority being given to field force units. Training within these units additionally suffered from a continuing lack of uniformity, with tactical training still often lacking realism, while many were also hampered by the extra burdens placed upon them. The War Diary of 1st London Division's 1st Bn (City of London) Royal Fusiliers noted on 4 September that "training was greatly interfered with by the number of guards which have to be found for all unit billets, battalion headquarters and stores, as well as a permanent guard of seven men on the Corps Stop Line, a weekly guard for Brigade headquarters and for all crashed aircraft in our area". Another factor influencing training programmes was the almost continuous threat of air attack that units based in the southeast had to contend with.

Responsibility for implementing training was further disrupted when GHQ Home Forces became the major operational headquarters and its Home Commands were transformed into operational Army Commands. To further complicate the situation, while the Home Commands were responsible for training all operational units in the country the War Office retained direct control of recruit training units and the training of field units earmarked for overseas operations. Training manuals and guidelines continued the pre-War practice of providing general principles while allowing commanders much latitude on interpreting them. In June 1940 the General Staff issued a pamphlet to commanders on training their battalions asserting that "Variation and originality in method of instruction should be encouraged provided that they produce good results". However, many unit commanders continued to feel that tactical drills would inhibit their officers from using their intelligence and knowledge from adapting principles to situations, though it was soon accepted that with the huge increase in the Army's size the ablest of officers and their knowledge would be in shorter supply. Senior officers like Generals Alexander, Montgomery and Dill suggested that the best way to train this new conscript Army was through tactical drill, so that everyone would know their role and the tempo of operations maintained. It is not well known that the main author of the tactics volume in the 1930 revised Infantry Training Manual was a certain Lieutenant Colonel Bernard Montgomery.

On return from the Continent, General Alexander recommended drawing up "lines of conduct - simple guides for simple soldiers" so that men would have answers to battlefield problems when faced with them. In all, about ten types of minor operations were presented, such as village clearing and attacking strong points, with over 30,000 copies of these "Tactical Notes" being printed. Even before this, in March 1940, 2nd London Division began developing battle drills based on a pamphlet entitled "Training in Fieldcraft and Elementary Tactics", by analysing each movement and operation of war and breaking it down to bare essentials, working out an ideal plan for dealing with these under ideal conditions and teaching that plan as a drill with variations to ensure the latter did not become an end in itself. It assumed that the imaginative commander could work out an adaptation that would fit the tactical circumstance; the unimaginative could "just carry out the drill woodenly and still not do too badly". In the Division all training was performed at the double and with ruthless application to ensure the highest possible standard of physical fitness, while also paying strict attention to weapon handling. After June 1940 many Corps and Divisional commanders established their own tactical schools, many drawing their own lessons from the BEF campaign but again there was a complete lack of uniformity in training. Adoption of universally accepted tactical drills in the Army's training regime was not to be implemented until 1941-42. In April 1941 a brigade training instruction from 2nd London Division still noted that "the British soldier generally is lamentably ignorant of the enemy he is training to meet, and until he understands the enemy's capabilities he will get a false sense of the enemy's superiority". It then looked at morale, fitness and technique in detail suggesting improvements.

During late summer the Army began to prepare for training during the coming winter months. The new schedule was due to begin at the start of October. An example of what this was to include and how it was to be implemented can be seen in 3rd Division's training memorandum. The stated objective was:

- First to provide a hundred per cent reserve of specialists
- To complete personal weapon training
- Train the bulk of junior leaders
- Then conduct more advanced training.

The training was to enhance the basic qualities required for every soldier. This was to be achieved through discipline, morale, fitness, drill, dress, saluting and cleanliness. It expected that the whole Division was to be able to march up to twenty five miles and still be fit enough to fight. The memorandum then focused on anti gas training, night driving, manoeuvre training for artillery units, wireless operations, clerks, snipers and mortars. It expected that the training should vary and be stimulating, while field exercises should be held at least weekly for small units and fortnightly for larger ones. It believed that "once his interest is aroused and his imagination stimulated, self reliance, initiative, inquisitiveness and rapid dissemination of information will follow automatically." It strongly believed that the continued interchange of information was vital. Suggestions to stimulate the men included motor transport and motorcycle rallies, speed and endurance tests, battle drill and runs, military plays (demonstrating the right and wrong ways to undertake training and roles), war talks, visits to industry and other units, use of models, competitions, evening classes and live firing tactical exercises.

Official records show that since the declaration of war in September 1939 1,166,800 men had been enrolled under the National Service Act, while another 654,500 had volunteered for service with the armed forces. Whilst this might sound good there were real problems with absorbing the numbers. Concern in increasing the size of the Army was not seriously addressed until August 1940 when Ernest Bevin, the Minister of Labour, reported that continued large manpower increases for the Army would result in industry being unable to fulfil war production quotas due to skills and manpower shortages. Despite this warning the Government abandoned its policy of balancing the manpower needs of industry and Army by allotting 324,000 men to the Army between June and August, overruling the objections of the Adjutant General who knew that the training system could not cope with such numbers. At the end of June the War Office issued a letter about authorising this increase; it read "In view of great pressure the Cabinet has decided to increase the size of the Army for Home Defence, interfering as little as possible with Field Army units. A scheme whereby training, holding and home defence units will absorb a very great input largely within sixty new battalions has been evolved. During June 1940, instead of the normal 70,000 intake, the figure will be 165,000. In July it will rise to 180,000. The new units will be rather in the form of `Kitchener Army` units, officers being selected and Regimental Associations and others being asked to help."

122 new infantry battalions were raised to take these new men after they completed basic training, with many of these units later forming new coast defence brigades in the autumn in order to release the field units assigned to that role. In addition, further infantry battalions (70 series) were formed at the start of September by taking the companies comprising young soldiers aged between 16 and 18 from existing home service battalions. Their immediate role was to take over the guarding of vulnerable places, so as to release more men for the Field Army, while the long-term view was to train these soldiers for later service in the Field Army. With this increase in manpower the Army was, on paper at least, large enough to cope with an invasion; however, this increase did not take into account the large numbers assigned to non combat or support roles (increasingly necessary for a modern fighting machine and something that Churchill, among others, constantly failed to grasp) and the ability of the Army to properly train and equip them.

The British Army was still the only truly mechanised Army in Europe, albeit with much civilian transport impressed into military service. Although the RASC was able to replace the vehicle losses sustained on the Continent by late summer many units still had a significant number of civilian vehicles in their charge, especially those lower down the priority list. Many of these units had shown initiative in sourcing such vehicles in early summer and were loath to give them up. By 26 August the War Office, whilst reporting that only five field divisions had received their establishment of first line transport, also raised concerns (mostly financial) about the amount of civilian transport still held by many units. The provision of vehicles was not helped by the continuing demand from all Commands for even more transport, especially for troop carrying vehicles; this was shown by the official requests between July and September for over 7200 cars and lorries. In the same period the War Office issued 23,266 motorcycles, 7174 cars, 21,200 lorries and 2340 coaches and buses. The increase in the number and type of road transport units also meant an increase to the three main types of maintenance units - the Vehicle Reserve Depot (VRD), Motor Transport Stores Depot (MTSD) and Heavy Repair Shop (HRS). The first two were tripled in number, though the HRS was more of a problem due to the requirement of specialist machinery and skilled personnel. To assist the RASC in maintaining its vehicle fleet the Ministry of Supply allocated a number of civilian 'Army Auxiliary' workshops. The Home Guard also helped by providing a number of transport and specialist recovery units.

Supported by leading industrialists, a range of civilian cars and trucks were further adapted to military use, resulting in the production of a range of ad hoc lightly armoured and armed vehicles as a short term solution to the lack of proper armoured vehicles. The most famous of these were the Beaverette and Ironside, both based on a motorcar chassis, with about 2800 of the former and 3600 of the latter being produced. These "armoured" motor cars typically weighed two tons, with armour plate between 10-12 mm thick, had a road speed of up to 45mph, a crew of three and were generally armed with a light machine gun and/or anti tank rifle. The light armoured brigades charged with undertaking local counter attacks, were equipped with these vehicles. Another private development was the Armadillo, an ad hoc "armoured" lorry mostly used for airfield defence, with over 940 being adapted. The Home Guard also took advantage of this situation by producing their own local varieties. Some, including General Alan Brooke, saw these ad hoc vehicles as a detriment to the growth of Britain's war industry, taking up valuable materials and tools to produce.

Another example of the desperate need for armoured support in the invasion period was the pressing into service of some First World War tanks, several being rescued from scrap merchants and one or two even made mobile after a lot of dedicated care (an example being a memorial removed by Royal Navy ratings in Portsmouth and renovated to working condition). Other obsolete tanks from the 1920's made up the bulk of the armour in adhoc striking forces formed from the training units of Southern Command.

On 13 July General Headquarters confirmed its priority in re-equipping the British Army:

- The first priority was that all field units were to equally have their full establishment of personal equipment plus 25% of the war establishment scale of other equipment for training needs.
- The second priority was for the following formations to have all their war establishment of equipment - IV and VII Corps; 1st Canadian, 1st and 2nd Armoured, 3rd and 43rd Divisions; the NZEF; 1st Armoured Reconnaissance, 29th and 31st Infantry Brigades.
- The third priority was for holding, home defence and auxiliary pioneer (AMPC) units to have all their personal equipment and a minimum scale of other requirements.
- The fourth priority was for all field formations to have a full war establishment of equipment.

During the invasion period the need to provide the maximum number of weapons and equipment to the troops took priority over the production of the best possible weapons and equipment, a concern compounded by the time and extra resources needed to retool and provide new production facilities within Britain's growing war industry. Even in November 1940, when the immediate invasion threat was over, Churchill insisted that "at this stage in tank production numbers count above everything else. It is better to have any serviceable tank than none at all." As such, the troops often received what the Ministry of Supply could most easily mass produce, what the War Office could provide from outdated stocks and what could be sourced locally. This was demonstrated in the War Diary of 1st Bn Queen Westminster Rifles in 1st London Division, which dryly noted on 19 August "Received two new (Bren gun) carriers. The fact that they could only be used in reverse in no way dampened the carrier platoon commander's ardour".

An example of utilising existing stocks were the armoured trains, the Royal Armoured Corps initially being responsible for manning these trains. Headquarters Scotland Command had started the ball rolling with its request for a number of trains to patrol the desolate regions in the north. Eventually twelve trains were authorised for the whole country in late May, the GHQ Home Forces and Ministry of Transport co-ordinating efforts to improvise them from existing rolling stocks. A standard pattern was adopted of an engine, two wagons and two armoured trucks, with armament consisting of two 6-pounder guns, two anti tank rifles and six machine guns. The intended roles for these trains were reconnaissance, added firepower with a quick response time and, as a last resort, acting as a mobile road or railway block. Their vulnerability was recognised but accepted given the state of the national defences. The lack of a tender reduced their range to 30 miles on the flat or 15 miles over hilly ground. Trials advocated the addition of a tender and better armour protection, amid continual demands for training ammunition (the 6-pounders were initially provided with only armour piercing ammunition). The Corps decided to man the trains with personnel from 23rd and 24th Army Tank Brigades, as these unequipped formations could most readily spare them. Each train had an officer and twenty five men to man the armament with seven Royal Engineers from their Railway services to run the train. An additional twenty nine men were assigned as reserve crew or in an administrative capacity. Four armoured train group headquarters were established to better administer the trains, three being assigned to each group. On 21 September it was decided that the Polish forces would replace the RAC personnel once they were trained. A number of privately run trains, like the Romney, Hythe and Dymchurch Light Railway, were also adapted to military use and included in local defence plans.

Over the centuries the British Army had built up a strong logistical pedigree in its operations throughout the world and was able to implement a high degree of improvisation when required. It was clearly understood that a properly organised and efficient administrative infrastructure was an essential prerequisite for success. However, the logistics administration organisation at home was still not designed to operate at the higher and faster combat tempo required (many depots had civilian labour that worked "office hours") and it would be a challenge to integrate it with the combat logistics organisation within the same country, both operating over a relatively short distance but under greater threat of direct enemy land and air action. It was quickly confirmed in May 1940 that while GHQ Home Forces would have operational command of the logistics network, the executive command of administrating the network would remain with the War Office and each Army Command headquarters, with a clear delineation of the responsibility between them: The War Office was to be responsible for the establishing, controlling and maintaining of war stocks in depots and for all rail and sea movements. The Command headquarters were to be responsible for administration within their own area; supplies issued from the Command supply depots were to be replenished by civilian contractors, Ministry of Food and the NAAFI; petrol was to be supplied by either the War Department pumps or contracted civilian ones, themselves filled by the Petroleum Board and controlled by the RASC; Commands were to hold a small reserve of small arms and minor equipment but heavy weapons and large equipment were to be held by the War Office; ammunition was to be held in Command depots to War Office scales; the Commands were not to have a reserve of vehicles, as this remained the responsibility of the War Office, but the Commands were to be responsible for vehicle maintenance and repair once issued.

On 1 July the movement control organisation was reorganised. This organisation had been instituted just before the outbreak of war to facilitate the efficient movement of troops, equipment and supplies around the country and from the various embarkation ports for service overseas; but by early summer it was recognised that this potentially vital organisation had not adapted to the new realities of impending invasion. The reorganisation was to ensure that there was greater decentralisation of command and a closer liaison with the civilian railway companies. Medium to large-scale movements through London was to remain the responsibility of the Metropolitan Police. Small organisational staffs were to be co-located with the Command

and Area headquarters, while liaison officers would be available at Corps and divisional level headquarters and other representatives would be placed at ports, depots and important railway stations. A report dated 6 July noted that the railways, under the new war conditions, presented great difficulties as it meant altering the established routeing of imports from the seaports while coping with the abnormal level of military traffic, civilian evacuations and air interference. It concluded that the dense network and high efficiency of the railways should enable them to meet all military requirements. To ensure efficiency it was important that the earliest possible warning of future movements be issued to all concerned, together with fuller information on details, timing and routeing when decided. One area where the movement control organisation was not to have a role was in the battle zone itself, with the RASC and Military Police retaining responsibility there. It was agreed that arranging large or complex rail movements was best done by conference between the movement control staff at the War Office and the railway company head offices in London; it was recognised that this may not be possible in some circumstances (like moving combat formations from the north of the country to the invasion zone) and therefore arrangements would be agreed and confirmed by using teleprinters. In the southeast movement control District staffs were established at Redhill and Orpington (for Eastern Command), Aldershot and Woking (for Aldershot Command), Salisbury (for Southern Command) and Dorking (War Office).

It was established practice for stores and supplies to be moved from depots by railway to railheads where they would be transported forward by road through several different stages before reaching the troops. For ammunition the War Office was responsible for delivery to the Command depots, then Commands took responsibility for delivery to planned railheads near Corps or divisional sub depots, with motor transport available at 24 hours notice in case the former method broke down. This supply system was designed to act as a conveyor belt so obviating the need to build large supply dumps close to the front, while small mobile units were provided by depots and repair units to better provide initial support to combat units. Each field division had companies specifically roled to provide ammunition, POL (Petrol, Oil and Lubricants) and supplies, while each Army Corps had at least two companies holding mobile reserves of fuel and ammunition. Additional companies were allocated as required from GHQ or Command resources, including troop transport, ambulance, engineer and artillery support units. In terms of ammunition supply XII Corps had the use of the War Office controlled 12th Ammunition Supply Depot in Staffhurst Wood, near Edenbridge, and three Corps Ammunition Depots - 1st in Foxden Wood near Pluckley for 1st London Division, 2nd in Burrswood near Tunbridge Wells for 45th Division and the 3rd at Rowhook near Horsham for Broc Force; in addition an ammunition train was based at Tongham, near Aldershot. V Corps had the use of the Command Ordnance Sub Depot at Grateley (near Andover) and its own Corps Ammunition Depots at Holnest (near Sherborne), New Alresford (near Winchester) and Damerham (near Fordingbridge). A smaller Corps Sub Depot was established at Shalfleet on the Isle of Wight.

XII Corps reported in June that it intended to hold seven days reserves of rations in its area, while the divisions under its command would also hold three days reserves. It was expected that the normal supply system would continue to operate as long as possible but if communications with Corps headquarters failed the field units were authorised to contact the nearest supply depot or dump to achieve its supply requirements. All reserve stocks were to be replaced at the first opportunity. Each main supply depot was to be able to meet the supply needs of 500,000 men. The Corps had the use of the War Office Main Supply Depot and

Eastern Command's Reserve Supply Depot, both in Reigate, and eight normal issue depots (Woolwich, Lingfield, Brighton, Chichester, Chatham, Canterbury, Dover and Shorncliffe), one normal issue sub depot at Tenterden and four reserve dumps of preserved rations (Bromley, Dorking, Lindfield and Lenham). Southern Command had use of the Main Supply and POL Depots at Newbury and Banbury. A number of food reserve depots were also established at strategic places in case the normal distribution channels were dislocated.

After the BEF returned home the importance of providing POL (Petrol, Oil, Lubricants) was upgraded with reserve canned petrol stocks provided for each Command or District and the opening of petrol depots at eight strategic locations. At the same time the RASC was responsible for co-ordinating plans to destroy or disable fuel stocks if they were in danger of being captured, including the individual petrol pumps at all civilian motor garages; however, inland fuel depots were not to be destroyed but immobilised in anticipation of their quick recapture. In XII Corps area the petrol supply, in terms of depots, was organised as follows: one War Office depot (120,000 gallons) was at Buckland near Dorking; twelve Petroleum Board bulk depots at Gravesend (50,000 gallons), Rochester (250,000 gallons), Aylesford (700,000 gallons), Faversham (160,000 gallons), Ashford (50,000 gallons), Hawkinge (35,000 gallons), Tunbridge Wells (120,000 gallons), Portslade (Brighton) (2 million gallons), Horsham (85,000 gallons), Haslemere (35,000 gallons), Guildford (130,000 gallons) and Redhill (74,000 gallons) and five Corps dumps at Cale Hill (south west of Ashford) (20,000 gallons), Tenterden (20,000 gallons), Somerhill (Tunbridge Wells) (50,000 gallons), Wilderwick (north east of East Grinstead) (50,000 gallons) and Newlands Corner (east of Guildford) (60,000 gallons) - the last dump was also made available to VII Corps. If the POL depots were not available a POL railhead was to be opened either at Gomshall or Dorking. There were also three kerosene depots at Bexhill, Folkestone and Broadstairs. The Petroleum Board depots were only to be used by the Army as a last resort. The armed forces were well served by the Petroleum Board, who had ensured that stocks remained high enough to provide sufficient fuel reserves for operational requirements. Cabinet papers at the end of June reported that fuel stocks for the armed forces were 2,278,000 tons for the Navy, 606,000 tons for the RAF and 218,000 tons for the Army. It noted that consumption between March and May had been 261,700 tons, 23,400 tons and 16,000 tons respectively, plus an additional 14,300 tons by the Army overseas.

On 9 July the Petroleum Board established the Petroleum Warfare Department to investigate the potential of using petrol in a defensive way. Among the more successful experiments were the flame traps, flame fougasses and beach mines. On 20 July the first flame trap was constructed, with 200 eventually being installed in the coastal regions. Each flame trap consisted of a 500 gallon tank, ideally located 200 yards from a critical road and connected to perforated steel pipes. Ignition was typically by throwing a Molotov Cocktail on to the released petrol. Mobile versions were also produced. The flame fougasses consisted of a 40 gallon barrel with a small explosive charge. These had an average range of 30 yards and were generally arranged in a battery of four fougasses. Some 50,000 barrels were soon issued to 7000 sites, again mostly in the coastal area.

Since the outbreak of War the Army and civilian authorities had initiated long formed plans to ensure that the full resources of the country's medical system could support the military effort. These medical arrangements had been simplified and strengthened during the invasion period, with the Royal Army Medical Corps liaising closely with the Ministry of Health. It had been agreed at the outset that both the Army and civilian facilities would treat and evacuate casualties within its care, irrespective of their status. Evacuation of casualties from hospitals to those outside the immediate zone of operations would be by hospital train and road convoy. The senior medical officers in the Command sub areas were responsible for the hospitals, depots and stores in their area, while the senior medical officers at Corps and Divisional level were responsible for their field ambulance and hygiene units. In XII Corps area there were military hospitals at Sheerness, Maidstone, Dover and Hellingly (Hailsham); there was a Command medical store at Maidstone and medical sub depots at Haywards Heath, Hellingly, Goodwood, Chartham and Willsborough.

The Army had been forced to leave behind all its bridging equipment on the Continent (much of which was to be used by the Germans in the invasion, especially in making their tanks amphibious). In July 1940 there was still not a great deal of this specialist equipment available: 1500 feet of pontoon bridging (in twenty two foot sections and capable of bearing a load of 18 tons), 40 steel spans (semi mobile) and 14 Hamilton heavy bridges (capable of spanning 140 feet). The more modern Inglis heavy bridges were on order but were not high on the production schedule. The War Office felt that requests for tactical bridging were unlikely to be needed in cases of sabotage or air attack, so it released the available equipment for tactical operations in support of the Field Army. This was influenced by the fact that repairs to railway bridges were the responsibility of the relevant railway company, supported by the Royal Engineer railway units, and repair of road bridges the responsibility of the Ministry of Transportation, with Royal Engineer road construction units available for designated tactical roads. Concern was felt that the standard of training in constructing heavy bridges was very low and needed addressing; the War Office noted that during the recent campaigns the Germans had been very quick to bridge crossings and so allow the momentum to continue unabated; the reason, it felt, was not that the German equipment was better but that the troops were better trained and their deployment more efficient. The Army had three Bridging Companies, though two of these (4th and 5th Companies) only received their equipment by the end of July. 3rd Company was assigned to GHQ Reserve, 4th Company went to Northern Command, while 5th Company was split between IV and VII Corps. Each Company had a mix of RASC and RE personnel, the part assigned to VII Corps comprising 3 officers and 146 men (only 11 were RE) with 56 3-ton and 8 1-ton or 30-cwt lorries, organised around two pontoon sections. The War Office required that this equipment be located up with the leading elements assigned to an assault crossing so as to reduce the construction time and congestion involved.

In addition to the Bartholemew Committee, The War Office formed the Howard Committee, under the chairmanship of Lieutenant General Sir Guy Howard. Its task was to look at the Army operations following the Dunkirk evacuation and, in particular, the ability of the lines of communication organisation to adapt to fluid operations. The subsequent report noted that the normal, more complacent, attitude within the lines of communication had been changed irrevocably by the blitzkrieg; at short notice organisations, like Headquarters Lines of Communication, found itself charged with functions previously performed by the General Headquarters. The report found that it was essential that any headquarters, however far to the rear, be prepared to improvise and adapt to new and rapidly changing situations; it recommended that the standard of competence of headquarters staffs within the lines of communication organisation should be as high as that expected in normal combat formations. The report also found it vital that the commander in chief of the field force regards the lines of communication as being of equal importance as the field units (it noted that General Gort never visited the lines of communication units or associated headquarters). The report also found that the BEF's lines of communication organisation had been too complicated and tried to provide for all contingencies. The Committee recommended that a more flexible and less congested lines of communication organisation would provide a more efficient service. Most of these recommendations were taken aboard; for example, the base supply depots were adapted and provided with their own dedicated transport and labour saving machinery that could also be used in the field while self contained and adaptable detail issue depots were also created.

The failure to integrate air support to the Army was recognised as an important problem that needed both the Army and RAF to co-operate fully. While the 1935 Army Regulations recognised the need to have air superiority over the battlefield, it had failed to develop a coherent strategy to work to achieve it. This was also the fault at the time of the RAF that was more concerned with pursuing its own strategic objectives, Army air cooperation thus being regarded as a low priority. The lack of a properly organised and resourced air support system had reduced the effectiveness of the BEF and enabled the enemy to dominate the battlefield from the air, a vital aspect of the blitzkrieg doctrine. These experiences led to a clearer appreciation of the need to secure closer and more effective ground-air co-operation, though in reality there still remained a significant difference between the Army and RAF in how best to achieve it - the Army wanted a system comparable to that enjoyed by the Germans while the RAF thought that effective co-operation only required a willingness to work together with the aid of a more efficient signals system. In August 1940 a workable scheme was devised - a mobile operations room, known as an Air Support Signals Unit, was to be located at Army level headquarters and supported by officers in radio equipped cars that were to be located with forward troops. However, this scheme took a long time to set up and train and would not have been truly effective in time to meet the invasion in September 1940. The RAF's 22 (Air Co-operation) Group, mainly using Lysander aircraft, was supposedly dedicated to this role but had also been allocated other roles during the actual invasion, notably potential chemical warfare operations. The Group did conduct artillery co-operation trials with the Royal Artillery's School of Artillery between September and December (some pre-War trials were held in 1938 and a few were held with the French in May 1940, just before the campaign began) that would eventually lead to airborne observation posts. Operations with the BEF had shown that the air co-operation aircraft were extremely vulnerable to both anti aircraft fire and fighter attack, and that to be effective (or at least, to survive) such aircraft required fighter escort (experiences of the First World War should have made that much clear, at least).

A review of the War Office organisation in August 1940 recommended that its own Military Operations (MO) and Military Intelligence (MI) Departments be merged to provide a more efficient use of the resources available. It noted with concern that the length of an officer's posting in these intelligence posts was too short, not helped as intelligence postings were seen to be a detriment to career advancement. It confirmed that little or no time was devoted to intelligence instruction at the Staff College, with the result that staff officers graduating knew little if anything about this vital work. It was agreed during the summer of 1940 that the War Office would be responsible for providing intelligence on the strategy and order of battle for the German Army while GHQ Home Forces was to be responsible for gathering intelligence on how the German forces were to be used, especially the strategy and tactics adopted after the landings. To help provide this latter intelligence GHQ Home Forces had its own reconnaissance unit (also known as "Phantom") which had worked well with the BEF; in addition to reporting to GHQ Home Forces this unit was also expected to keep Commands informed directly and was organised to be self sufficient and mobile. More about this unit, now called the GHQ Liaison Regiment is provided in Appendix 5.

In terms of interrogators it was recognised that the War Office's MI9 had the pick of those undergoing training. While MI9 were charged with examining captured enemy soldiers at the Command Transit Cages, GHQ Home Forces aimed to have interpreters down to divisional level on the scale of three at Command headquarters, two at Corps headquarters and one at divisional headquarters. It was expected that tactical interrogation would happen at divisional prisoner of war cages, while a fuller interrogation would happen at Command cages. The number of prisoner of war camps was to be increased from the present three, presently holding mostly Luftwaffe prisoners, with additional sites being identified at York (550 capacity), Bury (2000), Kempton Park (1500) and Oldham (1500); 2000 prisoners could also be accommodated in Dumfriesshire, 2000 in Perthshire, 2500 in West Riding, 1500 in Shropshire, 3000 in Northamptonshire and 3000 in Oxfordshire. Prisoners were to be moved mainly by rail or road to a collecting camp near Sutton Coldfield, itself capable of holding 4000 prisoners once the Czech contingent had been moved out, before being sent onto one of the camps. The racecourses at Kempton Park, Lingfield and Ascot, as well as the other Command cages, could be used as transit camps if required. Each Command had their own prisoner of war cage, each capable of holding 500 prisoners; Eastern Command's cage was located at Shipley, near Horsham, while 1st London Division's was at Pluckley and 45th Division's was near Hawkhurst, while Southern Command's cage was in Swindon.

Despite its shortcomings the Corps proved invaluable during the "Phoney War" period and subsequent campaign, performing largely in the much needed liaison and personal reconnaissance roles. However, the structure at GHQ level was less of a success, not least when the Director of Military Intelligence, Major General Mason-Macfarlane, was detailed to form an ad hoc defensive force (Mac Force) on 17 May as a result of the German breakthrough and took his security chief (Lieutenant Colonel Templer, recently promoted) as his chief staff officer, thus stripping the GHQ Command Post of all its senior intelligence officers at this critical time. Even having the correct intelligence could be hindered by human frailties: at 10.30 in the morning on 22 September 1940 5 Commando, near Dover, received intelligence that 'invasion of Great Britain due to start at 15.00 hours; preliminary bombing expected to start at 12.00 hours. All posts to be manned completely by 13.00 hours'. At 13.10 hours a further message was received stating 'For England read Indo China. All troops to stand down'!

It is appropriate to note here the British signals interception organisation and its efforts to decode the German Enigma coding system. It is well known that the Poles had led the effort in cracking this system, which the Germans relied upon to safeguard all their military and political communications. Poles within the French signals interception service continued this work after Poland fell, though with little French participation. In Great Britain this work was initially carried out by the Admiralty, which had created a signals interception section during the First World War; however, after that War the Admiralty's refusal to grasp the nature and value of such intelligence meant that the work of this section existed in a vacuum - there were no systematic procedures for processing, evaluating and distributing the information gleaned from code breaking. This section was transferred to the Foreign Office and re-named The

Government Code and Cypher School. This School was moved out of London to Bletchley Park in Buckinghamshire, to be joined by the three services own Sections, on the outbreak of War and where a growing number of intellectuals were gathered under the administration of MI6. Its efforts to break Enigma reached its peak in the spring of 1940 and was conducted along three lines - firstly, the intercepted signals were intensively studied for clues, the Luftwaffe being the most helpful; secondly, using the Polish technical achievements they developed their own data processor to handle the huge amount of possible cipher computations; thirdly, rigorous rules were established for the methodical recording and analysis of all traffic such as pattern, call signs and mistakes. An integral part of this work was establishing a secure method of distributing the intelligence gained to the appropriate staffs and commanders. It was this concentration of mechanical sophistication, intellectual ability and financial backing that allowed the British to take the lead, though a working communications was established with their French allies. In early April 1940 the first real signals were deciphered, though as Enigma came in several varieties due to the needs of its user not all could be quickly read (the Naval variant remained unbroken until 1941). When the blitzkrieg broke in May some groups of deciphered signals had already started the process of accurately reading the enemy's mind, however the collating and disseminating of this intelligence was still not geared to the needs of the Armed Forces. Within a short space of time the RAF and Army intelligence services were encouraged to provide German speaking intelligence officers to provide both a direct link between the two levels and additional manpower to improve output. At this time distribution of the intelligence could be both simple and secure - to the Prime Minister, Chiefs of Staff, the Directors of Intelligence in the three services, Fighter Command and Commander in Chief Home Forces.

To provide secure distribution overseas a number of Special Liaison Units (SLU) were organised and located at field headquarters, each consisting a specially picked officer and a small section of cipher clerks and signallers. A Unit had served with both GHQ BEF and the RAF Advanced Air Striking Force and used a cipher system not dissimilar to Enigma (though, this was never broken by the enemy). Here, then, was at least the skeleton of a complete intelligence system: a source of information and an organisation for processing and disseminating it. The code name "Ultra" was assigned to this system, which did not include the Royal Navy at this time, whose own Section left Bletchley Park for the Admiralty in London; the main reason for this move was the lack of German naval signals being broken, while a wide range of existing intelligence gathering facilities were able to provide a better service through the Navy's efficient Operational Intelligence Centre.

Although the tempo of blitzkrieg operations demonstrated Ultra's shortcomings many lessons were learnt, in particular the need to have a deciphering system that was swift and continuous. Although the French service managed to evacuate to Algiers (it moved back to Vichy France in October) communication was covertly maintained with the British through the Poles still attached to the French. It was a major failure of Germany's own intelligence services that even with the fall of France they remained unaware that Enigma was being progressively infiltrated.

June 1940, therefore, found Ultra intact but still striving for maturity. At the start of the Battle of Britain in July a SLU was formed at Fighter Command's headquarters to ensure a more efficient method of communication. The information it provided was mainly used to endorse or disprove existing intelligence gathering methods but did also provide an insight into the Luftwaffe's strategy, order of battle and daily operational orders. As the German Army was more secure in its Enigma use and tended to use land lines rather than radio, Ultra intelligence relied on the Luftwaffe to provide information on invasion preparations, for example the parachute forces available, trials of new equipment and tactics to support landings and timings related to Luftwaffe operations in England after an invasion. This ability to listen in on its enemy during its preparations was of immense value; indeed, by September the British had managed to piece together with considerable accuracy the pattern of events likely to follow the invasion. However, Ultra could not on its own provide information on when or where this invasion would come, at least not until the time that hopefully such orders would be sent out through Enigma, the Luftwaffe signals intercepted, decoded, assessed and then passed on - even then, it would probably be a matter of hours before the event occurred. The importance of Ultra at this time, particularly for the Army, was its ability to monitor most of the German preparations as they evolved and provide guidance on how operations after S Day was expected to be carried out.

The Army's organisational structure at home had hardly changed since the Victorian era. The War Office, led by the Chiefs of Staff, was responsible for the strategic overview of all operations worldwide but, in terms of home defence and administration, command was delegated to the General Headquarters, Home Forces (GHQ). The country was traditionally split up into six Command and two District Headquarters, each responsible for the administration and training of Army units within its area. However, after the Army was ejected from the Continent these Commands were suddenly thrust into the frontline. Each Command headquarters now had in a very short period of time to change completely into an operational Army level field headquarters, whilst still retaining its traditional administrative role. Headquarters Southern Command papers show that it would move to a secret tented location (referred to only as "the Wood") should the traditional headquarters site become untenable. This headquarters was to be split into an administrative operations headquarters, about 70 strong, and an echelon of nearly 350 personnel to carry on the main administrative work. Other Command headquarters may have had similar plans.

Although the three BEF's Corps (and later the Norway Expeditionary Force) headquarters had been formed from within these same Command structures at the outbreak of War, the Army had never had to consider the effects associated with the radical transformation now required. This metamorphosis was to be achieved without additional resources being allocated and would put a great strain on the General Officers Commanding and their staffs, most of whom had been recalled from retirement to release more active officers and personnel when War was declared. Northern Ireland District was treated differently as its troops remained under direct control of the War Office.

Eastern Command, in particular, found itself in the unenviable position of being responsible for the two areas of the country most likely to see invasion landings - Kent/Sussex and East Anglia - this situation being further complicated as its area of responsibility was cut in two by the Thames Estuary and London. Given the expectations that the Germans would invade on the east coast this Command needed to be the best that the British could provide, in terms of units, reserves, equipment and command. Although Headquarters Eastern Command was charged with commanding the defence of both East Anglia and the southeast it is likely that it would quickly lose responsibility for XII Corps and the invasion sector, with GHQ taking over direct operational command, so allowing the Command's Headquarters to concentrate its attention on defending East Anglia, where the bulk of its forces were deployed. Indeed this concern had already been noted by GHQ, who would establish a separate Command Headquarters, based at Aldershot, covering the southeast in February 1941 (it would include the Aldershot Command).

In its review of October 1940 GHQ Home Forces identified the threat to individual Commands. It agreed that Eastern Command faced the greatest threat due to its geographical position; Southern Command faced a potential sea borne attack by up to three divisions as far west as Portland or from large scale airborne landings inland; Western Command faced a negligible threat, except from local airborne landings or if Ireland was invaded; Northern and Scottish Commands also faced negligible threats from sea or air landings.

In May 1940 it was acknowledged that these Command and District headquarters could not be expected to carry out all its functions throughout its area of responsibility, given the many new responsibilities it had to contend with. The War Office agreed to establish a number of sub-area headquarters, each with a small staff, to ensure both an effective decentralisation of command and the continued quality of control at a local level. A major problem found in the new Command structure was that too many officers and senior non commissioned officers in these regional commands were unable to comprehend the changes required for such a transformation, not surprising, as many of them had been recalled from retirement on the outbreak of War.

On his return from France in June, General Alan Brooke once again took over command of Southern Command. He soon noted that "the Command had a long way to go to be put on a war footing... The more I see of conditions at home, the more bewildered I am as to what has been going on in this country since the war started. There are masses of men in uniform but they are mostly untrained". To change this most senior commanders, and in particular those like Alan Brooke who had recently returned from the Continent, took the lead in trying to instil a greater war atmosphere, including spending a great deal of time touring their areas, visiting defences and units and changing the many unsuitable officers found. Montgomery went even further by banning officers` wives and dependants from his command area as he felt they would distract the officers from their duties!

To better co-ordinate and control these many headquarters the War Office decided to the enlarge the existing General Headquarters Home Forces (GHQ) at the end of May 1940 under the command of General Sir Edmund Ironside. He was a former General Officer Commanding Eastern Command and Inspector General of Overseas Forces before replacing Lord Gort as Chief of the Imperial General Staff (CIGS), when the latter was appointed to command the British Expeditionary Force in 1939. General Ironside's appointment to be Commander in Chief Home Forces was strongly supported by Churchill and, though he was regarded as a very capable officer (on 29 May he recorded that Churchill had said to him that "we all depend on you because you don't lose your head in crisis"), he never seemed happy to hold this position according to several close colleagues. He commented in his diary that he was "now in command and not hampered by a machine made for peace conditions and not fit to function in war." He felt that the Home Defence Executive, set up to co-ordinate all matters relating to national defence and involving ten Government Ministers and their staff, was nothing more than a debating society. He was able to eventually get this Executive greatly scaled down.

GHQ would be pre-eminent as it was charged with directly commanding all the Army's forces available to defeat the invasion. GHQ had decided at an early stage that it would retain overall command of the Home Forces, excluding the Anti Aircraft Command who remained under the RAF's Fighter Command. It would act in the capacity of an Army Group level field headquarters in order to counter the invasion and as such, would most importantly have direct control over the major counterattack forces. General Ironside faced many of the problems that Lord Gort had had to contend with as BEF commander, namely having to command his forces in the field while also having to placate the politicians and senior officers behind him. Given the vital role expected of it, it was important that the staff of the GHQ Headquarters would need to be the best that the Army had available. However, on appointment General Ironside raised concern over the improvised nature of the Headquarters staff. It was due to him that this vital Headquarters was to expand as its responsibilities increased and eventually comprised a number of branches and sections including administration, movements, intelligence as well as attachments from various corps of the Army (it took longer still to get the War Office to authorise a civilian electrician, desperately needed for the out of hours work required to keep its signals network operational at all times). An important element of the Headquarters set up were the sixty nine liaison officers who were to ensure that an effective method of communications existed - there were originally thirteen of these, one each for the Home Commands, II Corps, IV Corps, VII Corps, VIII Corps, XI Corps, XII Corps and 3rd Division.

War Office planners had identified the three likely stages of enemy invasion and the needs of countering them:

- First was the ability to destroy attempts at landing a sizeable enemy force either by sea or air. This was considered to be outside the remit of the Army
- Second was the ability of the Army to conduct effective counter attacks against any enemy beachheads
- Third was the ability to prevent enemy breakouts into the rest of the country so allowing the rest of the Army to re-organise and re-equip before going on the offensive to push the Germans out of the country.

When he was appointed to command of GHQ Home Forces, General Ironside commented in his diary that "a defending commander is largely unaware of the attackers' plans. He cannot tell where the crucial stroke will fall. He must guard all his vital points against both ground and airborne attack. A measure of dispersal over a large area will be necessary, but he must not unduly weaken his reserves, for they will be his only means of influencing the battle. He must be constantly on alert to avoid surprise, must not be misled by feint attacks and, when the main stroke is identified, he must counter attack at once. His opportunity may be fleeting. He must therefore be skilful in placing his reserves and he must retaliate at the right place and time. He can have no cut and dried plan and must largely improvise. He must possess imagination, intuition, powers of deduction and agility of mind." Such was the reasoning behind his plans.

He expected three stages of attack - firstly, widespread bombing to break the morale of the people, concentrating air attacks on ports and shipping to cripple the Navy and block supplies; secondly, intense attacks on the RAF and industry in order to gain air supremacy; thirdly, invasion from sky and sea, with paratroopers securing airfields and landing spaces so additional forces could be flown in and attack beach and port defences from the rear so that the main forces could land largely intact.

On taking over command, he noted a number of immediate concerns in addition to his military ones that could influence operations. These were:

- That there were too many alien nationals still living in the coastal areas
- There was too much petrol available in the coastal areas, much of which was unguarded
- There was unrestricted movement at weekends in the coastal areas
- Civil organisations were too slow in their methods and did not appreciate the value of time in military operations and, importantly, a need for more realisation on the serious nature of England's position.

On 4 June he noted in his diary that "eternal preaching of the defensive has been the curse of our tactics; the call for no more Somme's has deluded our population. Nobody has been educated in the horrors of modern war. I do not believe people understand it yet. We must brutalise the whole population to stand up to this menace. If they do not stand staunch it means the loss of the whole Empire. We can do it. We must be ruthless with weakness." On 11 June he further noted "We are fighting for all we hold dear, liberty and the right to live as we wish to live." This appreciation was in tune with Winston Churchill's minute of 3 June to the Chiefs of Staff, which began "The completely defensive habit of mind, which has ruined the French, must not be allowed to ruin our initiative."

On 25 June Home Forces Instruction No. 3 was submitted to the Cabinet to convey the Army's anti invasion plan. It proposed to defend the coast with a thin crust of infantry, supported by coastal artillery, with the aim of disrupting the enemy landings long enough to allow the arrival of local reinforcements. The most important aspect of this coastal defence was that ports be denied to the enemy for as long as possible. There was general agreement that the ports be immobilised and their facilities removed inland rather than be destroyed, unless circumstances demanded it; this was in line with the Army's main objective to recapture any port within ten days.

Should the enemy succeed in breaking through this "crust", a large number of defended localities and nodal points, especially important communication centres, extending deep inland would aim to further disrupt and canalise the enemy advance. These defended localities and nodal points would typically feature road and railway blocks complemented by anti tank obstacles, multiple barbed wire entanglements and minefields all covered by pillboxes and other defensive positions. An idea of the layout of smaller nodal points can be judged by looking at the plans for Lydd in Kent (see page 337), which shows the village split into several sectors, each with interlocking fields of fire and obstacles, and a final keep based on the parish church. The Instruction noted that the general plan of defence would feature a combination of mobile columns and static defences. However, a War Office intelligence memorandum produced in

August 1940 commented that experience on the Continent had shown that the use of villages as strongpoints was largely rendered impossible due to the extensive use of dive-bombers. The Instruction recognised that static defence only provided limited protection of the most vulnerable points and must be supplemented by the mobile columns, which required time to deploy in order to properly counter enemy penetrations. In addition, local reserves would be responsible for countering parachute landings or minor breakthroughs. A Kent Home Guard exercise involving the Tunbridge Wells nodal point in 1943 noted the importance of providing a regular flow of information to both headquarters, reserve troops and observation posts, the continuation and duplication of communications and the weakness of outlying posts if split up into too small a force. It confirmed the need to ensure that friendly troops could freely move through the nodal points and that their defenders should continue to harass the enemy even if bypassed.

A further set of defended stop lines was to be produced in depth over a wide area covering London and the industrial centres of the Midlands. This system would aim to prevent the enemy from running amok among the vital industrial and political centres of the country, as had happened in France and Belgium. This latter network was called the General Headquarters (GHQ) Stop Line and was to be supplemented by similar stop lines devised at Command, Corps and Divisional levels (five were in eastern England and three in the southeast) and a demolition zone where bridges were prepared for demolition and roads and railways for cratering. More details of these defensive lines can be found in Appendix 8. Construction work began in June, with the strongest part of the Line being west of London. The defensive lines should not be confused with France's Maginot Line or Germany's Siegfried Line as they mainly consisted of widely spaced pillboxes defending anti tank ditches or natural obstacles where possible. To be truly effective the defences needed to be located in depth, capable of mutual support, supported by artillery, have good communications and, above all else, manned by determined and properly equipped personnel; in few places was this possible to achieve at the outset, but the lines could still provide the field forces with something tangible to regroup behind.

Counter attack forces were to be created, whether they were at brigade level or at the strategic Corps level. They had to be mobile and self contained but had little in the way of heavy weapons at their disposal. On 28 June Churchill said in a Cabinet meeting that the battle would be won or lost not on the beaches but by the mobile brigades and main reserves. In a 3 July memo General Ironside noted his concerns over a desire to move his GHQ Reserves closer to the coast as this would then restrict their own liberty of manoeuvre.

The Imperial General Staff concluded at the beginning of July (in agreement with the German High Command) that should the Germans succeed in establishing an effective force in England, the Army had not the offensive power to drive it out. The Instruction was seriously flawed from the outset by concentrating on a defensive and reactionary strategy, primarily due to the lack of properly equipped and trained mechanised formations to lead the counter strokes. The Instruction was also heavily influenced by what had recently happened to France, Holland and Belgium - notably that these countries had been defeated by terror, with mobile columns that simply ran riot through the interior of these countries. In truth, General Ironside was not able to propose the anti invasion scheme that he truly wanted, as he had neither the equipment nor quality of troops, properly trained and deployed.

General Ironside, however, constantly strived to encourage an aggressive mentality, promoting ideas that would assist his forces; this attitude however did not apparently get across to everyone. Brigadier Horrocks, commanding a brigade in 3rd Division deployed along the East Sussex coast in June noted "There was a curious atmosphere along the south coast. Everyone seemed to expect an invasion at any moment, but nobody was doing very much about it, and there was still an atmosphere of the peacetime holiday resort about Brighton. It proved a very difficult problem to organise our defence with the utmost care, so as to make up for our lack of numbers, because an enormous town like Brighton is laid out primarily to provide holidays by the sea, not as a fortress from which to repel an invasion. Montgomery used to pay constant visits and, on finding that a particular house was partially masking the fire from one of our machine gun posts, demanded that the owners be moved out and the house blown up, stating that defence must come first. He was, of course, correct, but it was not always as simple as it sounded. My predecessor had positioned troops on the two piers without allowing the civilian firms responsible for the entertainment booths to remove their possessions. Some months afterwards I received a bill for many thousands of pounds for compensation."

The British plans were also seriously affected by three understandable fears that quickly grew to endemic proportions. Firstly, like everyone in the country, officials and commanders believed that the Germans had the ability to drop parachute troops anywhere in the country and, given the well publicised recent successes of such forces, expected them to be foremost in the invasion, either by seizing airfields or ports so as to allow other invasion forces to be landed with little opposition. Much thought, planning and resources were allocated to constructing defences across the country to counter this type of operation and destroying those forces landed. This fear did, however, have a positive side in that it encouraged commanders and troops at all levels to develop a quick reaction and aggressive ethos in order to stop such an attack before it could take hold. General Karl Student, the father of Germany's paratrooper force, commented later that "We heard later that the people in Britain had a parachute psychosis. That amused us, but there is no doubt it was the best defensive precaution, properly directed."

The second fear was also a product of the blitzkrieg, namely the epidemic of reports and incidents attributed to "Fifth Columnist" activity, whether real or imagined. Such activity was designed to assist the German advance and hamper allied defences and movements, either through the actions of traitorous civilians or Germans in disguise. Although many of these reports were false the concerns they raised seriously infected military and civilian authorities and individuals, with the effect of further hampering their potential effectiveness. Much consideration had been given to controlling the population after invasion (discussed in more detail later) and in tackling treason. Already many people had been taken in to custody for their views and political stance. The lack of any significant fascist organisation or sympathy for their views among the general populace helped reduce the opportunity for a real "Fifth Column".

Since May, both these concerns had seriously infected Great Britain, with reports and scares making almost daily appearances in the press; the authorities sought to minimise their effect but recognised the importance of mentally preparing everyone to counter them. In this way, every citizen could take an active part in the defence of the United Kingdom.

The third fear lay in the recognition that the British coastline was extremely vulnerable to seaborne invasion due primarily to its length; there was a real concern that invasion forces, even in small numbers, could land at almost every port, bay and beach around the country and that all these places would need defending. It is not surprising to note that serious concern was even raised over the vulnerability of the Isle of Man to a seaborne invasion! Despite this concern many senior officials, including Churchill, noted that the invasion was most likely to occur in either East Anglia or north Kent, due to their proximity to Germany and the occupied countries. On 29 June General Ironside recorded that "The coast line is terrific in length and could be attacked at any point, air landings can take place anywhere in Great Britain or Ireland with even less warning than for seaborne landings".

The Germans did indeed plan diversionary operations from Norway, Denmark and the Bay of Biscay against South East Scotland, the Tyne, Yorkshire, East Anglia and the Irish Republic to take advantage of this vulnerability. As such, the British leaders had to plan for all contingencies, including moving into the Irish Republic from Northern Ireland and Wales should the Germans invade that neutral state. To properly organise against these threats, allow for the planning requirements and available resources to be properly allocated, the country was divided into categories of likely invasion zones - Kent, Sussex and East Anglia being awarded the highest priorities.

By the end of June Admiral Sir Frederic Dreyer had completed a survey of all likely landing areas around the entire coast of Great Britain. It was confirmed that the Royal Navy were responsible for all defences extending seawards from the high water mark, while the Army was responsible from the foreshore inland. While the senior Royal Engineer officers at Command level and below co-ordinated resources and plans, implementation of the Army's defensive measures was expected to be left to local units and civilian contractors, supplemented by Royal Engineer and Auxiliary Military Pioneer Corps (AMPC) troops.

Beach defence can be covered in four phases:

- Firstly, the Navy organised lightly armed small ex-civilian vessels to patrol up to seven miles off the most likely beaches. These were expected to report invasion fleets before trying to engage them. In the invasion areas these were based at Ramsgate (28 craft), Dover (25), Newhaven (20) and Littlehampton (12). The craft varied in size and capabilities and were largely manned with reservists and civilian volunteers. At sea each vessel was assigned a patrol line of between five and eight miles wide; in most areas these lines were duplicated to ensure coverage of the sector. Usually the larger vessels stayed at sea for six days at a time, while the smaller craft had a reduced endurance. Additionally, anti submarine trawlers were deployed to use their sonar equipment to pick up approaching craft.
- Secondly, where suitable, net booms were laid offshore with the aim of snagging the propellers of invasion craft. These were laid and maintained by the Navy's harbour boom detachments. In July a number of small defensive minefields were also laid to protect most harbours, ports and major estuaries along the south and east coasts.
- Thirdly, the actual beaches along these coasts were covered with various obstructions set at low tide, supplemented by mines - 50,000 anti tank mines having been laid by

July with another 200,000 ordered, while the Navy offered 100,000 beach mines in June, 74,400 of which were issued by 20 September - 47,800 (32,700 laid) in East Anglia and 26,000 (12,300 laid) to XII Corps - anti tank obstacles and barbed wire, all covered by pillboxes and other defensive positions. The naval beach mines contained 20 pounds of amatol explosive each and were to be placed about 20 feet apart in groups of six to eight for maximum effect. It was planned to place lines of scaffolding poles, draped with mines and explosives, along vulnerable beaches to prevent invasion craft from landing but work was hampered by tides and the composition of the beaches themselves. It was not until February 1941, however, that Naval trials at Felixstowe showed that the scaffolding as placed would not stop barges or trawlers from crashing through them; it was subsequently decided to move the scaffolding further up the beach and double their strength. In any case, by the time of the expected invasion, very little construction had actually been completed - only a third of the 15 mile stretch between Hythe and Dungeness, mostly at Hythe, Dymchurch and Littlestone, and only a quarter of the 12 miles between Pevensey and St Leonards.
- Fourthly, the exits from the beaches were prepared with further defensive positions, obstacles, demolitions and anti tank flame traps. Of course, all of these preparations varied in quality and quantity, depending on the resources available and type of beach involved. For example, records show that in Southern Command beach defences included over 4 miles of anti-tank ditches, 72 miles of concrete anti-tank obstacles, about 720 pillboxes, 65 miles of barbed wire and 15 miles of anti-tank mines; by 8 October Eastern Command had completed 440 miles of anti-tank obstacles, 1340 pillboxes, 1700 miles of barbed wire and 73 miles of anti-tank mines.

In many places on the east and south coasts field artillery was also placed close to the beaches so as to support the coastal batteries; but it was noted by artillery commanders that this was not an ideal situation for such an important asset, the artillery on Romney Marsh being particularly vulnerable as the flat terrain would have hindered redeployment. To complement the coastal artillery the Army also deployed its heavy artillery to cover most key harbours or beaches. The only harbour not covered so was Newhaven. Half of its available super heavy artillery and a third of its heavy artillery pieces were deployed to the Kent and Sussex coasts, most of the former around Dover.

No additional trained infantry was likely to become available for beach defence until late autumn set in when 134 fresh battalions were to be assigned - comprising 60 newly formed infantry battalions, 59 infantry holding battalions and the 15 pioneer battalions - in new coastal infantry brigades, that were being formed from the infantry training groups, so that the infantry divisions currently in place could be released from this static task; this would take time to arrange and the first units were not to become ready until the end of September. In early October a War Office report on the 9th Bn King's Own, one of the pioneer battalions due for re-rolling, noted that it had not been able to conduct normal collective training as it was often split up, with no company level exercises conducted. It believed that the battalion needed three to four months of uninterrupted training to be able to properly take its place in the field force. The War Office had decreed that these brigades would have only half their expected scale of heavy weapons and armoured carriers, though even supply of these would be a low priority. Until ready for their deployment, these new brigades were assigned static area defence roles.

The Army had also taken on responsibility for the ground defence of airfields, radar stations and supply depots so freeing the RAF and Royal Navy from this task. Every airfield was graded in vulnerability and importance and allocated both a defensive element and nearby counter attack force. In January 1941 General Student, father of Germany's airborne forces, recommended that his troops be assigned to seize airfields well inland where infantry forces could then be landed by plane. As noted, the British had already assessed this opportunity. Other than airfields, potential airborne landing zones were identified with those around London and within five miles of a major port, airfield or open beach being noted as a priority for obstruction and, if necessary, defence. By September demolition plans at ports and around likely landing zones were 90% complete. An additional 2,800 vital points, notably factories and transport centres, were also identified with Army Commands being responsible for finding the necessary guards; all this meant tying up 58,000 much needed troops including 17,000 from the Field Army.

One issue that was to remain a great unknown and had the gravest consequences was the use of chemical weapons. Despite the 1925 Geneva Protocol forbading its use, the British had been indoctrinated since before the War to the possibility of large scale gas attack on its civil population and detailed preparations had been in place to cope with such an eventuality. Experience during the First World War had also left the strong implication that chemical warfare on the battlefield would again be an integral part of operations. The War Office and Air Ministry had jointly agreed before the War that the principal chemical weapon would be mustard gas, which would be released in two forms - HS (shell/bomb) and HT (aerial spray). The War Office had requested production of 40 tons of HS and 2 tons of HT per week for the Army while the Air Ministry's requirement was 290 tons of HS and 180 tons of HT per week, with all production centralised at Randle, near Runcorn. Due to Treasury constraints the pre-War production capacity was to be 300 tons per week (ratio of 50:250 tons in favour of the Air Ministry) in order to maintain a reserve of 2,000 tons; however, delays meant that when War was declared only 500 tons were available. The Army lost most of its chemical weapons stock in France and the single factory producing them (new facilities were then being built in north Wales) was still not able to replace them quickly. By 20 June production was 200 tons of mustard gas and 12 tons of phosgene gas per week respectively. From July weekly production increased to 500 mustard gas filled Livens drums, 500 phosgene gas filled Livens drums, 10 bulk contamination tanks, 300-500 chemical mines and 10,000 chemical ground bombs, while 6,000 25-pounder gas shells were to be produced per month.

Both the Army and RAF did retain the capability to deploy such weapons, mostly by air or artillery. A report on 21 June felt that substantial airborne operations by the RAF were possible but ground-based operations were limited. By the end of June 1940 the British had 450 tons of mustard gas, with 1000 spray tanks and 39,000 bombs available to deploy it by air; the Army had 950 Livens projectors with 4000 mustard gas and 2000 phosgene gas filled drums, 10 mustard gas filled bulk contamination tanks, 1000 mustard gas filled mines and 15,000 6-pound mustard gas ground bombs. The War Office estimated that the Germans had a stockpile of 10,000 tons of poison gas.

The decision to use these weapons would have been political. In mid June General Sir John Dill, the Chief of the Imperial General Staff, proposed pre-emptive gas attacks by air on any landings but was overruled by those who urged caution on the basis that it was believed

Germany's own stocks were larger and that the level of British stocks meant that such action could not be sustained. In late December 1940 Churchill recorded he was anxious that gas warfare should not be adopted at the present time. He felt that the enemy may have it in mind and that their use could be imminent. Despite this reluctance there was some discussion over when and where attacks by the British should take place, if authorised. It was felt that attacks on the beaches and beachheads offered the best results, as this would be when the Germans would be more concentrated so offering a better target. The concerns about appropriate weather conditions being necessary and the effect on the British civil population in those overrun areas were also noted as being factors to be considered in such an attack. If used it was agreed that non-persistent agents would be preferred so as not to inhibit their own forces operations.

On 5 August Churchill sent the Chiefs of Staff a minute detailing his thoughts on the overall defence against invasion. It started "Bearing in mind the immense cost in war energy and the disadvantages of attempting to defend the whole coast of Great Britain, and the dangers of being unduly committed to systems of passive defence, I should be glad if the following notes could be considered:

- Our first line of defence against invasion must be the enemy ports. Air reconnaissance, submarine watching and other means of obtaining information should be followed by resolute attacks with all our forces available and suitable upon any concentrations of enemy shipping.
- Our second line of defence is the vigilant patrolling of the sea to intercept any invading expedition and to destroy it in transit
- Our third line is the counter attack upon the enemy when he makes any landfall, and particularly while he is engaged in the act of landing. This attack must be reinforced by air action and both sea and air attacks must be continued so that it becomes impossible for the invader to nourish his lodgements
- The land defences and the Home Army are maintained primarily for the purpose of making the enemy come in such large numbers as to afford a proper target to our sea and air forces
- However, should the enemy succeed in landing at various points, he should be made to suffer as much as possible by local resistance on the beaches, combined with attack from the air and sea. The defence of any part of the coast must be measured not by the forces on the coast but by the number of hours within which strong counter attacks by mobile forces can be bought to bear upon the landing places. Such attacks should be hurled with the utmost speed and fury upon the enemy at his weakest moment, which is not, as is sometimes suggested, when actually getting out of his boats, but when sprawled upon the shore with his communications cut and his supplies running short. It ought to be possible to concentrate 10,000 men fully equipped within six hours, and 20,000 men within twelve hours, upon any point where a serious lodgement has been effected. The withholding of the reserves until the full gravity of the attack is known is a nice problem for the Home Command
- It must be admitted that the task of the Navy and Air Force in preventing invasion becomes more difficult in the Narrow Seas (*English Channel*), namely from the Wash to Dover. This sector of the coast front is also nearest to the supreme enemy objective, London. The sector from Dover to Land's End is far less menaced, because the Navy

and Air Force must make sure that no mass of shipping, still less protecting warships, can be passed into the French Channel ports. At present the scale of attack on this wide front is estimated by the Admiralty at no more than 5,000 men. Doubling this for greater security, it should be possible to make good arrangements for speedy counter attack in superior numbers, and at the same time to achieve large economies of force on this southern sector, in which the beach troops should be at their minimum and the mobile reserves at their maximum. These mobile reserves must be available to move to the southeastern sectors at short notice.

The Chiefs of Staff replied on 13 August that, following consultation with the Commander in Chief Home Forces, they were in complete agreement with the principles contained above. They further noted that the paramount importance of immediate counter attack upon the enemy had been impressed on all ranks and that it was the policy of the Commander in Chief Home Forces to bring back divisions from static coast defence roles into reserve as soon as they were adequately trained and equipped for offensive operations.

A massive change in the Army's strategy in opposing the invasion occurred with a change in leadership. General Alan Brooke took over command of the Home Forces on 19 July and shared Churchill's vision of an aggressive and mobile defence. He noted in his diary "I knew well enough the dangers we were exposed to, the probability of an attempt to invade these islands, the unpreparedness of our defences, the appalling lack of equipment and the deficiency of training and battle worthiness in the majority of our formations. The idea of failure was enough to render the load of responsibility almost unbearable. Perhaps the hardest part of it all was the absolute necessity to submerge all one's innermost feelings and apprehensions and maintain a confident exterior. To find oneself daily surrounded by one's countrymen, who may at any moment be entirely dependent for their security on one's ability to defend them, to come into continuous contact with all the weaknesses of the defensive machinery at one's disposal, to be periodically racked with doubts as to the soundness of one's dispositions, and with it all to maintain a calm and confident exterior is a test of character, the bitterness of which must be experienced to be believed."

The General's credentials were impressive. He had distinguished himself during the First World War and spent the inter war years as an instructor at both the Staff College and Imperial Defence College before holding a succession of appointments that affected every branch of the Army - Commandant of the School of Artillery, command of an infantry brigade, Inspector of Artillery, Director of Military Training, commander of the experimental Mobile Division and commander of the Anti Aircraft Command. Even during the short existence of the BEF he had once more distinguished himself, first as commander of II Corps and then as the Commander in Chief of the new BEF, formed from the British Army units still left in France during June. It is no exaggeration to say that his diversity of experience was unrivalled; he was one of the few senior commanders in the Army at the time that was both an efficient administrator and effective field commander. Horrocks, after the War, recorded that "this alert, seemingly iron, man without a nerve in his body and who gave out his orders in short, clipped sentences, was a great soldier. We regarded him as a highly efficient military machine. It is only after reading his diaries that I appreciated what a consummate actor he must have been. Behind the confident mask was the sensitive nature of a man who hated war. Yet he never gave us the slightest indication of those moments of utter despair when it seemed to him almost impossible that any of us would ever escape from Dunkirk".

On assuming his new post he immediately ordered a halt to further work on the GHQ and other defensive lines, though by August the GHQ Line running from the Bristol Channel to Cambridge via London was largely complete as were many of the lesser lines (see Appendix 8 for details). He did allow the continuing development of nodal points for all round defence at important road and rail junctions as well as centres of communication, though rear area troops and Home Guard units were now expected to man these defences, so freeing the Field Army from such distractions. He made it clear that all troops were expected to engage German forces where they found them, irrespective of their own limitations, and all formations were allocated to either defensive or counter attack roles accordingly. He also had combined operations rooms set up at Command and Corps level to better co-ordinate command and communication at these important levels.

General Alan Brooke noted that a number of important defects must be improved as a priority:

- An increase in both motorised and infantry mobility
- Improvement in the general fitness of all troops
- All brigade groups were to be trained offensively, not just those allocated to counter attack roles
- Improvement in the standard of use of anti tank weapons
- Bolder training methods.

He accepted that junior officers were the weak link and that their training must be improved, as these leaders needed to demonstrate the new offensive spirit to their men. Despite this change in emphasis it took a while for those formations involved to adapt. Montgomery noted in his initial inspection of 50th Division at the end of July that "the result of concentrating entirely on defensive works and neglecting other matters is going to reflect adversely on the battle efficiency of the Division unless we are careful. I met rifle companies who had been in the same place for one month, doing nothing but working on defences. The men had done no drill or training and did not seem to be on their toes. I did not see the light of battle in their eyes. The best defences in the world are in themselves of little value unless the troops in them are full of beans and mentally alert." This did not mean that Montgomery had a low opinion of the Division or of the Territorial Army, as he was well aware of its performance with the BEF, but referred more to the inability to conduct offensive operations by being tied to a coastal defensive task. Montgomery also agreed with the change in emphasis from defensive to offensive action, stating "in the invasion battle the enemy has the initiative, therefore initially our operations tend to have a defensive bias... but the successful defeat of invasion can only be achieved by offensive not defensive action. This being the case our worst enemy is a defensive mentality. We have to develop the offensive spirit in our officers and men ... this does not mean that we will knock our heads against every snag that the enemy likes to prepare for us, regardless of the situation, but that although initially we may be forced to act on the defensive we are on the watch all the time for opportunities to take offensive action. The opportunity when it does come may be fleeting so immediate advantage must be taken before the chance passes. Nothing is ever hopeless so long as hearts are stout and men have the weapons with which to fight. I therefore say that the first requirement in the successful defeat of invasion is proven, well trained and well led soldiery who are mentally alert, skilled in fieldcraft, expert in the use of their weapons and are offensively minded." Montgomery also noted that defensive positions should be seen as the springboard for offence, command should be properly organised with the chain of command understood by all, forces should not be dispersed unduly, proper use must be made of engineer resources including demolitions and minefields, whilst communications must be effective and flexible.

General Alan Brooke visualised a lighter line of defence along the beaches, expected to hamper and delay the landings as much as possible, with highly mobile forces trained to immediate aggressive action that were intended to concentrate and attack any landings before they became too established. With this in mind he ordered most of the anti tank guns allocated to the stop lines to be moved to more forward locations. He also relied heavily on the RAF being able to attack the invasion forces with the greatest possible force, in accordance with Churchill's wishes. He regarded that the safety of the country depended on the mobile forces, which were to be strengthened as more gun-armed tanks became available (though these were still likely to be outnumbered by those the Germans expected to have ashore on the first day). He was determined that the infantry tanks would be used in mass and that the armoured formations must not be tied to the infantry formations but be free to strike at the enemy's flanks and rear. This wish, however, failed to understand that tanks alone were bound to have a limited effect on the enemy; experience had already proved that a combined assault offered the best chance of success. General Alan Brooke was aided by a stronger artillery base, aided by a shipment of several hundred surplus First World War 75mm guns (each supplied with 1000 rounds of ammunition) from the USA under the lend lease programme; many of these guns initially had limited mobility, having wooden wheels and no ammunition limbers, and had to be mounted on trucks until their tyres could be replaced by pneumatic ones and limbers provided. On 15 September Alan Brooke noted in his diary that "The suspense of waiting is very trying especially when one is familiar with the weakness of our defence! Our exposed coastline is just about twice the length of the front the French were holding in France with about eighty divisions and a Maginot Line! Here we have twenty two divisions of which only about half can be looked upon as in any way fit for any form of mobile operation! Thank God the spirit is now good and the defeatist opinions expressed after Dunkirk are now no longer prevalent. But I wish I could have six months now to finish equipping and training the force under my command."

His plans would be hindered by Churchill's brave decision to send trained and equipped troops, especially valuable tanks, to North Africa as soon as they became available - 3rd Hussars (light tanks), 2nd (52 cruiser tanks) and 7th RTR (50 infantry tanks) sailed in a large troop convoy from Liverpool on 20 August. Such troop movements were to be expected as General Ironside, supporting Churchill's constant desire to take the offensive, commented on 8 July that "It is our business to evolve the best kind of Army for home defence, with a proportion ready to serve abroad offensively". The War Office however believed that it was better to take risks in the Middle East rather than at home, especially with its meagre armoured resources, until the onset of autumn 1940. In September Winston Churchill changed his mind, noting 'by the middle of September the invasion menace seemed sufficiently glaring to arrest further movement of vital units to the East, especially as they had to go round the Cape'. On 17 September he suggested to General Ismay that it would be impossible to withdraw the New Zealand forces from their forward position in Kent and that it would be better to keep the

Australians back, so delaying the large reinforcement convoy to North Africa until late October. He commented that 'none of these forces going round the Cape can possibly arrive in time to influence the impending battle in Egypt (both the British and Axis were already looking at operations in North Africa). But they may play a big part here. Anyhow, we cannot afford to make sure that these forces are out of action throughout October in either theatre'.

The Cabinet Office produced a "Most Secret" memorandum on 18 June entitled "Need for Organisation of Civil Resistance". It started "An invasion of this country is probably imminent. The extent to which our preparations to meet it will succeed depend upon the extent to which clear decisions have been taken and consistent plans made in accordance with those decisions. An important question is the extent to which the civilian population is to be asked to resist the invader during or after actual military operations. The answer to this question depends on the lines upon which we are to organise civilian authorities, encourage industrial opposition, acts of sabotage and espionage in our civilian population, and whether behind our troops we are to leave regular or irregular units entrusted with the task of making a German occupation difficult and even dangerous. It should be pointed out that in this connection, if such units are left behind the enemy will take reprisals on the population as surely as if the whole population were effectively organised for resistance."

It suggested only two possible views:

- Either the population should not be encouraged to resist, either actively or passively, as any opposition would lead to the most terrible reprisals
- They should be encouraged to resist by all practical means whatever the cost.

In the event of the second view being adopted then the question of how this could be carried on, should the Government and armed forces be forced to leave the country, would need to be considered.

The memo suggested that the first view be rejected and adequate preparation be put in hand for the organisation required for the second. It noted that the first view had been adopted in those countries already overrun and was in line with the traditional view of warfare that resistance should be left to the fighting forces. Supporting the second view, it was acknowledged that during actual military operations the existence of constant organised civilian opposition in both the back areas and fighting zone would clearly be of great assistance to their own troops and an embarrassment to the enemy. It noted that the enemy lines of communication was the Achilles Heel of an invading force, and which had never been adequately exploited to date.

It prompted that after enemy occupation of any locality, or even the whole country, some form of resistance and of secret organisation would be essential in order to contain as many Germans as possible, threaten the economic and military structure of the new regime as well as to keep alive the spirit of resistance in the population, so preventing the mental development of a subject people. It accurately presupposed the German intentions to strip the country of its wealth and economy. It believed that it was reasonably certain that a sufficient proportion of the civilian population would act on their own, even if there was no lead given by their leadership, and that this would inevitably lead to reprisals. The memo also stated that civil unrest in India, Ireland and Palestine had shown the value of such tactics. In addition to organising the authorities it believed that the public should be clearly told that there would be no-one who may not be called to give their life for their country, that the secret of success lies in the offensive spirit by the nation as a whole and that the only method of achieving this is for everyone to place themselves unreservedly in the hands of the military authorities.

When the German blitzkrieg began in May, representatives of the War Office and the Ministry for Home Defence met the Chiefs of Staff about setting up a home defence force to foil parachutists and cope with fifth columnist activity. They agreed that every male between 17 and 65 who had handled a weapon and was not physically disabled could serve as a Local Defence Volunteer (LDV) in a force organised under military rules and under the command of GHQ Home Forces. Each volunteer was expected to serve ten hours per week for an initial six months, though this contract could be terminated with two weeks notice. On the evening of 14 May the War Secretary, Anthony Eden, made a radio broadcast announcing the new force and asked for volunteers. The result was overwhelming with men reporting to their local police station before he had even finished speaking. This response coupled with the complete absence of an administration or prior experience to draw on meant confusion on a massive scale for all concerned, though on the practical side a number of volunteers spent that night on guard armed with little more than a good pair of eyes and a steely determination. This determination to serve often came into conflict with the army, local authorities and civilians as roadblocks sprang up interfering with military and official traffic while anyone was likely to be stopped and questioned - even the King was not safe, as his car was once stopped during a factory visit by an enthusiastic sentry from the factory's own unit. General Ironside recorded that "I have the greatest belief in the strength of the LDV, given only a little time for organisation. We have an inexhaustible supply of experience and courage in the country." One of the benefits of this force was the close-knit relationship forged through its members, especially as many were organised in factories, public utilities, towns and villages. Despite the problems and public ridicule the Home Guard, as it was renamed on 23 July, became a valuable resource to the Army as it provided a comprehensive observation and guard force, with members using local knowledge to enhance their capabilities, and allowed the Army's field forces to redeploy more of their troops from a static to mobile role.

A lunch meeting at Chequers on 30 June involving Winston Churchill and Lieutenant General Thorne, commanding XII Corps, revived the idea of creating a guerrilla resistance force at home. The War Office department Military Intelligence (Research) (MI(R)) had spent much of its time developing weapons useful to a guerrilla force. In 1939 it reported that "if guerrilla warfare is co-ordinated and also related to main operations it should, in favourable circumstances, cause such a diversion of enemy strength as eventually to present decisive opportunities to the main forces." One of MI(R)'s personnel was Major Colin Gubbins, who spent the spring of 1939 working on the Guerrilla Field Service Regulations, comprising three booklets: The Partisan Leader's Handbook, The Art of Guerrilla Warfare and How to Use High Explosives. Teams were sent to Finland and Poland to study operations, the former leading to the establishment of Independent Companies. During the Norwegian Campaign investigations on the potential for guerrilla operations at home were conducted. It was soon recognised that the new resistance organisation was beyond the capabilities of MI(R), so it was agreed that it would come under the direct control of GHQ Home Forces.

The result was the Auxiliary Units. A secret document written on 8 August set out role of the Units. They were to act offensively on the flanks and in the rear of enemy troops, in particular against tank and lorry laagers, supply dumps and small defended posts; they were also charged with providing a system of intelligence by either wireless or field telephone on what was happening behind the enemy front line. It was expected that their activities be carried out mainly at night so its members be intimately familiar with the countryside. Where the units may remain active for a longer period, reserves of food and water would be provided in caches. The country was split into 12 sectors and sub divided into Units and then Patrols, numbers varying according to location. Patrol leaders were selected by intelligence officers with patrol members nominated for their local knowledge and dedication. It was essential that these people were confident and adaptable, as their role was to form the basis of a guerrilla force in the event of a successful German invasion. They were prepared to remain concealed for up to two weeks after invasion before emerging to conduct their role. Twelve Intelligence Officers were assigned to maintain contact with all the patrols and to liaise with relevant military authorities. The existence of the Units was very secret, as were their hides, to ensure security and maximum effectiveness. After invasion the Units were to operate either on general instructions or if the situation permitted on the orders passed through their Intelligence Officer.

1940 had seen the beginning of the development of so called special forces within the British Army to conduct offensive operations. This move was passionately supported by Winston Churchill, who wanted a force of 5,000 men capable and willing to attack the enemy as soon as possible, but opposed by the military traditionalists who felt discomfort in adopting the "un-gentlemanly" methods advocated. It was accepted by the War Office in 1939, that if guerrilla warfare was co-ordinated with the main Army operations it should, in favourable circumstances, present decisive opportunities. Although an initial "special service" force had been formed to support Finland's defensive actions against Russia, the first units to see combat were five Independent Companies, organised from infantry divisions at home in April 1940 with the aim of establishing the basis of a guerrilla force in Norway following the German invasion. These units contained good quality personnel but had few heavy weapons and poor equipment and, although they acquitted themselves well, were unable to fulfil their role.

It was important to the development of special forces that both Sir John Dill and Sir Alan Brooke supported the premise of attacking the enemy wherever they may be found; however, these officers did not welcome the dilution of resources and quality personnel from existing formations who desperately required them. The officer tasked with developing new "raiding forces" was the South African Lieutenant Colonel Dudley Clarke, an assistant to Sir John Dill and one passionate about the potential of developing such a force. On 6 June the War Office agreed to support this development as long as no existing military unit was re-rolled and that there was a minimum of demands on weapons and equipment. To co-ordinate this work a new section - MO9 - was established under the secretariat of Military Operations within the War Office, with Clarke in charge. Although MO9 had the support of the Royal Navy it was clear that the bulk of the new forces would have to come from within the Army. The most obvious place to start were the now largely redundant Independent Companies and an 11th Company was authorised. By 15 June the Navy had set up a base of operations on the River Hamble near Southampton and began collecting various small craft. On 12 June Churchill had decided that this new raiding initiative required a senior officer to head a combined staff from all services, with Lieutenant General Sir Allan Bourne, the Adjutant General of the Royal Marines, being chosen. He had under command the Royal Marine infantry brigades, Independent Companies and new striking companies when formed. In addition to the pre war amphibious warfare centre (up till then a neglected backwater), Bourne also oversaw in May the establishment of the new Irregular Warfare School in western Scotland. The Navy established small boat bases at Warsash, Brightlingsea and Falmouth and a training centre at Hayling Island. In mid July Admiral of the Fleet Sir Roger Keyes was appointed Director of Combined Operations.

On 20 June the War Office instructed each of its Military Commands to nominate officers prepared to volunteer for special service of an undefined nature. This was the start point for the formation of new striking companies that were to develop into the Army Commando units. The guiding principle was that a commanding officer, once selected, chose his troop commanders who, in turn, chose their junior officers and they choose the other ranks who were to serve in their unit. In all cases, the selected personnel had to be physically fit, intelligent and self-reliant. Two other aspects marked them from established Army units - each commando was to be reliant on its own resources in terms of accommodation, billeting its personnel within the civilian community it found itself in, and transport as it had none allocated. These aspects were to reinforce the desire to develop a force and ethos for raiding operations. There were three main operational characteristics of a commando unit: that it could operate independently for 24 hours, that it could operate widely dispersed, that it should not be used either to directly attack formed bodies of enemy troops or expect to defend positions against direct attack by such bodies.

On 22 June Churchill suggested the formation of a parachute-trained force that could also be used as shock troops, having seen the impact that Germany's own force had recently had. Two days later a training school was authorised at RAF Ringway, south of Manchester and the hunt for anyone who knew anything about parachute jumping began. In early July the first special service units arrived at the school and began training alongside potential instructors. Thus the Parachute Regiment was born.

While these units began their formation the first raid on the Continent by the Army, since being harshly evicted, was undertaken. It was a sign of the times that everything seemed improvised when on the night of 22 June (the day France capitulated) 115 men of 11 Independent Company, carried in a steam yacht and seven RAF launches, set out to raid the French coast north of Boulogne. Only one of the four groups was able to claim any success but it did prove a propoganda boost. On 14 July 100 men from 11 Company and the new 3 Commando set out to raid Guernsey. The raid was a failure as only one group landed and probed inland but found no enemy while another mistakenly landed on Sark, where they had time for a drink with the locals in the pub before heading back! Although these two raids had indifferent results they did help to stimulate an offensive spirit and derail some of the more ludicrous proposals, such as seizing Denmark. In October the Independent Companies and Commandos were reorganised into new special service battalions, themselves grouped within a brigade structure. In its review on 29 October 1940 GHQ Home Forces stated that `we should be able decrease the likelihood of an invasion by an offensive policy of raiding along the whole extent of the enemy coast in order to force him to build and occupy defences and to keep him in a state of uncertainty`.

Many of these special forces were used as "enemy" during field exercises during the summer and autumn and it was in this role that they were able to further develop and hone their skills. Their successes in getting into the rear areas before attacking supply lines, depots and headquarters demonstrated their potential so much so that they were allocated vital counter attack and penetration roles in countering an invasion.

Despite all the change of emphasis to a forward defence there were still only a mere two infantry divisions guarding the planned invasion zone. As can be seen from the Order of Battle in Appendix 1, 1st London Division was the largest in the British Army at the time and was deployed in east Kent with four infantry brigades plus the garrisons at Dover, Shorncliffe and Deal under its operational command. As the British expected that a main sea-borne force would land on the northeast Kent coast, between Whitstable and Margate, the Division deployed its troops and developed its stop lines accordingly. This deployment meant that Divisional Headquarters and its administrative units would in reality be closer than most of its fighting troops to the enemy forces upon invasion! A serious concern was that the bulk of the Division was spread across the villages and towns in the region to both counter parachute landings and reduce its vulnerability to air attack; it was fortunate that sufficient transport was available to move them to the actual landing zone and many units had movement plans ready but this process would take time.

Most of the forces deployed with the coastal garrisons were able to make use of the existing military barracks and facilities. Shorncliffe Garrison had the unenviable task of defending the area around Hythe and Folkestone and would have been tasked with preventing the crucial connection between the seaborne and airborne forces. However, the Garrison had few trained infantry as the bulk of its personnel came from the Royal Engineers and relied heavily on its exposed infrastructure. Dover Garrison was well supplied with fighting troops, coastal artillery (much of which could fire inland) and a developed defence plan, given its vital strategic role. Deal Garrison was the responsibility of the Royal Marines and could be counted upon to support the defence of Dover.

The other division to face the onslaught would be the 45th Infantry Division, a former training formation now finding itself in the most unenviable location of all. This Division was responsible for the coast between Dymchurch and Brighton, a distance of about eighty miles. It had only three infantry brigades and the support of the motor machine gun brigade on its right flank to stop almost the entire German invasion force! Very few of these troops or their commanders had any modern fighting experience, as the Division's existence to date had been to train soldiers to become infantrymen. Due to the length of coastline it was expected to defend the Division had little choice but to deploy most of its combat strength close up against the shoreline. It was strongest on its left (Romney Marsh) and weakest on its right (Newhaven). It was only able to produce a small mobile divisional reserve based on the motorised 5th Loyals; this reserve could only provide a covering force, using the defensive stop lines, behind which more substantial reserves could hopefully form up for counter attack.

The reserve of XII Corps rested largely on the two infantry brigade strong New Zealand Expeditionary Force (NZEF), largely located east of Maidstone in an anti paratroop posture; it had formed an advance guard called Milforce, containing the Force's heaviest weapons and was strategically placed near Ashford. The 29th Independent Infantry Brigade coverd the Corps' right flank but was inexperienced and lacked the power to conduct strong counter attacks on its own.

Irrespective of the strengths and weaknesses of these divisions, it would still be up to them to either stop an invasion on the beaches or delay any breakout by enemy forces before the main counter attack forces had the chance to arrive and deploy. Having been in place early on they did have the advantage of knowing the terrain and building links with neighbouring units and authorities. The vulnerability of the Ashford sector was recognised in late summer, with the 31st Independent Infantry Brigade due to move there from IV Corps on 28 September; however, this move would have been too late in the circumstances.

45th Infantry Division, like the others, produced a Defence Scheme. This ran to several pages and covered all aspects of its intended operations, in accordance with Corps instructions. In its intelligence summaries the second half of September was frequently mentioned as a likely invasion period, though it was admitted that it would be difficult to see how the date could be decided until the last possible moment on account of the weather, Moon and tides. It believed that the main attack would be delivered at the narrowest part of the Straits of Dover with diversionary attacks elsewhere. Invasion would be preceded by a struggle for air supremacy in which Germany would employ all its available air force.

The Scheme noted that:

- As the Divisional area extended for over a thousand square miles it was clear that available resources were insufficient to provide strength everywhere. The policy would be that the Division's main strength would be concentrated to prevent the enemy landing from the sea and as such it would provide some depth to forward defences
- In order to prevent small detachments scattered around the Divisional area from being quickly overrun by airborne forces, such strength as available was to be concentrated to hold nodal points and stop lines
- It was recognised and accepted that in certain places considerable gaps in the beach defences would occur and that some defensive depth was essential within the forward companies. Mines placed on beaches would be laid above the high water mark
- All troops and commanders must be well trained in all possible operational options in their area, especially counter attack - there was to be only one degree of resistance: to the last man and last round of ammunition
- It noted that there was no reason to suppose that the enemy's tactics on land would differ from those used in the recent campaigns. It believed that in the event of a landing the enemy was expected to push out in widely scattered columns without consideration of support or flank protection
- To counter this, the Divisional area was split into a grid of stop lines, supplemented by nodal points. It was important that these delay and disorganise any enemy advance. The nodal points were to have both an inner and outer line, the outer made up of defensive posts covering all possible approaches and sited to complement roadblocks. These posts were to be sited from an offensive not defensive point of view and be well camouflaged; the inner line or keep was to be surrounded by a continuous anti tank obstacle with the objective of holding to the last
- Civilians were to stay put unless there was an opportunity to evacuate them

- When necessary the local railway and bus companies would evacuate their rolling stock and vehicles to pre-arranged localities inland
- Communications within the Division would be handled mainly through the Post Office system and supplemented by cable laid by the Royal Signals.

The Scheme confirmed the alert status within the Division - during the night forward defences would be completely manned, with mobile reserves at thirty minutes notice to move; during the day the forward defences would be thirty percent manned, the remainder at an hour's notice to move while mobile reserves were to be at two hour's notice.

The XII Corps instructions enhanced this Defence Scheme by developing a defence in depth concept by also adopting a grid system, linked to but not necessarily a part of the stop lines. It noted that German success in France was due largely to the absence of an organised system of defences behind the front line but suggested that the more enclosed nature of the countryside in the southeast of England offered considerable facilities to check any rapid armoured penetration inland. The grid system comprised "fences", which bounded areas carefully chosen to give maximum protection against attacks, and "crossings" which would be defended by small local garrisons from the Home Guard in order to provide an initial check. These garrisons must be organised so as to deal with attempts to cross the "fences" and "crossings" from either side. Preparation of these "fences" and "crossings" would be arranged under the respective Division or Sub Area command and be generally confined to roadblocks; these would have an anti tank "Molotov" grenade post on either side and be covered by an infantry section or platoon sized defensive position. Concealment, economy of manpower and good field of fire were essential. It noted that even if the "fences" fail to hold they can do much to break up, disorganise and delay the enemy's advance. To aid quick and accurate reporting each fence, crossing and nodal point were given a code letter.

In line with Churchill and Alan Brooke's views, it was essential that the major counter offensive forces (notably VII and IV Corps) be deployed quickly and decisively, once the decision had been made by GHQ where and how they were to be employed; generally speaking, VII Corps was kept on eight hours notice to move, reduced to four hours during high risk periods. In July GHQ Home Forces confirmed that both of these Corps were to be organised and equipped into mobile brigade groups; training was to emphasise infantry-armour co-operation, RAF co-operation and movement of troops and vehicles, especially vehicle control and protection from air attack. However, there were no divisional level exercises and as such there remains concern over the ability of divisional headquarters staff to effectively command and control their various brigade groups in their vital role. It would certainly be a mistake to allow these brigade groups to operate without proper co-ordination, especially regarding artillery and logistics support, with recent experiences in France serving as a salutory lesson.

VII Corps was the most important of the two counter offensive formations as it contained most of the available armour and was closest to the invasion zone. It was also unique in that it contained most of the Canadian forces in the country. However, there were concerns over its commander, Lieutenant General McNaughton. He was Canada's most senior officer and had commanded the 1st Canadian Division until promoted to command the newly formed Corps in July. In 1932 he was described (admittedly not by one of his supporters) as "a super engineer and college professor by profession. He is a gunner in the Canadian Militia and, technically, a good one. He is cold, calculating, touchy and determined to pursue his own schemes, inclined to do everything himself and will not take advice." In June 1941 Alan Brooke noted that he felt that he did not have the required qualities to make a success of commanding the Corps; whilst he was somewhat of a hero in Canada it was considered that he lacked the required qualities of command and lacked a modern tactical outlook. Even as late as 1943 he seemed to prefer traditional limited attritional battles rather than modern mobile operations and failed to recognise how swiftly the enemy would react to any attack. This all seems at odds with the training instructions he issued to 1st Canadian Division in March 1940; these placed much emphasis on mobility, including the need to make quick decisions and have a good organisation and discipline, so allowing a unit to move rapidly and without confusion at short notice. The Corps War Diary also records the efforts he made to improve the combat potential of the troops under command and his positive involvement in most exercises. Certainly, Alan Brooke had already shown his willingness to replace unsuitable officers but General McNaughton's case was politically influenced as VII Corps was already earmarked to become the 1st Canadian Corps and, as such, would require a senior Canadian officer in command. Having an unsatisfactory commander in charge of the most important force that the British Army had available at that time was probably the most serious command concern that Alan Brooke would have to face immediately following an invasion.

Of the formations within the Corps, 1st Canadian Division was commanded by Major General Pearkes VC. He had won the Victoria Cross in the First World War but had not experienced higher command before he was appointed to command the 2nd Brigade in 1939. He was subsequently promoted to command the Division in July 1940 and enjoyed considerable reputation as the most experienced Canadian field commander at that time. The Division had proved its organisational abilities in its short-lived excursion to Normandy in June 1940 and was eager for action. Major General Norrie, commanding 1st Armoured Division, had considerable experience of armoured warfare, having previously been with the Tank Corps in the First World War and briefly the Inspector of the Royal Armoured Corps; however he had no actual experience of actual modern tank warfare and was to be criticised for his cavalry approach to armoured warfare when commanding XXX Corps during the ill fated Battle of Gazala in 1942. The 1st Armoured Division had faced many challenges during its short time with the Second BEF and had gained much needed combat experience. Brigadier Watkins had succeeded to command of 1st Army Tank Brigade in July, his predecessor having commanded it in the BEF, including through the famous Arras counter attack. Brigadier Watkins was to lead this brigade in action for the next two years in North Africa.

IV Corps was commanded by Lieutenant General Nosworthy, who was to successfully lead a Corps through the northwest African campaign in 1942-43. This Corps was deployed in such a way that it could move into East Anglia to counter any invasion there. It was notionally a strong Corps, with one armoured and two infantry divisions under command; however, only the 42nd Infantry Division had seen recent combat with the BEF while the 2nd Armoured Division, supposedly the Corps' punch, was hardly combat effective as it was almost entirely equipped with obsolete light tanks. None of the senior commanders in the Corps had yet experienced modern combat. Nevertheless, on 14 July General Ironside reported that the Corps was in fine order and had an efficient leader in General Nosworthy, who, he said, was full of enthusiasm and confidence.

It is worth noting here how these armoured forces fared in equipment by September. The most important armoured formation was 1st Armoured Division. Although it notionally had three armoured brigades, the 20th Brigade was only equipped with heavy armoured cars, the 3rd Brigade only had a single cruiser regiment while the 2nd Brigade, its strongest though under strength cruiser formation (two of its regiments had barely a squadron's worth of tanks each by mid October), was effectively detached from the Division as it was located in Wiltshire; even by 12 October the Division had less than half of its potential armoured strength. 2nd Armoured Division, in IV Corps, was even less well equipped, with a single cruiser regiment and the other tank regiments having the obsolete light tank. The most effective armoured formation in either Corps was likely to be the veteran 1st Army Tank Brigade, equipped with two full strength infantry tank regiments. 8th RTR, attached to the New Zealand Milforce from that Brigade in early September, had a squadron (C) of the potent mark II tanks and two with the machine gun armed mark I infantry tank. The only other armoured formation of note was the 21st Army Tank Brigade, Southern Command's strike force and mostly equipped with the new mark III Valentine infantry tanks. The armoured training units at Bovington organised a number of local "strike" groups with a mix of all tank types. The War Office was already starting to create three new armoured divisions (6th, 8th and 9th), but these would have to wait until almost winter before the units assigned to it received any tanks, let alone had any semblance of formation (the 6th Division was not expected to be operational before the spring of 1941).

A Home Forces report dated 29 June listed the status of the various mobile forces available at that time:

- 1st Army Tank Brigade had only 8th RTR at full strength
- 1st Canadian Division had two of the three brigade groups mobile
- The New Zealand Force had little transport and no signals or heavy weapons
- 2nd Armoured Division had only the cruiser equipped 3rd RTR with a full complement, while its 1st Armoured Brigade was 75% complete and partly operational, 22nd Armoured Brigade was only 30% complete and not considered operational but the Support Group was fully operational
- 43rd Infantry Division was fairly complete, with a brigade needing troop carrying capacity
- 3rd Armoured Brigade had 47 cruiser tanks but little wheeled transport.

A report on 10 July reported that the following formations were available for mobile operations: 1st and 2nd Armoured Divisions, 3rd, 5th, 42nd, 43rd, 44th, 52nd and 1st Canadian Infantry Divisions, the NZEF and the 1st, 2nd and 3rd Motor Machine Gun Brigades. The Australian Imperial Force was in reserve but not yet equipped or trained for offensive operations. However, another Home Forces report, dated 11 August, reported 1st Canadian and 43rd Divisions as fully mobile, NZEF was 50% mobile, 3rd Division was mobile (though its artillery was only 66% mobile), 5th Division had a brigade fully mobile and the rest at 50%, 42nd Division was 30% mobile, 44th Division was 30% mobile, 52nd Division was 60% mobile; 29th and 31st Brigade Groups were fully mobile. It was clear that throughout the summer mobility remained a serious concern.

Wherever VII Corps was directed it did not have the resources to effectively mount more than one major counter offensive at a time. Its units would have to move under the threat of air attack, initially relying on the railways due to the absence of road transporters, assemble and then co-ordinate attacks between armour, infantry and artillery units. The Army had only undertaken large counter attacks twice for real during the war - the Arras counterattack and 1st Armoured Division's counterattacks against the German bridgeheads over the River Somme in June - and both these had quickly broken down, despite initial success. The four most serious concerns relating to the Arras attack were:

- First, that briefings were not co-ordinated to ensure that the different combat arms knew what was to occur and provide clarification of how different combat units operated
- Secondly the chain of command was not confirmed so both infantry and armour commanders believed they were in charge
- Thirdly, close co-operation between infantry and armour was hindered by lack of training, incompatible methods of communication and lack of time to get to know each other and
- Fourthly, poor intelligence on the enemy's strengths and movements.

The result was that both infantry and armour fought independent actions. Since then, although hampered by the lack of equipment and spares for much of June and July, training between infantry, armour and artillery in close co-operation operations improved in the later summer months. Although the infantry-armour training was conducted with enthusiasm the same problems continued to exist. An example was an exercise conducted in early August between the tanks of 8th RTR and the infantry of the Canadian 22nd Regiment; the post exercise report noted that:

- The forming up places were too congested with units paying too little attention to camouflage and concealment
- There was a lack of signals from tanks to infantry
- An unwillingness of infantry to help suppress anti tank defences
- The infantrymen were generally not kept aware of how the operation was proceeding
- There was insufficient fire and movement by the infantry
- Lack of sufficient time was given to conducting proper reconnaissance
- It further noted that junior commanders must show more initiative.

There had been an increasing number of exercises at both staff and troop level to ensure better levels of training and command, the most common form of exercise being long distance road movements of units up to brigade strength. The decision to keep the brigade as the main operational formation meant that both divisional and Corps commanders would need to closely co-ordinate the activities of their headquarters and those formations to ensure that they moved and fought as part of a whole rather than in piecemeal actions - the success or failure of these few units would dominate the ability of the British Army to hold and defeat their enemy. This co-ordination was not helped by the fact that by September, although it had a full complement of despatch riders, VII Corps signals had only four out of the expected twelve wireless sets, while 1st Armoured Division signals had only half the complement of Number 9 wireless sets (but all of its Number 11 sets).

To the west of the invasion zone was Montgomery's V Corps. Only 4th Infantry Division, one of its two infantry divisions, could be expected to be released quickly for operations outside the Corps area. It would be under strength as one of its three brigades had effectively been detached to garrison the Isle of Wight. The other division, 50th Infantry Division, would have been faced with countering almost alone the German Sixth Army's landing in Lyme Bay, should this have occurred. This Corps could be a potent force, as both divisions had served well with the BEF and its senior commanders had experienced modern combat. Southern Command's GHQ Reserve comprised a potentially strong counter attack force, with 21st Army Tank Brigade being re-equipped with the more modern Valentine infantry tank and an allocated Australian infantry brigade. This force would have received the full support of the Command's resources on its deployment but still faced two problems that should have hampered its operations - the lack of a single senior commander for the strike force and its size, which would have reduced its potential for offensive action if deployed in isolation from other field force formations.

It is interesting to note here the disposition of the units that had made up the original British Expeditionary Force (BEF) and so gained crucial battlefield experience. The closest ones to the invasion area were 1st Armoured Division and 4th Infantry Division (the 35th Infantry Brigade in 1st London Division had reformed after being destroyed while serving with the 12th Infantry Division in May 1940). Three divisions were in the southwest (3rd, 48th and 50th Infantry Divisions), one in GHQ Reserve North (42nd Infantry Division), three in the northeast (1st, 2nd and 44th Infantry Divisions) and all of those in Scotland (5th, 46th and 51st Infantry Divisions). Both part of the 1st Canadian Division in VII Corps and 52nd Infantry Division in II Corps had spent a few days in Normandy back in June but had seen very little combat - the 1st Canadian Brigade's Anti Tank Company recorded in its War Diary that "the Company returned to barracks, ending up just where we had started from almost to the hour, seven days later. No sight of the enemy, no action, no casualties, eight men under arrest" (it was noted that many had taken the opportunity to fill their water bottles with wine, with the inevitable consequences!). The 52nd Division had experienced more combat (through its 157th Brigade) defending positions west of the River Seine and around the base of the Cotentin Peninsula. In addition there had been a large scale transfer of former BEF personnel within the Army, especially the artillery and headquarters staff, with the aim of helping to spread the valuable and hard won experience as far as possible.

Much depended on the senior field commanders expected to take the initial brunt of the invasion. Many of the senior officers who had gained valuable operational experience during the 1940 campaigns, and who were to lead and train the new Army, remained in command of their units during this period while others had been promoted. Lieutenant General Thorne, commander of XII Corps, had been the commander of the 48th Infantry Division in the BEF and, as such, had experience of modern combat as a senior field commander. He would be, at least initially, responsible for opposing the invasion. General Thorne was a good choice for command of this vital Corps as, although only recently promoted to Lieutenant General, he had already demonstrated the high level of skills needed and was highly regarded by all who met him. He had become one of the youngest brigade commanders during the First World War and from the outset was interested in ensuring that troops and officers under his command were well trained and inspired (as a Grenadier Guards platoon commander he had radically conducted tactical training in Hyde Park among the strolling civilians). He was regarded as a forward thinking officer at the Staff College, sufficiently so as he returned there as an instructor barely a year after graduating, with his career being enhanced when later selected as Military Attaché in both America and Germany. It was in this latter post that he tried to instil in the War Office a true appreciation of the rise in Germany's military developments and effectiveness. During the inter war years he had promoted the need for proper passive air defence system through the application of camouflage and was one of the first to promote an understanding of the psychology of modern warfare. As commander of the 48th Infantry Division in the BEF he had been responsible for holding much of the open right flank during the withdrawal to Dunkirk, maintaining a position of inspiration and level headiness during that crucial time. Very soon after taking over the Corps he promoted the setting up of guerrilla forces that became known as Auxiliary Units (he got the idea from his time as Military Attaché in Germany).

Like Montgomery, he advocated the need for commanders and soldiers to be both physically and mentally tough. This position was supported by General Ironside, who told him on his appointment that "You will find plenty to do down in your sector. There is no time to keep weaklings or men who cannot work a full twenty-four hours. I want you to be absolutely brutal in turning people out and getting better in".

General Thorne had been friends with Alan Brooke since their days in the Staff College so when Alan Brooke replaced Ironside the relationship between the Commander in Chief Home Forces and one of his most important Corps commanders continued to flourish. In 1970 Peter Fleming, also closely linked with the Auxiliary Units, wrote that "it was in great part due to Thorne's tireless energy, his powers of leadership and his imaginative use of scanty resources that, if Operation Sea Lion had been launched in September 1940, Hitler's Wehrmacht would (with any luck) have suffered its first defeat."

Of the three Divisional commanders under Thorne's command, Generals Liardet and Freyberg knew their troops well, having been in command since the start of the War; Generals Liardet had been the first Major General of the Territorial Army and was widely respected and immensely popular within his Division; General Freyberg had been chosen by the New Zealand Government to lead its first expeditionary force of the War, partly influenced by praise from both Ironside and Churchill. From the outset, General Freyberg insisted that the "New Zealand forces were not an integral part of the British Army - they are a distinct New Zealand force, proud of their own identity." This is an interesting statement from a British General, but one that properly identifies him with his command responsibilities. General Freyberg was a very active and forceful person who suffered from natural impulsiveness, often being found at the front line. W G Stevens, who served under him, commented that if he disagreed firmly with plans and did not want to take part in them he would not; however, once he agreed he would co-operate wholeheartedly. With regard to divisional planning conferences utmost care was taken to ensure the plan was sound, with all involved aware of what was expected. He would then allow formation commanders make their own plans within the overall Divisional plan. He was a firm believer in aggressive tactics and radiated confidence among all he met. It was later commentated that he was a good Divisional commander but generally unsuitable to command at higher level. General Schreiber, commanding 45th Infantry Division, had gained valuable experience as the commander of the BEF's II Corps' artillery and was thought highly enough to later command IV Corps and then 1st Army in Tunisia in 1943. Brigadier Leese, commanding

29th Independent Infantry Brigade, was later to be described by Montgomery as the best soldier in North Africa - high praise indeed.

The adjacent Southern Command was led by Lieutenant General Claude Auchinleck. Although he had been appointed to command the Expeditionary Force in Norway he had not been able to exert much influence during the campaign due to the circumstances involved. His approach to command was very different to that of his main subordinate, Lieutenant General Montgomery. Though these two rarely saw eye to eye, Auchinleck was later to have an exceptional tribute paid to him by none other than Field Marshal Rommel, who said of his handling of the 8th Army at the First Battle of El Alamein that "he conducted the battle with remarkable skill and tactically much better than Ritchie (the Army commander he replaced). His appreciation of the situation seemed admirably cool; he did not allow himself to be impressed by any of our measures, remaining unmoved by the demand of the fleeting moment." Enough has been written about Montgomery's particular style and abilities of a commander; certainly he was regarded by many as the Army's most effective and aggressive senior field commander at that time. In his V Corps, Major General Eastwood, commanding 4th Infantry Division, had been regarded as a rising star just before the War broke out. He had served as Vice Chief of the General Staff in the BEF, having arrived to take over 4th Division just as the German offensive broke, but was able to gain much experience in commanding ad hoc formations set up to cover the withdrawal to Dunkirk. After evacuation he was appointed Chief of Staff for the Second BEF on Alan Brooke's recommendation. Major General Martel had commanded 50th Infantry Division from the outset and had also played a major part in the BEF's operations, notably during the Arras counter-attack. As mentioned, the Command's Strike Force was not under any specific field commander, though Major General Wynter, commanding the Australian Imperial Force, could have been a candidate; however, as his career path was to be more administrative than combat it is questionable whether he could have been the best choice for such an offensively orientated force. Brigadier Morshead, commanding the 18th Australian Brigade, was a better choice for such a command and, as he was later to show, he was to prove one of Australia's best field commanders. Brigadier Drake-Brockman, commanding the well-equipped 21st Army Tank Brigade, was untried in battle to date.

The British Army did not, however, expect to fight alone on the ground. Each RAF airfield had its own ad-hoc defence force in addition to assigned Army troops; these forces being found from station personnel and equipped with whatever could be supplied, scrounged or built. The Royal Navy organised a small number of "infantry" battalions from their shore and training establishments to assist in the defence of their main naval bases, while other personnel continued to man some of the emergency coastal batteries until the autumn. Records kept by the Flag Officer Portsmouth show an example of the Navy's contribution. On 12 May Portsmouth was able to provide 130 Maxim medium and 102 Lewis light machine guns and 3680 rifles, but only 300 men trained as soldiers. On 25 May that Flag Officer authorised "landing parties" for local defence (see the Army Order of Battle for Portsmouth for details) and by 7 June two companies of Collingwood Battalion were trained. By 11 July only the HMS Excellent force was permanently established, the others ready to form at short notice; at this time there were 1200 men trained and ready to move at two hours notice - a battalion of 600 men were at the Royal Naval Barracks, 300 in two companies in HMS Excellent and 300 in two companies in HMS Collingwood. There were also 1850 partly trained men - 1200 men in two battalions in the Royal Naval Barracks, 300 in HMS Collingwood, 250 in HMS Vernon and 100 in HMS Excellent. In addition 1850 men were assigned to unarmed working parties - 1000 men in the Royal Naval Barracks, 800 in HMS Collingwood and 50 in HMS Vernon. The Flag Officer made it clear that while he would co-operate with the Army, he would retain control of the movement of naval personnel assigned defence duties. This was wise given that the personnel had little tactical training and weapons handling, so would be suitable for mostly static defensive operations. Another concern was that most of the units were only formed when required so the officers and men assigned had little if any experience of operating together. One restriction on the use of Naval personnel was the need to ensure that the fleet had sufficient replacement and re-victualling personnel available to keep the ships operational with as quick a turn around as possible.

The Royal Marines, though already stretched with their traditional role of supporting the Navy, were also able to provide a number of trained men and equipped units. During the winter of 1939-1940 the first of three infantry brigades was formed as an amphibious strike force, despite the Chiefs of Staff originally considering in September 1939 that potential for amphibious raids was too remote to devote resources. These brigades were organised on Army lines, each battalion also having a machine gun company and a mobile company equipped with motorcycles and Bren gun carriers; personnel in these brigades were drawn from new recruits and were taught infantry skills in their units and the training battalion, following the initial six weeks basic training at the reserve depot near Exeter. Initially these brigades were under the operational command of the Chiefs of Staff and administered by the Admiralty (in August 1940 a Royal Marines divisional headquarters was authorised but not established until early 1941). They were warned to be ready for operations in the Irish Republic, the Azores or Cape Verde Islands if Germany had sought to occupy them; however, by early September two of the brigades had left for Freetown in Sierra Leone to co-operate with Free French operations at Dakar in Senegal (Operation Menace). They returned home in October 1940.

The Royal Marines also had its unique Marine Naval Base Defence Organisation (MNBDO), established in January 1940 to provide anti aircraft, searchlight and coastal artillery units for overseas operations but were now deployed around the country. The recruits joining these units received additional specialist training at Army establishments. Those destined for sea service with the Royal Navy received basic training, in accordance with Army training manuals, at the Main Depot at Deal in Kent or the Reserve Depot near Exeter before receiving additional training at the three "Divisions" at Chatham, Portsmouth and Plymouth (all Royal Navy ships were assigned to one of these as its home port and received naval and marine personnel from them accordingly). These divisions formed ad hoc rifle companies for local defence. Importantly, the Royal Marines Depot at Deal also formed the majority of troops within that Garrison. By December 1940 the Royal Marines had increased in size from 16,000 to 24,000 (4,300 in the MNBDO, 8,800 in the divisions and 9,800 at sea or in naval shore establishments), these additional resources helping to relieve some of the pressure on the Army in providing troops and equipment to defend these areas.

On 21 June Churchill asked the War Office to consider raising a foreign legion from those elements of the allied forces that had been evacuated from the Continent. Although the War Office traditionally rejected such ideas it was felt that given the immediate threat to the country such formations could be practical, with a role garrisoning Iceland being considered. It was recommended, at least initially, that the French be kept separate from the others due to concerns over their true desire to continue the fight, not least due to the repercussions of the recent naval actions. By the end of June there were over 25,000 foreign troops in the United Kingdom, though few of these were in formed units capable of combat. The best of these contingents, not least in morale, were the Poles, now based in Scotland. It contained the remains of three infantry divisions and an armoured cavalry brigade, which had been formed within the French Army at the fall of Poland and had been determined to escape from France. It was felt by the War Office that they could be deployed anywhere, including the Irish Republic "if there is a proper rough house". Despite their obvious enthusiasm and hatred of the Germans the main problem faced was the need to change their operational structure as they had been previously trained and equipped to French Army standards and so had little knowledge of British Army doctrine and equipment, let alone the English language. The priority in equipping the foreign troops was to be firstly the Poles then the Belgians, Czechs and then the French.

The Czechs were located near Chester and represented the remains of the 1st Czech Infantry Division that had also been formed, trained and equipped by the French; this formation was reorganised as an independent infantry brigade but suffered greatly from internal political unrest. The French troops were mainly from the 13th DBLE (Foreign Legion Brigade) that had fought well in Norway. It had been located in Staffordshire and Merseyside until the end of August, when most of them left for the abortive operations at Dakar in West Africa (2500 men in two infantry battalions, with tank, engineer and artillery elements were dispatched). On 25 September only 809 Army and Foreign Legion personnel were left in this country, based in Farnborough. The Norwegians formed a "brigade" in late August from volunteers and was located in Dumfries, while a ski company also served in Iceland; the Dutch and Belgians were located in South Wales - a "Belgian Military Regroup Camp" providing three infantry companies totalling 682 trained men by the end of August, while the Dutch were forming two battalions for airfield defence in early July.

The Government had long recognised the need to give some legitimacy to the presence of foreign troops on British soil. The result was the Allied Forces Act, based upon the Visiting Forces (British Commonwealth) Act of 1933, which made `visiting` governments responsible for the conduct of their forces while they were on British territory. This was rushed through Parliament on 21 August and stated that foreign armies would be allowed to train under their own flags, their own commanders and their own military law. This form of autonomy was important, as it would provide a potent propaganda tool to stimulate resistance in the occupied countries and aid recruitment overseas. Those countries able to produce and maintain their own air force squadrons were able to further reinforce their status as allies, rather than being thought of as refugees. Assurance was given during the debate in Parliament that there was no provision for conscription into these forces, though in many cases military law included this possibility.

The main combat support given to the British Army from overseas was to be that provided from the Commonwealth and Empire forces; the value of these forces can be gauged by the fact that they were assigned to the crucial counter attack formations. In the 1930's the leading Commonwealth countries had sought a legal status for how their forces would operate with the British armed forces in the event of another World War, the issue greatly influenced by their experiences of the First World War. In 1933 Canada passed the Visiting Forces (British

Commonwealth) Act. This provided for two types of relationship - serving together and acting in combination. The former permitted foreign (i.e. British) command whilst the latter permitted serving with such forces for a common purpose. In January and March 1940 the New Zealand and Australian Governments respectively informed their field commanders in the United Kingdom of the status under which they were permitted to serve. In both cases they were to insist that the Commonwealth forces were to be employed as a whole and separate force, with the General Officers Commanding having direct recourse to their respective national government. It was agreed, though, that their forces should be placed under operational command of the Commander in Chief of the theatre they were serving in (in this case the Commander of Chief Home Forces). The forces were not, however, to be engaged on operations unless adequately equipped for the purpose assigned. It was tacitly agreed that both the New Zealand and Australian formations would be moved to the Middle East as soon as conditions permitted in order to join the bulk of their forces already there. The Commonwealth forces all looked to emulate the British Army in organisation, equipment, doctrine and tactics. The three countries contributing significant forces to the defence of Great Britain had all needed to quickly build up a large trained force from a miniscule Regular force and a volunteer reserve or militia force. The troops despatched at this time represented most of the trained strength available in these countries, but in all cases, still required further training and almost a complete provision of equipment, these being provided from British Army and industrial stocks, to make them suitable for operations.

The Australian Army was modelled on its First World War organisation but had been reduced to the bare essentials during the 1920's by Government neglect. Moves to address this took off in 1938 and in early 1939 it was re-organised into four Area Commands, each responsible for the training of units under its care. This training was often well prepared, arduous and thoughtful and had the aim of ensuring that the Militia could take on the role of building up a citizen army once again. In August 1939 the Government decided not to form a regular field force but intensified the Militia's training. By the outbreak of War the Army had over 3500 Regular and about 70,000 Militia enrolled; however, it was largely equipped with obsolete weapons and equipment, as orders with Britain's industry in 1936 had still not been filled and Australia as yet lacked its own war industry. The Chiefs of Staff agreed to form an Australian Imperial Force (AIF) of one infantry division totalling 20,000 volunteers, with the raising of a second AIF being considered in October 1939. In November 1939 the British Chiefs of Staff suggested the first AIF be sent to the Middle East, with Government agreement, once a suitable level of training had been achieved. It was interesting to note that only one field artillery regiment could be mobilised and sent overseas at that time (equipped with sixteen 18 pounders and eight 4.5-inch howitzers), on the understanding that once it reached the Middle East the guns would be returned to Australia and the regiment re-equipped from British sources. In January 1940 the first part of this AIF left Australia for the Middle East but its second element was diverted to the United Kingdom in May 1940. This element was initially at brigade strength but largely deficient in heavy equipment; it was assigned to the Southern Command's strike force, a role that suited its temperament as, like their compatriots, what they lacked in training and equipment was made up for in morale and aggression. In November it was released from its role and shipped to rejoin its compatriots in North Africa.

New Zealand faced a similar situation to the Australians. During the 1920's its Territorial Force was reduced from 20,000 men to 3,000. In late 1930 a Regular Cadre was reformed and the Territorial Force built up to nearly 8,000 by 1932. However, the Army was starved of funds as most money was diverted to the Singapore defences, to which scheme both Australia and New Zealand were committed due to the rising threats from Japan's expansionism. On the outbreak of War the Army comprised 510 Regular and 7100 Territorial Force personnel. Immediately a special force of three infantry battalions was authorised, one from each of the Military Districts, and manned by volunteers. In October 1939 a National Militia Reserve was raised to supplement the Territorial Force, with four battalions and fourteen independent companies being raised by that November. In January 1940 the first echelon of the expeditionary force left New Zealand for the Middle East. As with the Australians, the second echelon left on 2 May but was diverted to the United Kingdom; a third echelon was sent to Egypt in August. The New Zealand Expeditionary Force diverted to the United Kingdom was nearly at divisional strength and represented most of its country's trained personnel available at the time. It had only moved from Aldershot to join XII Corps in Kent early in September. This formation also had a key counter attack role. This Force was later to rejoin other elements already in North Africa and reform as the 2nd New Zealand Infantry Division.

It is generally overlooked that there was also a small Indian force in the country at this time, having been deployed with the BEF with its mule transport capabilities. However, it was very much in operational limbo as, after being evacuated from France in June 1940, no consistent policy on their deployment had been agreed.

Given that Canada, of all the Commonwealth and Empire countries, was to be in a position to play a major part in Britain's defence, both in terms of numbers and deployment, it is worth commenting in more detail than the others on the state of Canada's Army. Canada's pre war defence posture reflected Great Britain's; accordingly its Army was accorded the lowest level of spending. In 1931 General McNaughton commented that a citizen militia, backed by a small regular force acting as an instructional corps, was the proper type of land defence force for Canada. The militia was expected to undertake at least twelve days training a year but this was rarely achieved. Institutionally there was little provision for keeping the art of war fighting alive, with many in the Army and political arena assuming that military knowledge was mainly a matter of technical efficiency that any properly educated person could master probably better than a regular officer. In 1936 the reorganisation of the militia began and in 1937 agreement in principle was reached to form a mobile force for operations either in Canada or overseas. However, preparing such a force was less well conducted, with a regular arm that was a mere skeleton (it was only about 4200 strong, while the militia was nominally 55,000 strong); its summer exercises in 1938 found inter-arm co-operation to be the main problem, though some light tanks and modern artillery guns were deployed for the first time.

As with its antipodean colleagues the Canadian expeditionary force dispatched largely relied on the British for its equipment, training, organisation and operational doctrine. In September 1939 the Canadian Government initially agreed not to dispatch a force larger than one infantry division, though it was accepted that an Army Corps would ultimately be required. High unemployment levels throughout the country complemented the volunteer spirit in 1939. As the Militia Act specified that no soldier could be compelled to serve continuously overseas for more than a year (and as the Government was against national conscription), volunteers were encouraged to enlist for the duration of the War in the newly created Canadian Active Service Force, which incorporated the activated reserve units and regular force (in September 1939 about half of the 58,337 volunteers were either serving or former regulars and reservists). In December 1939 regulations were altered to permit the enlistment of resident foreign nationals, so allowing American nationals to join. In June 1940 the National Resources Mobilisation Act was passed, imposing conscription for home defence service. In July 1940 General Crerar was appointed Canada's Chief of the General Staff and was tasked with producing an appreciation of the military situation, the outcome of which was to prepare a Canadian Army based on mechanised power. This work was to form the basis of the Army's Programme for 1941.

In July 1940 Canada's leaders acknowledged that Britain was Canada's best line of defence and as such Britain should be given every possible assistance by it. They believed that this strategy was sounder than building up a local defence apparatus in Canada. With this in mind Canada was to be the biggest contributor in providing two infantry divisions, representing most of its available Army strength, for overseas operations. It was agreed that these formations be organised on the basis of proportional representation of the major territorial regions of Canada; for example, in 1st Division, units from Ontario made up the 1st Brigade, units from the western provinces the 2nd Brigade and units from Quebec and the eastern provinces the 3rd Brigade.

The Canadian Army was a virtually untrained citizen force of limited military proficiency, with most training expected to be conducted within the formations after they were deployed overseas. With this in mind, the High Command agreed to send units overseas irrespective of the availability of equipment and weapons only when there was a reasonable prospect of completing their equipment and after the unit's initial training period was completed. It was expected that, for the 1st Division, individual training was to be completed by the end of February 1940 and to complete unit training by April, when brigade and divisional exercises were to be undertaken. This schedule was, of course, dependent on the course of the War - before the blitzkrieg broke most of the training was based on the expected trench warfare. However, by early summer 1st Division was conducting many exercises at all levels, in line with its expected anti invasion role, earning it the nickname of "McNaughton's Flying Circus". However, Major General Pearkes, the new 1st Divisional Commander in July, noted that it was difficult to train beyond battalion level and that there was still too much of the militia camp attitude toward training. An example of the Canadian's training regime can be found in the War Diary of the 2nd Canadian Division's Royal Hamilton Light Infantry. It recorded that for the week beginning 7 September 1940 its A Company's programme was:

> Monday - Duty Company for the Battalion
> Tuesday - Conduct map reading and map marching exercises plus Defence against Gas (DAG) training
> Wednesday - Undertake physical exercise, patrolling and Passive Air Defence (PAD) training
> Thursday - Conduct a field exercise involving a deliberate company scale attack
> Friday - Undertake further physical exercise, conduct weapons and bayonet training, parade drill and perform a tactical route march.
> Saturday - Further physical exercise and drill, followed by inspection, while the afternoon was dedicated to sports.
> Sunday - Rest day.

As with all military formations in Britain at this time training was greatly retarded by the lack of proper equipment, while those located in the southeast had the added problems of having to react to the frequent air raids and air combat that took place in the skies above. Despite these problems, General McNaughton advised the Canadian Prime Minister on 8 June that he considered the Canadian force to be battleworthy. The 1st Division held its first Divisional scale anti invasion exercise in February 1941, involving moving to a concentration area before advancing to contact and deploying for attack. The result was disappointing with much traffic congestion due to poor staff planning and inadequate traffic control. General McNaughton remarked that the exercise had "shaken the complacency of everyone participating, from the Corps Commander to the lowest private soldier." Similar problems were experienced by 2nd Division in its first major exercise, held in March 1941. The first Corps level exercise was held in June 1941 and, although there was improvement in many areas, many shortcomings were revealed at the command and staff officer level (the provision of competently trained staff officers was already a serious concern identified in April 1940).

On 17 May 1940 the Canadian Cabinet's War Committee decided to authorise the formation of a Canadian Corps overseas. Headquarters VII Corps was selected to be this Canadian Corps, fulfilling Canada's wishes to have all its own troops under its own command, and was undergoing that transition during the summer of 1940. In April 1940 General McNaughton noted that "a Corps was probably the smallest organisation through which the Canadian forces in the field could be effectively administered and fought." The British request for heavy artillery units to be sent with the Canadian Expeditionary Force was to serve as the catalyst of arguments between the War Office and Canadian High Command over command of non-divisional formations. These arguments were largely influenced by the Canadian Government's reluctance to finance such units unless under Canadian command. On 1 September the Canadian Government finally accepted financial responsibility for all Canadian troops. On the outbreak of War Canada set up a military headquarters in London as a first step in maintaining autonomy over its own armed forces overseas. With the support of the War Office it was agreed that this headquarters was to be responsible for all administrative arrangements relating to Canadian forces, ensure a close liaison flourished with the War Office and Canada's National Defence Headquarters and command all Canadian forces in Britain not assigned to a higher command. For operational matters Lieutenant General McNaughton, now commander of VII Corps, was placed in overall command of these forces.

With the onset of autumn and the realisation that the main threat of large scale invasion had passed for the time, Alan Brooke was fortunate enough to be able to re-distribute his growing forces, in particular relieving his front line divisions with the newly formed coastal defence brigades, before moving them to winter quarters where they were better placed to carry out the mobile training and complete the re-equipping that they still desperately needed; other formations were sent overseas - mostly to North Africa. There was also a further overhaul of the higher command structure and co-ordination between the different services.

Even during the invasion period the Prime Minister and Chiefs of Staff were looking at the future strategy of the War. On 3 September Churchill submitted a memorandum to the War Cabinet on the munitions and equipment situation; this included the following:
- The decision to raise the Army to a strength of fifty-five divisions as rapidly as possible does not seem to require reconsideration. Within this we should aim for ten armoured

- divisions, five by the spring, seven by the summer and ten by the end of 1941. The execution of these programmes will tax our munitions industry to the full.
- Intense efforts must be made to complete the equipment of our Army both at home and in the Middle East. Surely, as large numbers of our Army proceed abroad the need of the Home Guard and of garrison troops for home defence will be felt on a far larger scale than at present.
- The danger of invasion will not disappear with the coming of winter, and may confront us with novel possibilities in the coming year. The enemy's need to strike down this country will naturally increase as the war progresses, and all kinds of devices for crossing the seas not existing may be devised. Actual invasion must be regarded a perpetually threatened, but unlikely to materialise as long as strong forces stand in this island. Apart from this, the only major theatre of war that can be foreseen in 1940-41 is the Middle East. Here we must bring into action British and Commonwealth forces on a scale that should only be limited by sea transport and local maintenance. We must expect to fight in Egypt, the Sudan, Turkey, Syria, Palestine and possibly Iraq and Persia. Fifteen British, six Australasian and at least six Indian divisions should be prepared for these theatres. Air power and mechanised troops will be dominant factors.
- There remain the possibilities of amphibious warfare against enemy held territory in Europe or North Africa. The needs of such operations will be provided by existing arms and supplies.
- This war is not a war of masses of men hurling masses of shells at each other, but it is by devising new weapons and, above all, by scientific leadership that we shall best cope with the enemy's superior strength.

On 15 October he amended the memorandum by noting 'at present we are aiming at five armoured divisions and armoured brigades equivalent to three more. This is not enough. We cannot hope to compete with the enemy in numbers of men and must therefore rely upon an exceptional proportion of armoured fighting vehicles. For this purpose the Army must review their demands for mechanised transport, large purchases of which must be made in the United States. The Home Army, working in this small island with highly developed communications of all kinds, cannot enjoy the same scale of transport which divisions on foreign service require. Improvisation and makeshift must be their guides.'

The result of the Army's experience of combat operations on the Continent between April and June 1940, and overcoming of its initial shock following the failure of these operations, meant that the Army in September 1940 was quite different from that found in July. In just a few months it had become better equipped, better organised, had been able to consider the lessons painfully learnt by the BEF and had high morale. It had used this valuable time to consider its defensive options and how to make the best use of what resources it had, strengthening its defences and training its personnel in aggressive and mobile warfare, ensuring the start of a move by the Army from a defensive reactionary posture to a more offensive one. There were still many problems to overcome - the lack of well armed and reliable tanks in sufficient numbers; a still developing and modernising command and communications organisation; the lack of sufficient mobile anti aircraft weapons; lethargy and complacency among those officers and other ranks who had still not modernised their approach to war and the red tape of bureaucracy which still afflicted military and civilian organisations alike. Not all of the lessons of recent combat had been implemented or understood fully as records show that many senior officers preferred to wait until the invasion scare was over before devoting time and resources to properly adapt the lessons.

1941 allowed the British Army the first opportunity to test their operational readiness in large scale anti invasion exercises. Although these should be seen as the initial attempts to put theory into practice, with many units released from coastal defence and generally free from air attack, they are also useful in showing how a British Army at that time could have fared against an equally determined enemy. The GHQ conducted Exercise Dragon, a staff exercise, in January 1941. It findings included:

- Co-operation between the Army Tank Brigade and motorised units had not been really practised
- Confirmation that the main task of an Armoured Division was to destroy enemy tanks and that the orders given to it by senior commanders must be clear and concise, but that its tactical deployment must be left to the field commander
- Corps commanders should expect to give an indication of further action by armoured divisions
- Signals jamming (by the British) was unlikely to be effective as the resources were not yet available to make it worthwhile; however, it reinforced the view that commanders must make more use of the radio for communications

It recommended that field divisions should conduct at least one field exercise a month, as divisional level training was still rare. The Royal Armoured Corps staff exercise in late January 1941 observed that "owing to restrictions enforced during peacetime training, armoured formations still tend to be very road bound. Commanders are to ensure that their men are accustomed to the idea of cross-country moves. No opportunity should be lost in moving off road."

Eastern Command conducted its first field exercise in April 1941. Exercise Thunderbolt was held over three days around Newmarket by II Corps, comprising 6th Armoured Division and 45th Infantry Division, while 42nd Infantry Division and 21st Army Tank Brigade provided the enemy. For the first time about 150 men of the new parachute training squadron were to be dropped. The post exercise report highlighted the following concerns:

- <u>Command and control</u>. It was evident that the handling of armoured formations by higher command needed further study. Delays in passing important orders was due to a lack of close liaison between staff and signals. Passage of information from the front to the rear was poor. There was a lack of co-operation between the support and combat arms, especially between the artillery and infantry, noting that many commanders were located too far apart from each other to ensure efficient control
- <u>Movement</u>. It was noted that the march discipline of the armoured units was better than the infantry; however, the rear echelon's discipline on both march and in harbour was poor. The need to separate the movement of tracked and wheeled vehicles was made apparent. Infantry tended to bring their buses and coaches too far forward before de-bussing, something that was bound to lead to heavy casualties and greater confusion in combat. It was observed that night movement of small groups of vehicles was the

best option as this allowed for greater control. Special attention was required to the routing and control of road traffic
- Artillery. The need to deploy survey units at an early stage was vital as this enabled artillery units to come into action quicker and more efficiently. Battery commanders also needed to make more use of their forward observers
- Reconnaissance. It was important that these units be assured decent rest periods. However, their concealment needed more attention when on patrol
- Engineers. The arrangements for demolitions were poor as on too many occasions orders were not correctly passed on or not enough time was given to get the explosives in place
- Anti parachutist. It was important that continual vigilance be employed as it was noted that some units in the immediate area of the drop did not see anything. It was reinforced that co-ordinated and aggressive action must be undertaken in these circumstances
- Prisoners. These must be passed back quickly as the best chance of getting information from them was through proper interrogation
- Security. Wireless security was still poor as was personal security, with too much loose talk with strangers and civilians. Staff officers should be reminded that operational orders and maps should not be taken into the combat area
- Signals. The cipher unit must be located with the advance headquarters. Signals units must be kept informed of troop movements
- Air. The time lag in passing requests for air support still took too long, while there was widespread misuse of air recognition and information signals. It was noted that many troops took little notice of aircraft, either friendly or "enemy", which tended to reduce their exercise value.

The Command conducted its next exercise in June 1941. Exercise Bulldog involved 6th and 9th Armoured Divisions, 1st, 42nd, 45th and 46th Infantry Divisions and 24th Guards Brigade. This was a much larger exercise with the units that had been involved in Exercise Thunderbolt performing better than their counterparts, especially in movement control and security. The effectiveness of all units was, however, tempered with the need to reduce the impact on the vital agriculture of the region. The post exercise report recorded the following issues:

- Commanders needed accurate, quick and up to date information in order to make better use of their resources; this included information on the topography and local knowledge but commanders also failed to make vigorous use of reconnaissance
- The use of ad-hoc formations should be discouraged, though the main reason was administrative rather than operational
- It was important not to over tax both tanks and their crews during road movements. The best way to achieve this was to reduce the mileage they were expected to cover in one bound
- Demolition tasks were still not acceptable; many failed as either they were left to the last minute or due to imprecise or unclear orders being given
- There was too long a time lag in getting engineering equipment and materials to those units who had not previously considered this problem
- The use of radio communications was still insufficient

- Chemical warfare was still regarded as a novelty and more attention to individual training was required
- A closer liaison with the Home Guard was required, especially with respect to their capabilities; unit commanders often overlooked this valuable asset
- Staff officers needed to be aware that working without relief in operations lasting more than two days was not viable. Mostly this was due to overconfidence by the officers themselves
- Liaison between military and civilian authorities was too often non-existent.

Between 27 September and 3 October 1941 GHQ Home Forces oversaw another large field exercise, Exercise Bumper, involving 250,000 troops of Eastern Command. Twelve divisions and two Army Tank Brigades took part: 6th and 9th Armoured, 1st, 43rd, 46th and 54th Infantry Divisions were the defenders while 8th Armoured, 3rd, 4th and 48th Infantry Divisions, 1st and 2nd Canadian Divisions represented the enemy. The three objectives for this Exercise were to give higher command the opportunity to handle large modern mechanised formations in the field, examine the composition and organisation of a force suitable for overseas operations and test the defensive organisation against a large-scale lodgement in Britain. General Alan Brooke published his post Exercise report and started by reminding all concerned that this was the first time higher command had had the opportunity to command large numbers of troops in the field and that the armoured formations taking part had been formed for less than a year. He recognised that the Exercise had been limited by the impossibility to reproduce the firepower of a battlefield, the commanders not being faced with life and death decisions and the restrictions imposed in order to reduce damage to the environment. He said that the exercise had demonstrated the influence that armoured formations have on any battlefield and that those armoured divisions involved had achieved a high standard of efficiency. He was satisfied with the fighting efficiency of the troops and expected the levels attained to be maintained; he was impressed with the marked fighting spirit demonstrated by all. Although the Home Forces had made significant advances he was concerned that some serious problems still existed. These included:

- <u>Command and control</u>
    - Many headquarters were located too far to the rear
    - Passage of information and intelligence was far too slow
    - Concern that staff officers still attempted to produce the perfect written order, delaying its issue and execution. He re-iterated that reliance must be on verbal orders and conferences, confirmed if possible at a later stage
    - Concern that many senior commanders were caught up in the staff work of their headquarters and that they must be free from all distractions to plan operations
    - He felt that many field commanders operated at too slow a tempo during operations, with the result that many opportunities were lost. He noted that, in particular, 9th Armoured Division had been mishandled as too many of its operations involved so called cavalry charges, instead of using the ground and supporting weapons.
    - Concern that the opportunity to mount Divisional level attacks had been largely ignored as it was felt Brigade group operations were the answer to all situations

- The extrication of forces in contact with the enemy had been well handled, no doubt due to the experiences of the British forces on the Continent. He also noted that 54th Division, in particular, had performed well in its defensive operations
- He accepted that in a withdrawal the length of the frontages occupied was likely to be decided by the enemy but, in attack, these should be selected to suit the strength of the force used. In too many cases during the exercise the frontages were too large and impracticable, with infantry divisions being asked to attack on a nine-mile front to a depth of eight miles.

- Armour
  - Tanks too often got involved in fighting for towns and villages, rather than bypassing them.
- Reconnaissance
  - The armoured car regiments had been poorly handled, with little appreciation of their value. They were overworked and lacked proper rest
  - Signals transmission was poor
  - Armoured cars lacked the weaponry to perform their tasks more effectively.
- Artillery
  - Both the Army and Corps level artillery were generally decentralised too early, so reducing their effectiveness
  - It was still not appreciated that use of high explosive shells in indirect fire will not stop tank attacks
  - Anti aircraft defence of road movements was still poorly conducted (though it was accepted that the lack of a real threat during the Exercise was a mitigating point).
- Engineers
  - Divisional engineers were decentralised to brigade level, contrary to instructions and reducing their efficiency
  - Demolitions were often found to be haphazard and premature, requiring firmer control by higher comman
  - Too little was made of the chemical warfare staff.
- Obstacles
  - There was a tendency to place defences behind tanks obstacles rather than astride them, so reducing the effect of supporting fire and aiding enemy reconnaissance.
- Air
  - Control of the air effort should remain concentrated at as high a level as long as possible
  - During the advance to contact the headquarters of the air units should be located with Army headquarters but once in contact this should be moved to the Corps headquarters involved
  - Whilst selection of targets was good the air effort was too often inadequate
  - Little photographic reconnaissance was undertaken as none was requested by the Army
  - There was poor passing of information, especially relating to RAF unit movements, while a mutual programme of understanding Army and RAF signals procedures was recommended

- Less reliance should be made of the telephone network by RAF units
- It was felt that the vehicle echelon of RAF units during moves needed revision, as they tended to be cumbersome.
- Security
  - There was still too much loose talk.
- Administration
  - There was a lack of imagination in the planning of the exercise, especially the absence of reality
  - The supply organisation was too elaborate and tended to over supply units at the front rather than exercise control of the system
  - The internal administration of many units was poor with many troops not having hot food for several days
  - There was too often a premature destruction of stores, especially when isolated enemy vehicles were in the area
  - The railheads were overloaded, with too many units allotted to the same one
  - The traffic control organisation was too static.

It was clear that to defeat an invading German Army, with its quality and experience, the British Army would still have to perform much better in many crucial areas - notably command, communications, all arms co-ordination, air support and logistics. Equally as important, its commanders at all levels needed to modernise their outlook and regain belief, let alone exude confidence to subordinates, in their ability to counter the coming storm. Those who would not or could not meet these requirements would need to be replaced by younger more energetic officers. Morale was also critical and would remain so as circumstances developed; although the British were willing to fight in order to retain their way of life, it would not be enough just to repeat the exhortation to "take one with you", especially after the initial shock of invasion had passed. It was crucial that the Army change from being defensively minded to that of aggressive offence; without this it could never hope to win and maintain the strategic initiative vital to successfully defeating an invasion.

Nevertheless, it is important to remember that the morale of the British people most often rises most in adversity and never more so than when fighting with their backs to the wall as now. The Army did have another two things in its favour - it was fighting on its own territory and had the full support of the population, as demonstrated by the overwhelming recruitment of the Home Guard. The importance of these two aspects could not be under-estimated, as any invader would have to face everywhere a hostile people who continued to believe in ultimate victory. General Alan Brooke noted in his diary on 15 September that "It should not be thought that I considered our position a hopeless one ... far from it. We should certainly have had a desperate struggle and the future might well have hung in the balance, but I felt that, given a fair share of the fortunes of war, we should certainly succeed in finally defending these shores."

CHAPTER SIX: INVASION DAY

The projected German invasion can be split into four geographical areas, in line with the invasion areas picked by the Germans: Hythe to Dungeness, Rye and Winchelsea, Bexhill to Eastbourne and Cuckmere to Rottingdean.

Landing Zone B: Hythe to Dungeness

Topography
This area is popularly known as Romney Marsh. The crescent shaped St Mary's Bay runs for about ten miles and shelves gradually, with the beach alternating between shingle and sand that is also very wide at low tide (100 metres to the north and 1000 metres in the south). Between Dymchurch Redoubt and St Mary's Bay settlement a significant concrete coastal wall backs the beach and regularly spaced wooden groynes (designed to protect the beach) extend from it across the beach to the low water mark. The coastal fringe contains a number of small settlements, while several small villages lie across the marshes further inland. The whole area is flat and crisscrossed by many small water channels and as a result, contains few roads across it and one running directly parallel behind the beaches. The exits from this area are controlled by the Royal Military Canal, a Napoleonic defensive work that could delay but not, by itself, prevent German advances. The town of Hythe lies at the eastern end of this zone and straddles the Canal, with Army rifle ranges facing the beach directly to the south, while the towns of Lydd and New Romney lie at the southern end. Ancient coastal cliffs rise up immediately behind both Hythe and the Canal, permitting good defensive and observation positions, but again are no serious obstruction to a German advance by themselves. Further inland the ground is more undulating and heavily wooded with many small roads running inland towards Ashford and Tenterden and a couple running parallel to the Canal. The Ashford to Hastings railway crosses the Royal Military Canal near Ham Street before following the Canal to Rye; the private small gauge railway runs from Hythe to Dungeness almost directly behind the beach, whilst another railway was built running from near Appledore to south of New Romney for the railway guns mounted there. It had been previously agreed that Romney Marsh would not be flooded prior to any invasion due to its agricultural significance, but plans to do so were well prepared.

The area where most of the German paratroopers expected to land was generally one of slightly rolling farm and pasture land with some woods, bisected by the main Ashford to Folkestone road and railway. High ground marked by long ridges, forming part of the North Downs, rises to the northeast and is cut by several valleys running north or northeast towards Canterbury. These provide the main routes of communication from that city, including a railway along the Elham valley. The area where Battle Group Steinzler was expected to land is near the top of the North Downs but has more severe contours, making such an operation rather hazardous, but few settlements.

The land running from Folkestone to Ashford follows the south facing slopes of the North Downs and provides easier lines of communication, both road and railway, with Ashford providing an important communications hub at the southern end of the Stour valley. The airfield at Lympne was constructed close to the old cliff line running behind the Royal Military

Canal, while Hawkinge airfield was constructed on the edge of the North Downs overlooking Folkestone.

German Naval intelligence stated that "between Folkestone and Dungeness the coast forms a wide bay sheltered against westerly winds, with a flat beach that shelves gently. The approach to the bay is hindered by the Varne and the Ridge sandbanks, which can only be crossed high tide."

The German Plans
Transport Fleet B comprised two tow convoys and two transport convoys. Tow Convoy 1 had 75 tows escorted by the 3rd Minesweeping, 3rd Patrol and 11th R Boat Flotillas and was to sail from Dunkirk at S-9½ hours; Tow Convoy 2 had 25 tows escorted by the 2nd Patrol and 3rd R Boat Flotillas and was to sail from Ostend at S-14 hours. Both these convoys were to sail in three columns at an average speed of 5 knots. The Fleet was to rendezvous west of Dunkirk and cross the Channel, aiming at Folkestone, then turn west into St Mary's Bay. This formation was to be over 16 kilometres long. Three gunboats were to be placed at the west end and another six at the east, supported by four and five AA ferries respectively. Minesweepers were to be employed from the force to sweep and mark the routes. Transport Convoy 1 had 8 ships escorted by the 16th Minesweeping Flotilla and was to sail from Ostend at S-13 hours, while Transport Convoy 2, with 49 ships and 98 barges escorted by the 4th Minesweeping Flotilla, was to sail from Rotterdam at S-18 hours. These two convoys were to sail in two columns and comprised the bulk of the first echelon. They were due to arrive in St Mary's Bay at about S+2 hours.

The German XIII Corps (17th and 35th Infantry Divisions) planned to land in three parts - the advance detachments, first echelon and second echelon. Up to 10,000 men per division were to land on the first day. The three advance detachments, each comprising a reinforced infantry battalion formed from the assaulting regiments, were to land from 0615 and had the vital task of overcoming the initial coastal defences. The detachment from 35th Division had 1300 men in four rifle companies, four heavy machine gun and four anti tank platoons and eight engineer groups. This force was carried in four escorts, eight minesweeper trawlers and three barge tows and was to land near Littlestone. The two advance detachments from 17th Division totalled 1900 men in two reinforced infantry battalions, supported by four mountain guns, five light field guns, six anti tank guns, sixteen heavy mortars, twenty heavy machine guns plus two flame thrower tank platoons and twenty engineer groups. These were carried in twenty-seven escort craft and four barge tows and were to land either side of Dymchurch Redoubt. 1st Brandenburg Company was organised into two platoons - one was to land with the 35th Division advance detachment and the other with Tank Detachment D. Each division also had a panzer battalion attached (B and D respectively, the latter with only two companies), totalling 98 tanks and carried in nine and six barge tows respectively; these were expected to land immediately after the advance detachments, with one company landing at a time. These advance detachments were allowed to use the light railway line running behind the beaches to reorganise before moving forward to cross the Royal Military Canal and meet up with the airborne troops. By this action it was hoped that the rest of the first echelon would avoid having to become involved in the initial fighting on the beaches or on the marshes.

According to surviving plans by 07.30 the advance detachments were to have completed their landing, whilst the barge tows of the first echelon were to start landing and transports were to have arrived; for each division these troops would include its headquarters, four infantry battalions, an artillery battalion, an engineer battalion and its bicycle battalion; in 35th Division these forces were carried in 74 barges, most armed with either a 75mm (20 barges), 47mm (15 barges) or 20mm (13 barges) gun, while 17th Division had 17 barges fitted with a 75mm gun and others with a 20mm gun. The transports were to carry another forty-five 75mm guns. All these extra weapons were to be landed later to supplement the divisional artillery, much of which was due to be landed the following day together with the remaining divisional and Corps fighting troops; further support troops planned to land over several days, making another 27,000 men. The German Navy calculated that it could put 200 barges, with a gap of about 125 metres between each, ashore at one time.

17th Infantry Division was tasked with clearing Hythe and linking up with 7th Air Division. Battle Group Hoffmeister, led by the commander of the 21st Infantry Regiment, was to form in the Stanford-Sandling area, to the north west of Hythe, in the afternoon of S Day. It was to consist of Tank Detachment B, a machine gun battalion, 1st Brandenburg Company, an assault gun battery, two mechanised anti tank companies, an anti aircraft company, a mechanised artillery battery and an engineer company. Many of these units were from the Corps Troops and were due to land with the first or second echelons. The battle group was to move behind Folkestone with the objective of capturing Dover before the end of S Day. 21st Infantry Regiment was to prepare for an advance either on Dover with this battle group or to the River Stour south of Canterbury; if the latter move was ordered then elements from 7th Air Division were to be assigned to Group Hoffmeister. Given the topography of the area there are only two feasible routes for these mechanised forces - the first would link up with the airborne Assault Regiment before moving onto Hawkinge and then Dover; the second involved forcing a way past the Shorncliffe Garrison and then moving through Folkestone's western and northern suburbs before climbing the steep North Downs to the north east of the town, all the time being at least under observation.

The Division's other infantry regiment (55th) was to move towards Ashford and Wye whilst the Divisional cycle battalion was to patrol towards Canterbury and Ashford; this cycle battalion was initially to move behind the tanks to Aldington, where it was to help guard the left flank. The first operational objective of the Division was to secure a small ridge running from Etchinghill to Lympne by Sandling. The Division was eventually to establish an extended bridgehead between Chilham and Ashford along the River Stour and between Chilham and Dover just north of the main A2 road.

35th Infantry Division, supported by Panzer Battalion D, was to cross the marshes and Royal Military Canal on a broad front between Bilsington and Appledore in order to establish a beachhead extending from south of Ashford to Sissinghurst, this line running through Bethersden, High Halden and Biddenden; 109th and 111th Infantry Regiments were to be responsible for the eastern and western sectors of this line respectively, backed by strong anti tank defences.

In an independent action a Brandenburg Special Forces company was tasked with raiding Dover harbour and coastal batteries from the sea in fast boats with the purpose of disrupting the defences and their port demolition tasks (an airborne option had been discounted due to obstacles and anti aircraft defences in the area of the coastal batteries). Corps headquarters was to be established at Hythe. The boundary between the two divisions was to run from Dymchurch to east of Bilsington and then north to Kingsnorth, south of Ashford, and Great Chart, whilst the Corps left boundary ran from New Romney through Appledore and Tenterden.

7th Air Division, though not under Corps command, was to land in two waves to coincide with the Corps programme. The first wave, consisting of two battle groups, was to land at about the same time the advance detachments. Battle Group Meindl, consisting of two reinforced battalions led by the new commander of the Assault Regiment, was to land north west of Hythe and clear the defences around the bridges over the Royal Military Canal in and west of Hythe, before forming a defensive flank between Hythe and Saltwood; Battle Group Steinzler, also two reinforced battalions strong and led by the commander of the Assault Regiment's second battalion, was to land near Paddlesworth, west of Hawkinge, with the objective of securing the high ground around its landing zone. There is some indication that it also proposed to move to the southeast and engage defenders in the Sandgate area. The second wave was Battle Group Brauer - led by the commander of the 1st Parachute Regiment and comprising the remainder of the 1st Parachute Regiment, including part of its anti tank company, the divisional engineer battalion and the 2nd and 3rd Parachute Regiments - planned to land an hour later northwest of Hythe. 2nd and 3rd Parachute Regiments were to provide flank protection to the north and west respectively, having taken the high ground north of Postling and securing Lympne airfield respectively. At least one battalion of the 1st Parachute Regiment and its gun company would have remained in divisional reserve. It is not clear from remaining documents as to which part of the Division the assaulting battalions would come from, though given the command structure it is likely that the Assault Regiment would have formed most of it. There was no indication as to when and how divisional headquarters would land but it is likely that Colonel Brauer would have exercised control of the Division that landed until it did. It is also not clear which elements of the Division were to support Group Hoffmeister if required, or how many heavy weapons would be dropped with the paratroopers. The subsequent development of the operation would dictate whether any additional divisional units were to be landed, or indeed whether elements of the 22nd Air Landing Division would be involved.

<u>The British defences</u>
This was the strongest of the invasion sectors covered by coastal artillery; 519th Coast Regiment defended Dover (two 9.2-inch and nine 6-inch guns), two coastal batteries covered Folkestone (four 6-inch guns) and one 18-inch, two 14-inch, two 13.5-inch, four 12-inch and seven 9.2-inch railway mounted guns were deployed around these two ports. These were expected to supplement the five emergency coastal batteries (eight 6-inch and two 4.7-inch guns) located along the coast between Dungeness and Hythe. Although there was an integrated fire control system in place covering Dover, this did not extend to the intended landing zones along the coast; there the newly formed 12th Coastal Artillery Group headquarters near Hythe co-ordinated the emergency coastal batteries and was linked to the Dover coastal artillery command. The coastline of the Bay was broken up into sectors each of 1000 yards wide to facilitate co-ordinated artillery defensive fire. The artillery fire plan indicated that heavy artillery was to open up on targets 500 yards before the beach while field artillery would begin firing on targets 200 yards out. The established coastal artillery was

cleared to engage targets up to three miles from the coast. This would permit the invasion fleet to be engaged before it entered St Mary's Bay.

Land forces immediately available to counter the airborne landings would mostly come from 1st London Division: Headquarters 2nd London Infantry Brigade, its Brigade Anti Tank Company and 1st Bn London Rifle Brigade, 64th Field Regiment RA (fourteen guns just north of Hawkinge) and 501st Field Company RE. These were deployed behind Hythe and Folkestone and which would almost certainly have been tied up with opposing the airborne attack, as would the troops of the neighbouring Corps heavy artillery units, the troops assigned to defend both Lympne and Hawkinge airfields plus the Home Guard from Kent's 1st, 7th and 8th Battalions.

The bulk of the coastal defence was supplied by 45th Infantry Division, which had its 135th Brigade deployed mostly along the coast between Dymchurch and Lydd, supported by 18th Royal Fusiliers (Pioneers), the machine guns of 7th Devon's D Company (a platoon each in Aldington, New Romney and Greatstone), 55th Field Regiment RA (twenty two guns), three anti tank batteries (sixteen guns deployed to New Romney, Lydd and Greatstone) and the Home Guard from Kent's 1st and 8th Battalions. Although there are no detailed dispostions recorded by 135th Brigade the units that relieved it later in the year did record theirs and it is very likely that they would have retained much of the initial layout. Therefore 7th Somerset Light Infantry would have been responsible for the sector from south of Lydd on Sea, inland to Snargate and back to the coast east of New Romney. Each of the nodal points was surrounded by triple thickness barbed wire obstacles, minefields and anti tank obstacles (See maps). At Greatstone and St Mary's Bay the defending companies each deployed two platoons along the seafront with one in reserve. Dymchurch was split into two separate sectors: 6th Somerset Light Infantry's B Company covering the north end and its HQ Company in the centre around the Martello Towers, each with two platoons deployed along the sea front, all positions being self contained. The nodal point at St Mary in the Marsh was based on three platoon locations: Heffonden Farm, the church/pub and around the school. The nodal point of Burmarsh had three platoon localities – the village, Chapel Farm and Gammon's Farm (both farms are to the west of the village); New Romney was split into six sub sectors, each self contained. 338 Battery from 34th Searchlght Regiment had a series of sites along the coast and along the Royal Miltary Canal.

Both 6 Commando and 3 Independent Company had counterattack roles from Littlestone and Lydd, ostensibly to protect the Canadian heavy artillery at Dungeness. 135th Brigade had a reserve near the Royal Military Canal consisting most of 18th Royal Fusiliers (Pioneers), D Company of 6th Somerset Light Infantry, a machine gun platoon from 7th Devon's D Company, the sound ranging battery of 1st Survey Regt RA, 259th Field Company RE and the Home Guard from Kent's 1st and 2nd Battalions. There would also be an infantry reserve available in Lydd as the Canadians were deploying a rifle company to the rifle ranges there for a few days each at that time.

Shorncliffe Garrison was a mix of units containing five infantry companies and three specialist engineer battalions in an infantry role, mostly deployed along the coastline, but these had limited counterattack capabilities due to the lack of heavy equipment and infantry training. The Small Arms School was to defend its rifle ranges that lay between Hythe and Dymchurch

Redoubt, while 5th Stevedore Battalion's 17th Company was deployed in Dymchurch Redoubt, at Botolph's Bridge and at Lympne. This Garrison lacked any organic artillery and would have been reliant on the 2nd London Brigade's artillery at Acrise until reinforcements arrived.

In terms of fortifications the only major works featured Dymchurch Redoubt, a major moated concrete fortification lying between Hythe and Dymchurch, and a number of Martello Towers extending along the coast from Dymchurch to Folkestone. These latter structures were still largely shell proof and used as command posts, heavy machine gun posts and artillery observation posts while the Redoubt housed a coastal battery and a stevedore platoon; both could be expected to hold out for some time. These fortifications were supplemented by pillboxes and other improvised defensive works covering the beaches and inland exits, including beach mines, beach scaffolding, anti tank obstacles and barbed wire. Another line of pillboxes ran along the top of the old cliff line behind Folkestone. The Royal Military Canal had been deepened and improved as an anti tank obstacle and was also covered by an extended line of pillboxes while others were built on the escarpment behind. Most bridges across the Canal were removed leaving the following, all prepared for demolition: Iden lock, Appledore, Ham Street (including the railway bridge), Bilsington, Goldenhurst Farm and West Hythe. All these were covered by defensive positions and fortifications. A number of drainage channels on the Marsh plus the River Rother at the western end had also been deepened and improved as anti tank obstacles. 501st Field Company RE was assigned the vital role of demolishing the remaining crossings over the River Rother and Royal Military Canal, while a company of the 1st Training Battalion RE at Shorncliffe was assigned demolition roles at Dover Harbour. Although plans had been prepared all equipment and personnel would only be activated on the issuing of a specific codeword; if this was not received in time then these troops, especially 501st Field Company as it was located close to a parachute drop zone, may not be able to reach their positions in enough time to carry out their assignments. A Corps Stop Line was nearly complete running from Ham Street to Ashford along the railway line, facing east, but this really only consisted of widely spaced pillboxes. In the immediate invasion area Sellindge, Burmarsh, St Mary on the Marsh, New Romney, Lydd, Ham Street and Appledore were prepared as nodal points and were expected to hold to the last man and round of ammunition. All had stocks of mines either already deployed or immediately available, if time and circumstances permitted. Forces manning Burmarsh, New Romney and Lydd also had limited counter attack capabilities.

Reinforcements at short notice, excluding from Dover Garrison, would be expected to include the remainder of 2nd London Brigade and possibly 1st London Brigade, supported by two field regiments (thirty six guns), an anti tank battery and a machine gun company; these would be able to move south from the Canterbury area and had transport at hand to achieve this. 1st London Division headquarters at Ashford could also provide the divisional reserve of 2/5th Queens, two machine gun companies and an anti tank battery plus Milforce (8th RTR with fifty infantry tanks, a light reconnaissance squadron, an infantry company, two artillery troops (eight guns), an anti tank battery, a machine gun company and a light anti aircraft battery) from the New Zealand Expeditionary Force (NZEF). The rest of the NZEF would be available as soon as it could move from the Maidstone area. A number of minor units would have been responsible for protecting vital points and defending nodal points in order to prevent or hinder any enemy penetration inland.

Dymchurch Redoubt

Dymchurch with a Martello Tower

This is where the 17th German Infantry Division was to land

Greatstone beach

Littlestone beach

This is where the 35th German Infantry Division was to land

Landing Zone C: Rye Bay and Fairlight

Topography
Rye Bay is split by the River Rother, which flows around the town to the north and east before reaching the sea to the south at Rye Harbour. Camber, to the east, has a sandy beach that extends seawards for a considerable distance at low tide. The beach is backed by tall dunes along its western half and a steep shingle bank along the eastern half; directly behind both lie marshes and gravel works and the only road that leads to both Rye and Lydd. There was only one beach exit for vehicles, at the eastern end of the dunes. Rye Harbour is very narrow with few port facilities, with most development along its western side. The harbour mouth had been barred with concrete piles driven in and steel hawsers placed across the entrance. The beach to the west of the harbour has steep shingle banks behind which lie more marshes and the ancient Camber Castle. The town of Rye lies over a mile inland on a hill, with the River Rother

and the Royal Military Canal protecting it to the east and south. High ground lays to the west either side of the Rivers Tillingham and Brede, both of which form shallow and broad valleys perpendicular to the coast, and to the north before dropping to the River Rother at the Isle of Oxney. Rye, Winchelsea and Cliff End and the ridges inland provide good observation, while Rye dominates the road and rail communications in the area. From Rye the main road inland runs along the high ground to the north west towards Hawkhurst while smaller roads runs across the Isle of Oxney to Tenterden, along the Udimore ridge behind Hastings and to Hastings through Winchelsea.

Winchelsea beach also has a high continuous shingle bank, which is reinforced by a sea wall behind which there is a small settlement and a single road, which runs directly behind the beach from Winchelsea through Pett Level before climbing into the hilly ground leading to Fairlight and Hastings. The beach continues westward to the small village of Cliff End where the cliffs rise steeply from the sea. The military survey noted that the beach was suitable for landing troops and armoured vehicles at all times of tides. Winchelsea lies on a wooded hill about a mile inland. It has the River Brede running around its northern side while the Royal Military Canal flows around its southern side before continuing to the sea at Cliff End. The marshy area behind this beach was known as Pett Level and had been flooded since May 1940, when three gaps were made in the sea wall. The main Ashford to Hastings railway runs along the Brede valley at this point.

The terrain gets hillier going westwards towards Hastings. The small and steep Fairlight Cove lays a couple of miles from Winchelsea and is quite isolated and totally unsuitable for motor vehicles. The British military survey noted that the beach was only suitable for the landing of small groups of troops.

German Naval intelligence stated that "the coast between Dungeness and Cliff End is low lying and forms Rye Bay, where depths offshore increase very slowly. West of Cliff End as far as Hastings there is no possibility of landing, as the coast is steep and rocks and reefs are found offshore."

<u>The German Plans</u>
Transport Fleet C consisted of three elements: Convoy C was to sail from Gravelines and Calais with 100 tows in three columns at S-8½ hours before crossing the Channel at 5 knots in a westwards direction before turning north into Rye Bay at S-2 hours. This Convoy would be over 14km long and protected by the 1st and 32nd Minesweeper, 4th R Boat and 7th Patrol Flotillas. On the approach to the beaches four or five AA pontoon ferries would deploy to guard each flank, with two smoke screen boats assigned to the western end. Secondly, Convoy 3 consisting of 57 transports and 114 barges was to leave Antwerp at S-11 hours, escorted by eight trawlers of the 15th Minesweeper Flotilla. This was due to arrive off Rye by S+2 hours. Thirdly, a group of seven steamers was due to sail from Ostend at S-11 hours and join Convoy 3. It was planned that the barges arriving with the transports would land at S+3½ hours, whilst the transports were not expected to be fully unloaded until late at night on S+2. The vessels carrying the tanks were to sail with the transport fleet and pull ahead to join the advance detachment vessels when close to the coast. The rest of the first wave was unlikely to arrive until S+4. By S+3hours 5 of 1st and all of 15th Minesweeper and 7th Patrol Flotillas were to form a picket line

protecting the unloading transports, 4th R Boat Flotilla was to conduct anti submarine or minesweeper duties and 32nd Minesweeper Flotilla was to help the unloading.

The German VII Corps (7th Infantry and 1st Mountain Divisions) was to land on a similar basis to XIII Corps above but with four advance detachments (two per division) and one panzer battalion (A). The advance detachments of the two Mountain Regiments were each allocated three R Boats, eight auxiliary minesweepers and a tow (each minesweeper carried about twenty two infantry, six engineers and five men for the infantry or anti tank gun carried, plus a crew of twenty two); In 7th Infantry Division's sector 19th Infantry Regiment's advance detachment was to land west of the harbour and was assigned four patrol boats, ten minesweepers and two tows, while 62nd Infantry Regiment's advance detachment was to land at Camber and was carried in four patrol boats, ten minesweepers and one tow. Both of 7th Division's detachments would have to cross up to 800m of gently shelving pebble beach or flat open beach, whilst 99th Mountain Regiment's detachment would have between 200-700m of pebble beach to cross. The advance detachments (except 98th Mountain Regiment's) each also had a flame-thrower tank platoon assigned. Panzer Battalion A was carried in sixteen tows, the tanks expected to be put into the water three kilometres off the beach and involving a half hour transit under water, unless circumstances did not allow this, in which case they were to be landed directly onto the beach. There was a sandbank about 700m offshore which would expose the submersible tanks. These advance detachments were to advance two kilometres inland to Winchelsea and Rye with the tank detachment in support (a tank company was assigned to 1st Mountain Division). The minimum objective of the first echelon was to secure up to the River Rother. Once the bulk of the first echelon was landed Panzer Battalion A was to become a Corps asset and be located around Winchelsea.

7th Infantry Division was to land either side of Rye, its 19th and 62nd Infantry Regiments landing to the west and east of the harbour entrance respectively, with the aim of capturing both Rye and Winchelsea before pushing forward to the River Rother; once across this it was to establish a line between Sissinghurst and Cranbrook, if circumstances permitted. Lydd and Dungeness were to be taken from the rear by reserve forces of the Division.

1st Mountain Division would land near Winchelsea (99th Mountain Regiment) and at Fairlight (98th Mountain Regiment), the latter requiring the use of rocket assisted climbing lines, and aimed to move behind Hastings to Battle, before moving north to establish a line between Cranbrook and Burwash, over halfway between Tunbridge Wells and Hastings. Hastings was to be taken from the east and north. It planned to arm the seventy six barges of the First Wave with forty-four 75mm artillery guns and eighteen 47mm anti tank guns, which would be landed as soon as possible to supplement the Divisional artillery. Corps headquarters controlled 41st Artillery Brigade with two motorised battalions, each with twelve 100mm guns; an engineer regiment with six battalions, three of which were bridging units. The boundary between the two divisions was to run inland from Winchelsea Beach to east of Icklesham then to Broad Oak, south of Staple Cross and Salehurst and on to Etchingham. It was expected that each division would have up to 10,000 men landed by the end of the first day, including two infantry regiments, divisional headquarters, an artillery battalion, engineer battalion and ant tank units each.

The German Navy calculated that it could put 200 barges, with a gap of about 110 metres between them, ashore at one time. Due to the nature of the beaches the assault forces would have to expect to cross up to 800 metres of shallows and open beach either side of the harbour but only 300 metres at Cliff End. 14,000 men were to land on the first day, with another 27,000 coming in over the next few days.

The British defences
There was only a single coastal artillery battery with two 6-inch guns in this area (as the battery at Hastings was not sited to be able to engage targets to the east), supported by a single 9.2-inch and two 6-inch guns of 56th Heavy Regiment RA sited to the north west of Rye. Coast defence was the responsibility of 45th Infantry Division's 134th Brigade, with 1st Royal Irish Fusiliers primarily responsible for this sector, supported by D Company 1/6th Devons and two platoons of A Company 7th Devon (machine gun) (at Pett and Rye Harbour/Camber respectfully). Defence was organised in two lines, with companies and a machine gun platoon deployed at Camber, Rye Harbour and Winchelsea Beach, with other companies deployed to defend Rye and Winchelsea inland. Only half of 1/6th Devons, 205th and 262nd Field Companies RE together with the 19th (Rother), 22nd (Seddlescombe) and 23rd (Hastings) Sussex Home Guard Battalions were readily available to oppose any penetration behind Hastings and Rye. 302 Battery from 34th Searchlght Regiment had a series of sites between Winchelsea and Hastings, all of which had one or two taxis available for mobile defence. Forces at Lydd were well positioned to counter from the east the landings at Camber. 142nd Army Field Regiment RA (seventeen guns around Rye and Pett) provided the only field artillery support, though the guns of 55th Field Regiment RA at Lydd and Old Romney could have supported, if permitted. There were no significant numbers of troops immediately available to counter attack, although 45th Division's reserve based on its motorcycle battalion (5th Loyals) at Wadhurst could have been made available. At Fairlight, other than the Home Guard and infantry detachment at the radar station, there was a company from 11th Sussex, a platoon of 1/6th Devon's D Company and a searchlight detachment from 302 Battery. 1/6th Devons C Company group was its mobile reserve for the area, together with its carrier, mortar, motorcycle and tank hunter platoons.

Other than a line of pillboxes covering the defensive entanglements at both Camber and Winchelsea beaches there were a couple of large pillboxes at the mouth of Rye Harbour and some more to cover the entrances to Rye and Winchelsea further inland. The derelict Camber Castle was also adapted for defence. A number of defensive posts had been constructed along the beaches and high ground to further supplement the defence. The Rivers Rother and Brede plus the Royal Military Canal had been deepened and adapted to become anti tank obstacles. Beach mines were laid to supplement the defences - 119 covering Rye Harbour, 106 about Cliff End on the western flank, 42 covering Pett Level and 484 at Fairlight; scaffolding, barbed wire and anti tank obstacles were heavily used along this whole sector. The bridges leading into Rye and Winchelsea had been prepared for demolition, with 205th Field Company RE assigned this role. In May three gaps had been cut in the sea wall at Pett to flood the levels just inland, with those gaps invested with anti tank and other obstacles.

There were two radar stations close to the beaches in this sector - a low level one near Brookland, east of Rye, and a high level one just inland west of Fairlight. Both were assigned a detachment from 2/8th Sussex for ground defence, Rye also having a troop of three 40mm guns from 147th Battery, 43rd LAA Regiment, while Fairlight had B Company 11th Sussex and a troop of 302nd Battery, 34th Searchlight Regiment available nearby for its defence. In this area Rye, Winchelsea, Brede and Baldslow were prepared as nodal points and protected by minefields.

Camber beach

Rye Beach

This is where the 7th German Infantry Division was to land

Winchelsea beach seen from above Cliff End

Fairlight Glen

This is where the 1st German Mountain Division was to land

Landing Zone D: Bexhill to Eastbourne

Topography
Bexhill has a narrow shingle beach with a railway line running close behind the coast to Eastbourne. Pevensey Bay lies to the west and has a wide shingle beach with small coastal

settlements at Normans Bay and Pevensey Bay. The village of Pevensey lies at least a mile inland and includes an ancient castle that dominates the southern approaches. The ground behind the coastline consists of a large marshy flood plain, generally known as Pevensey Levels, with few roads crossing it. The town of Hailsham dominates the western flank of these Levels. Eastbourne also has a small shingle beach and is heavily built up, the urban area extending northwestwards to Polegate, a major communication centre. The steep ridges of the South Downs, running north from Beachy Head, dominate this urban area. The seaside piers in this stretch of coast had all had been damaged to prevent them from being readily used to land troops and equipment.

The military survey noted that the beaches between Hastings and Pevensey were suitable for landing troops for three hours either side of high water but landing of armoured vehicles was considered hazardous due to the presence of offshore rocks. The beaches between Pevensey and Eastbourne were suitable for landing troops at all times, although armoured vehicles would be restricted to an hour either side of high water due to the shelving of the beach. The German Navy calculated that it could put ashore at one time 100 barges, with a gap varying 90 to 120 metres between them.

German Naval intelligence stated that the coast between Bexhill and Beachy Head was low lying with a flat beach; but offshore there were a number of reefs and rocky shallows, which restricted the area of coast suitable for a landing to about 7 miles.

The German Plans

Transport Fleet D was to sail from Boulogne and assemble off that port by S-10 hours before crossing the Channel at 16.00 on S-1 day, heading westwards and then turning north into Pevensey Bay. It was to consist of 165 tows in four columns and be over 20km long and 2km wide, escorted by 2nd and 18th Minesweeper, 2nd R Boat, 15th 16th and 19th Patrol Flotillas. The planned formation on approaching the beaches was to have the support of ten light gunboats (half concentrated off the Bexhill sector), twenty-nine escort boats, four Herbert and six pontoon AA ferries. The advance detachments were to be carried in the patrol boats and fifty-eight tugs, while the tanks took up nine barge tows. The remainder of the assault force was carried in one hundred and forty barge tows. All of the Fleet was to return across the Channel to reload with the rest of the first wave.

The German XXXVIII Corps (26th and 34th Infantry Divisions) was to land on a similar basis to XIII Corps, with three advance detachments. The two from 34th Infantry Division each had six companies (comprising three rifle, one engineer and one mortar platoons), two assault guns, two mobile anti tank guns and two mobile 20mm anti aircraft guns; the 26th Infantry Division detachment was similarly formed with the infantry coming equally from 39th and 78th Regiments though without the mobile artillery. The one amphibious panzer battalion (C) was assigned to support the detachments (two companies with 34th Division and one with 26th Division).

34th Division was to land between Norman's Bay and western end of Bexhill and aim to make a rapid advance inland to Lunsford Cross, south of Ninfield; it was then to expand this beachhead by consolidating a line from Lunsford Cross to Rickney (on Pevensey Levels) via Wartling. As soon as possible this line was to be expanded towards the high ground north and northeast of the Levels. The Division was also expected to link up with 1st Mountain Division around Battle, from Ninfield, before clearing Bexhill from the rear. It was estimated that 10,000 men of the division would be landed on the first day, based on 80th and 107th Infantry Regiments, the divisional cycle battalion, a reinforced artillery battalion, two engineer battalions, an anti tank battery and four anti aircraft batteries. Most of the divisional artillery would be landed in the second echelon, togther with the 253rd Infantry Regiment, four engineer companies, an anti tank battalion and the remaining divisional services.

26th Division was to land between Pevensey and Langney Point and penetrate inland to establish a line running from Rickney to Wilmington via Hankham and Willingdon. As soon as possible Eastbourne was to be sealed off and the assault extended northward to a line along the River Cuckmere running from Arlington to Hellingly (west and north of Hailsham). Eastbourne was to be seized only when these lines were firmly in German hands and there were enough forces to achieve its capture. It was estimated that only 7,000 men of the division would be landed on the first day, based on 39th and 78th Infantry Regiments, cycle battalion, assault gun battery, an anti tank battery, a rocket battery, five anti aircraft batteries, two engineer battalions, a signals company and a medical company. As with 34th Divison, most of the divisional artillery would be landed in the second echelon, togther with the 77th Infantry Regiment, four engineer companies, an anti tank battalion and the remaining divisional services.

General von Manstein, the Corps Commander, had recognised the vital importance of securing the high ground towering over Eastbourne and had initially requested that he be given the 6th Mountain Division in place of the 34th Division or at least a reinforced mountain infantry battalion to secure this high ground but had not been successful in either case.

Corps troops included 507th Engineer Regiment (with five battalions), 609th Artillery Regiment (with three battalions), headquarters and two batteries of 9th Rocket Regiment, two mechanised companies each of 521st Anti Tank Battalion and the 605th Anti Aircraft Battalion. A Corps defensive line was to be established between Burwash and Uckfield.

<u>The British defences</u>
There were three coastal artillery batteries (totallng two 6-inch, two 4.7-inch and four 4-inch guns), supported by the six 9.2-inch guns of D Battery 56th Heavy Regiment RA behind Bexhill; this battery had observation posts on Galley Hill (east of Bexhill) and at Constable's Farm (north of Bexhill).

45th Infantry Division was responsible for the defence of the area, with its 134th Brigade providing the 1/8th Devons at Bexhill and 136th Brigade the 1/4th DCLI and 1/9th Devon. These battalions were supported by 7th Devons (machine gun) (five platoons of B and C Companies (at Pevensey Castle, Friday Street, Langney Point Pevensey Bay and Eastbourne sea front) and a platoon of A Company at Cooden/Bexhill) and C Company 11th Sussex at Bexhill. 96th Field Regiment RA (eighteen guns at Stone Cross and Willingdon and six more in anti tank roles along the seafront between Langney and Pevensey) supported 136th Brigade while a troop from 142nd Army Field Regiment RA (four 4.5-inch guns) with the two 6-inch medium guns of A Battery 56th Heavy Regiment RA supported 8th Devons around Bexhill. C Company 8th Devons defended Norman's Bay having deployed platoons in the settlement, at the railway level crossing and at Cooden Beach railway station, with a reserve position at Culver Croft Bank.

There were few reserves available for counter attack outside of these Brigades, with the (unlikely) exception of 29th Infantry Brigade or 45th Division's own mobile reserve force, located to the north east of this sector; each infantry battalion in this sector had a company assigned a quick reaction role, supported by their carrier and motorcycle platoons. 10 Platoon of 7th Devon (MG) was also available to support counter attacks. The 20th (Hailsham), 21st (Eastbourne), 23rd (Bexhill and Hastings) Sussex Home Guard Battalions would have been directly involved from the outset.

Beach defences comprised almost entirely of pillboxes, two lines of concrete "dragon's teeth" anti tank obstacles, barbed wire entanglements and other improvised beach defences, including scaffolding, along the coast, supplemented by the Martello Towers at Eastbourne, Pevensey and at Norman's Bay (utilised either as machine gun posts, artillery observation and command posts. An anti tank ditch had been dug to the rear of Langney Point while Bexhill and Cooden golf courses were mined. Eastbourne pier had been damaged to prevent easy landings at it. The remains of Pevensey Castle had been prepared for defence and was the battle headquarters of 1/4th DCLI, with 9 Platoon 7th Devon (MG) assigned to the castle. Bexhill beach also had beach scaffolding, beach mines (Cooden beach had 660 naval beach mines emplaced), barbed wire and anti tank obstacles proected by pillboxes. The towns and villages covering the exits to the Pevensey Levels were also prepared for defence as nodal points, notably Ninfield, Wartling, Pevensey, Hailsham, Polegate and Willingdon.

There were also two radar stations close to the beaches in this sector - a low level one just north of Pevensey and a high level one at Beachy Head. It was also vital not to let these or their personnel fall to the enemy intact (remember that both these were targeted by German special forces). Both were assigned a detachment from 2/8th Sussex (B Company 70th Sussex was also at Beachy Head, while C Company 11th Sussex was at Pevensey) for ground defence, Pevensey also had a troop of three 40mm guns from 147th Battery, 43rd LAA Regiment RA. There was also a Naval Shore Signals Station at Beachy Head.

Cooden beach, Bexhill looking towards Pevensey   Langney Point, looking towards Bexhill

This is where both German infantry divisions were to land

Norman's Bay
(from the rear defence post)

Pevensey Bay from the Castle
(With concealed defences in the Castle)

Landing Zone E: Cuckmere to Rottingdean

Topography

Cuckmere Haven is a narrow meandering river valley running into the sea between two steep cliffs. The beach is formed by a steep shingle bank with only a small track running back nearly two kilometres to meet the coastal road at Exceat, while the ground in between is generally marshy. From Exceat another road continues north along the valley through Litlington and Alfriston, where the valley narrows as it meets the South Downs, before meeting the main road and railway running between Lewes and Polegate. A similar geological formation called Birling Gap can be found just up the coast nearer to Beachy Head. The British military survey reported that there was no suitable place for large bodies of troops or any armoured vehicles to be landed between Seaford and Eastbourne.

The town of Seaford lies at the eastern end of a wide shingle beach that runs from the River Ouse to a rocky promontory that separates the town from Cuckmere Haven. The town is spread out with many gaps in between the buildings. The railway from Newhaven to Seaford largely runs along a tall embankment across the flood plain to Bishopstone, with the only vehicle exits being at Bishopstone and Tide Mills, where behind the shingle bank the terrain drops down to an exposed flood plain leading to Denton. Higher, undulating ground forming part of the South Downs lies immediately inland. The only roads leading inland from Seaford are the coastal road to Denton and one to Alfriston. From Newhaven the River Ouse runs inland along a narrow valley before entering a broad flood plain below Lewes, where the Glynde Reach branches off to the northeast. Newhaven lies mostly on the western bank with its small harbour lying on the eastern bank, all overshadowed by Newhaven Fort, a major 19th Century fortification at the top of a steep cliff. The main road inland to Lewes runs along the railway up the eastern part of the valley, crossing the Glynde Reach before entering the town along the base of Mount Caborn. Another road runs along the western side of the valley to Lewes, via a number of villages. Lewes lies in a gap of the South Downs where the river cut through it, so forming a significant natural defensive position. The military survey noted that troops could be landed at Seaford at all times while armoured vehicles could only land an hour and a half either side of high water.

Rottingdean lies at one of the few gaps in the coastal cliffs running from Newhaven to Brighton, lying at least 5 miles from Newhaven and three miles from Brighton. The gap is very narrow with a small exit into the village and features a small shingle beach. Other than the coastal road there is a minor road running northwest to Falmer, at least four miles away on the Lewes-Brighton road. The terrain running to Brighton consists of generally undulating ground, but the chalk ridges of the South Downs dominate the whole area. The military survey noted that the beaches between Newhaven and Shoreham were suitable for landing troops and armoured vehicles at all times of tides.

German Naval intelligence stated that the coast between Beachy Head and Brighton was mostly cliffs, with the chain of hills making up the South Downs comes right up to the coast. From the beach access inland was possible only at a few places. They considered a major landing in this sector to be impossible due to the steep foreshore, rocky beach and offshore obstacles.

The German Plans

The landings in this sector were the most hazardous as they involved the longest crossing time and had the most exposed flank, being mostly outside the main mine barrier deployed to the southeast of Beachy Head. To overcome this problem the invasion fleet preferred to use transports, coasters and trawlers (only the tank company being carried in barges). They were the only ones permitted to remain in or return to harbour if threatened. Transport Fleet E comprised three parts: Convoy 4 had 25 transports, 25 trawlers and 125 empty barges carrying the first echelon and was to sail from Le Havre at S-11 hours. It was to sail north in two columns at 7 knots and be escorted by 12th Minesweeper Flotilla; Convoy 5 had 25 transports and 50 empty barges and was to sail from Le Havre at S-15 hours. It was also to sail north in two columns at 7 knots and be escorted by 14th Minesweeper Flotilla; Convoy E had 100 coasters, 200 fishing vessels and 4 Herbert AA Ferries and was to sail from Le Havre at S-11½ hours carrying the advance detachments. It was to sail north in a group 2km long and 2.6km wide, at 7 knots and be escorted by the 1st R Boat, 4th, 13th, 20th Patrol Flotillas and five heavy auxiliary gunboats. One Herbert anti aircraft ferry was assigned to both the advance detachments of 6th Mountain and 8th Infantry Divisions, while 28th Infantry Division had two Herbert ferries. Fecamp, Caen and Rouen were also used for loading the assault forces. The convoys were only to continue sailing to their landing zone if it was considered safe to do so, otherwise they would be re-routed to the Eastbourne sector and arrive by S+2 hours. The second echelon was expected to sail from Boulogne. The empty barges were due to be left at the landing zone to aid unloading.

The German X Corps provided only 6th Mountain Division for the assault, but initially under the command of VIII Corps; X Corps Headquarters was to cross with the first echelon. This Mountain Division was to land at Cuckmere Haven with the assault led by 141st Mountain Regiment as the Advance Detachment (assisted by the remaining tank company of Panzer Battalion D, two engineer companies, three artillery batteries, a motorised anti aircraft battery, signals company and a medical company); 143rd Mountain Regiment formed the rest of the first echelon with three engineer companies, an assault gun battery, two anti tank batteries, one artillery battalion, a mechanised anti aircraft company, the Divisional cycle battalion, signals company and divisional service elements. The Division's second echelon comprised further specialist engineer companies, a mechanised anti aircraft battery, an artillery battalion and a signals company). Some 6,000 men were expected to be landed on the first day. The Division was expected to link up with XXXVIII Corps behind Beachy Head before moving up through Alfriston to secure a line between Lewes and Uckfield.

The German VIII Corps (8th and 28th Infantry Divisions) would land either side of Newhaven. 8th Infantry Division would be responsible for clearing Seaford and Newhaven with its advance detachment (comprising the 28th Infantry Regiment, an engineer battalion, part of an assault gun battery, three artillery batteries and a mixed anti aircraft group (two batteries) before moving up the Ouse valley to seize Lewes with the rest of the first echelon; this comprised 84th Infantry Regiment, the Divisional cycle battalion, the rest of the assault gun battery, three engineer companies, one bridging company, a mechanised anti tank battery, four anti aircraft batteries, two medical companies, some divisional services and a Luftwaffe signals unit. Its second echelon had the rest of its artillery (9 batteries), 38th Infantry Regiment, one anti aircraft battery, two ant tank batteries and two reinforced engineer battalions. Some 6,000 men were also expected to be landed here on the first day.

28th Infantry Division was responsible for protecting the Army's west flank by landing at Rottingdean. Its reinforced 49th Infantry Regiment formed the advance detachment with a battalion of the 83rd Infantry Regiment, an artillery battalion (three batteries), a mortar battery, a mechanised anti tank battery, part of an assault gun battery, two anti aircraft batteries, Divisional cycle battalion, signals company, three engineer companies and a Luftwaffe signals unit. It was to move along the coast to Brighton and inland to Falmer with the first echelon. This comprised the 7th and 83rd Infantry Regiments (less a battalion each), two artillery battalions, two anti aircraft batteries, two anti tank batteries, the rest of the assault gun battery, six engineer companies, two medical companies, a signals company and Divisional service units. The second echelon included the remaining infantry battalion, one reinforced engineer battalion, an artillery battalion, an anti aircraft battery and a signals company. Some 8,000 men were expected to be landed here on the first day.

VIII Corps troops included an artillery regiment of two battalions, a rocket battalion of three batteries, four engineer battalions, a mechanised anti tank battalion of three batteries, an anti aircraft battalion of four batteries and a signals battalion. X Corps troops included a mechanised anti aircraft battalion (three batteries), three artillery battalions, a rocket battery and three engineer battalions. Many of these troops would cross with the second echelon forces.

<u>The British defences</u>
The British had three coastal artillery batteries (totalling six 6-inch guns) available at Seaford, Newhaven and in eastern Brighton, supported by two 8-inch guns of B Battery 56th Heavy Regiment RA inland at Alfriston. A coastal artillery radar station was located just west of Newhaven fort.

The defence at Cuckmere Haven comprised a company of 50th Sussex (a home defence battalion), 276th Anti Tank Battery (four 2-pounder guns) and a machine gun platoon from B Company 7th Devon. 133rd Company AMPC at Seaford had been working on the defences at the Haven for the past three months and would have been well placed to support its defence. The searchlight site on Seaford Head (from 326 Battery, 31st Searchlight Regiment) had orders to witdraw into Seaford on invasion. The 20th (Hailsham) Sussex Home Guard Battalion had platoons inland at Alfriston, Berwick and Willingdon and was responsible for the bridge at Exceat, which was prepared fro demolition.

136th Brigade's 1/5th DCLI was the core of the defence at Newhaven. It had 11th Sussex's A Company, a platoon of 7th Devon's C Company (machine gun), with sections at Bishpstone railway station and in Newhaven Fort, and was supported by the bulk of 50th Sussex in Seaford. The 16th (Lewes) Sussex Home Guard Battalion had a company each at Newhaven and Seaford. Artillery support was provided by B Troop (four 4.5-inch howitzers) at Denton and a section from F Troop (two 75mm guns), both from 96th Field Regiment RA.

1/5th DCLI's War Diary is rare in that it records in detail the defensive preparations of Newhaven. In addition to the coast artillery the fort's garrison was made up by its own D Company, its mortar platoon and a MG section from 7th Devon's C Company, with 8th Sussex's D Company deployed outside the perimeter and at the harbour, being assigned the role of protecting the port area from the east. B Company was deployed at East Beach, with 11 Platoon at Tide Mills. A Company was deployed at Bishopstone, with 7 Platoon in reserve at Hill Rise Road. C Company was in reserve at South Heighton, with 13 Platoon at Denton and 15 Platoon at Mount Pleasant. The Battalion's mobile reserve comprised a cycle mounted 14 Platoon, its Carrier Platoon (five carriers) and Motorcycle Platoon (ten motorcycles). The Battalion's rear headquarters and echelon was based at Beddingham.

As mentioned above, the defence of Seaford rested heavily on 50th Sussex, which had two companies deployed on the seafront from Bishopstone to Seaford Head and one in reserve in the northeast part of the town. The pioneers and Home Guard formed a reserve in depth, though the former had about a third of its men detached elsewhere. It would up to these troops to derail the plans of the German 8th Infantry and 6th Mountain Divisions.

Broc Force was responsible for the defence of Rottingdean. 50th Queens held this sector, with its headquarters just along the coast before Brighton; other than a company in Lewes its deployment is not known, but the eastern boundary of Broc Force, to which it belonged, ran from Saltdean to Falmer, so it is likely that the Battalion had most of its strength within a short distance of Rottingdean. This Battalion was supported in Rottingdean by a company from the 10th (Brighton East) Home Guard Battalion, 251st Battery of 88th Field Regiment RA and three armoured cars. 31st Searchlight Regiment had sites at Telscombe and Peacehaven.

Of all the landing zones Rottingdean and, to a lesser extent Cuckmere Haven, offered the best chance of stopping the invasion on the beaches due to the terrain; even a small number of determined troops in good defensive positions could be expected to achieve this, something demonstrated during the Dieppe raid in 1942.

The principal counter attack force available in this sector was the 29th Independent Infantry Brigade, which was spread out north and northwest of Lewes, and the mobile units of 1st Motor Machine Gun Brigade (Broc Force), deployed along the South Downs north and northwest of Brighton. 562nd Field Company RE at Alfriston would no doubt be drawn in to preventing German advances inland from Cuckmere Haven. These forces would be supported by the rest of the Sussex Home Guard in the area. In addition a Canadian pioneer company had just arrived in Brighton.

The most important defensive fortification was Newhaven Fort, overlooking the harbour and Seaford beach. This contained the main coastal battery, protective pillboxes and observation sites. Two light coastal guns were located below the fort guarding the entrance to the port. The beaches and seafronts contained the usual lines of mines, barbed wire and anti tank blocks. Martello Towers would be found at Bishopstone and eastern end of Seaford. Little is known about the coastal defences at Rottingdean, though the usual beach defences would have been found here as well.

Newhaven was also the start of the GHQ Line extension running along the left side of the Ouse valley and through the centre of Lewes, itself a nodal point, and continuing up to Uckfield; This line featured a large number of pillboxes and other defensive positions, including minefields and prepared demolitions of the bridges. The Home Guard was largely responsible for manning this Line.

Cuckmere Gap also had a large number of anti tank and infantry pillboxes covering the beach defences, supplemented by an anti tank wall and three anti tank ditches. The natural features of a high shingle bank, river and the sloping river valley lent themselves to the defence.

The beach defences included a number of beach mines laid above the high water mark to supplement the double line of barbed wire defences and anti tank obstacles, with 166 mines laid east of Newhaven, 104 west of Newhaven and 647 at Cuckmere.

In the area, Friston and Alfriston were also designated nodal points. In addition to Newhaven Fort a "final stand" keep was established in Newhaven town centre, close to the main bridge over the Ouse.

Looking toward the Haven from above Exceat Bridge

The Haven from Seaford Head

Cuckmere Haven, where 6th German Mountain Division was to land

View of the approach to Newhaven, with the harbour and fort on the left and Seaford on the right

Newhaven fort looking over East Beach   View over the harbour to Denton and Lewes

East Beach is where the 8th German Infantry Division was to land

Rottingdean from the South Downs	Rottingdean Beach

This is where the 28th German Infantry Division was to land

In the centre, Lewes from the south west, showing Mount Caborn on the horizon in the centre, the Ouse valley below it and Firle Beacon on the to the right

CHAPTER SEVEN: S DAY AND BEYOND

We have now seen what the expected line up would have been on S Day for both sides. But what of S Day and beyond? Based on the plans, objectives, expectations and recent combat experience of both sides it is possible to realistically consider the potential development of the Operation. This Operation can best be split into three distinct phases - firstly, the day of the invasion and those days immediately following; secondly, the period of British counter offensive and German build up and, thirdly, the period beyond that.

Invasion Day and immediate aftermath

Anyone involved with military operations will be aware that plans rarely survive contact with the enemy and, especially with the large scale amphibious operations of this nature and at that time; it is dubious at best whether the invading German forces could have been delivered to the beaches as planned, in the right order and refreshed from the crossing. However, should the Royal Navy have been unable to prevent the invasion convoys from crossing the rather calm Channel in late September, it is likely that the German Army would have been brought to the landing zones in a state that would make an invasion attempt a realistic proposition.

It was clear that this first critical period of the Operation would greatly influence its development and outcome; even with an uncontested crossing the German assault forces would still need to quickly recover from the stress of the crossing and slow approach to the beaches. Their formation would have been tested, with tow ropes breaking, collisions and mechanical unreliability an almost certainty. Then they would finally come into contact with the British defenders, whose dispositions and resources were largely unknown and in circumstances they could not fully expect to control for some time. It was impressed on these assaulting forces that they must take their initial objectives before reorganising and that any delays were likely to further compromise the all important landing schedules. For their own part the British forces would need to react quickly to the landings from land, sea and air, ensuring that any lodgements made were eliminated or contained, while senior commanders built up an accurate and timely assessment of what was happening so as to respond more effectively with the resources at hand. Certainly this would have been a very confused and desperate time for all on both sides.

The first line of defence for the British was the surveillance of the embarkation ports, conducted by both air and sea. The RAF's Coastal Command operated the following airborne patrol lines:
- 'Bust', covering Brest to Guernsey twice daily though preferably at dusk
- 'Hatch', covering Cherbourg to Le Havre once a day
- 'Dundee', between Dieppe and Dunkirk daily
- 'Hookos', covering Dunkirk to Rotterdam after dusk and again before dawn, continuously in moonlight
- 'Moon 1, 2 and 3' covered mid Channel from south of Falmouth to northwest of Dieppe, operating at dusk and after nightfall if conditions allowed.

On 23 September six British destroyers undertook a night sweep northwards along the French coast from Brest, while another four destroyers were searching the Channel for a reported

German merchantman. The next night four motor torpedo boats from Dover swept the coast from Ostend to Dunkirk (one was sunk by a mine during their return). Submarines were also tasked with patrolling off the deep water ports, but due to losses had largely been withdrawn to ports further away. Given that components of the German invasion fleets were expected to be at sea during the day before S Day observation should have picked them up, though some could be misinterpreted as coastal traffic. The heightened air activity by the Luftwaffe in protecting these convoys would also have been picked up.

Even if the shipping was reported at sea there are significant doubts whether the British chain of command involving all three services would have acted upon them in time to catch them at their most vulnerable - crossing the Channel. This situation did indeed arise during the "Channel Dash" in 1942 when two major German warships and their escorts audaciously made their way through the English Channel and North Sea against uncoordinated and delayed British opposition. In 1940 British Naval Intelligence felt that the majority of the invasion fleet would need to come from the German ports, especially the Baltic, as they felt the Channel ports actually to be used would take a longer time to recover from the damage inflicted during the recent campaign than was the actual case. The fact that the invasion convoys were to be extended over many kilometres when fully deployed meant that the German escort and gunfire support craft would be spread out and vulnerable. Unlike warships, these formations had to be slow (between 5-7 knots) in order that the craft maintained position and the towing craft were not placed under undue pressure. Despite these precautions it would have been inevitable that many craft would have lost their tows or broken down, causing even more stress on the formation. The presence of early morning fog during the invasion period would have both helped and hindered the invasion fleets. If the intelligence gained from such sightings had been properly interpreted then naval strike groups from Portsmouth, Dover and possibly Harwich could have intercepted some of the convoys in mid Channel. German air support would likely have been negligible, given that the Luftwaffe was still unused to night naval operations. The resulting confusion and terror could have put paid to the invasion, with the convoys scattered. A key concern to these naval striking groups would have been the German minefields, torpedo craft and submarines, most of which would have been unknown until they hit. Local naval forces would be kept busy in defeating the submarines off the key ports while small minesweeping vessels cleared lanes out of them and then fight to break through the German minefields. The need for bold action by the striking forces could also require them to accept heavy losses to the defensive barriers as minesweeping was a slow process. Much would depend on the courage of the naval commanders to accept these risks. Another source of attack on these convoys could have come from the air, as both Coastal Command and Bomber Command were already active against the continental ports, so some of these forces could have taken the opportunity of attacking the large convoys below them. If this had happened at the same time that the Roal Navy engaged them then the invasion could have ended in mid Channel, even without heavy losses on the invasion craft, as surprise would have been lost several hours before the landings were timed and the fleets broken up.

Unless they were engaged crossing the Channel, the first real contact with the invasion force would then most likely have been with the small craft of the Auxiliary Patrol or anti submarine trawlers stationed a few miles off the actual beaches. These craft were too lightly armed to seriously disrupt the enemy, but their crews would hope that their pre-arranged signals to shore would be reported and acted upon without delay, enabling the defensive preparations to be put into action. The crews would then aim to do as much mischief to the Germans as possible. For their part the Germans would have been very nervous and although there would have been strict naval orders to hold their fire and to restrict manouvering there would undoubtably been uncontrolled outbreaks. The efficiency of the escorts would have been hampered by the troops of the advance detachments they were carrying. The heavy coastal guns of the British could have been permitted to open fire as soon as the convoys entered their effective range, especially from around Dover.

As already mentioned the British had penetrated the German Enigma codes but still had to rely mainly on the Luftwaffe to provide them with the information they required. Records of the time show that the British intelligence staff involved felt that they were not yet able to determine when the invasion would occur with sufficient advance warning.

Of the four landing zones the toughest proposition facing the Germans would no doubt have been Landing Zone B, west of Hythe, as the heaviest concentration of defending troops and coastal artillery was to be found here, coupled with significant reserves readily available.

17th Infantry Division faced the most onerous of tasks and due to the shipping plans would have been under strength from the start, with the assault regiments only two thirds strong for the first couple of hours until their reserve battalions could land. 21st Infantry Regiment was expected to land at the rifle ranges west of Hythe, take Dymchurch Redoubt and move via either Hythe or Lympne to Sandling. Its subsequent role as part of the strike force against Dover could be in doubt, especially if it was still engaged around Hythe in the afternoon when Group Hoffmeister (the Regimental commander) was expected to be formed around Sandling. The other assault regiment of the Division was the also reduced 55th Infantry Regiment. This was to land between the Redoubt and village of Dymchurch, cross Romney Marsh on a broad front and then the Royal Military Canal west of Lympne before advancing through the airborne forces towards Ashford. Before reaching the Canal the Regiment would need to overcome the nodal point defences at Burmarsh, as this could dominate the few roads running inland in the area, and hope to take intact the important bridges at Botolph's Bridge and West Hythe, Falconhurst Farm and Bilsington. Panzer Battalion B was to land and move with 55th Infantry Regiment until it reached the assembly area for Battle Group Hoffmeister between Stanford and Sandling. The tanks would, however, require significant engineer support to get over the sea wall and would provide a good target for artillery and aircraft while waiting on the beach. Once moving inland, and even with some retaining their submersible equipment, these tanks would be restricted to the roads, given the many steep sided and deep ditches crisscrossing the marshes. German intelligence had already noted the problems that both Romney Marsh and the Pevensey Levels provided them, saying both were unfavourable for high-speed units due to the many waterways and commanding heights. To add to their concerns the British had plans to open the sea sluices that would hopefully flood much of Romney Marsh at high tide. Where this Battalion was due to cross the Canal is not known but the defenders would have mostly been poorly equipped Home Guard. 6th Somerset Light Infantry holding this sector would have the support of a machine gun platoon and its mortars but other than the Martello Towers had few positions from where it could engage targets directly on the beach as the ground directly behind the sea wall dropped significantly. Much would have depended on the Redoubt and those Towers. The location of its headquarters in the front line was a strange choice for this battalion, as the probable loss of its commander so early in the battle could have severely hampered its defensive role. It was crucial for the Germans to knock out the coastal guns in the Redoubt and at Hythe quickly as they could cause much damage, and it was no doubt with this in mind that the heavy gunboats were placed on the eastern flank. The Redoubt may also have been the target of attacks on coastal defences.

Until the rest of the Division could be landed, especially its third infantry regiment, survival of the Division would have rested largely on the 7th Air Division to protect its open flanks to the north, as it only had its divisional cycle battalion available. With its two infantry regiments going in two completely different directions it would be very difficult for the Division to undertake co-ordinated action.

As mentioned above, Battle Group Hoffmeister was to be the key striking force of the Sixteenth Army, charged as it was with the capture of the port of Dover, preferably intact. This formation would need significant protection during its formation in the afternoon, especially as this was unlikely to go un-noticed by British observers on the high ground. Although no plans remain to confirm the route this force was to take in order to reach Dover, there are only two viable options:

- The first was to reach Etchinghill before climbing the road up the steep escarpment and moving through the Storm Regiment to capture Hawkinge airfield; it could then take either an inland or coastal route to Dover; this option, if successful, would reduce the need to fight through a hostile urban area while also securing a vital airfield. A smaller lane runs up to the high ground through Peene, but this is not suitable for armoured vehicles
- The second option was to take the main A20 road running below the escarpment and then through the back suburbs of Folkestone, before climbing the escarpment by either of the main roads running north to Hawkinge or along the coast at Capel le Ferne; this option would involve fighting a continuous battle with Shorncliffe Garrison and relying largely on its own resources to secure the roads leading out of Folkestone, all of which had been prepared specifically with the stopping of tanks in mind.

In any case, the Battle Group would have been very fortunate to have reached Dover before the end of the day, let alone capture it, hampered as they would have been by defenders, terrain and the late start. This timing is strange, given the strategic importance of taking Dover intact, as much precious time would have been lost. Maybe the senior commanders expected it would take a lot of time to land and assemble the mechanised elements of this Group and have the intelligence from the paratroopers of the best route to take. Another factor to be considered would be the presence of Milforce with its heavy infantry tanks likel to be threatening from the Sellindge area. The Battle Group could also easily have become isolated as it lacked the resources to properly secure its own lines of communication and would have to rely on 7th Air Division to retain contact with it. If the former route was taken then the Battle Group could have been required to support Battle Group Steinzler's efforts to secure Hawkinge airfield, however securing this could then provide Battle Group Hoffmeister with a secure base of operations. It is not known whether the Germans knew that there was a significant fuel depot near Hawkinge. Its capture intact wouldhave greatly aided this Battle Group's operations. However, even with dedicated armoured and air support it should have taken a great deal of time to secure Dover port, which by then should have been thoroughly wrecked and blocked.

The proposed attack on Dover by German Brandenburg special forces in small fast boats on S Day was unlikely to have had much success (even the Germans thought this would have been a suicidal operation). The capture of the port at Dover was top of the German requirements and so securing this objective would have required the other Corps operations to most likely suffer as a consequence, as more resources would have been dedicated to it. Even after capturing Dover the Battle Group would still be vulnerable and isolated as neither 7th Air or the rest of 17th Infantry Divisions had the resources to reinforce it in strength; German plans showed that V Corps, due to land in the Second Wave, was to take over responsibility for clearing northeast Kent.

The capture of Folkestone harbour was a lower priority and one likely to be assigned to the 7th Air Division; though remaining records are not precise on this matter there would be no other unit available for such a task (in my opinion the Division's Battle Group Meindl would have been the most likely choice, once it had cleared the Hythe area, but would have required the destruction of Shorncliffe Garrison before undertaking this task). Even so, this port had already been decommissioned, blocked and mined.

As already indicated, success and, indeed survival, of 17th Infantry Division would have been largely down to the presence of the 7th Air Division. This elite formation would have been vital, as it was to provide troops to carry out a number of vital tasks, such as containing and hopefully eliminating Shorncliffe Garrison, taking responsibility for clearing the Hythe and Folkestone areas and covering the exposed German flanks north of Folkestone against counter-attacks; it would also have the only really viable reserve available to XIII Corps.

Although the Division's initial assault forces were quite likely to land relatively intact at S Hour, the rest of the Division would need the full protection of the Luftwaffe to survive the attention of the now alert and vengeful defenders in both the air and on the ground. The paratroopers were most vulnerable at the time of dropping as they jumped with only light weapons, depending on quickly finding the containers dropped at the same time to provide them with the heavier weapons and equipment essential to complete their roles. Using a static line parachute meant that these troops could be dropped from heights as low as 90 metres, reducing their vulnerability in the air. However, they would not be able to steer the parachutes and would be dependent on the wind and navigational skills of the aircrew to land in as compact a force as possible. Other factors of concern to the Germans was that they had not trained or been operational above the company level and were therefore only used to small unit tactics, rather than at regimental or divisional level; the second factor was that the Division was still going through a massive enlargement and re-equipment procedure, which was to continue well into 1941. It is possible that what happened to the German parachutists dropped on Crete in May 1941 could have happened here, with many units either cut off or destroyed as they tried to regroup and recover their containers having landed among an alert Army and hostile civilian population. The glider-borne units were better placed to react quickly as they carried their heavier equipment with them and landed as a compact unit; however, there is no information available as to who they would have been and, their intended role or where they were to land.

Another factor against them was the timing of the assault. With the initial airborne assault coming in around dawn, to coincide with the seaborne landings, surprise and confusion to the defenders could have been largely reduced. Two reasons why the Germans never tried night time drops were the poor navigational skills of the aircrew and the ability of the troops to recover the all important containers in the dark. Nevertheless, the main effect of the airborne landings would have been to distract defending troops from the beaches, endanger much of the heavy artillery positioned to counter the beach landings and probably absorb most of the local counter attack forces readily available (as was to happen in Normandy).

Battle Group Meindl was expected to land around the village of Pedlinge, northwest of Hythe with two reinforced battalions. Its primary responsibilities were to secure road crossings across the Royal Military Canal at Hythe and to its immediate west. Depending on how well the Battle Group landed these tasks were well within their capabilities as the closest British forces was 501st Field Company RE at Sandling Park just to the north (unless already deployed to carry out their demolition tasks), the Army units and RAF defence force deployed at RAF Lympne to the west, two stevedore companies at Saltwood to the east and the local Home Guard, though other troops from Shorncliffe Garrison could be redeployed quickly to meet the threat. Once 21st Infantry Regiment had passed through this Battle Group was to secure a line along the railway running from Hythe station to Saltwood.

The other assault force was Battle Group Steinzler, with its two reinforced battalions due to land on the heights west of Hawkinge. Its orders were to secure this high ground and provide a defensive flank. However, no detailed plans remain to better explain this role. Given its planned landing zone there are three potentially vital actions this Battle Group could undertake within the general scope of its orders:

- Secure the road climbing up the escarpment from Etchinghill for possible use by Battle Group Hoffmeister
- Attack and seize Hawkinge airfield
- Secure from the south the high ground dominating the vital village of Lyminge, possibly even attacking it.

These potential operations would have stretched this Battle Group greatly, especially as it was to be the most exposed paratroop force once landed. An advance on Sandgate, west of Folkestone, is mentioned in some sources as an objective though this would be inadvisable as it would mean significant numbers of men surrendering the high ground and then fight its way through built up areas and through the Shorncliffe Garrison to reach the sea at Sandgate, where there was nothing of vital importance to either side. The surrender of the high ground and all this entails would not have been worth the potential meagre gains. The 1st London Rifle Brigade would be principally responsible for denying success to this Regiment, especially its company at Arpinge which, if properly deployed, could significantly inhibit the German ability to attack the airfield; the Battalion's headquarters was located at Lyminge with its reserve company, though if it deployed up onto the escarpment it would leave the village exposed to any German advances from the southwest. No doubt the Battalion commander, with the support of his Brigade commander nearby, would have demanded the release of his other two companies from Shorncliffe Garrison, with these either directed to join the company at Arpinge, secure Etchinghill to isolate the Storm Regiment or counter the parachute landings by moving on Sandling. In any case, it was important that the strength of these companies not be dissipated by being expected to undertake too many tasks, or sidetracked by isolated groups of

German parachutists; much would depend on the local intelligence, communications and transport available to direct these companies so that they could be most effective. The defence of RAF Hawkinge seemed well catered for, with each unit assigned specific defence roles and locations and the station commander being in direct communications with Headquarters 1st London Division. The availability of the 64th Field Regiment RA nearby would have greatly enhanced the defence, as long as the guns could be free to operate.

An important consideration that would have had to be addressed by the German Army commanders was that the extended role of this unique Division would have been tempered by Luftwaffe demands for its early return, allowing it to be made available for other missions. It was, after all, a Luftwaffe resource on loan to the Army and without any significant heavy weapons or logistics.

35th Infantry Division would also have found it difficult to reach its final objective across the Royal Military Canal but, once it had broken the resistance of the coastal defences, it is unlikely to have met sufficient co-ordinated opposition inland to halt its progress, except on its left flank in the New Romney-Lydd area where the bulk of the local reserves were found. The advance detachment of 111th Infantry Regiment was to be the first to land (from 0615), between Littlestone and Greatstone and was expected to clear New Romney largely unaided as the rest of the Regiment was not due to land for another hour. 7th Somerset Light Infantry, supported by 6 Commando, led the defence and was aided by significant artillery and anti tank guns. Most of the defenders at Littlestone and Greatstone were deployed along the seafront but each had a final "keep" to fall back on, whilst nearby New Romney would initially have to rely on its own resources. The ability of the defenders at Greatstone and Littlestone to retain most of their positions would also greatly aid the defence of vital New Romney. This advance detachment was probably the one most likely to fail to clear its beach, given the strength of the coastal defence here. With Greatstone and Littlestone protecting its front the mobile forces and artillery in New Romney could help draw in the German forces landing to its east to attack it and so restrict moves inland behind it.

Assuming the Regiment was able to secure the New Romney area it was then to advance across the Marsh with the road running inland from New Romney to Appledore as their left boundary. This task was made even more difficult as the defences of Lydd and Dungeness were outside the Division's area of responsibility and as such could only be attacked if the Army commander authorised it. Given the landing plans in this area it is surprising that the Division had not been assigned responsibility for at least taking Lydd as it was in a better geographical position to do so. The longer this Division could be kept on the Marshes the better chance the British had of deploying enough resources to the area and contain them in a position still favouring the defence.

The second major unit to land was to be the under strength Panzer Battalion D, at St Mary's Bay, west of Dymchurch. This was to start landing thirty minutes after the advance detachment down the coast, but would have little support except for the Brandenburg commando and attached engineers. This would be its most vulnerable time until 109th Infantry Regiment began landing forty five minutes later opposite Dymchurch. This Regiment did not have an advance detachment and so would be required to fight its way off the beaches. Once the coastal defences had been overcome the Regiment was to cross the marsh on a broad front and then cross the Royal Military Canal between Ham Street and Bilsington, while Panzer Battalion D advanced through Ivychurch to Ham Street. The only obstacle to this progress would be from the nodal point defences at St Mary in the Marsh and the artillery nearby at Honeychild Manor, while defence of the Canal would be mostly down to the Home Guard and pioneers. Due to the landing schedule the defenders at Dymchurch and St Mary's Bay would have a little longer to prepare their response, however, this sector was the weakest for the British and it is unlikely that they could prevent the panzers moving inland.

Certainly, the success of 35th Division would have caused consternation to General Liardet at 1st London Division Headquarters as, despite the Romney Marsh sector being outside his command, it threatened his right flank and administrative rear and both he and General Schreiber had few reserves immediately available to cope with it properly (that is what the belated deployment of 31st Brigade from Oxfordshire was supposed to provide for).

With the exception of three nodal points - Lydd, St Mary in the Marsh and Burmarsh, a couple of miles inland, almost all of 135th Brigade was assigned to the coastal defences. Once these were overrun there was little left to form another strong defensive line inland, such as along the Royal Military Canal; the forces at the eastern end of the Canal would no doubt already be engaged with the airborne forces. With the exception of the forces in the Lydd and New Romney areas, there is little that the small local counter attack forces located in the nodal places, despite their mobility and firepower, could be expected to achieve in preventing moves inland (and this includes the famous light railway). All the units deployed along the coast had strict orders not to withdraw from their localities, though the need to ensure resupply and casualty evacuation was retained.

Shorncliffe Garrison was already tasked with denying Hythe to the enemy and countering the airborne landings. Unfortunately, it would probably have very little artillery able to support it; the heavy railway mounted guns and the nearest field artillery regiment (the 64th near Lyminge) would have been in the immediate area of the airborne landings and could become pre-occupied with dealing with those German troops and safeguarding their own weapons. The Garrison would need to rely heavily on the Home Guard to report accurately on the German movements and engage the airborne troops, so allowing the Garrison to make the most effective use of its few properly combat trained elements. The Garrison would need to move forward, particularly along the A20 road, to engage the enemy rather than wait for the Germans to come to them. Doing so could further help isolate Battle Group Steinzler above it and contain the movement of Battle Group Hoffmeister. Other elements could reinforce the defenders in Saltwood and Hythe.

The ability of 2nd London Infantry Brigade to operate effectively may well have been compromised from the outset as its Headquarters would be isolated at Postling, on the northern edge of the proposed landing area for the bulk of the German airborne forces; as such this Headquarters would have to re-deploy quickly or be overrun; either way this could hamper the effectiveness of the rest of the Brigade. An alternative headquarters site had already been identified in the hamlet of Skeete, on the North Downs above Postling, which would have been better. As already mentioned, the 1st London Rifle Brigade was in an unenviable position, with half of its strength deployed with Shorncliffe Garrison and another company deployed to protect Hawkinge on the heights above. Unless its commander was given the authority to react as he saw fit, and mount a co-ordinated counter attack against either the parachute or glider landings much valuable time could be lost in deciding its priorities and deploying accordingly. Maybe the best option the Battalion had was to hold Lyminge until the rest of the Brigade arrived as, although overlooked by the high ground where Battle Group Steinzler was due to land, the village controlled the entrance to one of the main routes to Canterbury. The garrisons of both RAF airfields should have been strong enough to repel all but the most determined and supported assaults, with the light anti aircraft guns being crucial to the defence.

It was the expectation that both 135th Infantry Brigade and Shorncliffe Garrison would provide General Liardet with enough time to redeploy the two London infantry brigades from around Canterbury south to protect Hawkinge airfield, Dover and Ashford. These brigades had the transport resources at hand to rapidly re-deploy. Given its geographical split, 2nd London Brigade could best move down the Elham Valley and via Denton to secure Hawkinge and push the Germans off the high ground, while 1st London Brigade could move south along Stone Street to protect Ashford from the North Downs escarpment to the north of Sellindge. However, if the latter Brigade was ordered to advance south from the Downs and attack the paratroops it would need significant fire support and anti aircraft protection. If it was defeated then there would be little left to prevent an advance towards the key communications hub of Ashford.

General Thorne could also make the decision to quickly deploy the NZEF. As previously mentioned, its role was either to move from Ashford to counter attack penetrations north west of Folkestone or to move south and resecure the defensive line along the Royal Military Canal east of Ham Street. In either case Milforce was to cover the deployment of the 5th NZ Infantry Brigade and then support its advance, with the 7th NZ Infantry Brigade being in reserve. Given the probable deployment of the two London infantry brigades northwest of Folkestone the NZEF would likely be released for the Canal option, one of the most vulnerable sectors XII Corps would have faced. An additional role could have included re-securing Lympne airfield, taking up the 135th Brigade reserves in the area, as denial of any airfield was a high priority to the British high command. This deployment would have also covered the relocation of the exposed and vulnerable 1st London Division's rear services to the north. However, any deployment along the Canal would leave the NZEF vulnerable on its left flank, where the airborne landings would have occured. If the NZEF moved quickly and reached the Canal before the 35th Division could move inland then it would release Milforce to form a mobile striking force to cover this flank. An important consideration for offensive operations was the slow speed of the infantry tanks of 8th RTR, who would form the cornerstone of such operations. Whilst these tanks were feared for their armour protection, they were vulnerable to swift counter measures due to their slow speed and required regular maintenance (most tanks lost in France were due to breakdowns). The chance to recover or replace these tanks would have been unlikely.

Of all the landing zones envisaged it is probable that VII Corps, landing in Rye Bay, would have had the easiest task of all in breaking through the coastal defences, though it would have been very difficult to link up with XIII Corps to its east by nightfall due to the defences in the Lydd-Dungeness-New Romney area. One major concern to the Germans would no doubt have been the delayed landing time at Rye, with the Corps' landing plans suggesting an initial landing starting at 0700, whilst XIII Corps planned to begin landings at about 0615. Although the timings were dictated by the tides this delay would have served to warn the British and so give them more time to man their positions and prepare their response. If this situation was repeated down the coast then the Ninth Army formations were likely to receive a more severe welcome than they would with the surprise approach that they desired.

7th Division's 62nd Infantry Regiment was to land at Camber and move on Rye from the south east, being charged with its capture. The beach defenders were concentrated at the western end, near the harbour entrance, and would have been aided by the distance the Germans would have to cross the beach (similar to what the Americans faced at Omaha Beach on D Day). These defenders would hope to have the support of the forces in Lydd, even after the landings had occurred, as there was little else available to aid them. If deployed in time they could also decimate the Germans landing or if not then, if handled well, they could attack penetrations behind the dunes. The Regiment was expected to detach an element to clear or cover the defences at Lydd and Dungeness, especially the coastal artillery believed to be on the west facing shoreline of the ness (actually a dummy battery). It might also be attracted to the towers of the nearby radar station, further diluting its power to cross the Canal and secure the vital town. The approach from Camber is several miles of low lying marshland and flooded gravel workings, giving the defenders time and knowledge to better prepare their response. With all this in mind, this Regiment would have had its work cut out to achieve all its objectives and its advance detachment would have to be very lucky to capture Rye on its own, as planned.

The Division's other regiment, 19th Infantry Regiment, was to land west of Rye Harbour with most of Panzer Battalion A, capture both Winchelsea and Rye Harbour before penetrating up to the River Rother to the northwest of Rye. The Panzer Battalion was vital to the success here given the lack of anti tank weapons available to the British, but it would largely be restricted to the one road leading inland to Winchelsea from the coast and so easier to halt. It would also be landing opposite the coastal battery. Although the field regiment covering this sector had a number of guns deployed in an anti-tank role none were located at Winchelsea, though it did have an OP there and the road from the coast was already pre-registered for the guns further inland. Even with tank support it would be a major achievement for the Division to take both towns before the day was out; of the two towns Winchelsea was to be taken first, the defence of this place hopefully allowing the defenders at Rye more time to seek further improvements to their own situation. The importance of holding Rye and Winchelsea was not lost on the British as these two places control the area; Rye in particular controls the road network running inland. It was intended that these were to be the cornerstone of the defence, their natural defences contributing greatly to the ability to resist the assault. It would be interesting to see if the battalion commander would allow or be able to withdraw his troops and supporting arms from the harbour area once it was clear that the Germans were moving inland; these troops could further bolster the defence of the town, which dominates the narrow harbour in any case. If not withdrawn then those troops could easily be isolated and contained. Although the harbour could be quite easily cleared and reopened by the Germans it was not a proper port as it lacked facilities and was, in any case, tidal and narrow, making it unsuitable for transports to use.

1st Mountain Division's 99th Mountain Regiment was to land between Winchelsea Beach and Cliff End, cross the marshes of Pett Level and Royal Military Canal to reach the high ground at Icklesham, then turn west to hopefully meet its sister regiment landing at Fairlight. It was then expected to move behind Hastings, taking that town from the rear. With all due respect to the defenders, it is unlikely that this Division would have met little concerted resistance after landing, due in part to 7th Infantry Division landing on its right and the absence of any significant British reserves in the area. The bulk of the defence was located at Cliff End and Pett but did not have the strength to hold the enemy for any significant length of time. Some of the mountain troops could be drawn into the fighting around Winchelsea, especially if the 7th Division was struggling, as this overlooked their landing zone and could not be allowed to interfere with the landing of the follow on forces. The 98th Mountain Regiment landing at Fairlight could have had significant problems in crossing the beach and scaling the cliffs but, given their skills and the lack of heavy weapons available to the defenders they should have been expected to soon be moving inland. The defenders of the radar station inland would also not be able to hold up an advance towards Hastings for long either.

The British infantry deployed along the Hastings seafront would need to redeploy to meet the threat from the mountain troops, hopefully guided by Home Guard reporting of the German movements inland. With this in mind XIII Corps should have been able to establish a beachhead west of Rye, though a quick link up with the neighbouring Corps to the west would be unlikely to occur that day, due more to the terrain involved rather than the British defence. It is probable that both Fairlight and Rye radar stations would have been lost on the first day, due to their closeness to the landing sites and lack of significant troops available to defend them. This gap in the reporting network would have to be filled by the Observer Corps until mobile radar stations could be deployed inland.

Even if the landing in Pevensey Bay went to plan, XXXVIII Corps would have had a difficult time, especially 26th Infantry Division landing at Pevensey, in achieving their objectives. While the few British reserves immediately available could not have prevented a beachhead being formed, the Corps was also likely to find itself isolated from its neighbouring Corps due to the terrain. Pevensey controlled the road network in this sector and was prepared to hold out for days. Pevensey radar station nearby was also well protected by defences but it would most likely have been made non operational very quickly, its towers providing an easily recognisable objective to draw the Germans to it. The British would hope to draw the German troops into fighting in the urban areas of Bexhill and Eastbourne as well as the nodal points, despite the German intentions to take these two towns from the rear after securing their initial objectives. 34th Infantry Division could have been better placed to reach Battle than 1st Mountain Division, but this town was outside the Army's boundary and was therefore out of bounds. Such a decision would be of great help to the British, once they became aware of it, as the forces around Battle would not worry about having to fight on two flanks and could concentrate on stopping the advance of the Mountain Division to its east.

The key to preventing the Germans from breaking out from this landing zone was to hold the Hailsham and Polegate areas. 9th Devon's War Diary insisted that the Battalion was to hold both Stone Cross and Friston (the later probably by using the company stationed at Birling Gap) at all costs. The Brigade and Battalion commanders would need to take the important step of quickly re-positioning the troops not in action, particularly those defending the seafronts of both Bexhill and Eastbourne. Certainly, the ability of the Germans to overcome these defenders and maintain their momentum would have been severely tested. It was critical for the defenders in this landing zone that higher command be simplified, especially as the boundary between two brigades of 45th Division ran through the area - 134th Brigade covering the east sector with one battalion and 136th Brigade covering the west sector with two battalions. Divisional Headquarters could decide to concentrate its efforts in ths sector. Without a proper command structure it is likely that the overall defence would have been largely uncoordinated, with the surviving defenders likely to fall back on their own Brigade areas if heavily pressed. It was hoped that the marshy Pevensey Levels would mitigate this command issue, as it could hinder German penetration through its middle, if properly prepared for flooding and demolition. Much would depend on the effectiveness and mobility of the deployed British artillery, however the heavy guns deployed inland from Bexhill would have been very vulnerable to German advances, given their static nature.

X and VIII Corps landing the other side of Beachy Head would also have had a difficult, though not insurmountable, task. The Germans recognised the vulnerability of landing in this sector by assigning their second echelon to land in Pevensey Bay. However, this decision would deprive the assault divisions of vital artillery, infantry and support elements until the ground in between had been cleared and secured. If the first echelon was also directed to land in Pevensey Bay on S Day they would probably have had a profound effect on the landing schedules of all the forces using this zone and lead to further congestion on and off the beaches as units sought to create sufficient room for elements of an additional three assault divisions and one Corps troops to deploy. Little thought seems to have been given to this aspect of the landing and so it would be up to the senior commanders on the spot to sort out the resulting mess. Certainly these divisions would still be expected to carry out their operational orders of securing Lewes, Newhaven and the South Downs; the only way of doing this from Pevensey Bay would have been an advance along the main road from Polegate to Lewes and then deploying accordingly.

Assuming that the landings occurred as planned then the key to all three landings in this area was the port of Newhaven, dominated by the fortifications overlooking the port and sea approach. Given the plans and dispositions of the assaulting forces available it is doubtful whether this fortification would have been taken before nightfall and the longer it engaged the invaders the greater the opportunity there was to disrupt the overall German plans. The Luftwaffe planned to subject Newhaven Fort to heavy air attack from the outset and much would depend on their abilities to neutralise this place. There was only one bridge, already prepared for demolition, across the River Ouse in the area and the part of the town there as designated as the Nodal Point's "keep" (it was about a mile from the shore, while the next was over four miles to the north at Southease). The failure to cross this river could most likely result in the destruction of 28th Infantry Division at Rottingdean and the formation of a strong British defensive flank based on the GHQ Line along the River Ouse for the British. It is surprising that, as far as is known, there were no plans to land troops west of the harbour mouth or send assault forces into the harbour. The Germans had given much importance to seizing intact working ports, such as Dover, but appeared to have ignored the potential of Newhaven, relying on the use of Pevensey Bay as Ninth Army's main conduit for its follow on forces; this could have been down to their worries about the western flank being too exposed to Royal Navy counter strokes. Unless the Luftwaffe was successful, the British plans to block the port would have been completed before the landing began. Even after landing the troops of 8th Division would be restricted in its move towards Newhaven by the terrain and roads and would be under constant observation. The 1/5th DCLI reserve, with its little artillery support, would be the last opportunity to hold the lower Ouse valley. Its counter attack role would have to be forgotten due to its clear lack of strength but its manouverability gave it many other options to hold up an enemy advance; the only likely support could have been those elements of its A Company who could be spared from the defence at Bishopstone. The ability of the forces in Seaford to distract and engage 8th Division could also be crucial. In itself the seaside town was not important but the longer its defenders could actively hold out then the fewer troops on either flanking assault division would be available to penetrate inland and attain their own objectives. It would be important not to let these defenders be cut off and isolated in Seaford as the Germans advanced inland on either side of it, though any extraction could be costly if the Germans held a cordon to its north.

The advance on and seizure of Lewes, vital to both sides as it controlled access to and from the area from the north and west, would also probably have been too much for 8th Division to achieve by nightfall. The Ouse valley was already well organised for defence as it formed part of the GHQ Stop Line, with the Home Guard largely responsible for the fortifications and prepared demolitions. The terrain also favoured the defender in terms of the observation it provided across and down it. The ability of the coastal defences to hold long enough to give time to start moving reserve formations was key here. The few troops in Lewes lacked the ability to hold this vital town and the high ground either side of it without reinforcement and heavy weapons. Although the defence was directed along the river through the town Mount Caborn, the high ground to the east, would offer a good bastion to protect the town from the south and east (it was later prepared as such), if sufficient forces could be found. 29th Independent Infantry Brigade was prepared to move at short notice and could be expected to reach this area in time, unless XII Corps Headquarters directed it to the Hailsham area. This Brigade was still largely untested and was not expected to do more than hold an area until stronger reinforcements arrived. Broc Force was nominally assigned the role of protecting Lewes but would already be heavily engaged with the containment of 28th Division at Rottingdean. At best it could provide some of its mobile units to help protect the western side of the Ouse valley to the south of the town. However, it was fortunate that the Force had planned an exercise to test its ability to counter an invasion around Newhaven at the same time as the actual projected invasion!

6th Mountain Division was to land in force at Cuckmere Haven, with an entire mountain infantry regiment, artillery, engineers and a panzer company forming the advance detachment. It was well suited to fighting up the rolling valley sides but would have needed the support of the panzers to overcome the initial beach defences, which were the strongest along the invasion coast in terms of fortifications in such a small enclosed area. It is likely that the tanks would have had great difficulty manoeuvring across the shingle beach due to its gradient and composition, the earthen and shingle bank as well as the significant anti tank ditch just behind it, all covered by fixed defences. However, once these defences were overcome there was little inland to hold up any advance up the Cuckmere valley until they reached the nodal point village of Alfriston, about six kilometres inland. The reserve company of 50th Sussex would have had to be deployed to the Haven from Seaford to counter any pentration from the beach, though it and the Home Guard platoon at Exceat Bridge would be unlikely to have the resources to do more than delay such an advance. It is surprising that, given its traditional role, this Division was not assigned the task of securing Beachy Head, a task assigned instead to 26th Infantry Division. It would hope to avoid having to fight in Seaford, immediately to its west, but whether it could ignore the British defenders there would be questionable, especially as 8th Infantry Division did not appear to propose attacking it in strength. It is also likely that elements from the Mountain Division could become engaged at the nodal point of Friston, though they would be unlikely to commit more than a covering force here. Not noted in any of the plans was the seizure of the civilian airfield (and RAF emergency landing ground) located between Cuckmere Haven and Friston.

The landing of 28th Infantry Division at Rottingdean was fraught with potentially disastrous problems for the Germans. The use of an entire reinforced infantry regiment (49th) assaulting a narrow opening in the cliffs could lead to severe congestion on the beach, though numbers should suffice in overcoming the few defenders there, unless those defenders were well supplied and in sound defensive positions (a small garrison at Puys, near Dieppe, held a numerically stronger Canadian force on the beach with few heavy weapons). The survival of the field battery in the village would have been crucial to the long term defence of this sector. With this Regiment due to move west along the coast and inland towards Falmer, much would depend on the rest of the first echelon landing quickly and moving inland. It is surprising that no mention is made of moving elements east along the coast to link up with 8th Division around Newhaven, especially as without this link 28th Division would be completely isolated. The other key to success would be securing the high ground of the South Downs just inland as this dominates the entire sector. For the British, Broc Force would need to contain this sector and was fortunate in having artillery, heavy machine guns, a variety of light armoured vehicles and a few heavy infantry tanks at hand. However, it was spread out as far west as Bognor Regis and would require time and transport to reposition itself, especially as there are few roads running parallel to the coast allowing ease of movement to this sector. Units would likely have to be fed into battle piecemeal initially as speed was of the essence to secure the high ground and seal off any penetrations inland. If this could be achieved then it is quite likely that 28th Infantry Division could be destroyed, as there was little room to manoeuvre and even less chance of reinforcement, re-supply or naval or air support. If the first echelon could be prevented from landing as planned then the advance dertachment should certainly have been too weak to survive before it could be reinforced overland.

The initial days would have seen the greatest effort in the air to date, with both sides aiming to control the skies over the invasion beachheads and anchorages. Daylight RAF bomber operations to date had already painfully demonstrated the vulnerability of its bombers without proper fighter support. The desire to strike quickly would have to mean accepting heavy losses, potentially crippling this important force in the early stages. There could never be enough fighters for all the demands placed on them. Co-operation between the arms of the RAF would need to be tightened. The advent of evening would have been the best time to release the Operation Banquet aircraft to hit key locations, dependent on intelligence of such targets being gathered, assessed and graded and the ability of aircrew to find their targets. With such demand aircrews would quickly become tired, though rotating units could help alleviate this.

The Navy would also be operating at a high tempo, with its striking forces aiming to force their way into the anchorages and reinforcement convoys, its minesweepers breaking down the minefields and anti submarine craft harrying their prey. Other vessels would be striving to keep their own ports open. All this activity would be under the constant threat of air attack. Naval high command would also be seeking clarification as to the location of the German battle fleet and likely be sidetracked for a short time by the diversionary operations, as was intended. Additional naval forces could be tasked to prepare for a move to the invasion area, to either replace losses or reinforce the effort. Operations would continue around the clock and could also feature night bombardment of the German embarkation ports.

The immediate period of the invasion would have severely tested the ability of the British Army to provide an effective command and control structure. At the highest operational level Eastern Command Headquarters would nominally be in charge of all field operations in the invasion area; however, it is unlikely that this would have been able to provide effective command of the defensive and counter attack forces to be engaged there as most of its forces were deployed in East Anglia awaiting invasion there; at best it would have been able to control the administrative processes supporting XII Corps. As already mentioned, this senior command issue had already been recognised by GHQ Home Forces and a South Eastern Command was in the early stages of being planned (it was formed in February 1941 taking over responsibility for Kent, Sussex, Surrey and the Aldershot Command, with headquarters in Aldershot). Headquarters Southern Command could have been a viable option, especially as it could provide many of the initial out of area reserves. Although General Brooke had confidence in General Auchinleck`s abilities, he would have been reluctant to re-assign that Headquarters and so leave the rest of the south coast vulnerable. The only other choice was Headquarters Aldershot Command, the home of the British Army, but its commander was too junior to be expected to play such a vital role. It could, however, take over the administration responsibilities from Eastern Command, which could then concentrate on East Anglia.

GHQ Home Forces was the body responsible for the defence of the entire country and in preparing troops and units for deployment overseas. As such it was not suited to operate as an Army level headquarters responsible for operations against the invasion area. Its most effective role would be to co-ordinate logistics and reinforcement to the invasion area, ensuring that fresh units adequately equipped and trained could replace worn out units, with those units being sent to quiet areas to hopefully rest and re-equip. General Alan Brooke would also be best placed to link between the tactical and strategic level, helping his senior commanders retain the initiative and co-ordinate efforts with the other services. It is less likely that an ad-hoc Army level headquarters would have been formed to control operations covering the invasion area, as this would have taken time to organise and be more likely to fail; the creation of lower level ad-hoc headquarters in the BEF in May had already been recognised as a failure. The decision of establishing a suitable senior command structure would certainly have been one of the most crucial decisions facing General Brooke at this early stage.

At the Corps level command would have been easier to clarify. Initially Headquarters XII Corps would have been responsible for conducting the defence but with landings on such a wide front it would have been a major effort to undertake this role alone for more than a few days. Indeed with the deployment of VII Corps in its counter attack role, most likely through the middle of the XII Corps area, General Brooke may have felt a reorganisation of the command structure was required. After the initial few days he would be convinced that this was the only point of invasion and should be able to focus his attention and energy to the area. He would also be very well informed through the various reporting and intelligence structures as to the scale and content of the invasion. From the pre-invasion dispositions three Corps could be deployed initially to counter the invasion. XII Corps could best continue to focus its efforts on the eastern part of the beachhead, while V Corps could be expected to take responsibility for the western part. VII Corps could cover the centre, at least until another corps headquarters arrived to again free them for the counter offensive work they were designed for.

Of the formations in XII Corps, 1st London Division would be better able to retain a strong command and control structure, as the formation was more compact and could concentrate its efforts on destroying the Germans on the eastern flank. Due to its extensive frontage and lack of reserves, the ability of Headquarters 45th Infantry Division to provide effective command and control over all its units could likely have seen this structure fracture very quickly, General Schreiber having little but advice and moral support to offer his brigade commanders at this stage. It would be up to these brigadiers to fight their own battle before reinforcements hopefully arrived. The problems faced by 135th Brigade would have been eased by the arrival of the New Zealanders in their rear, though General Schreiber may have be reluctant to allow command of this Brigade to be transferred to General Freyberg; however, until it could be relieved from the Royal Military Canal to regroup, this would probably have been the best course of action for General Thorne to countenance as it would simplify the command structure in the area and allow General Schreiber to concentrate on holding the Pevensey Marshes area with his remaining brigades. The survival of this Brigade would have depended largely on the exfiltration of those forces from the Lydd/New Romney area as no counter attack could be mounted to reach it quickly.

The commanders of both Broc Force and 29th Infantry Brigade would need to co-ordinate their operations with each other, if the latter was deployed to cover Lewes. Both would report directly to Headquarters XII Corps, at least initially. Further operations in this part of the battlefield, especially after the deployment of VII Corps on their left, would best require a dedicated divisional or Corps level commander; the best options available would either be Headquarters 4th Division or its parent, V Corps.

The first fortnight would have probably dictated the outcome of the campaign. For the Germans the need to establish a significant beachhead linking all landing zones, coupled with the desire to secure both working ports and airfields so the remainder of the First Wave could be landed quickly and effectively supplied, was all-important. For the British it was the need to keep the invaders penned back to the coast and isolated by land, air and sea, so allowing time for the major counter attack forces to be bought forward for the decisive blows. The terrain would favour the British, with the escarpments of the North and South Downs overlooking a countryside that generally resembled the Bocage found in Normandy, notably an abundance of small fields, thick hedgerows and sunken lanes plus large swathes of dense woodland. It was this type of terrain that would help the Germans contain the Allies for three months in 1944 and could do the same for the British in 1940, providing enough men and equipment could be quickly and properly deployed and maintained. For both sides the seizing and maintaining of the initiative at all levels was to be vital - the Germans would need to land the remainder of the assault divisions quickly, especially their artillery, without which they would have to continue relying heavily on the Luftwaffe; these additional combat resources were vital to keep the momentum of advance going until it reached the line assigned for the final beachhead and then prevent the British from mounting significant counter attacks before they were ready to meet them; the British had to ensure that the Germans were engaged everywhere so as not to allow them time to rest and regroup, while ensuring their own troops already fighting were able to regroup and making sure the few reserves were correctly used to maximise their effect. The reluctance of the German Army to fight at night, preferring to use this time for rest and reorganisation, could also be a major factor aiding the defence should the British maximise the opportunities offered.

In the east 1st London Division's main task was preventing the loss of Dover and Hawkinge, while maintaining Ashford as a base of operations and, if possible, reaching and reinforcing Shorncliffe Garrison. In doing this it could support the Garrison's efforts in denying Folkestone harbour, which had already been put out of action with a blockship in place, the sea approaches mined and port installations removed or disabled. At the same time the Division would need to switch its operational axis around completely, moving its combat resources to the new front and its administrative resources to a new, less vulnerable, rear area; Divisional papers do not indicate whether this need had been considered in any of the staff exercises ran over the summer, but such a move would be vital to the survival of the Division as a combat formation. If all went well the Division and Garrison could then push on to Hythe and Lympne, forcing the Germans back onto Romney Marsh and into an untenable situation, as they would be overlooked everywhere. Other than the assets previously mentioned, General Liardet would have been able to reinforce Dover Garrison with troops from Deal Garrison, and Dover Garrison could then support Shorncliffe Garrison. He would be reluctant to move the other two infantry brigades (198th and 35th) from their role in protecting the north Kent coast. However, it is plausible that 35th Brigade Headquarters and 2/7th Queens could have been brought to the Ashford area, joining that Brigade's 2/5th Queens presently in Divisional reserve, to provide a better local command structure and much needed depth for the divisional reserve once the strength of the German landings was fully appreciated. 198th Brigade could be used to relieve a worn out brigade in due course.

As already discussed, the presence of the German 35th Infantry Division south of Ashford would need the deployment of the New Zealand Expeditionary Force (NZEF) to counter it, as it was the only force of suitable strength that was readily available to General Thorne. This would, of course make it largely unavailable to work with other Corps assets to drive into and destroy the German airborne landings. As mentioned above, this deployment may have included taking what remained of 135th Infantry Brigade under its command, again simplifying command in this sector. It was crucial that the supply depots around Tenterden be removed quickly to both deny them to the Germans and free up the area to reserves moving up. It was already prepared as a nodal point, but it was recognised that the broken ground surrounding the town would better suit the attackers than the defenders. Although 135th Brigade's orders were to hold its coastal positions to the last man and round of ammunition, it would have been tempting to withdraw some of it, especially the artillery, to reinforce the few elements left covering the Royal Military Canal, once it became clear that it could not prevent both a penetration inland from the beaches and contain the airborne landings. There would have been a real danger of the bulk of the Brigade being contained and isolated in the New Romney-Lydd area and so being unavailable for the equally crucial battle for the Royal Military Canal. 31st Infantry Brigade Group in IV Corps was earmarked to move down to the vulnerable Ashford sector in late September and had already made initial preparations for this, with two battalions to be deployed along the Canal from Iden to Ham Street and one in reserve north of Tenterden; given this, it is possible that this formation would have been moved into the area as quickly as possible and attached to XII Corps as a further reserve.

134th Infantry Brigade's main aim would still be to keep the Germans either side of Hastings apart, though this Brigade would have little, if any, additional support for some days and would have had to depend heavily on the local Home Guard to provide the additional resources required. Certainly those troops guarding the seafront in the Hastings area would need to be redeployed to maximise their usefulness. With this in mind the Home Guard could be tasked to fight in their own town while the regular troops present withdrew to provide a decent local counter attack force. General Schreiber at 45th Infantry Division had a small, though more mobile reserve that could provide blocking positions inland, but was faced with a similar problem as General Liardet - where and when to commit it? Most likely this would have had to be either in support of the troops north of Hastings and Bexhill or covering the Pevensey Levels. However, pre invasion plans for this force to man the appropriate defensive lines was the wrong approach to adopt as it negated their real ability to probe and contain the German advances inland by using their mobility and firepower to the maximum effect. 136th Infantry Brigade's operations would most likely been split, with 1/5th DCLI at Newhaven almost certainly having to fight a separate battle. The rest of the Brigade would need to avoid being contained within Eastbourne and aim to hold the Polegate and Hailsham area, thus providing cover for VII Corps as it deployed behind it. It might also have to find troops to contain the 6th Mountain Division as it broke out from the Cuckmere Valley.

On the western flank of the German invasion more substantial reserves were readily available to XII Corps – Broc Force could be quickly freed from its positions behind Brighton and the Corps reserve of 29th Infantry Brigade could be deployed to cover Lewes. These forces lacked the strength to defeat three German divisions, even if those remained significantly understrength. What they could do was to continue to deny the use of Newhaven port by the Germans and hold the important town of Lewes until stronger forces arrived to push the Germans back. The success of 6th Mountain Division would be critical to both sides. It is unlikely that it would be held up long by the defenders of Alfriston and would likely reach the northern end of the Cuckmere Valley by the end of the first day. However, unless reinforced by the rest of the first echelon and any elements detached on the flanks (against Seaford and Beachy Head) were returned it was unlikely to push on to reach its objective – a line between Lewes and Uckfield – as this would leave both its flanks exposed. Assuming it was reinforced it could be tasked with initially moving on to attack Lewes from the east in support of 8th Division fighting its way up from the south. This would further stretch 29th Brigade's resources and could then leave the GHQ Line (also running between Lewes and Uckfield) dangerously exposed and under defended, with the Home Guard being almost solely responsible for holding it unless a mobile force from Broc Force was despatched early on to arrive from Lewes. The Mountain Division could also be used to probe along the main road to Polegate, vital to the German plans to reinforce its divisions from Pevensey Bay. It is unlikely to have the strength or resources to do both. It would though have the capability to secure the northern escarpment of the South Downs south east of Lewes, providing them with observation over a wide area to the north, including where the British VII Corps might likely move into and advance from when conducting its counter offensive. The main role of Broc Force would be to isolate the 28th Division and had the resources and mobility to achieve that. The lack of many east-west running roads behind Brighton could hinder the movement of its forces from the west and would require a strong movement control organisation to alleviate this. For many days it would be rather likely that these three understrength divisions would have to fight isolated; as such they would be less likely to conduct strong combat operations for long periods as they would be conscious of the need to husband their ammunition and other supplies. This could allow the British to more easily retain the initiative here than anywhere else.

Of course, operations of all the German assault divisions would be tempered by the ability to reinforce and re-supply them during the following days. German naval and coastal artillery preparations would need to be in place quickly to cover both sides of the Channel and be strong enough to help cope with the attentions of the Royal Navy while the anti aircraft deployments would once again need to be effective to prevent the RAF's bombers from destroying the logistics network that would be developing around the landing zones. Above all, the Luftwaffe needed to be able to continue operations at very intense levels in support of both Kriegsmarine and Army. Even without combat losses its operational strength would have started to drop unless its repair and replacement organisation improved its performance.

It was computed that during the invasion of France the German infantry divisions had a daily requirement of 600 tons of supplies, while the panzer divisions required more. For the invasion almost all of this had to be shipped over and initially landed on the open beaches. British military intelligence confirmed that the success of the invasion relied on the ability of the Germans to maintain their forces after the supplies landed with the assault forces had been expended. They estimated that the invading forces would as a whole need between 8,000 to 10,000 tons a day, these figures based on an estimate of 300 tons a day for a German infantry division (a British infantry division in 1940 required about 350 tons a day). They mirrored the German High Command view that the continued supply of the invading forces could only be carried out through properly equipped ports, in view of the reducing numbers of adapted landing craft, improvised landing facilities on the open beaches, likelihood of worsening weather and the need to accommodate the large armoured formations of the Second Wave.

Until the Second Wave formations could be landed the German infantry would need to rely heavily on the panzer tanks remaining from the landings to counter British attacks. Mobile "fire brigades" were to be formed under direct command of the respective Corps headquarters and deployed according to their need. The Royal Navy could not be expected to maintain a continuous presence in the Channel given both the Kriegmarine's defences and attention of the Luftwaffe during the day. However, this might not be necessary as long as it could operate during the night, bombarding ports and landing zones, laying new minefields and generally upsetting the German re-supply and reinforcement schedules. In July Churchill asked the Admiralty to consider the potential of laying minefields behind the invading forces following a successful landing in order to isolate them. The Admiralty opposed this option, as they believed it would hamper their own offensive operations, stating that the smaller minelayers were incapable of producing a suitable minefield during the night, while the few destroyers equipped as minelayers would be desperately needed as destroyers. With the losses in warships likely to grow quickly this option may have needed reconsidering. The RAF would need to continue to operate around the clock in support of such operations.

Much would depend on the ability of the British to move reinforcements and supplies around the country. Naval, air and Army units would need replacing and those units relieved would need quiet parts of the country to rest. Britian's war industry would also need to maximise its output. Above all, the transport, communications, maintenance and repair infrastructures would need to be kept operating at peak efficiency. The German invasion troops would not have the luxury of being relieved and it was hoped that neither would they have rest areas in the beachheads. Constant exposure to fighting would certainly have the effect of degrading their combat effectiveness, even after only a few days.

It is often overlooked how similar Operation Sea Lion was to Operation Overlord, the allied landings in Normandy in 1944. Many of the plans for and concerns of both the invading and defending forces were mirrored - the Germans having to consider the defence of a long and exposed coastline with troops of limited capability and equipment and the allies planning to assault a defended coast, with airborne forces covering their flanks, naval and air forces protecting the invasion craft as well as providing artillery support. There is some merit in transposing the experiences of the Germans in June 1944 to those of the expectant British in 1940. David C Isby, in his book "The German Army at D Day - Fighting the Invasion", notes that many of the German soldiers had already experienced combat, where they had seen not only how devastating defeat could be but that, if properly executed, effective defensive tactics could defeat even skilfully delivered attacks from a numerically superior opponent. The units defending the invasion beaches did a surprisingly good job, considering how little time and how few resources they had available. The Germans had similarly decided that the Main Line of Resistance was to be the high tide line, with belts of barbed wire, other obstructions and mines placed on the beach, all covered by strongpoints and artillery placed inland. Possible air landing zones were identified and obstructed. However, unit training was often neglected as the burdens of construction increased. The German 352nd Infantry Division, covering the Omaha and Gold Beaches, produced an evaluation of the fighting on 6 June, which could also quite easily be transposed to that of the British divisions defending the Kent and Sussex coasts. It noted that, in general:

- The infantry in the permanent concrete battle installations were protected from the effect of enemy fire, though their field of view was limited and the troops inside became isolated as the communications system often broke down
- The infantry employed in local counter attack roles were too weak in numbers and weapons to be truly effective
- Divisional reserves were not properly effective as they were too often misdirected and delayed by air attacks
- The artillery performed well, although its effectiveness was reduced by air attacks and a limited ammunition supply, while the anti tank guns deployed along the coast were fairly successful
- The signals interception service was able to obtain valuable intelligence by listening to enemy transmissions.
- The command structure operated well, though concern was noted that armoured (panzer) units often came under command of formations already in combat, the commanders of which had no real understanding of how best to commit them.

The British Counter Offensive

Returning to 1940 and with the Germans ashore and striving to establish a continuous beachhead, General Alan Brooke would have to rely on his VII Corps to quickly engage and hopefully destroy the most important of the enemy's penetrations as quickly as possible and before they became too established. This would start the second phase of the invasion. It remained vital that no working port remained in the enemy's hand and so offensive operations in the Dover, Folkestone and Newhaven areas would be required, whether by using what local reserves remained or by committing the GHQ Reserve. The key concern to Brooke was that VII Corps lacked the strength to take on more than one counter offensive at a time and would therefore need to be used against the most serious threat until such a time as other forces could be brought into the region to support it. It would be for General Brooke to decide where to commit VII Corps and provide General McNaughton with the desired outcome and parameters, who would then plan the most important operation of his career.

It is not known what sort of relationship would have developed between these two senior commanders but it would certainly have been made clear to VII Corps what was expected of them. Normally GHQ Home Forces would have released its reserves to the Army level command covering that sector for it to control the operations; however, for reasons already given, it was unlikely that Eastern Command Headquarters would have that role. Certainly, General Brooke would keep a very close eye on how the Corps proposed to attack and follow its progress accordingly. General McNaughton would know that he could have whatever he needed to support him but he would also know the price of failure, with General Brooke probably ignoring the political ramifications of replacing him.

Given that the British expected part of the invasion to come in eastern Kent, VII Corps' main consideration had been focused on Dover with 1st London Division providing the screen behind which it could deploy. Although Dover was indeed the Germans primary target the British forces available in that sector should have been enough to hold it for the immediate future, whilst the need to move a Corps across the front of an active battlefront on its right flank in order to reach Dover would pose many more worries.

Depending on the tactical situation at the time the main counter offensive was likely to be focused on the German's left flank, aiming to destroy the enemy forces west of Hastings. Although not operating to recapture a lost port, this sector offered the best chance of success in ultimately destroying the invasion by maximising the potential of the formations available. An attack on Newhaven would have meant moving armoured forces along a narrow valley but only after Lewes was secured; of the significant ports mentioned above Newhaven was of least interest to the Germans as it lay outside its protective cross Channel corridor. That would leave the centre of the invasion zone. We know that the Germans planned to concentrate on Pevensey Bay for reinforcement for the entire Ninth Army and that the inter-Army boundary lay here. As such, success here would pay better dividends for the British.

The key consideration was the timing of the counter offensive. There would no doubt be great pressure to undertake the offensive quickly before the Germans became too established and it would be crucial that Alan Brooke deflected this pressure from his Corps commander until he was ready. To be most effective the Corps' commanders needed time to gather intelligence and conduct their planning. It would also need to move to laying up areas behind the agreed start line and, crucially, move its main armoured brigade from Salisbury Plain to rejoin the Armoured Division. It is likely that it would rely on XII Corps to screen its move up and secure its start line as any of its own forces used for this important role would not likely be available for the actual attack. All this would take time and as such the offensive would unlikely start until the start of S+2 at the earliest. Secrecy was vital during this period so the Germans would not know where the main attack would come from. Therefore radio security was vital, while air reconnaissance and observation from the captured high ground of the South Downs must be denied to the Germans.

Any counter offensive here would also need to factor in the presence of 6th Mountain Division coming out of the Cuckmere valley to the west. Although this Division was tasked with moving northwest to a line between Lewes and Uckfield, it is likely that it would find itself supporting 8th Division's capture of Lewes. Nevertheless once the British counter offensive started it would also find itself looking to its vulnerable right flank. Wth this in mind, VII Corps would need to find something to protect its own right flank without diluting its own offensive power or, if it had additional forces, to take the opportunity to also attack that Division. If the German 26th Division attained its objective of securing a line between Arlington and Hellingly then the offensive would have to focus on retaking Hailsham, probably by attacking from the Heathfield and East Hoathly area. This ground was mostly open and low lying with small woods and streams interspersed with small villages and hamlets to the west, while to the north of Hailsham the ground is more broken and wooded.

It is possible that the 1st Armoured Division would operate separately from the 1st Canadian Division as they had different equipment and capabilities. The Armoured Division could best be successful by using its mobility in attacking north of the Pevensey Levels and on to Bexhill, while the Canadian Division and the slower heavier armour of the 1st Army Tank Brigade attacked towards Pevensey and Eastbourne, via Hailsham. It is likely that there would still be British defenders holding out in and around Eastbourne and these would be only too happy to assist in attacking the Germans, while the local Home Guard could provide much needed local knowledge, supported by the reconnaissance elements of VII Corps and 5th Loyals, in identifying weaknesses in the German line. It is possible that a brigade from the 2nd Canadian Division could be attached to provide further infantry strength for the Corps, especially as the Armoured Division lacked any organic infantry support. It is not likely that XII Corps could provide much support, other than with those forces presently fighting there. Would General Brooke have identified the lack of VII's strength before it deployed, given the scale of the invasion? If so, he could have decided to reinforce it with another infantry division, the 3rd around Bristol or the 52nd in East Anglia being the most likely candidates as they were well equipped.

The way VII Corps went in to action would largely determine its potential success. The consideration of using brigades independently could lead to a dissipation of effort, something not truly appreciated by British field commanders until 1942. Its commanders would need to be able to respond quickly to developments in order to retain the initiative, ensuring appropriate resources were deployed to achieve success and reserves moved up and introduced effectively. The knowledge of local forces and Home Guard could prove of emense value in the achievement of this.

Success would also be reliant on what the Germans had to counter it. Both divisions of XXXVIII Corps had experienced little combat before the invasion and would have hoped to have the bulk of their forces, weapons and supplies ashore, together with those elements of the other Ninth Army assault divisions that would have been directed to land at Pevensey, before the British offensive began. The Corps Commander, General von Manstein, would have wished to land as soon as he was allowed and his skills and experience could have been crucial.

The counter offensive would likely run for a few days and would see renewed heavy air battles over the area as both sides would know the importance of its outcome. For the British it would mean destruction of one of the invading Corps and the logistics base for the entire Ninth Army, meaning the ultimate destruction of the German forces to the west. If this occurred, could Sixteenth Army hold enough land to bring in additional forces to re-launch a successful invasion? Failure of the counter offensive would give the Germans the time to land more of the First Wave, link its landing zones and secure its initial defensive line. It would also serve as an important morale booster.

The fact that McNaughton was to suffer a nervous breakdown that November suggests that the strain of conducting the crucial counter offensive could have been too much for him. If that was the case, then who would Brooke choose as his replacement? Whoever, it would be someone that Brooke had the utmost confidence in them being aggressive and would most likely have commanded in the BEF. Generals Alexander (I Corps) or Holmes (X Corps) could have been strong contenders and be readily available; General Montgomery was likely to be already heavily engaged with V Corps while General Pearkes, commanding 1st Canadian Division and destined to be the temporary Corps commander, was unlikely as this would have meant too many senior command changes within this Corps at a crucial time.

It is not inconceivable to consider that IV Corps may have also been moved to the region, in part if not as a whole, to contribute to ensuring the success of the counter-offensive or to conduct its own counter offensive into east Kent. However, an important consideration in using this Corps was the additional timescale involved in moving these forces south into the invasion area in a manner that would ensure that it could deploy effectively. Another major factor influencing such a coordination of effort was that neither IV, VII nor XII Corps' had exercised together at any level and so did not know each other's strengths and weaknesses. If IV Corps had also been deployed to the south east even more strain would have been placed on the command capabilities of General Headquarters, in the absence of an Army level headquarters, to co-ordinate and support the efforts of two attacking Corps at the same time.

Although operating with an integrated transport network, it would still be an enormous feat to move such a large force with all the equipment and supplies involved and under air attack, whilst trying to maintain operational surprise; fortunately, much time had been spent by the Army in planning tactical movements by road and railway and the system should have been able to cope. Records show that 1st Army Tank Brigade planned to move by train, entraining either near East Grinstead or Crawley and detraining either at Pluckley, Robertsbridge, Eridge or Penshurst for operations in Kent or to the north of Hastings, or detraining either at Rudgwick, Horsham or Billingshurst for operations near Brighton. For operations north of Hastings or in east Kent VII Corps established routes by road that ran through East Grinstead and then either:

- Through Crowborough, Wadhurst and Ticehurst to Rolvenden
- Through Tunbridge Wells, Lamberhurst and Cranbrook to Tenterden, or

- Through Tunbridge Wells, Pembury and Goudhurst to Biddenden.

For operations in Kent and East Sussex the Corps also established a "position of readiness" in the area bound by Tonbridge-Staplehurst-Hawkhurst-Hartfield, where it could assemble.

Headquarters V Corps could also be linked to this counter offensive. Although its main objective was to protect the ports of Portsmouth and Southampton, it would not have been wise to leave it in place to await a German breakout. As already mentioned, it could be redeployed along the coast to take responsibility for the western sector of the invasion, taking over command of both Broc Force and 29th Independent Infantry Brigade already there. The redeployment of 50th Infantry Division with V Corps in Sussex would be a calculated risk, as it would leave the Dorset coast seriously undefended. While no plans remain there is some merit in the suggestion that VIII Corps could have taken over responsibility for the Dorset coast, taking 50th Infantry Division under its control, thereby allowing the rest of V Corps to concentrate on the threats in Sussex. Although the British did not know it, the Germans had largely discounted landing their Sixth Army there, as its selected landing zone was well outside the Kriegmarine's defensive area and the shipping carrying this force would be very vulnerable to attack whilst at sea. 4th Infantry Division would remain under strength as its brigade on the Isle of Wight would most likely have been left in place, while the garrisons of the above ports would not have enough resources to provide additional troops or equipment to support the field forces outside their own area. The GHQ Reserve in Southern Command could be allocated to reinforce this Corps, notably with the rather well equipped 21st Army Tank Brigade, and the 18th Infantry Brigade of the Australian Imperial Force.

If not already re-deployed with VII Corps the 3rd Infantry Division, in VIII Corps, could be transferred to V Corps command (Montgomery may have lobbied hard for, given his recent experience as its commander in the BEF) to provide a second infantry division. Other divisions and Corps could be warned to prepare to move down to the invasion zone to relieve those forces already in action there. A major concern would have been the lack of reserve armoured forces. 2nd Armoured Division in IV Corps was effectively combat ineffective as it had only one cruiser regiment, while the other "armoured" formations lacked any tanks as yet. Tank losses would be heavy during the counter offensive and unless the knocked out or broken down tanks could be recovered replacements would have to come from the meagre stocks or fresh from the factories. The same would be the case with the artillery. For both, production and repair facilities would need to be working at maximum levels, otherwise the Army would have to rely on its infantry formations to conduct the attacks.

The third phase

If the counter offensive succeded then, as mentioned before, Ninth Army would be doomed with only those elements able to break through to Sixteenth Army around Hastings being available for further operations. Those divisions west of Beachy Head, even if they managed to form a continuous front, could easily be contained as they would have little chance of significant resupply and so be incapable of conducting anything more than small local attacks. Without supply or support these formations would not survive into the winter The British could assign tired or lower grade formations to watch over them, so releasing their stronger units for employment against Sixteenth Army. If it had not already done so, that Army would need to put more effort in capturing a workable port, notably Dover, without which it would also not likely be able to survive the year.

Given the topography in the Sixteenth Army's area of operations, its two Corps could still be fighting largely independently of each other due to the Isle of Oxney and Tenterden largely controlling movement between Hastings and Romney Marsh. The ground north of Hastings is heavily broken and wooded, allowing good opportunities for infiltration by those knowing the area. IV Corps, assuming it was still fresh if deployed to support the VII Corps offensive, could then move on to destroy the German VII Corps, using the light tanks of its 2nd Armoured Division to probe weaknesses and conduct raids. In the meantime fresh infantry divisions and artillery could also have been brought in to relieve the XII Corps ones and these could conduct their own attacks, though without the likelyhood of any real armoured support. Their key role, however, would be to maintain the defences stretching from Tenterden to Dover via Ashford, with the heaviest fighting likely to be around Ashford and the North Downs to the west of Dover. Without a working port or secured anchorage the German High Command would be unlikely to commit the landing of its second wave. Therefore, if the high ground west of Folkestone could be held by the British and its heavy artillery stay in range of the beaches then the German XIII Corps would also be doomed. The Germans would have the advantage of a shorter and better controlled sea crossing and greater air support direct from the Continent, whilst the 22nd Airlanding Division could possibly be flown in, either in part or as a whole. If this was done then the Luftwaffe would also seek to have its airborne troops relieved, even if this meant at the expense of Army operations.

If the British Army's counter offensive failed to achieve all or most of its objectives there is likely to have been a lull in offensive operations by both sides, unless IV Corps was then committed if it had not already done so. The Germans would most likely still be trying to shuttle their armoured forces and the rest of the Second Wave across the Channel and then preparing them for the breakout, while husbanding their present resources. Records show that in Sixteenth Army, XLI Panzer Corps was to embark from Antwerp and V Corps from Rotterdam, with these forces planning to land at Dover, Folkestone, Rye and Hastings; the latter was to have its pier repaired and breakwater utilised. As the German plans estimated this would take nearly a month, the British would be need to use this time to reorganise and re-equip, no doubt replacing worn out units with fresh reserves from around the country.

Again, it would have been important for both sides to retain the initiative during this period, including operations behind the front lines. This is when the Auxiliary Units needed to show their worth, carrying out their range of destructive operations and hopefully reporting on German movements. In the air there is unlikely to be any real lull as both sides would continue in their attempts to secure supremacy over the battlefield; in addition the Luftwaffe would also be seeking to further destroy Britain's will and capacity to resist by attacking the cities, transport hubs and vital factories while the RAF would be attacking the embarkation ports, airfields and supply infrastructure. Both air forces would already be seeking a compromise between the level of operations demanded and the hope of husbanding their dwindling resources. By this time, the Navy would also need to consider husbanding their ships, especially the destroyers and cruisers, while continuing to disrupt the German supply chain across the Channel. The shipyards would be very busy, hoping to produce new warships and quickly repair damaged ones. Hopefully most of these shore facilities would still be out of the range of the Germans.

The third phase would begin when the German Army felt itself ready to resume the offensive in order to gain their First Operational Objective, a line running from the Thames Estuary to Southampton. Given the shipping plans available, this would be unlikely before mid October at the earliest. It was expected that the two Panzer Corps would lead the breakout - XLI Panzer Corps (Sixteenth Army) probably aiming for the Tunbridge Wells-Tonbridge area and XV Panzer Corps (Ninth Army) aiming for the Guildford area.

Sixteenth Army plans show that the newly arrived V Corps would be responsible for clearing the north Kent coast, including the Isle of Thanet, and the A20 road corridor up to and including Maidstone; XIII Corps was to cross the Kentish Weald, aiming for Sevenoaks and Tonbridge, while VII Corps would concentrate on taking Tunbridge Wells before moving on to Redhill. Opposing these breakout forces would be the responsibility of XII Corps, unless it had been relieved, though it is doubtful whether any of its original units would still be under its command.

Although Ninth Army plans do not remain it is likely that they would have been similar to those of Sixteenth Army, with XXXVIII Corps aiming for the Guildford area, X Corps the Haslemere area and VIII Corps along the coast and South Downs to Portsmouth. To oppose these forces there would still be V Corps, probably reinforced by the Southern Command Reserve. In addition the GHQ Reserve would probably be located southwest of London, their losses hopefully replaced and units re-invigorated. Eastern Command may well have provided more forces in operations south of London; XI Corps Headquarters, 15th and 52nd Divisions being the best placed to intervene. Other reinforcing divisions would no doubt be readily available, as could a fresh Corps headquarters.

The ability of the Army to prevent a breakout would not only depend on the strength and leadership of the defending forces but also on the frontages these units would have to cover; too often in the defensive battles fought by the BEF had the infantry battalions been forced to deploy along too wide a front, with inadequate defensive obstacles or support in depth. They had however, been able to contain most of the frontal attacks that they had faced and, in doing so, had once more earned the grudging admiration of their enemy for their tenacity. The War Diary of the German XLI Corps on 27 May could very easily be transposed to this period. It read "Fighting for individual houses and villages prevented the Corps from gaining ground. Losses in men and equipment are grievous. The enemy fights with determination and stays in his positions until the last moment; if he is expelled from one point then appears a little later at some other and takes up the fight again". It would be vital that the remaining British armoured forces once again be able to counter the most serious penetrations, operating as a cohesive force rather than distributed in small packets supporting the infantry.

With the intelligence facilities still at his disposal, Alan Brooke would be aware of this impending offensive and, as such, would be faced with two stark choices - either order his remaining forces to hold their lines as best as possible while organising such local counter attack forces that could still be mustered, or conduct a fighting withdrawal to the nearest GHQ and Command stop lines, using the nodal defence points and demolitions to slow or canalise

German advances, allowing for time to bring up whatever reserves could be found. Given the fighting instructions he had previously issued and his style of command it is probable that he would have allowed his commanders at the front the flexibility to conduct their own operations so as to make the best of the situation they faced. Certainly, the choices made would further increase the heavy political pressure on Churchill and Alan Brooke to succeed in preventing such a breakout. With the landing of the main panzer forces and the rest of the Second Wave any concerns that the British may have had that other major landings were still likely to occur would have had to be finally discarded. If they were not already of the opinion that the beachhead already carved out must be destroyed at all costs, they would be now.

The Army Commands would be required to give up their best equipped units, while still being required to prepare for operations in their region, if they had not already done so. From the dispositions of the rest of the Army outside the southeast, Northern Command could most readily provide 44th Division in I Corps (and possibly its 2nd Division) and possibly X Corps' 42nd Division. In addition Western Command's III Corps could be moved southeast and concentrated so as to cover Bristol and the West Midlands, relieving Southern Command of that responsibility. Neither London District nor Aldershot Command would have been able to provide any major combat formations but would have been better suited to provide much needed administrative support for those fighting and those arriving in the area. Alan Brooke would also be forced to take vital equipment, especially artillery, from those divisions remaining in place around the country to replace the heavy losses that would already have been incurred. He would also need Britain's war industry to continue production and delivery as quickly as possible; fortunately most of the armaments industry had already been relocated away from the southeast and the transport network was expected still to be flexible enough to cope with the demands laced on it.

As mentioned, the panzer divisions were to be at the forefront of the German offensive, in accordance with the blitzkrieg doctrine. However feared these were, and there was a healthy fear of them rampaging across the country, it was clear to all that they were only effective as long as they had fuel, ammunition and spare parts, all of which had to be shipped over and kept safe against saboteurs. It was well known that if these tanks were isolated they became increasingly vulnerable and, as such, much emphasis was placed on engaging these at every occasion with tank hunting parties. These tactics could work if properly co-ordinated and supported, with the troops and commanders needing to keep their composure in the face of such an onslaught and proper use of the defence stop lines. In any case, it is very unlikely that the British Army would have collapsed in the way their Continental allies had. Even in the face of defeat they would mean to fight on, supported by the people, but only if they retained the means to do so.

Even at this late stage not all would necessarily be lost. The main factor influencing British resistance at this time would have been political, and revolved around the ability of Churchill to have withstood the undoubtedly growing opposition to his leadership. Certainly, it is unlikely that any other senior political figure would have kept the British fighting for so long. Morale would have been an important factor. It would hope to remain quite high, as the British character tends to grow through adversity. Certainly, this period would have been the most testing that it would have to face. This, coupled with the British armed forces still fighting desperately, would have meant that the Germans would have faced armed opposition wherever they went, even behind their lines, despite the obvious reprisals this would have entailed for the civilian population remaining in the overrun areas. The Waffen SS had already committed atrocities in its campaigns, notably of captured soldiers, where they had been repulsed or suffered heavy casualties; given the ferocity of the fighting expected it would not be long before such atrocities occurred again, the Army's leadership being powerless to interfere, as the Waffen SS and security forces were not responsible to them in matters of discipline.

Given the terrain and numbers of German troops available a continuous front would not be practical and so, using local knowledge supplied by the Home Guard, slipping reinforcements and additional special forces, such as the Army Commandos and Independent Companies, into the German rear would have been feasible. The Royal Signals had already trained special "stay behind" parties equipped with radios that would report on enemy movements and help bring down artillery fire on them. The Germans might also have been feeling frustrated that their vaunted superiority had so far been thwarted, as well as being concerned at the heavy losses in both manpower and equipment they must have suffered so far. Above all, there would have been a growing concern over the time lag in their planning. The longer the Operation took to complete the worse the weather would get, leaving its forces in Great Britain more dependent on what could be transported across the Channel in shipping, already reduced by losses, largely to beaches exposed to the elements; the handful of ports captured would most likely still be blocked and their installations destroyed or at least severely damaged and which could still be under continuing attacks.

In their appreciation of the German preparations for an invasion, produced in 1942, the War Office estimated that initial port capacity for Dover and Folkestone once captured would be about 150 tons a day, rising to 800 and 600 tons respectively after seven days; equally they estimated that 5200 tons of supplies could be landed a day across the beaches from Dungeness to Hythe, based on 52 barges unloading at a time. Bringing in supplies and reinforcements by air would have been easier though this alone could not keep an Army operational as the heavy equipment needed could not be easily airlifted; indeed, General von Rundstedt later agreed that the system of air supply was not sufficiently developed in 1940 for this possibility to be considered. Given detailed preparations by the British to destroy anything likely to be of value to the enemy, especially fuel, and the obvious enthusiasm such activity would have warranted, it is hoped that little of use would likely have been captured or be in immediate working order.

Even if the Germans achieved their First Operational Objective it is feasible that they would be unwilling or unable to proceed with further offensive operations unless the political or military situation warranted it. They could have thought that the ground gained would be sufficient for them to defend through the coming winter, so allowing for another build up of forces to complete Operation Sea Lion. By now, Sixteenth Army would have closed up to London, the Capital protected by the high ground of the North Downs lying to its south. In doing so they would have broken the main GHQ Line, leaving very little in the way of field fortifications to bar the way. However, it would be wary of getting sucked in to fighting within the metropolis. Ninth Army would need to concentrate on capturing Portsmouth, though the Royal Navy would have abandoned this port (its spiritual home) as a main base of operations by this time and prepared it for demolition, while the garrison continued to strengthen its defences. No doubt some of the British would be looking at the Isle of Wight to become a fortress island, even if

Portsmouth fell. It would need significant increases in resources to make this viable and that is unlikely to have happened.

The Second Operational Objective involved the occupation of London and securing a line running from Maldon in Essex to Gloucester, via St Albans and Oxford, with the boundary between the two armies extending from to Banbury via Windsor. Of these towns Sixteenth Army was to be responsible for Windsor and Ninth Army for Banbury. Sixteenth Army was to act as the pivot, with Ninth Army moving in a north-westerly direction. Sixteenth Army was expected to force its way, still led by its Panzer Corps, through a narrow corridor to the west of London before looping around the north of the Capital, while other forces from the Army would aim to penetrate the Capital from the south. These operations would entail a considerable amount of urban fighting; although Headquarters London District only had an initial force of three infantry brigades, plus garrison units, Anti Aircraft Command and Home Guard, to protect the Capital, it would likely have other units that would have been forced back into it, especially from the south and west. These forces, together with the terrain involved, would require all the resources of the Sixteenth Army to overcome. London, unlike Paris and Brussels, would not be declared an "Open City" and so would be defended with all the tenacity and ingenuity that the defenders could muster.

The London Area Home Defence Scheme dated 4 July provides detail of how the Capital was to be defended. There were three continuous defence lines – an outer perimeter line, an intermediate line up to five miles inside the outer line and an inner line running from the River Lea in the east, along the River Thames to Hammersmith then north through East Acton, then along the Grand Junction Canal and the River Brent to Dollis Hill and Finsbury Park. In addition there were three switch lines: along the River Thames from Hammersmith to Kingston, along the River Lea from Walthamstow to Waltham Abbey and along the River Thames from the junction of the River Lea to Erith. The Home Guard was tasked with manning the perimeter and intermediate defences and road/rail blocks, while the London District troops would be responsible for the inner line. Instructions were to hold all posts to the last man, noting that the success of defending a built up area was to force the enemy to fight continuously, with the network of small posts creating an effective defence, if held with determination. North and South Sub Area headquarters were authorised to initiate and conduct operations with their own available resources, until either of the assigned infantry brigades were instructed to take over. The three infantry brigades would be held as the District's strategic reserve.

Ninth Army would be faced with crossing the River Thames to the west of London and breaking through the GHQ Blue and Red Lines, the last real defensive barrier in the south for the British. However, this Army might not be strong enough to achieve this Objective and protect its open left flank at the same time. With these considerations in mind the Army Group would probably have to delay major offensive operations to achieve the Second Operational Objective until the Third Wave had been landed and deployed. As already mentioned, these forces could include the Sixth Army, who could then carry out its intended role of securing southwest England, thereby protecting the Ninth Army's left flank.

Given such considerations it is not beyond the realms of possibility that the Operation could have stalled, with the onset of winter producing a stalemate, as neither side could have been strong enough to destroy the other. The British Army would have been exhausted and desperately short of essential equipment like tanks and artillery. These could be replaced; the manufacturing plants should still have been largely safe as they were mostly away from the threatened areas and duplicated, while manpower was easier to replace, albeit with much reduced training and experience. The Royal Navy was still likely to be a major threat that could be reinforced from its overseas stations (the first four of the US Lend-Lease destroyers arrived at Belfast from Canada on 26 September); if not already done so Force M, recovering from the unsuccessful Dakar operation, could be recalled and committed as it was the other main strike force the Royal Navy possessed outside the Home Fleet and Mediterranean Fleet. The RAF could also still have the capacity to regenerate, as its training facilities and aircraft factories were also mainly located away from the southeast, though they would now be probably well within bomber range.

By now, the reality of the Operation is that the British could not aim to destroy the invading forces on land during 1940, although it could continue limited offensive operations throughout the winter months. The key of the defence remained preventing the Germans from establishing or maintaining an efficient supply system. It could do this by continuing to constantly attack the Continental embarkation ports and shipping, preventing the capture of a working port or the putting of one back into operation and attacking any airfields lost or newly established. Although the German Army was later to demonstrate an ability to maintain operations with a greatly reduced tonnage of supplies, it would have been tested severely in this scenario.

If Operation Sea Lion had succeeded?

If the Germans had been successful in attaining most of their objectives and Winston Churchill replaced by a less warlike leader the British may have had to accept a ceasefire, similar to that imposed on the French and which allowed for a Vichy style Government to be installed. This would certainly have been preferable to many in the political establishments of both sides - the British would claim to have retained some of their sovereignty while the Germans would have avoided the problem of committing large numbers of troops and resources to subjugating a hostile population for an indefinable period of time.

If Britain had fallen, or a puppet government installed, could its armed forces continue the war outside of the United Kingdom if there remained the political and moral will to do so? Plans had already been drafted to move much of the Royal Navy to eastern Canada, to join the Royal Family and the country's economic reserves, whilst other units would have gone to the Mediterranean, to strengthen the Fleet already there. The Navy's traditional role was to ensure the Empire's maritime communications were kept intact and it would still be tasked to continue that vital role, as without secure maritime routes communication and military deployments would be impossible (By March 1941 over 600,000 service personnel had been shipped safely throughout the world); to achieve this role it had invested in fleet bases in the Mediterranean (Gibraltar covered the North Atlantic), at Colombo (Sri Lanka, covering the East Indies), Freetown (Sierra Leone,covering the South Atlantic), Simonstown (South Africa) and Singapore (with Hong Kong, responsible for the Far East). In addition, Bermuda was the station responsible for the United States and West Indies, supported by the key convoy base at Halifax in Canada). These could now be expected to play increased roles in maintaining the security at sea. The following table provides a list of the British and Commonwealth main warships by area in late September 1940:

Area	Main bases	Ships
Mediterranean	Alexandria, Malta	5 battleships, 1 aircraft carrier, 2 heavy cruisers (*), 2 AA cruisers, 4 light cruisers (1 RAN), 22 destroyers (5 RAN), 11 submarines
North Atlantic	Gibraltar	1 battlecruiser, 9 destroyers
North Atlantic	At sea	1 aircraft carrier, 2 light cruisers, 8 destroyers (1 RCN)
USA/Canada	Halifax	9 armed merchant cruisers, 20 destroyers (9 RCN)
Caribbean	Bermuda, Trinidad	2 light cruisers, 4 armed merchant cruisers, 2 sloops
South Atlantic	Freetown, Simonstown	1 battlecruiser, 1 heavy cruiser, 3 light cruisers, 13 armed merchant cruisers, 2 sloops
Red Sea	Aden	1 battleship, 1 heavy cruiser, 5 light cruisers (1 RAN), 1 armed merchant cruiser, 3 destroyers, 1 submarine, 8 sloops (3 RIN)
Indian Ocean	Colombo	1 aircraft carrier, 1 heavy cruiser (RAN), 4 light cruisers, 3 armed merchant cruisers (2 RAN)
Far East	Singapore, Hong Kong	6 light cruisers (2 RAN, 1 RNZN), 6 armed merchant cruisers (2 RNZN, 1 RAN), 5 destroyers, 1 sloop (RAN)

Notes:
(*) HMS Kent had been badly damaged and required extensive repairs
RAN =Royal Australian Navy, RCN = Royal Canadian Navy, RNZN = Royal New Zealand Navy, RIN= Royal Indian Navy

In addition to the surviving ships of the Home Fleet there were a significant number of warships that had been launched and were being completed throughout this period, mainly in the major shipbuilding centres of the Tyne, Clyde, Barrow in Furness, Belfast and Birkenhead. These included three battleships, two aircraft carriers, seven cruisers, fifteen destroyers and six submarines. It is safe to assume that the Navy would have made significant efforts to move these vessels across the Atlantic, so they could be completed.

The French ships immobilised in Alexandria since July 1940 could in theory have been taken over but would have required the support of the French crews and officials to achieve this. Assuming this was successful an old battleship, four cruisers, three destroyers and several small vessels could have been added to the operational Mediterranean Fleet.

Many of the Royal Air Force's aircraft had the range to reach Iceland and some possibly Canada; however, at the main airport at Reykjavik reconstruction from a grass runway to one capable of taking large aircraft only began in October 1940, while facilities were basic and unable to cope with large numbers of aircraft for some time. In addition, Iceland would have been within range of the larger German bombers and fighters. Arrangements to evacuate vital machine tools, skilled personnel and construction plans to rebuild this vital force would have been made (plans to create a major RAF training organisation in Canada and other territories were already well advanced by this time), but there were no existing facilities to enable this to happen yet in either Iceland or Canada. The RAF in the Middle East was its largest deployment outside the United Kingdom. In June 1940 twenty nine squadrons (including fourteen bomber, four coastal and five fighter squadrons) were deployed to cover the Middle and Near East, totalling about three hundred first line aircraft (eighty aircraft were in Kenya, fifty in Sudan and fifty in Aden). Half of these were based in Egypt but only nine Blenheim and two Sunderland equipped squadrons could be considered as having modern aircraft, the fighters depending on the Gloster Gladiator biplane and the bombers on a varied collection of largely obsolete aircraft. Its primary task was the defence of Egypt and the Suez Canal and maintenance of communication through the Red Sea and was to prove effective against the Italian forces. It did not however yet have a local aircraft industry to help with keeping the air force operational. The RAF had already began addressing the need to provide reinforcements – long range aircraft could reach Egypt via Gibraltar and Malta, while from 5 September shorter range aircraft were shipped to Takoradi in the Gold Coast for re-assembling then flying across the continent, reducing the risks and time of shipping them around South Africa. This cross-country route could still provide the lifeline should the RAF be forced to relocate to Canada, for example.

The War Office conducted a secret review early in summer, asking senior commanders how the British Army would react to being evacuated if the country fell. Their response was that whilst they felt the Regular Army would obey the main bulk of the Army would probably opt to remain so as to be with their families. Certainly, there would have been enough shipping space for all those wishing to leave but the Army would have been almost entirely without the equipment, supplies and industrial base to remain operational, at least until alternatives had been acquired or built.

In late September the British Army had over 173,000 men serving overseas, a figure nearly matched by the Empire and Commonwealth troops deployed outside India; of these, the largest number -155,300 men - were located in the Middle and Near East and had been steadily reinforced throughout 1940. Middle East Command was set up before the war to provide a centralised Army command structure encompassing the Middle East, East Africa and eastern Mediterranean theatres; General Sir Archibald Wavell commanded it. A triumvirate was established to form a High Command, bringing together the three services, to co-ordinate military activities in this most vital region. All three senior commanders got on well, were highly regarded and would prove to be very successful. The Middle East provided the British Army's only other sizeable and active field force, including its third operational armoured division (7th), but it had very little in the way of a military or industrial base to continue a struggle alone (in January 1940 the British Cabinet agreed to establishing base organisations in Egypt and Palestine) and was beginning to look at India to provide an alternative source of logistical support. On 13 September the Italians began their brief advance into both Egypt and East Africa. Significant Indian, South African and African forces were quickly sent to Kenya and Sudan to counter the minor advances and prepare for its November counter offensive, whilst the Western Defence Force did the same in western Egypt. Additionally, the British were faced with significant Egyptian unrest due to its occupation of the country – although the country remained neutral many of its people were pro German.

The Empire and Commonwealth was already providing significant military forces in the region. In February 1940 Australian and New Zealand units had began arriving; in April the 4th

Indian Infantry Division was expected to be ready for operations in the region by the start of July, though this was dependent on the ability of the Indian authorities to devote the whole of the military production capacity to equip it. Later the War Office accepted a pledge from the Indians to create and maintain a three division Corps in the Near East in order to protect the vital oilfields in the region (2nd Division was formed in Iraq and 5th Divison sent to Sudan in early September), while an Australian Corps of two divisions (6th and 7th) would also be available, initially in Palestine from October. Two African divisions (1st and 2nd) had been formed in July 1940 for service in East Africa, while the 1st South African Division was formed in August and reached Kenya in November (the 2nd Division was formed in October 1940). In May 1940 three South African Airforce squadrons flew into Kenya.

The War Office produced the following table in September 1940, showing the army's actual garrison strength overseas and what was considered necessary for their survival.

Present Garrison	**Garrison considered necessary**	**Reinforcements proposed**
Middle East (includes Egypt, Palestine, Sudan, Aden and East Africa): One armoured division (7th in Egypt) One cavalry division (1st in Palestine) One infantry division (6th in Egypt) One African division (1st in East Africa) One under strength Indian division (4th in Egypt) One under strength Australian division (6th in Palestine) One under strength New Zealand division (2nd in Egypt) One under strength South African division (1st in East Africa) One British, African and Indian brigade each 23 local defence battalions	Two armoured divisions One cavalry division Three infantry divisions Two infantry brigades	One Corps headquarters One armoured division (2nd) One Indian division (5th) The rest of the Australian and New Zealand divisions Two Indian brigades One British brigade Three African brigades
West Africa: Local garrison troops only	Four infantry brigades	Four African and one British brigades

| Far East: One under strength division (9th Indian) | Three infantry divisions | Two divisions, one from Australia |

GHQ India, commanded by General Sir Robert Cassels since 1935, was also largely a garrison organisation and was charged with preparing a growing Indian Army for overseas operations (9th and 11th Divisions were formed in mid September for deployment to Malaya and 7th and 8th Divisions formed in early October). Traditionally the Indian Army was deployed on its northwest frontier, was available for operations in the Middle, Near and Far East. Malaya Command, commanded by Lieutenant General Sir Lionel Bond, was mainly a garrison organisation, which had had some of its best units removed and replaced by largely untrained Indian Army units, headed by III Indian Corps.

In June 1940 the War Office took over responsibility for the defence of West Africa, with an Army Command being established at Accra, Gold Coast. In the region, the port of Freetown was considered strategically most vital.

An important, yet often ignored, base to potentially continue resistance was Iceland, the Army having a division sized garrison in occupation since mid May. This garrison was largely made up from the 49th (West Riding) Infantry Division, whose units had already served in the Norwegian Campaign, and was known as Alabaster Force. A much smaller group, Valentine Force, garrisoned the Faeroe Isles. Both territories were Danish sovereignty and their Government, which had remained with the Royal Family in occupied Denmark, denounced this occupation. The British had decided to occupy the islands to both deny the enemy from using them and to establish a potential advance base for naval operations on Iceland. Indeed, the Germans had also seen the potential of Iceland and had considered plans to seize it after the fall of Norway in June. The island could have made a suitable advanced base of operations for the British against its own homeland as it was sufficiently removed from Europe to protect it from heavy sea and air attack, yet well positioned to support offensive and clandestine operations. As already mentioned, it was not, however, even partly developed at this stage to undertake such a role, lacking both port and airfield facilities and often had to contend with bad weather.

Undoubtedly, the embryo of a resistance organisation would have been in place in the United Kingdom, using the Auxiliary Units as a basis, though how long this could remain effective would be another of those great unknowns. Even those elements of the armed forces who sought the protection of a neutral Irish Republic, notably the 64,000 troops already in Northern Ireland, may not have been safe as it is unlikely that the Germans would have allowed these to remain a potential threat and so rejoin the war effort. The Irish Republic was a member of the British Commonwealth but recognised the reality of its position. Whilst the United Kingdom remained an unconquered nation it was happy to covertly support its war effort, but with a successful invasion it would have had to acquiesce to German demands, such as the surrender of any British troops, aircraft and vessels within its territory and which could also have included the stationing of naval and air units within its territory. After the fall of France in June British political envoys secretly mooted the proposal of ending the partition of Ireland if the Republic was to join the war effort against the Axis nations. This failed as it would have required Ulster political support, which would never have been given. However, with the imminent fall of the United Kingdom, would such a proposal have been accepted? It would not be worth the Germans effort to countermand this move as they would still have a degree of overlordship of Ireland in any case and so it could work in their favour, leaving it to the Dublin Government to control a hostile Ulster without requiring a significant garrison of their own.

It would also have been essential to establish new supply and support bases for the forces already overseas quickly, as these had traditionally relied on Britain's industrial base to provide them with most of their requirements and, without these they would have been hard put to defend themselves. Indeed, Canada had already been emptied of most of its weapons and equipment (it was already buying old or obsolete equipment from America) and its Army, though receiving a large influx of volunteers, was in no real state to defend itself let alone conduct any offensive operations (a 3rd Infantry Division was still forming in late 1940 while a 4th Division had been authorised. An Armoured Corps was established in August 1940 and as a result an armoured brigade was despatched to the United Kingdom in June 1941).

Nevertheless, those British and Commonwealth forces in Canada would have been left in relative peace by the axis forces, given the distance from Europe; but they would be heavily reliant on the political and economic support of the United States to sustain them. Those in the Mediterranean and East Africa theatres would no doubt have faced the combined power of Germany and Italy; whilst the British and Commonwealth forces were to demonstrate their ability to overcome the Italians they would have faced a severe challenge to defeat both with a much reduced supply base. Forces elsewhere around the world would continue to be sidelined, hoping at best to check the expansion designs of an increasingly bold Japan. The Empire and Commonwealth would also have to contend with an unhappy Vichy France. Although its navy had largely been made ineffective due to the July attacks it retained potentially strong colonial forces in territories around the world that could impact significantly on the integrity of the far flung British Empire, particularly in Syria, western Africa and in closing the western Mediterranean.

Despite all this, the most important factor would have been the will to continue the War, both in political and military terms, wherever necessary and whatever the cost.

Appendix 1

BRITISH ARMY ORDER OF BATTLE

The British Army in the Home Forces can be split into two types of formation - the Field Army and Home Command Troops. The former were the combat troops organised into formations from Brigade up to Corps level; the latter were mainly training or support units under the operational control of Command, District or Sub Area headquarters. All units were expected to have an anti invasion role, the most common being anti parachute operations.

For ease of reference the information provided below includes the unit's title, major location, personnel strength and equipment state. Those senior officers marked with an asterix had served with the British Expeditionary Force, many having been promoted since their return.

Glossary of terms

The following abbreviations have been used:
GOC: General Officer Commanding   CO: Commanding Officer

KOSB = King's Own Scottish Borderers   KOYLI = King's Own Yorkshire Light Infantry
KRRC = King's Royal Rifle Corps
OBLI = Oxford and Buckinghamshire Light Infantry

RHA = Royal Horse Artillery   RTR = Royal Tank Regt

ATS = Auxiliary Territorial Service (Womens Army service)

Regt = Regiment   Bn = Battalion
Coy = Company   Bty = Battery
Plt = Platoon   Stn = Section

ADS = Advanced Dressing Station   CCS = Casualty Clearing Station

A/T = Anti Tank   A/A = Anti Aircraft

EOD = Explosive Ordnance Disposal (Bomb Disposal)

HAA = Heavy Anti Aircraft   LAA = Light Anti Aircraft

IPTC = Infantry Pioneer Training Centre   ITC = Infantry Training Centre

LAD = Light Aid Detachment

LofC = Line of Communications

MG = Machine Gun   M/C = Motor Cycle
MGTC = Machine Gun Training Centre

MNBDO = Marine Naval Base Defence Organisation
OCTU = Officer Cadet Training Unit

THE WAR OFFICE
Whitehall, London

Chief of the Imperial General Staff: General Sir John Dill
Vice Chief of the Imperial General Staff: Lieutenant General Sir Robert Haining
Director of Military Operations and Plans (DMO): Major General R Drewing
Adjutant General: Lieutenant General Sir Walter Venning
Quartermaster General: Lieutenant General H Wemyss
Director of Military Intelligence (DMI): Major General F Beaumont-Nesbitt
Director of Military Training (DMT): Major General C Maldern

NOTES:
- *General Sir John Dill had been Deputy CIGS from April 1940 until he replaced General Ironside in early June. Before April he had been commander of the BEF's I Corps*
- *The Vice CIGS had been appointed on 27 May. He retired in 1942*
- *The Adjutant General, DMO, DMI and DMT had all been in post since the start of the War.*

GENERAL HEADQUARTERS, HOME FORCES
HQ: St Paul's School, Hammersmith, London (Advance HQ -Office of Works, Whitehall)
(170+488, including 150 ATS and civilians)

Commander in Chief: General Sir Alan Brooke* (from 20 July)
Chief of the General Staff: Lieutenant General B Paget
Adjutant General: Lieutenant General Sir W Lindsell
Master Gunner: Major General S Archibald

NOTE:
- *General Paget had commanded British forces in the Aandalsnes sector of Norway. He was to take over from General Brooke in 1941*
- *General Lindsell had been the BEF's Quartermaster General. In 1942 he was to take over command of administration in the Middle East.*

EASTERN COMMAND (GOC: Lieutenant General Sir Guy Williams)
HQ: Luton, Bedfordshire

NOTE:
Sir Guy Williams had commanded the 5th Division until 1938 when appointed to this command. He retired in 1941.

XII CORPS (GOC: Lieutenant General Andrew Thorne*)
HQ: Tunbridge Wells, Kent (HQ: 50+685)

NOTES:
- *The two Corps stop lines ran from Graveney (near Faversham) to Dover via Blean and Adisham and was positioned to cover the north east Kent coast, while the other ran along the*

Royal Military Canal from Hythe to near Rye before following the River Rother to near Uckfield. A branch stop line ran from Ham Street to Charing via Ashford
- On 2 August 29th Brigade Group came under command as Corps reserve
- On 5 September the NZEF moved to the Maidstone area and came under command
- On 28 September 31st Brigade Group arrived in the Tenterden area, becoming responsible for the defence of the Royal Military Canal
- On 4 November the NZEF moved back to Aldershot
- General Thorne had held a wide variety of posts before the War, notably GOC London Command (1938-39) before commanding 48th Division in the BEF. In June he was promoted to command this Corps. In 1941 he was appointed to command Scottish Command.

- 1st London Division (GOC: Major General Claude Liardet)
HQ: Eastwell Park, Ashford, Kent (Rear HQ: Pett Place, Charing)
1st London Brigade: *(HQ: Kent College, Canterbury)* (GOC: Brigadier C Britten)
1 (City of London) Royal Fusiliers *(Herne Bay; Z Coy: Beltinge) (36+882)*
2 (City of London) Royal Fusiliers *(Sturry; A Coy: Ickham, B Coy: Stodmarsh, C Coy: Chislet, D Coy: Tyler Hill) (32+827)*
1 London Irish *(Hernhill; A Coy: Goodnestone, B Coy: Boughton, C Coy: Seasalter, D Coy: Graveney) (32+832)*
Brigade A/T Coy *(Harbledown)*, LAD RAOC *(Sturry)* plus D Coy 70 Buffs *(Whitstable)*.
2nd London Brigade: *(HQ: Postling Court)* (GOC: Brigadier G Portman)
1 London Scots *(Bridge; A and B Coys: Broome Park, C Coy: Goodnestone, D Coy: Eastry) (33+865)*
1 London Rifle Brigade *(Lyminge; A and D Coys: Shorncliffe, C Coy: Arpinge) (37+904)*
1 Queen`s Westminster Rifles *(Shepherdswell; HQ Coy: Denton, A Coy: Coldred, B Coy: Eythorne, D Coy: Kingsdown) (30+777)* (Mobile column consisted C Coy, M/C Plt (28 m/c), Carrier Plt *(7 carriers)* and Tank Hunter Plt (27 cycles))
Brigade A/T Coy *(Horton Park)*; LAD RAOC *(Elham)*.
35th Infantry Brigade: *(HQ: Norton Court, Faversham)* (GOC: Brigadier E Hayes)
2/5 Queens *(Kennington; A Coy: Eastwell Park, Ashford, B and C Coys: Wye racecourse; D Coy: Olantigh, Wye) (35+969)*
2/6 Queens *(Minster, Sheppey; A Coy: Eastchurch, C Coy: Kingsferry Bridge) (35+966)*
2/7 Queens *(Ospringe; A Coy: Painter`s Forstal, B and E Coys: Teynham, C Coy: Oare, D Coy: Faversham) (33+1003)*
Brigade A/T Coy *(Newnham)*, C2 Mobile Field Bty *(Sheerness) (2+60) (2x12-pdr, 2x3-pdr)*, C6 Mobile Field Bty *(Warden, less 1 Section at Faversham) (4+127) (4x4-inch)*.
198th Infantry Brigade: *(HQ: Sarre)* (GOC: Brigadier J Rawcliffe)
1/6 Border *(St Nicholas at Wade; C Coy: Birchington, D Coy: Manston) (32+874)*
1/7 Border *(Margate; A and D Coys: Westgate, C Coy: Broadstairs) (34+801)*
1/8 Kings *(Ramsgate; B Coy: Sandwich, D Coy: Pegwell Bay) (32+894)*
Brigade A/T Coy *(Sarre)*; Brigade Coy RASC *(Westbere) (8+183)*
5 Independent Coy *(Manston) (300)*
Plus B Coy 6 Buffs *(Ramsgate)*.
Divisional Troops:
RA: 64 Field Regt *(Acrise) (253 and 254 Btys: 8x75mm, 4x25-pdr, 8x4.5-inch, 2x13-pdr) (39+538)*,
90 Field Regt *(Petham) (35+564) (357 and 258 Btys: 4x25-pdr, 2x13-pdr, 4x4.5-inch, 4x75mm)*,
113 Field Regt *(St Nicholas at Wade, Minster) (2x18-pdr, 4x4.5-inch) (34+536)*; 115 Army Field Regt *(Ashford) (50+874) (5 mobile Btys: C1: London, C2: Chatham, C4: Boughton - 2x12-*

pdr, 2x3-pdr each), C5: Barham(4x4-inch) and C6: Isle of Sheppey (4x4-inch) and X Static Bty (Whitstable, A Stn: Kingsdown, B Stn: Ramsgate) (4x4-inch) (6+110) (also an infantry group of the Regt at Gatwick (5+202); 67 A/T Regt (Smeeth - 265 Bty (Barham (4x6-pdr) and Sandwich (2x6-pdr), 266 Bty (Willesborough), 267 Bty (Godinton), 268 Bty (Detling, infantry role)) (28+468) (16x2-pdr, 6x6-pdr); 74 Medium Regt (Sutton Valence) (32+671) (A Bty: Sutton Valence as mobile reserve (4x60-pdr), B Bty:Ash (4x60-pdr) with 198 Bde; C Bty: Hernhill (4x6-inch) supporting 1*st* London Bde; D Bty: Faversham (4x60-pdr) as mobile reserve);

1 Kensingtons (MG) (36+772) (Hothfield, A Coy: Whitstable (4 and 5 Plts), Horton Park (6 Plt), Westgate (7 Plt); B and C Coys: Hothfield; D Coy: Dover, Minster (Sheppey) (13 Plt); Reserve Plt: Leysdown) (12 MMG per coy); 15 Royal Fusiliers (Pioneer) (Dover/Deal) (27+804);

RE: 220 Field Coy (Harbledown) (5+232), 501 Field Coy (Sandling Park) (5+234), 563 Field Park Coy (Charing) (3+162);

RASC: 10 Coy (Canterbury) (3+114), Divisional Ammunition Coy (Pluckley) (6+374), Divisional Petrol Coy (Little Chart; Workshops at Charing and Petrol Plt at Stone Street) (5+301), Divisional Supply Coy (High Halden, 2nd Echelon at Godmersham and Depot at Tenterden) (15+432), 5 Troop Carry Coy (Womenswold) (9+338), 6 Troop Carry Coy (Faversham, sections at Herne, Whitstable and Kennington) (8+352);

RAMC: 140 Field Ambulance (Smeeth with ADS at Barham and Etchinghill) (11+239), 167 Field Ambulance (Canterbury with ADS at Boughton, Herne and Wingham) (9+236), 204 Light Field Ambulance (Ramsgate with ADS at St Nicholas and Broadstairs) (2+53), 214 Field Ambulance (Harrietsham with ADS at Otterden and Doddington) (11+245);

RAOC: Divisional LAD`s (Charing) (9+172);

CMP: Divisional Provost Coy (Ashford) (1+106).

NOTES:

- *This Division was a Territorial Army formation, which was allocated to home defence when the War began*
- *The Divisional rear boundary ran from Dymchurch Redoubt to the Isle of Sheppey via Headcorn, Sutton Vallence, Hollingbourne, Bredgar and Borden*
- *The Divisional reserve consisted of 2/5 Queens, 2 companies of 1 Kensington (mg) and a troop of 113 Field Regt. C Section 6 Troop Carry Company assigned*
- *Divisional roles were: 1.Defend beaches, 2.Occupy the Corps Line, 3.Prepare operations east and west of the Corps Line. The Division expected invasion to come along the north east Kent coast and disposed troops accordingly*
- *1*st *Brigade's role was, in order of priority, to defend the beaches in their area and conduct anti parachute operations (especially along the A2). It was also expected to occupy the Corps line, if required*
- *2*nd *Brigade's role was, in order of priority, to defend the beaches, defend Hawkinge, conduct anti parachute operations, counter attack towards Hythe, Dymchurch or St Margaret's Bay as appropriate, and occupy the Corps Line*
- *35*th *Brigade's role was split with the HQ and one battalion defending Faversham, conducting anti parachute operations; one battalion to defend the Isle of Sheppey to the last! (especially Eastchurch airfield and beaches) and one battalion to act as Divisional reserve*
- *198*th *Brigade's role was to defend Thanet, especially Manston airfield*
- *On 2 July 1 Kensington (MG) arrived at Ashford from London District. It had served with the ill fated 51*st *Highland Division in France but had escaped largely intact*

- By 13 July the Division had 98% Personnel, 45% artillery pieces, 0% A/T guns (June = 11x25-pdr, 4x18-pdr, 8x4.5-inch)
- 501 Field Company RE tasked with demolition of bridges over Royal Military Canal
- By 7 September the Division had 100% Personnel, 96% artillery pieces, 20% A/T guns
- Infantry battalions each had mortar, carrier, motorcycle and cycle mounted tank-hunting platoons. When on alert in September two thirds of the men slept at their battle positions while headquarters and supporting echelons were more dispersed due to dive bombing threat. Battalion headquarters were usually split into advanced and rear elements, the former consisting of the CO, Adjutant, RSM, most of the Signals Platoon and an intelligence group, totalling 2 officers and about 50 men carried in one armoured car, one car, 2 trucks, 3 buses and 3 motorcycles
- 1st London Brigade expected to move by the following routes if ordered to support 2nd London Brigade: to Dover or Folkestone via Watling Street (A2); to Lympne or Hythe via Stone Street and to Romney Marsh via the Ashford Road (A28), all staging through Canterbury
- On 30 September 115 Army Field Regt moved to Horsmonden and Paddock Wood to train new coast defence batteries, the mobile batteries being disbanded. Also, 4 Cheshire (MG) relieved 1 Kensington along the coast, allowing that unit to concentrate at Hothfield
- In early November the Division was replaced by 43rd Division and moved to Maidstone as Corps Reserve where it was renamed as 56th (London) Division
- The Commanding Officer had been in charge since 1938, having previously been in command of 2nd London Division and was the first Territorial officer to attain divisional command. The commanding officers of both the London and 198th Brigades had also been in charge since the outbreak of War. Brigadier Hayes replaced Brigadier V de Cordova on 9 August. General Liardet was appointed Inspector General of airfield defence in January 1941; Brigadier Hayes had previously commanded the Infantry Company Commander's School.

- 45th Infantry Division (GOC: Major General Edmond Schreiber)
HQ: Hawkhurst, Kent
134th Brigade: *(HQ: Mountfield)* (GOC: Brigadier W Michelmore)
1/6 Devons *(Battle; A Coy: Hastings, B Coy: St Leonards, C Coy: Baldslow with Mortar, Carrier, M/C and Tank Hunter Plts, D Coy: Pett and Cliff End) (34+890); (Plt A Coy 7 Devon (MG): Pett Level)*
1/8 Devons *(Little Common, Bexhill; A Coy: west Bexhill, B Coy: Cooden (reserve), C Coy: Normans Bay, D Coy: east Bexhill; Carrier Plt: Polegate; M/C Plt: Cooden) (35+891); (5 Plt A Coy 7 Devon (MG) along Bexhill sea front and Cooden)*
1 Royal Irish Fusiliers *(Rye; A Coy: Winchelsea, B Coy: Rye Harbour, C Coy: Camber, D Coy: Rye, X Coy: Winchelsea Beach; Carrier, M/C and Mortar Plts: Rye; B Echelon: Peasmarsh) (27+956); (Plt A Coy 7 Devon (MG) at Rye Harbour and Camber)*
Brigade A/T Coy *(Robertsbridge).*
135th Brigade: *(HQ: Ham Street)* (GOC: Brigadier A Newth)
1/5 Somerset Light Infantry *(Lydd; A and D Coys, Mortar, Carrier and M/C Plts: Lydd; B Coy: Brick Wall Farm, C Coy: Dungeness; B Echelon: Brookland) (32+832)*
1/6 Somerset Light Infantry *(Dymchurch; A Coy: St Mary's Bay, B Coy, HQ Coy and the Mortar Plt: Dymchurch; C Coy with the Carrier and M/C Plts and Rear HQ: Burmarsh, D Coy: Court at Street) (33+859)*
1/7 Somerset Light Infantry *(New Romney; A Coy: Greatstone, B and D Coys: Littlestone, C Coy: St Mary's in Marsh; Carrier and M/C Plts: New Romney; B Echelon: Ivychurch) (34+853)*
Plus 6 Commando *(Littlestone) (37+406)*; 3 Independent Coy *(Lydd) (300)*; 18 Royal Fusiliers

(Pioneers) *(Ham Street; A Coy: Appledore, B Coy: Bishops Wood, C Coy: Lydd, D Coy: Aldington)* *(27+843); (D Coy 1/7 Devon (MG) Dymchurch; plts at Aldington (13 Plt), New Romney (14 Plt), Greatstone (15 Plt), section at Littlestone).*

136th Brigade: *(HQ: Upper Dicker)* (GOC: Brigadier G Whitfield)

1/4 Duke of Cornwall`s Light Infantry *(Pevensey; A Coy: Langney Point, B and C Coys: Pevensey Beach, D Coy: Westham) (33+856); (7 Devon (MG): C Coy- Pevensey Castle (9 Plt) and two plts B Coy - Langney Point and Pevensey Bay)*

1/5 Duke of Cornwall`s Light Infantry *(Denton; A Coy: Bishopstone, B Coy: Newhaven East Beach and Tide Mills, C Coy: Denton, D Coy: Newhaven town and Fort; 14 Plt C Coy, Carrier and M/C Plts: South Heighton; B Echelon: Beddingham) (35+911) (C Coy 7 Devon (MG): 11 Plt at Bishopstone and at Newhaven Fort, B Coy - Plt at Cuckmere Haven (west side))*

1/9 Devon *(Willingdon; A Coy: Eastbourne (Martello Tower to Coastguard Station), B Coy: Birling Gap, C Coy: Eastbourne (Martello Tower to Langney Point), D Coy: Polegate, Stone Cross) (34+850) (Carrier, M/C and Tank Hunter Plts assigned to Brigade reserve) (7 Devon (MG): C Coy- 10 Plt at Friday Street, 12 Plt on Eastbourne sea front).*

Divisional Troops:

1/7 Devons (MG) *(Hawkhurst; A Coy: Bexhill to Rye (HQ at Brede), B Coy: Eastbourne to Pevensey and Cuckmere Haven, C Coy: Eastbourne to Newhaven, D Coy: Dymchurch to Littlestone (HQ at Dymchurch)) (34+801);*

5 Loyals (M/C) *(Wadhurst) (32+628) (Divisional reserve with 3 m/c coys and 4 scout car plts);*

RA: 55 Field Regt *(Woodchurch) (32+579) (373 Bty: A Troop - Lydd (4x75mm), B and C Troops – Honeychurch Farm (8x75mm); 374 Bty: D Troop - Old Romney (4x25-pdr), E Troop - New Romney (2x4.5-inch) and Burmarsh (2x4.5-inch), F Troop - Dungeness and Littlestone (1x18-pdr each) (Total: 4x4.5-inch, 12x75mm, 4x25-pdr, 2x18pdr));* 96 Field Regt *(Hailsham; Advanced HQ: Hankham) (36+554) (381Bty: A Troop (4x18/25-pdr) and C Troop (2x4.5-inch, 2x75mm) - Stone Cross, B Troop (4x4.5-inch) - Denton; 382 Bty: D and E Troops - Hampden Park, Willingdon (10x75mm), F Troop - Langney (2x75mm) & Seaford (2x75mm) (total: 6x4.5-inch, 14x75mm, 4x18/25-pdr,2x6-pdr),* 142 Army Field Regt *(Northiam) (33+530) (383 Bty: Northiam, A Troop - Gotham, Bexhill (4x4.5-inch), B Troop - Northiam (infantry role, 1x75mm at Rye lock in A/T role), C Troop - East Guldeford (2x4.5-inch) and French Court Farm, Pett (2x4.5-inch); 384 Bty: Playden, D Troop - Camber Castle (2x75mm) and Rye Harbour (2x75mm), E Troop - Rye (4x75mm), F Troop - Playden (4x18/25-pdr) (Total: 8x4.5-inch, 9x75mm, 4x18/25-pdr));* 69 A/T Regt *(Mayfield) (27+427) (273 Bty: Greatstone (8x4-inch), 274 Bty: New Romney (4x2-pdr), 275 Bty: Lydd (4x2-pdr), 276 Bty: Cuckmere (4x2-pdr); 1 Sound Ranging Bty/1 Survey Regt (Appledore)*

Plus E Armoured Train *(Tonbridge) (46) (2x6-pdr, 6 lmg and 2 a/t rifles) (operating east and south of Tonbridge);*

RE: 205 Field Coy *(Battle) (5+234),* 259 Field Coy *(Tenterden) (6+237);* 562 Field Coy *(Alfriston; sections at Upper Dicker, Newhaven, Seaford and Pevensey) (5+257),* 261 Field Park Coy *(Lamberhurst) (3+194);*

RASC: Divisional Supply Column *(East Grinstead) (13+440),* Divisional Petrol Coy *(Tenterden) (7+315),* Divisional Ammunition Coy *(Speldhurst) (8+384);*

RAMC: 190 Field Ambulance *(Hawkhurst; ADS: Rye) (12+238);* 191 Field Ambulance *(Tenterden) (11+238);* 192 Field Ambulance *(Cuckfield) (12+239);*

Divisional HQ Troops *(Hawkhurst) (16+233).*

NOTES:
- This Division had started the War as a training formation
- In May the 12th Division's artillery, which had been left in the UK when it joined the BEF, came under command
- The Division moved to the Sussex coast from the West Country and was allocated a home defence role
- General Schreiber took command on 12 May, having been the artillery commander of the BEF's II Corps until late April, then promoted briefly to the command of 61st Infantry Division. He later rose to command First Army in 1942 before being appointed to Western and then South Eastern Commands in 1942 and 1944 respectively. The commanding officers of 134th and 135th Brigades had been in charge since the outbreak of War, while Brigadier Whitfield replaced Brigadier R Money on 27 August. Brigadier Michelmore rose to Divisional command in 1941
- Defensive stop lines covered Newhaven at Lewes, the northern exits from the Pevensey Levels and Udiam-Newenden-Rolvenden
- By 31 May the Divisional artillery consisted 12x25-pdr, 6x18-pdr, 12x4.5-inch and 6 AT guns (plus the 12th Division's artillery, comprising 8x25-pdr, 24x18-pdr and 16x4.5-inch guns, which had not gone overseas with that Division)
- The Romney, Hythe and Dymchurch Light Railway had been taken over, with an armoured engine and two trucks, carrying four light machine guns and two anti tank rifles, being created. The track runs directly behind the beaches between Hythe and Dungeness
- In June the Divisional reserve consisted of 5 Loyals, part of 7 Devons (MG), 274 A/T Bty (6x6-pdr) and a troop of 55 Field Regt. Their role was to man blocking positions either north east of Lewes, at Hailsham or the along the River Rother. Most of these forces were re-assigned during the summer
- On 21 June The Division's area of responsibility moved east when 3rd Division left the south coast, the eastern boundary became Jury's Gut on Romney Marsh
- On 1 July 1 Sound Ranging Bty arrived to assist countering the German long-range artillery
- By 13 July the Division had 100% Personnel, 45% artillery pieces, 0% A/T guns
- 134th Brigade reserve consisted of the Brigade Anti Tank Company (one plt with 10 armoured lorries, one infantry plt and two bren carrier sections) based at Vinehall School
- 136th Brigade reserve consisted the 9 Devon's carrier, tank hunting and motorcycle platoons
- 6 Commando arrived on 16 September from Scarborough. Its role was to protect the Littlestone coastal and super heavy batteries; 3 Independent Company arrived from Hampshire on 13 September to protect the Dungeness coastal battery. Both these included counter attack roles
- By 7 September the Division had 100% Personnel, 100% artillery pieces, 20% A/T guns
- 5 Loyals main role was to hold stop lines dismounted. Its dispositions were to be as follows: Pevensey exits (HQ: Wilmington, A Coy: Polegate, B Coy: Hailsham, C Coy: in centre), Rye (HQ: Northiam, A Coy: Brede/Broad Oak, B Coy: Beckley/Four Oaks, C Coy: Wittersham), Royal Military Canal (HQ: Woodchurch, A Coy: Ham Street, B Coy: Appledore, C Coy: reserve)
- On 27 September the 31st Independent Brigade came under command in the High Halden-Bethersden area
- On 27 October 136th Brigade was relieved by 219 Coast Brigade (15 Queens, 11 Buffs, 11 East Surrey, 10 Sussex); The Brigade moved back to the Uckfield-Wadhurst area
- In November the Division was relieved by 44th Division and moved to I Corps.

- **2nd New Zealand Expeditionary Force** (GOC: Major General B Freyberg VC)
HQ: Linton, Maidstone, Kent
5th Infantry Brigade: *(HQ: Gore Court, Otham, Maidstone)* (GOC: Brigadier Hargest)
21 (Auckland) Bn (less C Coy) *(Leeds)*, 22 (Wellington) Bn *(Hollingbourne)*, 23 (Otago) Bn *(Milgate Park)*; 5 A/T Coy *(Leeds) (10 armoured lorries)*.
7th Infantry Brigade: *(HQ: Wichling, Faversham)* (GOC: Brigadier H Barrowclough)
28 (Maori) Bn *(Doddington)*, 29 (Composite) Bn; 4 A/T Coy *(Doddington) (10 armoured lorries)*;
Milforce: *(HQ: Eastwell Park, Ashford)* (GOC: Brigadier R Miles)
8 RTR *(Challock) (34+553) (23 Matilda Mk II, 27 Matilda I on 3 September)*, C Sqn 2 Divisional Cavalry Regt *(4+100) (8 light tanks, 14 carriers)*, C Coy 21 Infantry Bn, coy 27 MG Bn *(Challock)*, B and F Troops, 5 Field Regt *(Challock) (8x25-pdr)*; 32 Bty 7 A/T Regt *(Challock) (4x2-pdr)*; C Troop 157 LAA Bty (53 LAA Regt) *(4x40mm)*.
Divisional Troops:
RNZA: 5 Field Regt *(Mote Park, Maidstone) (27 and 28 Btys: 16x25-pdr)*, 7 A/T Regt *(Mote Park, Maidstone) (20x2-pdr)*;
NZE: 7 Field Coy;
RNZMC: 4 Field Ambulance;
RNZASC: Ammunition Coy, Petrol Coy *(Gore Court)*, Supply Column *(Elsfield)*.

NOTES:
- In mid June the NZEF arrived in the UK, 7,000 strong; it changed its name from Second Echelon to this title on 29 June
- 7th Brigade Headquarters was formed from Headquarters 6th Brigade, 29 Bn was formed from 5th Brigade reinforcements
- By 13 July it had 50% Personnel, 10% artillery pieces, 10% A/T guns (total of 3x18-pdr, 3x4.5-inch; 2x2-pdr)
- On 25 July 16x75mm field guns were received with the lorries they were to be carried in. 5 Field Regt was reformed on 28 July
- On 9 August 7 A/T Regt was reformed, with guns
- On 27 August 14 and 15 Forestry Companies joined the NZEF
- On 31 August Alan Brooke inspected the Force and was much impressed with what he saw
- On 5 September it moved to Maidstone from Aldershot
- On 6 September 8 RTR was attached to Milforce from 1st Army Tank Brigade. One of its assigned tasks was to counter attack north west of Folkestone from Sellindge. Its road movement density was ten vehicles per mile at a convoy speed of 8mph
- The NZEF's role was primarily to support 1st London Division's operations to secure the Dover and Folkestone areas; 5th Brigade was to be supported by Milforce; 7th Brigade also to conduct anti parachute operations in Maidstone-Sutton Valence-Charing area, if required, or act as Divisional reserve. It had a secondary task to restore the Royal Military Canal defences east of Ham Street and cover the deployment of VII Corps at the line: Ham Street- Ashford-Charing-Faversham
- On 7 September it had 50% Personnel, 40% artillery pieces, 25% A/T guns
- On 9 September it received 16x25pdr field guns to replace the older guns
- On 9 September HQ Milforce moved from Linton to Eastwell Park
- On 10 and 11 September 21 Bn moved from Kingswood to Leeds and 22 Bn from Warren Wood to Hollingbourne and were billeted with local families

- On 12 September 157 LAA Bty joined Milforce having just received their guns
- The NZEF was due to return to Aldershot in late September, but this was postponed until 4 November
- On 27 September 5 Field Regt (less B and F Troops) moved to Stonebridge Green, 7 A/T Regt (less 32 Bty) moved to Hothfield and 4 A/T Company to Linstead Lodge. On 29 September 23 Bn moved to Bearsted, with 23 Bn moving to Hollingbourne the next day. The Supply Column moved into Hollingbourne House
- 7th Brigade was disbanded on 8 October, 28 Bn was attached to Milforce
- In January 1941 the Division left for Egypt to join the other New Zealand forces already there
- Major General Freyberg had been retired in 1937 but was recalled to command the Salisbury Plain Area until appointed to command of the NZEF, which he commanded throughout the war. Brigadier Barrowclough rose to divisional command; Brigadier Miles was the Force's Artillery Commander and was to be captured on Crete, escaped when Italy surrendered, but died in Spain in 1943. Brigadier Hargest had a similar experience but was killed in Normandy whilst a liaison officer.

-Broc Force:
1st Motor Machine Gun Brigade: *(HQ: Steyning (3+186))* (GOC: Brigadier M Burrows)
16/5 Lancers *(Arundel; A Sqn: Madehurst, B Sqn: Angmering) (33+491)*
2 Lothian and Border Horse *(Ditchling; A Sqn: Withdean Hall, Preston, B Sqn: Upper Beeding, C Sqn: Stanmer) (37+486)*
17/21 Lancers *(Ashington; A and B Sqns: Findon, C Sqn: Storrington) (31+492);*
RA: 60 Army Field Regt *(Findon) (34+591) (237 Bty: Angmering, 239 Bty: Findon – 24x18/25-pdr, 8x25-pdr)*; 88 Army Field Regt *(Hurstpierpoint) (34+599) (351 Bty: Brighton, 352 Bty: Rottingdean - 6x4.5-inch, 18x75mm)*; 69 Medium Regt *(Horsham) (29+661) (241 Bty: Worthing, 242 Bty: Horsham - 16x6-inch mortar)*, 41 Survey Training Regt *(Brighton) (27+1001) (4 btys in infantry role supported by 3x13-pdr – B Bty (5 plts): West Pier, C Bty (6 plts): Black Rock and (2 plts): Shoreham Harbour; A Bty (2 plts) and D Bty (3 plts) in reserve)*; 45 A/T Bty RM *(Littlehampton) (4+256) (7x6-pdr) (relieved at end of September);*
9 East Surrey *(Littlehampton; B Coy: Felpham, D Coy: Barnham) (24+662);* 2/8 Sussex (Home) *(Uckfield; A Coy: Rowfant aviation fuel depot, B Coy: Chichester fuel distribution depot, Thorney Island, C Coy: Slindon, RNAS Ford, D Coy: RAF Tangmere, E Coy: Hove, Shoreham) (80+1211) (8 Sussex split on 25 September with 1/8 merging at Cowfold with 70 Sussex)*, 50 Buffs *(Hove) (23+922)*, 50 Queens *(Roedean) (23+827) (HQ: Roedean School; responsible for the Brighton Black Rock to Rottingdean sector; D Coy: Lewes);*
1/5 Argyll and Sutherland Highlanders (MG) *(Portslade; A Coy: Yapton, E Coy attached to 29th Brigade) (35+945);* 5 Devons (MG) *(36+875) (Goring; A and C Coys: Worthing, B Coy: Lancing)* (D Coy detached to 31st Brigade);
RE: 263 Army Field Coy *(Bramber) (5+259);*
RASC: Brigade Coy *(Billingshurst) (9+331)*, 13 Motor Coach Coy *(Wadhurst) (10+174)*, 1 Recruit Training Bn *(Brighton) (5+272);*
RAMC: 165 Field Ambulance *(Horsham) (8+114).*

NOTES:
- *The Brigade was formed on 30 May and also known as Broc Force. Eastern sub area HQ was in Hurstpierpoint and Western sub area HQ in Pulborough*
- *On 14 July 1st Motor Machine Gun Brigade replaced 3rd Infantry Division. The Brigade was also tasked with the defence of Lewes*
- *Regiments in the Brigade had three squadrons of three troops, each troop had 6 lightly armoured cars equipped with a total of two Vickers MMG and two Bren LMG guns and 2 anti tank rifles. The rest of the Regiment were carried in trucks as mobile infantry. 2 Lothian and Border recorded having 72 Austin "armoured" cars, 17 3-ton Bedford lorries, 15 15-cwt Fordson trucks and 41 motorcycles. In May it recorded having 11 light tanks and 11 carriers*
- *Broc Force was operationally disposed in two lines - along the coast with most of 9 East Surrey plus a MG company from both 5 ASH and 5 Devon in the right hand sector; most of 5 Devon with a company of 9 East Surrey in the centre; 50 Queens with most of 5 ASH, 41 Survey Training Regt and 1 Recruit Training Bn in the left hand sector. The rear line was along the South Downs with 16/5 Lancers assigned the right hand sector, a sqn 17/21 Lancers in the centre and 2 Lothian and Border in the left hand sector*
- *The Brigade reserve consisted of part 17/21 Lancers and 69 Medium Regt RA*
- *The Brigade's western boundary ran from Bognor Regis to Eastergate; its eastern boundary ran from Saltdean to Falmer; its inter sub area boundary ran along the River Adur*
- *50 Buffs arrived on 31 August, while 88 Army Field Regt arrived on 5 August from Tunbridge Wells*
- *On 19 September the first Mark III infantry tanks were delivered to 1 Motor Machine Gun Brigade (17/21 Lancers). By the end of September 18 had been delivered, 6 per regiment)*
- *On 24 September the Brigade undertook an exercise to recapture Newhaven*
- *On 9 October 50 Queens was reformed as 15 Queens and on 25 October moved to the Newhaven sector with the newly formed 219th Coast Brigade*
- *On 12 October 1st Motor Machine Gun Brigade reformed as the 26th Armoured Brigade and on 9 November joined 6th Armoured Division, forming around Salisbury Plain from 12 September under Major General J Crocker, a former BEF armoured brigade commander. Responsibility for its coastal sector passed to the new West Sussex County Division on 9 November*
- *On 21 October 41 Survey Training Regt RA moved to Larkhill*
- *Brigadier Burrows had previously been Military Attaché in Rome and Budapest. He was promoted to command the new 9th Armoured Division in December.*

29th Independent Infantry Brigade (GOC: Brigadier Sir O Leese)
HQ: Staplefield, Sussex
1 Royal Scots Fusiliers *(Haywards Heath) (33+876)*, 2 Royal Welch Fusiliers *(Horsham)*
 (29+925), 2 East Lancashire *(Maresfield) (35+942)*, 2 South Lancashire *(Wych Cross)*
 (27+910);
RA: 17 Field Regt *(East Grinstead) (35+554)* (*10/26 Bty – East Grinstead, 13/92 Bty - Forest Row*)
 (24x25-pdr); 204 A/T Bty *(Uckfield) (7+144) (12x2-pdr);*
E Coy 1/5 Argyll and Sutherland Highlanders (MG);
RE: 236 Field Coy *(Nutley) (6+247);*
RAMC: 154 Field Ambulance *(Lindfield) (10+188).*

NOTES:
- *The Brigade was formed on 14 July in Aldershot; 17 Field Regt re-equipped with 25pdr guns in Aldershot*
- *On 2 August it arrived as Corps Reserve. At this time its commander rated the Fusilier battalions highly, the artillery as efficient but the rest as poor. However, by 3 September General Alan Brooke noted his satisfaction with its efficiency*
- *Its tasks in order of importance were to recapture Newhaven (with 45th Division), control penetration from Pevensey and Romney Marsh (with 45th Division) and occupy the Rother Line, if required*
- *On 16 August the Brigade conducted its first full exercise - a simulated counter attack on Rye, gauged a moderate success. Between 22-24 August and 12-13 September it conducted exercises to occupy defensive lines around Lindfield and Mayfield*
- *By 7 September the Brigade had 45% Personnel, 40% artillery pieces, 25% A/T guns*
- *On 23 October it took over 1st Motor Machine Brigade's coastal role*
- *Brigadier Leese had been the BEF's deputy chief of operations staff and was to command the West Sussex County Division that replaced Broc Force. He was destined to command Eighth Army in Italy and end the War as Commander in Chief South East Asia.*

31st **Independent Infantry Brigade** (HQ: Tenterden)
(For more details see IV Corps)
2 South Staffordshire (Bethersden), 2 OBLI (Wittersham, with coys at Iden, Appledore and Ham Street), 1 Royal Ulster Regt (Aldington, with coys at Ruckinge and Court at Street)
D Coy 5 Devons (MG) (Great Chart)
RA: 75 Field Regt (Woodchurch) (12x4.5-inch, 8x18-pdr), 223 Bty / 57 A/T Regt (High Halden) (12x2-pdr), Brigade A/T Coy (High Halden)
RE: 237 Field Coy (Leigh Green)
RAMC: 152 Field Ambulance (St Michaels, Tenterden)
RASC: Brigade Coy (Stanhope, Ashford), 39 Motor Coach Coy (Cranbrook).

NOTES:
- *On 27 September the Brigade arrived from IV Corps to replace the NZEF*
- *On 14 October its headquarters moved to Tenterden*
- *Its role was to cover the 45th and 1st London Divisional boundaries north of the Royal Military Canal and prevent penetration plus the recapture high ground north of Hythe. It planned to defend the Canal in platoon localities*
- *On 11 November it left to rejoin IV Corps.*

Corps Troops:
RA: 56 Heavy Regt *(31+805)* (Cuckfield, A Bty: *Normanshurst (2x6- inch), Eastry (2x6-inch),* B Bty: *Peasmarsh (Pelsham Farm) (1x9.2-inch), Aldington (1x9.2-inch), Alfriston (2x8- inch),* C Bty: *Udimore (2x6-inch), Westernhanger (2x6-inch),* D Bty: *Bexhill (2x9.2-inch each at Wartling, Picknill Green and Sidley Green, OP in the Martello Tower at Norman's Bay);* **4 Super Heavy Bty** *(Hythe) (4+89) (1x9.2-inch rail each at Sandling and Folkestone);* **5 Super Heavy Bty** *(Shepherdswell) (7+109) (2x12-inch Rail);* 37 Super Heavy Bty (27 Army Field Regt) *(8+186) (1x12-inch each Eythorne and Lyminge),* X Super Heavy Bty RCA *(Littlestone) (2x9.2-*

inch) (5+80) (Formed 6 September, guns in place 17 September); Y Super Heavy Bty RCA *(Bridge) (1x9.2-inch rail), Golden Wood, Ashford (1x9.2-inch rail)) (4+78) (Formed 6 September, guns in place 17 September);* 59 Heavy Regt (Newfoundland) *(Ardingley: 3 Btys at Crawley in infantry role as part of Tunbridge Wells defences);* 5 Medium Regt *(Farningham) (38+1031) (15/17 Bty and 20/21 Bty: 16x6-pdr - Maidstone to Penshurst, 6x6-pdr - Hoo Peninsula, 2x6-pdr - Rochester) (GHQ Line role);*

RE: HQ Corps Troops *(Hurstpierpoint);* HQ 1 Chemical Warfare Group HQ *(Bodiam) (4+40),* 62 Chemical Warfare Coy RE *(Robertsbridge) (5+240);* 221 Army Field Coy *(Sheldwich) (6+246),* 262 Army Field Coy *(Bognor Regis) (4+249),* 264 Army Field Coy *(Mayfield) (4+233);* 569 Army Troops Coy *(Haywards Heath) (6+299);* 265 Corps Field Park Coy *(Tenterden) (4+165),* 655 General Construction Coy *(Hawkinge) (6+230) (airfield repair),* 718 General Construction Coy *(Tunbridge Wells) (6+267),* 160 and 161 Rail Operating Coys *(Littlestone) (160 supporting Y Super Heavy Bty, 161 supporting X Super Heavy Bty) (12+550);*

RAOC: 20 Army Field Workshop *(Ashford) (6+238),* 1 Corps Ammunition Dump *(Pluckley),* 2 Corps Ammunition Dump *(Groombridge);* 3 Corps Ammunition Dump *(Rowhook);*

RAMC: 224 Field Ambulance *(Tunbridge Wells) (5+186),* 7 Casualty Clearing Station *(Cranbrook) (9+86);*

CMP: 108 Provost Coy *(Tunbridge Wells) (106).*

Dover Garrison: *(235+6834) (HQ: Dover Castle)* (GOC: Brigadier C Gotto)
Training Bn Irish Guards *(Grand Shaft Barracks, Citadel; Beach Defence Coy at Archcliffe Fort, plts at Marine Rail Station and Eastern piers) (24+614),* 9 Green Howards *(Kearsney; one coy along the harbour front) (25+652),* 50 Royal West Kent *(Citadel - 4 coys, tank hunt plt at Lydden) (23+704);* A Coy 6 Buffs *(Duke of York School / Swingate radar station),* B Coy 70 Buffs *(St Margarets Bay);*

5 Commando *(St Margarets Bay) (37+422) (arrived 14 September);*

15 Royal Fusiliers (Pioneer) (HQ, A and D Coys) *(Duke of York School; from 1st London Division);*

D Coy 1 Kensington (MG) *(Duke of York School; from 1st London Division);*

RA: 5 Field Training Regt *(Fort Burgoyne and Connaught Barracks) (33+1266) (2x4.5-inch, 6x13-pdr, rest in infantry role);* 34 Signal Training Regt *(Castle Barracks) (26+913) (infantry role);* 29 Independent A/T Bty *(Duke of Yorks School) (4+258) (6x2-pdr);*

RE: 13 Cinque Ports Fortress Unit *(Archcliffe Fort);*

AMPC: 158 Coy *(Kearsney) (4+249).*

Plus HMS Lynx (Royal Navy Base) *(2 rifle platoons: Prince of Wales Pier and Submarine Basin, each =1+18 strong)*

<u>NOTES:</u>
- *Brigadier Gotto assumed command on 20 June*
- *5 Commando had 2 troops each at Guston, Langdon and Martin Mill, protecting the super heavy guns; 1 troop at St Margarets' beach and 3 troops in reserve at St Margaret at Cliffe*
- *A defensive perimeter was built to cover the land approaches to the town, with all likely routes covered by defensive positions including pillboxes. The line ran through Old Park Barracks-Minnis Lane-River Bottom Wood-Coombe Farm-Elms Vale-Coney Hill-Shakespeare*

Cliff. 50 RWK was assigned the western sector with two companies; 9 Green Howards was responsible for the northern sector. The Garrison held seven days of supplies
- In November 130th Brigade (43rd Division) took over responsibility for Dover Garrison.

Deal Garrison *(4,318 Royal Marines)* (GOC: Brigadier R Sturges RM)
11 Bn RM *(Upper Deal)*, Depot Bn RM *(Depot)*; part 15 Royal Fusiliers (Pioneer) *(B Coy: Depot, C Coy: Walmer)*; 4 Independent Coy *(Sandwich) (300)*, D Coy 6 Buffs *(Sandwich)*;
A Section 56 Heavy Regt RA *(Kingsdown) (2x6-inch)*.

NOTES:
- *11 Bn was formed in February 1940 as part of the MNBDO and moved to Deal in June*
- *In November the Depot Bn RM was relieved*
- *Sandwich, Eastry and Wingham were prepared as nodal points*
- *Brigadier Sturges was promoted to command forces on Iceland by the end of 1940 and rose to command the RM's Special Service Group (Commando) in 1943*
- *In February 1941 11 Bn sailed for Egypt.*

Shorncliffe Garrison *(226+6200)*: (GOC: Brigadier H Schomberg)
6 Buffs (Home) *(34+1585)* *(Folkestone: HQ and C Coy)*, 70 Buffs *(West Folkestone; A Coy: Hawkinge, C Coy: Folkestone) (36+886) (formed 19 September from the Young Soldier companies of 6 Buffs)*, Small Arms School *(Hythe) (20+118)* plus unattached Royal Fusiliers *(232)*;
RA: 2 Flash Spotting Bty / 2 Survey Regt *(Seabrook)*, Y Troop 2 Survey Bty / 2 Survey Regt *(Seabrook)*;
RE: 1 Training Bn *(Napier Barracks) (47+2008)*; 163 OCTU *(St Martin's Plain) (28+550)*; 4 Docks Group (1005, 1006, 1008 and 1009 Operating Coys) *(Moore Barracks) (55+1411)*, 5 Stevedore Bn *(Hythe; 17 Coy: Dymchurch Redoubt and RAF Lympne, 18 and 20 Coys: Saltwood, 19 Coy: Seabrook) (22+793)*; 6 Field Sqn *(6+30)*;
RASC: 10 Coy *(2+76)*.

NOTES:
- *The primary role was to defend Folkestone and Lympne, whilst co-ordinating counter attacks with 2nd London Brigade to recapture Hythe and Dymchurch*
- *70 Buffs moved to Westenhanger, northwest of Hythe, on 11 October. This would have placed it in the middle of the proposed airborne landings. 6 Buffs were tasked as Garrison Reserve*
- *1 Training Bn RE was also tasked with providing demolition parties for Dover and Folkestone harbours. It was estimated that 3 officers and 132 men needed six hours to complete the task at Dover alone*
- *Brigadier Schomberg had been in post since the start of the War. In November 1940 he was appointed commander of the newly raised 222nd Infantry Brigade*
- *4 Docks Group replaced 141 OCTU on 16 August. It was tasked with coastal defence between Folkestone and Sandgate*
- *On 23 August 2 Flash Spotting Bty arrived to assist countering the German long-range artillery*
- *5 Stevedore Bn was formed on 31 August from 1 Stevedore Centre, based at Lympne since June. The Centre had been deployed as follows: HQ Coy: Westenhanger, A Coy: Saltwood,*

B Coy: Seabrook, Depot Coy: Folkestone
- By 10 November 129th Infantry Brigade (43rd Division) arrived and took over the Garrison's responsibilities
- 6 Field Sqn joined the newly formed 8th Armoured Division on 27 November
- The Garrison held seven days of supplies.

Sheerness Garrison (CO: Lt Col Mitchell RE)

8 East Surrey (-) *(A Coy: Eastchurch, Z Coy: Fletcher Bty, Warden (4+65))* plus 2/6 Queens *(see 35 Infantry Brigade, 1st London Division)*; two MG plts 1 Queen Westminster Rifles *(Minster and Leysdown) (see 1st London Division)*;

RE: Kent Fortress Unit *(9+172) (Sheerness and Grain) (HQ, 2 and 3 Coys: 31 coastal defence searchlights)*, 7 Advance Depot;

RA: C6 Mobile Bty *(4x4-inch) (see 115 Army Field Regt, 1st London Division)*.

NOTE: In November 221st Coast Brigade took over defence of the Isle of Sheppey (9 Green Howards, 7 Dorset, 10 RWK)

Chatham Garrison: *(5,200)* (GOC: Major General A Goschen)
 (Brigadier G Seath, GOC Royal Marines` Chatham Division)

8 East Surrey (-) *(63+1095) (Aylesford; B Coy: Chatham, D Coy: Shornmead, E Coy: Rochester, X and Y Coys: Gravesend)*;

RA: 15/17 Bty, 5 Medium Regt *(Rochester Bridge: 2x6-pdr, Aylesford: 2x6-pdr)*;

RE: Royal School of Military Engineering (RSME) *(Brompton) (37+342)*, 1 Depot Bn *(Brompton) (11+575)*, 2 Depot Bn *(13+760)*, 3 (LofC) Depot Bn *(Chatham) (20+1303)*, 4 (Field) Depot Bn *(Luton)*, 5 (LofC) Depot Bn *(Bridgewood)*; 3 Tunnel Group *(Rochester) (8+166)*; 1 and 2 Base Workshops Coy *(Chatham) (12+304)*, 126 Electrical and Mechanical Coy *(6+303)*;

RASC: 9 Training Coy *(3+127)*;

RAOC: 2 Ordnance Field Park *(Gillingham) (3+27)*.

Plus RAF Air Ammunition Park *(Snodland)*; RN Troop *(Fort Horsted) (2x12-pdr)*, RN Troop *(Aylesford) (2x4-inch)*;

Plus Royal Marines` Depot, Chatham Division *(Dockyard) (6 companies)*; Naval Bn (HMS Pembroke) (700).

NOTES
- *Chatham was developed as a nodal point with two lines - the outer along the line of Napoleonic forts to the south and east of Rochester with either end located on the River Medway; the inner one covered Rochester bridge and Chatham dockyard*
- *General Goschen had been in post since the start of the War, having been recalled from retirement*
- *Brigadier Seath retired in 1942.*

Eastern Command Troops:

South East:
- Chatham Sub Area *(HQ: Chatham)*
- Home Counties Sub Area *(HQ: Sevenoaks)* (GOC: Brigadier S Davenport)

7 Dorset (Home) *(Warlingham; A Coy: Warlingham, B and D Coys: Biggin Hill, C Coy: Gatwick)* *(27+663)*, 8 Royal West Kent (Home) *(38+358)* *(Brasted; 8 coys: Halstead Ammunition Depot, West Malling, Biggin Hill and Penshurst airfields, Westerham, Bletchingley and Tatsfield)*, 50 East Surrey *(Dorking; A Coy: Beare Green, B Coy: Gatwick, C Coy: Newdidgate, D Coy: Brooklands)* *(26+734)*, 50 Sussex *(Seaford; A Coy: Cuckmere, B Coy: reserve, C Coy: east Seaford, D Coy: west Seaford)* *(26+786)* *(9 October reformed as 10 Sussex and joined 219 Brigade)*, 70 Royal West Kent *(Tonbridge; A Coy: West Malling, C Coy: Penshurst, D Coy: Gravesend)* *(29+1041)* *(formed 19 September)*, 11 Sussex *(Cowfold: A Coy: Newhaven, B Coy: Fairlight Radar station, C Coy: Pevensey Radar Station)*; 70 Sussex *(Cowfold; A Coy: Reigate, B Coy: Beachy Head, C Coy: Bexhill, D Coy: Newdidgate, E Coy: Westerham, F Coy: RNAS Ford)* *(1095)* *(formed 19 September from 8 Sussex)*, Buffs ITC *(Canterbury)* *(51+1707)*, Royal West Kent ITC *(Maidstone)* *(41+1827)*;

RA: 8 Reserve A/A Regt *(Deepcut)* *(37+1118)*, 101 OCTU *(Sandhurst)* *(11+315)*;

RE: 8 Training Bn *(Isle of Oxney)* *(15+673)*, 12 EOD Coy *(Tunbridge Wells)* *(10+257)*, 1 Stevedore Centre *(Worthing)* *(31+703)* (from 4 September), 158 Rail Construction Coy *(Redhill)* *(6+268)*, 170 Tunneling Coy *(Ringmer)* *(5+134)*, 58 and 61 Chemical Warfare Coys *(Heathfield)* *(11+470)*, 717 Artisan Works Coy *(Gatwick)* *(6+265)*, 721 Artisan Works Coy *(Camberley)* *(5+272)*;

RAOC: 18 Army Field Workshops *(Crowborough)* *(5+232)*, 12 Ammunition Sub Depot *(Edenbridge)* *(7+202)*, 12 Main Supply Depot *(Reigate)* *(6+60)*, Command Workshops *(Sevenoaks)*, Command Workshops *(Crawley)*;

RASC: 4 Driver Training Centre *(Bognor Regis)* *(22+684)*, 5 LofC Motor Transport Coy *(Sevenoaks)* *(7+276)*, 7 Reserve Motor Transport Coy *(Bognor Regis)* *(10+275)*, 8 Station Transport Coy *(Rowfant)* *(3+157)* (role was to move Main Supply Depot supplies), 19 Reserve Motor Transport Coy *(Westerham)* *(10+463)*;

RS: 12 Division Signals Regt *(Caterham)* *(28+533)*;

RAMC: 5 General Hospital *(Goodwood)*, 10 Training Coy *(Hollingbourne)* *(83+351)*;

AMPC: 33 Group (133, 206 and 207 Coys) *(Burgess Hill)* *(15+564)*; 16 Group (10, 102, 204 Coys) *(Tunbridge Wells)* *(17+827)*, 5 Coy *(Cuckfield)* *(5+273)*, 61 Coy *(Horley)* *(4+283)*, 127 Coy *(Crawley)* *(4+258)*, 132 Coy *(Whitstable)* *(4+263)*, 133 Coy *(Seaford)* *(4+265)* (arrived in June to build the Cuckmere Haven defences. By mid September it also had 2 sections at Pevensey, one at Goring, one at Worthing and one at Lewes).

XI CORPS (GOC: Lieutenant General H Massy)
HQ: Bishops Stortford, Hertfordshire

NOTES:
- On 1 July 157th Brigade (52nd Division) came under command, covering the Stradishall-Clare-Haverhill area

- The Corps was responsible for the defence of the Essex and Suffolk coastlines
- On 10 October 157th Brigade returned to 52nd Division command
- In mid October the Australian Imperial Force (AIF) joined the Corps at Colchester as its reserve
- In mid October the 1st Armoured Reconnaissance Brigade left the Corps
- General Massy had been promoted to the command in October 1939. He was sacked late in 1941 as it was felt that he was inadequate to the task.

- 15th Infantry Division (Scottish) (GOC: Major General R Money)

HQ: Colchester, Essex

44th Infantry Brigade: *(HQ: Kelvedon)* (GOC: Brigadier J Campbell)
1/8 Royal Scots *(Abberton) (33+911)*, 1/6 KOSB *(Colchester) (36+887)*, 1/7 KOSB *(St Osyth) (31+881)*.

45th Infantry Brigade: *(HQ: Ardleigh)* (GOC: Brigadier D Davidson; Brigadier J Russell from 26 September)
1/6 Royal Scots Fusiliers *(Frinton) (32+820)*, 9 Cameronians *(Clacton) (33+919)*, 10 Cameronians *(Harwich) (33+914)*.

46th Infantry Brigade: *(HQ: Billericay)* (GOC: Brigadier H Clark)
2 Glasgow Highlanders *(Rayleigh) (35+878)*, 10 Highland Light Infantry *(Purleigh) (34+835)*, 11 Highland Light Infantry *(Southend) (32+867)*.

Divisional Troops:
RA: 129 Field Regt *(Ramsden Heath) (34+553) (311 Bty: 8x4.5-inch; 312 Bty: 16x75mm)*, 130 Field Regt *(Great Bentley) (31+545) (315 and 316 Btys: 16x75mm, 8x4.5-inch)*, 131 Field Regt *(Kelvedon) (32+535) (319 and 320 Btys: 16x18-pdr)*; 64 A/T Regt *(West Bergholt) (18+533) (253, 254, 255, 256 Btys; 253 to North Weald as infantry) (10x2-pdr)*
1/7 Middlesex (MG) *(Coggeshall;* A Coy: *Frinton,* B Coy: *Dovercourt,* C Coy: *St Osyth,* D Coy: *Southminster (42+793)*;
8 York and Lancaster (Pioneer) *(Brentwood) (26+794)*;
RE: 278 Field Coy *(Wickford) (5+230)*, 279 Field Coy *(Dedham) (5+226)*, 280 Field Coy *(Fordham) (5+250)*, 281 Field Park Coy *(Felstead) (3+156)*;
RASC: Divisional Ammunition Coy *(Braintree) (9+392)*, Divisional Petrol and Supply Coys *(Maldon) (23+719)*, 15 Coach Coy *(Little Leighs) (9+175)*;
RAMC: 193 Field Ambulance *(Nayland) (12+239)*, 194 Field Ambulance *(Witham) (10+234)*, 195 Field Ambulance *(Ingatestone) (13+239)*;
RS: Divisional Signals Regt *(Great Leighs) (25+479)*;
CMP: Divisional Provost Coy *(Dunmow) (99)*.

NOTES:
- The Division was a Territorial Army formation assigned to home defence when the War began
- In July C and D Btys 53 Heavy Regt *(Thorrington and Burnham) (4x9.2-inch, 4x6-inch)*, 221 Bty/56 Medium Regt *(8x6-inch)*, part of 5 RHA and C Troop 72 Medium Regt *(4x6-inch)* were allocated from Corps Troops
- By 13 July the Division had 100% Personnel, 40% artillery pieces, 10% A/T guns
- On 2 August Alan Brooke on a visit found the Division was good but required a great deal more training

- *General Money replaced Major General Le Fanu on promotion on 23 August. The commanders of 44th and 46th Brigades had been in charge since the outbreak of War. General Money had commanded the Senior Officer's School (1939-40); he was posted to India in 1942*
- *By 7 September it had 100% Personnel, 100% artillery pieces, 20% A/T guns*
- *The Division was responsible for the defence of the Essex coastline*
- *In late October 207th (Coastal) Infantry Brigade joined the Division.*

- 55th Infantry Division (West Lancashire) (GOC: Major General V Majendie)
HQ: Diss, Norfolk (13+393)
164th Infantry Brigade: *(HQ: Aldeburgh)* (GOC: Brigadier A Miller)
9 Kings *(Aldringham) (32+885)*, 1/4 South Lancashire *(Wrentham) (34+870)*, 2/4 South Lancashire *(Halesworth) (33+869).*
165th Infantry Brigade: *(HQ: Ipswich)* (GOC: Brigadier R Brett)
1/5 Kings *(Felixstowe) (32+909)*, 1 Liverpool Scots *(Needham Market) (29+878)*, 2 Liverpool Scots *(Woodbridge) (31+886).*
199th Infantry Brigade: *(HQ: Beccles)* (GOC: Brigadier L Mandleberg)
2/8 Lancashire Fusiliers *(Lowestoft) (32+948)*, 2/6 Manchester *(Beccles) (33+843)*, 2/7 Manchester *(Lowestoft) (32+856).*
Divisional Troops:
2 Kensingtons (MG) *(Claydon) (34+787)*;
RA: 87 Field Regt *(Woodbridge) (31+510)*, 109 Field Regt *(Beccles) (32+594) (204 Bty: 8x4.5-inch, 369 Bty: 8x75mm)*, 136 Field Regt *(Yoxford) (32+523) (347 Bty: 4x4.5-inch, 4x75mm; 348 Bty: 12x75mm)*, 66 A/T Regt *(Heveringham) (32+504) (261 (Halesworth), 262, 263 (Clopton) and 264 Btys (Blythburgh) – 12x6-pdr, 10x2-pdr);*
RE: 55 Field Coy *(Bungay) (5+241)*, 557 Field Coy *(Woodbridge) (6+247)*, 558 Field Coy *(Aldeburgh) (6+241)*; 559 Field Park Coy *(Bury St Edmunds) (4+155);*
RASC: Divisional Ammunition Coy *(Bury St Edmunds) (10+398);*
RAMC: 177 Field Ambulance *(Framlingham) (11+233)*, 178 Field Ambulance *(Colchester) (11+236);*
CMP: Divisional Provost Coy *(Thorndon) (102).*

NOTES:
- *The Division was a Territorial Army formation assigned to home defence when the War began*
- *General Majendie had been in command since the start of the War, as had the commanders of 164th and 199th Brigades; Brigadier Brett had been appointed in February. General Majendie rose to command Northern Ireland District in 1941*
- *The Division was responsible for the defence of the Suffolk coastline*
- *In June the Divisional artillery had 8x25-pdr, 4x18-pdr, 18x4.5-inch and 2 A/T guns*
- *In June 199th Brigade joined from 66th Division*
- *In July A and B Btys 53 Heavy Regt (Sternfield and Uggleshall) (8x9.2-inch), 59 Medium Regt and 115 Bty of 32 Field Regt were allocated from Corps Troops*
- *By 13 July the Division had 100% Personnel, 50% artillery pieces, 25% A/T guns*
- *By 7 September it had 100% Personnel, 90% artillery pieces, 25% A/T guns*
- *In mid October 21st Army Tank Brigade (42, 43, 48 RTR) and 208th (Coastal) Infantry Brigade came under Divisional command*

- *In November the Division moved to the Oxfordshire / Gloucestershire area as IV Corps mobile reserve, with its HQ at Moreton in Marsh.*

Corps Troops:
RA: 53 Heavy Regt *(Saxmundham) (32+809) (8x9.2-inch, 2x6-inch)*, 56 Medium Regt *(Colchester) (31+648) (174 Bty: A Tp: Harwich (5x6-pdr), B Tp 174 Bty: Shoeburyness (4x4-inch, 2x13-pdr, 2x75mm); 221 Bty: 8x6-inch mortars)*, 59 Medium Regt *(Leiston) (30+652) (GHQ Line role: 236 Bty at Duxford with 8x6-inchmortars and 235 Bty at Leiston with 13x6-pdr)*, 72 Medium Regt *(Coddenham) (32+643) (A and B Btys at Ipswich with 16x6-inch)*, X Super Heavy Bty (27 Army Field Regt) *(4+93) (1x12-inch Rail at Wrabness (15 Div), 1x12-inch Rail at Orwell (55Div))*, V and W Btys (27 Army Field Regt) *(Tollesbury) (6+100) (4x6-inch with 15 Div)*, 5 RHA *(Dunmow) (27+479) (G Bty: Chelmsford (6x6-pdr), K Bty: Coggleshall (6x6-pdr, 2x3-pdr, 2x12-pdr)* (GHQ Line role), 32 Army Field Regt *(Dunmow) (36+463) (115 Bty (8x4-inch), 107, 120 and 121 Btys: 12x12-pdr and 18x6-pdr)* (GHQ Line role), 147 Army Field Regt *(Wetheringsett) (34+593) (413 and 431 Btys: 4x4.5-inch, 2x18pdr)* (attached to 55 Division), 1 and 2 Coast Defence Btys *(Southend) (36+111) (forming)*, 1 and 2 Army Observation Btys *(Felixstowe) (3+174)*;

1/6 Suffolk *(Ipswich) (67+1541)*, 7 York and Lancaster (Pioneer) *(Woodbridge) (28+815)*;

7 Commando *(Felixstowe) (27+347)*, 8 Commando *(Burnham) (28+357)*;

RE: 228 Army Field Coy *(Lavenham) (5+256)* (GHQ Line role), 229 Army Field Coy *(Sudbury) (5+253)*, 230 Army Field Coy *(Bury St Edmunds) (6+259)* (GHQ Line role), 231 Corps Field Park Coy *(Bartlow) (5+189)*, 15 Road Construction Coy *(Thaxted) (3+104)*, 117 Road Construction Coy *(Castle Hedingham) (4+102)*, 118 Road Construction Coy *(Bishops Stortford) (4+98)*, 709 General Construction Coy *(Wattisham) (6+276)*, 135 Mechanical Equipment Coy *(Bishops Stortford) (13+361)*;

AMPC: 4 Centre *(Clacton) (5+208)*, 11Coy *(Felsted) (4+230)*, 92 Coy *(Woodbridge) (4+269)*, 122 Coy *(Wickford) (4+264)*, 134 Coy *(Southwold) (6+262)*, 169 Coy *(Brentwood)*, 192 Coy *(Felsted) (6+272)*, 198 Coy *(Halesworth) (4+279)*, 226 Coy *(Fordham)*;

RAC: C Armoured Train *(Saxmundham) (46) (covered Felixstowe and Lowestoft)*

RASC: 36 Motor Coach Coy *(Clare) (10+175)*, 568 Army Troops Coy *(Chelmsford) (5+298)*, 6 Armoured Division Coy *(Lambourne End) (3+161)*, 13 Divisional Ammunition Coy *(Braintree) (9+393)*;

CMP: 107 Provost Coy *(Bishops Stortford) (109)*;

RS: Corps Signals Regt *(Much Hadham) (19+621)*.

1st Armoured Reconnaissance Brigade (GOC: Brigadier C Norman*)
HQ: Halstead, Essex

13/18 Hussars *(Epping) (31+457)*, 4/7 Dragoon Guards *(Colne) (37+467)*, 12 Lancers *(Halstead) (34+481) (93 Beaverettes)*, East Riding Yeomanry *(Witham) (33+476)*;

RA: 12 RHA *(Sudbury) (27+525) (C Bty: 4x4.5-inch, D Bty: 4x18-pdr, 2x25-pdr)*; A Bty 5 RHA *(2x13-pdr, 2x12-pdr)*;

RAMC: 14 Light Field Ambulance *(Halstead) (10+184)*;

RASC: 11 Coy *(Halstead) (4+297)*.

NOTES:
- *The Brigade had been formed in France on 30 March and served in the BEF under its present commander*
- *The Brigade's main role was to counter attack the airfields in Essex if attacked by airborne troops*
- *On 7 August 12 RHA joined the Brigade*
- *The Brigade was equipped with "Beaverrettes" (ad hoc lightly armoured vehicles)*
- *On 1 November 12 RHA joined the newly formed 6th Armoured Division's Support Group*
- *In late November the Brigade reformed as 27th Armoured Brigade (9th Armoured Division) and moved to Northampton for re-equipping.*

Colchester Garrison (CO: Colonel J French) *(351+6799)*
4 Cavalry Training Regt *(23+636)*;
RA: 36 Signals Training Regt *(27+987)*;
RE: 4 Training Bn *(154+1786)*, 280 Field Coy *(5+250)*;
RAMC: 164 and 166 OCTU *(55+1183)*; 9 Training Coy *(65+331)*;
RAOC: 23 and 24 Field Workshops *(9+328)*, 53 Training Section *(2+756)*;
AMPC: 126 and 169 Coys *(11+542)*.

II CORPS (GOC: Lieutenant General E Osborne*)
HQ: Newmarket, Suffolk

NOTES:
- *The Corps HQ had served with the BEF*
- *Inter Corps boundary was Wells-Fakenham-Swaffham-Mundford-Thetford*
- *The Corps was responsible for the defence of the Norfolk coastline and the protection of the East Midlands*
- *General Osborne had commanded 44th Division in the BEF. He was promoted to command on 25 June but was sacked late in 1941 as it was felt that he was inadequate to the task.*

- 18th Infantry Division (Eastern) (GOC: Major General M Beckwith-Smith*)
HQ: Norwich, Norfolk
53rd Infantry Brigade: *(HQ: Kelling)* (GOC: Brigadier S Collingwood)
1/5 Norfolks *(Blakeney) (33+931)*, 1/6 Norfolks *(Cromer) (36+852)*, 2 Cambridge *(Sherringham) (33+875)*.
54th Infantry Brigade: *(HQ: Caister)* (GOC: Brigadier E Backhouse)
1/4 Norfolks *(Hemsby) (34+931)*, 1/4 Suffolks *(Seacroft) (34+879)*, 1/5 Suffolks *(Great Yarmouth) (33+864)*.
55th Infantry Brigade: *(HQ: Westwick)* (GOC: Brigadier W Ozanne)
1/5 Bedford and Hertford *(North Walsham) (33+810)*, 1 Cambridge *(Mundesley) (31+892)*, 1/5 Sherwood Foresters *(Drayton) (33+877)*.
37th Independent Infantry Brigade: *(HQ: Norwich)* (GOC: Brigadier R Wyatt)
2/6 East Surrey *(Swaffham) (35+777) (B coy at Wells, others defending RAF bases)*, 6 Sussex *(Great Shelford) (32+914)*, 7 Sussex *(Huntingdon) (34+894)*; 182 Field Ambulance RAMC *(Cambridge) (12+226)*; Brigade Coy RASC *(Cambridge) (7+182)*.

Divisional Troops:
9 Northumberland Fusliers (MG) *(Coltishall) (32+793)*;
13 South Staffordshire (Pioneer) *(Kings Lynn) (29+850)*;
RA: 118 Field Regt *(Worstead) (33+536) (259 Bty: 2x4.5-inch, 2x18-pdr, 260 Bty: 8x75mm)*, 135 Field Regt *(Holt) (36+459) (336 Bty: 8x75mm, 344 Bty: 4x75mm, 2x18-pdr, 2x4-inch)*, 148 Field Regt *(Loddon) (38+519) (419 Bty: 8x18-pdr, 4x4.5-inch, 420 Bty: 4x4.5-inch)*, 125 A/T Regt RA *(Norwich) (33+489)* (A, B, C and D Btys: infantry role, 4x6-pdr and 8x2-pdr);
RE: 287 Field Coy *(Cawston) (6+242)*, 288 Field Coy *(Cawston) (6+245)*, 560 Field Coy *(Brundall) (6+253)*, 251 Field Park Coy *(Shotesham) (3+152)*;
RAMC: 196 Field Ambulance *(Norwich) (10+185)*, 197 Field Ambulance *(Hetherset) (10+183)*, 198 Field Ambulance *(Reepham) (9+179)*;
RASC: Divisional Supply Column *(Bawdeswell) (14+430)*, Divisional Petrol Coy *(East Dereham) (5+290)*, Divisional Ammunition Coy *(Shipham) (11+388)*;
RS: Divisional Signals Regt *(Wroxham) (26+512)*;
CMP: Divisional Provost Coy *(Norwich) (2+111)*.

NOTES:
- *The Division was a Territorial Army formation assigned to home defence when the War began*
- *By 13 July the Division had 95% Personnel, 50% artillery pieces, 5% A/T guns*
- *37th Independent Brigade arrived mid July and came under Divisional command*
- *By 7 September the Division had 100% Personnel, 80% artillery pieces, 20% A/T guns*
- *The Division was responsible for the defence of the Norfolk coastline*
- *In mid October the Division was replaced by miscellaneous units and 213th (Coastal) Brigade (Caister) before taking over 52nd Division's area*
- *General Beckwith-Smith had been promoted in June from command of 1st Guards Brigade in the BEF's 1st Division. He was to lead the Division into captivity at Singapore in 1942. The commanders of 54th and 55th Brigades had been in charge since the start of the War; Brigadier Wyatt was appointed on 11 June, while Brigadier Collingwood was in charge from 28 May to 25 October.*

- 52nd Infantry Division (Lowland) (GOC: Major General J Drew)
HQ: Diddington, Huntingdonshire
155th Infantry Brigade: *(HQ: Swaffham)* (GOC: Brigadier T Grainger-Stewart)
7/9 Royal Scots *(Massingham) (34+925)*, 1/4 KOSB *(Kings Lynn) (36+918)*, 1/5 KOSB *(Swaffham) (36+927)*.
156th Infantry Brigade: *(HQ: Freckenham)* (GOC: Brigadier I Grant)
4/5 Royal Scots Fusliers *(Wymondham) (36+829)*, 1/6 Cameronians *(Dereham) (37+977)*, 1/7 Cameronians *(Thetford) (34+934)*.
157th Infantry Brigade: *(HQ: Clare)* (GOC: Brigadier Sir J Laurie)
1 Glasgow Highlanders *(Newmarket) (36+889)*, 1/5 Highland Light Infantry *(Cambridge) (37+836)*, 1/6 Highland Light Infantry *(St Neots) (35+829)*.
Divisional Troops:
RA: 78 Field Regt *(Beechamwell) (34+572) (A, B and C Btys: 24x25-pdr)*, 79 Field Regt *(Fordham) (41+601) (A, B and C Btys: 24x25-pdr)*, 80 Field Regt *(Haverhill) (39+585) (P, Q and R Btys: 24x25-pdr)*, 54 A/T Regt *(Mundford) (28+554) (213, 214, 215 and 216 Btys: 48x2-pdr)*;

RE: 202 Field Coy *(Didlington)* *(6+252)*, 241 Field Coy *(Kings Lynn)* *(6+259)*, 554 Field Coy *(Watton)* *(6+249)*, 243 Field Park Coy *(Thetford)* *(3+154)*;
RAMC: 155 Field Ambulance *(Thetford)* *(9+176)*, 156 Field Ambulance *(Mundford)* *(10+176)*, 157 Field Ambulance *(Haverhill)* *(12+231)*, 205 Field Ambulance *(Bungay)* *(10+237)*;
RASC: Divisional Ammunition Coy *(Mundford)* *(8+385)*;
CMP: Divisional Provost Coy *(Thetford)* *(2+111)*.

NOTES:
- *The Division was a Territorial Army formation assigned to home defence when the War began, though it was sent briefly to Normandy with the second BEF. General Drew had been in command since the start of the War as had the commander of 155th Brigade. Brigadier Laurie was appointed on 23 April while 156th Brigade had Brigadier Fitzgerald from 21 May to 19 August. General Drew was made responsible for combined operations training in 1941*
- *In 1 July 157th Brigade came under XI Corps operational command*
- *By 13 July the Division had 100% Personnel, 100% artillery pieces, 100% A/T guns*
- *By 7 September the Division had 100% Personnel, 100% artillery pieces, 100% A/T guns*
- *On 19 September Alan Brooke found the Division to be in good form but still very short of transport*
- *The Division was responsible for the defence of Cambridgeshire but was allocated a mobile role within the Corps*
- *In mid October the Division was replaced by 18th Division.*

Corps Troops:

RA: 57 Heavy Regt *(Wolferton)* *(34+857)* *(A Bty: Burgh St Margarets (4x9.2-inch); B Bty: Dersingham (6x6-inch); C Bty: Holt (4x9.2-inch), D Bty: Freethorpe (2x6-inch)) (a total of 8x9.2-inch, 8x6-inch static guns)*, 2 Medium Regt *(Brandon)* *(32+614)* *(4/7 and 8/12Btys: 4x60-pdr, 12x6-inch)*, 70 Medium Regt *(Brandon)* *(26+617)* *(Infantry role, A and B Btys in training)*, 2 Survey Regt *(Newmarket)* *(24+442)* (from Larkhill 26 August) *(Survey Bty: Brandon, Flash Spotting Bty: Shorncliffe, Kent)*;
RE: 234 Army Field Coy *(Cambridge)* *(6+237)* *(GHQ Line role)*, 240 Army Field Coy *(Ely)* *(5+233)* *(GHQ Line role)*, 292 Army Field Coy *(Cambridge)* *(6+248)*, 678 General Construction Coy *(Duxford)* *(5+268)*, 691 General Construction Coy *(Coltishall)* *(6+264)*, 716 General Construction Coy *(Feltwell)* *(6+269)*, 108 Corps Field Park Coy *(Everton)* *(3+160)*, 14 Corps Field Survey Coy *(Hayes)* *(7+122)*;
RASC: Corps Ammunition Coy *(Huntingdon)* *(8+333)*, Corps Troops Supply Column *(St Ives)* *(18+481)*, 14 Motor Coach Coy *(Drinkstone)* *(9+183)*, 16 Motor Coach Coy *(Swaffham)* *(8+170)*, 17 Motor Coach Coy *(Newmarket)* *(9+167)*;
RAMC: 219 Field Ambulance *(Cambridge)* *(5+161)*;
RAOC: 12 Army Field Workshops RAOC *(Newmarket)* *(13+478)*;
AMPC: 76 Coy *(Melbourn)* *(5+265)*, 97 Coy *(Yarmouth)* *(4+274)*, 130 Coy *(Ludham)* *(5+273)*, 199 Coy *(Newmarket)* *(4+279)*, 215 Coy *(Ampthill)* *(6+278)*.

Eastern Command Troops:

East Anglia:
- Cambridge Sub Area *(HQ: Cambridge)* (GOC: Brigadier J Griffin)
- Hertford Sub Area *(HQ: Hertford)* (GOC: Brigadier W Buckley *from 23 June*)

7 Essex (Home) *(North Weald; Canvey, Tilbury) (52+1087)*, 8 KRRC (Home) *(Barnsbury) (54+1182)*, 8 Norfolk (Home) *(Thetford) (53+1283)*, 50 Lincolnshire (Hold) *(Spalding) (21+849)*, 50 Suffolk *(Saxmundham) (27+945)*, 50 Essex *(Billericay) (24+838)*, 50 Northampton *(Thetford) (22+774)*, 50 Bedford and Hertford (Hold) *(Cromer) (21+734)*, 50 Norfolk (Hold) *(Norwich) (24+880)*, 70 Essex *(Ingatestone) (28+663)*, 70 Norfolk *(Norwich) (31+853)*, 70 Suffolk *(Ipswich) (forming 19 September with 2 coys)*, Essex ITC *(Worley) (38+1334)*, Bedford and Hertford ITC *(Bedford) (37+1591)*, Norfolk ITC *(Norwich) (37+1687)*, Suffolk ITC *(Bury St Edmunds) (46+1554)*;

RA: 4 Reserve A/T Regt *(Bury St Edmunds) (46+491)*, 4 A/T Training Regt *(Culford) (50+457)*, 22 Medium and Heavy Training Regt *(Shoeburyness) (34+1172)*, 21 Heavy Bty *(Shoeburyness) (5+74) (infantry role)*;

RAC: G Armoured Train *(Heacham) (46) (covered Hunstanton, Kings Lynn and Wells)*;

RE: 1 Coy Kent Fortress Unit *(Southend; Canvey, Shoeburyness) (8 coastal searchlights)*, 115 Road Construction Coy *(Thaxted) (3+104)*, 117 Road Construction Coy *(Castle Headingham) (4+102)*, 657 General Construction Coy *(Hatfield) (6+267)*, 710 General Construction Coy *(Peterborough) (6+260)*, 713 General Construction Coy *(Henlow) (6+263)*, 3 Bore Section *(Billingsworth) (2+91)*, 150 Rail Construction Coy *(Cambridge) (7+277) (GHQ Line role)*, 4 EOD Coy *(Cambridge) (11+421)*;

RASC: 4 Coy *(Cosmore) (10+170)*, 30 Coy *(Biggleswade) (5+124)*, Training Centre *(Luton) (47+1566)*, 10 Driver Training Centre *(Cromer) (18+921)*;

RAMC: 18 and 22 Casualty Clearing Stations *(Leighton Buzzard) (17+180)*, 34 General Hospital *(Hatfield) (24+162)*, Military Hospital *(Shenley) (17+132)*;

RAOC: 15 Division Field Workshop *(Norwich) (3+186)*, 27 Advanced Supply Depot *(Shefford) (17+245)*.

GHQ Reserve (South)

VII CORPS (GOC: Lieutenant General The Honourable A McNaughton)
HQ: Aldershot, Hampshire (Rear HQ: Leatherhead) (21+208); Main HQ: Burgh Heath) (79+251)

NOTES:
- The Corps was the GHQ Reserve South, one of the Army's major counter attack groups
- General McNaughton was promoted to command on 19 July and was a former Canadian Chief of General Staff and was to suffer a nervous breakdown in November. He later commanded 1st Canadian Army but retired in 1944. Major General The Honourable P Montague was the Senior Officer of the Canadian Military Headquarters in London, promoted to that post after General Crerar was promoted in early July. The Brigadier General Staff (Operations) was Brigadier M Dempsey, who was to command 2nd British Army in 1944, while the Canadian Brigadier General Staff was Brigadier G Turner, who had recently held that post in 1st Canadian Division. Brigadier J Stewart was the

Commander Canadian Artillery and Brigadier C Hertzberg was the Canadian Chief Engineer.

- 1st **Armoured Division** (GOC: Major General Charles Norrie)

HQ: Dorking, Surrey (12 October = 3 cruiser and 5 light tanks); (Advance HQ: Brockham Park, Dawes Green)

2nd Armoured Brigade: *(HQ: Warminster)* (GOC: Brigadier R McCreery*)
(12 October = HQ: 4 cruiser and 6 light tanks)
2 Dragoon Guards (Queen's Bays) *(35+551) (12 October = 52 cruiser tanks)*, 9 Lancers *(30+540) (12 October = 15 cruiser and 11 light tanks)*, 10 Hussars *(Longbridge Deverill) (30+506) (12 October = 14 cruiser and 11 light tanks)*.

3rd Armoured Brigade: *(HQ: Aldershot)* (GOC: Brigadier R Rimmington from 21 September)
(12 October = HQ: 4 cruiser and 6 light tanks)
5 RTR *(Elstead) (45+742) (27 July = 29xA10, 18xA13, 4xA9 cruiser tanks)*.

20th Armoured Brigade: *(HQ: Rudgwick) (2+270)* (GOC: Brigadier E Fanshawe)
1 Northamptonshire Yeomanry *(Chiddingford) (33+443)*; 2 Northamptonshire Yeomanry *(Pallinghurst) (36+427)*; 1 Gloucestershire Hussars *(Cranleigh) (35+450)*;
(15 September: Brigade had 64 heavy armoured cars; by 29 September it also had 9 mark III infantry tanks)

Support Group: (GOC: Brigadier F Morgan*)
11 RHA *(Abinger) (28+461) (HQ, A and B Btys: 16x18/25-pdr)*, 101 AT/LAA Regt *(Bramley) (36+836) (43+44 A/T, 237+239 LAA Btys: 24x2-pdr, 48 AAMMG)*; Saskatoon Light Infantry (MG) *(Ockley) (32+770) (from 1 Canadian Division)*;

Divisional Troops:
RE: 1 Field Sqn *(Dorking) (9+297)*, 1 Field Park Troop *(Abinger) (4+181)*; 186 Transport Construction Coy *(Elstead) (14+246)*;
RS: Divisional Signals Regt *(Betchworth) (21+618)*;
RASC: Divisional Troops Coy *(Cranleigh) (9+352)*, 2 Armoured Brigade Coy *(Ewshott) (10+332)*, 3 Armoured Brigade Coy *(Frensham) (8+335)*;
RAMC: 1 Light Field Ambulance *(Warminster) (10+182)*, 2 Light Field Ambulance *(Abinger) (9+86)*, 188 Light Field Ambulance *(Abinger) (8+118)*.

NOTES:
- *The Division had gone to France in May and fought with the French and 51st Highland Division along the Somme front in June before evacuating, having left behind most of its equipment but gaining much valuable battle experience*
- *The Division's role was firstly to cover the Corps advance and then strike at the enemy's rear and flanks. In particular, operations in east Kent were initially to cover the Corps concentration along the line Ham Street-Ashford-Charing; In Sussex they were initially to cover the Corps concentration along the line of the River Rother*
- *Convoy movement speed was 25 miles per two hours, density of 20 vehicles per mile. If conditions permitted tracked vehicles were to move by rail to forward assembly areas*
- *At the start of July the Division had 81 medium tanks on strength*
- *At the end of July 1st Army Tank Brigade (Betchworth) came under VII Corps direct command*

- On 11 August 2 RTR came under War office command and prepared to move to North Africa, sailing from Liverpool on 20 August with 7 RTR and 3 Hussars
- General Norrie replaced Major General Evans on 23 August, having previously commanded 1st Armoured Brigade. Brigadier McCreery was appointed in January, while the commanders of 20th Armoured Brigade and the Support Group had been in charge since the outbreak of War. 3rd Armoured Brigade had Brigadier Crocker in charge from 20 April to 21 September; his successor, Brigadier Rimmington, had been the chief instructor at the armoured fighting vehicle school's gunnery wing, but was die of his wounds after being captured in Libya in 1941. General Norrie rose to Corps command in 1941, Brigadier McCreery rose to command 8th Army in 1944, Brigadier Fanshawe was made responsible for training armoured forces in 1942, while Brigadier Morgan rose to command 1st Corps in 1942 and made Chief of Staff to General Eisenhower in 1943
- On 15 September the Division had 99 cruiser and 25 light tanks (125 and 23 respectively by 29 September)
- 2nd Armoured Brigade had a strike force consisting HQ and B Sqn Bays and C Sqn 9 Lancers
- On 12 October the Division's strength consisted 59 cruiser tanks, 154 light tanks, 93 Beaverettes, 16x18/25-pdr, 24x2-pdr
- On 16 October 22nd Armoured Brigade (from 2nd Armoured Division) replaced 20th Armoured Brigade, which left to join the newly formed 6th Armoured Division
- On 25 October 3rd Armoured Brigade left the Division to prepare for a move to the Middle East. This move had been postponed until the onset of autumn made invasion unlikely.

- 1st Canadian Infantry Division (GOC: Major General George Pearkes VC)

HQ: Reigate, Surrey. (Advance HQ: Merstham)
1st Brigade: *(HQ: Horley)* (GOC: Brigadier A Smith)
48 Highlanders *(Newdidgate) (31+688)*, Royal Canadian Regt *(Reigate) (30+744)*, Hastings and Prince Edward Regt *(Betchworth) (37+749)*;
2nd Brigade: *(HQ: Westerham)* (GOC: Brigadier A Potts)
PPCLI *(Godstone) (28+742)*, Seaforth Highlanders *(Godstone) (24+742)*, Loyal Edmonton Regt *(Oxted)(31+743)*;

3rd Brigade: *(HQ, Bookham, Leatherhead)* (GOC: Brigadier C Price)
22ieme Regt *(Caterham) (30+691)*, Carleton and York Regt *(Caterham) (26+742)*, West Nova Scotia Regt *(Woldingham) (30+749)*;
Divisional Troops:
RCA: 1RCHA *(Ewshot) (39+596) (24x18/25-pdr)*, 2 Field Regt *(Westerham) (37+572) (24x18/25-pdr)*, 3 Field Regt *(Bookham) (38+609) (24x18/25-pdr)*, 1 A/T Regt *(Gatton Park) (21+534) (27, 51, 57 and 90 Btys: 48x2-pdr)*;
MG: Saskatoon Light Infantry *(see 1Armoured Division)*; Toronto Scots *(Chipstead) (27+759) (B Coy with 3 Brigade, C Coy with 2 Brigade, D Coy with 1 Brigade)*;
RCE: 1 Field Company *(Charlwood) (5+234)*, 3 Field Company *(Oxted) (6+229)*, 4 Field Company *(Caterham) (5+229)*; 2 Field Park Company *(Alderstead Heath) (4+168)*;
RCASC: Divisional Supply Column *(Blindley Heath) (13+429)*, Divisional Petrol Coy *(Ifield) (6+265)*, Divisional Ammunition Coy *(Great Bookham) (9+354)*; 1 Troop Carry Company

RASC (assigned to 2 Brigade), 10 Motor Coach Coy RASC *(Charlwood) (9+170)* (assigned to 1 Brigade), 12 Troop Carry Company RASC (Assigned to 3 Brigade);
RCAMC: 4 Field Ambulance *(Upper Gatton Park, Reigate) (12+225)*, 5 Field Ambulance *(Gatton Park, Reigate) (13+218)*, 9 Field Ambulance *(Gatton Hall Park, Reigate) (12+218)*;
RCMP: 1 Provost Company *(Reigate).*

NOTES:
- *The Division had arrived in the United Kingdom by December 1939, containing most of the trained units available in Canada at the start of the War. In June it had briefly gone to Normandy but had seen little if any action*
- *On its return from France it went to Oxfordshire before moving to Surrey at the start of July*
- *By 13 July the Division had 30% Personnel, 100% artillery pieces, 100% A/T guns*
- *Each Brigade formed a reconnaissance company (headquarters and 4 motorcycle troops, 10+206 strong with 26 motorcycle and 20 motorcycle combinations)*
- *Divisional concentration areas were either around Tunbridge Wells or East Grinstead, depending on the objective*
- *By 7 September the Division had 100% Personnel, 100% artillery pieces, 100% A/T guns*
- *In autumn 1 Survey Regt and 2 LAA Regt RCA joined.*
- *In mid September the Division began moving to winter quarters from tented camps*
- *Between 20-25 October it moved to the Worthing-Newhaven Sector, 3rd Brigade moved to the Hurstpierpoint-Shoreham-Stanmer area*
- *General Pearkes was promoted in 1940 after commanding 2nd Brigade and returned to Canada in 1942. Brigadier Potts rose to divisional command in 1942 and Brigadier Price rose to command 3rd Division in 1941. Brigadier Smith was severely injured in a vehicle accident in late 1940 and as a result retired in 1941.*

Corps Troops:
- 1st Army Tank Brigade (GOC: Brigadier H Watkins)
HQ: Betchworth, Surrey
4 RTR *(East Grinstead) (33+544) (50 Matilda Mk II)*, 44 RTR *(Reigate) (33+545) (50 Matilda Mk II);*
5 Light Field Ambulance RAMC *(Leatherhead) (8+114);* Brigade Coy RASC *(Reigate).*

NOTES:
- *The Brigade had served with the BEF and had led the counterattack at Arras in May*
- *In July the Brigade was detached from 1st Armoured Division, in support of 1st Canadian Division.*
- *Brigadier Watkins replaced Brigadier D Pratt on 19 July*
- *In August 4 RTR joined the Brigade*
- *By the end of August the Brigade had its full complement of Matilda Mk II infantry tanks*
- *Movement by train would require six trains per tank battalion, with 8-9 tanks per train. East Grinstead and Lingfield stations were earmarked for the Brigade's use. Movement by road transport was regulated at 10 vehicles to a mile and at a speed of 20mph, with units moving independently of each other. It was estimated that it would take the Brigade three hours to move to any of its preparatory assembly areas*

- On 6 September 8 RTR was attached to the NZEF in Kent. It had previously been located in the Horley-Springfield-Charlwood area
- On 12 September 44 RTR joined the Brigade. On 19 August it had swapped with 7 RTR 26 Matilda MkII for 10 Matilda MkII and 16 Valentine tanks
- By 15 September the Brigade had 126 Matilda Mk II, 27 Matilda Mk I infantry and 16 light tanks.

Corps HQ Protection Company (Lorne Scots) *(Aldershot)*;
RCA: 8 Army Field Regt *(Nork Park) (24x18/25-pdr)*, 11 Army Field Regt *(Banstead) (24x18/25-pdr)*, 1 Medium Regt *(West Horsley) (12x6-inch)*; 1 Survey Bty *(Weybridge)*; 2 LAA Bty *(AAMG)* (Attached to 53 LAA Regt RA for training);
RCE: 2 Army Field Company *(Buckles Gap) (6+218)*, 12 Army Field Company *(Burgh Heath) (6+235)*; 1 Tunnelling Company *(Mickleham Hall) (8+274)*; 2 Road Construction Coy *(Mickleham Wood) (9+338)*; 1 Corps Field Survey Company *(Cobham)*; 3 Bridge Coy RE *(Dorking) (part of unit)*;
MG: Royal Montreal Regt *(Sutton) (34+754)*;
1 Canadian Pioneer Bn *(Wentworth Hall) (30+779) (A Coy to Brighton on 25 September, C Coy at Weybridge)*;
RCASC: 1 Corps Troops Ammunition Company *(Worth Park) (8+292)*, 1 Canadian Troops Supply Column *(Pound Hill, Crawley) (18+472)*, 1 Corps Petrol Park *(Ifield) (10+318)*, 1 Corps Ammunition Park *(Pound Hill, Crawley) (20+659)*; Corps Ammunition Dump *(Three Bridges)*;
RCCS: Corps Signals Company *(Aldershot) (21+412) (arrived from Canada on 5 September)*;
RCAMC: 8 Field Ambulance *(Leatherhead)*; 6 Motor Ambulance Convoy *(Ashtead)*; 4 Casualty Clearing Station *(Ashtead)*;
RCAOC: Corps Ordnance Dump *(Horley)*; 1 Corps Ordnance Field Park *(Epsom)*; 2 Army Field Workshop *(Epsom)*;
RCCS: Corps Signals Company;
RCMP: 2 Provost Company *(Walton on the Hill)*.

ALDERSHOT COMMAND (GOC: Major General D Johnson)
<u>NOTE:</u> *Major General Johnson had taken command on 25 June, having commanded 4th Division in the BEF. He became Director of Infantry in 1941 and retired in 1944.*

- 2nd Canadian Infantry Division (GOC: Major General V Odlum)
HQ: Aldershot
4th Brigade: (GOC: Brigadier C Topp DSO)
Essex Scottish *(Aldershot) (29+802)*, Royal Hamilton Light Infantry *(Aldershot) (31+879)*, 2 Canadian Pioneer Bn *(Aldershot) (35+885) (arrived from Canada 4 September)*.
5th Brigade: (GOC: Brigadier P Leclerc)
Black Watch of Canada *(Aldershot) (32+937)*, Calgary Highlanders *(Aldershot) (26+864)*, Regt du Maisonneuve *(Aldershot) (33+823)*.
2nd Division Artillery Group: (GOC: Brigadier R Frazer)
4 Field Regt *(Ewshott) (40+586) (2/14 and 26/53 Btys: 4x75mm)*, 5 Field Regt *(Aldershot)*

(40+588) (5/73 and 28/89 Btys: 3x75mm), 6 Field Regt *(Aldershot) (39+582)* (*13x21 and 91/11 Btys: 8x75mm*), 2 A/T Regt RCA *(Farnborough) (24+552) (20, 23, 108 Btys - infantry role).*

Divisional Troops:
RCE: 7 Field Coy *(Aldershot) (6+250) (Arrived from Canada on 5 September)*, 11 Field Coy *(Aldershot) (5+249) (Arrived from Canada on 5 September);* 1 Field Park Coy *(Aldershot) (2+10) (Advance party, which arrived from Canada on 4 September);*
CRAMC: 10 Field Ambulance *(Aldershot) (12+229) (Arrived from Canada on 4 September)*, 11 Field Ambulance *(Aldershot) (12+230) (Arrived from Canada on 4 September)*, 18 Field Ambulance *(Aldershot) (3+12) (Advance party, which arrived from Canada on 4 September);* 1 General Hospital CRAMC *(Aldershot);*
RCASC: Divisional Supply Column *(Aldershot) (14+438)*, Divisional Petrol Coy *(Aldershot) (3+32) (Advance party, which arrived from Canada on 5 September)*, Divisional Ammunition Coy *(Aldershot) (2+24) (Advance party, which arrived from Canada on 5 September);* Composite Troop Carry Company;
CRMP: Divisional Provost Coy.

NOTES:
- *The headquarters and two infantry battalions of 6th Infantry Brigade and one MG battalion were detached in Canada and sent to Iceland in June as Force Z under Brigadier L Page*
- *Most of the Division arrived from Canada in August*
- *On 4 September 5th Infantry Brigade arrived from Canada*
- *In September the Division's role was local defence in the Aldershot area, notably defending the Odiham (4th Brigade) and Hogs Back (5th Brigade) areas. 4 Brigade was also available for operations with VII Corps*
- *The Division had had no field training before arriving in the country and was poorly equipped. As such, the Artillery Group was assigned an infantry role. Between 21 and 24 September the first artillery pieces (15x75mm guns) were received*
- *On 10 September a Composite Troop Carry Company RCASC was formed from VII Corps RCASC troops. The Supply Column was reformed as 4 and 5 Composite Companies to supply 4th and 5th Brigades' needs*
- *By 13 September the Division was nominally attached to VII Corps in order to bring all Canadian troops under a unified command*
- *On 25 September 9/15 Bty (11 Army Field Regt RCA) was attached from VII Corps troops with 12x18/25 pdr*
- *General Odlum left for Australia in 1941; Brigadier Leclerc rose to divisional command in Canada*
- *By 5 November Divisional artillery contained 28x75mm guns*
- *Force Z arrived from Iceland in December 1940.*

- 1st Infantry Training Group *(HQ: Bisley)* (GOC: Brigadier A Lawrence)
13 Queens *(28+961) (Cowshott Camp)*, 14 Queens *(28+941) (Stony Castle Camp)*, 9 Hampshire *(28+952)*, 10 Hampshire *(31+950)*.

NOTES:
- *The Group was assigned the defence of the Pirbright - Brookwood area on its formation in early July*
- *14 Queens was formed on 6 July*
- *9 Hampshire was formed on 3 July on the Isle of Wight but moved to the Aldershot area on 9 July*
- *Group reformed as 201st (Coastal) Infantry Brigade on 4 October*
- *On 21 October it replaced 10th Infantry Brigade at Selsey Bill in its coastal defence role.*

Aldershot Command Troops:
Sub Area HQ`s: Blackdown and Deepcut; North Aldershot, South Aldershot, Bordon and Longmoor

11 Queens *(56+1271) (A Coy: Ascot, B Coy: Woking and Odiham, C Coy: Croydon, D and E Coys: Aldershot, F Coy: Command HQ, G Coy: Guildford)*, 50 OBLI *(Church Crookham) (19+697) (GHQ line role east of Odiham)*, 50 Wiltshire *(Basingstoke) (21+729) (9 October reformed as 7 Wiltshire and joined 203 Brigade)*, Grenadier Guards Training Bn *(Windsor) (65+2669)*, Queens ITC *(Guildford) (27+1703)*, Guards Depot *(Caterham) (48+3085)*, Scots Guards Training Bn *(Pirbright) (55+1808)*, Coldstream Guards Training Bn *(Pirbright) (75+2355)*, 167, 168, 169 and 170 Infantry OCTU`s *(111+2193) (GHQ line role)*, Infantry Wing OCTU *(Sandhurst) (27+743)*;
RA: 121 OCT Regt *(40+658) (GHQ line role, north and south of Aldershot: 8x4.5-inch, 12x13-pdr)*, 23 Field Regt *(53+335) (GHQ line role, South Aldershot: 12x75mm)*, 50 A/T Training Regt *(24+1177) (Aldershot) (GHQ Line role, Bordon and S Aldershot: 12x2-pdr)*;
RAC: 55 Armoured Training Regt *(Farnborough) (48+1871)*;
RE: 141 and 142 OCTU`s *(72+1193)*; 1 Motor Transport Depot *(29+1346)*; 293 Corps Field Park Coy *(5+165)*, 4 Field Sqn *(9+306)*, 214, 216 and 217 Army Field Coys *(17+717)*, 290 Army Troops Coy *(7+279)*, 514 Army Survey Coy *(7+137)*, 143 Field Park Troop *(6+187)*, 715 General Construction Coy *(Farnborough) (6+267)*;
RS: 151 OCTU *(38+680)*;
RASC: 1 Depot Bn *(3+376)*, 12 Training Bn *(23+1275)*, 8 and 9 Motor Coach Coys *(17+328) (assigned to VII Corps)*;
RAMC: 9 Light Field Ambulance *(Church Crookham) (6+115)*, 1 and 2 Training Coys *(120+753)*, 1 Depot *(Church Crookham) (119+2953)*, 12 Depot *(10+688)*;
AMPC: 26 Group (37,186,504,505, 507 Coys) *(25+1316)*, 185 Coy *(Farnham) (4+264)*;
RAOC: 1 Base Ordnance Depot *(5+310)*.

Blackdown and Deepcut Garrison (GOC: Brigadier H McCarthy-O'Leary)
RAC: 102 OCTU *(Blackdown) (25+425)*;
RA: 1 and 2 Reserve Field Regts *(Ascot) (114+1575) (GHQ line role, Blackdown, Ascot and Bordon: 8x4.5-inch, 16x18-pdr, 8x13-pdr)*;
RASC: 1 Training Bn *(Blackdown) (38+1474)*;
AMPC: 75 Coy *(Blackdown) (4+301)*.

NOTE: Brigadier McCarthy had been in command since the War began

Bordon and Longmoor Garrison (GOC: Brigadier Daunt)
RA: 12 Field Training Regt *(Bordon) (29+1071)* (*GHQ line role, S Aldershot: 8x13-pdr, 8x18-pdr, 8x4.5-inch*), Holding Unit RCA (*GHQ line role, Bordon and Longmoor: 6x4.5-inch, 3x18-pdr*);
RE: 16 Depot Bn *(Bordon) (54+1959)*, 7 Rail Bn *(Longmoor) (46+1303)*, 14 and 15 Transport Training Bns *(Longmoor) (41+1733)*, 604, 607 and 608 Rail Construction Coys *(Longmoor) (10+277)*, 192 and 193 Rail Operating Coys *(Woolmer) (10+345)*, 601-603 Rail Construction Coys *(Woolmer) (15+548)*, 11,14,15 Forestry Coys NZE; Rail, Construction and Maintenance Group NZE *(9 Rail Survey and 10 Rail Construction Coys) (Woolmer)*;
RASC: 156 Transport Coy *(Longmoor) (5+228)*;
HQ Canadian 2nd Echelon *(Bordon)* (included Infantry Base Depots and other training units).

NOTE: Brigadier Daunt had been in command since the War began.

SOUTHERN COMMAND (GOC: Lieutenant General Claude Auchinleck)
HQ: Salisbury

NOTES:
- *General Auchinleck had been promoted to command from V Corps on 20 July, having commanded the expeditionary force sent to Norway in April. He rose to become Commander in Chief, India*
- *HQ 6th Armoured Division began forming at Andover from 27 September, moving to Chippenham on 10 October. It was expected to be operational by the spring of 1941.*

V CORPS (GOC: Lieutenant General B Montgomery*)
HQ: Tidworth, Wiltshire

NOTES:
- *In June the Corps HQ was formed from the Norway Expeditionary Force HQ*
- *The Corps was responsible for the defence of the Hampshire and Dorset coasts*
- *On 14 August only a third of the Corps was considered mobile, mostly in 4th Division*
- *Corps stop lines were Salisbury-Ringwood-Christchurch (West facing); Stalbridge-Blandford-Wimborne-Christchurch (South West facing) and Yeovil-Sherborne-Stalbridge (North facing)*
- *General Montgomery replaced General Auchinleck on 24 July. He had commanded 3rd Division in the BEF.*

- 4th Infantry Division (GOC: Major General R Eastwood)
HQ: Horndean, Hampshire
10th Brigade: *(HQ: Chichester)* (GOC: Brigadier E Barker*)
2 Bedford and Hertfordshire *(Chichester) (35+844)*, 2 Duke of Cornwall's Light Infantry *(Wittering) (33+858)*, 1/6 East Surrey *(Selsey) (33+805)*.
11th Brigade: *(HQ: Hursley, Winchester)* (GOC: Brigadier J Grover)
2 Lancashire Fusiliers *(Ringwood) (28+901)*, 1 East Surrey *(Winchester) (33+847)*, 1/5 Northampton *(Winchester) (34+858)*.

Divisional Troops:
RA: 22 Field Regt *(Waterlooville) (32+549) (4x18-pdr, 4x4.5-inch)*, 30 Field Regt *(West Wittering)*
(36+557) (104/111 Bty: Nutbourne, 112/117 Bty: Runcton) (22x75mm, 4x25-pdr, 4x18/25-pdr),
77 Field Regt *(Ringwood) (34+542) (A, D and G Tps (4x75mm each) and E Tp (2x25-pdr,*
2x75mm) on beaches between Bournemouth and Portsmouth; C and F Tps on Isle of Wight (4x18-
pdr, 4x4.5-inch) and B Tp (4x25-pdr) as mobile reserve), 14 A/T Regt *(Romsey) (26+511) (38, 61,*
68 and 88 Btys) (Regt concentrated at Romsey with 6x2-pdr, rest as infantry);
RE: 7 Field Coy *(Chichester) (6+237)*, 59 Field Coy *(Havant) (6+250)*, 225 Field Coy *(Ringwood)*
(6+241), 18 Field Park Coy *(Bishop Waltham) (3+151)*;
RAMC: 10 Field Ambulance *(Chichester) (9+172)*, 11 Field Ambulance *(Bishop Waltham)*
(12+217);
RAOC: Divisional LAD`s *(Havant) (14+374)*;
RASC: Divisional Ammunition Coy *(Owslebury) (10+385)*, Divisional Petrol Coy *(Warnford)*
(5+292), Divisional Supply Column *(Warnford) (15+418)*;
RS: Divisional Signals Regt *(Rowlands Castle) (24+467)*.

NOTES:
- *The Division was a Regular Army formation that had served in the BEF*
- *General Eastwood was in command from 25 June to 4 October before becoming Director General Home Guard; he was promoted to command Northern Command in 1941. Brigadier Barker had served since the start of the War and rose to command Eighth Army in 1945, while Brigadier Grover was appointed on 14 June*
- *The Division's main role was to protect the important ports of Portsmouth and Southampton; 12th Brigade Group was assigned to the Isle of Wight (see below)*
- *In July the Division was allocated 2x9.2-inch and 2x6-inch (D Bty) and 4x9.2-inch (C Bty 54 Heavy Regt) and 24x25-pdr (144 Army Field Regt) from Corps Troops*
- *By 13 July the Division had 100% Personnel, 40% artillery pieces, 45% A/T guns*
- *By 7 September it had 100% Personnel, 100% artillery pieces, 40% A/T guns*
- *In mid October 10th Brigade was relieved by 201st (Coastal) Infantry Brigade.*

- 50th Infantry Division (Tyne Tees) (GOC: Major General G Martel*)
HQ: Blandford, Dorset
69th Brigade: *(HQ: Lytchett Heath)* (GOC: Brigadier J Barstow)
1/5 East Yorkshire *(Studland) (38+902)*, 6 Green Howards *(Swanage) (34+847)*, 7 Green
  Howards *(Wimborne) (36+850)*.
150th Brigade: *(HQ: Weymouth)* (GOC: Brigadier C Haydon*)
1/4 East Yorkshire *(Weymouth) (35+895)*, 1/4 Green Howards *(Weymouth) (34+860)*, 1/5 Green
  Howards *(Lulworth) (35+880)*.
151st Brigade: *(HQ: Cattistock)* (GOC: Brigadier J Churchill*)
6 Durham Light Infantry *(Maiden Newton) (36+862)*, 8 Durham Light Infantry *(Yeovil)*
  (34+885), 9 Durham Light Infantry *(Sherborne) (36+888)*.
Divisional Troops:
1/4 Northumberland Fusiliers (m/cycle) *(Boscombe) (33+524)*;
2 Middlesex (MG) *(Poole/Frome) (35+771)*;
RA: 72 Field Regt *(Weymouth) (35+567) (285 and 286 Btys: 12x18/25-pdr, 8x25-pdr)*, 74 Field Regt

(Weymouth) (34+581) (286 and 386 Btys: 24x25-pdr), 124 Field Regt (Studland) (41+601) (287 Bty: 7x75mm, 2x4-inch, Corfe Castle, 288 Bty: 6x75mm, Parkstone), 65 A/T Regt (Child Okeford) (25+558) (257Bty: Durweston (8x2-pdr), 258 Bty: East Moores, 259 Bty: Chideock and 260 Bty: Winterbourne) (10x6-pdr, 8x2-pdr);

RE: 232 Field Coy (Weymouth) (5+246), 233 Field Coy (Wimborne) (6+230), 505 Field Coy (Bridport) (5+251), 235 Field Park Coy (Spettisbury) (3+164);

RAMC: 149 Field Ambulance (Beaminster) (12+218), 150 Field Ambulance (Sturminster) (10+238), 186 Field Ambulance (Wimborne) (12+235);

RASC: Divisional Ammunition Coy (Sedgehill) (10+404), Divisional Supply Column (Yeovil) (13+460), Divisional Petrol Coy (Marnhull) (6+303);

RS: Divisional Signals Regt (Blandford) (25+437);

RAOC: Divisional LADS (Blandford) (10+188);

CMP: Divisional Provost Coy (Blandford) (1+110).

NOTES:

- The Division was a Territorial Army formation which had served in the BEF, 69th Brigade with BEF's 23rd Division. General Martel had commanded since the start of the War, having previously been Deputy Director of Mechanisation. Brigadier Barstow had been in charge since 24 June, Brigadier Haydon since 26 April and only Brigadier Churchill since the start of the War
- The Division's main role was coastal defence in Dorset
- In July it was allocated 2x9.2-inch and 2x6-inch (B Bty 54 Heavy Regt) and 24x25-pdr (143 Army Field Regt) from Corps Troops
- By 13 July the Division had 100% Personnel, 30% artillery pieces, 10% A/T guns
- By 7 September it had 100% Personnel, 100% artillery pieces, 40% A/T guns
- In mid October 210th (Coastal) Infantry Bde arrived, with 9 Royal West Kent (Swanage), 7 Suffolk (Poole), 9 Essex (Lyme Regis) and 8 Essex (Chesil).

Corps Troops:

1 Lothian and Border Yeomanry (Bovington) (26+143) (ad hoc light armoured vehicles);

4 Commando (Weymouth) (36+460);

2 Northumberland Fusiliers (MG) (Lyndhurst) (26+798);

9 Kings Own (Pioneer) (Bournemouth and Beaulieu) (28+1083);

RA: 5 Survey Regt (Hindon) (28+408), 54 Heavy Regt (Romsey) (32+775) (12x9.2-inch, 4x6-inch) (A Bty (4x9.2-inch) as Corps reserve), 4 Medium Regt (Ringwood) (23+650) (9/13 and 14/16 Btys: 4x6-pdr), 63 Medium Regt (Mere) (29+622) (anti tank role) (214 Bty: Selsey (4x4-inch and 3x6-pdr), ThorneyIsland (4x4-inch), Havant (3x4-inch), Boscombe (1x4-inch), Portsdown (2x4-inch, 2x6-pdr), Hayling Island (2x6-pdr); 216 Bty: Bognor Regis (6x6-pdr), Lee on Solent (2x6-pdr and 1x4-inch), Horndean (2x12-pdr and 2x3-pdr mobile) (Attached to 4th Div), Whiteparish (2x12-pdr and 2x3-pdr mobile), Ringwood (4x6-pdr (Command Line)), 143 Army Field Regt (Hursley) (40+589) (24x25-pdr) (allocated to 50 Division), 144 Army Field Regt (39+443) (24x25-pdr) (allocated to 4th Division), 203 A/T Bty (Hermitage) (6+116); Corps Ammunition Depot (New Alfresford), Corps Ammunition Depot (Holnest), Corps Ammunition Depot (Damerham), Corps Ammunition Sub Depot (Shalfleet);

RE: 577 Army Field Coy (Wimborne) (6+266), 579 Army Field Coy (Wimborne) (8+418), 564 Army Field Coy (Romsey) (6+243), 751 Army Field Coy (Poole) (7+235), 64 Chemical

Warfare Coy *(Southampton) (5+233)*, 65 Chemical Warfare Coy *(Cosham) (5+237)*, 516 Corps Field Survey Coy *(Teffont) (6+135)*, Dorset Fortress Coy *(Weymouth) (1+37)*, 576 Corps Field Park Coy *(Wimborne) (4+294)*, 575 Army Troops Coy *(Warminster) (7+293)*;

RASC: 19 Motor Coach Coy *(Maidenhead) (9+149)*, 25 Motor Coach Coy *(Gillingham) (11+173) (assigned to 50th Division)*, 26 Motor Coach Coy *(Winchester) (8+170) (assigned to 4th Division)*;

RAOC: 14 Army Field Workshop *(Wimborne) (12+235)*;

RAMC: 4 Casualty Clearing Station *(Winchester) (8+86)*;

RS: Corps Signals Regt *(Tidworth) (27+712)*.

Portsmouth Garrison *(including Southampton) (425+11,534)* (CO: Lt Col J Harter)
(GOC Royal Marines Portsmouth Division: Brigadier T Hunton; GOC MNBDO: Brigadier E Weston)

HQ: *Fort Wallington, Fareham*

342 MGTC *(Gosport) (81+1017)*;

RA: 3 Training Regt *(Fort Brockenhurst) (30+817) (4x4.5-inch at Gosport)*, 31 Howitzer Bty RM *(Hayling Island) (135) (6x3.7-inch)*;

RE: 137 Artisan Works Maintenance Section *(Portsmouth) (4+187)*, Survey Training Centre *(Fort Southwick) (30+772)*, Hampshire Fortress Unit *(Portsmouth)*;

RASC: 20 Station Transport Coy *(5+145)*, 3 Station Maintenance Coy *(4+106)*;

RAOC: 4 Training Bn *(Hilsea) (45+2301)*, Command Supply Depot *(Portsmouth)*;

AMPC: 58 Coy *(Southsea) (4+337)*.

Royal Navy:
- Barracks (Anson, Benbow and Cornwallis Bns) *(Anson Bn to Portsbridge; Benbow Bn to Pitt Street, Portsea; Cornwallis Bn – C and D Coys to Forts Nelson and Wallington, rest to Fareham)*
- HMS Excellent *(A Coy: Farlington, B Coy: Whale Island, C Coy: Cosham, X Coy: Portsea)*
- HMS Collingwood *(Coy: outpost line Fort Fareham and Stubbington; Coy: reserve)*
- HMS Vernon *(Coy: Portsea)*
- HMS St Vincent *(Coy: Gosport)*
- HM Dockyard *(Naval Guard (80 men) and RM Police)*
- RM Reinforcement Depot *(Hayling Island) (plus 300 RN)*
- HQ MNBDO *(Fort Cumberland, Portsea) (inc. training wing, signals company and landing, transport and workshop companies)*
- HQ Coast Defence Group *(Eastney) (defence platoon and signals company)*
- Portsmouth Division RM *(Eastney Barracks, Southsea) (6 companies)*.

NOTES:
- *Brigadier Hunton rose to be Commandant General in 1943. Brigadier Weston retired in 1943*
- *Fortress Headquarters was established in the West Bastion*
- *The July Defence Scheme allotted the Navy responsibility for west Pitsea, including the Dockyard, and the Gosport Peninsula. The Gosport line (commanded by the Senior Naval Officer at HMS St Vincent) ran from Fort Elson to Browndown Point, with an outpost line*

running between Fort Fane, Fort Stubbington and Lee on Solent. Anson Bn was on two hours notice to mobilise, while Cornwallis Bn was on 4 hours notice
- Fort Blockhouse was to be a cornerstone of the defences, with 300 men, 1x4-inch, 2x12-pdr and 1x2-pdr guns assigned
- Anson Bn was disbanded on 9 October
- In February 1941 the Naval Force was reduced to Benbow Bn, two companies in HMS Excellent, one coy in HMS Cornwallis and local forces in HMS St Vincent (Gosport) and HMS Dolphin (Haslar)
- In February 1941 HQ Marine Naval Base Defence Organisation was sent to Egypt.

Southampton Garrison: (CO: Colonel G Thomson from 7 August)
8 Hampshire (Home) *(41+1320) (10 October split into two battalions. C Coy: Fort Fareham)*,
  70 Hampshire *(1202) (formed 19 September with two young soldier coys from 8 Hampshire and four companies from 6 Dorset; A Coy at Lee on Solent)*;
RE: 1 Docks Group (991-994 Dock Operating Coys) *(42+1615)*;
RAMC: 3 Training Coy *(1+243)*;
AMPC: 172 Coy *(5+279)*, 172 Coy *(4+266)*,
 RASC: Command Supply Depot *(Southampton)*, Command Supply Depot *(Stockbridge)*

Isle of Wight Garrison *(278+7648)* (GOC: Brigadier D Beak from 18 June) *(HQ: Newtown)*
12th Brigade (4th Division):
2 Royal Fusiliers *(Newport) (33+809)*, 1/6 Black Watch *(Wooton, Haven Street) (35+866)*,
  1 Royal West Kent *(Ventnor-Bembridge) (36+753)*, 11 Hampshire *(Wooton) (18+307)*;
RAMC: 12 Field Ambulance *(East Cowes) (10+182)*;
RE: 578 Army Field Coy *(Cowes) (7+263)*.

50 Hampshire (Hold) *(Freshwater) (24+734)*, Hampshire ITC *(Parkhurst) (36+1669)*, D Coy
  8 Hampshire (Home) *(Sandown)*;
RA: 1 Coast Defence Training Bty *(Yarmouth) (20+326)* plus C & F Troops, 77 Field Regt
  (4th Division) (4x18-pdr, 4x4.5-inch), detachment 63 Field Regt *(2x6-pdr)*;
AMPC: 30 Coy *(Sandown) (6+255)*;
RAOC: Command Supply Depot *(Newport)*.

NOTES:
- It was recorded that the troops assigned to defend the Isle of Wight should be of the highest calibre as they were unlikely to be either reinforced or relieved once operations were underway
- 50 Hampshire included men of the Royal Jersey Militia.

Bulford Garrison *(285+12,410)* (CO: Colonel G Fleming from 23 May)
6 Wiltshire (Home) *(34+772)*, 162 Infantry OCTU *(28+554)* *(assigned to Salisbury Plain Area Strike Force as a reserve with 4 coys)*;
RA: 4 Field Training Regt *(33+1474) (4x4.5-inch)* *(assigned to the GHQ Blue Line Salisbury Plain Area Strike Force reserve)*;
RASC: 3 Driver Training Bn *(24+1241)*, 10 Artificer Training Bn *(53+2793)*, 11 Artificer

Training Bn *(50+1841)*, 2 Station Maintenance Coy *(4+145)*, 5 Station Transport Coy *(5+152)*, G Coy *(7+1976)*;
CMP: Command Provost Coy *(132)*;
AMPC: 203 Coy *(5+277)*.

Tidworth Garrison *(404+8,959)* (CO: Colonel H Hawtrey)
1 Rifle Brigade *(31+835)*, 2 KRRC *(37+861)* (Garrison reserve: 14 scout cars, 14 carriers, 26 m/c, 50 lorries), 1 Queen Victoria Rifles *(28+606)* *(14 scout cars, 14 carriers, 26 m/c, 50 lorries)*, 10 Green Howards *(18+283)*, 2 Rifle Brigade Motor Training Bn *(54+1561)* (*assigned to the GHQ Blue Line and Salisbury Plain Area Strike Force, with one scout and one motor infantry coy based on Amesbury*);
RAC: 53 Light Armoured Training Regt *(64+1804)* (*assigned to Salisbury Plain Area Strike Force based on Marlborough with 5 medium tanks, 20 light tanks and 12 carriers in 1 tank and 1 infantry sqn*);
RAMC: 8 Casualty Clearing Station *(10+87)*, 20 Training Coy *(137+689)*;
RAOC: 61 Training Section *(7+1071)*;
CMP: 110 Provost Coy *(108)*;
AMPC: 145 Coy *(5+263)*, 506 Coy *(5+252)*.

Blandford Garrison *(88+4,312)* (GOC: Brigadier H Woodhouse)
11 South Staffordshire (Pioneer) *(29+866)*, 302 Essex ITC *(27+1816)*; 309 Berkshire ITC *(26+1542)*;
18 Coy RASC *(5+188)*.

Southern Command Troops:
- Salisbury Plain Sub Area: *(HQ: Bulford)* (GOC: Brigadier M Studd)
1 KRRC Motor Training Bn *(Chisledon) (63+1612)* (*one scout and one motor infantry coy formed the Chippenham strike force*), 4 Berkshire *(Shirehampton) (31+876)*, 6 Dorset (Home) *(Salisbury) (56+754)*, Motor Infantry Battalions` Depot *(Winchester) (24+2780)*, Sussex ITC *(Chichester) (61+1657)*;
RAC: Household Cavalry Training Regt *(Windsor) (26+492)*, 54 Light Armoured Training Regt *(Perham Down) (48+1871)* (*assigned to the GHQ Blue Line and Salisbury Plain Area Strike Force, with one tank and two infantry sqns based on Swindon*), 57 Heavy Armoured Training Regt *(Warminster) (46+1890)* (*assigned to Salisbury Plain Strike Forcebased on Warminster with a sqn of 10 medium and 3 light tanks, 3 MG troops and 1 rifle troop*);
RA: 133 OCTU *(Shrivenham) (293+2378)* (*GHQ Line and RAF Brize Norton defence roles*), Command Ordnance Sub Depot *(Grateley)*;
RE: 187 Transport Construction Coy *(Stockbridge) (14+360)*, Home Depot Postal Section *(Bournemouth) (18+541)*, 5 Movement Control Group *(Salisbury) (42+193)*, 3 Chemical Warfare Group (11, 12, 13 Bns, 66, 70 and A Depot Coys) *(Barton Stacey) (156+4780)*, 67, 68 and 69 Chemical Warfare Coys *(Winterbourne) (16+664)*, 165 Rail Survey Coy *(Alton) (7+66)*, 669 Artisan Works Coy *(Alverstoke) (6+270)*, 698 General Construction Coy *(Old Sarum) (6+262)*, Chemical Warfare Group *(Porton) (47+430)*;
RASC: 28 Troop Carry Coy *(Marlborough) (7+155)*, 40 Motor Coach Coy *(Fawley) (9+160)*,

1 Armoured Reconnaissance Brigade Coy *(Swindon) (10+386)*, 3 Bulk Petrol Coy *(Manton) (5+178)*, 1 Reserve Motor Transport Coy *(Marlborough) (11+482)*, 25 Reserve Motor Transport Coy *(Swindon) (9+154)*, 27 Reserve Motor Transport Coy *(Wroughton) (8+216)*, 1 Holding Coy *(Marlborough) (334)*, 12 Ammunition Coy *(Bramley) (3+100)*, 4 Driver Training Bn *(Perham Down) (21+1284)*, HQ and Depot Coy IMCC *(Chilton Foliat) (25+527)*;

RAMC: 1 Ambulance Train *(Netley) (1+13)*, 13 General Hospital *(Malmesbury) (15+226)*, 4 Training Coy *(Netley) (108+885)*;

RAOC: 2 Base Ammunition Depot *(Corsham) (209)*, 22 Ammunition Supply Depot *(Marlborough) (12+212)*, 5 Ordnance Field Park *(Bournemouth) (8+241)*, Command Supply Depot *(Tidworth)*, Command Supply Depot *(Bulford)*, Command Supply Depot *(Warminster)*, Command Supply Depot *(Devizes)*, Command Supply Depot *(Shrivenham)*, 4 Supply Reserve Depot *(Swindon)*, 63 Training Section *(Corsham) (18+625)*;

AMPC: 14 Group (16, 21, 99 and 124 Coys) *(Corsham) (27+1050)*, 81 Coy *(Chichester) (6+277)*, 125 and 159 Coys *(Bramley) (9+524)*, 142 Coy *(Warminster) (4+247)*, 154 Coy *(Marlborough) (4+251)*, 184 Coy *(Winchfield) (4+260)*, 216 Coy *(Marlborough) (4+273)*;

RS: 3 Command Signals *(Salisbury) (29+956)*;

CMP: 101 Provost Coy *(Salisbury) (1+102)*.

- Southern Sub Area *(HQ: Sherborne)* (GOC: Brigadier J Lumley)

50 Dorset *(Weymouth) (22+828)*, Dorset ITC *(Dorchester) (34+1830)*, 305 Welch ITC *(Portland) (26+1260)*;

RAC: 52 Heavy Armoured Training Regt *(Bovington) (58+2019)*;

RA: Ammunition Sub Depot *(Marston Magna)*, Command Ammunition Depot *(Grenham)*;

RE: 671 General Construction Coy *(Weymouth) (5+249)*, 672 Artisan Works Coy *(Weymouth) (5+253)*;

RASC: 5 Mobile Ambulance Coy *(Fordingbridge) (8+211)*, 2 Reserve Motor Transport Coy *(Aldbourne) (6+408)*, 21 Reserve Motor Transport Coy *(Yetminster) (11+426)*, 23 Reserve Motor Transport Coy *(Haslemere) (11+447)*, 1 Armoured Brigade Coy *(Farringdon) (5+168)*, Regimental Training and Officer Producing Centre *(Boscombe) (220+753)*, Petrol Reserve Depot *(Blandford)*, Petrol Reserve Depot *(Southampton)*;

RAMC: 216 Field Ambulance *(Gillingham) (13+236)*, 21 Training Coy *(Shaftesbury) (105+325)*;

RAOC: 16 Army Field Workshop *(Wootton Bassett) (6+213)*, Command Supply Depot *(Yeovil)*, Command Supply Depot *(Taunton)*, Command Supply Depot *(Bath)*, Command Supply Depot *(Blandford)*, Command Supply Depot *(Bovington)*, Command Supply Depot *(Wimborne)*;

AMPC: 39 Coy *(Wincanton) (4+259)*, 51 Coy *(Chilmark) (7+277)*, 82 Coy *(Wilton) (4+252)*, 90 Coy *(Crondall Lodge) (4+251)*, 137 Coy *(Yeovil) (4+274)*.

VIII CORPS (GOC: Lieutenant General H Franklyn*)

HQ: Taunton, Somerset

NOTES:
- *Corps formed in August and was responsible for the defence of southwestern England*
- *General Franklyn had commanded 5th Division in the BEF and was promoted to this command on 19 July. He rose to be Commander in Chief Home Forces in 1943.*

- 3rd Infantry Division (GOC: Major General J Gammell)
HQ: Bridgwater, Somerset (Forward HQ: Cannington)
7th Guards Brigade: *(HQ: Frome)* (GOC: Brigadier A Cazenove)
1 Grenadier Guards *(Frome) (38+897)*, 2 Grenadier Guards *(Castle Cary) (35+900)*,
    1 Coldstream Guards *(Midsomer Norton) (34+915)*.
8th Brigade: *(HQ: Blagdon)* (GOC: Brigadier C Woolner)
1 Suffolk *(Cheddar) (32+898)*, 2 East Yorkshire *(Clevedon) (30+888)*, 1 South Lancashire
    (Weston Super Mare) (34+901).
9th Brigade: *(HQ: Tiverton)* (GOC: Brigadier B Horrocks)
2 Lincolnshire *(Tiverton) (36+876)*, 1 KOSB *(Wellington) (32+904)*, 2 Royal Ulster Regt
    (Taunton) (33+906).
Divisional Troops:
RA: 7 Field Regt *(Tiverton) (26+539) (9/17 and 14/63 Btys: 24x18/25-pdr)*, 33 Field Regt *(Frome)*
    (35+535) (114/109 and 101/113 Btys: 24x18/25-pdr), 76 Field Regt *(Weston Super Mare)*
    (39+534) (302 Bty: 8x18-pdr, 303 Bty: 4x18/25-pdr, 4x18-pdr), 20 A/T Regt *(Langport)*
    (26+474) (41, 45, 67 and 99 Btys: 24x2-pdr);
RE: 246 Field Coy *(Shepton Mallet) (6+272)*, 253 Field Coy *(Whimple) (6+252)* 15 Field Park
    Coy *(Weston Super Mare) (3+160)*;
RAOC: Divisional LADS *(Street) (309)*;
RASC: Divisional Petrol Coy *(Glastonbury) (7+352)*, Divisional Supply Column *(Coombe Down)*
    (15+506), Divisional Ammunition Coy *(Glastonbury) (9+440)*, 7 Motor Coach Coy *(Weston*
    Super Mare) (9+137), 38 Motor Coach Coy *(Brutun) (9+170)*, 43 Motor Coach Coy
    (Adlestrop) (10+149);
RAMC: 7 Field Ambulance *(Beckington) (12+210)*, 8 Field Ambulance *(Yatton) (14+231)*, 9 Field
    Ambulance *(Bampton) (12+236)*;
RS: Divisional Signals Regt *(Bridgwater) (23+464)*;
CMP: Divisional Provost Coy *(Glastonbury) (102)*.

NOTES:
- *The Division was a Regular Army formation that had served in the BEF*
- *It was in the Brighton area until 10 July, when it moved to Wiltshire as Command Reserve*
- *By 13 July the Division had 100% Personnel, 60% artillery pieces, 100% A/T guns*
- *General Gammell took over command from General Montgomery on 25 July; Brigadier Cazenove replaced Brigadier Whitaker on 18 August, while Brigadier Woolner had been in charge since February and Brigadier Horrocks since 17 June. General Gammell was promoted to command Eastern District in 1942 and then Chief of Staff to the Supreme Allied Commander Mediterranean in 1944. Brigadier Horrocks rose to be a Corps commander*
- *Its primary role was counter offensive either in the Poole/Portland, Southampton, Exeter, Avon or Gloucester areas*
- *It was not expected to leave the Corps area unless it was clear that no major threat existed in it*
- *9th Brigade was responsible for GHQ Green Line around Bristol*

- On 14 August two thirds of the Division was considered mobile, though another motor coach company was assigned for 7th Guards Brigade on 18 August
- On 4 September 8th Brigade moved to the Western Super Mare - Cheddar area, with 9th Brigade going to the Tiverton area
- On 7 September it had 100% Personnel, 100% artillery pieces, 100% A/T guns
- On 9 September it came under VIII Corps command
- On 20 September the HQ moved from Chippenham. Its primary counter offensive role was now reduced to either Portland / Wareham or Exmouth
- In November Divisional HQ moved to Blandford.

- 48th **Infantry Division (South Midlands)** (GOC: Major General R Petrie)
HQ: Lydford, Devon
143rd Brigade: *(HQ: Great Torrington)* (GOC: Brigadier J Muirhead*)
1 OBLI *(Okehampton) (37+888)*, 1/7 Warwickshire *(Great Torrington) (32+905)*,
  1/8 Warwickshire *(Bridstowe) (35+921)*.
144th Brigade: *(HQ: Liskeard)* (GOC: Brigadier J Hamilton*)
2 Warwickshire *(Bodmin) (38+919)*, 1/5 Gloucester *(Bodmin) (35+861)*, 1/8 Worcestershire
  (Falmouth) (35+861).
145th Brigade: *(HQ: Bovey Tracey)* (GOC: Brigadier Viscount Bridgeman)
1/4 OBLI *(Bovey Tracey) (34+861)*, 1Buckingham *(Ashburton) (35+810)*
Divisional Troops:

RA: 18 Field Regt *(Chagford) (32+557) (59 Bty: 8x25- pdr, 94 Bty: 8x4.5-inch)*, 24 Field Regt *(Lostwithial) (34+550) (22/56 Bty: 8x25-pdr; 50/70 Bty: 6x4.5-inch)*, 68 Field Regt *(Okehampton) (35+568) (269 Bty: 6x4.5-inch; 271 Bty: 7x25-pdr, 2x18-pdr)*, 53 A/T Regt RA *(Budleigh Salterton) (27+536) (209 and 210 Btys (Okehampton), 211 Bty (Exmouth), 212 Bty (Budleigh Salterton) (211 and 212 Btys manned coast defence guns. Regt also had 12x2-pdr, 8x6-pdr)*;
1/9 Manchester (MG) *(31+797) (Okehampton; coys: Bodmin, Witheridge and Falmouth)*;
RE: 9 Field Coy *(Bude) (6+228)*, 224 Field Coy *(Liskeard) (7+255)*, 226 Field Coy *(Thorverton) (6+248)*, 227 Field Park Coy *(Lifton) (3+158)*;
RAMC: 143 Field Ambulance *(Bridstowe) (10+167)*, 144 Field Ambulance *(Launceston) (10+217)*, 145 Field Ambulance *(Totnes) (11+157)*;
RASC: Divisional Petrol Coy *(Chillaton) (6+279)*, Divisional Ammunition Coy *(South Zeal) (7+377)*, Divisional Supply Column *(Exeter) (14+415)*;
RS: Divisional Signals Regt *(Lewdown) (25+475)*;
CMP: Divisional Provost Coy *(Okehampton) (104)*.

NOTES:
- The Division was a Territorial Army formation that had served with the BEF
- General Petrie took command on 18 June, having briefly commanded 12th Division in France. The commanders of 143rd and 144th Brigades had been in charge since the War began, while Brigadier T O`Donovan had commanded 145th Brigade between 29 June and 13 August. Brigadier the Viscount Bridgeman rose to be Deputy Adjutant General in 1944
- In July it moved to Bristol from Wiltshire
- By 13 July the Division had 100% Personnel, 40% artillery pieces, 30% A/T guns

- The Division's roles were anti parachute in the Cirencester-Wantage-Salisbury area *or* defend coastal areas
- In August the Division moved to Devon; 143rd Brigade was the Divisional reserve
- On 17 August 144th Brigade replaced 101st and 102nd Royal Marine Brigades
- On 14 August two thirds of the Division were considered mobile
- On 31 August 2 Gloucester was placed under 70th Brigade command
- By 7 September it had 100% Personnel, 66% artillery pieces, 30% A/T guns
- On 9 September 9th Brigade replaced 145th Brigade
- On 1October Divisional HQ moved to Crediton
- In November the following Coastal Infantry Brigades arrived: 203rd Brigade (Cornwall) (HQ: Bodmin), 209th Brigade (Torbay), 211th Brigade (Plymouth).

- 70th Brigade *(HQ: Totnes, Devon)* (GOC: Brigadier P Kirkup*)
11 Durham Light Infantry *(Newton Abbot) (42+960)*, 1 Tyneside Scots *(Kingsbridge) (38+882)*,
    2 Gloucester *(Bishop Steignton) (34+883)*;
8 Kings Own (Pioneer) *(Sidbury) (27+1031)*;
RA: D4 Mobile Field Bty *(2x12-pdr, 2x3-pdr)*;
RE: 2 Docks Group *(Paignton)* (995 Maintenance and 996-999 Operating Coys) *(37+1753)*;
RAMC: 187 Field Ambulance *(Newton Abbot) (11+242)*;
RASC: Brigade Coy *(Newton Abbot) (5+182)*.

NOTES:
- The Brigade had served with the 23rd Division in the BEF before being largely destroyed in May. Brigadier Kirkup was in command during this period
- The Brigade was responsible for the Salcombe -Lyme Regis coast
- On 31 August 2 Gloucester under command from 48th Division
- On 5 September it was relieved by 102nd Royal Marines Brigade, HQ moved to Newton Abbot in preparation for a move to Iceland.

Corps Troops:
RA: 51 Heavy Regt *(Morchard Bishop) (28+718)* (*infantry role)*, 53 Medium Regt *(Yelverton)*
    (30+736) (*209 Bty: 2x6-inch at Falmouth, 4x6-pdr, 8x4-inch at Barnstaple, Start Bay, St Ives, Padstow and Marazion; 210 Bty: 16x6-inch mortars between Seaton and Hayle; D4 Mobile Bty: 2x12-pdr and 2x3-pdr at Totnes*), 58 Medium Regt *(Minehead) (28+621)* (*Anti tank training role plus 16x6-pdr on Taunton Stop Line*); Corps Ordnance Depot (Washaway);
8 Northumberland Fusiliers (m/cycle) *(Helston) (29+537)*;
1 and 7 Independent Coys *(Scilly Isles) (600)*, 6 Independent Coy *(Porthcurno) (300)*,
    8 Independent Coy *(Truro and St Ives) (300)*, 9 Independent Coy *(Penzance) (300)*;
8 Somerset Light Infantry (Home) *(Taunton) (45+828)*;
RE: 570 Corps Field Park Coy *(Ottery St Mary) (4+227)*; 571 Army Field Coy *(Sidmouth) (8+288)*; 572 Army Field Coy *(Ottery St Mary) (5+272)*; 573 Army Field Coy *(Exmouth) (8+262)*; 592 Army Troops Coy *(Axminster) (7+296)*; 593 Army Troops Coy *(Ilminster) (7+296)*;
RAC: A Armoured Train *(Newton Abbot) (47)* (*Covered Exeter to Kingsbridge*); D Armoured Train *(Wadebridge) (46)* (*Covered Wadebridge to Padstow*); F Armoured Train *(Barnstaple) (47)* (*Covered to Bideford and Braunton*);

RASC: 11 Motor Coach Coy *(Bideford) (9+162) (attached to 48th Division)*, 12 Motor Coach Coy *(Exeter) (10+173) (attached to 48th Division)*, 17 Troop Carry Coy *(Bradninch) (8+361) (attached to 3rd Division)*, 148 Brigade Coy *(Newton Abbot) (6+184)*;
RAOC: 19 Army Field Workshop *(Wells) (4+228)*;
RAMC: 6 Casualty Clearing Station *(Okehampton) (7+869)*, 23 Casualty Clearing Station *(Honiton) (7+89)*.

Plymouth Garrison *(333+9480)* (GOC: Major General C Allfrey)
(GOC Royal Marines Plymouth Division: Brigadier C Glynicke;
GOC Exton Depot: Brigadier A Dawson)
10 Devon (Home) *(68+1220)* (1st Cornish *(VIP Cornwall)*, E Coy *(Plymouth)*, H Coy *(Wembury)*),
    303 Duke of Wellington's Regt ITC *(27+1615)*, 304 York and Lancaster ITC *(29+1390)*;
3 Commando *(Plymouth) (38+447)*;
RA: 23 Medium and Heavy Training Regt *(30+1250)*; 70 Coast Defence Training Regt *(28+950)*;
RASC: 1 Station Maintenance Coy *(Devonport) (3+78)*, 17 Station Transport Coy *(Devonport) (2+156)*;
RAMC: 9 Casualty Clearing Station *(11+88)*, 22 Training Coy *(Devonport) (65+245)*;
AMPC: 6 Group (Spanish, 187 and 211 Coys) *(13+789)*.

Plus RN Barracks (*a battalion of 700 men and a labour coy of 350 men for the Inner defences*); HMS
    Raleigh (*6 to 7 coys to defend Torpoint*)
Plus Plymouth Division RM *(Stonehouse Barracks)* (6 coys) (30 September = 183+4133);

<u>NOTE:</u> *General Allfrey was appointed on 19 July. He rose to command V Corps in 1942.*

- 9th Infantry Training Group:
7 Buffs *(Saltash) (29+962)*, 9 Buffs *(Saltash) (28+927)*, 10 Buffs (Home) *(Plympton) (30+946)*.

<u>NOTES</u>:
- *Plymouth was divided into 6 sectors: 1 (Fort Stamford; 70 Coast Defence Training Regt with 1½ coys 10 Devon, 2 RN coys and a RN MG plt), 2 (Plympton; 10 Buffs), 3 (Crown Hill; 303 ITC, coy 10 Devon, RN MG plt, troop 269 Bty 68 Field Regt (2x4.5in), RN pom-pom troop), 4 (Crown Hill; 304 ITC, RM MG plt), 5 (Saltash; 9 Buffs (-)), 6 (Fort Scaesdon; 7 Buffs (-2 coys), coy 9 Buffs, 2 RM plts) + coastal sector (2 coys 7 Buffs), Inner Sector (23 Medium and Heavy Training Regt). Sub area troops available for counter attack (3 Commando, B Coy 8 Northumberland Fusiliers, 143 Brigade A/T Coy)*
- *9th Infantry Group was formed in mid July and reformed as 209th Infantry Brigade on 13 October and assigned a coast defence role.*

- 102nd Brigade RM: *(HQ: Elburton, Plymouth)* (GOC: Brigadier R Campbell RM) *(66+1364)*
2 Bn RM *(Modbury)*, 3 Bn RM *(Plympton)*.

<u>NOTES</u>:
- *The Brigade was formed by splitting the original RM Brigade on 12 July*
- *On 18 August it moved to Liverpool for overseas operations*
- *On 26 August the Brigade returned to Plymouth*

- On 5 September it replaced 70th Brigade
- On 28 September the Brigade HQ sailed to Freetown for overseas operations.

11th Infantry Training Group: *(HQ: Minehead)*
9 Somerset Light Infantry (Home) *(Watchet) (28+959)*, 10 East Surrey *(Bideford) (25+965)*, 11 Devon *(Ilfracombe) (32+928)*.

NOTE: *The Group was formed in mid July and reformed as 211th Infantry Brigade on 11 October and assigned a coast defence role.*

Bristol Garrison (CO: Colonel R Cherry)
Gloucester ITC *(44+1798)*;
RE: 17 Field Coy *(5+249)*, 154 Rail Operating Coy *(6+336)*.

Larkhill Garrison (GOC: Brigadier H Fitzgibbon)
RA: 21 Medium and Heavy Training Regt *(31+1221)*, 12 Field (Depot) Regt *(33+22) (provided a gun section to each of the six Salisbury Plain strike groups = 12x18-pdr)*, 122 OCTU *(42+877)*, 7 Practice Camp *(at least 21 field guns and 7 A/T guns were assigned to the GHQ Blue Line defence)*.

Southern Command Troops:
South Western Sub Area: *(HQ: Plymouth)*
3 Tower Hamlets Rifles *(Bridgwater) (26+929)*; 8 Buffs (Home) *(Burnham on Sea) (22+949) (to Paignton with 209 Coast Bde in October)*, 50 Duke of Cornwall's Light Infantry *(Truro) (19+796)*, 10 Devon *(Newton Abbot) (23+900)*, 50 Warwickshire *(Barnstaple) (25+917)*; 50 Somerset Light Infantry *(Weston Super Mare) (19+799)*, 70 Somerset Light Infantry *(Burnham on Sea) (28+796)*, Somerset Light Infantry ITC *(Taunton) (35+1629)*, Devon ITC *(Exeter) (38+1619)*, Wiltshire ITC *(Devizes) (37+1730)*, Duke of Cornwall's Light Infantry ITC *(Bodmin- Mevagissey-St Austell) (41+1679) (HQ, 2 rifle,1 special coys)*, 308 ITC *(Devizes) (29+1577)*;
RA: 16 Field Training Regt *(Exeter) (26+1013) (8x4.5-inch)*; Command Ordnance Sub Depot *(Latchley)*;
RS: 20 Corps Signals Unit *(Taunton) (1+228)*, Special Operations Training Bn *(Trowbridge) (12+626)*, 1 Special Wireless Coy *(Trowbridge) (8+336)*;
RE: 700 General Construction Coy *(Exeter) (5+295)*, 725 General Construction Coy *(Launceston) (6+269)*, 670 Artisan Works Coy *(Truro) (5+271)*, 723 Artisan Works Coy *(Launceston) (6+280)*, 726 Artisan Works Coy *(Launceston) (6+293)*, 727 Artisan Works Coy *(Launceston) (6+278)*, 7 EOD Coy *(Brislington) (6+164)*;
RASC: 9 Independent Brigade Coy *(Scilly Isles) (253)*, 8 Mobile Ambulance Coy *(Winkleigh) (7+203)*;
RAOC: Command Supply Depot *(Devonport)*, Command Supply Depot *(Exeter)*, Command Supply Depot *(Cleeve)*, Command Supply Depot *(Okehampton)*, Command Supply Depot *(Barnstaple)*, Command Supply Depot *(Truro)*;
RAMC: 41 General Hospital *(Bishops Lydeard) (20+152)*, 52 General Hospital *(Bridgwater) (10+97)*;

AMPC: 6 Group (*87 and 167 Coys*) *(Chard) (14+557)*, 25 Coy *(Taunton) (5+255)*, 46 Coy *(Taunton) (6+273)*, 55 Coy *(Penzance) (6+260)*, 64 Coy *(Malpas) (7+258)*, 65 Coy *(Falmouth) (6+259)*, 69 Coy *(Ilminster) (6+271)*, 96 Coy *(Axminster) (5+252)*, 179 Coy *(Somerton) (4+262)*, 193 Coy *(Taunton) (6+278)*, 3 Centre *(Westward Ho) (54+1118)* (to Ilfracombe at end of September);
RM: Special Reserve Depot *(Exton, Lympstone)*.

Southern Command Troops:
South Midland Sub Area: *(HQ: Oxford)* (GOC: Brigadier H MacMullen)
8 Gloucester (Home) *(Gloucester) (44+972)*, 8 Berkshire (Home) *(Oxford) (53+1075)*, 70 Berkshire *(Oxford) (33+822)* (*all these had GHQ Red Line role*), 70 Gloucester *(Gloucester) (29+804)*, OBLI ITC *(Oxford) (55+1898)*, Berkshire ITC *(Reading) (38+1984)*;
RE: 565 Army Field Coy *(Wallingford) (6+237)*, 215 Corps Field Park Coy *(Wallingford) (4+208)*, 659 General Construction Coy *(Brize Norton) (4+264)*, 664 General Construction Coy *(Abingdon) (5+273)*, 680 General Construction Coy *(Minchinhampton) (6+270)*, 722 Artisan Works Coy *(South Cerney) (5+285)*, 129 Forestry Coy *(Cinderford) (4+143)*, 1 Bore Section *(Reading) (2+90)*, 152 Rail Construction Coy *(Steventon) (5+270)*, 191 Rail Operating Coy *(Reading) (9+149)*; 6 EOD Coy *(Reading) (9+270)*;
RASC: 19 Troop Carry Coy *(Tewkesbury) (9+287)*, 41 Motor Coach Coy *(Winchcombe) (9+128)*, 2 Mobile Ambulance Coy *(Chesham) (6+168)*, 6 Armoured Division Supply Column *(Swindon) (3+159)*, 4 Bulk Petrol Coy *(Newbury) (6+173)*, 6 Armoured Division Troops Coy *(Wantage) (3+183)*, 6 Armoured Division Petrol Supply Park *(Russley Park) (3+153)*, 3 Bridging Coy *(Wallingford) (12+514)* (*GHQ Red Line and RAF Benson defence roles*), 5 Bridging Coy *(Aylesbury) (10+445)*, 1 Motor Boat Coy *(Bourton on the Heath) (9+112)*, 2 Motor Boat Coy *(Moreton in Marsh) (7+145)*, 16 Reserve Motor Transport Coy *(Campden) (10+430)*, 11 Reserve Motor Transport Coy *(Chipping Norton) (14+352)*, 18 Reserve Motor Transport Coy *(Witney) (11+453)*, 20 Reserve Motor Transport Coy *(Basingstoke) (12+406)*, 26 Reserve Motor Transport Coy *(Wantage) (8+320)*, 9 Main Supply Depot *(Newbury) (7+70)*, 2 Motor Transport Stores Depot *(Slough) (34+72)*, 3 Motor Transport Stores Depot *(Ashchurch) (21+535)*, 3 Motor Transport Depot *(Tewkesbury)*, 2, 3 and 4 Vehicle Reserve Depots *(Slough) (18+571)*, 1 Vehicle Reserve Depot *(Ashdown Park) (6+369)*, 5 Vehicle Reserve Depot *(Ashchurch) (7+64)*, 6 Vehicle Reserve Depot *(Ashchurch) (9+110)*, Petrol Reserve Depot *(Newbury)*, Petrol Reserve Depot *(Tetbury)*, Petrol Reserve Depot *(Avonmouth)*, HQ and 2 Depot Coy BACC *(Banbury) (24+633)*;
RAOC: 9 Main Supply Depot *(Newbury) (2+30)*, 10 Main Supply Depot *(Banbury) (2+30)*, 11 Main Supply Depot *(Lidlington) (2+30)*, Central General Stores Ordnance Depot *(Didcot)*, Command Supply Depot *(Tetbury)*, Command Supply Depot *(Slough)*, 60 Training Section *(Didcot) (5+871)*;
AMPC: 19 Coy *(Monkton Farleigh) (7+265)*, 91 Coy *(Didcot) (5+254)*, 93 Coy *(Newbury) (4+257)*, 94 Coy *(Hullavington) (4+256)*, 107 Coy *(Didcot) (6+223)*, 165 Coy *(Cirencester) (5+280)*, 170 Coy *(Reading) (5+282)*, 189 Coy *(Gloucester) (5+275)*, 190 Coy *(Bradford on Avon) (4+280)*, 201 Coy *(Deddington) (6+275)*;
RAMC: 225 Field Ambulance *(Reading) (5+140)*, Military Hospital *(Bath) (15+72)*, 14 General Hospital *(Newbury) (16+200)*, 16 General Hospital *(Oxford) (19+151)*, 61 Ambulance Train *(Kidlington) (2+20)*, 65 Ambulance Train *(Weston Super Mare) (2+20)*;
RS: 1 Special Wireless Group *(Harpenden) (12+215)*, 1 Special Signals Unit *(Whaddon)*

(26+245), 6 Armoured Division Signals Regt *(Tytherington) (13+134)*, 8 Armoured Division Signals Regt *(Tetbury) (12+126)*.

GHQ RESERVE (SOUTHERN COMMAND):

21st Army Tank Brigade
(GOC: Brigadier G Drake-Brockman; Brigadier R Naesmyth from 26 September)
HQ: West Lavington, Wiltshire
42 RTR *(38+538) (13 Matilda II, 9 medium, 13 light tanks)*, 48 RTR *(35+545) (41 Valentine infantry, 7 light tanks)*;
6 Light Field Ambulance RAMC *(Longbridge Deverill) (9+166)*;
Brigade Coy RASC *(Codford) (11+328)*;
Brigade Workshop RAOC *(Tidworth) (5+194)*.

NOTES:
- *The Brigade had a counter attack role, primarily within Southern Command*
- *In July Brigade units reformed as 99 and 100 RTR respectively*
- *On 19 August 48 RTR reformed as 100 RTR disbanded when the new Valentines (Mark III infantry tanks) arrived*
- *On 26 August 44 RTR reformed*
- *On 10 September 44 RTR moved to 1st Armoured Division, 99 RTR disbanded and 42 RTR reformed (10 medium, 11 light, 5 Infantry tanks)*
- *On 15 September the Brigade had 65 infantry and 17 light tanks (80 and 20 respectively by 29 September)*
- *In mid October it came under 55th Division command in Suffolk.*

Australian Imperial Force (GOC: Major General H Wynter)
HQ: Tidworth
18th Infantry Brigade *(HQ: Lobscombe Corner)* (GOC: Brigadier L Morshead)
2/9 (Queensland) Bn, 2/10 (South Australia) Bn, 2/12 (Queensland/Tasmania) Bn.
25th Infantry Brigade *(HQ: Tidworth)* (GOC: Brigadier W Bridgeford)
70 (Queensland) Bn, 71 (Victoria) Bn and 72 (New South Wales) Bn.
Force Troops:
RAA: 3 Field Regt *(5 Bty: 12x25-pdr; 6 Bty: 3x18-pdr, 3x4.5-inch)*, 1 A/T Bty RAA *(22x2-pdr)*; Coy 1 MG Bn;
RAE: 3 Engineer Coy;
RAAMC 3 Field Ambulance;
RASC: 27 Motor Coach Coy (Bulford) *(9+164)*.

NOTES:
- *In June the AIF arrived in the UK (Field artillery = 5 Bty: 12x25-pdr, 6 Bty: 3x18-pdr, 3x4.5-inch)*
- *On 25 June 25th Brigade was formed from drafts, its battalions given provisional numbers. Each battalion had only three infantry companies*
- *By 13 July the AIF had 60% Personnel, 10% artillery pieces, 5% A/T guns*

- By the end of July vehicle strength was: infantry (50%), armoured carriers (25%), MG (90%), engineers (25%), signals (40%), artillery (20%)
- On 14 August two battalions were considered mobile
- In August 18th Brigade's role was Southern Command strike force together with 21st Army Tank Brigade and 12 Field Regt RA. 25th Brigade's role was local defence within Tidworth Garrison
- 18th Brigade Group included 3 Field Regt, an anti tank section (2x2-pdr), the MG Company, 3 Engineer Company and 3 Field Ambulance
- By 7 September the AIF had 60% Personnel, 25% artillery pieces, 5% A/T guns
- In Mid October the AIF joined XI Corps (Colchester) with 18th Brigade (9, 10, 12 Bns), 25th Brigade (31, 32, 33 Bns), 3 Field Regt, 1 A/T Regt, 1 MG Bn, 3 Field Ambulance, 11 Field Ambulance
- On 23 October 70, 71 and 72 Battalions were reformed as 2/31, 2/32 and 2/33 Battalions
- On 18 December this force was reformed as 9th Australian Infantry Division
- Although General Wynter commanded this Division on formation he went on to hold senior administrative positions in the Far East. Brigadier Morshead was to command this Division in North Africa and rose to command Australia's 2nd Army.

GHQ RESERVE (NORTH)

IV CORPS (GOC: Lieutenant General Francis Nosworthy)
HQ: Amersham, Buckinghamshire

NOTES:
- The Corps was the GHQ Reserve North, one of its major counter attack groups
- General Nosworthy had been Deputy Chief of the General Staff, Indian Army, until promoted to command on 31 May. He went on to command IX Corps in Tunisia in 1942.

- 2nd Armoured Division (GOC: Major General J Tilly)
HQ: Cambridge
1st Armoured Brigade: *(HQ: Newmarket)* (GOC: Brigadier H Charrington)
1 Kings Dragoon Guards *(Stetchworth) (38+592) (October: 52 light tanks)*, 4 Hussars *(31+591) (October: 52 light tanks)*, 3 RTR *(Cambridge) (45+748) (September: 52 cruiser tanks)*; Brigade Coy RASC *(Walton) (8+290) (October: 114 light tanks in the Brigade)*.
22nd Armoured Brigade: *(HQ: Sawston)* (GOC: Brigadier J Scott-Cockburn)
2 Gloucestershire Hussars *(33+516) (December: 45 light tanks)*, 3 City of London Yeomanry *(40+518) (December: 44 light tanks)*, 4 City of London Yeomanry *(37+527) (December: 46 light tanks)*; Brigade Coy RASC *(Northampton) (8+354)*.
Support Group: *(HQ: Harston)* (GOC: Brigadier H Latham)
1 Derbyshire Yeomanry *(Harston) (30+332) (38 Humber armoured cars)*; 1 Tower Hamlets Rifles *(Hinxton) (40+845)*, 1 Rangers *(Pampisford) (40+849)*; 102 LAA/AT Regt *(Northampton) (38+722) (16x2-pdr)*; 2 RHA *(Linton) (28+480) (H/I and L/N Btys: 4x4.5-inch, 4x18-pdr)*.
Divisional Troops:
RE: 3 Field Sqn *(Histon) (9+298)*, 142 Field Park Troop *(Brixworth) (5+176)*;
RAMC: 3 Light Field Ambulance *(Great Abington) (8+116)*, 4 Light Field Ambulance *(Orwell)*

(10+188);
CMP: Divisional Provost Coy *(Thorndon) (110)*.

NOTES:
- *Since its formation in Spring it had been allotted to home defence*
- *General Tilly had been appointed on 10 May; Brigadier Charrington was appointed on 11 May and Brigadier Latham in February, while Brigadier Scott-Cockburn had held his appointment since the start of the War*
- *In June the Division had 149 light tanks (excluding 22 Armoured Brigade), 8x4.5-inch, 8x18-pdr, 6x2-pdr and 9 armoured cars*
- *In June the Division was relieved by 1st Division in Lincolnshire and moved to IV Corps*
- *The Division's role was to recapture airfields in the Lincolnshire/Cambridgeshire area*
- *3 RTR joined 1st Armoured Brigade on 16 August*
- *By 15 September the Division had 55 cruiser and 258 light tanks*
- *In October the Division was ordered to prepare for an overseas move to North Africa. 1st Armoured Brigade moved to the Northampton area. 1 Derbyshire Yeomanry transferred to the newly formed 6th Armoured Division on 10 November.*

- 42nd Infantry Division (East Lancashire) (GOC: Major General H Willcox)
HQ: Newbury, Berkshire
125th Brigade: *(HQ: Newbury)* (GOC: Brigadier G Sutton*)
1 Border *(Kingsclere) (29+695)*, 1/5 Lancashire Fusiliers *(Newbury) (29+932)*, 1/6 Lancashire Fusiliers *(Highclere) (33+918)*.
126th Brigade: *(HQ: Taplow)* (GOC: Brigadier L Bootle-Wilbraham, from 20 September)
1 East Lancashire *(Henley) (30+902)*, 1/5 Kings Own *(Maidenhead) (30+907)*, 1/5 Border *(Bisham) (32+789)*.
127th Brigade: *(HQ: Wheatley)* (GOC: Brigadier J Smyth*)
1 Highland Light Infantry *(Great Milton) (32+854)*, 1/4 East Lancashire *(Headington) (36+926)*, 1/5 Manchester *(Holton) (35+926)*.
Divisional Troops:
RA: 52 Field Regt *(Newbury) (36+581)* (*207 and 208 Btys: 19x75mm*), 53 Field Regt *(Maidenhead) (34+594)* (*209 and 210 Btys: 6x4.5-inch*), 111 Field Regt *(Wheatley) (36+588)* (*211 Bty: 8x75mm, 4x18/25-pdr, 212 Bty: 8x75mm, 2x6-inch*), 56 A/T Regt *(Speen) (31+592)* (*221 Bty (Pangbourne), 222 Bty (Benham), 223 Bty (Sonning), 224 Bty (Wheatley): 48x2-pdr*);
RE: 200 Field Coy *(Newbury) (5+247)*, 201 Field Coy *(Twyford) (6+247)*, 250 Field Coy *(Wheatley) (7+245)*, 203 Field Park Coy *(Wickham) (4+187)*;
RAMC: 125 Field Ambulance *(Newbury) (12+227)*, 126 Field Ambulance *(Hare Hatch) (12+236)*, 127 Field Ambulance *(Wheatley) (11+225)*;
RASC: Divisional Supply Column *(Arbourfield) (15+451)*, Divisional Ammunition Coy *(Basildon) (10+376)*, Divisional Petrol Coy *(Hungerford) (5+282)*;
RS: Divisional Signals Regt *(Newbury) (22+489)*;
RAOC: Division LAD`s *(Darlington) (7+116)*;
CMP: Divisional Provost Coy *(Newbury) (1+105)*.

NOTES:
- *This Division was a Territorial Army formation that had served with the BEF*

- General Willcox had been appointed to command on 18 June; Brigadier Sutton had been in charge from the start of the War and Brigadier Smyth from February. Brigadier E Miles had commanded 126th Brigade from January. General Willcox rose to command Central India in 1942
- By 13 July it had 100% Personnel, 20% artillery pieces, 0% A/T guns
- By 7 September it had 100% Personnel, 50% artillery pieces, 20% A/T guns
- On 10 September it joined the Corps from X Corps
- The Division's Anti Tank Regiment was allocated initially to the GHQ Line in the Thames Valley
- On 17 September Alan Brooke reported that the Division was good but required a good deal more training.

- 43rd Infantry Division (Wessex) (GOC: Major General R Pollock)
HQ: Ware, Hertfordshire
129th Infantry Brigade: *(HQ: Saffron Walden)* (GOC: Brigadier W Leader)
1/4 Somerset Light Infantry *(34+848)*, 1/4 Wiltshire *(32+905)*, 1/5 Wiltshire *(Newport) (37+931)*.
130th Infantry Brigade: *(HQ: Harpenden)* (GOC: Brigadier B Young)
1/7 Hampshire *(33+863)*, 1/4 Dorsets *(Berkhampstead) (36+871)*, 1/5 Dorsets *(St Albans) (35+798)*.
Divisional Troops:
RA: 94 Field Regt *(Huntingford) (38+569) (218 and 224 Btys: 18x18/25-pdr)*, 112 Field Regt *(Baldock) (37+585) (217 and 220 Btys: 14x18/25-pdr)*, 59 A/T Regt RA *(Welwyn) (30+561) (233 (Great Dunmow), 234 (Saffron Walden), 235 and 236 Btys: 48x2-pdr)*;
RE: 204 Field Coy *(Baldock) (7+261)*, 260 Field Coy *(Dedham) (6+243)*, 553 Field Coy *(Feldon) (6+246)*, 207 Field Park Coy *(Harlow) (3+146)*;
RAMC: 129 Field Ambulance *(Luton) (11+219)*, 130 Field Ambulance *(Great Dunmow) (11+170)*;
RASC: Divisional Ammunition and Petrol Coys *(Watford) (17+692)*, Divisional Supply Coy *(Hertford) (14+470)*, 6 Motor Coach Coy *(Great Dunmow) (10+162)*;
CMP: Divisional Provost Coy *(Watton) (1+105)*.

NOTES:
- *This Division was a Territorial Army formation assigned to home defence when the War began*
- *General Pollock had taken charge on 29 April, having commanded Northern Ireland District. He retired in 1941; Brigadier Young was appointed in January while Brigadier G Whittuck had commanded 129th Brigade from the beginning to 13 September, when Brigadier Leader took over. Brigadier Young rose to be Chief Engineer Middle East in 1941*
- *In July the Divisional artillery consisted 48x25-pdr and 8 A/T guns*
- *By 13 July the Division had 100% Personnel, 100% artillery pieces, 100% A/T guns*
- *In July 129th Brigade was made available to the defence of London*
- *The Division's anti tank regiment was allocated initially to the GHQ Line in East Anglia*
- *4 Somerset Light Infantry had the capability to move by air transport for up to a range of 150 miles*
- *By 7 September the Division had 100% Personnel, 100% artillery pieces, 100% A/T guns*
- *In November the Division replaced 1st London Division in Kent.*

- 128th Independent Infantry Brigade (GOC: Brigadier F Browning)
HQ: Hitchin, Hertfordshire
1/4 Hampshire *(36+865)*, 2/4 Hampshire *(33+875)*, 1/5 Hampshire *(Royston) (37+855)*;
128 Field Ambulance RAMC *(Bygrave) (10+239)*.

NOTES:
- *Brigadier Browning took command on 14 May, having been the Commandant of the Small Arms School. He rose to be the Deputy General Officer Commanding 1st Airborne Army in 1944 and ended the War as the Chief of Staff of South East Asia Command*
- *The Brigade was detached from 43rd Division in July.*

- 31st Independent Infantry Brigade (GOC: Brigadier H Smyth)
HQ: Harpenden, Hertfordshire
2 South Staffordshire *(St Albans) (33+855)*, 2 OBLI *(Berkhampsted) (38+909)*, 1 Royal Ulster Regt *(Harpenden) (34+951)*;
D Coy 5 Devons (MG) *(Hemel Hempstead)*;
RA: 75 Field Regt *(St Albans) (35+602) (299 and 300 Btys: 12x4.5-inch, 8x18-pdr)*, 225 Bty / 57 A/T Regt *(Kings Langley) (12x2-pdr)*;
RE: 237 Field Coy *(Hemel Hempstead) (7+251)*;
RAMC: 152 Field Ambulance *(Hemel Hempstead) (11+187)*;
RASC: Brigade Coy *(Oxford) (8+250)*, 39 Motor Coach Coy *(St Albans) (9+169)*

NOTES:
- *The Brigade was formed on 17 July*
- *On 4 August it came under Corps command*
- *By 7 September the Brigade had 33% Personnel, 33% artillery pieces, 25% A/T guns*
- *On 9 September the Brigade moved from the Oxford area*
- *On 28 September it was transferred to XII Corps at Ashford.*

Corps Troops:
1/7 Bedford and Hertfordshire *(Hertford) (23+1273)*, 2/7 Bedford and Hertfordshire *(Hertford) (26+794)*, 14 Royal Fusiliers *(Peterborough) (29+674)*, 16 Lancashire Fusiliers *(Newbury) (33+918) (GHQ Line role)*, 10 Berkshire *(Witney) (35+650)*;
RA: 64 Medium Regt *(High Wycombe) (34+646) (211 Bty (8x4.5-inch): Mildenhall and Hardwick; 212 Bty (8x6-inch): St Ives)*, 66 Medium Regt *(Amersham) (33+699) (227 and 228 Btys: 8x6-inch, 8x4.5-inch) (airfield counter attack role)*, 67 Medium Regt *(High Wycombe) (34+651) (231 and 232 Btys: 8x6-inch, 8x4.5-inch) (airfield counter attack role)*, 68 Medium Regt *(Booker Common) (32+669) (233 Bty at St Ives and 234 Bty at Worlington. 8x6-inch, 8x4.5-inch) (airfield counter attack role)*, 141 Army Field Regt *(St Albans) (33+584) (infantry role)*, 144 Army Field Regt *(Amersham) (39+442) (preparing for a move to Egypt in November)*; 4 Survey Regt *(Penn Street) (25+420)*, 3 Army Observation Bty *(White Waltham) (2+84)*;

RE: 295 Army Field Coy *(Newport) (6+252)*, 582 Army Field Coy *(Pangbourne) (6+224)*,
 583 Army Field Coy *(Pangbourne) (5+233)*, 584 Army Field Coy *(Pangbourne) (6+270)*,
 219 Corps Field Park Coy *(Hitchin) (4+181)*, 297 Corps Field Park Coy *(Pangbourne)
 (3+215);* part 3 Bridge Coy *(Aylesbury);*
RASC: 5 Motor Coach Coy *(Saffron Walden) (10+161)*, 35 Motor Coach Coy *(Oxford) (10+177)*,
 39 Motor Coach Coy *(Oxford) (9+169)*, 20 Troop Carry Coy *(Witney) (7+154)*, 12 Coy
 (Oxford) (4+111), 19 Coy *(Oxford) (4+120);* Corps Ammunition Coy *(Beaconsfield)
 (7+358)*, Corps Troops Supply Column *(Beaconsfield) (19+591)*, Corps Troops Petrol Park
 (Beaconsfield) (15+488);
RAOC: Corps Troops Ammunition Park *(Newport Pagnell) (18+636);* 6 Army Field Workshop
 (Aspley Guise) (12+509);
RAMC: 217 Field Ambulance *(Chesham) (10+189)*, 34 General Hospital *(Hatfield) (23+160);*
 119 Coy *(Shefford) (5+280)*, 121 Coy *(Bletchley) (5+276)*, 123 Coy *(Lidlington) (7+242)*,
 166 Coy *(Cheshunt) (6+265)*, 180 Coy *(Henlow) (5+285)*, 197 Coy *(Aylesham) (3+280);*
CMP: 103 Provost Coy *(Cambridge) (100)*, 106 Provost Coy *(Chesham) (104);*
RS: Corps Signals Regt *(Chalfont St Giles) (26+610).*

LONDON DISTRICT (GOC: Lieutenant General Sir Bertram Sergison-Brooke)
HQ: Queens Gate, Kensington (Operational HQ: Horse Guards, Whitehall)

NOTE: The GOC had been recalled from retirement in October 1939.

- 20th Guards Brigade
HQ: *Woking, Surrey* (GOC: Brigadier W Fox-Pitt)
2 Irish Guards *(Woking) (37+950)*, 2 Welsh Guards *(Byfleet) (35+944)* 1 Norfolk *(Ashtead)
 (35+897);*
RA: 52 Light Bty *(Weybridge) (20+475) (6x3.7-inch howitzers)*, C1 A/T Bty *(Norwood) (2x12-pdr,
 2x3-pdr);*
RASC: Brigade Coy.

NOTES:
- *Much of the Brigade had fought at Boulogne in May 1940 before being evacuated. Brigadier Fox-Pitt was appointed on 10 May*
- *The Brigade's role was to defend southwest London and was in District Reserve*
- *On 15 September 1 Norfolk and 52 Light Battery RA joined.*

-24th Guards Brigade
HQ: *Barnes, Surrey* (GOC: Brigadier W Fraser)
1 Scots Guards *(Norwood) (31+972)*, 1 Irish Guards *(Wimbledon) (36+957)*, 1 Welsh Guards
 (Northwood) (37+959);
RA: Brigade A/T Coy;
RAMC: 137 Field Ambulance *(Wimbledon) (8+185).*

NOTES:
- *The Brigade had fought in Norway in May and June 1940 before being evacuated. Brigadier Fraser was appointed in February and rose briefly to divisional command before retiring in 1941*
- *The Brigade's role was to defend the southwest and was a South London Sub Area Reserve.*

-3rd London Brigade
HQ: *Woodford, Essex* (GOC: Brigadier H Coombe)
2 Rangers *(Goodmayes) (33+806)*, 2 Tower Hamlets *(Chigwell) (31+746)*; 2/8 Middlesex *(Woodford) (35+769)* (MG)
RA: 51 Light Bty *(North east London) (24+490) (6x3.7-inch howitzers)*, 53 Light Bty *(Golder's Green) (18+464) (6x3.7-inch howitzers)*, 120 Field Bty *(Snaresbrook) (4x4-inch)*;
RE: 260 Field Coy *(Ongar) (6+243)*;
RAMC: 223 Field Ambulance *(Epping) (5+42)*.

NOTES:
- *Brigadier Coombe had been in charge since the start of the War*
- *The Brigade was to defend Outer Line A, running from Dagenham to Kinsgwear on the River Lea. It was a North London Sub Area Reserve*
- *On 20 September D Troop 51 Light Bty arrived from Larkhill. The Battery's Horse troops remained at Larkhill.*

Woolwich Garrison (CO: Colonel N Sherbrooke) *(367+6921)*
7 Rifle Brigade *(43+765)*; RA Depot *(239+3229)*; 12 Training Coy RAMC *(61+547)*, 1 Training Bn RAOC *(44+2380)*

London District Troops:
HQ Northern Sub Area *(Regent's Park Barracks)*, HQ Southern Area *(Duke of York's Barracks)*

Grenadier Guards Holding Bn *(Wellington Barracks) (57+1828) (mobile column at Hayes, responsible for River Thames sector)*, Coldstream Guards Holding Bn *(Regents Park Barracks) (49+1837) (mobile column at Elstree, responsible for River Brent sector)*, Scots Guards Holding Bn *(Tower of London) (39+1139) (mobile column at Greenwich, responsible for the east Thames switch line)*, Welsh Guards Training Bn *(Esher) (76+1463) (role to defend the Staines and Thames Ditton areas)*, M Coy Scots Guards *(Whitehall) (4+87)*, 12 Queens (Home) *(Clapham) (56+899) (A Coy: Dulwich, B Coy: Blackfriars, C Coy: Battersea, E Coy: Deptford, F Coy: Croydon, G Coy: Battersea, H Coy: Kempton and Walton)*, 10 Middlesex (Home) *(Southall) (60+1548) (A Coy: Wimbledon, C Coy: Clapham, F Coy: Tower of London)*, 13 Royal Fusiliers (Home) *(London Docks) (55+1299)*, 7 KRRC (Home) *(Totteridge; coys at Enfield, Waltham Abbey, Blackfriars, Holborn) (68+1230)*, 50 Royal Fusiliers *(Stanmore) (25+729)*, Irish Guards Training Bn *(Lingfield) (50+1065)*, East Surrey ITC *(Kingston) (46+1800) (District reserve role, also to defend Richmond, Bushey and Hampton Court parks against airborne attack)*, Royal Fusiliers ITC *(Hounslow) (61+1976) (District reserve role)*;
Middlesex MGTC *(MillHill) (115+1640) (District reserve role)*;

Household Cavalry Reserve Regt *(Hyde Park) (15+265) (District reserve role);*
GHQ Liaison Regiment *(Richmond) (48+407) (4 squadrons located around the south and in East Anglia);*
RA: 3 Reserve Medium Regt *(Watford) (63+1195);*
RASC: 2 and 24 Station Transport Coys *(6+276)*, 8 Station Maintenance Coy *(4+590)*, 1 Holding and 2 Training Bn`s *(Woking) (131+3350)*, Y Armoured Petrol Park and Supply Group *(Walton) (8+219)*, Y Armoured Divisional Troops Coy and Armoured Supply Park *(Weybridge) (7+295)*, 2 Heavy Repair Shop *(Hampton) (8+294)*, Depot *(Feltham) (103+1679)*, Vehicle Reserve Depot *(Kensington Olympia);*
RE: 5 EOD Coy *(56+58)*, 101 and 507 Army Field Coys *(11+435)*, 223 Field Park Coy *(Penge) (3+126)*, 508 Field Park Coy *(Pinner) (4+154)*, 719 General Construction Coy *(Acton)*, 720 General Construction Coy *(Beckenham)*, 724 General Construction Coy *(Mill Hill) (16+252)*, 159 Rail Construction Coy *(6+273);*
RAMC: 18 Training Coy *(Millbank) (146+692)*, 1 NZ General Hospital *(Pinewood)*, 10 General Hospital *(Watford) (20+160);*
AMPC: 28 Group (66, 80 Indian, 117 Coys) *(26+1386)*, 95 Coy *(Elstree) (4+250)*, 28 and 208 Coys *(Beckenham) (11+1024);*
RS: 2 Air Formation Signals Unit *(Hendon) (1003)*, 1 Command Signals Unit *(Weybridge) (40+997);*
RAOC: 3 Ordnance Field Park *(Eastcote) (15+413)*, 4 Petrol Depot *(Pinner) (6+199)*, 6 Ordnance Field Park *(Hendon) (5+338)*, 12 Technical Training Centre *(Acton) (3+296)*, 15 Technical Training Centre *(Park Royal) (3+319)*, 16 Technical Training Centre *(Isleworth) (3+372).*

Whitehall defence: Admiralty Detachment RM (1+53), part Grenadier Guards Holding Bn (2+158), Kings Life Guard *(Horse Guards)*. Six sites were specially designated in this scheme - the Admiralty, the War Office, the Air Ministry, the Ministry of Home Security plus the Ministry of Information, located in London University, and London's Civil Defence Headquarters, located in the Geological Museum in South Kensington. (Pillboxes = Admiralty Arch, Trafalgar Square, St James's Park (2), Westminster Bridge)

London Defence Lines:
Outer: Woolwich-Bromley-Mitcham-Kingston-Hounslow-Uxbridge-Rickmansworth-Potters Bar-Waltham Abbey-Chigwell-Barking
Intermediate: Greenwich-Clapham-Hammersmith-Brent-Stanmore-Barnet-Enfield-Redbridge
Inner: Thames-Ealing-Golders Green-Hackney

Defensive sectors were organised using the Metropolitan Police areas as a template.
- North East District comprised Central (Finsbury, Blackfriars and Farringdon), H (Barking and Ilford), J (Hackney), K (West Ham and Silvertown) and Port of London Authority Sectors.
- North West District comprised DN (Finsbury and Stoke Newington), S (Barnet, Edgware and Golders Green), X (Wembley, Ruislip, Uxbridge and Harrow) and Y (Enfield and Highgate) Sectors.
- South East District comprised LM (Lambeth and Camberwell), P (Dulwich, Lewisham and Catford), R (Eltham, Woolwich, Blackheath and Erith) and Z (Streatham, Purley and Croydon) Sectors.
- South West District comprised Westminster, F (Chelsea, Fulham and Hammersmith),

T (Staines, Hounslow, Brentford, Acton and Southall), V (Wandsworth, Malden, Wimbledon, Richmond and Kingston) and W (Battersea, Balham, Tooting, Sutton and Epsom) Sectors.

NORTHERN COMMAND (GOC: Lieutenant General Sir Ronald Adam*)
HQ: York

NOTE:
Lieutenant General Sir Ronald Adam had been III Corps commander with the BEF and before that was Commandant of the Staff College in 1937 and Deputy Chief of the Imperial General Staff between 1938-39. He was promoted to command on 8 June. He became Adjutant General in 1941.

I CORPS (GOC: Lieutenant General Harold Alexander*)
HQ: Doncaster, West Riding

NOTES:
- *The Corps HQ had served with the BEF*
- *General Alexander had commanded the BEF's 1st Division and was temporary commander of I Corps during the evacuation. In December he was promoted to command Southern Command as the youngest Army commander to date and ended the war as Supreme Allied Commander, Mediterranean*
- *The Corps was responsible for the defence of Humberside and the Lincolnshire coastline.*

- 2nd Infantry Division (GOC: Major General D Watson)
HQ: Pocklington, East Riding
4th Infantry Brigade: *(HQ: Tibethorpe)* (GOC: Brigadier E Warren*)
1 Royal Scots *(36+924)*, 2 Norfolks *(35+814)*, 2 Derbyshire Yeomanry *(Driffield) (27+436)*.
5th Infantry Brigade: *(HQ: Skirlaugh)* (GOC: Brigadier G Gartlan*)
1 Camerons *(Patrington) (34+907)*, 2 Dorsets *(Sigglesthorne) (31+903)*, 1/7 Worcestershire *(Patrington) (35+857)*.
6th Infantry Brigade: *(HQ: Kilham)* (GOC: Brigadier H Hayman-Joyce)
1 Royal Welch Fusiliers *(Skipsea) (35+892)*, 1 Berkshire *(Hunmanby) (33+806)*, 2 Durham Light Infantry *(Carnby) (34+853)*.
2nd **Division Counter Air Group RA**: *(HQ: Market Weighton)*
121 Field Regt *(Malton) (36+696)*, 122 Field Regt *(North Cave) (37+524)*, 61 Medium Regt *(Malton) (27+585)*.
Divisional Troops:
RA: 10 Field Regt *(Skirlaugh) (36+604) (30/46 and 51/54 Btys: 16x25-pdr, 10x18-pdr)*, 16 Field Regt *(Walton) (31+585) (27 and 34 Btys: 4x25-pdr, 6x18/25-pdr, 2x13-pdr, 86 Bty: 6x18-pdr in coast defence role)*, 99 Field Regt *(Langstoft) (38+589) (A, B and C Btys: 5x25-pdr)*, 123 Army Field Regt *(Burton Agnes) (36+533) (283 and 284 Btys: 6x4.5-inch, 4x18-pdr)*, 13 A/T Regt *(Elton) (26+599) (2, 8, 44 and 82 Btys: 24x2-pdr)*;
2 Manchester (MG) *(Malton;* A and B Coys: *Hornsea,* C Coy: *Thornholme* and D Coy: *Driffield) (34+755)*;

RE: 5 Field Coy *(Leconfield) (5+249)*, 208 Field Coy *(Hornsea) (7+252)*, 506 Field Coy *(Bridlington) (5+255)*, 21 Field Park Coy *(Lowthorpe) (4+159)*;
RAMC: 4 Field Ambulance *(Beverley) (15+292)*, 5 Field Ambulance *(Bishop Burton) (10+175)*, 6 Field Ambulance *(Sledmore) (9+236)*;
RASC: Divisional Supply Column *(Middleton) (14+489)*, Divisional Petrol Coy *(Sledmore) (6+302)*, Divisional Ammunition Coy *(Market Weighton) (8+364)*;
CMP: Divisional Provost Coy *(Pocklington) (112)*;
RS: Divisional Signals Regt *(Pocklington) (22+450)*;
RAOC: Divisional Field Workshop *(Retford) (5+221)*, Divisional LAD`s *(Pocklington) (9+202)*.

NOTES:
- *The Division was a Regular Army formation that had served with the BEF*
- *The Division was assigned to the defence north of the River Humber*
- *By 13 July it had 100% Personnel, 40% artillery pieces, 33% A/T guns*
- *In August four infantry battalions were allocated to beach defence.*
- *By 7 September it had 100% Personnel, 80% artillery pieces, 50% A/T guns*
- *General N Irwin had commanded until 12 August and Brigadier Gartlan was in charge between 15 August and 18 September, when General Watson took over. Brigadier Warren was appointed in February and Brigadier Gartlan had commanded 5th Brigade since the start of the war. Brigadier D Furlong had commanded 6th Brigade from 20 May until his death on 5 September 1940 in a minefield accident. He was the most senior officer killed on active service during this period. General Watson rose to command Western Command in 1944*
- *2 Derbyshire Yeomanry joined the new 8th Armoured Division on 27 November.*

- 44th Infantry Division (Home Counties) (GOC: Major General A Percival)
HQ: Doncaster, West Riding
131st Infantry Brigade: *(HQ: Spalding)* (GOC: Brigadier J Utterson-Kelso*)
2 Buffs *(Sutterton) (37+934)*, 1/5 Queens *(Gedney) (38+835)*, 1/6 Queens *(Boston) (32+852)*.
132nd Infantry Brigade: *(HQ: Bawtry)* (GOC: Brigadier J Steele*)
1/4 Royal West Kent *(Wiseton) (33+796)*, 1/5 Royal West Kent *(Epworth) (33+809)*, 1/7 Queens *(Rossington) (34+833)*.
133rd Infantry Brigade: *(HQ: Snaith)* (GOC: Brigadier E Beard)
2 Sussex *(Selby) (31+911)*, 1/4 Sussex *(Goole) (35+912)*, 1/5 Sussex *(Thorne) (36+905)*.
Divisional Troops:
RA: 57 Field Regt *(Pontefract) (37+577) (225 and 226 Btys: 16x75mm)*, 58 Field Regt *(Doncaster) (32+518) (229 and 230Btys: 14x25-pdr, 6x75mm)*, 65 Field Regt *(Knottingly) (32+551) (257 and 258 Btys: 8x75mm, 4x25-pdr, 4x18/25-pdr)*, 57 A/T Regt *(Campsall) (22+449) (225, 226, 227 and 228 Btys: 9x2-pdr, 8x6-pdr)* *(225 Bty was with 31 Independent Brigade in IV Corps)*;
1/6 Cheshire (MG) *(Louth) (31+790)*;
RE: 11 Field Coy *(Fosdyke) (4+275)*, 209 Field Coy *(Tickhill) (7+281)* (GHQ Line role), 210 Field Coy *(Castleford) (6+271)* (GHQ Line role), 211 Field Park Coy *(Adwick) (3+165)*;
RAMC: 131 Field Ambulance *(Pontefract) (11+185)*, 132 Field Ambulance *(Tickhill) (11+215)*, 133 Field Ambulance *(Castleford) (11+238)*;
RASC: Divisional Ammunition Coy *(Darrington) (9+368)*, Divisional Petrol Coy *(Upton) (8+278)*, Divisional Supply Column *(Pontefract) (15+432)*;

CMP: Divisional Provost Coy *(Doncaster) (106)*;
RS: Divisional Signals Regt *(Hooton Pagnell) (25+451)*;
RAOC: Divisional Field Workshop *(Doncaster) (3+215)*, Divisional LAD`s *(Doncaster) (13+338)*.

NOTES:
- The Division was a Territorial Army formation that had served with the BEF
- General Percival was appointed on 25 June, having previously served as Brigadier, General Staff in the BEF`s I Corps. He later commanded at Singapore, where he went into captivity. The commanders of 131st and 132nd Brigades were appointed in November 1939, while Brigadier Beard was appointed on 19 June. Brigadier Steele rose briefly to a Corps Command in 1942 before becoming Deputy Chief of General Staff in the Middle East
- The Division was assigned to the defence south of the River Humber
- By 13 July it had 100% Personnel, 20% artillery pieces, 5% A/T guns
- On 25 August it was 45% mobile and had 48 field guns, 9 anti tank guns and 66 armoured carriers.
- By 7 September it had 100% Personnel, 66% artillery pieces, 20% A/T guns
- In November it moved to XII Corps, replacing 45th Division in Sussex.

- 1st Infantry Division (GOC: Major General K Anderson*)
HQ: Lincoln
1st Guards Brigade: *(HQ: Louth)* (GOC: Brigadier F Copland-Griffiths)
3 Grenadier Guards *(Louth) (35+907)*, 2 Coldstream Guards *(Immingham) (37+926)*, 2 Hampshire *(Louth) (38+877)*.
2nd Infantry Brigade: *(HQ: Bourne)* (GOC: Brigadier C Hudson*)
1 Loyals *(Horncastle) (32+871)*, 2 North Staffordshire *(Horncastle) (33+894)*, 1/6 Gordons *(March) (32+831)*.
3rd Infantry Brigade: *(HQ: Spilsby)* (GOC: Brigadier T Wilson*)
1 Duke of Wellington's Regt *(35+898)*, 2 Sherwood Foresters *(Spilsby) (30+842)*, 1 Kings Shropshire Light Infantry *(Wrangle) (30+902)*.
Divisional Troops:
RA: 2 Field Regt *(Louth) (25+599) (35/87 and 42/53 Btys: 16x25-pdr)*, 19 Field Regt *(Remby) (29+575) (29/97 and 39/96 Btys: 16x18/25-pdr)*, 67 Field Regt *(Sleaford) (33+599) (265 and 266 Btys: 10x18/25-pdr)*, 153 Army Field Regt *(Wrangle) (35+545) (A Bty: 8x4.5-inch, B Bty: 8x75mm)*, 154 Army Field Regt *(Utterby) (32+627) (A&B Btys: 8x75mm, 6x4.5-inch)*, 21 A/T Regt *(Woodhall Spa) (30+589) (BB, Q, Y and Z Btys: 12x2-pdr, 8x6-pdr)*;
RE: 23 Field Coy *(Wainfleet) (5+256)*, 238 Field Coy *(Louth) (6+254)*, 248 Field Coy *(Lincoln) (6+253)*, 6 Field Park Coy *(Wragby) (3+172)*;
RAMC: 1 Field Ambulance *(Stenigot) (11+231)*, 2 Field Ambulance *(Thurlby) (12+242)*, 3 Field Ambulance *(Horncastle) (12+236)*;
RASC: Divisional Petrol Coy *(Lincoln) (7+274)*, Divisional Ammunition Coy *(Woodhall Spa) (11+382)*, Divisional Supply Column *(Collingham) (13+450)*;
CMP: Divisional Provost Coy *(Leeds) (111)*;
RS: Divisional Signals Regt *(Lincoln) (21+454)*;
RAOC: Divisional LAD`s *(Lincoln) (17+332)*.

NOTES:
- *The Division was a Regular Army formation that had served with the BEF*
- *The Division was assigned to the defence of the Lincolnshire coastline*
- *By 13 July it had 100% Personnel, 66% artillery pieces, 45% A/T guns*
- *In August eight infantry battalions were allocated to beach defence*
- *On 25 August it was 90% mobile and had 46 field guns, 20 anti tank guns and 90 armoured carriers.*
- *By 7 September it had 100% Personnel, 66% artillery pieces, 45% A/T guns*
- *General Anderson had commanded 11th Brigade in the BEF before taking temporary command of 3rd Division during the Dunkirk evacuation; he later rose to command the First Army in Tunisia. He was promoted to command of this Division on 13 June. Brigadier Hudson had been in charge since the outbreak of War, Brigadier Wilson since December and Brigadier Copland-Griffiths since 14 July.*

Corps Troops:
2 Cheshire (MG) *(Spilsby) (32+809)*, 4 Cheshire (MG) *(Brigg, Spurn Head, Hull, Grimsby) (32+786)*;
6 Kings Own (Pioneer) *(York) (25+838)*, 7 Kings Own (Pioneer) *(Newark) (23+977)*;

3rd Infantry Training Group:
7 East Yorkshire *(Otley) (29+903)*, 11 West Yorkshire (Home) *(Otley) (24+925)*, 8 Bedford and Hertfordshire (Home) *(Otley) (25+944)*, 8 Duke of Wellington's Regt (Home) *(Otley) (27+931)*.

4th Infantry Training Group:
7 South Lancashire (Home) *(Whitwell) (25+940)*, 8 South Lancashire (Home) *(Ollerton) (25+923)*, 12 Sherwood Foresters (Home) *(Thoreby) (29+937)*, 7 Leicester (Home) *(Nottingham) (29+933)*.

5th Infantry Training Group:
7 Norfolk (Pioneer) *(Nottingham) (24+998)*, 7 Lincoln *(Nottingham) (25+929)*, 8 North Staffordshire (Home) *(Arnold) (29+934)*.

6 KOYLI (Home) *(Doncaster) (36+807)*, 6 Leicester (Home) *(Grantham) (63+1329)*, 6 Kings Shropshire Light Infantry (Home) *(Worksop) (25+945)*, 1/10 Sherwood Foresters *(Nottingham) (33+720)*, 1/10 West Yorkshire (Home) *(York) (21+1154)*, 2/10 Sherwood Foresters *(Nottingham) (28+721)*, 12 Warwick *(Sheffield) (24+765)*, 13 West Yorkshire (Home) *(York) (18+404)* *(formed 25 September from 10 Bn with 3 coys - B: Doncaster, C: Sheffield, D: Goole)*;

RA: 1 Survey Regt *(Wentbridge) (24+534)* *(Flash Spotting Bty: Alford, Survey Bty: Northern Command, Sound Ranging Bty: Eastern Command)*, 6 Super Heavy Bty *(Little Weighton) (5+97)* *(2x12-inch rail)*, 3 Medium Regt *(Market Rasen) (25+700)* *(infantry role)*, 79 Medium Regt *(Laceby) (27+614)* *(P Bty: Grimsby, Q Bty: Kingston upon Hull) (4x6in)*, 80 Medium Regt *(Mansfield) (28+545)* *(A&B Btys training: 6x60-pdr)*, 27 Army Field Regt *(Melton Mowbray) (40+919)* *(most of regt detached to super heavy and heavy units)*, 69 Field Regt *(Horncastle) (33+599)* *(1x4.5-inch, rest as infantry)*, 140 Army Field Regt *(Sleaford) (33+784)* *(366 Bty: 9x75mm, 367 Bty: 11x75mm)*, FM1 Bty *(Alford) (4x4-inch)*, D5 Bty *(North Somercotes) (4x4-inch, 2x12-pdr, 2x3-pdr)*, H5 Bty *(Skegness) (8x6-pdr)*;

RAC: H Armoured Train *(Market Weighton) (48) (covered York, Selby and Hull);*
RE: East Riding Fortress Coy *(Spurn Point) (8+162)*, 3 Cheshire Field Sqn *(Kettering) (9+298)*, 102 Army Field Coy *(Louth) (6+231)*, 107 Army Field Coy *(Worksop) (6+224)*, 213 Army Field Coy *(Worksop) (7+228) (GHQ Line role)*, 103 Army Troops Coy *(Withernsea) (5+271)*, 104 Army Troops Coy *(Tadcaster) (6+261)*, 105 Corps Field Park Coy *(Bawtry) (4+150)*, 13 Corps Field Survey Coy *(Tadcaster) (7+128);*
RASC: 2 Bulk Petrol Coy *(Edmondthorpe) (6+180)*, 18 Troop Carry Coy *(Chesterfield) (8+338)*, 18 Motor Coach Coy *(Stocksfield) (10+173)*, 23 Motor Coach Coy *(Horncastle) (9+176)*, 27 Motor Coach Coy *(Worksop) (5+153)*, 29 Motor Coach Coy *(Great Driffield) (10+166)*, 30 Motor Coach Coy *(Doncaster) (10+185)*, 34 Motor Coach Coy *(Louth) (9+172)*, 926 Coy *(Winthorpe) (6+257)*, 1 and 2 Ambulance Car Coys *(Malton) (12+557)*, 3 Ambulance Car Coy *(Thwing) (7+254)*, 5 Ambulance Car Coy *(Sowerby Bridge) (8+269)*, 6 Ambulance Car Coy *(Thurner) (9+311);* 1 and 2 Cypriot mule companies *(Melton Mowbray);*
RAMC: 1-5 Casualty Clearing Stations *(Rotherham) (43+434)*, 17 Casualty Clearing Station *(Riccall) (9+88)*, 21 Casualty Clearing Station *(Nocton) (8+88)*, 218 Field Ambulance *(Worksop) (5+140);*
CMP: 102 Divisional Provost Coy *(Doncaster) (105);*
RAOC: 1 Army Field Workshop *(Retford) (10+332).*

NOTES:
- *3rd Infantry Group was formed in mid July and reformed as 203rd Infantry Brigade on 10 October in a coastal defence role in the South West*
- *4th Infantry Group was formed in mid July and reformed as 204th Infantry Brigade on 12 October and remained in the North Midlands*
- *5th Infantry Group was formed in mid July and reformed as 205th Infantry Brigade on 10 October and was attached to 1st Infantry Division in a coast defence role.*

X CORPS (GOC: Lieutenant General W Holmes*)
HQ: Darlington, Durham

NOTES:
- *The Corps was responsible for the defence of the North East coastline*
- *General Holmes had commanded 42nd Division in the BEF and was promoted to this command on 17 June. He rose to command Ninth Army in the Levant in 1942.*

- 54th Infantry Division (East Anglian) (GOC: Major General J Priestman)
HQ: Morpeth, Northumberland
161st Brigade: *(HQ: Chatton)* (GOC: Brigadier J Hobart)
1/4 Essex *(Wooler) (39+959)*, 1/5 Essex *(Beal) (39+959)*, 2/5 Essex *(Eglingham) (39+991).*
162nd Brigade: *(HQ: Felton)* (GOC: Brigadier R Reford)
1 Hertford *(Rothbury) (32+803)*, 2 Hertford *(Felton) (32+841)*, 1/6 Bedford and Hertfordshire *(Alnmouth) (30+784).*
163rd Brigade: *(HQ: Fencehouses)* (GOC: Brigadier R Moseley)
2/4 Essex *(Fulwell) (32+894)*, 1/5 Berkshire *(Earsden) (35+813)*, 1/7 Berkshire *(Castle Eden) (35+834).*

2nd Motor Machine Gun Brigade: *(HQ: Chatton)* (GOC: Brigadier T Murray)
43 RTR *(Ellingham) (42+504)*, 49 RTR *(Low Lynn) (42+474)*, 51 RTR *(Belford) (39+416)*; Brigade Coy RASC *(York) (9+331)*;

Divisional Troops:
RA: 85 Field Regt *(Gosforth) (35+600)* (*337 Bty: 4x18/25-pdr, 2x75mm, 338 Bty: 8x18-pdr, 6x75mm*), 86 Field Regt *(Felton) (32+603)* (*341 Bty: 8x75mm, 2x4.5-inch, 342 Bty: 4x18/25-pdr, 2x60-pdr*), 134 Field Regt *(Chester le Street) (32+580)* (*213 and 340 Btys: 12x75mm, 4x4.5-inch, 3x6-inch, 4x18/25-pdr*), 55 A/T Regt *(Ponteland) (27+541)* (*217 (Morpeth), 218 (Blyth), 219 and 220 Btys: 16x2-pdr*);
1/4 Gordons (MG) *(Morpeth) (41+829)*;
RE: 249 Field Coy *(Newton on Moor) (5+218)*, 286 Field Coy *(Bridlington) (5+229)*, 556 Field Coy *(Lowick) (6+239)*, 289 Field Park Coy *(Pegswood) (4+149)*;
RAMC: 151 Light Field Ambulance *(Lilburn) (8+172)*, 161 Field Ambulance *(Corbridge) (12+234)*, 162 Field Ambulance *(Thropton) (11+178)*, 163 Field Ambulance RAMC *(Chester le Street) (11+246)*;
RASC: Divisional Supply Coy *(Mitford) (15+432)*, Divisional Petrol Coy *(Capheaton) (6+309)*, Divisional Ammunition Coy *(Alnwick)*;
RS: Divisional Signals Regt *(Whalton) (25+455)*;
CMP: Divisional Provost Coy *(Morpeth) (2+112)*.

NOTES:
- *This Division was a Territorial Army formation assigned to home defence when the War began. General Priestman had been in command since the start of the War, as had Brigadier Moseley; Brigadier Hobart was appointed in November 1939 and Brigadier Reford succeeded Brigadier J McCreedy on 27 August. General Priestman retired in 1941*
- *By 13 July the Division had 100% Personnel, 66% artillery pieces, 45% A/T guns*
- *On 30 August 2nd Motor Machine Gun Brigade arrived from York and relieved 161st Brigade. Regiments in the Brigade had three squadrons of three troops, each troop had six lightly armoured cars equipped with a total of two Vickers medium, two Bren light machine guns and two anti tank rifles. The rest of the Regiment were to be carried in trucks as mobile infantry*
- *By 7 September the Division had 100% Personnel, 100% artillery pieces, 25% A/T guns*
- *The Division was responsible for the defence of Northumberland and Tyneside*
- *In November 2nd Motor Machine Gun Brigade left for Derbyshire to become 25th Army Tank Brigade.*

- 59th Infantry Division (Staffordshire) (GOC: Major General F Witts)
HQ: Carleton, North Riding
176th Infantry Brigade: *(HQ: Stockton)* (GOC: Brigadier J Short)
1/7 South Staffordshire *(Stockton) (34+829)*, 1/6 North Staffordshire *(Croft) (35+902)*, 1/7 North Staffordshire *(West Hartlepool) (31+890)*.
177th Infantry Brigade: *(HQ: Guisborough)* (GOC: Brigadier A Hawkins)
1/5 South Staffordshire *(Kirk Yealtham) (34+824)*, 1/6 South Staffordshire *(Yarm) (35+875)*, 2/6 South Staffordshire *(Guisborough) (32+810)*.

197th Infantry Brigade: *(HQ: Snainton)* (GOC: Brigadier S Lucey)
2/5 Lancashire Fusiliers *(Scarborough) (33+911)*, 2/6 Lancashire Fusiliers *(Pickering) (35+901)*, 1/5 East Lancashire *(Whitby) (35+888)*.

Divisional Troops:
RA: 61 Field Regt *(Croft) (39+514) (241 Bty: 4x75mm, 4x4.5-inch, 242 Bty: 8x75mm)*, 110 Field Regt *(East Harsley) (33+564) (207 and 208 Btys: 9x75mm, 4x18/25-pdr, 2x18-pdr)*, 116 Field Regt *(Sedgefield) (37+603) (243 Bty: 8x75mm, 244 Bty: 4x4.5-inch, 4x75mm, 2x18-pdr)*; 68 A/T Regt *(Hutton Rudby) (28+483) (269, 270, 271 and 272 Btys: 12x2-pdr, 8x6-pdr)*;
RE: 257 Field Coy *(Scarborough) (6+225)*, 509 Field Coy *(Redcar) (5+230)*, 510 Field Coy *(Seaton) (6+250)*, 511 Field Park Coy *(Eaglescliffe) (5+182)*;
RAMC: 203 Light Field Ambulance *(Ormesby) (10+234)*, 210 Field Ambulance *(Thornton) (9+193)*, 211 Field Ambulance *(Billingham) (10+182)*;
RASC: Divisional Ammunition Coy *(Rushyford) (9+363)*, Divisional Supply Column *(Hovingham) (13+431)*, Divisional Petrol Coy *(Crosby Court) (7+291)*;
RAOC: Divisional Field Workshop *(Darlington) (4+220)*;
RS: Divisional Signals Regt *(Hutton Rudby) (24+506)*;
CMP: Divisional Provost Coy *(Stokesley) (112)*.

NOTES:
- *This Division was a Territorial Army formation assigned to home defence when the War began. 1/6 South Staffordshire had served with the BEF*
- *General Witts had been in command since 11 May, having previously been the BEF Deputy Chief of Staff; he retired in 1943. All three Brigadiers had served since the outbreak of War*
- *By 13 July the Division had 98% Personnel, 50% artillery pieces, 10% A/T guns*
- *By 7 September the Division had 100% Personnel, 100% artillery pieces, 40% A/T guns*
- *The Division was responsible for the defence of Teeside and North Yorkshire coastline.*

Corps Troops:
RAC: B Armoured Train *(Morpeth) (48) (covered Kelso, Berwick and Newcastle)*;
6 Loyals *(Thirsk) (29+564) (Corps mobile reserve)*;
1/6 Argyll and Sutherland Highlanders (MG) *(Middlesborough) (39+713)*
17 Royal Fusiliers (Pioneer) *(Amble) (28+790)*, 12 South Staffordshire (Pioneer) *(Saltburn) (33+813)*;
10 Northumberland Fusiliers (Home) *(Gosforth) (43+1919) (split into 2 battalions 25 September)*, 13 Durham Light Infantry *(Gateshead) (42+1444)*, 8 Green Howards (Home) *(Neasham) (39+1395) (split into 1/8 and 2/8 Bns on 25 September)*, 50 Durham Light Infantry (Hold) *(West Hartlepool) (21+743)*, 70 Northumberland Fusiliers *(Newcastle) (38+373)*;
RA: 1 Medium Regt *(West Auckland) (34+648) (1/3 Bty: Howden (2x6-inch), 5/22 Bty: Hildon (4x60-pdr and 3x6-inch)*, 65 Medium Regt *(Newcastle) (35+891) (222 Bty: Redcar, 223 Bty: Alnmouth) (34x6-pdr, 3x6-inch)*; 50 Army Field Regt *(Hunwick) (39+508) (434 Bty: 6x4.5-inch, 435 Bty: 2x4.5-inch, 2x18-pdr)*, 6 Survey Regt *(Gateshead) (2+21)*;
RE: North Riding Fortress Coy *(Redcar) (7+107)*, 242 Army Field Coy *(East Ayton) (5+236)*, 55 Army Field Coy *(Bedlington) (5+248)*, 256 Army Field Coy *(Stockton) (5+264)*, 258 Corps Field Park Coy *(Darlington) (4+160)*, 212 Army Troops Coy *(Harlington) (6+293)*, 91 Army Troops Coy *(Darlington) (6+272)*, 580 and 588 Army Troops Coys *(Scarborough) (16+612)*, 127 Electrical and Mechanical Coy *(Scarborough) (4+238)*;

RASC: 1 Bulk Petrol Coy *(Barnard Castle) (6+173)*, 20 Motor Coach Coy *(Matfen) (10+188)*, 26 Station Transport Coy *(Bedale) (5+147)*;
RAMC: 222 Field Ambulance *(Darlington) (8+169)*, 20 Casualty Clearing Station *(Otterburn) (7+92)*;
RAOC: 4 Ordnance Field Park *(Darlington) (14+476)*, 7 Divisional Workshops *(Durham) (4+209)*;
CMP: 105 Divisional Provost Coy *(Darlington) (106)*.

- 24th Army Tank Brigade *(HQ: Harrogate)* (GOC: Brigadier A Kenchington)
41 RTR *(Oldham) (36+507)*, 45 RTR *(Leeds) (32+518)*, 47 RTR *(Oldham) (32+502)*;
5 Field Sqn RE *(Ripon) (5+30)*;
8 Light Field Ambulance RAMC *(Ilkley) (7+113)*;
Brigade Workshop RAOC *(Ilkley) (2+165)*.

NOTES:
- *In 8 September the HQ moved from Ilkley*
- *By 15 September the Brigade had three Mark III infantry tanks allocated. Each battalion manned two armoured trains (each with 2x6pdr and 6 lmg)*
- *Brigadier K Stewart had commanded until 19 September*
- *On 30 September the Brigade moved to Boroughbridge, with 41 RTR at Knaresborough*
- *On 1 November the Brigade was reformed as 24th Armoured Brigade and assigned to the new 8th Armoured Division.*

- Catterick Garrison *(810+22,141)* (GOC: Brigadier J Gordon)
2nd Infantry Training Group: 7 East Lancashire *(26+961)*, 11 Kings *(24+930)*, 12 Kings *(27+949)*, 11 Green Howards *(21+903)*

RAC: 51 Light Armoured Training Regt *(77+1762) (19 Carriers)*, 56 Armoured Training Regt *(48+1672)*;
RA: 123 OCT Regt *(65+642)*, 51 A/T Training Regt *(20+1104)*, School of Super Heavy Artillery *(36+139)*,
RE: 697 General Construction Coy *(6+301)*, 121 Road Construction Coy *(4+111)*;
RASC: 11 Station Maintenance Coy *(5+100)*, 12 Station Transport Coy *(8+292)*, H Coy *(1+1611)*;
RS: 1 Depot Bn *(16+1191)*, 1 General Trades Training Bn *(20+1397)*, 1 Operational Training Bn *(17+1242)*, 1 Holding Bn *(60+1126)*, 152 OCTU *(39+662)*;
RAMC: 7 Training Coy *(157+499)*;
RAOC: 56 Training Section *(3+642)*;
AMPC: 70 Coy *(6+274)*.

NOTE: 2nd Infantry Group was formed in mid July and reformed as 202nd Infantry Brigade on 20 October in a coastal defence role in Northern Command.

- Hull Garrison (CO: Colonel W Bradley-Williams from 5 July)
1/8 Lancashire Fusiliers *(Brough) (36+888)*, 6 East Yorkshire *(Hull) (43+897)*, 50 KOYLI *(Hull) (21+968)*.

Northern Command Troops:
- Northumbria Sub Area: *(HQ: Darlington)* (GOC: Brigadier P Shears)
Northumberland Fusiliers MGTC *(Newcastle) (71+1753)*, 1 Machine Gun Training Bn *(Whitley Bay) (72+694)*;
Durham Light Infantry ITC *(Brancepeth Castle) (60+1835)*;
RA: 52 A/A Driver Training Regt *(Auckland) (22+1272)*;
RE: 679 Artisan Works Coy *(Alnwick) (6+255)*, 707 General Construction Coy *(Hexham) (6+251)*; 1 Australian Forestry Coy *(Seahorses)*;
RASC: 6 Driver Training Bn *(Barnard Castle) (24+889)*;
RAOC: 7 Divisional Field Workshop *(Durham) (4+209)*;
AMPC: 12 Group HQ *(Darlington) (4+12)*, 34 Group HQ *(Gosforth) (4+14)*, 4 Coy *(Darlington) (6+12)*, 15 Coy *(Newcastle) (6+24)*, 33 Coy *(Hudswell) (7+269)*, 45 Coy *(Redcar) (5+270)*, 48 Coy *(Haydon Bridge) (4+277)*, 49 Coy *(Bellasize) (7+265)*, 54 Coy *(Darlington) (7+246)*, 60 Coy (Alnwick and *Morpeth) (7+349)*, 138 Coy *(Hartlepool) (4+266)*, 164 Coy *(Durham) (4+263)*.

-Yorkshire Sub Area: *(HQ: York)* (GOC: Brigadier E Dorman)
341 Cheshire MGTC *(Sheffield) (39+1358)*;
50 York and Lancaster (Hold) *(Doncaster) (18+819)*, 50 East Yorkshire (Hold) *(Beverley) (22+818)*, 50 West Yorkshire *(Wetherby) (21+896)*, 50 Green Howards *(Ripon) (23+898)*, 50 Duke of Wellington's Regt *(Rotherham) (25+768)*, 70 KOYLI *(Doncaster) (18+672)*, 70 West Yorkshire *(Leeds) (17+504)*, Green Howards ITC *(Richmond) (45+1689)*, KOYLI ITC *(Strensall) (31+1742)*, East Yorkshire ITC *(Beverley) (44+1762)*, West Yorkshire ITC *(York) (39+1673)*, Duke of Wellington's Regt ITC *(Halifax) (46+1677)*, York and Lancaster ITC *(Pontefract) (34+1776)*;
RA: 9 Field Training Regt *(Harrogate) (25+1166)*, 25 Medium and Heavy Training Regt *(Marske) (25+1147)*, 37 Signal Training Regt *(Scarborough) (21+792)*, 39 Signal Training Regt *(Wakefield) (23+840)*, 125 OCTU *(Ilkley) (128+498)*;
RE: 3 Training Bn *(Ripon) (36+1771)*, 921 Water Transport Group *(Ripon) (21+559)*; 29 Rail Survey Coy *(York) (7+64)*, 800-805 and 808-809 Road Construction Coys *(Halifax) (31+796)*, 125, 851, 853 and 854 Quarry Coys *(Halifax) (16+590)*, 113 Road Construction Coy *(Hornsea) (4+106)*, 131 Forestry Coy *(Halifax) (3+153)*, 153 Rail Operation Coy *(York) (5+257)*, 157 Rail Construction Coy *(York) (6+271)*, 197 Training Sts Coy *(Breedon) (5+257)*, 677 General Construction Coy *(Rawcliffe) (5+253)*, 681 General Construction Coy *(Linton on Ouse) (6+268)*, 685 Artisan Works Coy *(Holmfield) (6+278)*;
RS: Rail Telegraph Coy *(Milton) (4+191)*. Rail Signals Training Bn *(Milton) (13+393)*, Training Bn *(Harrogate) (24+649)*, 3 Holding Bn *(Kirkburton) (34+2256)*, 3 Depot Bn *(Ossett) (10+1198)*, 3 Operations Training Bn *(Huddersfield) (17+1258)*, 3 General Trades Bn *(Huddersfield) (17+1066)*;
RAMC: 8 Training Coy *(York) (128+606)*, 1 General Hospital *(York) (7+192)*, 2, 4, 6, 7, 11, 17 and 28 General Hospitals *(Leeds) (94+1413)*, 18 General Hospital *(Ashby St Ledger) (14+227)*, 11 Depot *(Leeds) (75+1698)* RAOC: 23 Advance Supply Depot *(Bedale) (12+214)*;
RASC: 17 Reserve Motor Transport Coy *(Kirkhammerton) (9+468)*, 2 LofC Training Centre *(Halifax) (13+276)*, 2 Motor Transport Training Depot *(Halifax) (25+1315)*, 2 Movement and Control Group *(Aberford)*, 5 Driver Training Centre *(Sheffield) (31+1729)*, 4 Station

Transport Coy *(York)* *(5+376)*, 4 Station Maintenance Coy *(York)* *(4+259)*, 5 and 6 Reserve Motor Transport Coy *(Darley Dale)* *(19+745)*;
RAOC: Main Supply Depot *(York)* *(2+30)*;
AMPC: 8 Group HQ *(Stainforth)* *(4+15)*, 9 Group HQ *(Kirkby Fleetham)* *(5+7)*, 12 Coy *(Masham)* *(5+255)*, 17 Coy *(Dishforth)* *(6+253)*, 29 Coy *(Monk Frystone)* *(5+243)*, 40 Coy *(York)* *(4+277)*, 43 Coy *(Leeming)* *(7+298)*, 44 Coy *(Cleethorpes)* *(5+283)*, 56 Coy *(Leeds)* *(6+257)*, 85 Coy *(Rudston)* *(6+276)*, 104 Coy *(Hatfield)* *(7+264)*, 106 Coy *(Topcliffe)* *(7+322)*, 110 Coy *(Selby)* *(7+266)*, 6 Centre *(Bradford)* *(58+1913)*, 906 Reinforcement Coy *(Bradford)* *(7+233)*.

- North Midlands Sub Area: *(HQ: Nottingham)* (GOC: Brigadier A Hopwood *from 18 July*)
50 Sherwood Foresters *(Derby)* *(14+712)*, 70 Sherwood Foresters *(Nottingham)* *(18+489)*, Lincolns ITC *(Lincoln)* *(45+1852)*, Sherwood Foresters ITC *(Derby)* *(45+1750)*;
6 Cavalry Training Regt *(Ollerton)* *(44+908)*;
RE: 2 Training Bn *(Newark)* *(44+2176)*, 9 Rail Bn *(Derby)* *(34+1213)*, 10 MU Training Bn *(Donnington)* *(20+661)*, 18 Technical Training Bn *(Derby)* *(15+1001)*, 19 Technical Training Bn *(Weston)* *(17+1057)*, 7and8 Movement Control Groups *(Derby)* *(72+299)*, 130 Forestry Coy *(Ollerton)* *(8+143)*, 199 Rail Mobile Workshop *(Derby)* *(6+383)*, 290 General Construction Coy *(Bramcote)* *(5+242)*, 600 Rail Construction Coy *(Derby)* *(6+261)*, 653 General Construction Coy *(Hemswell)* *(6+268)*, 654 Artisan Works Coy *(Lincoln)* *(5+277)*, 673 Artisan Works Coy *(Newark)* *(5+255)*, 686 General Construction Coy *(Cranwell)* *(6+269)*, 694 Artisan Works Coy *(Hornsea)* *(6+252)*, 4 Bridge Coy RE *(Derby)*;
RASC: 3 Recruit Reception and Training Centre *(Sutton on Trent)* *(9+2604)*, 5 Driver Training Bn *(Mansfield)* *(42+1167)*, 7 Driver Training Bn *(Chesterfield)* *(20+1290)*, 8 Driver Training Bn *(Matlock)* *(27+1246)*; 9 Driver Training Bn *(Alfreton)* *(30+1366)*, 11 Recruit Reception and Training Centre *(Sutton on Ashfield)* *(5+311)*, 12 Driver Training Centre *(Eckington)* *(2+614)*, 2 Works Motor Transport Coy *(Chesterfield)* *(8+400)*, 4 Bridge Coy *(Derby)* *(12+478)*, 3 and 4 Reserve Motor Transport Coy *(Staveley)* *(22+854)*;
RIASC: Force K6 *(Ashbourne)* (*29 Indian Animal Transport Coy (Doncaster), 32 Indian Animal Transport Coy (Ashbourne)) (Force was a packhorse unit that had served with BEF. In early October this Force moved to St Austell and Bulford*);
RAOC: 2 Training Bn *(Chillwell)* *(48+1984)*, 13 Technical Training Centre *(Derby)* *(5+243)*, Main Supply Depot *(Derby)* *(2+30)*;
AMPC: 42 Coy *(Nottingham)* *(5+285)*, 47 Coy *(Skegness)* *(5+297)*, 63 Coy *(Keadby Bridge)* *(6+283)*, 78 Coy *(Warsop)* *(6+277)*, 79 Coy *(Hornsea)* *(6+264)*, 84 Coy *(Boston)* *(5+295)*, 139 Coy *(Mablethorpe)* *(5+280)*, 160 Coy *(Worksop)* *(5+268)*, 202 Coy *(Weedon)* *(6+280)*.

- East Midlands Sub Area: *(HQ: Leicester)* (GOC: Brigadier R Abbott from 12 July)
50 Seaforth (Hold) *(Market Harborough)* *(23+711)*, 50 Royal Scots Fusiliers (Hold) *(Melton Mowbray)* *(21+802)*, 50 Leicester *(Hinckley)* *(24+730)*, 50 KOSB *(Nuneaton)* *(19+776)*, 50 Camerons *(Loughborough)* *(18+753)*, Leicester ITC *(Swigston)* *(33+1666)*, Northamptons ITC *(Northampton)* *(41+1744)*;
110 Cavalry OCTU *(Weedon)* *(4+136)*;
RAOC: 3 Train Bn *(Leicester)* *(76+1326)*, 14 Technical Training Centre *(Gainsborough)* *(5+301)*;
AMPC: 163 Coy *(Leicester)* *(6+267)*, 191 Coy *(Leicester)* *(6+272)*

WESTERN COMMAND (GOC: General Sir Robert Gordon - Finlayson)
HQ: Chester

NOTE: The GOC had been appointed on 10 June, having previously been the Adjutant General. He retired in 1941.

III CORPS (GOC: Lieutenant General J Marshall-Cornwall)
HQ: Whitchurch, Shropshire

NOTES:
- *The Corps HQ had served with the BEF*
- *The GOC was promoted to command on 24 June. In 1941 he became GOC British Troops in Egypt and retired in 1943.*

- 38th Infantry Division (Welsh) (GOC: Major General A Williams)
HQ: Knutsford, Cheshire
113th Brigade: *(HQ: Northwich)* (GOC: Brigadier L Alston)
2/5 Welch *(Crewe) (29+875)*, 4 Monmouth *(Northwich) (31+824)*, 15 Welch *(Stafford) (34+871)*.
114th Brigade: *(HQ: Croxteth, Liverpool)* (GOC: Brigadier T Perkin)
1 Brecknock *(Haydock) (32+844)*, 2 Hereford *(Aintree) (33+803)*, 1/5 King's Shropshire Light Infantry *(Formby) (31+846)*.
115th Brigade: *(HQ: Blackburn)* (GOC: Brigadier C Price-Davies)
8 Royal Welch Fusiliers *(Bury) (32+802)*, 9 Royal Welch Fusiliers *(Rochdale) (28+763)*, 10 Royal Welch Fusiliers *(Blackburn) (32+738)*.
Divisional Troops:
RA: 102 Field Regt *(Southport) (34+544) (405 and 406 Btys: 12x75mm)*, 132 Field Regt *(Macclesfield) (30+498) (321 and 322 Btys: 12x75mm, 8x4.5-inch)*, 146 Field Regt *(Middleton) (36+508) (407 and 408 Btys: 12x75mm)*, 70 A/T Regt *(Stockport) (21+267) (277, 280, 281 and 282 Btys: 10x2-pdr)*;
RE: 283 Field Coy *(Huyton) (5+229)*, 284 Field Coy *(Rugeley) (4+237)*, 561 Field Coy *(Ramsbotham) (4+256)*, 247 Field Park Coy *(Burton Manor) (3+144)*;
RAMC: 207 Field Ambulance *(Tytherington) (11+238)*, 208 Field Ambulance *(Southport) (11+232)*, 209 Field Ambulance *(Rambsbotham) (10+238)*;
RASC: Divisional Petrol Coy *(Tarporley) (6+270)*, Divisional Supply Column *(Tarporley) (13+418)*; Divisional Ammunition Coy *(Tarporley) (7+362)*;
RAOC: Divisional LAD`s *(Chester) (5+112)*;
RS: Divisional Signals Regt *(Neeston) (25+553)*;
CMP: Divisional Provost Coy *(Chester) (1+93)*.

NOTES:
- *The Division had been assigned to home defence at the start of the War and was responsible for the northwest. It joined III Corps on 15 July*
- *General Williams was appointed on 11 May, but retired at the end of October 1940, being replaced by Major General N Irwin; all three brigadiers had served since the outbreak of War*

- By 13 July it had 100% Personnel, 40% artillery pieces, 5% A/T guns
- By 7 September it had 100% Personnel, 80% artillery pieces, 20% A/T guns
- In October the Division moved to the Aldershot Command.

- **2nd London Division** (GOC: Major General H Willans)
HQ: Whitney on Wye, Herefordshire
4th London Brigade: *(HQ: Saundersfoot)* (GOC: Brigadier W Bradshaw)
11 Royal Fusiliers *(Tenby) (35+823)*, 12 Royal Fusiliers *(Pembroke) (37+784)*, 2 London Irish Rifles *(Haverfordwest) (35+851)*.
5th London Brigade: *(HQ: Bridgend)* (GOC: Brigadier H Freeman-Attwood)
2 Queen's Westminster Rifles *(Llantwit) (30+708)*, 2 London Scots *(Llantwit) (36+909)*, 2 London Rifle Brigade *(Porthcawl) (31+835)*.
25th Infantry Brigade: *(HQ: Kington)* (GOC: Brigadier W Ramsden*)
2 Essex *(33+808)*, 4 Buffs *(39+869)*, 4 Border *(36+842)*; 222 Army Field Coy *(7+223)*, 180 Field Ambulance *(11+235)*.
Divisional Troops:
2 Queen Victoria Rifles (motorcycle) *(Hereford) (32+577)*;
RA: 114 Field Regt *(Presteign) (37+534) (231 and 232 Btys: 12x75mm)*, 117 Field Regt *(Carmarthen) (35+456) (255 and 256 Btys: 16x75mm, 8x4.5-inch)*, 138 Field Regt *(Neath) (31+480) (359 and 360 Btys: 16x75mm, 8x4.5-inch)*; 62 A/T Regt *(Hereford) (30+545) (245 (Kington), 246 (Wormelow), 247 (Cowbridge) and 248 Btys (Saundersfoot): 8x6-pdr, 6x2-pdr)*;
RE: 502 Field Coy *(Stoneleigh) (6+236)*, 503 Field Coy *(Portcawl) (6+251)*, 504 Field Park Coy *(Abergavenny) (3+150)*;
RAMC: 199 Field Ambulance *(Pontyclun) (12+180)*, 200 Field Ambulance *(Saundersfoot) (11+211)*;
RASC: Divisional Ammunition Coy *(Llantrissant) (10+349)*, Divisional Petrol Coy *(Weobley) (5+281)*, Divisional Supply Column *(Llandilo) (15+372)*;
RS: Divisional Signals Regt *(Hay on Wye) (26+508)*;
CMP: Divisional Provost Coy *(Hay on Wye) (100)*.

NOTES:
- *The Division was a Territorial Army formation assigned to home defence at the start of the War*
- *General Willans and Brigadier Bradshaw had been in command from the outbreak of War, while Brigadier Ramsden was appointed in November 1939 and Brigadier Freeman-Attwood on 27 July. Brigadier Ramsden rose briefly to a Corps command in 1942*
- *The Division moved from Cambridge in June. 25th Brigade joined after serving with the 50th Division in the BEF*
- *114 Field Regiment and 180 Field Ambulance had originally formed part of 12th Division*
- *By 13 July it had 90% Personnel, 33% artillery pieces, 5% A/T guns*
- *On 6 August the Division moved to the South Wales / Hereford area from Staffordshire and was responsible for South Wales and West Midlands*
- *By 7 September it had 90% Personnel, 80% artillery pieces, 20% A/T guns*
- *In early October 4 Buffs moved overseas to Malta.*

- 23rd Army Tank Brigade (GOC: Brigadier W Murrogh)
HQ: Welshpool
40 RTR *(Warwick) (30+539)*, 46 RTR *(Prescot) (38+646)*, 50 RTR *(Glamorgan) (33+538)*;
7 Light Field Ambulance RAMC *(Llansantffraid) (7+117)*;
Brigade Workshop RAOC *(Caernarfon) (5+35)*

NOTES:
- *Brigadier Murrogh had been in command since the outbreak of War*
- *By 15 September 3 Mark III infantry tanks with Brigade. Each battalion manned 2 armoured trains (each with 2x6pdr and 6 lmg)*
- *On 22 November the Brigade reformed as 23rd Armoured Brigade and joined the new 8th Armoured Division.*

- 3rd Motor Machine Gun Brigade (GOC: Brigadier H Lumsden)
HQ: Newcastle under Lyme, Staffordshire
15/19 Hussars *(33+505)*; 1 Fife and Forfar Yeomanry *(28+513)*, 5 Royal Irish Dragoon Guards *(Builth Wells) (27+526)*;
201 Light Field Ambulance RAMC *(Newastle under Lyne) (10+188)*;
Brigade Coy RASC *(Madeley) (10+343)*.

NOTES:
- *The Brigade was reformed on 23 June from the BEF`s 2nd Light Reconnaissance Brigade, when Brigadier Lumsden took command. He rose to command Eighth Army in 1942*
- *Regiments in the Brigade had 3 squadrons of 3 troops, each troop had 6 lightly armoured cars equipped with a total of 2 Vickers and 2 Bren guns and 2 anti tank rifles. The rest of the Regiment were carried in trucks as mobile infantry*
- *In December the Brigade reformed as 28th Armoured Brigade in the new 9th Armoured Division.*

- 36th Independent Infantry Brigade (GOC: Brigadier A Kent-Lemon)
HQ: Malvern, Worcestershire
5 Buffs *(35+881)*, 6 Royal West Kent *(35+730)*, 7 Royal West Kent *(34+681)*;
149 Army Field Regt RA *(29+599) (432 and 433 Btys: 16x25-pdr)*;
181 Field Ambulance RAMC *(13+216)*;
Brigade Coy RASC *(Pershore) (8+182)*.

NOTES:
- *The Brigade had served with the 12th Division in the BEF but was largely destroyed on 20 May in the Somme*
- *Brigadier Kent-Lymon was appointed on 1 July, having commanded 15th Brigade in Norway.*

Corps Troops:
1/8 Middlesex (MG) *(Liverpool) (33+767)*;
2 Commando *(Knutsford) (20+329)*;

5 South Wales Borderers *(Newport) (35+961)*, 6 South Lancashire (Home) *(Frodsham) (57+1067)*, 6 East Lancashire (Home) *(Pendleton) (5+1017)*, 8 Border (Home) *(Kendal) (61+1421)*, 8 Cheshire (Home) *(Birkenhead) (37+626)*, 8 Royal Ulster Rifles (Home) *(Holyhead) (21+769)*, 9 South Staffordshire (Home) *(Burton on Trent) (69+1471)*, 9 Gloucester (Home) *(Barry) (25+690)*, 9 Sussex *(Ross on Wye) (25 Sept to Mumbles to join 212 Infantry Brigade)*, 2/9 Manchester (Home) *(Tenby) (30+763)*, 1/10 Kings (Home) *(Wavertree) (30+791) (formed 25 September when 10 Kings split)*, 2/10 Kings (Home) *(Liverpool) (383) (formed 25 September when 10 Kings split)*, 1/11 Warwickshire (Home) *(Redditch) (31+652)*, 2/11 Warwickshire (Home) *(Nuthurst) (30+682) (formed 25 September from 11 Bn)*, 11 Manchester (Home) *(Lancaster) (47+999)*, 11 Royal Welsh Fusiliers (Home) *(Shrewsbury) (63+1979)*, 16 Welch (Home) *(Cardiff) (48+1047)*, 17 Welch (Home) *(Milford Haven) (42+1060)*;

RA: 51 Medium Regt *(Ellesmere) (29+664) (manned emergency coast batteries in the northwest and Wales)*, 73 Medium Regt *(Oswestry) (28+647) (forming)*, 75 Medium Regt *(Oswestry) (27+607) (Training: 12x6-inch)*, 76 Medium Regt *(Oswestry) (30+600) (Forming: 4x60-pdr)*, 77 Medium Regt *(Pontypridd) (25+615) (Training)*, 78 Medium Regt *(Fishguard) (23+573) (8x6-inch)*, 102 RHA *(Hoylake) (34+544)*, 97 Army Field Regt *(Swansea) (31+477) (coast defence role)*, 98 Army Field Regt *(Hightown) (32+828) (Mersey coast and airfield defence) (391and 392 Btys: 10x4-inch, 28x6-pdr, 12x13-pdr)*, 137 Army Field Regt *(Knowsley) (33+552) (349 and 350 Btys: 10x75mm)*, 139 Army Field Regt *(Malvern) (30+528) (362 and 364 Btys: 28x18-pdr, 4x4.5-inch)*, 71 A/T Regt *(Huyton) (26+261) (278, 279, 283 and 284 Btys: 4x-2pdr, rest as infantry) (formed 18 Sept)*, 3 Survey Regt *(Coed y Brein) (25+432) (A&B Btys)*;

RE: 517 Corps Field Survey Coy *(Cargwyle) (5+118)*, 100 Army Field Coy *(Monmouth) (6+235)*, 567 Army Troops Coy *(Ross on Wye) (7+303)*, 568 Army Troops Coy *(Haverfordwest) (7+319)*;

RASC: Corps Troops Ammunition Coy *(Welshpool) (7+258)*, Corps Troops Supply Coy *(Market Drayton) (18+461)*, 192 Coy *(Tamworth) (7+207)*, 913 Coy *(Liverpool) (17+387)*; 914 Coy *(Penarth) (6+190)*, 31 Motor Coach Coy *(Porthcawl) (8+166)*; 32 Motor Coach Coy *(Shugborough) (9+144)*, 37 Motor Coach Coy *(Buckwell) (8+169)*;

RS: 3 Corps Signals *(Salop) (26+565)*;

RAOC: 9 Army Field Workshop *(Rhyl) (8+235)*, 15 Army Field Workshop *(Manchester) (5+268)*;

RAMC: 159 Field Ambulance *(Penmaenmawr) (11+236)*, 55 Ambulance Train *(Hanwood) (2+19)*, 56 Ambulance Train *(Ruabon) (2+20)*, 59 Ambulance Train *(Burton on Trent) (2+18)*, 60 Ambulance Train *(Blackpool) (2+20)*, 66 Ambulance Train *(Aberdare) (2+20)*, 10 Casualty Clearing Station *(Denbigh) (7+87)*, 11 Casualty Clearing Station *(Porthmadoc) (9+88)*, 12 Casualty Clearing Station *(Llandeilo) (11+89)*, 13 CCS *(Bangor) (9+89)*.

1st Czech Infantry Brigade Group *(HQ: Cholmondley)* (GOC: Brigadier General J Cihak) *(670+2337)*

Three rifle battalions, 1field artillery bty *(4x75mm)* and a depot company.

NOTES:
- *By 12 August a Brigade Group was formed from the remains of the 1st Czech Infantry Division that had fought with the French*

- *Allocated local airfield defence role*
- *General Cihak had been the acting commander of the 1st Czech Division in France and became the Chief of Staff, Ministry of National Defence, before the end of 1940.*

10th Infantry Training Group *(HQ: Redditch, Worcestershire)*
7 Suffolk *(Leamington)* *(26+940)*, 8 Essex *(Redditch)* *(28+951)*, 9 Essex *(Kidderminster)* *(27+958)*, 9 Royal West Kent *(Malvern)* *(28+906)*.

NOTES:
- *The Group was to defend Birmingham: the battalion's respective areas were the River Avon, Kidderminster, River Severn and the Warwick - Oxford canal*
- *The Group was formed in mid July and reformed as 210th Infantry Brigade on 10 October and assigned to V Corps in a coast defence role in Dorset.*

12th Infantry Training Group *(HQ: Cwmbran)*
6 South Wales Borderers (Home) *(Crickhowell)* *(23+963)*, 10 Gloucester (Home) *(Caerlon)* *(24+910)*, 18 Welch (Home) *(Monmouth)* *(6+81)*.

NOTE: *The Group was formed in mid July and reformed as 212th Infantry Brigade on 7 October and assigned a coast defence role.*

13th Infantry Training Group *(HQ: Hereford)*
9 Berkshire *(28+951)*, 11 Worcester (Home) *(27+945)*, 13 Warwickshire (Home) *(29+931)*, 14 South Staffordshire *(28+909)*.

NOTE: *The Group was formed in mid July and reformed as 213th Infantry Brigade on 30 September and assigned a coast defence role with II Corps.*

14th Infantry Training Group *(HQ: Northwich, Cheshire)*
19 Royal Fusiliers *(27+986)*, 20 Royal Fusiliers *(29+939)*, 21 Royal Fusiliers *(31+924)*, 6 OBLI *(28+919)*.

NOTE: *The Group was formed on 4 July and reformed as 214th Independent Infantry Brigade on 11 October and moved to the South Midlands on 27 October.*

15th Infantry Training Group *(HQ: Caernarfon)*
7 Loyals *(Caernarfon)* *(28+949)*, 8 Loyals *(Caernarfon)* *(27+954)*, 9 Loyals *(Caernarfon)* *(26+919)*, 12 Royal Welsh Fusiliers *(Abergele)* *(26+962)*.

NOTE: *The Group was formed in mid July and reformed as 215th Independent Infantry Brigade on 10 October and moved to West Lancashire on 10 October. 7 Loyals moved to Liverpool on 28 September.*

Isle of Man *(142+2386)* (GOC: Brigadier C Ford from 12 August)
50 Kings *(Douglas)* *(21+901)*;
AMPC: 3 Group (52 and 101 Coys) *(Douglas)* *(18+492)*, 7 Coy *(Ramsey)* *(7+246)*, 9 Coy *(Peel)*

(7+291);
Plus 2x75mm guns loaned from 2nd London Division

NOTE: *Main role was to guard 11,000 internees. Home Guard on the Isle had 2,348 men in July, organised in three battalions, who also aided in the guard role.*

Western Command Troops:

- East Lancashire Sub Area *(HQ: Manchester)* (GOC: Brigadier J Fitzgerald from 30 August)
Manchester MGTC *(Ashton under Lyne) (94+1481)*;
50 Loyals *(Clitheroe) (21+890)*, 50 Lancashire Fusiliers *(Rochdale) (22+849)*, Lancashire
    Fusiliers ITC *(Bury) (38+1738)*;
RE: 112 Coy *(Manchester) (8+237)*;
RAOC: 7 Main Supply Depot *(Radcliffe) (2+30)*;
AMPC: 11 Centre *(Oldham) (60+1650)*, 105 Coy *(Bury) (7+236)*, 118 Coy *(Manchester) (4+276)*.

- West Lancashire Sub Area *(HQ: Chester)* (CO: Col A Macdougall from 19 August)
Cheshire MGTC *(Chester) (109+1596)*;
8 Argyll and Sutherland Highlanders *(Liverpool) (prepared for overseas move, but moved to Scotland
    in October)*, 50 Kings Own *(Morecombe) (19+876)*, 50 East Lancashire *(Blackburn)
    (21+851)*, 50 Border *(Workington) (22+826) (9 October reformed as 9 Border and joined
    225 Brigade)*, 50 South Lancashire *(Huyton) (21+745)*, 70 Kings *(Liverpool) (30+800)
    (formed 19 September from 10 Kings with 3 coys)*, Border ITC *(Carlisle) (50+1857)*, Kings ITC
    (Formby) (44+1610), Kings Own ITC *(Lancaster) (42+1687)*, Loyals ITC *(Preston)
    (44+1623)*, East Lancashire ITC *(Lytham St Annes) (36+1804)*, South Lancashire ITC
    (Warrington) (37+1732), 310 ITC *(Carlisle) (28+1745)*, 311 Royal Welsh Fusiliers ITC
    (Chester) (28+1523);
3 York and Lancaster IPTC *(Kirkham) (8+196)*;
RE: 1 Movement Control Group *(Chester) (42+195)*, 3 MT Group *(Crewe) (23+1063)*, 3 Docks
    Group *(1000 Maintenance, 1001-1004 Operating Coys) (Blackpool) (42+1632)*, 5 Training Bn
    (Chester) (33+1778), 171 Tunnelling Coy *(Halton) (6+201)*, 172 Tunnelling Coy *(Chester)
    (6+199)*, 190 Rail Operating Coy *(Nantwich) (6+435)*, 712 General Construction Coy
    (Tern Hill) (6+348);
RASC: 5 Coy *(Preston) (4+79)*, 6 Coy *(Preston) (4+164)*, I Coy *(Chester) (12+1764)*, 1 Bulk Petrol
    Store Coy *(Lavernock) (13+78)*, 13 Reserve Coy *(Chester) (11+475)*, 4 Motor Transport
    Stores Depot *(Preston) (10+136)*, 4 Base Petrol Filling Centre *(Carlisle) (7+261)*, 6 Main
    Supply Depot *(Carlisle) (6+55)*;
RAOC: 62 Training Section *(Burscough) (2+687)*, 67 Training Section *(Longtown) (26+364)*,
    6 Main Supply Depot *(Carlisle) (2+30)*;
RAMC: 20 General Hospital *(Ormskirk) (21+253)*, 19 Training Coy *(Chester) (243+387)*;
RS: 4 Command Signals *(Chester) (29+729)*;
CMP: 104 Provost Coy *(Nantwich) (98)*, Command Provost Coy *(Chester) (373)*;
AMPC: 5 Centre *(Huyton) (70+2370)*, 12 Centre *(Liverpool) (62+1709)*, 1 Coy *(Huyton) (6+266)*,
    2 Coy *(Carlisle) (5+257)*, 59 Coy *(Speke) (5+263)*, 109 Coy *(Ormskirk) (7+246)*, 112 Coy
    (Preston) (4+281), 115 Coy *(Overton) (5+275)*, 136 Coy *(Liverpool) (4+280)*, 175 Coy
    (Macclesfield) (4+280).

- North Wales Sub Area *(HQ: Shrewsbury)* (GOC: Brigadier A Gernier)
2/11 Royal Welch Fusiliers *(Llandudno) (forming 25 September)*, 50 Royal Inniskilling Fusiliers *(Newtown) (22+913)*, 50 Royal Ulster Regt *(Anglesey) (21+777)*, 50 Royal Welsh Fusiliers *(Denbigh) (22+854)*, 50 South Wales Borderers *(Aberystwyth) (21+837)*, 50 Welch *(Towyn) (19+822)*, 70 Royal Welch Fusiliers *(Rhyl) (23+361) (formed 19 September from 11 Bn)*, Kings Shropshire Light Infantry ITC *(Shrewsbury) (50+1877)*, 301 Warwickshire ITC *(Oswestry) (26+1884)*, Royal Welsh Fusiliers ITC *(Wrexham) (44+1559)*;
RA: 11 A/A Driver Training Regt *(Rhyl) (21+1178)*, 35 Signals Training Regt *(Rhyl) (23+804)*;
RE: 173 Tunnelling Coy *(Dolgellau) (5+202)*;
RASC: 22 Coy *(Newport) (3+94)*, 29 Coy *(Shrewsbury) (5+167)*, 11 Mobile Ambulance Coy *(Llandudno) (5+194)*;
RAMC: 17 Training Coy *(Shrewsbury) (68+389)*;
RS: 2 Holding Bn *(Llandudno) (25+1270)*, 2 Training Centre *(Prestatyn) (56+3455)*, 4 LofC Signals *(Rhos on Sea) (30+980)*;
AMPC: 11 Group *(Shrewsbury) (30+567)*, 1 Centre *(Pwllheli) (36+1592)* (disbanded 15 October), 3 Coy *(Pwllheli) (4+256)*, 178 Coy *(Wrexham) (4+282)*, 194 Coy *(Wrexham) (4+279)*.

- South Wales Sub Area *(HQ: Abergavenny)* (GOC: Brigadier A Mascall)
South Wales Borderers ITC *(Brecon) (40+1721)*, Welch ITC *(Cardiff) (32+1673)*;
RA: 2 Coast Defence Training Bty *(Milford Haven) (11+279)*, 1 OCT Regt *(Llandrindod Wells) (52+938)*;
RE: 151 Rail Construction Coy *(St Mellons) (6+252)*;
RASC: 1 and 2 Petrol Filling Coys *(Cardiff) (13+506)*, 1 Petrol Depot *(Cardiff) (5+138)*;
RAOC: 2 Supply Reserve Depot *(Barry) (107+486)*, 5 Training Bn *(Chepstow) (21+2001)*;
AMPC: 24 Coy *(Swansea) (8+242)*, 38 Coy *(Cardigan) (8+239)*, 53 Coy *(Chepstow) (6+341)*, 72 Coy *(Haverfordwest) (6+248)*, 74 Coy *(Llavaches) (5+279)*, 171 Coy *(Barry) (5+279)*.

- Central Midlands Sub Area *(HQ: Leamington)* (CO: Colonel J Blakiston-Houghton from 24 May)
50 Gloucester *(Ludlow) (23+805)*, 50 Worcester *(Burton on Trent) (29+717)*, 50 South Staffordshire *(Penkridge) (19+799)*, 50 Kings Shropshire Light Infantry *(Church Stretton) (21+769)*, 50 North Staffordshire *(Alton Towers) (21+812)*, North Staffordshire ITC *(Lichfield) (41+1558)*, South Staffordshire ITC *(Lichfield) (40+1518)*, Worcester ITC *(Worcester) (39+1755)*, Warwickshire ITC *(Warwick) (41+1747)*;
2 IPTC *(Birmingham) (20+248)*, Kings Own IPTC *(Great Barr) (26+1333)*;
RE: 9 EOD Coy *(Birmingham) (7+248)*, 162 Rail Construction Coy *(Trench) (6+271)*, 651 Artisan Works Coy *(Trench) (5+275)*, 652 Artisan Works Coy *(Weston on Trent) (6+266)*, 693 Artisan Works Coy *(Donnington) (5+297)*, 689 General Construction Coy *(Cowbridge) (5+262)*, Stores Depot *(Donnington) (9+96)*;
RASC: 13 Coy *(Lichfield) (3+87)*, 21 Coy *(Lichfield) (4+150)*, 14 Reserve Coy *(Evesham) (11+504)*, 15 Reserve Coy *(South Littleton) (11+492)*, Petrol Reserve Depot *(Stratford on Avon)*;
RAOC: 66 Training Section *(Branston) (6+162)*, 1 Armament Stores Section *(Donnington) (3+172)*, 6 Ordnance Field Park *(Birmingham) (8+102)*, 8 Main Supply Depot *(Hereford) (2+30)*, 21 Advanced Supply Depot *(Ledbury) (10+205)*, Command Supply Depot *(Stratford on Avon)*, Command Supply Depot *(Solihull)*;
RAMC: 22 General Hospital *(Glasbury on Wye) (18+239)*, 16 Training Coy *(Davyhulme)*

(61+267);
AMPC: 23 Group *(20, 77, 129, 149, 153, 162, 176, 177 Coys) (Donnington) (37+2154)*, 18 Coy *(Essington) (4+260)*, 22 Coy *(Coventry) (7+159)*, 41 Coy *(Kenilworth) (7+239)*, 57 Coy *(Wormelow) (7+263)*, 83 Coy *(Wolverhampton) (7+235)*, 88 Coy *(Berrington) (4+256)*, 100 Coy *(Coventry) (5+251)*, 103 Coy *(Stratford on Avon) (4+261)*, 116 Coy *(Atcham) (4+256)*, 135 Coy *(Hereford) (4+265)*, 161 Coy *(Craven Arms) (6+334)*.

SCOTTISH COMMAND (GOC: Lieutenant General R Carrington)
HQ: Edinburgh (Advance HQ: Currie)

NOTES:
- *The Command Stop Line ran from Dysart (on the Firth of Forth) to Newburgh; Perth to Dunkeld via Stanley, then to Loch Ranoch*
- *General Carrington had been the Deputy Adjutant General at the War Office before being appointed to this role in 1940. He retired in 1941.*

- 51st Infantry Division (Highland) (GOC: Major General A Cunningham)
HQ: Banff, Banffshire
152nd Brigade: *(HQ: Halkirk)* (GOC: Brigadier D Wimberley from 13 September)
1/5 Camerons *(Wick) (32+783)*, 2 Seaforth Highlanders *(Tain) (35+808)*, 4/5 Seaforth Highlanders *(Thurso) (35+869)*.
153rd Brigade: *(HQ: Aberdeen)* (GOC: Brigadier D Graham)
1 Gordon Highlanders *(Old Deer) (37+837)*, 1/5 Black Watch *(Aberdeen) (33+800)*, 10 Gordon *(Aberdeen) (40+887)*.
154th Brigade: *(HQ: Orton, Morayshire)* (GOC: Brigadier A Stanley-Clarke*)
7/10 Argyll and Sutherland Highlanders *(Gordonstoun and Forres) (33+796)*, 11 Argyll and Sutherland Highlanders (Home) *(Fochabers) (31+778)*.
15th Brigade: *(HQ: Turriff)* (GOC: Brigadier H Greenfield)
1 KOYLI *(34+868)*, 1 York and Lancaster *(35+876)*, 1 Green Howards *(33+870)*.
Divisional Troops:
RA: 126 Field Regt *(Craigellachie) (35+485) (297 Bty: 8x4.5-inch, 298 Bty: 12x75mm)*, 127 Field Regt *(Inverurie) (35+527) (301 and 304 Btys: 12x75mm, 8x4.5-inch)*, 128 Field Regt *(Tain) (33+458) (307 and 308 Btys: 12x75mm, 8x4.5-inch)*, 61 A/T Regt *(Rothes) (26+538) (241, 242 (Halkirk), 243 and 244 (Peterhead) Btys) (4x18-pdr with 241 Bty, rest as infantry or manned coastal guns)*;
RE: 274 Field Coy *(Craigellachie) (6+278)*, 275 Field Coy *(Alness) (5+271)*, 276 Field Coy *(Old Meldrum) (6+278)*, 277 Field Coy *(Aberdeen) (3+178)*, 239 Field Park Coy *(Grantown) (3+161)*;
RASC: Divisional Ammunition Coy *(Boat of Garten) (10+408)*, Divisional Petrol Coy *(Boat of Garten) (5+286)*, Divisional Supply Column *(Dulnain Bridge) (12+451)*;
RAMC: 174 Field Ambulance *(Old Meldrum) (10+182)*, 175 Field Ambulance (Lybster) *(12+183)*, 176 Field Ambulance *(Aberlour) (13+205)*;
RS: Divisional Signals Regt *(Rothes) (23+490)*;
CMP: Divisional Provost Coy *(Keith) (1+104)*.

NOTES:
- The Division was a Territorial Army formation that was detached from the BEF and fought with the French until largely destroyed south of the River Somme in June. Its remains returned to Scotland where it began reforming alongside the 9th Division
- The Division's role was to protect north eastern Scotland
- By 13 July 9th Division had 90% Personnel, 33% artillery pieces, 33% A/T guns
- On 27 July General Brooke reported that the Division was in a poor state of training and deficient of officers
- On 19 August 15th Brigade (5th Division) came under command at Huntly
- In August the Division was reformed from 9th Division
- General Cunningham had commanded 9th Division from 26 June, while Brigadier Graham had commanded 9th Division's 27th Brigade from April; 152nd Brigade had been led by Brigadier H Stewart until 7 August, then by Brigadier I Thomson until 13 September; only 154th Brigade retained its same commander. Brigadier Greenfield was appointed on 25 July. General Cunningham briefly commanded the Eighth Army in 1941 and ended the War commanding Eastern Command; Brigadier Wimberley rose to be Director of Infantry in 1944 and Brigadier Graham a divisional commander in 1943
- On 4 September 2 Seaforth Highlanders transferred from 154th Brigade to 152nd Brigade
- By 7 September it had 100% Personnel, 80% artillery pieces, 20% A/T guns.

- **5th Infantry Division** (GOC: Major General H Berney-Ficklen)
HQ: Auchterarder, Perthshire
13th Brigade: *(HQ: Crieff)* (GOC: Brigadier V Russell)
2 Camerons *(34+953)*, 2 Royal Inniskilling Fusiliers *(37+937)*, 2 Wiltshire *(31+869)*.
17th Brigade: *(HQ: Callander)* (GOC: Brigadier M Stopford*)
2 Royal Scots Fusiliers *(55+529)*, 2 Northampton *(Doune) (37+897)*, 1/6 Seaforth *(Doune) (34+805)*.
Divisional Troops:
RA: 9 Field Regt *(Dunblane) (36+556) (19/28 and 20/76 Btys: 6x25-pdr, 6x18/25-pdr)*, 91 Field Regt *(Crieff) (37+539) (361 and 363 Btys: 16x75mm)*, 92 Field Regt *(Huntly) (36+567) (365 and 368 Btys: 8x75mm, 6x25-pdr)*, 52 A/T Regt *(Invermay) (28+548) (205, 206, 207 and 208 Btys: 20x2-pdr)*;
1/7 Cheshire (MG) *(Braco) (34+791) (attached from Corps troops)*;
RE: 38 Field Coy *(Callander) (5+249)*, 245 Field Coy *(Auchterarder) (6+273)*, 252 Field Coy *(Crieff) (6+254)*, 254 Field Park Coy *(Auchterarder) (3+189)*;
RASC: Divisional Ammunition Coy *(Auchterarder) (8+396)*, Divisional Petrol Coy *(Bridge of Earn) (6+301)*, Divisional Supply Column *(Dunning) (15+455)*;
RAMC: 137 Field Ambulance *(Selkirk) (1+54)*, 141 Field Ambulance *(Callander) (11+228)*, 164 Field Ambulance *(Crieff) (12+240)*;
CMP: Divisional Provost Coy *(Auchterarder) (1+110)*.

NOTES:
- The Division was a Regular Army formation that had served with the BEF, while 15th Brigade also served in Norway
- By 13 July it had 100% Personnel, 33% artillery pieces, 33% A/T guns

- The Division's role was to provide the mobile reserve or defend the Command Line, as appropriate
- The GOC replaced General H Franklyn on 19 July. 13th Brigade had been commanded by Brigadier M Dempsey until 19 July, then Brigadier D Wimberley until 12 September. Brigadier Stopford had been in command since October 1939 and ended the War commanding Twelvth Army in Burma
- On 19 August the 15th Brigade came under 51st Division command and moved to Huntly
- By 7 September it had 100% Personnel, 80% artillery pieces, 40% A/T guns
- At the end of October the Division replaced 38th Division in Western Command.

- 46th Infantry Division (North Midland and West Riding) (GOC: Major General D Anderson)
HQ: Stirling
137th Brigade: *(HQ: Stirling)* (GOC: Brigadier T Daly)
2/5 West Yorkshire *(Denny) (32+910)*, 2/6 Duke of Wellington's Regt *(Clackmannan) (33+862)*, 2/7 Duke of Wellington's Regt *(Forfar) (36+897)*.
138th Brigade: *(HQ: Cupar)* (GOC: Brigadier G Bucknall)
1/6 Lincolns *(32+905)*, 2/4 KOYLI *(St Andrews) (35+888)*, 1/6 York and Lancaster *(Kirkton) (32+924)*,
139th Brigade: *(HQ: Haddington)* (GOC: Brigadier R Chichester-Constable*)
2/5 Leicester *(Gullane) (33+775)*, 2/5 Sherwood Foresters *(Haddington) (36+852)*, 9 Sherwood Foresters *(Dunbar) (32+820)*.
Divisional Troops:
RA: 70 Field Regt *(Haddington) (35+552)* *(A Bty: 4x75mm, 4x18/25-pdr, 2x18-pdr; B Bty: 8x75mm, 4x18/25-pdr)*, 71 Field Regt *(Arbroath) (35+572)* *(281 Bty: 8x75mm, 4x18-pdr; 282 Bty: 12x75mm)*, 151 Army Field Regt *(Leuchars) (28+569)* *(A&B Btys: 12x75mm, 6x4.5-inch, 2x18-pdr)*, 58 A/T Regt *(Bridge of Allan) (20+560)* *(229 (Stirling), 230 (Haddington), 231 (Stirling) and 232 (Ceres) Btys: 20x2-pdr)*;
2/7 Middlesex (MG) *(Stirling) (36+782)*;
RE: 270 Field Coy *(Newport) (6+246)*, 271 Field Coy *(Kelso) (6+254)*, 272 Field Coy (Kelso) *(5+241)*, 273 Field Park Coy *(Luncarty) (3+152)*;
RASC: Divisional Ammunition Coy *(Bridge of Allan) (10+387)*, Divisional Petrol Coy *(Ochtertyre) (7+294)*, Divisional Supply Column *(Thomanean) (13+449)*
RAMC: 183 Field Ambulance *(Gifford) (11+176)*, 184 Field Ambulance *(Freuchie) (11+184)*, 185 Field Ambulance *(Stirling) (12+190)*;
RS: Divisional Signals Regt *(Stirling) (22+542)*;
CMP: Divisional Provost Coy *(Stirling) (1+110)*.

NOTES:
- The Division was a Territorial Army formation that had served with the BEF
- The Division's role was to protect southeastern Scotland
- General Anderson was appointed on 5 July. Brigadier J Gawthorpe commanded 137th Brigade until 10 August and Brigadier E Grinling 138th Brigade until 8 August. 139th Brigade Commander was appointed on 22 May. General Anderson was promoted to command III Corps by the end of 1940
- By 13 July it had 100% Personnel, 20% artillery pieces, 45% A/T guns

- On 27 July Alan Brooke reported the Division was in a lamentably backward state of training, barely fit to do platoon training and deficient of officers
- By 7 September it had 100% Personnel, 66% artillery pieces, 45% A/T guns
- On 16 September 51 Field Regt was replaced by 151 Army Field Regt.

Corps Troops:
1/7 Northumberland Fusiliers (motorcycle) *(Duddington) (28+951);*
11 Commando *(Brechin) (34+488)*, 2 Independent Coy *(Mallaig) (300)*, 10 Independent Coy *(Corpach) (300);*
9 York and Lancaster (Pioneer) *(Montrose) (28+797)*, 10 South Staffordshire (Pioneer) *(Forfar) (29+792)*, 14 Durham Light Infantry (Pioneer) *(Duddington) (30+984);*
RA: 71 Medium Regt *(Kettleholm) (33+642) (A and B Btys at Lockerbie with 6x6-inch) (also manned 2 coast defence btys)*, 152 Army Field Regt *(Grangemouth) (27+576) (A and B Btys: 8x4.5-inch, 4x18-pdr)*, 155 Army Field Regt *(Lanark) (25+540) (A and B Btys: 8x75mm, 6x4.5-inch, 2x18-pdr)*, 156 Army Field Regt *(Beattock) (29+562) (A and B Btys: 8x75mm, 4x4.5-inch)*, 45 A/T Regt *(Invermay) (145) (forming);*
RE: 23 Field Coy *(Kircudbright) (7+237)*, 586 Army Field Coy *(Carlingnose) (6+150)*, 587 Army Field Coy *(Carlingnose) (6+93)*, 106 Army Troops Coy *(Newport) (8+301)*, 110 Army Troops Coy *(Falkland) (7+296)*, 585 Corps Field Park Coy *(Carlingnose) (4+115);*
RASC: 21 Motor Coach Coy *(Crieff) (9+143)*, 22 Motor Coach Coy *(Turriff) (10+167)*, 23 Motor Coach Coy *(Callander) (9+140)*, 24 Motor Coach Coy *(Tain) (10+135)*, 33 Motor Coach Coy *(Plean) (8+168);* 1 Pack Transport Coy *(Helmsdale) (6+314)*, 13 Station Transport Coy *(St Boswells) (3+84)*, 14 Station Transport Coy *(Leith) (3+155)*, 15 Station Transport Coy *(Stirling) (3+123)*, 31 Station Transport Coy *(Port of Monteith) (6+133)*, 6 Station Maintenance Coy *(Leith) (3+102);*
RAMC: 158 Field Ambulance *(Turriff) (12+235).*

Polish Forces (HQ: *Montrose*) (GOC: General M Kukiel)
- Armoured Group *(HQ: Forfar)* (GOC: Major General K Dworak)
    (1 Bn, 2 Bn, Training Bn)
- 10th Armoured Cavalry Brigade *(HQ: Forfar)* (GOC: Major General S Maczek)
    (24 Lancers, 10 Mounted Rifles) *(ex French tankettes)*
- 1st and 2nd Infantry Brigades (GOC 1st - Major General G Paszkiewicz; 2nd - Major General R Dreszer) *(500+8000 each)*
- 3rd, 4th and 5th Cadre Brigades and a Training Centre (3rd - Major General W Langner; 4th – Major General S Sosabowski; 5th - *not known*)
- One engineer Bn *(1200 men).*

NOTES:
- *In June the Polish units gathered at Haydock before moving to Crawford, Scotland*
- *2 Tank Bn landed at Liverpool on 30 June and moved to Crawford on 18 July*
- *On 5 August Polish forces came under official British command*
- *By 20 August 8x75mm field guns, 1x2pdr anti tank gun and 16 armoured carriers had been delivered*
- *On 2 September the Armoured Group and Cavalry Brigade moved to Forfar, with other units going to Blairgowrie*

- In August 1st and 2nd Brigades were formed, each with 8500 men in three battalions, three field and one AT batteries, 3rd, 4th and 5th Brigades were formed as cadre training formations in Moffat
- General Kukiel had been recalled from retirement and was briefly the Vice Minister of War for the Government in exile; in 1943 he became the Minister of War. General Dworak had been the Deputy Commander of the 10th Polish Armoured Brigade in France and ended the War as the Deputy Commander of the 1st Polish Armoured Division. General Maczek had commanded his brigade in France and rose to command 1st Polish Corps in 1945. General Paszkiewicz had been the Deputy General Officer Commanding Krakow Army in 1939 and rose to be Deputy Commander of I Polish Corps in 1943. General Dreszer had commanded the 4th Polish Division in France. General Langner had been a Corps Commander in 1939 and rose to be the Inspector of Military Training (Polish Forces) in 1943. General Sosabowski had commanded the 1st Polish Division in France and later famously commanded the Polish Parachute Brigade at Arnhem
- On 1 October I Polish Corps formed, HQ at Perth; the Corps Reconnaissance Unit (with two reconnaissance and one tank squadrons) and 1st Armoured Regt (two battalions) were also formed. Units at Crawford moved to Blairgowrie.

Norwegian Infantry Brigade *(HQ: Dumfries)* (GOC: General C Fleischer)
Three rifle companies, one MG company, a mixed arms company, one field artillery bty *(4x75mm)* and a depot company.

NOTES:
- In June Norwegian volunteers gathered at Dumfries
- The Brigade was allocated a local airfield defence role during this period
- In October force moved to Coatbridge for further training
- General Fleischer had commanded Norwegian forces in Northern Norway; he became Military Attache in Washington but died in 1942.

Orkney Garrison *(HQ: Stromness)* (GOC: Major General G Kemp) *(140+5057)*
5/9 Gordon Highlanders *(Kirkwall) (34+811)*, 7 Gordon Highlanders *(Kirkwall) (35+749)*, E Coy 13 Cameronians *(Kirkwall) (4+96)*, D Coy 12 Highland Light Infantry *(Kirkwall)*;
RE: Orkney Fortress Coy *(Stromness) (6+127)*, 119 Road Construction Coy *(Stromness) (4+98)*, 683 General Construction Coy *(Kirkwall) (5+258)*, 701 General Construction Coy *(Stromness) (6+266)*, 696 Artisan Works Coy *(Longhope) (6+261)*, 1010 Docks Operating Coy *(Stromness) (3+261)*;
RASC: K Coy *(Stromness) (1+183)*;
AMPC: 19 Group (68, 128 Coys) *(Kirkwall) (5+260)*, 141 and 144 Coys *(Stromness) (23+1071)*;
Plus: Auxilliary Bn RM *(Lyness and Skeabrae) (6+516)* *(labour duties)*.

Shetlands Garrison *(HQ: Lerwick)* (GOC: Brigadier C Stockwell from 29 May)
7 Black Watch *(Lerwick) (37+900)*, 7 Seaforth Highlanders *(Sumburgh) (35+831)*, Shetland Defence Bn; C Coy 8 Gordon Highlanders (MG) *(5+110)*;
RA: 32 Howitzer Bty RM *(Lerwick) (2+38)* *(2x3.7-inch howitzer)*;
RE: 116 Road Construction Coy *(Lerwick) (4+110)*, 675 Artisan Works Coy *(Kirbister) (6+258)*;
AMPC: 98 Coy *(Lerwick) (5+268)*.

Scottish Command Troops:
- North Highland Sub Area: *(HQ:Inverness)* (GOC: Brigadier F Chalmer from 1 July)
1 Black Watch *(Callander) (34+757) (support area troops in Western Highlands)*, 8 Gordon Highlanders (Home) (Dufftown) *(31+748)*, 8 Seaforth Highlanders (Home) *(Golspie) (32+639)*, 50 Gordon Highlanders *(Keith) (21+723)*, Royal Scots ITC *(Glencorse) (35+1965)*, Cameron Highlanders ITC *(Inverness) (44+1799)*, Seaforth Highlanders ITC *(Inverness) (46+1917)*;
RAC: L Armoured Train *(Kittybrewster) (47) (covered Inverness and Peterhead)*;
RE: 6 Training Bn *(Elgin) (44+1709)*, 674 Artisan Works Coy *(Inverary) (6+259)*, 656 General Construction Coy *(Wick) (5+243)*, 660 General Construction Coy *(Elgin) (6+255)*, 661 General Construction Coy *(Inverurie) (6+259)*, 668 General Construction Coy *(Dingwall) (5+254)*, 684 General Construction Coy *(Kinloss) (4+249)*, 692 General Construction Coy *(Wick) (4+253)*, 702 General Construction Coy *(Evantown) (6+255)*;
RIASC: 25 Animal Transport Coy *(Lairg)* (*This Indian unit was detached from Force K6 in Northern Command. Rejoined the Force in early October*);
RAOC: 10 Field Workshop *(Inverness) (4+243)*;
AMPC: HQ 22 Group *(Inverness) (4+14)*, HQ 30 Group *(Aberdeen) (4+14)*, 31 Coy *(Thurso) (7+305)*, 50 Coy *(Aberdeen) (5+302)*, 67 Coy *(Fraserburgh) (4+260)*, 73 Coy *(Peterhead) (5+236)*, 114 Coy *(Watten) (4+279)*, 146 Coy *(Thurso) (4+277)*, 147 Coy *(Tain) (5+271)*, 150 Coy *(Forres) (6+275)*, 200 Coy *(Forres) (5+274)*, 209 Coy *(Dingwall) (5+268)*, 217 Coy *(Stonehaven) (4+273)*;

- South Highland Sub Area: *(HQ: Perth)* (GOC: Brigadier W Grey-Wilson)
6th Infantry Training Group
16 Durham Light Infantry *(Dunfirmline) (28+951)*, 17 Durham Light Infantry *(Moreton Hall) (29+944)*.

8 Black Watch (Home) *(Ladybank) (43+1158)*, 9 Black Watch (Home) *(Dundee) (38+871)*, 12 Argyll and Sutherland Highlanders (Home) *(Stirling) (47+839)*, 50 Black Watch *(Broughty Ferry) (23+737)*, 50 Argyll and Sutherland Highlanders *(Alloa) (21+699)*, Black Watch ITC *(Perth) (40+1842)*, Argyll and Sutherland Highlanders ITC *(Stirling) (46+1833)*;
RAC: J Armoured Train *(Stirling) (47) (covered Stirling, Dundee and Edinburgh)*;
RE: 662 General Construction Coy *(Auchtermuchty) (6+30)*, 665 General Construction Coy *(Montrose) (5+265)*, 682 General Construction Coy *(Leuchars) (5+270)*;
RAOC: 58 Training Section *(Stirling) (2+464)*, 11 Field Workshop *(Stirling) (2+57)*, 21 Field Workshop *(Stirling) (5+211)*;
AMPC: HQ 7 Group *(Perth)*, 6 Coy *(Aberfoyle) (4+273)*, 14 Coy *(Dunfirmline) (5+276)*, 27 Coy *(Arbroath) (4+278)*, 131 Coy *(Dunkeld) (6+274)*, 155 Coy *(Newport) (4+266)*, 156 Coy *(Guardbridge) (5+265)*, 157 Coy *(Lindores) (4+278)*, 195 Coy *(Montrose) (5+279)*, 196 Coy *(Lunan Bay) (4+281)*.

- Edinburgh Sub Area: *(HQ: Edinburgh)* (GOC: Brigadier H Maitland-Makgill-Crichton)
10 Royal Scots (Home) *(Edinburgh) (63+1192)*, 50 Royal Scots *(Edinburgh) (22+789)*, 165 ITC *(Dunbar) (28+596)*, KOSB ITC *(Berwick) (42+2100)*;
3 Cavalry (Horse) Training Regt *(Edinburgh) (34+1252)*;

RA: 6 Field Train Regt *(Longniddry) (24+1269)*, 38 Signals Training Regt *(Edinburgh) (18+742)*;
RAC: K Armoured Train *(Longniddry) (47) (covered Longniddry to Berwick)*;
RE: 4 Movement Control Group *(Edinburgh) (40+188)*, 667 Artisan Works Coy *(Kelso) (5+228)*, 695 General Construction Coy *(Turnhouse) (5+247)*;
RASC: J Coy *(Leith) (7+1126)*, 3 MA Centre *(Falkirk) (6+193)*;
RS: 5 Command Signals *(Edinburgh) (30+733)*;
RAMC: 33 General Hospital *(Peebles) (22+247)*, 13 Training Coy *(Edinburgh) (330+1115)*, 2 Depot *(Dalkeith) (16+1477)*;
CMP: Command Provost Coy *(Edinburgh) (110)*;
AMPC: HQ 4 Group *(Edinburgh)*, 8 Coy *(West Linton) (7+240)*, 62 Coy *(Edinburgh) (6+222)*, 152 Coy *(Kelso) (6+275)*.

- Glasgow Sub Area: *(HQ: Glasgow)* (GOC: Brigadier F Witts from 19 June)

7th Infantry Training Group
7 KOYLI *(Glasgow) (29+956)*, 9 Duke of Wellington`s Regt *(Glasgow) (29+918)*, 10 York and Lancaster *(Paisley) (28+916)*, 13 Sherwood Foresters *(Renfrew) (28+915)*.

8th Infantry Training Group:
9 Lancashire Fusiliers *(Coatbridge) (30+929)*, 10 Lancashire Fusiliers *(Coatbridge) (29+922)*, 13 Kings *(Glasgow) (25+936)*, 22 Royal Fusiliers *(Kirkintilloch) (29+933)*.

8 KOSB (Home) *(Stranraer) (13+240)*, 10 Royal Scots Fusiliers (Home) *(Ayr) (31+569)*, 1/11 Cameronians (Home) *(Glasgow) (22+516)*, 2/11 Cameronians (Home) *(Stevenston) (20+466)*, 13 Cameronians (Home) *(Bogside) (22+516) (formed 25 September from 2/11 Bn with 5 coys)*, 13 Argyll and Sutherland Highlanders (Home) *(Dalmuir) (37+686)*, 14 Argyll and Sutherland Highlanders (Home) *(Paisley) (39+571)*, 50 Cameronians *(Lanark) (22+1003)*, 50 Highland Light Infantry *(Dumbarton) (22+913)*, 70 Argyll and Sutherland Highlanders *(Clydebank) (26+693)*, 306 ITC *(Troon) (26+1642)*, Cameronians ITC *(Hamilton) (39+2003)*, Highland Light Infantry ITC *(Glasgow) (33+1712)*, Royal Scots Fusiliers ITC *(Ayr) (49+1812)*;
RE: 658 General Construction Coy *(Stranraer) (5+254)*, 2 Bore Section *(Garelochhead) (2+79)*;
RASC: 1 Vehicle Reserve Depot *(Glasgow) (12+494)*;
RAOC: 5 Main Supply Depot *(Kilmarnock) (2+30)*;
RAMC: 3 General Hospital *(Glasgow) (11+217)*, 57 Ambulance Train *(Glasgow) (2+20)*;
AMPC: 2 Centre *(Glasgow) (18+892) (disbanded 1 October)*, 71 Coy *(Kilmarnock) (6+295)*, 120 Coy *(Thornliebank) (4+276)*, 148 Coy *(Castletown) (4+262)*, 168 Coy *(Buddon Camp) (5+281)*, 181 Coy *(Stranraer) (5+284)*, 182 Coy *(Stranraer) (4+279)*.

NOTES:
- *6th Infantry Group was formed in mid July and reformed as 206th Independent Infantry Brigade on 12 October, with 14 Durham Light Infantry and 7 Northumberland Fusiliers*
- *7th Infantry Group was formed in mid July and reformed as 207th Independent Infantry Brigade on 10 October*
- *8th Infantry Group was formed in mid July and reformed as 208th Independent Infantry Brigade on 6 October. It was attached to 55th Division between 16 October and 6 November, after when it came under 42nd Division.*

NORTHERN IRELAND DISTRICT
(GOC: Major General R Packenham-Walsh from 14 July)
HQ: Belfast

VI CORPS (GOC: Lieutenant General Sir H Pownall)
HQ: Belfast

NOTES:
- *Inter Divisional boundaries ran from Cookstown to Lisnakea via Fintona*
- *General Packenham-Walsh had been the BEF`s Engineer in Chief*
- *General Pownall had been the BEF`s Chief of General Staff and took over at the start of October. He rose through staff appointments to be Chief of Staff to the Supreme Allied Commander in South East Asia.*

- 53rd Infantry Division (Welsh) (GOC: Major General B Wilson)
HQ: Belfast
158th Infantry Brigade: *(HQ: Crossgar)* (GOC: Brigadier J Duke)
1/4 Royal Welch Fusiliers *(Downpatrick) (40+898)*, 1/6 Royal Welch Fusiliers *(Ballynahinch) (37+888)*, 1/7 Royal Welch Fusiliers *(Newtonards) (39+903)*.
159th Infantry Brigade: *(HQ: Derry)* (GOC: Brigadier J Bruxner-Randall)
3 Monmouth *(Derry) (31+893)*, 1 Hereford *(Portrush) (33+874)*, 1/4 Kings Shropshire Light Infantry *(Coleraine) (34+881)*.
160th Infantry Brigade: *(HQ: Armagh)* (GOC: Brigadier R Rose)
2 Monmouth *(Armagh) (29+893)*, 1/4 Welch *(Banbridge) (34+901)*, 1/5 Welch *(Newry) (35+890)*.
Divisional Troops:
16 Royal Fusiliers (Pioneer) *(Cookstown, Dungannon) (21+841)*;
1/5 Cheshire (MG) *(Warrenpoint) (31+778)*;
RA: 81 Field Regt (Balleymoney) *(35+581) (323 and 324 Btys: 8x18-pdr, 4x4.5-inch)*; 83 Field Regt *(Bangor) (34+571) (329 Bty: 4x18-pdr, 330 Bty: 4x4.5-inch)*, 133 Field Regt *(Portadown) (34+584) (331 and 332 Btys: 10x18-pdr, 6x4.5-inch)*; 63 A/T Regt *(Lisburn) (31+529) (249, 250, 251 and 252 Btys: 24x2-pdr, 12x75mm)*;
RE: 244 Field Coy *(Limavady) (7+233)*, 282 Field Coy *(Banbridge) (7+231)*, 555 Field Coy *(Lurgan) (8+244)*, 285 Field Park Coy *(Hillsborough) (4+152)*;
RAMC: 202 Field Ambulance *(Dromore) (10+234)*, 212 Field Ambulance *(Benburb) (10+239)*, 213 Field Ambulance *(Culleybackey) (10+182)*;
RASC: Divisional Ammunition Coy *(Lenaderg) (8+345)*, Divisional Supply Column *(Lurgan) (3+428)*, Divisional Petrol Coy *(Tenderog) (6+324)*;
CMP: Divisional Provost Coy *(Belfast) (112)*;
RAOC: Divisional LAD`s *(Belfast) (9+206)*;
RS: Divisional Signals Regt *(Belfast) (26+489)*.

NOTES:
- *This Division was a Territorial Army formation that had been assigned to home defence at the start of the War and moved to Northern Ireland in April, responsible for Counties Down and Armagh)*

- General Wilson and the commanders of 158th and 159th Brigades had been in post since the outbreak of War. Brigadier Rose was appointed on 10 May. General Wilson retired in 1941
- By 13 July it had 100% Personnel, 50% artillery pieces, 33% A/T guns
- By 7 September it had 100% Personnel, 50% artillery pieces, 50% A/T guns.

- 61st Infantry Division (GOC: Major General A Carton de Wiart VC)
HQ: Ballymena
182nd Infantry Brigade: *(HQ: Londonderry)* (GOC: Brigadier E Williams)
2/7 Warwickshire *(35+876)*, 9 Warwickshire *(34+889)*, 9 Worcester *(Strabane) (36+828)*.
183rd Infantry Brigade: *(HQ: Belfast)* (GOC: Brigadier G Watson)
1/7 Gloucester *(38+869)*, 10 Worcester *(38+850)*, 4 Northampton *(34+921)*.
184th Infantry Brigade: *(HQ: Antrim)* (GOC: Brigadier C Fullbrook-Leggatt)
1/5 OBLI *(Coleraine) (37+865)*, 6 Berkshire *(Larne) (34+921)*, 2 Buckingham *(Carrickfergus and Ballymena) (39+801)*.
Divisional Troops:
RA: 119 Field Regt *(Londonderry) (36+560) (267 Bty: 8x75mm, 268 Bty: 8x4.5-inch)*, 120 Field Regt *(Balleymoney) (37+565) (270 and 271 Btys: 12x75mm, 2x4.5-inch)*, 145 Field Regt *(Antrim) (36+604) (395 and 396 Btys: 12x75mm, 2x4.5-inch)*;
RE: 266 Field Coy *(Limavady) (5+231)*, 267 Field Coy *(Coleraine) (6+239)*, 268 Field Coy *(Coleraine) (6+236)*, 269 Field Park Coy *(Coleraine) (3+157)*;
RAMC: 171 Field Ambulance *(Londonderry) (12+239)*, 172 Field Ambulance *(Coleraine) (9+180)*, 179 Field Ambulance *(Rostrevor) (11+225)*;
RASC: Divisional Ammunition Coy *(Kilrea) (10+413)*, Divisional Supply Column *(Clandeboys) (15+248)*, Divisional Petrol Coy *(Clandeboys) (7+180)*;
CMP: Divisional Provost Coy *(Ballymena) (107)*;
RAOC: Divisional LAD`s *(Ballymena) (206)*;
RS: Divisional Signals Regt *(Ballymena) (27+494)*.

NOTES:
- This Division was a training formation that had moved to Northern Ireland in June, after providing the headquarters of Mauriceforce in the Norwegian Campaign. It was responsible for Counties Antrim, Londonderry and Tyrone
- The GOC was appointed in November 1939 and Brigadier Williams in February, while Brigadier Fullbrook-Leggatt had held his post since the outbreak of war; Brigadier Watson had taken command on 16 July
- By 13 July it had 95% Personnel, 33% artillery pieces, 0% A/T guns
- The Division`s primary role was training, though it was available to support the 53rd Division in operations
- By 7 September it had 95% Personnel, 60% artillery pieces, 0% A/T guns.

Corps Troops
North Irish Horse *(Enniskillen) (30+457) (7 armoured cars and ad hoc light armoured vehicles)*, 2 Fife and Forfar Yeomanry *(Dungannon) (34+456) (7 Mk VI light tanks and bren gun carriers)*;

2 South Wales Borderers *(Omagh) (32+885)*, 1/5 Leicester *(Caledon) (36+860)*, 1/8 Sherwood Foresters *(Enniskillen) (36+839)*, 5 Royal Irish Fusiliers *(Ballykinler) (11+399)*, 5 Royal Inniskilling Fusiliers *(Belfast) (23+562)*, 6 Royal Ulster Regt *(Belfast) (30+844)*, 7 Royal Ulster Regt *(Belfast) (27+678)*;
12 Commando *(Crumlin) (21+244)*;
RA: Army Observation Bty *(Aldergrove) (2+114)*;
RE: Antrim Fortress Coy *(Carrickfergus) (6+63)*, 218 Army Troops Coy *(Randalstown) (6+286)*, 515 Corps Field Survey Coy *(Bangor) (6+135)*, 704 General Construction Coy *(Limavady) (6+268)*, 676 General Construction Coy *(6+278)* and 705 General Construction Coy *(Newtonards) (6+236)*, 10 Troop Carry Coy *(Aghadowey) (9+338)*, 120 Road Construction Coy *(Limnavady) (4+102)*, 122 Road Construction Coy *(Limnavady) (4+106)*, 806 Road Construction Coy *(Limnavady) (3+89)*, 807 Road Construction Coy *(Limnavady) (4+105)*, 6 Movement Control Group *(Magherafelt) (47+195)*;
RASC: 1 Motor Coach Coy *(Ballywillwill) (9+172)*, 2 Motor Coach Coy *(Saintfield) (9+163)*, 3 Motor Coach Coy *(Market Hill) (9+165)*, Corps Troops Ammunition Park *(Bangor) (27+1294)*, Corps Troops Petrol Park *(Bangor) (17+585)*, Corps Troops Supply Column *(Lisburn) (17+534)*, 7 Mobile Ambulance Coy *(Holywood) (8+228)*;
RAMC: 20 General Hospital *(Carrickfergus) (16+141)*, 24 General Hospital *(Belfast) (30+236)*, 25 General Hospital *(Bangor) (21+149)*, 31 General Hospital *(Belfast) (19+150)*, 16 Casualty Clearing Station *(Belfast) (10+88)*, 19 CCS *(Holywood) (9+90)*, 147 Field Ambulance *(Irvinestown) (11+240)*, 206 Field Ambulance *(Lisburn) (10+238)*, 14 and 15 Ambulance Trains *(Whitehead) (3+47)*, 15 Training Coy *(Holywood) (80+471)*;
RAOC: 3 Army Field Workshop *(Lisburn) (11+420)*, 5 Army Field Workshop *(Comber) (13+468)*;
CMP: 109 Provost Coy *(Lisburn) (108)*;
RS: Corps Signals Regt *(Lisburn) (24+521)*.

District Troops:
70 Royal Ulster Regt *(Belfast) (24+302)*, 70 Royal Inniskilling Fusiliers *(Belfast) (24+199)*, 307 ITC (Durham Light Infantry) *(Holywood) (28+1592)*, 407 Infantry Holding Bn *(Holywood) (20+741) (2 coys; 9 October reformed as 6 Royal Inniskilling Fusiliers)*, Royal Irish Fusiliers ITC *(Ballykinler) (40+1829)*, Royal Ulster Regt ITC *(Ballymena) (37+1663)*, Royal Inniskilling Fusiliers ITC *(Omagh) (31+1980)*;
RE: 8 Rail Construction and Operating Coy *(Belfast) (6+269)*, 109 W and P Coy *(Ballyclare) (10+274)*, 136 Airplane Maintenance Section *(Limnavady) (4+180)*;
RASC: 23 Coy *(Belfast) (4+146)*, 32 Coy *(Antrim) (5+120)*, 10 Reserve Motor Transport Coy *(Hillsborough) (11+496)*, 2 Advance Motor Transport Depot *(Belfast) (12+232)*, 3 Base Petrol Centre *(Carrickfergus) (8+259)*, 3 Heavy Repair Workshop *(Belfast) (7+189)*;
RAOC: 5 Ordnance Field Park *(Belfast) (14+143)*, 66 Training Section *(Kinnegar) (207)*, Command Reserve Depot *(Larne) (1+15)*;
AMPC: HQ 29 *Group (Belfast) (4+12)*, 108 Coy *(Newtonards) (3+287)*, 173 Coy *(Lisburn) (4+273)*, 174 Coy *(Belfast) (4+267)*, 183 Coy *(Carrickfergus) (4+276)*;
RS: Northern Ireland District Signals Coy *(Belfast) (8+102)*, 1 Air Formation Signals *(Belfast) (18+239)*, 6 Command Signals *(Belfast) (13+315)*.

Appendix 2

HOME GUARD

- *Local Defence Volunteers were renamed the Home Guard on 23 July. The battalions were initially grouped into county zones and split into groups; later regional districts were organised. Battalions varied widely in strength and equipment. Zone headquarters were purely administrative, while the Group headquarters was responsible for training and liaison*
- *Strengths: 13 July - 1,166,212; 1 August - 1,472,505; 30 September - 1,682,303*
- *In March 1942 the breakdown by Command was as follows: Eastern - 129,864; Northern - 254,936; Scottish - 144,678; South Eastern - 82,113; Southern - 178,620; Western - 432,460 (Wales - 121,532); London - 185,880*
- *The battalion strengths recorded below are that recorded in March 1942, the first time centralised records were kept, while the formations are those existing at or after November 1941. A large number of these battalions had been formed after 1940 from existing units*
- *Army ranks were not used until May 1941. To identify commanders the following was widely observed: zone commander had four stripes, battalion commanders had three stripes, company commanders had two stripes and section commanders had three chevrons*
- *40% were veterans of the First World War and earlier. The average age was 35*
- *Its main role was to observe and delay enemy movements and guide Army units. Secondary role was defence of GHQ Line and nodal points, conduct anti parachute operations and, if necessary, organise guerrilla operations*
- *By mid July 82,878 rifles and 56,000 guns had been issued; by 1 August this had risen to 483,924 rifles and 63,440 guns, though with an average of only 10 rounds per weapon. By the end of September 847,000 rifles, 46,629 guns and 48,750 sub machine guns (smg) had been issued, with 50 rounds per rifle and 750 rounds per smg*
- *In August battalions were affiliated to their local county infantry regiments*
- *In November the battalions were numbered.*

South East

- Aldershot District (including Bordon and Woking)
- East Kent District (including Maidstone, Sittingbourne, Tonbridge and Tunbridge Wells. HQ was at Harrietsham)
- North Kent and Surrey District (including Chatham, Gravesend, Sevenoaks and Dorking to Guildford. HQ was in Oxted)
- Sussex District (HQ in Haywards Heath) (formed in September 1941 by merging the East and West Sussex Zones)

Initially the Kent Zone was administered from Maidstone and the East Sussex Zone from Lewes. In Kent HQ 1 Group was at Ashford and covered East Kent, HQ 5 Group was at Sevenoaks and covered South Kent. In East Sussex HQ South East Group was at Seddlescombe and covered from Bexhill eastwards, while HQ North Group was at Crowborough

- Kent

(21, 22, 24 Bns manned the GHQ Line)

1st Bn *(Ashford)* *(5 coys: A Coy - Ashford, B Coy - Aldington and Sellindge, C Coy - Dymchurch (10 Plt), Lydd and New Romney (11 Plt); D Coy - Ashford; also at Wye) (890)*

2nd Bn *(Hothfield)* *(7 coys: B Coy - Pluckley, Smarden, C Coy - Bethersden, High Halden, Biddenden, Woodchurch, Shadoxhurst, D Coy - Tenterden, Rolvenden, Wittersham, Appledore, E Coy - Great Chart, Kingsnorth; others covered Charing and Hothfield) (888)*

3rd Bn *(Canterbury)* *(4 coys) (543)*

4th Bn (St Augustine) *(HQ: Canterbury)* *(5 coys: A Coy - Herne Bay, B Coy - Whitstable)*

5th Bn *(Wingham)* *(5 coys covering Sandwich and the East Kent collieries. Coy - Alkham, D Coy – Sandwich) (By 1 Aug it had 767 rifles) (1541)*

6th Bn (Thanet) *(HQ: Margate)* *(5 coys: A Coy - Margate, Westgate, B Coy - Birchington, C Coy – Broadstairs, D Coy - Ramsgate, E Coy – Minster, Sarre, Monkton) (2,000)*

7th Bn *(Lyminge)* *(HQ: Bridge)* *(5 coys covering Lyminge, Stelling Minnis, Elham, Barham, Swingfield) (485)*

8th (Cinque Ports) Bn *(HQ: Folkestone)* *(7 coys: A Coy – Hythe, Saltwood and Lympne, B Coy – Folkestone Gas, Cheriton, Capel and Sandgate, D Coy - Hawkinge, E Coy - Deal; others covered Dover and St Margaret`s Bay) (1268)*

9th Bn *(Faversham)* *(10 coys covering Boughton, Doddington) (1010)*

10th Bn *(Sittingbourne)* *(8 coys including Teynham) (1929)*

11th Bn *(Maidstone)* *(9 coys) (1233)*

12th Bn *(Chatham, Gillingham)* *(HQ: Dock Road, Chatham; 7 coys covering the eastern part of the MedwayTowns: C and D Coys - Gillingham, E Coy - Rainham, L and M Coys - Chatham) (2066)*

13th Bn *(Rochester)* *(HQ: Castle Hill, Rochester; 7 coys covered Strood and the southern part of the Medway Towns. A and D Coys - Rochester, B Coy - Blue Bell Hill, C Coy - Burham, Snodland, E Coy - Frindsbury, F Coy - Strood) (1321)*

14th Bn *(Hoo, Higham)* *(3 coys) (605)*

15th Bn *(Cobham)* *(3 coys) (460)*

16th Bn *(Gravesend)* *(5 coys) (775)*

17th Bn *(Northfleet)* *(6 coys) (1186)*

18th Bn *(Dartford)* *(7 coys) (942)*

19th Bn *(Farningham)* *(4 coys: A Coy - Longfield, B Coy - Farningham, C Coy - Swanley, D Coy – Darenth) (8 Aug 1940: 708 strong)*

20th Bn *(Sevenoaks)* *(HQ at Knole Park; (9 coys: A Coy - Sevenoaks; B Coy - Kemsing, Seal; C Coy – Sundridge, Brasted; D Coy - Edenbridge; E Coy - Chelsfield; F Coy - Biggin Hill, Knockholt; G Coy - Riverhead, Dunton Green; H Coy - Westerham; K Coy - Penshurst, Hildenborough) (2015)*

21st Bn *(Tonbridge)* *(7 coys: B Coy - Speldhurst, D Coy - Southborough, Coy - Pembury; Coy - Langton, Groombridge, Ashurst, E Coy - Penshurst) (855)*

22nd Bn *(Tunbridge Wells)* *(3 Coys: A Coy - St John`s, B/C Coy - Crescent Road, D Coy - Pantiles) (882)*

23rd (Weald) Bn *(Goudhurst)* *(10 coys: D Coy: Lamberhurst, Coy - Hawkhurst, Coy - Cranbrook) (1164)*

24th Bn *(Malling)* *(9 coys) (HQ at Ightham) (1491)*

25th (GPO) Bn *(HQ at Tunbridge Wells; 4 coys: A Coy - Tunbridge Wells, B Coy - Canterbury, Ashford, Herne Bay, Whitstable, Margate, Ramsgate, Dover and Folkestone, C Coy - Maidstone, Rochester, D Coy - Hastings) (1396)*

26th Bn *(Orpington) (1 Southern Railways)* *(10 coys: C Coy - Ashford Works, D Coy - Ashford, Wye, Chilham, Chartham, Charing, G Coy - Sandwich to Ashford and Canterbury to Lyminge lines, H Coy - Canterbury to Sandwich line (1 Plt: Birchington to Whitstable, 2 Plt: Margate, 3 Plt: Ramsgate, 4 Plt: Selling and Canterbury; Bn includes Hastings) (2921)*

29th (Mid Kent) Bn *(HQ: Hollingbourne; 6 coys) (860)*

30th (Sheppey) Bn *(HQ: Sheerness; 9 coys)*
31st (Dockyard) Bn *(HQ: Chatham; 8 coys) (was original 14th Bn until December 1940; reformed as 31st Bn in July 1942)*
32nd Bn *(Edenbridge) (5 coys) (Formed November 1942 from the Tonbridge Bn)*
33rd (Short Brothers) Bn *(Rochester) (8 coys: HQ, A, B and C Coys - Fort Clarence, D Coy - Fort Horsted, E Coy – Fort Bridgewood, F Coy - Strood works)*

51st Bn *(Bromley) (7 coys) (1417)*
52nd Bn *(Farnborough) (4 coys) (628)*
53rd Bn *(Orpington) (5 coys) (782)*
54th Bn *(Chislehurst) (5 coys) (706)*
55th Bn *(Beckenham) (7 coys) (1099)*
56th Bn *(Erith) (6 coys) (1207)*
57th Bn *(Sidcup) (6 coys) (1598)*
1st Bn *(Kent Bus Company) (733)*
Kent Electrical Power Company *(Rochester) (433) (Formed 27th Bn with 4 coys in 1941)*

- Sussex
(In September 1940 there were 14,000 men in West Sussex, 60% of whom were armed)
1st Bn *(Chichester) (4 coys) (1123)*
2nd Bn *(Petworth) (4 coys) (704)*
3rd Bn *(Horsham) (6 coys: E Coy - Rudgwick) (1661)*
4th Bn *(Billingshurst) (6 coys: D Coy - Henfield) (1104)*
5th Bn *(Worthing) (7 coys: B Coy - Goring by Sea, C Coy - Worthing, Coy - Findon) (1319)*
6th Bn *(Arundel) (5 coys) (1025)*
7th Bn *(Midhurst) (6 coys: E Coy - Fernhurst) (731)*
8th Bn *(Bognor Regis) (6 coys; HQ: Chichester) (856) (formed November 1941)*
9th Bn *(Shoreham) (4 coys) (700) (formed February 1943)*
10th Bn *(Brighton East) (6 coys: A Coy - Rottingdean) (formed from the Brighton Bn (4 coys) in February 1943)*
11th Bn *(Brighton) (39th GPO) (6 Coys: A Coy - Brighton, B Coy - Guildford, C Coy - Eastbourne, D Coy – Horsham, E Coy - Worthing, G Coy - Aldershot) (896)*
12th Bn *(Brighton) (Southdown Bus) (5 Coys: 301 Coy - Bognor Regis, Midhurst, Petworth, Chichester, Selsey, Wittering, 302 Coy Worthing, Littlehampton, 303 Coy - Eastbourne, Alfriston, East Grinstead, Heathfield, Uckfield, Seaford; others covered Brighton, Hilsea (Hampshire)) (1113)*
13th Bn *(Haywards Heath) (HQ: Cuckfield; 5 coys: C Coy - Hassocks, Hurstpierpoint, D Coy – Burgess Hill) (1742)*
14th Bn *(Hove) (HQ: Cricket Ground; 7 coys: A Coy - Cricket Ground, B & C Coys - Old Shoreham Road, D Coy – The Drive, Hove, E & F Coys - Portslade, G Coy - Greyhound Stadium) (1177)*
15th Bn *(Brighton West) (5 coys) (1702) (formed from the Brighton Bn (4 coys) in February 1943)*
16th Bn *(Lewes) (6 coys, including Newhaven; B Coy - Seaford, D Coy - Ditchling; 16 Plt: Barcombe Mills) (1322)*
17th Bn *(East Grinstead) (5 coys: C Coy: Withyam, E Coy - Hartfield) (1166)*
18th Bn *(Crowborough) (3 coys: A Coy - Wadhurst, Mayfield, Frant, B Coy - Crowborough, Rotherfield, Groombridge, C Coy - Heathfield, Framfield, East Hoathly) (1200)*
19th Bn *(Rother) (HQ: Battle; 6 coys: F Coy - Battle) (583) (By January 1941 this and the 22nd Bn were the same formation)*
20th Bn *(Hailsham) (HQ: Hailsham; A Coy - Alfriston, Wilmington, Berwick; B Coy - Polegate, Willingdon, Pevensey; C Coy - Wartling, Windmill Hill, Warbleton; D Coy - Heathfield, Chiddingly, Laughton; E Coy - Hellingly, Upper Dicker, Arlington) (1062)*

21st Bn *(Eastbourne)* *(6 coys: A Coy - North, B Coy - South (promenade and town centre), C Coy - East (Langney), D Coy - West) (Beachy Head) (652)*

22nd Bn *(Brede)* *(HQ: Seddlescombe; 5 coys: Q Coy - Rye and Winchelsea (205), R Coy - Peasmarsh, Beckley, Udimore, Iden and Playden (311), S Coy – Battle and Crowhurst (14 Plt) (213), T Coy – Seddlescombe, Brede, Staple Cross and Ewhurst (373), U Coy - Ninfield, Catsfield (15 Plt) and Hooe (17 Plt), Penhurst/Ashburnham (18 Plt) (191)) (1034) (formed from 19 Bn by January 1941, when it was known as the Battle Bn)*

23rd Bn *(Hastings)* *(HQ: Priory Avenue; 7 coys: A Coy - Pett, Fairlight, Icklesham (192), B Coy - Baldslow (138), C Coy - Filsham Rd, St Leonards (242), D Coy - Holmsdale Gardens, Hastings (123), E Coy - Station Road, Hastings (107) (1227)*

24th Bn *(Uckfield)* *(5 coys: D Coy - Uckfield, Isfield, Buxted) (formed June 1943 from 18th Bn) (was previously the Bexhill Bn, amalgamated on 1 March 1941 with the Hastings Bn. Bexhill Bn organised as follows: HQ: Drill Hall (58); A Coy - Little Common (60), B Coy - Albany Rd, Central Bexhill (47), C Coy - Cantelupe Rd, East Bexhill (48), D Coy - Dorset Rd, East Bexhill (52), E Coy – Dalmeny Rd, West Bexhill (53), F Coy - Cooden (50) (368 in January 1941)*

25th Bn *(Redhill)* *(2nd Southern Railways) (9 Coys: A and D Coys - Redhill, Purley, Sutton, Coulsdon (A Coy was the Brighton Line), B Coy - Deepdene (Southern Railway Head office), C (HQ) Coy - East Croydon, E Coy - Horsham, F Coy - Worthing, G Coy - Brighton, H Coy - Hassocks, J Coy - Lewes, K Coy - Eastbourne, Hailsham, East Grinstead) (2906)*

26th Bn *(Worth Forest)* *(HQ-Selsfield; 4 coys: A Coy - Selsfield, Turners Hill, Rowfant; B Coy - Crawley, Ifield; C Coy - Handcross, Balcombe; D Coy - Rusper, Lower Beeding, Colgate) (Formed January 1943)*

- Surrey

1st Bn *(Camberley) (5 coys) (2254)*
2nd Bn *(Farnham) (6 coys) (2140)*
3rd Bn *(Weybridge) (6 coys) (1730)*
4th Bn *(Guildford) (4 coys: A - Tilehurst, Stoughton; B - Burpham, Merrow; C - Pewley Downs; D - Ridgemount) (1394)*
5th Bn *(Bramley) (7 coys) (1611)*
6th Bn *(Leatherhead) (8 coys) (1737)*
7th Bn *(Dorking) (7 coys) (1721)*
8th Bn *(Reigate) (6 Coys: A, B and C - Reigate, D - Redhill, E - Merstham, F - Kingswood) (931)*
9th Bn *(Oxted) (7 coys) (1077)*
10th Bn *(Chertsey) (8 coys) (1502)*
11th Bn *(Woking) (6 coys)*
12th Bn *(Woking) (3 Southern Railways) (7 coys) (1634)*
13th Bn *(Haslemere) (6 coys, including the Admiralty Signals Establishment)*

- County of Surrey

(2, 4, 6, 7, 8 and 9 Bns manned the GHQ Line)

31st Bn *(Streatham) (5 coys)*
32nd Bn *(Purley) (5 coys)*
33rd Bn *(Croydon) (4 coys)*
51st Bn *(Malden) (7 coys) (1728)*
52nd Bn *(Surbiton) (7 coys) (2159)*
53rd Bn *(Weston Green) (6 coys) (1685)*
54th Bn *(Wimbledon) (7 coys) (1562)*
55th Bn *(Sutton) (5 coys) (1683)*
56th Bn *(Epsom) (7 coys) (2221)*
57th Bn *(Mitcham) (5 coys) (2005)*
58th Bn *(Purley) (5 coys) (1295)*
59th Bn *(Addington) (5 coys) (1266)*

60th Bn *(Croydon) (6 coys) (1805)*
61st Bn *(Norwood) (5 coys) (813)*
62nd Bn *(Norbury) (5 coys) (1250)*
63rd Bn *(Richmond) (5 coys) (886)*
64th Bn *(Kingston) (4 coys)*

London

District HQ was at Curzon Street, Westminster

- County of London

1st Bn *(Westminster) (7 coys) (848)*
2nd Bn *(Chelsea) (6 coys) (903)*
3rd Bn *(Fulham) (6 coys) (948)*
4th Bn *(Victoria) (5 coys) (435)*
5th Bn *(St Marylebone) (8 coys) (1248)*
6th Bn *(Hammersmith) (7 coys) (1646)*
7th Bn *(Chiswick) (7 coys) (1575)*
8th Bn *(Islington) (7 coys) (2264)*
9th Bn *(Stoke Newington) (5 coys) (1138)*
10th Bn *(Finsbury) (5 coys) (1416)*
11th Bn *(Poplar) (6 coys) (1397)*
12th Bn *(Aldgate) (6 coys) (823)*
13th Bn *(Camberwell) (4 coys) (1393)*
14th Bn *(Lambeth) (5 coys; HQ: Brixton) (1464)*
15th Bn *(Bermondsey) (5 coys) (1065)*
16th Bn *(Bermondsey) (5 coys) (1253)*
17th Bn *(Bermondsey) (5 coys) (952)*
18th Bn *(Dulwich) (5 coys) (1091)*
19th Bn *(Sydenham) (Gas Coy) (390)*
20th Bn *(Lewisham) (5 coys; HQ: Forest Hill) (571)*
21st Bn *(Eltham) (6 coys) (1194)*
22nd Bn *(Woolwich Arsenal) (5 coys) (1195)*
23rd Bn *(Deptford) (6 coys) (1193)*
24th Bn *(Erith) (5 coys) (1192)*
25th Bn *(Greenwich) (7 coys) (1461)*
26th Bn *(Woolwich) (5 coys) (1122)*
27th Bn *(Roehampton) (5 coys) (1130)*
28th Bn *(Wandsworth) (7 coys; HQ: Putney) (1207)*
29th Bn *(Battersea) (7 coys) (1118)*
30th Bn *(Tooting) (6 coys) (1078)*
31st Bn *(Streatham) (5 coys) (1416)*
34th Bn *(Greenwich) (Thames; HQ: Charlton) (825)*
35th Bn *(2nd Civil Service) (7 coys; HQ: Somerset House, Westminster; A Coy – Air Ministry, B Coy – Customs and Excise, C Coy – Ministry of Information, D Coy – Postal Censorship, E Coy – Ministry of War Transport and Economic Warfare, F and G Coys – Ministry of Supply) (1610) (Formed May 1941)*
36th Bn *(Railway) (6 Southern Railways) (HQ: Waterloo) (2199)*
37th Bn *(St Pancras) (London Midland Service) (4 coys) (1162)*
38th Bn *(Paddington) (Great Western Railway) (3 coys) (811)*
39th Bn *(Finsbury) (Water Company) (6 coys) (1562)*
40th Bn *(Westminster) (Gas Company) (10 coys) (2572)*
41st Bn *(Ilford) (Transport) (7 coys) (2295)*
42nd Bn *(East Sheen) (Transport) (6 coys) (1636)*
43rd Bn *(Chiswick) (Transport) (5 coys) (1213)*
44th Bn *(Camberwell) (Transport) (4 coys) (1706)*
45th Bn *(Isleworth) (Transport) (5 coys) (1222)*
46th Bn *(Finchley) (Transport) (6 coys) (2300)*
47th Bn *(Lambeth) (London County Council) (6 coys) (1258)*
48th Bn *(Lambeth) (London County Council) (8 coys)*
49th Bn *(Peckham) (Gas Company) (5 coys) (1256)*
50th Bn *(Victoria) (Electricity Company) (3 coys) (686)*
52nd Bn *(Wandsworth) (Gas Company) (4 coys) (801)*
54th Bn *(New Broad Street) (Electricity Company) (6 coys) (1254)*

55th Bn *(Southall) (Electricity Company) (2 coys) (366)*
56th Bn *(Balham) (7 coys) (1043)*
57th Bn *(Catford) (5 coys) (1376)*
58th Bn *(Civil Service) (4 coys, Whitehall) (1176)*
60th Bn *(Transport) (London Underground) (6 coys) (1559)*
61st Bn *(Civil Service) (2 coys, including the War Office)*
62nd Bn *(University) (10 coys, South Kensington)*

- City of London
1st Bn *(Finsbury) (4 coys) (267)*
2nd Bn *(Civil Service) (8 coys, HQ: Somerset House) (1407)*
3rd Bn *(Farringdon) (5 coys; HQ: Lincolns Inn) (993)*
5th Bn *(Blackfriars) (Press) (5 coys; HQ: The Times Newspaper) (698)*
6th Bn *(Silvertown) (8 coys) (1758)*
7th Bn *(Barking) (6 coys) (1549)*
8th Bn *(Hackney) (7 coys) (946)*
10th Bn *(Woodford) (5 coys) (865)*
11th Bn *(Dagenham) (4 coys) (1435)*
12th Bn *(Ilford) (7 coys) (2299)*
13th Bn *(West Ham) (6 coys) (1826)*
14th Bn *(Aldgate) (Port of London Authority- PLA) (6 coys) (1307)*
15th Bn *(East Ham) (PLA) (4 coys; HQ: Royal Albert Dock) (429)*
16th Bn *(Broad Street) (London Midland Railway) (6 coys) (1680)*
17th Bn *(Shoreditch) (1 London North East Railways) (4 coys) (3743)*
18th Bn *(St Pauls) (1 General Post Office - GPO) (912)*
19th Bn *(St Pauls) (2 GPO) (4 coys) (880)*
20th Bn *(Cannon Street) (3 GPO) (7 coys) (1701)*
21st Bn *(Acton) (4 GPO) (6 coys) (1254)*
22nd Bn *(Crouch End) (5 GPO) (8 coys) (1332)*
23rd Bn *(Poplar) (6 GPO) (6 coys) (1026)*
24th Bn *(Fenchurch Street) (PLA) (6 coys)*
28th Bn *(City-East City) (GPO - Post) (6 coys)*
29th Bn *(City-South East) (GPO - Post) (5 coys)*
31st Bn *(City-North West) (GPO - Post) (8 coys)*

- Middlesex
1st Bn *(Staines) (6 coys) (1390)*
2nd Bn *(Hounslow) (5 coys) (1655)*
3rd Bn *(Twickenham) (5 coys) (1387)*
4th Bn *(Haryes) (6 coys) (1598)*
5th Bn *(Sunbury) (4 coys) (866)*
6th Bn *(Brentford) (6 coys) (2048)*
7th Bn *(Acton) (8 coys) (1656)*
10th Bn *(Southall) (7 coys) (1144)*
11th Bn *(Wealdstone) (6 coys) (1638)*
12th Bn *(Wembley) (5 coys) (1399)*
13th Bn *(Ruislip) (4 coys) (1375)*
14th Bn *(Uxbridge) (9 coys) (1165)*
15th Bn *(Harrow) (4 coys) (1120)*
16th Bn *(Harrow) (1785)*
17th Bn *(Harrow) (1920)*
18th Bn *(North Wembley) (1204)*
19th Bn *(Elstree) (8 coys) (1681)*
20th Bn *(Golders Green) (4 coys) (1645)*
21st Bn *(Barnet) (7 coys) (1159)*
22nd Bn *(Stanmore) (7 coys) (1045)*
23rd Bn *(Edgware) (6 coys) (2123)*
24th Bn *(Mill Hill) (8 coys) (1931)*

25th Bn *(Enfield) (5 coys) (1579)*
26th Bn *(Wood Green) (5 coys) (1687)*
27th Bn *(Enfield) (5 coys) (1224)*
28th Bn *(Hornsey) (4 coys) (1125)*
29th Bn *(Highgate) (5 coys) (1236)*
30th Bn *(Enfield) (5 coys) (1088)*
31st Bn *(Sunbury) (Thames Patrol) (4 coys) (634)*
32nd Bn *(Harrow) (4 coys)*
33rd Bn *(Holloway) (5 London North East Railways) (4 coys)*

Battalions based in London were allocated to the various defence sectors as follows:
- Central Sector (Lincoln's Inn): 1, 3 and 5 City of London
- H Sector (Mile End): 8, 11 and 12 County of London
- J Sector (Woodford Green): 51 to 56 Essex
- K Sector (Barking): 6, 7, 11 12 and 13 City of London
- Port of London (PLA) Sector (Trinity Square, EC3): 14, 15 and 24 City of London
- DN Sector (Euston): 5, 9 and 10 County of London
- S Sector (Hampstead): 19 to 24 Middlesex
- X Sector (Wembley): 11 to 15 and 32 Middlesex, 6 Hertford
- Y Sector (Enfield): 25 to 30 Middlesex
- LM Sector (Kennington): 13 to 15 County of London
- P Sector (Bromley): 51 to 55 Kent, 18 to 20 and 57 County of London
- R Sector (Eltham): 56 and 57 Kent, 21 to 26 and 34 County of London
- Z Sector (Croydon): 58 and 59 Surrey, 31 to 33 County of London
- Westminster Garrison: 1 County of London and 2 City of London
- F Sector (Hammersmith): 2, 3, 6 and 7 County of London
- T Sector (Ealing): 1 to 7, 10 and 31 Middlesex
- V Sector (Kingston): 27 and 28 County of London, 51 to 54 Surrey
- W Sector (Cheam): 29, 30 and 56 County of London; 55 to 57 Surrey

South

HQ for Hampshire and Dorset District was in Salisbury

- Hampshire

1st Bn *(Andover) (1540)*
2nd Bn *(Whitchurch) (1221)*
3rd Bn *(Basingstoke) (1 Borough Coy: south of railway, Western Coy: Monk Sherborne, Silchester, Southern Coy: Preston Candover, 2 Borough Coy: Thorneycroft factory, 3 Borough Coy: factory, Winchester Road, 4 Borough Coy) (1172)*
4th Bn *(Alresford) (339)*
5th Bn *(Winchester) (1377)*
6th Bn *(Bournemouth) (1857)*
7th Bn *(Boscombe) (1374)*
8th Bn *(Avon Valley) (HQ- Fordingbridge) (1227)*
9th Bn *(New Forest) (HQ- Hythe) (2097)*
10th Bn *(Romsey) (1149)*
11th Bn *(Eastleigh) (992)*
12th Bn *(Southampton East) (2599)*
13th Bn *(Itchen) (HQ: Bitterne) (1591)*
14th Bn *(Fareham) (C Coy: Gosport) (2033)*
15th Bn *(Petersfield) (1342)*
16th Bn *(Havant) (1385)*
17th Bn *(Portsmouth) (2353)*
18th Bn *(Portsmouth Dockyard) (4 coys; HQ: Southern Railway Jetty) (2438)*
19th Bn *(West Isle of Wight) (1252)*
20th Bn *(East Isle of Wight) (HQ: Brading) (1433)*
21st *(Southampton) (4 Southern Railways) (2166)*
22nd Bn *(GPO - Bournemouth) (1018)*
23rd Bn *(GPO - Southsea) (699)*
24th Bn *(Alton) (1224)*

25th Bn *(Rotherwick) (HQ: Fleet; C Coy – Ewshot) (2424)* 26th Bn *(Southampton West)*
27th Bn *(Farnborough)* 28th Bn *(New Milton)*
30th Bn *(Droxford) (HQ-Bishop Waltham)* 31st Bn *(Cosham)*
32nd Bn *(Connaught) (HQ: Fareham).*

- Berkshire
1st Bn *(Abingdon) (2034)* 2nd Bn *(Maidenhead) (1379)*
3rd Bn *(Newbury) (1962)* 4th Bn *(Pangbourne) (1204)*
5th Bn *(Wantage) (1486)* 6th Bn *(Bracknell) (1260)*
7th Bn *(Reading) (2523)* 8th Bn *(Windsor) (520)*
9th Bn *(Windsor Castle) (318)* 10th Bn *(GPO - Reading) (1078)*
11th Bn *(Crowthorne) (1405)* 12th Bn *(Thames - Reading) (665)*

South West

HQ South West District was in Taunton

- Dorset
1st Bn *(Bridport) (2034)* 2nd Bn *(Dorchester) (1426)*
3rd Bn *(Poole) (1741)* 4th Bn *(Sherborne) (1551)*
5th Bn *(Weymouth) (1539)* 6th Bn *(Wimborne) (1701)*
7th Bn *(Wareham) (1106)*

- Wiltshire
1st Bn *(Chippenham) (1986)* 2nd Bn *(Malmesbury) (1208)*
3rd Bn *(Warminster) (1736)* 4th Bn *(Trowbridge) (HQ: Melksham)*
 (2247)
5th Bn *(Swindon) (1704)* 6th Bn *(Marlborough) (1206)*
7th Bn *(Salisbury) (HQ: Bulford) (1645)* 8th Bn *(Salisbury) (564)*
9th Bn *(Cricklade) (1810)* 10th Bn *(Pewsey) (883)*
11th Bn *(Stratton St Margaret) (657)* 12th Bn *(Corsham)*
13th Bn *(Great Western Railway- Swindon)*

- Gloucestershire
1st Bn *(Cheltenham) (1997)* 2nd Bn *(Bourton on Water) (1208)*
3rd Bn *(Cirencester) (2260)* 4th Bn *(Forest of Dean) (HQ: Lydney)*
 (1246)
5th Bn *(Gloucester) (2834)*
6th Bn *(South Gloucestershire) (HQ: Chipping Sodbury) (2112)*
7th Bn *(Stroud) (1592)* 8th Bn *(Dursley) (1898)*
9th Bn *(Bristol)* 10th Bn *(Bristol)*
11th Bn *(City of Bristol) (HQ: Clifton)* 12th Bn *(City of Bristol) (HQ: Whitehall)*
13th Bn *(City of Bristol) (HQ: Filton)* 14th Bn *(City of Bristol) (HQ: Avonmouth)*
15th Bn *(GPO - Bristol) (1156)* 16th Bn *(City of Bristol)*
17th Bn *(Wye Valley) (HQ: Coleford) (720)* 18th Bn *(City of Bristol) (HQ: Filton)*
19th Bn *(Churchdown)*

Defence of Bristol = 10,230 men, excluding the GPO Battalion.

- Somerset
1st Bn *(Minehead)*   2nd Bn *(Taunton)*
3rd Bn *(Yeovil)*   4th Bn *(Frome)*
5th Bn *(Bath)*   6th Bn *(Bath - Admiralty)*
7th Bn *(Long Ashton)*   8th Bn *(Weston Super Mare)*
9th Bn *(Wells)*   10th Bn *(Bridgwater)*
11th Bn *(Ilminster)*   12th Bn *(Somerton)*
13th Bn *(Axbridge)*

- Devonshire
1st Bn *(Exeter)*   2nd Bn *(Ottery St Mary)*
3rd Bn *(Cullompton)*   4th Bn *(Barnstaple)*
5th Bn *(Bideford)*   6th Bn *(Chumleigh)*
7th Bn *(Okehampton)*   8th Bn *(Holsworthy)*
9th Bn *(Newton Abbot)*   10th Bn *(Torbay) (HQ: Torquay)*
11th Bn *(South Hams) (HQ: Kingsbridge)*   13th Bn *(Totnes)*
14th Bn *(Moorside) (HQ: Bovey Tracey)*   15th Bn *(Plympton)*
16th Bn *(Plymouth) (HQ: Crownhill Fort)*   17th Bn *(Devonport)*
18th Bn *(Saltash)*   19th Bn *(Seaton)*
20th Bn *(Tiverton)*   21st Bn *(GPO - Plymouth)*
22nd Bn *(Southern Railway) (HQ: Exeter)*   23rd Bn *(Drakes) (HQ: Tavistock)*
24th Bn *(Hartland) (HQ: Northam)*   25th Bn *(Ilfracombe) (HQ: Barnstaple)*

- Cornwall
1st Bn *(Bude)*   2nd Bn *(Coastal) (HQ: Delabole)*
3rd Bn *(Launceston)*   4th Bn *(Wadebridge) (HQ: Padstow)*
5th Bn *(St Austell)*   6th Bn *(Liskeard)*
7th Bn *(Falmouth)*   8th Bn *(Helston)*
9th Bn *(Camborne)*   10th Bn *(Truro)*
11th Bn *(Newquay)*   12th Bn *(Land`s End) (HQ: Penzance)*
13th Bn *(Bodmin)*   14th Bn *(Hayle)*
Scilly Isles Independent Company *(St Mary`s)*

East
– HQ Essex and Suffolk District was in Felsted
– HQ Norfolk and Cambridgeshire District was in Newmarket

-Essex
1st Bn *(Rochford)*   2nd Bn *(Maldon)*
3rd Bn *(Stanford le Hope)*   4th Bn *(Romford)*
5th Bn *(Brentwood)*   6th Bn *(Chelmsford)*
7th Bn *(Witham)*   8th Bn *(Colchester)*
9th Bn *(Clacton)*   10th Bn *(Harlow)*
11th Bn *(Braintree)*   12th Bn *(Stansted)*
13th Bn *(GPO - Colchester)*   14th Bn *(West Thurrock)*

15th Bn *(Halstead)*   16th Bn *(Southend)*
17th Bn *(Colchester)*   18th Bn *(Blackheath)*
19th Bn *(Grays)*   20th Bn *(Hornchurch)*
51st Bn *(Chingford)*   52nd Bn *(Chigwell)*
53rd Bn *(Woodford Green)*   54th Bn *(Woodford)*
55th Bn *(Walthamstow)*   56th Bn *(Waltham Abbey)*

-Suffolk:
1st Bn *(Lowestoft)*   2nd Bn *(Bury St Edmunds)*
3rd Bn *(Bury St Edmunds)*   4th Bn *(Rendham)*
5th Bn *(Woodbridge)*   6th Bn *(Ipswich)*
7th Bn *(Stowmarket)*   8th Bn *(Saxmundham)*
9th Bn *(Ipswich)*   10th Bn *(Sudbury)*
11th Bn *(Ipswich)*   12th Bn *(Letchworth)*
13th Bn *(Hatfield - de Hailland)*   14th Bn *(Hatfield)*
15th Bn *(St Albans)*

- Norfolk
1st Bn *(East Dereham)*   2nd Bn *(Downham Market)*
3rd Bn *(Harleston)*   4th Bn *(Holt)*
5th Bn *(North Walsham)*   6th Bn *(Norwich)*
7th Bn *(Kings Lynn)*   8th Bn *(Swaffham)*
9th Bn *(Wymondham)*   10th Bn *(Norwich)*
11th Bn *(Great Yarmouth)*   12th Bn *(Brancaster)*
13th Bn *(Sheringham)*   14th Bn *(Hapton)*
15th Bn *(Setchey)*   16th Bn *(Norwich)*
17th Bn *(Reepham)*

- Cambridgeshire
1st Bn *(Cambridge City)*   2nd Bn *(Newmarket)*
3rd Bn *(Hildersham)*   4th Bn *(Cambridge West)*
5th Bn *(Cambridge)*   6th Bn *(GPO - Cambridge)*
7th Bn *(Cambridge University)*   8th Bn *(Cambridge)*

- Ely:
1st Bn *(Wisbech)*   2nd Bn *(Ely)*
3rd Bn *(March)*

- Huntingdonshire
1st Bn *(Fletton)*   2nd Bn *(St Ives)*
3rd Bn *(St Neots)*

East Midlands
- *HQ East Riding and Lincolnshire District was in Doncaster*
- *HQ North Midland District was in Nottingham*
- *HQ East Central District was in Dunstable*

- Hertfordshire
1st Bn *(Ware, Royston)*　　　　　　　　2nd Bn *(Hitchin, Stevenage)*
3rd Bn *(Hertford)*　　　　　　　　　　　4th Bn *(Welwyn)*
5th Bn *(Harpenden)*　　　　　　　　　　6th Bn *(Oxhey)*
7th Bn *(Hemel Hempstead)*　　　　　　　8th Bn *(Rickmansworth)*
9th Bn *(Abbots Langley)*　　　　　　　　10th Bn *(Watford)*
11th Bn *(Bishop Stortford)*　　　　　　　12th Bn *(Letchworth)*
13th Bn *(Hatfield - de Havilland factory)*　14th Bn *(Hatfield)*
15th Bn *(St Albans)*

- Bedfordshire
1st Bn *(Bedford)*　　　　　　　　　　　2nd Bn *(Biggleswade)*
3rd Bn *(Ampthill)*　　　　　　　　　　　4th Bn *(Luton)*
5th Bn *(Bedford)*　　　　　　　　　　　6th Bn *(Dunstable)*
7th Bn *(Luton)*　　　　　　　　　　　　8th Bn *(Bedford)*

- Buckinghamshire
1st Bn *(Aylesbury)*　　　　　　　　　　2nd Bn *(Wolverton)*
3rd Bn *(Buckingham)*　　　　　　　　　4th Bn *(Hughendon)*
5th Bn *(Beaconsfield)*　　　　　　　　　7th Bn *(High Wycombe)*
8th Bn *(Slough)*　　　　　　　　　　　　9th Bn *(Slough)*
10th Bn *(Iver)*　　　　　　　　　　　　11th Bn *(Amersham)*
12th Bn *(Mursley)*　　　　　　　　　　　13th Bn *(Langley - Hawkers aircraft factory)*

- Lincolnshire
1st Holland Bn *(Boston)*　　　　　　　　2nd Holland Bn *(Spalding)*
3rd Holland Bn *(Holbeach)*　　　　　　　1st City of Lincoln *(Lincoln)*
2nd City of Lincoln *(Lincoln)*　　　　　　3rd City of Lincoln *(Lincoln)*
1st Kesteven Bn *(Navenby)*　　　　　　　2nd Kesteven Bn *(Sleaford)*
3rd Kesteven Bn *(Grantham)*　　　　　　4th Kesteven Bn *(Bourne)*
1st Lindsey Bn *(Scunthorpe)*　　　　　　2nd Lindsey Bn *(Scunthorpe)*
3rd Lindsey Bn *(Epworth)*　　　　　　　4th Lindsey Bn *(Brigg)*
5th Lindsey Bn *(Grimsby)*　　　　　　　6th Lindsey Bn *(Cleethorpes)*
7th Lindsey Bn *(Laceby)*　　　　　　　　8th Lindsey Bn *(Caistor)*
9th Lindsey Bn *(Louth)*　　　　　　　　10th Lindsey Bn *(Skegness)*
11th Lindsey Bn *(Gainsborough)*　　　　　12th Lindsey Bn *(Saxilby)*
13th Lindsey Bn *(Horncastle)*

- Leicestershire
1st Bn *(Leicester North)*　　　　　　　　2nd Bn *(Leicester South)*
3rd Bn *(Leicester West)*　　　　　　　　4th Bn *(Leicester Centre)*
5th Bn *(Belvoir)*　　　　　　　　　　　6th Bn *(Melton Mowbray)*
7th Bn *(Market Harborough)*　　　　　　8th Bn *(Market Bosworth)*
9th Bn *(Loughborough)*　　　　　　　　10th Bn *(Charnwood)*
11th Bn *(Ashby de la Zouch)*　　　　　　12th Bn *(Leicester)*

13th Bn *(GPO - Leicester)*

- Rutland
1st Bn *(Oakham)*

- Northamptonshire
1st Bn *(Peterborough)*
3rd Bn *(Oundle)*
5th Bn *(Kettering)*
7th Bn *(Wellingborough)*
9th Bn *(Brixworth)*
11th Bn *(Hardingstowe)*
13th Bn *(Towcester)*
15th Bn *(Northampton)*

2nd Bn *(Peterborough)*
4th Bn *(Kettering)*
6th Bn *(Corby)*
8th Bn *(Rushden)*
10th Bn *(Daventry)*
12th Bn *(Northampton)*
14th Bn *(Brackley)*

- Nottinghamshire
1st Bn *(Nottingham)*
3rd Bn *(Beeston)*
5th Bn *(Colliery) (HQ: Daybrook)*
7th Bn *(Sutton in Ashfield)*
9th Bn *(Worksop)*
11th Bn *(Newark)*
13th Bn *(GPO-Nottingham)*

2nd Bn *(West Bridgford)*
4th Bn *(Bulwell)*
6th Bn *(Mansfield)*
8th Bn *(Chipstone)*
10th Bn *(Retford)*
12th Bn *(Worksop)*
14th Bn *(Trent - Newark)*

West Midlands

- HQ South Midlands District was in Oxford
- HQ Mid Western District was in Shrewsbury

- Oxfordshire
1st Bn *(Banbury) (1280)*
3rd Bn *(Chipping Norton) (2052)*
5th Bn *(Henley) (1286)*
7th Bn *(Oxford University) (837)*

2nd Bn *(Bicester) (1689)*
4th Bn *(Bullingdon) (1195)*
6th Bn *(Oxford) (2715)*

- Warwickshire
1st Bn *(Warwick)*
3rd Bn *(Nuneaton)*
5th Bn *(Solihull)*
7th Bn *(Rugby)*
12th Bn *(Coventry)*
14th Bn *(Coventry - Armstrong Whitworth factory)*
16th Bn *(Radford)*
18th Bn *(Coventry)*
21st Bn *(Birmingham - Edgbaston)*
23rd Bn *(Birmingham - Erdington)*
25th Bn *(Birmingham - Aston)*
27th Bn *(Birmingham - Kings Norton)*

2nd Bn *(Rugby)*
4th Bn *(Stratford)*
6th Bn *(Sutton Coldfield)*
11th Bn *(Coventry)*
13th Bn *(Coventry)*
15th Bn *(Coventry)*
17th Bn *(Coventry)*
19th Bn *(Coventry)*
22nd Bn *(Birmingham - Handsworth)*
24th Bn *(Birmingham - Moseley)*
26th Bn *(Birmingham - Acocks Green)*
28th Bn *(Birmingham - Edgbaston)*

29th Bn *(Birmingham - Edgbaston)*
30th Bn *(Birmingham - Edgbaston)*
31st Bn *(Birmingham - City)*
32nd Bn *(Birmingham - City)*
33rd Bn *(Birmingham - Edgbaston)*
34th Bn *(Birmingham - Edgbaston)*
35th Bn *(Birmingham - Edgbaston)*
36th Bn *(Birmingham - Erdington)*
37th Bn *(Birmingham - Small Heath)*
38th Bn *(Birmingham - Acocks Green)*
39th Bn *(Birmingham - Stechford)*
40th Bn *(Birmingham - Perry Barr)*
41st Bn *(Birmingham - Edgbaston)*
42nd Bn *(Birmingham - Hall Green)*
43rd Bn *(Birmingham - Longbridge)*
44th Bn *(Birmingham - Handsworth)*
45th Bn *(Birmingham - City)*
46th Bn *(Birmingham - Witton)*
47th Bn *(Birmingham - GPO)*
48th Bn *(Birmingham University)*
49th Bn *(Birmingham - Selly Oak)*
50th Bn *(Birmingham - Perry Barr)*
51st Bn *(Birmingham - Highfield)*
52nd Bn *(Birmingham - Castle Bromwich)*

- Worcestershire
1st Bn *(Worcester)*
2nd Bn *(Bromsgrove)*
3rd Bn *(Dudley)*
4th Bn *(Evesham)*
5th Bn *(Halesowen)*
6th Bn *(Kidderminster)*
7th Bn *(Malvern)*
8th Bn *(Oldbury)*
9th Bn *(Redditch)*
10th Bn *(Stourbridge)*
11th Bn *(Stourport)*
12th Bn *(Warley)*

- Hereford
1st Bn *(Leominster)*
2nd Bn *(Bromyard)*
3rd Bn *(Hereford-City)*
4th Bn *(Hereford-Rural)*
5th Bn *(Ledbury)*
6th Bn *(Harewood)*

- Staffordshire
1st Bn *(Stoke)*
2nd Bn *(Stoke-Burslem)*
3rd Bn *(Longton)*
4th Bn *(Hanley)*
5th Bn *(Leek)*
6th Bn *(Cheadle)*
7th Bn *(Uttoxeter)*
8th Bn *(Burton)*
9th Bn *(Lichfield)*
10th Bn *(Lichfield)*
13th Bn *(Cannock)*
14th Bn *(Stafford)*
15th Bn *(Newcastle under Lyme)*
16th Bn *(Newcastle under Lyme)*
17th Bn *(Stone)*
18th Bn *(Swynnerton - ordnance factory)*
20th Bn *(Wolverhampton)*
21st Bn *(Wolverhampton)*
22nd Bn *(Wolverhampton)*
23rd Bn *(Wolverhampton)*
24th Bn *(Wolverhampton - Tettenhall)*
25th Bn *(Brewood)*
26th Bn *(Willenhall)*
27th Bn *(Walsall)*
28th Bn *(West Bromwich)*
29th Bn *(West Bromwich)*
30th Bn *(Smethwick)*
31st Bn *(Smethwick)*
32nd Bn *(Aldridge)*
34th Bn *(Bilston)*
35th Bn *(Sedgeley)*
36th Bn *(Wednesbury)*
37th Bn *(Darlaston)*
38th Bn *(Brierley Hill)*
39th Bn *(Stourbridge)*
40th Bn *(Rowley Regis)*
41st Bn *(Tipton)*

- Derbyshire
1st Bn *(Bakewell)*
3rd Bn *(Chapel en le Frith)*
5th Bn *(Bolsover)*
7th Bn *(Chesterfield)*
9th Bn *(Ilkeston)*
11th Bn *(Repton)*
13th Bn *(Derby)*
15th Bn *(Calver - Peak)*

2nd Bn *(Buxton)*
4th Bn *(Eckington)*
6th Bn *(Chesterfield)*
8th Bn *(Alfreton)*
10th Bn *(Ashbourne)*
12th Bn *(Derby-Belper)*
14th Bn *(Derby Works)*

- Shropshire
1st Bn *(Shrewsbury)*
3rd Bn *(Market Drayton)*
5th Bn *(Wellington)*
7th Bn *(Craven Arms)*
9th Bn *(GPO - Shrewsbury)*
11th Bn *(Newport)*

2nd Bn *(Oswestry)*
4th Bn *(Bayston Hill)*
6th Bn *(Ironbridge)*
8th Bn *(Bridgnorth)*
10th Bn *(Shifnal)*

North East

- *HQ Northumberland District was in Gosforth*
- *HQ West Riding District was in Leeds*
- *HQ North Riding District was in Catterick*

- East Riding
1st Bn *(Hull)*
3rd Bn *(Hornsea)*
5th Bn *(Bridlington)*
7th Bn *(Withernsea)*

2nd Bn *(Brough)*
4th Bn *(Pocklington)*
6th Bn *(Malton)*
8th Bn *(Hull)*

- West Riding
1st Bn *(Bradford)*
3rd Bn *(Bradford)*
5th Bn *(Harrogate)*
7th Bn *(Leeds)*
9th Bn *(Leeds)*
11th Bn *(Wetherby)*
13th Bn *(Garforth)*
15th Bn *(GPO) (Sheffield)*
17th Bn *(GPO - Leeds)*
21st Bn *(Sowerby Bridge)*
23rd Bn *(Halifax)*
25th Bn *(Huddersfield)*
27th Bn *(Keighley)*
29th Bn *(Otley)*
31st Bn *(Settle)*
33rd Bn *(Skipton - Crosshills)*

2nd Bn *(Bradford - Odsal)*
4th Bn *(Bradford - Allerton)*
6th Bn *(Ripon)*
8th Bn *(Leeds)*
10th Bn *(Selby)*
12th Bn *(Aborford)*
14th Bn *(York)*
16th Bn *(GPO - Leeds)*
18th Bn *(Leeds)*
22nd Bn *(Brighouse)*
24th Bn *(Halifax)*
26th Bn *(Huddersfield)*
28th Bn *(Keighley)*
30th Bn *(Rawdon)*
32nd Bn *(Skipton)*
34th Bn *(Holmfirth)*

35th Bn *(Slaithwaite)*
40th Bn *(Batley)*
42nd Bn *(Stainforth)*
44th Bn *(Doncaster - Bentley)*
46th Bn *(Doncaster)*
48th Bn *(Castleford)*
50th Bn *(Wakefield)*
52nd Bn *(Wakefield)*
56th Bn *(Barnsley)*
59th Bn *(Rotherham)*
62nd Bn *(Sheffield - Aston)*
64th Bn *(Sheffield - Ecclesfield)*
66th Bn *(Sheffield)*
68th Bn *(Sheffield)*
70th Bn *(Skelmanthorpe)*
72nd Bn *(Ward Green)*

36th Bn *(Saddleworth)*
41st Bn *(Dewsbury)*
43rd Bn *(Tickhill)*
45th Bn *(Doncaster - Coldthorpe)*
47th Bn *(Goole)*
49th Bn *(Pontefract)*
51st Bn *(Wakefield)*
55th Bn *(Sheffield)*
58th Bn *(Rotherham)*
61st Bn *(Rawmarsh)*
63rd Bn *(Mexborough)*
65th Bn *(Sheffield)*
67th Bn *(Sheffield)*
69th Bn *(Sheffield)*
71st Bn *(Cudworth)*

- North Riding

1st Bn *(Northallerton) (HQ: Thirsk)*
3rd Bn *(Guisborough)*
5th Bn *(Southbank)*
7th Bn *(Malton)*
9th Bn *(Middlesborough)*
11th Bn *(Leyburn)*
13th Bn *(Saltburn)*

2nd Bn *(Whitby)*
4th Bn *(Redcar)*
6th Bn *(York-Bulmer)*
8th Bn *(Middlesborough)*
10th Bn *(Scarborough)*
12th Bn *(Richmond)*

- County Durham

1st Bn *(Blaydon)*
3rd Bn *(Consett)*
5th Bn *(Chester le Street)*
7th Bn *(Castle Eden)*
9th Bn *(Sunderland)*
11th Bn *(Durham)*
13th Bn *(South Hylton)*
15th Bn *(Bishop Auckland)*
17th Bn *(Staindrop)*
19th Bn *(Norton on Tees)*
21st Bn *(Gateshead)*
23rd Bn *(Washington)*
25th Bn *(Hebburn)*

2nd Bn *(Birtley)*
4th Bn *(Consett)*
6th Bn *(Durham-Stanley)*
8th Bn *(South Shields)*
10th Bn *(Gateshead)*
12th Bn *(Hornden)*
14th Bn *(Houlton le Spring)*
16th Bn *(Barnard Castle)*
18th Bn *(West Hartlepool)*
20th Bn *(Darlington)*
22nd Bn *(Wheatley Hill)*
24th Bn *(Sunderland)*
26th Bn *(Seaham)*

- Northumberland:

1st Bn *(Berwick)*
3rd Bn *(Morpeth)*
5th Bn *(Gosforth)*
7th Bn *(Tynemouth)*
9th Bn *(Newcastle Centre)*

2nd Bn *(Alnwick)*
4th Bn *(Hexham)*
6th Bn *(Blyth)*
8th Bn *(Wallsend)*
10th Bn *(Hexham)*

11th Bn *(Newcastle West)*   12th Bn *(Newcastle East)*
13th Bn *(GPO - Newcastle)*   14th Bn *(Bedlington)*
15th Bn *(Newcastle - Benton)*   16th Bn *(Amble)*
17th Bn *(Ashington)*   18th Bn *(Seaton Delavel)*

North West

HQ North West District was in Preston

- Cheshire
1st Bn *(Altrincham)*   2nd Bn *(Altrincham)*
3rd Bn *(Knutsford)*   4th Bn *(Birkenhead)*
5th Bn *(Chester-Broxton)*   6th Bn *(Chester)*
7th Bn *(Crewe)*   8th Bn *(Congleton)*
9th Bn *(Macclesfield)*   10th Bn *(Wilmslow)*
11th Bn *(Midlewich)*   12th Bn *(Northwich)*
13th Bn *(Sandiway)*   14th Bn *(Tarporley)*
15th Bn *(Runcorn)*   16th Bn *(Wallasey)*
17th Bn *(Heswall)*   18th Bn *(Ellesmere Port)*
19th Bn *(Shotton)*   20th Bn *(Great Sutton)*
21st Bn *(Great Bebington)*   22nd Bn *(GPO - Chester)*
23rd Bn *(Sale)*   24th Bn *(Nantwich)*
35th Bn *(Stalybridge)*   36th Bn *(Hyde)*
37th Bn *(Romiley)*   38th Bn *(Stockport)*
39th Bn *(Cheadle)*

- Lancashire
1st Bn *(Barrow)*   2nd Bn *(Ulverston)*
3rd Bn *(Lancaster)*   4th Bn *(Morecombe)*
5th Bn *(Preston)*   6th Bn *(Kirkham)*
7th Bn *(Blackpool)*   8th Bn *(Preston)*
9th Bn *(Blackburn County) (HQ: Wilpshire)*   10th Bn *(Blackburn)*
11th Bn *(Great Harwood)*   12th Bn *(Leyland)*
13th Bn *(Croston)*   14th Bn *(Bolton County) (HQ: Harwill)*
15th Bn *(Bolton)*   21st Bn *(Bury)*
22nd Bn *(Rochdale)*   23rd Bn *(Oldham)*
24th Bn *(Wigan County) (HQ: Hindley)*   25th Bn *(Leigh)*
26th Bn *(Wigan)*   27th Bn *(Rochdale)*
28th Bn *(Nelson)*   29th Bn *(Burnley)*
30th Bn *(Accrington)*   31st Bn *(Rossendale)*
32nd Bn *(Bacup)*   41st Bn *(Prestwich)*
42nd Bn *(Eccles)*   43rd Bn *(Salford)*
44th Bn *(Stretford)*   45th Bn *(Trafford Park)*
46th Bn *(South Manchester) (HQ: Didsbury)*   47th Bn *(Wythenshawe)*
48th Bn *(Ardwick)*   49th Bn *(Manchester)*
50th Bn *(Manchester-Ancoats)*   51st Bn *(Ashton under Lyne)*
55th Bn *(Colleries) (HQ: Walkden)*   56th Bn *(Manchester)*
57th Bn *(GPO - Manchester)*   58th Bn *(GPO - Manchester)*

59th Bn *(GPO - Manchester)*
61st Bn *(Manchester University)*
63rd Bn *(Moston)*
71st Bn *(Ormskirk)*
73rd Bn *(Maghull)*
75th Bn *(St Helens)*
77th Bn *(Bootle)*
79th Bn *(Newton le Willows)*
81st Bn *(Prescot)*
83rd Bn *(Liverpool - Anfield)*
85th Bn *(Liverpool - Childwall)*
87th Bn *(Liverpool - Airburth)*
89th Bn *(Liverpool - Works)*
91st Bn *(Liverpool – London Midland Railway)*
93rd Bn *(St Helens)*

60th Bn *(Heywood)*
62nd Bn *(Padiham)*
64th Bn *(Middleton)*
72nd Bn *(Crosby)*
74th Bn *(Southport)*
76th Bn *(Golborne)*
78th Bn *(Warrington)*
80th Bn *(Widnes)*
82nd Bn *(Liverpool - Toxteth)*
84th Bn *(Liverpool - Woolton)*
86th Bn *(Liverpool - Stoneycroft)*
88th Bn *(Liverpool - Bootle)*
90th Bn *(Liverpool Transport)*
92nd Bn *(Liverpool - GPO)*

- Cumberland and Westmoreland
1st Bn *(Longtown)*
3rd Bn *(Carlisle)*
5th Bn *(Workington)*
7th Bn *(Millom)*
9th Bn *(Lakes) (HQ: Keswick)*
11th Bn *(Kendal)*

2nd Bn *(Carlisle)*
4th Bn *(Cockermouth)*
6th Bn *(Whitehaven)*
8th Bn *(Penrith)*
10th Bn *(Appleby)*
12th Bn *(Warwick Bridge)*

Isle of Man
1st Manx Bn *(Douglas)*

2nd Manx Bn *(Douglas)*

Scotland

- *HQ Highland District was in Inverness*
- *HQ West Scotland was in Bridge of Weir*
- *HQ East Scotland was in Edinburgh*

-Aberdeenshire
1st Bn *(Buchan)*
3rd Bn *(Banchory)*
5th Bn *(Turriff)*
7th Bn *(Aberdeen - Works)*

2nd Bn *(Alford)*
4th Bn *(Aberdeen)*
6th Bn *(Aberdeen - GPO)*
9th Bn *(Aberdeen - University)*

- Angus
1st Bn *(Brechin)*
3rd Bn *(Arbroath)*

2nd Bn *(Forfar)*

- Argyll
1st Bn *(Oban)*
3rd Bn *(Cambletown)*

2nd Bn *(Dunoon)*

- Ayrshire
1st Bn *(Ardrossan)* 2nd Bn *(Beith)*
3rd Bn *(Irvine)* 4th Bn *(Kilmarnock)*
5th Bn *(Mauchline)* 6th Bn *(Maybole)*
7th Bn *(Ayr)* 8th Bn *(Ardeer-factory)*

- Banffshire
1st Bn *(Keith)* 2nd Bn *(Cullen)*

- Borders
1st Bn *(Hawick)* 2nd Bn *(Galashiels)*
3rd Bn *(Duns)* 4th Bn *(Kelso)*

- Caithness
1st Bn *(Wick)*

- Clackmannanshire
1st Bn *(Alloa)*

- Dumbartonshire
1st Bn *(Alexandria)* 2nd Bn *(Dalmuir)*
3rd Bn *(Bearsden)* 4th Bn *(Lenzie)*

- Dumfrieshire
1st Bn *(Locherbie)* 2nd Bn *(Dumfries)*
3rd Bn *(Annan)* 4th Bn *(Kirkconnel)*

- Dundee
1st Bn *(Dundee)* 2nd Bn *(Dundee)*
3rd Bn *(Dundee - GPO)*

- Edinburgh
1st Bn *(City)* 2nd Bn *(City)*
3rd Bn *(City)* 4th Bn *(Portobello)*
5th Bn *(City)* 6th Bn *(City)*
7th Bn *(Musselburgh)* 8th Bn *(City)*
9th Bn *(University)* 10th Bn *(3 London North East Railway)*
11th Bn *(GPO)*

- East Lothian
1st Bn *(North Berwick)* 2nd Bn *(Haddington)*

- Mid Lothian
1st Bn *(South Edinburgh)* 2nd Bn *(Dalkeith)*

- West Lothian
1st Bn *(West Edinburgh)* 2nd Bn *(Bathgate)*

- Fife
1st Bn *(Cupar)* 2nd Bn *(St Andrews)*
3rd Bn *(Anstruther)* 4th Bn *(Leven)*
5th Bn *(Kirkcaldy)* 6th Bn *(Lochgelly)*
7th Bn *(Dunfirmline)* 8th Bn *(Kirkcaldy)*
9th Bn *(Rosyth - docks)* 10th Bn *(Inverkeithing)*

- Glasgow
1st Bn *(City)* 2nd Bn *(City)*
3rd Bn *(City)* 4th Bn *(Works)*
5th Bn *(Langside)* 6th Bn *(Corporation)*
7th Bn *(London Midland Railway)* 8th Bn *(2 London North East Railway)*
9th Bn *(GPO)* 10th Bn *(GPO)*
11th Bn *(Ibrox)* 12th Bn *(Bridgeton)*
13th Bn *(GPO)* 14th Bn *(University)*

- Hebrides
1st Bn *(Sornoway)*

- Invernessshire
1st Bn *(Inverness)* 2nd Bn *(Fort William)*
3rd Bn *(Carrbridge)* 4th Bn *(Inverness)*

- Kirkcudbrightshire
1st Bn *(Castle Douglas)* 2nd Bn *(Dalbeattie)*
3rd Bn *(Gatehouse)*

- Lanarkshire
1st Bn *(Lanark)* 2nd Bn *(Aidrie)*
3rd Bn *(Wishaw)* 4th Bn *(Hamilton)*
5th Bn *(Rutherglen)* 6th Bn *(Motherwell)*

- Morayshire
1st Bn *(Elgin)* 2nd Bn *(Forres)*

- Peebleshire
1st Bn *(Peebles)*

- Perthshire
1st Bn *(Pitlochry)* 2nd Bn *(Blairgowrie)*
3rd Bn *(Auchterarder)* 4th Bn *(Perth)*
5th Bn *(Dunblane)* 6th Bn *(Perth)*

- Renfrewshire and Bute
1st Bn *(Greenock)* 2nd Bn *(Paisley)*
3rd Bn *(Newton Morris)* 4th Bn *(Renfrew)*

5th Bn *(Port Glasgow)*

- Rossshire
1st Bn *(Nigg)*   2nd Bn *(Garve)*

- Scottish Borders
1st Bn *(Hawick)*   2nd Bn *(Galashiels)*
3rd Bn *(Duns)*   4th Bn *(Kelso)*

- Shetlands and Orkneys
1st Zetland Bn *(Lerwick)*   1st Orkney Bn *(Kirkwall)*

- Stirlingshire
1st Bn *(Stirling)*   2nd Bn *(Falkirk)*
3rd Bn *(Larbert)*

- Sutherland
1st Bn *(Golspie)*

- Wigtownshire
1st Bn *(Stranraer)*   2nd Bn *(Newton Stewart)*

Wales

HQ South Wales District was in Abergavenny

- Anglesey
1st Bn *(Holyhead)*   2nd Bn *(Menai Bridge)*
3rd Bn *(Llangefni)*

- Brecknock
1st Bn *(Brecon)*   2nd Bn *(Builth Wells)*

- Caernarfonshire
1st Bn *(Conwy)*   2nd Bn *(Bangor)*
3rd Bn *(Carnarfon)*   4th Bn *(Criccieth)*
5th Bn *(Llandudno)*

- Cardiganshire
1st Bn *(Aberystwyth)*   2nd Bn *(Cardigan)*
3rd Bn *(Lampeter)*

- Carmarthenshire
1st Bn *(Carmarthen)*   2nd Bn *(Llanelli)*
3rd Bn *(Llanelli)*   4th Bn *(Llandilo)*
5th Bn *(Newcastle Emlyn)*   6th Bn *(St Clears)*
7th Bn *(Ammanford)*

- Denbighshire and Flintshire
1st Bn *(Colwyn Bay)*
3rd (Flint) Bn *(Rhyl)*
5th (Flint) Bn *(Hawarden)*
7th Bn *(Overton on Dee)*
9th Bn *(Ruthin)*
11th Bn *(Colwyn Bay)*

2nd Bn *(Denbigh)*
4th (Flint) Bn *(Mold)*
6th Bn *(Wrexham)*
8th Bn *(Chirk)*
10th Bn *(Marchweil - ordnance factory)*

- Glamorgan
1st Bn *(Aberdare)*
3rd Bn *(Bridgend)*
5th Bn *(Barry)*
7th Bn *(Pentre)*
9th Bn *(Merthyr)*
11th Bn *(Cardiff - Whitchurch)*
13th Bn *(Treharris)*
15th Bn *(Gower)*
17th Bn *(Cardiff - GPO)*
19th Bn *(Bargoed)*
21st Bn *(Cardiff)*
23rd Bn *(Bridgend - ordnance factory)*
25th Bn *(Pontypridd)*

2nd Bn *(Pontypridd)*
4th Bn *(Neath)*
6th Bn *(Caerphilly)*
8th Bn *(Swansea - Gorseinon)*
10th Bn *(Cowbridge)*
12th Bn *(Swansea - Sketty)*
14th Bn *(Swansea - Uplands)*
16th Bn *(Cardiff)*
18th Bn *(Swansea - GPO)*
20th Bn *(Port Talbot)*
22nd Bn *(Cardiff)*
24th Bn *(Porthcawl)*

- Merrioneth and Montgomery
1st Bn *(Ffestiniog)*
3rd Bn *(Machynlleth)*
5th Bn *(Llanfyllin)*
7th Bn *(Newtown)*

2nd Bn *(Dolgellau)*
4th Bn *(Corwen)*
6th Bn *(Welshpool)*

- Monmouthshire
1st Bn *(Chepstow)*
3rd Bn *(Newport - Docks)*
5th Bn *(Blackwood)*
7th Bn *(Ebbw)*
9th Bn *(Pontypool)*
11th Bn *(Abergavenny)*

2nd Bn *(Newport)*
4th Bn *(Monmouth)*
6th Bn *(Rhymney)*
8th Bn *(Abertillery)*
10th Bn *(Monmouth)*
12th Bn *(Usk - ordnance factory)*

- Pembrokeshire
1st Bn *(Tenby)*
3rd Bn *(Haverfordwest)*

2nd Bn *(Haverfordwest)*

- Radnorshire
1st Bn *(Knighton)*

2nd Bn *(Llandrindod Wells)*

Northern Ireland

- Antrim
1st Bn *(Ballymoney)*　　　　　　　　　　2nd Bn *(Ballymena)*
3rd Bn *(Carrickfergus)*　　　　　　　　　4th Bn *(Antrim)*

- Armagh
1st Bn *(Lurgan)*　　　　　　　　　　　　2nd Bn *(Portadown)*
3rd Bn *(Bessbrook)*　　　　　　　　　　　4th Bn *(Antrim)*

- Down
1st Bn *(Newtownards)*　　　　　　　　　 2nd Bn *(Downpatrick)*
3rd Bn *(Newry)*　　　　　　　　　　　　 4th Bn *(Banbridge)*

- Fermanagh
1st Bn *(Irvinestown)*　　　　　　　　　　2nd Bn *(Lisnakea)*
3rd Bn *(Enniskillen)*

- Tyrone
1st Bn *(Castlederg)*　　　　　　　　　　 2nd Bn *(Omagh)*
3rd Bn *(Cookstown)*　　　　　　　　　　 4th Bn *(Dungannon)*
5th Bn *(Augher)*

- City of Londonderry
1st Bn *(Limavady)*　　　　　　　　　　　 2nd Bn *(Garvagh)*
3rd Bn *(Magherafelt)*　　　　　　　　　　1st City Bn
2nd City Bn

Appendix 3

ANTI AIRCRAFT COMMAND

- Those units marked with an asterisk had served with the BEF
- There were four types of units within the Command, excluding those training. Heavy Anti Aircraft units (HAA) were equipped with 3-inch, 3.7-inch or 4.5-inch guns, many in a mobile role but all covering major population and industrial areas as well as naval and RAF bases. Light Anti Aircraft units (LAA) were equipped with a variety of 40mm, 20mm and 2-pounder automatic guns as well as multiple and single automatic machine guns (AAMG). These were located on a similar basis to the HAA units. Searchlight units (S/L) were larger in terms of personnel and equipped with either 90 or 150cm projectors; a battery having four troops, each with six searchlights. They also had sound locator equipment. These searchlight units were often distributed over a wide area in small groups or singly and were responsible for their own defence but were issued with two taxis per site for mobile defence. The fourth type was the experimental rocket units that had began to form in early autumn with single or double 3-inch rocket launchers
- The Command developed three operational belts: the outer or indicator belt largely consisted of single searchlight positions and was about 12 miles deep with searchlights 10,000 yards (9140 metres) apart; the intermediate or killer belt contained more searchlights and HAA guns with a depth of 16 miles and 6,000 yards (5500 metres) apart; the third was the gun defended areas, mostly around the capital, ports and main industrial centres with searchlights 12,000 yards (11,000 metres) apart. The central zone held the mobile units.
- The Command had 59 gun laying radar sets, with another 344 supplied by the end of 1940
- 120x3.7-inch HAA and 84x40mm LAA guns were allocated to GHQ in August to support the field forces in a mobile role mainly in defence of their lines of communications. Units were allocated but not transferred to the mobile brigades until authorised by GHQ, by issuing codeword "Bovril". Breakdown was: Eastern Command – East Anglia (1st AA Brigade): 24x3.7-inch, 12x40mm, Eastern Command - southeast (2nd AA Brigade): 24x3.7-inch, 36x40mm, Southern Command (3rd AA Brigade): 56x3.7-inch, 36x40mm, Northern Command (12th AA Brigade): 16x 3.7-inch
- 1st Division was formed in the mid 1930`s from London Territorial Army units, while the 2nd Division was formed from the 46th (North Midland) Infantry Division
- AA Command strengths:

	Heavy Guns	Light Guns	Searchlights	Manpower
24 July	1385:	497:	4087	157,319
	- 359 4.5-inch	- 135 3-inch		
	- 358 3.7-inch	- 366 40mm		
	- 310 3.7-inch (mobile)	- 152 2pdr (inc. 38 Naval)		
	- 226 3-inch	- 39 20mm Hispano		
		Plus over 3,000 AALMG		

Only 50% of HAA and 33% of LAA guns were available that was considered necessary before the fall of France.

	Heavy Guns	Light Guns	Searchlights	Manpower
25 September	1497:	603:	4246	269,000
	- 376 4.5-inch	- 116 3-inch		
	- 425 3.7-inch	- 477 40mm		
	- 357 3.7-inch (mobile)	- 152 2pdr (inc. 26 Naval)		
	- 225 3-inch	- 61 20mm Hispano		

- On 1 August the searchlight units transferred from the Royal Engineers to the Royal Artillery
- In late autumn the Command was reorganised and enlarged with the formation of corps headquarters and new divisions
- The General Officer Commanding the Command was General Sir Frederick Pile, appointed on the Command being established in March 1938 and who held this post until mid April 1945
- Where possible the gunsite identification code has been included below.

1st AA Division (HQ: Knightsbridge) (GOC: Major General F Crossman)
24 July: HAA = 103/London, 28/Slough (131); LAA= 33; S/L=240
25 September: HAA = 207/London, 28/Slough (235); LAA= 46; S/L=242

26th AA Brigade (HQ: Enfield)
- 1 HAA Regt *(Waltham Cross) (42+1119)*: 1 Bty (Edmonton (ZW2)), 2 Bty (Hampstead (ZE22), Mill Hill (ZW13)), 17 Bty (Hyde Park (ZW5)) (24x3.7-inch) (Joined Brigade 9 September)
- 4 HAA Regt * (Wanstead) (29+1328): 6 Bty (Cheshunt (ZE11) - 8x3.7-inch mobile), 202 Bty (Beeton – 4x3.7-inch mobile), 221 Bty (Highams (ZE10) - 8x3.7-inch mobile) (Joined Brigade 12 September)
- 8 HAA Regt (St John`s Wood) (31+920): 23 Bty (Wimbledon (ZS19) and Hurlingham (ZW8) - 8x3.7-inch mobile), 303 Bty (Finsbury Park (ZE13), Walthamstow (ZE19) - 8x3.7-inch mobile), 332 Bty (Dollis Hill) (ZW9), Brentham (ZW12) - 8x3.7-inch mobile) + Troop 313 Bty (Enfield (ZW1) - 2x3-inch) (Joined Brigade 12 September)
- 52 HAA Regt (Leyton) (41+1393): 154 Bty (Primrose Hill (ZE14), Isle of Dogs (ZE8) - 8x4.5-inch), 155 Bty (Barking (ZE2) and Chadwell Heath (ZE1) - 8x4.5-inch), 271 Bty (Hackney (ZE21) and Chase Side (ZW4) – 8x4.5-inch), 313 Bty (Cheshunt (ZE11) and Enfield (ZW1) - 6x3-inch)
- 86 HAA Regt (Bush Hill) (32+854): 273 Bty (Wanstead (ZE9) - 4x3.7-inch, 4x3-inch), 275 Bty (Buckhurst Hill (ZE4) - 4x3.7-inch), 274 Bty (non operational and to Towyn for training)
- 42 LAA Regt (Waltham Abbey) (38+726): 48 Bty (Waltham Abbey - 2x40mm, Enfield - 1x3-inch), 145 Bty (Radlett, Hatfield - 20 AAMG), 150 Bty (Enfield - 3x3-inch, Erith - 2x40mm), 4 Bty (Neasdon - 2x40mm)

38th AA Brigade (HQ: Harrow)
- 26 S/L Regt (Langley) (36+1784): 301 Bty (Woodford), 303 Bty (Putney), 321 Bty (Tottenham), 322 Bty (Dartford, Northfleet), 339 Bty (Grove Park)
- 27 S/L Regt (Hemel Hempstead) (45+1424): 304 Bty (Hatfield), 305 Bty (Watford), 306 Bty (Leighton Buzzard)

- 35 S/L Regt *(Marlow) (32+1377)*: 340 Bty *(Ruislip)*, 341 Bty *(Marlow)*, 343 Bty *(Thame)*
- 73 S/L Regt *(Bexleyheath) (37+1318)*: 322 Bty
- 75 S/L Regt *(Ealing) (46+1161)*: 470 Bty *(Ealing)*, 471 Bty *(Chigwell)*, 472 Bty *(Croydon)*, 473 Bty *(Thames Ditton)*
- 489 S/L Bty *(Ascot) (7+366)*

48th AA Brigade *(HQ: Chislehurst)*
- 6 HAA Regt *(Blackheath) (27+869)*: 12 Bty *(Eltham (ZS7), Grove Park (ZS22) - 8x3.7-inch mobile)*, 328 Bty *(Beckenham (ZS12) - 8x3.7-inch mobile)*, B Bty RM *(284)(Abbey Wood - 4x3.7-inch mobile, Bickley -3x3.7-inch mobile)* (Composite Regt formed 12 September)
- 54 HAA Regt *(Erith) (39+1368)*: 160 Bty *(Bexleyheath: Erith and Welling (ZS6) - 8x4.5-inch)*, 161 Bty *(Dulwich (ZS14), Clapham Common (ZS16) - 8x4.5-inch)*, 162 Bty *(Richmond Park (ZS20), Hayes Common (ZS10) – 4x3.7-inch)*, 312 Bty *(Woolwich Common (ZS8), Plumstead Marshes (ZS3) - 8x4.5-inch)*
- 97 HAA Regt *(Catford) (38+960)*: 298 Bty *(Dartford Heath (ZS2) - 4x3.7-inch)*, 299 Bty *(Raynes Park (ZS18) – 6x3.7-inch)*, 319 Bty *(Addiscombe, St Pauls Cray, Orpington (ZS5) - 8x3.7-inch)*
- 105 HAA Regt *(Grove Park) (31+731)*: 22 Bty *(Norbury (ZS15), Sydenham - 8x3.7-inch mobile)*, 188 Bty *(Mitcham Common (ZS17) - 8x3.7-inch mobile, detached from 67 HAA Regt 16 September)*, 326 Bty *(Wormwood Scrubs (ZW10) - 8x3.7-inch)*, 333 Bty *(Richmond Park (ZS20) - 4x3.7-inch, from 25 September)*. *(Regt forming 15 September)*

49th AA Brigade *(HQ: Kensington)*
- 84 HAA Regt *(Datchett) (35+1256)*: 260 Bty *(Bedfont, Uxbridge) (8x3.7-inch mobile)*, 261 Bty *(West Drayton – 2x3-inch, Langley - 4x3-inch)*, 262 Bty *(Burnham - 4x3-inch, Stanmore - 4x3-inch)*, 263 Bty *(Datchet - 4x3-inch, Windsor - 4x3-inch)*, 330 Bty *(Iver and Windsor - 6x3-inch)*
- 98 HAA Regt *(Cobham, Surrey) (28+748)*: 300 Bty *(Farnborough - 4x3.7-inch mobile, Tangmere – 4x3.7-inch mobile)*, 301 Bty *(Weybridge - 8x3.7-inch mobile)*, 320 Bty *(Weybridge - 8x3.7-inch mobile)*
- 1 LAA Regt *(Kingsbury) (27+704)*: 2 Bty *(Collindale - 12 AAMG)*, 3 Bty *(Stanmore - 5x40mm)*
- 36 LAA Regt *(Staines) (47+1149)*: 79 Bty *(Slough - 4x40mm, Langley - 8x40mm + 5 Troop: Benson – 12 AAMG, 6 Troop: High Wycombe - 12AAMG)*, 97 Bty *(Harrow: Northolt - 6x40mm, Hayes - 4x40mm)*, 128 Bty *(Feltham, Walton, Kempton and Hampton - 48 AAMG)*
- 53 LAA Regt *(Weybridge) (27+621)*: 157 Bty *(Lenham; A and B Troops: Detling - 8x40mm, C Troop: Wye 4x40mm)*, 158 Bty *(Thursley - 6x40mm, Swaffham Prior - 6x40mm)*, 159 Bty *(Gatwick - 8x40mm, Redhill -4x40mm)* (Regt had GHQ mobile role: 157 Bty with NZEF, 158 Bty with 1st and 2nd Armoured Divisions, 159 Bty with VII Corps) *(36x40mm)*
- 74 HAA Regt *(Wokingham) (37+1074)*: 230, 231 and 232 Btys (non operational - preparing for overseas move to North Africa)

- 1 AA `Z` Training Regt (formed September)

Divisional support troops: 900 Coy *(Dulwich) (11+249)*, 902 Coy RASC *(Finchley) (12+414)*.

2nd AA Division (HQ: *Cambridge*) (GOC: Major General M Grove-White)

24 July: HAA = 38/Humber, 27/Sheffield, 32/Derby, 16/Notts, 49/airfields, 4/Vital Points (166); LAA= 65; S/L=1251

25 September: HAA = 26/Humber, 28/Sheffield, 28/Derby, 21/Notts, 35/airfields, 8/ Vital Points (146); LAA= 68; S/L=1059

1st AA Brigade *(HQ: Stansted)* (Eastern Command Mobile Role)
(HQ to Ternhill in 4th AA Division in early October)
- 4 HAA Regt *(Wanstead)* - RHQ and 18 Bty allocated from 1st AA Division *(8x3.7-inch mobile)*
- 5 HAA Bty (allocated from 68 HAA Regt) *(Derby - 6x3.7-inch mobile)*
- 6 HAA Bty (allocated from 68 HAA Regt) *(6x3.7-inch mobile)*
- 31 LAA Bty (allocated from 16 LAA Regt) *(12x40mm)*

32nd AA Brigade *(HQ: Wittering)*
- 244 HAA Bty *(Stamford)* (part of 78 HAA Regt)
- 27 LAA Regt *(Stamford) (23+923):* 107 Bty *(Newark -16 AAMG, Grantham - 1x40mm, 2AAMG, Cranwell – 3x40mm, 12 AAMG),* 113 Bty *(Rugby - 14AAMG, Bramcote - 4 AAMG),* 149 Bty *(Stamford: Wittering – 6x40mm, Corby),* 300 Bty *(Peterborough)*
- 41 S/L Regt *(Wilford) (36+2169):* 362 Bty *(Brigstock),* 363 Bty *(Melton Mowbray),* 364 Bty *(Yaxley),* 365 Bty *(Oakham),* 125 Bty *(Rugby)*
- 44 S/L Regt *(Spalding) (43+2312):* 374 Bty *(Kings Lynn),* 375 Bty *(Boston),* 376 Bty *(Sleaford),* 377 Bty *(Spalding)*

39th AA Brigade *(HQ: Kirton in Lindsay)*
- 62 HAA Regt *(Hull) (34+925):* 172 Bty *(Hull - 4x4.5-inch)* + 198 Bty *(Hull - 6x4.5-inch)* (attached from 67 HAA Regt)
- 67 HAA Regt *(Rotherham) (34+1019):* 187 Bty *(Rotherham - 8x4.5-inch),* 189 Bty *(Immingham – 4x4.5-inch),* 173 Bty *(Sheffield)* (attached from 62 HAA Regt; non operational - training)
- 91 HAA Regt *(Ulceby) (30+1229):* 286 Bty *(Barton on Humber - 4x4.5in);* 270 Bty (non operational – training)
- 26 LAA Regt *(Sheffield) (31+838):* 114 Bty *(Doncaster),* 115 Bty *(Derby - 3-inch),* 116 Bty *(Rotherham, Chesterfield)* (Regt had a mobile role)
- 39 LAA Regt *(Bishop Norton) (32+933):* 109 Bty *(Doncaster),* 110 Bty *(Scunthorpe, North Coates – 2x40mm),* 111 Bty *(Grimsby, Cleethorpes - 16AAMG, Scampton - 12 AAMG)*
- 2 AA Regt RM *(Derby) (HQ-2+25):* D HAA Bty RM *(Mexborough) (8x3.7-inch)* (Battery to Derby 27 September)
- 30 S/L Regt *(Gainsborough) (39+1995):* 315 Bty *(Gainsborough),* 316 Bty *(Hatfield),* 318 Bty *(Gainsborough),* 323 Bty *(Rotherham)*
- 40 S/L Regt *(Hull) (40+2297):* 358 Bty *(Scawby),* 359 Bty *(Hull),* 360 Bty *(Skirlaugh),* 361 Bty *(Patringham)*

40th AA Brigade *(HQ: Sawston)*
- 78 HAA Regt *(Stradishall) (41+1704):* 243 Bty *(Watton, Feltwell, Marham and Duxford - 8x3-inch),* 245 Bty *(Thrapston and Leighton Buzzard - 4x3.7-inch)*
- 30 LAA Regt *(Newmarket) (28+933):* 117 Bty *(Duxford, Bassingbourn, Cranfield and Henlow – 4x40mm, 48AAMG),* 118 Bty *(Wyton, Upwood and Stradishall - 2x3-inch, 40 AAMG),* 120 Bty

(Honington, Mildenhall, Feltwell and Marham - 2x40mm, 2x3in, 40 AAMG)
- 52 LAA Regt *(Worksop)*: 154 Bty *(Elsham)*, 155 Bty *(Reepham)* (Regt deployed in infantry role along River Trent)
- 36 S/L Regt *(Newmarket) (40+1748)*: 317 Bty *(Newmarket)*, 345 Bty *(Ely)*, 346 Bty *(Royston)*, 424 Bty *(Mildenhall) (20 searchlights each)*
- 64 S/L Regt *(Whatlington) (39+1546)*: 441 Bty *(Wisbech)*, 442 Bty *(Ramsey)*, 443 Bty *(Thrapston) (20 searchlights each)*
- 72 S/L Regt *(Lingfield) (36+1373)*: 465 Bty *(St Neots)*, 467 Bty *(Northampton)*; 466 Bty (non operational) *(24 searchlights each)* (Regt moved from 6 Division, 17 September)
- 31 LAA Bty *(Wereham) (28+775) (12x40mm)* (part of 11 LAA Regt) *(GHQ Mobile role)*
- 131 Z Bty *(Brigstock)*
- 132 Z Bty *(Ely) (4+16)*
- 133 Z Bty *(Thrapston) (4+15)*

41st AA Brigade *(HQ: Coltishall)*
- 29 LAA Regt *(Weasenham, Norfolk) (31+726)*: 108 Bty *(Fakenham: Honington - 2x40mm, West Raynham – 2x3-inch, 16AAMG, Bircham Newton - 2x40mm, 12AAMG, West Bencham - 4x40mm, 4AAMG)*, 121 Bty *(Norwich: Coltishall - 16AAMG, Horsham St Faith - 2x3in, 16AAMG, Watton - 16AAMG)*, 126 Bty *(Collingham: Waddington, Scampton, Digby and Newark - 2x40mm, 40AAMG)* (Bty attached from 39 LAA Regt on 25 September)
- 60 S/L Regt *(Thetford) (40+1333)*: 429 Bty *(Thetford)*, 430 Bty *(East Harling)*, 431 Bty *(Narborough)*
- 65 S/L Regt *(Aylsham) (33+1725)*: 444 Bty *(Aylsham)*, 445 Bty *(Guist)*, 446 Bty *(South Raynham)*
- 69 S/L Regt *(Brundall, Norfolk) (33+1641)*: 456 Bty *(Brubdall)*, 457 Bty *(Cavick)*, 458 Bty *(Raveningham)*

50th AA Brigade *(HQ: Digby)*
- 68 HAA Regt *(Derby) (24+1765)*: 200 Bty *(Derby - 5x3.7-inch mobile)*, 276 Bty *(Nottingham - 8x3.7-inch)*, 277 Bty *(Nottingham - 8x3.7-inch)* + C Bty RM *(284) (Derby - 8x3.7-inch)*, 5 Bty *(Derby - 6x3.7-inch mobile)*, 18 Bty *(Bixley - 9x3.7-inch mobile)*, 409 HAA Bty *(Derby - 8x3.7-inch)*
- 28 LAA Regt *(Thornbury) (43+1517)*: 53 Bty *(Nottingham)*, 106 Bty *(Spilsby: Binbrook, Stenigot, Manby)*, 112 Bty *(Lowdham, Derby, Beeston)*, 115 Bty *(Derby)*
- 42 S/L Regt *(Newark) (38+1804)*: 366 Bty *(Louth)*, 367 Bty *(Woodhall Spa)*, 368 Bty *(Alford)*, 369 Bty *(Market Rasen)*
- 50 S/L Regt *(Oakham) (31+1675)*: 400 Bty *(Newark)*, 401 Bty *(Arnold)*, 402 Bty *(Nottingham)*, 403 Bty *(Derby)* plus 352 Bty *(Tuxford - 38 searchlights)*
- 58 S/L Regt *(Louth) (33+1375)*: 344 Bty *(Loughborough)*, 425 Bty *(Rugby)*, 426 Bty *(Louth)*

- 109 HAA Regt *(Weybourne, Norfolk) (25+269)*: 342 Bty and 343 Bty (Regt formed 26 September, 344 Bty at Aberporth, South Wales, for training)

- 2 AA `Z` Regt: 119 Bty *(Chilwell) (10+192)*, 120 Bty *(Derby) (10+138)*, 121 Bty *(Immingham) (12+174)* (Formed Derby 3 September)

Divisional support troops: 904 Coy *(Oundle)*, 926 Coy *(Scunthorpe)*, 929 Coy RASC *(Thetford)*.

3rd AA Division: (HQ: *Edinburgh (HQ: 53+768)*) (GOC: Major General H Martin)

24 July: HAA= 40/Forth, 24/Clyde, 4/Aberdeen, 7/NI, 12/Shetlands, 88/Scapa, 39/ Vital Points (214); 105 LAA; 312 S/L

25 September: HAA= 40/Forth, 38/Clyde, 4/Aberdeen, 12/NI, 12/Shetlands, 88/Scapa, 33/ Vital Points (226); 115 LAA; 412 S/L

36th AA Brigade *(HQ: Edinburgh)*
- 71 HAA Regt *(Dunfirmline) (30+1059)*: 227 Bty *(Inverkeithing)*, 229 Bty *(Dunfirmline)*, 325 Bty *(Winchburgh) (24x4.5-inch guns)*
- 94 HAA Regt *(Edinburgh) (28+748)*: 228 Bty *(Edinburgh)*, 291 Bty *(Dalmeny)*, 292 Bty *(Kyle of Lochalsh) (16x3.7-inch and 4x3-inch guns)*
- 108 HAA Regt *(Strathnaver, Nairn) (16+257)*: 338 Bty *(Aberdeen - 4x3.7-inch)*, 339 Bty *(Wick, Lossiemouth, Kinloss and Castletown - 8x3-inch)* (Regt formed 25 August; Replaced 101 HAA Regt 16 September)

42nd AA Brigade *(HQ: Glasgow)*
- 83 HAA Regt *(Winchburgh, West Lothian) (33+865)*: 257 Bty *(Kilcreggan)*, 258 Bty *(Bishopton and Aberdeen)*, 259 Bty *(Gourock) (8x4.5-inch and 6x3.7-inch guns)*
- 100 HAA Regt *(Hamilton) (31+959)*: 304 Bty *(Uddingston)*, 305 Bty *(Burrow Head)*, 321 Bty *(Paisley) (16x4.5-inch and 8x3.7-inch guns)*
- 316 HAA Bty *(Irvine and Stevenston) (8x3.7-inch guns)* (Detached from 102 HAA Regt)

51st AA Brigade *(HQ: Edinburgh)*
- 14 LAA Regt *(Baillieston) (33+575)*: 40 Bty *(Kinloss, Kilmarnock, Fort William, Lossiemouth)*, 57 Bty *(Kilmarnock, Kyle of Lochalsh) (8x40mm guns)*
- 18 LAA Regt *(Glasgow) (27+598)*: 56 Bty *(Johnstone, Greenock)*, 139 Bty *(Dumbarton) (10x40mm guns)*
- 19 LAA Regt *(Edinburgh) (29+872)*: 54 Bty *(Crombie)*, 60 Bty *(Stevenston)*, 104 Bty *(Dumfries) (3x40mm guns (54 Bty), rest AAMG`s)*
- 31 LAA Regt *(Perth) (30+871)*: 61 Bty *(Rosyth)*, 100 Bty *(Dundee, Montrose)*, 101 Bty *(St Andrews, Leuchars) (3x40mm (101 Bty) and 5x3-inch)*
- 32 LAA Regt *(Stirling) (31+822)*: 55 Bty *(Turnhouse)*, 98 Bty *(Haddington, Drem)*, 103 Bty *(Grangemouth) (7x40mm and 9x3-inch guns)*
- 40 LAA Regt *(Inverness) (29+889)*: 105 Bty *(Dingwall)*, 140 Bty *(Wick)*, 177 Bty *(Dyce, Aberdeen) (17x40mm guns)*

52nd AA Brigade *(HQ: Newbridge, Edinburgh)*
- 51 S/L Regt *(St Andrews) (33+1551)*: 319 Bty *(Dunearn)*, 320 Bty *(Auchtermuchty)* and 404 Bty *(St Andrews)*
- 52 S/L Regt *(Edinburgh) (33+1404)*: 405 Bty *(Haddington)*, 406 Bty *(Dreghorn Barracks, Edinburgh)* and 407 Bty *(Dalkeith)*
- 56 S/L Regt *(Stirling) (30+1421)*: 417 *(Dundee)*, 418 *(Dollar)* and 419 *(Balloch)* Btys
- 57 S/L Regt *(Polmont) (47+2040)*: 420 *(Kilmacolm)*, 421 *(Polmont)*, 422 *(Lenzie)* and 423 Btys

Northern Ireland Defences *(HQ: Belfast)*
- 102 HAA Regt *(Belfast) (34+865)*: 314 Bty *(Holywood)*, 315 Bty *(Belfast) (16x3.7-inch guns)*

- 175 LAA Bty *(Belfast) (10+220)*
- 176 LAA Bty *(Belfast) (8+213)*

Orkney and Shetland Defences
24 July: HAA = 88/Scapa, 12/Shetlands; 48/LAA
25 September: HAA = 88/Scapa, 12/Shetlands; 48/LAA; 108 SL

58th AA Brigade *(HQ: Kirkwall)*
- 70 HAA Regt *(Kirkwall) (35+905)*: 212, 216, 309 Btys *(16x3.7-inch, 12x4.5-inch)* (In process of changing places with 65 HAA Regt and moving to 4th AA Division)
- 65 HAA Regt: 181 Bty (arrived 17 September)
- 39 S/L Regt *(Stromness) (39+1692)*: 355, 356 and 357 Btys *(80 searchlights)* (Regt arrived 10 September)
- 178 HAA Bty *(Stromness: Herston, Burray, Kirkwall, Holm) (10+256) (8x3.7-inch)* (Left for Tyne, 25 September)
- 180 HAA Bty *(Flotta) (7+253) (8x4.5-inch)* (Detached from 64 HAA Regt)
- 266 HAA Bty *(Lyness: Kirkwall and Holm) (10+230) (8x3-inch)* (Replaced 178 Bty by moving from other Orkney sites on 25 September. In early October it also took over the sites of 216 Bty, 70 HAA Regt)
- 39 LAA Bty *(Shetlands) (11+236) (4x40mm guns)* (Detached from 14 LAA Regt)

59th AA Brigade *(HQ: Hoy)*
- 64 HAA Regt *(South Ronaldsway) (34+509)*: 174, 179 and 180 Btys *(32x3.7-inch)* (To 7th AA Division early October)
- 81 HAA Regt *(Longhope) (27+998)*: 253, 254, 255 Btys (Moved from 7th AA Division 16 - 21 September)
- 101 HAA Regt *(Lerwick, Shetlands) (21+914)*: 297 Bty *(Sumburgh - 4x3-inch)*, 317 Bty *(Sullom – 4x3-inch), Lerwick – 4x3-inch)* (from Inverness on 20 September)
- 38 S/L Regt *(Kirkwall) (31+1684)*: 350 Bty *(Longhope)*, 351, 352 and 353 *(North Hoy and Flotta)* Btys (Moved to Orkneys 6 September)
- 226 HAA Bty *(Lyness)* (Arrived 21 September)
- 99 LAA Bty *(Flotta) (11+236) (6x12-pounder)* (Detached from 14 LAA Regt)
- 142 LAA Bty *(Hoy) (10+203) (6x12-pounder)* (Detached from 22 LAA Regt)

- 3 AA `Z` Regt: 103 Bty *(Longniddry) (10+209)*, 107 Bty *(Halheath) (8+216)*, 115 Bty *(Longniddry) (9+210)*, 118 Bty *(Catterick) (9+215)* (Formed 3 September)
- 2 AA `Z` Training Regt *(Dunfirmline)*: 134 Bty *(4+32)*, 135 Bty *(4+22)* (Formed September)

Divisional support troops: 192 Coy *(Edinburgh) (10+297)*, 908 Coy *(Stromness) (8+393)*, 909 Coy RASC *(Bellahouston) (9+284)*.

4th AA Division: (HQ: *Chester*) (GOC: Major General C Cadell)

24 July: HAA = 52/Liverpool, 20/Manchester, 69/Birmingham, 32/Coventry, 14/Crewe, 15/ Vital Points (192); 50/LAA; 319 S/L

25 September: HAA = 60/Liverpool, 20/Manchester, 64/Birmingham, 24/Coventry, 8/Crewe, 8/Barrow, 15/ Vital Points (199); 77/LAA; 354 S/L

33rd AA Brigade *(HQ: Gatacre, Liverpool)*
- 93 HAA Regt *(Birkenhead) (38+1320)*: 288 Bty *(Liverpool - 8x3.7-inch)*, 289 Bty *(Wirral - 8x4.5-inch)*, 290 Bty *(Warrington - 8x3.7-inch)* and 267 Bty *(Birkenhead - 5x4.5-inch)*
- 103 HAA Regt *(Gatacre) (28+882)*: 322 Bty *(Kirkby, West Derby - 4x3.7-inch and 4x3.7-inch mobile)*, 323 Bty *(Penketh - 4x4.5-inch and 4x3.7-inch mobile)*, 327 Bty *(Bootle - 2x3.7-inch mobile)* (Attached from 105 HAA Regt 9 September), 324 Bty *(non operational - training)*
- 25 LAA Regt *(Birkenhead) (27+445)*: 82 Bty *(Birkenhead - 2x3-inch, 2x4-inch, 1x40mm, 8AAMG)*, 225 Bty *(Docks – 2x3-inch, 3x40mm, 16AAMG)* (mobile role)
- 33 LAA Regt *(Liverpool) (32+930)*: 67 Bty *(Speke, Hawarden)*, 68 Bty *(Ellesmere Port)*, 132 Bty *(Prescot, Speke)*
- 61 S/L Regt *(Liverpool) (41+1020)*: 432 Bty *(Maghull, Wirral)*, 433 Bty *(Crewe, St Helens)* and 434 Bty *(Warrington, Widnes)* (Left Orkneys 9-14 September)

34th AA Brigade *(HQ: Sutton Coldfield)*
- 60 HAA Regt *(Sutton Coldfield) (31+770)*: 168 Bty *(Waynesfield (E) - 3x3.7-inch, Walmley - 4x3.7-inch mobile)*, 169 Bty *(Minworth - 4x3.7-inch, Shard End (H65) - 4x3.7-inch)*, 194 Bty *(Parkhall - 4x3.7-inh, Warmley Ash (H54) – 4x3.7-inch)*, 409 Bty *(Erdington (L) - 4x3.7-inch, Stoke Cross (F) - 4x3.7-inch)*
- 69 HAA Regt **(Birmingham) (37+1655)*: 190 Bty *(Wolverhampton - 8x3.7-inch)*, 191 Bty *(Olton (O) – 4x3.7-inch, Tipton - 4x3.7-inch)*, 192 Bty *(Perry Bar (K) - 4x4.5-inch, Castle Bromwich (H61) - 2x4.5-inch, Handsworth – 2x4.5-inch)*, 199 Bty *(Dudley and Turner`s Hill (G) - 4x4.5-inch, Kings Heath - 2x4.5-inch, Harborne - 2x4.5-inch)*
- 95 HAA Regt *(Coventry) (32+708)*: 204 Bty *(Bedworth (A) and Walmley - 8x3.7-inch)*, 293 Bty *(Binley (C.) and Ryton (D) - 8x3.7-inch)*, 340 Bty *(Tipton and Bushbury from 23 September - 8x3.7-inch)*, 21 Bty *(Bubben Hall (E) and Gibbet Hill (F) - 4x3.7-inch)* (Moved from Orkneys 15-21 September)
- 107 HAA Regt *(Birmingham) (16+679)* - 334, 335, 337 Btys (not operational; 337 Bty detached to Towyn, North Wales, for training. Formed 11 September and to Brigade 25 September. Regt moved to Liverpool in October)
- 22 LAA Regt *(Meridien) (52+1009)*: 70 Bty *(Castle Bromwich - 12x40mm (8 mobile), 12 AAMG)*, 72 Bty *(Stourport – 12 AAMG, Redditch - 4x40mm, Leamington - 8 AAMG)*, 141 Bty *(Longford - 4x40mm, Hams Hall - 4x40mm)*
- 45 LAA Regt *(Albrighton) (27+470)*: 54 Bty *(High Ercall)*, 102 Bty *(Wolverhampton - 4x40mm, Tern Hill – 4x2in, Shawbury - 4x2-inch)*, 135 Bty *(Cosford - 4x2-inch, Donnington - 16 AAMG, Ironbridge - 8 AAMG, Stafford – 8 AAMG)*, 81 Bty *(Wolverhampton)* (attached from 25 LAA Regt until 27 September)

44th AA Brigade *(HQ: Manchester)*
- 65 HAA Regt *(Manchester) (41+1486)*: 182 Bty *(Belle Vue and Wilmslow - 4x3.7-inch)*, 183 Bty *(Charlton and Failsworth – 8x4.5-inch)* and 196 Bty *(Eccles and Pendleton - 8x4.5-inch)* (In process of changing places with 70 HAA Regt in 3rd AA Division)

- 70 HAA Regt *(Manchester)*: 211 Bty *(Crewe and Leighton)* (In process of moving from 3rd AA Division from 16 September)
- 106 HAA Regt *(Manchester) (24+714)*: 331 Bty *(Barrow - 4x3.7-inch)* (Forming from 15 September)
- 21 LAA Regt *(Preston) (33+1028)*: 69 Bty *(Preston and Accrington - 2x3-inch, 18 AAMG)*, 80 Bty *(Leyland, Blackburn, Chorley - 3x3-inch, 28 AAMG)* and 136 Bty *(Barrow - 30 AAMG)*
- 41 LAA Regt *(Carlisle) (35+1328)*: 133 Bty *(Barrow - 2x3-inch, 33 AAMG)*, 134 Bty *(Workington and Maryport - 2x2-pounder, 41 AAMG)*, 143 Bty *(Longtown - 40 AAMG)*
- 54 LAA Regt *(Altrincham) (21+863)*: 160 Bty *(Woodford)*, 161 Bty *(Ringway)*, 162 Bty *(Winnington)*

53rd AA Brigade *(HQ: Middleton)*
- 62 S/L Regt *(Manchester) (32+921)*: 435 Bty *(Preston)*, 436 Bty *(Lytham)*, 437 Bty *(Chorley)* (Regt arrived 10 September)
- 71 S/L Regt *(Failsworth) (37+1442)*: 462 Bty *(Little Moor)*, 463 Bty *(Tandlehill)*, 464 Bty *(Medlock Vale)*
- 78 S/L Regt *(Manchester) (24+1159)*: 498, 499 and 500 Btys (Regt formed 20 August; Btys split among other regts for training)
- 487 S/L Bty *(Ringway) (6+384)*

54th AA Brigade *(HQ: Sutton Coldfield)*
- 45 S/L Regt *(Birmingham) (35+1819)*: 378 Bty *(Sheldon)*, 379 Bty *(Halesowen)*, 380 Bty *(Shirley)*, 381 Bty *(Shenstone)*
- 59 S/L Regt *(Coventry) (31+1466)*: 399, 427 and 428 Btys *(61 searchlights)*
- 486 S/L Bty *(Whitchurch) (7+406)*
- 491 S/L Bty *(Coventry) (7+402)*

- 4 AA `Z` Regt: 104 Bty *(Exeter) (7+215)*, 108 Bty *(Barrow) (5+200)*, 116 Bty *(Exeter) (7+188)*, 122 Bty *(Salford) (11+190)* (Formed 3 September)
- 3 AA `Z` Training Regt: 132 Bty, 133 Bty (Formed September)

Divisional support troops: 912 Coy *(Tamworth) (7+307)*, 913 Coy RASC *(Liverpool) (17+387)*.

5th AA Division: (HQ: *Portsmouth (83+1211)*) (GOC: Major General R Allen)

24 July:	HAA = 44/Portsmouth, 39/Southampton, 34/Plymouth, 32/Bristol, 16/Cardiff, 14/Portland, 12/Falmouth, 12/Newport, 12/Swansea, 96/ Vital Points (311); 131/LAA; 840 S/L
25 September:	HAA = 40/Portsmouth, 32/Bristol, 32/Southampton, 30/Cardiff, 24/Plymouth, 24/Swansea, 22/Newport, 16/Portland, 8/Falmouth, 101/ Vital Points (329); 151/LAA; 914 S/L

3rd AA Brigade *(HQ: Cheltenham)* (Southern Command Mobile Role) (Moved to Belfast mid October)
- 88 HAA Regt (Allocated from 5 Brigade)
- 57 LAA Regt (Allocated from 35 Brigade)

5th AA Brigade *(HQ: Cheltenham)*
- 85 HAA Regt * *(Gloucester) (28+868)*: 175 Bty *(Painswick - 8x3.7-inch)* (Rest of Regt was detached to 45 AA Brigade); 231 Bty *(Gloucester) (8x3.7-inch)* (Attached)
- 88 HAA Regt *(Shurdington) (35+956)*: 281 Bty, 282 Bty *(Gloucester) (16x3.7-inch)* (Regt had GHQ Mobile role)
- 35 LAA Regt *(Oxford) (40+761)*: 70 Bty *(Reading - 3x3-inch)*, 89 Bty *(Upper Heyford, Brize Norton, Thorney Island – 32 AAMG)*, 144 Bty *(Abingdon and Ashton Keynes - 16 AAMG, Wroughton and Lyneham - 2x2-pounder)*
- 47 LAA Regt *(Stroud) (27+712)*: 66 Bty *(Hereford - 3x40mm, 20 AAMG)*, 85 Bty *(Kemble; Hullavington – 7 AAMG, Colerne - 2x3-inch, 4AAMG)*, 131 Bty *(Brockworth - 7x40mm, Churchtown - 5x40mm, Aston Down – 4 AAMG, Kemble - 4 AAMG)* (Regt formed 22 August)
- 37 S/L Regt *(Tewkesbury) (45+1927)*: 307 Bty *(Standish)*, 308 Bty *(Hanley Swan)*, 348 Bty *(Stanton)*
- 68 S/L Regt *(Bathford) (32+1460)*: 453 Bty *(North Nibley)*, 454 Bty *(Trowbridge)*, 455 Bty *(Botley)*
- 90 LAA Bty *(Brize Norton, Wroughton)* (Detached from 35 LAA Regt)

35th AA Brigade *(HQ: Fareham)*
- 57 HAA Regt *(Southsea) (38+1381)*: 213 Bty *(Nettlestone (IW 6) and Whippingham (IW 13) - 8x3.7-inch)*, 214 Bty *(Gosport - 8x4.5-inch)*, 215 Bty *(Southsea (P1) - 8x4.5-in)*, 219 Bty *(Morelands (P11) and Hayling Island (P5) – 8x3.7-inch)*
- 72 HAA Regt *(Hythe) (29+1097)*: 217 Bty *(Haxland (S15) and Nursling (S23) - 8x3.7-inch)*, 218 Bty *(Marchwood (S8) and Beaulieu (S7) - 8x4.5-inch)*, 310 Bty *(Hounsdown (S9) and Nursling (S23) - 6x3.7-inch)*
- 80 HAA Regt *(Burlesdon) (36+818)*: 249 Bty *(Bramley - 8x3.7-inch)*, 250 Bty *(Forts Nelson (P12) and Southwick (P21) – 8x3.7-inch)*, 251 Bty *(Bassett - 8x3.7-inch)*, 252 Bty *(Weston (S10) and Stoneham (S17) - 8x3.7-inch)* (Regt HQ, 250 and 251 Btys had mobile role within 5th Brigade, 6th AA Division)
- 15 LAA Regt *(Stubbington) (20+370)*: 42 Bty *(Swanick - 2x40mm, 6xAAMG)*, 129 Bty *(Haslar – 2x40mm, 6xAAMG)*
- 24 LAA Regt *(Southampton) (36+818)*: 71 Bty *(Southampton - 5x40mm)*, 86 Bty *(Southsea, Calshot – 6x3-inch)*, 87 Bty *(Ventnor, Bembridge, Yarmouth - 5x3-inch, 3x40mm)*, 88 Bty *(Hamble - 4x40mm)*
- 53 LAA Regt *(Portsmouth)*: 158 Bty *(HM Docks - 9x40mm)*
- 57 LAA Regt *(Botley) (29+705)*: 169 Bty *(Burlesdon - 12x40mm)*, 171 Bty *(Eastleigh - 8x40mm)* (Had GHQ mobile role)
- 1 AA Regt RM *(Fort Cumberland, Portsmouth)*: RHQ *(Langstone Harbour - 2x2-inch)*, 22 LAA Bty *(Hayling Island; RNAS Yeovilton, RNAS Ford, RNAS Lee on Solent, RNAS St Merryn, RNAS Worthy Down - 14 AAMG) (138)* (Bty also manned AA paddle steamers at Sheerness (2) and Harwich (1) - 1+29, each ship had 2x2-pounder, 6x20mm and 12 quadruple AAMG`s)
- 11 S/L Regt RM *(Alverstoke) (430)*: R Bty RM *(Gosport; Shanklin, Bembridge, Ryde, East Cowes, Fort Fareham, Portchester, Hillhead, Hook, Lee on Solent)* (22 searchlights)
- 48 S/L Regt *(Botley) (43+2217)*: 391 Bty *(Westbourne)*, 392 Bty *(Newport)*, 393 Bty *(Botley)*, 394 Bty *(Lyndhurst) (each had 12 searchlights)*
- 22 HAA Bty *(Southampton) (4x3.7-inch)* (Detached from 8 HAA Regt)
- 31 HAA Bty *(Arborfield) (245)* (Forming)

45th AA Brigade *(HQ: Cardiff)*
- 77 HAA Regt *(Cardiff) (41+1183)*: 239 Bty *(Barry - 8x3.7-inch)*, 240 Bty *(Newport - 8x3.7-inch, 2x3-inch)*, 241 Bty *(Rumney- 4x3.7-inch, Cardiff - 2x3-inch)*, 242 Bty *(Llandough - 4x3.7-inch, Lavernock - 6x3.7-inch, Llandaff – 2x3.7-inch)*

- 79 HAA Regt *(Swansea) (29+933):* 246 Bty *(Pembrey - 4x3.7-inch, Neath (N2) - 4x3.7-inch)*, 247 Bty *(Swansea – 8x3.7-inch, Morriston (N1) - 4x3.7-inch)*, 248 Bty *(Skelty ((N6) - 4x3-inch)*
- 85 HAA Regt *(-)*: 174 Bty *(Pembroke - 4x3.7-inch)*, 220 Bty *(Newport - 4x3.7-inch)*,
- 88 HAA Regt *(-)*: 220 Bty *(Newport - 4x3.7-inch)*, 283 Bty *(Newport - 4x3.7-inch, Nash - 8x3.7-inch)*
- 20 LAA Regt *(Cardiff) (40+622)*: 62 Bty *(Glascoed - 10 AAMG)*, 63 Bty *(St Athan - 4 AAMG, Pontypridd – 6 AAMG, Barry - 1x3-inch)*, 94 Bty *(Newport Docks - 2x3-inch, 14 AAMG)*
- 34 LAA Regt *(Newport) (37+824)*: 64 Bty *(Swansea Docks - 16 AAMG, Pembrey - 2x40mm, 12 AAMG)*, 65 Bty *(Llandarcy - 3x3-inch, 12 AAMG, Clydach - 8AAMG)*, 92 Bty *(Llandow – 14 AAMG, Bridgend - 16 AAMG)*
- 67 S/L Regt *(Cardiff) (33+1414)*: 450 Bty *(Castleton - 24 lights)*, 451 Bty *(Usk - 18 lights)*, 452 Bty *(Lydney – 15 Searchlights)*
- 77 S/L Regt *(Kilgetty) (33+1517)*: 495 Bty *(Carmarthen)*, 496 Bty *(Pembroke Dock)*, 497 Bty *(Haverfordwest)*
- 1 S/L Regt *(Swansea) (38+1434)*: 1Bty *(Swansea)*, 2 Bty *(Port Talbot)*, 7 Bty *(Carmarthen)*, 8 Bty *(Bridgend)* (Regt had an infantry role as it had no equipment)

46th AA Brigade *(HQ: Bristol)*
- 76 HAA Regt *(Bristol) (30+994)*: 236 Bty *(Avonmouth - 4x3.7-inch)*, 238 Bty *(Ashton Park - 4x3-inch, Avonmouth – 4x3-inch)*
- 23 LAA Regt *(Iron Acton) (42+902)*: 73 Bty *(Yeovil - 2x40mm)*, 74 Bty *(Portishead - 8 AAMG, Yate – 4x40mm)*, 130 Bty *(Corsham - 8 AAMG)*
- 66 S/L Regt *(Weston Super Mare) (31+1328)*: 447 Bty *(Rickford)*, 448 Bty *(Clevedon)*, 449 Bty *(Wedmore)*, 494 Bty *(Avonmouth and Hanham)*

47th AA Brigade *(HQ: Middle Wallop)*
- 46 LAA Regt *(Frimley) (31+729):* 76 Bty *(Poling - 3x40mm, Tangmere - 6x40mm)*, 137 Bty *(Farnborough – 4x40mm, Reading - 11 AAMG, Brooklands - 4x40mm, Weybridge - 8 AAMG)*
- 3 S/L Regt *(Kingsworthy) (45+1736)*: 9 Bty *(Bulford)*, 10 Bty *(Winchester)*, 11 Bty *(Alderbury)*, 12 Bty *(Basingstoke)*
- 63 S/L Regt *(Fernhurst) (32+1460)*: 438 Bty *(Farnham)*, 439 Bty *(Blackwater)*, 440 Bty *(Fernhurst)*, 490 Bty *(Southampton)*
- 70 S/L Regt *(Broadbridge Heath, Horsham) (31+1808)*: 459 Bty *(Horsham)*, 460 Bty *(Leatherhead)*, 461 Bty *(Storrington)*
- 78 LAA Bty *(Bramley) (3x3-inch)* (Detached from 35 LAA Regt)
- S S/L Bty RM *(Andover) (6+321) (22 searchlights)* (Attached 21 September, to Plymouth on 9 October)

55th AA Brigade *(HQ: Exeter)*
- 56 HAA Regt *(Plymouth) (41+2140)*: 165 Bty *(Seaton Barracks (4) - 8x3.7-inch)*, 201*(Down Thomas (2) – 4x3.7-inch static)*, 202 Bty *(Billacombe (6) - 4x3.7-inch, Yeovil - 4x3.7-inch)*, 203 Bty *(Maker Barracks (9) - 8x3.7-inch mobile)*
- 104 HAA Regt *(Bude) (25+751)*: 329 Bty *(Weymouth - 8x3.7-inch)*, 336 Bty *(Portland - 2x3-inch)* (Forming 15 September)
- 44 LAA Regt *(Weymouth) (30+877)*: 75 Bty *(Portland – 6 AAMG, Weymouth - 1x3-inch)*, 77 Bty *(Holton Heath – 4x40mm, Weymouth - 1x3in)*, and 91 Bty *(Plymouth - 4x3-inch)*, Troop 72 Bty (attached from 23 LAA Regt) *(Yeovil - 4x40mm)*

- 58 LAA Regt *(-) *(Camborne) (23+398)*: 172, 173, 174 Btys *(Scilly Isles - 2x40mm, rest in infantry role)*
- 3 HAA Bty *(Falmouth) (8x3-inch)* (Detached from 6 HAA Regt)
- 41 LAA Bty *(Stubbington) (8+176)* *(Worth Matravers - 3x40mm, Warmwell - 4x40mm, Christchurch – 4x40mm)* (Detached from 15 LAA Regt)
- 170 LAA Bty *(Plymouth - 4x40mm, Falmouth - 4x40mm, Exeter - 2x40mm, Porthcurno - 1x40mm)* (Detached from 57 LAA Regt)
- 2 S/L Regt *(Cranborne) (36+1491)*: 4 Bty *(Marston Magna)*, 5 Bty *(Wareham)*, 6 Bty *(Blandford)* and 475 Bty *(Ringwood) (24 searchlights per battery)*
- 76 S/L Regt *(Tisbury) (34+1530)*: 474 Bty *(Truro)*, 482 Bty *(Plymouth)*, 483 Bty *(Weymouth)*, 484 Bty *(Plymouth)*, 485 Bty *(Shaftesbury)*, 492 Bty *(Tisbury)*, 493 Bty *(Dorchester)*, 494 Bty
- 349 S/L Bty *(Market Lavington)* (detached from 37 S/L Regt 24 September)

- 5 AA `Z` Regt: 102 Bty *(Truro) (5+217)*, 114 Bty *(HM Docks) (8+217)* (arrived 24 September - 24 rockets), 123 Bty *(Bristol) (6+202)*. (Regt formed 3 September)
- 8 AA `Z` Regt: 111 Bty *(Cardiff) (5+214)*, 113 Bty *(Cardiff) (8+215)*, 124 Bty *(Cardiff) (10+139)*, 125 Bty *(Cardiff) (8+186)* (Regt formed Cardiff 2 September)
- 4 AA `Z` Training Regt (Formed September)

Divisional support troops: 914 Coy *(Penarth) (6+190)*, 915 Coy *(Keynsham) (8+255)*, 916 Coy *(Wickham) (7+255)*, 917 Coy RASC *(Charminster) (5+184)*.

6th AA Division: (HQ: *Sidcup (46+416)*) (GOC: Major General F Hyland)

24 July: HAA= 71/Medway, 48/Thames, 16/Dover, 15/Harwich, 33/airfields, 30/ Vital Points (213); 84/LAA; 568 S/L

25 September: HAA= 72/Medway, 48/Thames, 12/Dover, 8/Harwich, 45/airfields, 29/ Vital Points (214); 115/LAA; 670 S/L

2nd AA Brigade *(Pembury)* (XII Corps mobile role)
- 80 HAA Regt - 250 and 251 Btys *(Portsmouth - 16x3.7-inch)* (see 27th Brigade, 5th AA Division)
- 235 HAA Bty (89 HAA Regt) *(All Hallows - 8x3.7-inch)* (see 28th Brigade, 6th AA Division)
- 284 HAA Bty (89 HAA Regt) *(Littlehampton - 8x3-inch)* (see 37th Brigade, 6th AA Division)
- 31 LAA Bty (11 LAA Regt) *(Gillingham - 12x40mm)* (see 56th Brigade, 6th AA Division)

6th AA Brigade *(Debden)*
- 32 S/L Regt *(Woodbridge) (38+1279)*: 328 Bty *(Hadleigh)*, 329 Bty *(Woodbridge)*, 330 Bty *(Saxmundham)* and 562 Bty
- 33 S/L Regt *(Yeldham) (37+1255)*: 332 Bty *(Castle Headingham, Sudbury)*, 333 Bty *(Bishops Stortford)*, 34 Bty *(Debden)*
- 49 LAA Regt *(Debden) (12+364)*: 84 Bty, 90 Bty, 119 Bty (In process of forming)
- 285 HAA Bty *(Wattisham, North Weald, Belmont Castle) (8x3-inch, 4x3.7-inch)* (detached from 90 HAA Regt)
- 119 LAA Bty *(Debden, Wattisham, Dorsham) (4x40mm)* (detached from 49 LAA Regt)
- Troop 36 LAA Bty *(Debden) (4x40mm)* (detached from 11 LAA Regt)

27th AA Brigade *(HQ: Lingfield)*
- 12 LAA Regt *(Hildenborough) (36+1121):* 34 Bty *(West Malling, Crayford) (5x40mm)*, 35 Bty *(Hawkinge, Bekesbourne) (4x40mm)*, 152 Bty *(Seal; Gravesend - 4x40mm)* (attached from 51 LAA Regt)
- 43 LAA Regt *(Tonbridge) (24+864):* 147 Bty *(Pevensey and Rye RDF) (6x40mm)*, 148 Bty *(Kenley and Biggin Hill) (2x3-inch, 3x40mm)*
- 31 S/L Regt *(Plumpton, Lewes) (44+1738):* 324 Bty *(Forest Row, Heathfield, Mark Cross, Tillinghurst, Withyham, Colgate, Ardingley, East Grinstead, Crowborough, Mayfield, Hartfield)*, 325 Bty *(Lewes (Offham, Keymer, Chailey, Firle), Ringmer, Poynings, Brighton (Kemp Town), Peacehaven, Telscombe, Shoreham)*, 326 Bty *(Herstmanceux, Lower Dicker (Deanland), Hellingly, Hankham, Jevington, Rushlake, Boreham Street, Seaford Head, Pevensey)*, 327 Bty *(Bletchingley, Dorking, Charlwood, Caterham, Biggin Hill, Redhill, Rowfant, Edenbridge, Oxted) (on invasion RHQ to move to Forest Row. Regt linked to RAF Kenley)*
- 34 S/L Regt *(Staplehurst) (39+1760):* 302 Bty *(Hastings (St Helens)), Etchingham, Robertsbridge, Bodiam, Sandhurst, Flimwell, Ticehusrt, Whatlington, Mountfield, Brightling, Penhurst, Crowhurst, St Leonards, Ore, Westfield, Guestling, Winchelsea, Fairlight, Hollington, Staple Cross, Rolvenden, Four Oaks)*, 336 Bty *(Staplehurst, Marden, Sissinghurst, Egerton, Great Chart)*, 337 Bty *(Sevenoaks, Wrotham, Basted, Orpington Weald, Ightham, Nettlestead)*, 338 Bty *(Woodchurch, Warehorne, Tiffenden, Aldington, Wittersham, Hythe, Lydd, Honeychild Manor (New Romney), Dymchurch, Littlestone, Greatstone, Dungeness)*, 465 Bty *(Hildenborough, Brenchley, Bells Yew Green)* (from 72 S/L Regt) *(Regt linked to RAF Biggin Hill)*

28th AA Brigade *(HQ: Fort Luton, Chatham)*
- 53 HAA Regt *(Gillingham) (25+1160):* 157 Bty *(Biggin Hill - 8x3-inch)*, 158 Bty *(Rainham (TS4), Twydall (TS5) – 8x3.7-inch)*, 159 Bty *(Grain (TS11), All Hallows (TS12) - 8x3.7-inch)*
- 55 HAA Regt *(Strood) (48+1501):* 163 Bty *(Strood - Tower Hill (TS8) / Fenn Street (TS10) - 8x3.7-inch)*, 166 Bty *(Fort Borstal (TS7), Oak Street, Rochester (TS9) - 8x4.5-inch)*, 307 Bty *(Burham (TS24), Gibraltar Farm (TS6) –8x4.5- inch)*, 308 Bty *(Bell Farm (TS21) and Lower Hope (TS14) - 8x3-inch)*
- 58 HAA Regt *(Northfleet) (34+905):* 206 Bty *(Cobham (TS15) and Denton (TS16) - 8x4.5-inch)*, 207 Bty *(Iwade (TS2) and Wetham Green (TS3) - 8x4.5-inch)*, 208 Bty *(Sutton at Hone (TS19), Green Street Green (TS18) – 8x3.7-inch)*, 264 Bty *(Biggin Hill, West Malling - 6x3-inch)*
- 16 LAA Regt *(Gillingham) (38+1417):* 45 Bty *(Chattenden, Lodge Hill) (3x3-inch)*, 46 Bty *(Grain) (4x40mm, 1x3-inch)*, 83 Bty *(Detling, Maidstone, Rochester) (10x40mm)*, Troop 153 Bty *(Eastchurch) (2x40mm)*
- 55 LAA Regt *(Bobbing) (21+744):* 163 Bty *(Croydon - 2x40mm, Hawkinge - 4x40mm)*, 164 Bty *(Shotley)*, 165 Bty *(Redhill - 3x40mm, Hartlip - 3x40mm, Chatham - 2x40mm, Sheerness - 4x40mm)*
- 29 S/L Regt *(Faversham) (30+1335):* 313 Bty *(Gillingham, Hollingbourne, Sittingbourne, Minster)*, 314 Bty *(Molash, Sheldwich, Canterbury, Lyminge)*, 342 Bty *(Wingham, Birchington, Littlebourne) (9+437)*, 347 Bty *(Higham, Hoo, Lower Stoke, Bluebell Hill) (from 73 S/L Regt)*, 460 S/L Bty *(Chobham)*
- 451 LAA Troop *(Isle of Grain) (1x2-pounder)*

- **Dover:**
- 75 HAA Regt *(Dover) (22+823):* 223 Bty *(Langdon (D2) - 4x3.7-inch)*, 233 Bty *(Citadel (D7), Guston) – 8x3.7-inch)*, 272 Bty *(Coolinge (D14) - 2x3-inch, Minster, Thanet - 2x3-inch)*
- A HAA Bty RM *(Capel):* Hope Farm (D11), Arpinge Farm (D16), Hawkinge (D12)) *(238) (6x3- inch)*

- 138 LAA Bty (*Dover Castle and Radar Station*) *(12x40mm)* (detached from 16 LAA Regt)
- 468 S/L Bty (*Kearsney, Dover, Guston, Archcliffe Fort*)

29th AA Brigade *(HQ: Boxted)*
- 28 HAA Regt *(Brentwood):* 310 Bty *(Manningtree),* 311 Bty *(Danbury),* 312 Bty *(Benfleet),* 335 Bty *(Marks Tey),* 466 Bty *(Braintree) (32x3.7-inch)*
- 99 HAA Regt *(Felixstowe) (33+876):* 318 Bty *(Felixstowe - 8x3.7- inch),* 302 Bty *(Ipswich, Martlesham - 8x3-inch)*
- 48 LAA Regt *(Boxted) (33+873):* 49 Bty *(Manningtree - AAMG),* 95 Bty *(Harwich, Martlesham, Bawdsey – 1x3inch, 2x3-inch, 4x40mm and 3x40mm respectively)* (59 Bty to Aldershot 9 September to prepare for overseas move)
- 28 S/L Regt *(Brentwood) (29+1300):* 309 Bty *(Romford),* 311 Bty *(Danbury, Maldon),* 312 Bty *(South Benfleet, Shoeburyness),* 331 Bty *(Laindon, Ockenden, Grays, Stanford le Hope)*
- 74 S/L Regt *(Wakes Colne) (26+1293):* 310 Bty *(Manningtree),* 335 Bty *(Stanway, Peldon, Earls Colne),* 469 Bty *(Felixstowe)*
- 488 S/L Bty *(Bury St Edmunds) (7+372)*
- Troop 285 LAA Bty *(North Weald) (4x3 in)* (detached from 90 LAA Regt)

37th AA Brigade *(HQ: Stanford Le Hope)*
- 59 HAA Regt *(Benfleet) (24+753):* 164 Bty *(Hadleigh (TN9), Vange (TN10) - 4x4.5-inch, 4x3-inch),* 167 Bty *(Furtherwick (TN7), Northwick (TN8) - 8x4.5-inch),* 265 Bty *(Buckland (TN13), Orsett (TN14) - 8x4.5-inch)*
- 61 HAA Regt *(Orsett) (30+993):* 170 Bty *(Dagenham (TN20), Rainham - 8x4.5-inch),* 195 Bty *(Chadwell (TN15), Ockenden (TN17) - 4x4.5-inch and 4x3.7-inch)*
- 90 HAA Regt *(South Benfleet) (38+839):* 284 Bty *(Thorpe Bay (TN1), Rochford - 8x3-inch)*
- 17 LAA Regt *(Stanford le Hope) (34+895):* 50 Bty *(Rainham, Purfleet - 6x3-inch),* 96 Bty *(Canewdon, Canvey – 3x40mm, 2x3-inch),* 146 Bty *(Thames barges, Thameshaven, Coryton -1x40mm, 4x3-inch and 3x3-inch respectively)*

56th AA Brigade *(HQ: Barking)*
- 11 LAA Regt *(South Weald) (28+775):* 31 Bty *(Gravesend, Kenley, Tangmere - 12x40mm),* 32 Bty *(North Weald, Martlesham -10x40mm),* 33 Bty *(Hornchurch, Rochford – 3 and 2x40mm respectively)*
- 51 LAA Regt *(Romford):* 153 Bty *(Hornchurch)*

- 89 HAA Regt *(Sittingbourne) (33+753)* - 205 Bty *(Cooling, Decoy Farm, Isle of Grain),* 235 Bty *(Sutton at Hone, Whitehall Farm)* (Non-operational as preparing for an overseas move to North Africa on 15 September)

- 6 AA `Z` Regt: 101 Bty *(Ascot) (6+204),* 112 Bty *(Brentwood) (8+181),* 126 Bty *(Blackdown) (14+65)* (Formed September)
- 5 AA `Z` Training Regt (Formed September)

Divisional support troops: 919 Coy *(Mountnessing) (12+448),* 921 Coy *(Ditton) (10+370).*

7th AA Div: (HQ: *Newcastle (HQ: 58+948)*) (GOC: Major General R Pargitter)

24 July: HAA= 54/Tyne, 30/Tees, 20/Leeds, 14/airfields, 21/ Vital Points (139); 29/LAA; 557 S/L

25 September: HAA= 50/Tyne, 30/Tees, 20/Leeds, 14/airfields, 18/ Vital Points (132); 37/LAA; 595 S/L

12th AA Brigade *(HQ: Tadcaster)* (Northern Command Mobile Role)
- 177 HAA Bty *(4x3.7-inch)* (Allocated from 63 HAA Regt)
- 221 HAA Bty *(8x3.7-inch)* (Allocated from 4 HAA Regt - in London!)

30th AA Brigade *(HQ: Newcastle)*
- 63 HAA Regt *(Newcastle) (41+945):* 176 Bty *(Wallsend)*, 269 Bty *(Benton)*, 177 Bty *(Gosforth) (16x4.5-inch, 8x3.7-inch mobile)*
- 66 HAA Regt *(Washington) (42+879):* 185 Bty *(Whitburn)*, 197 Bty *(Sunderland)*, 209 Bty *(South Shields)*, 296 Bty *(Washington) (24x4.5-inch, 8x3.7-inch)*
- 46 S/L Regt *(Newcastle) (38+1820):* 382 Bty *(Durham)*, 383 Bty *(Morpeth)*, 384 Bty *(Rowlands Gill)*, 385 Bty *(Newcastle) (Btys had 24 searchlights each)*.

31st AA Brigade *(HQ: Church Fenton)*
- 96 HAA Regt *(Leeds) (46+1601):* 186 Bty, 287 Bty and 294 Bty *(Leeds)*, 295 Bty *(Driffield) (32x3.7-inch)*
- 43 S/L Regt *(Huddersfield) (39+1907):* 370 Bty *(Otley – 20 searchlights)*, 371 Bty *(Huddersfield – 12 searchlights)*, 372 Bty *(Methley, Church Fenton - 22 searchlights)*, 373 Bty *(Snaith – 16 searchlights)*
- 49 S/L Regt *(Selby) (43+2075):* 395 Bty *(Naburn, York)*, 396 Bty *(Snaith, Brough)*, 397 Bty *(Barton on Humber, Driffield)*, 398 Bty *(Brayton, Selby)*
- 54 S/L Regt *(Darlington) (34+1385):* 411 Bty *(Malton)*, 412 Bty *(Easingwold, Boroughbridge)*, 413 Bty *(Filey, Bridlington) (24 searchlights each)*
- 126 LAA Bty *(Rotherham) (10+324)* (Detached from 3 LAA Regt)

43rd AA Brigade *(HQ: West Hartlepool)*
- 87 HAA Regt *(Middlesborough) (32+975):* 278 Bty *(Middlesborough - 4x4.5-inch)*, 279 Bty *(West Hartlepool – 8x4.5-inch)*, 280 Bty *(Middlesborough - 6x3-inch)*
- 73 HAA Regt *(Norton on Tees) (33+776):* 210 Bty *(Ormesby - 4x3.7-inch)*, 311 Bty *(Stockton - 4x3.7-inch, 4x3-inch)*
- 47 S/L Regt *(Catterick) (41+1936):* 386 Bty *(Ripon)*, 387 Bty *(Thirsk)*, 388 Bty *(Catterick)*, 389 Bty *(Stokesley) (Btys had 24 searchlights each)*
- 53 S/L Regt *(Durham) (33+1365):* 408 Bty *(Durham)*, 409 Bty *(Darlington)*, 410 Bty *(Sedgefield)*
- 55 S/L Regt *(Guisborough) (35+1301):* 414 Bty *(Whitby)*, 415 Bty *(Guisborough)*, 416 Bty *(Pickering)*

57th AA Brigade *(HQ: Gosforth)*
- 13 LAA Regt *(Newcastle) (33+781):* 37 Bty *(Wallsend) (AAMG)*, 38 Bty *(South Shields) (2 Pounder)*, 122 Bty *(South Shields) (2 Pounder)*, 151 Bty *(Hebburn) (Hispano)*
- 37 LAA Regt *(Throckley) (44+811):* 52 Bty *(Heddon)*, 123 Bty *(Morsden)*, 127 Bty *(Durham)*
- 38 LAA Regt *(Thornbury) (36+805):* 51 Bty *(Mirfield)*, 124 Bty *(Harrogate)*, 125 Bty *(Bradford):* Leconfield – 2x3-inch, Brough - 4x40mm, Saxton Wold - 3x40mm)

- 50 LAA Regt *(Lanchester)* *(9+555)*: 58 Bty *(Lanchester)*, 93 Bty *(Burnhope)*, 178 Bty *(Lanchester)* plus 23 Bty RM *(138)* *(HQ: Seaham; A Tp: Seaham - 4x40mm; B Tp: Skinningrove - 3x3-inch, C Tp: Danby Beacon - 3x40mm, D Tp: Blyth - 2x2-pounder)* (Bty attached 14 September, to Middlesborough 27 September) (Regt preparing for overseas operations in early September; no guns)
- 56 LAA Regt *(Elton, Northumbria)* *(25+600)*: 166 Bty *(Elton: Billingham - 4x40mm)*, 167 Bty *(Norton: Redcar – 5x3-inch)*, 168 Bty *(Great Ayton: Cleveland - 2x3-inch)*
- 7 AA `Z` Regt: 106 Bty *(Marske)* *(5+211)*, 109 Bty *(Blackhill)* *(7+203)*, 110 Bty *(Catterick)* *(9+209)*, 117 Bty *(Marske)* *(10+214)*, 146 Bty *(Birtley)* *(4+25)*, 147 Bty *(Sedgefield)* *(1+28)*, 148 Bty *(Brayton)* *(3+12)* (Formed September)

Divisional support troops: 907 Coy *(Middleton)* *(8+195)*, 923 Coy *(Hexham)* *(8+257)*, 930 Coy *(Pontefract)* *(7+175)*, 920 Coy *(London)* *(5+247)*.

Training - AA:
- 2 LAA Training Regt *(Deepcut)* *(47+2225)*
- 7 Training Regt *(Oswestry)* *(31+1352)*
- 24 HAA Training Regt *(Blackdown)* *(29+1523)*
- 41 S/L Training Regt *(Carlisle)* *(35+1328)*
- 205 Training Regt *(Arborfield)* *(59+1300)*
- 206 Training Regt *(Arborfield)* *(41+1341)*
- 207 Training Regt *(Devizes)* *(58+1417)*
- 208 Training Regt *(Yeovil)* *(61+1524)*
- 209 Training Regt *(Blandford)* *(64+1706)*
- 210 Training Regt *(Oswestry)* *(67+1579)*
- 211 Training Regt *(Oswestry)* *(65+1612)*
- 212 Training Regt *(Chester)* *(59+1321)*
- 213 Training Regt *(Carlisle)* *(56+1382)*

Training - Searchlight:
- 216 Training Regt *(Abergele)* *(35+2379)*
- 217 Training Regt *(Hereford)* *(62+3394)*
- 220 Training Regt *(Yeovil)* *(66+2365)*
- 222 Training Regt *(Taunton)* *(56+2536)*
- 230 Training Regt *(Blandford)* (Forming at end of September)
- 231 Training Regt *(Blandford)* (Forming at end of September)
- 232 Training Regt *(Devizes)* (Forming at end of September)
- 234 Training Regt *(Carlisle)* (Forming at end of September)
- 235 Training Regt *(Ayr)* (Forming at end of September)
- 236 Training Regt *(Shrewsbury)* (Forming at end of September)
- 237 Training Regt *(Hollywood)* (Forming at end of September)

RDF (Radar) Stations in South and South East:
- North Foreland (north of Ramsgate) (CHH): Detachment of B Company 6 Buffs (15)
- Dunkirk (west of Canterbury) (CHL): Detachment from 50 Buffs (2+46)
- Dover (Swingate, north east of the Castle) (CHH): Detachment of A Company 6 Buffs (2+65)
- Rye (south east of Rye) (CHL): Detachment of 2/8 Sussex (2+68); Troop 147 LAA Battery (43 LAA Regt) (59) *(3x40mm)*
- Fairlight (On cliffs west of the village) (CHH): B Company 11 Sussex
- Pevensey (CHL): C Company 11 Sussex, Troop 147 LAA Battery (43 LAA Regt) *(3x40mm)*
- Beachy Head (CHH): B Company 70 Sussex
- Poling (north of Littlehampton) (CHL): Troop 76 LAA Bty (43 LAA Regt) *(3x40mm)*; Detachment from 2/8 Sussex (1+49)
- Ventnor (Isle of Wight) (CHH): Detachment of 1 RWK; troop 87 LAA Bty (24 LAA Regt) *(3x40mm)*

RAF personnel were provided by 60th (Signals) Group, formed on 23 March 1940 with its headquarters at Leighton Buzzard. Each radar station had an establishment of one officer and between 45 and 59 other ranks.

Airfield defence:
- In August the Inspector General of Fortifications, Major General Taylor, established a pattern of ground defences for RAF bases. All airfields were classified into one of three categories depending on likeliness of attack - A, B or C (most to least). Those in the south east were classified as follows:
    A: Eastchurch, Detling, West Malling, Manston, Hawkinge, Lympne, Tangmere, Thorney Island, Gosport, Middle Wallop, Gravesend, Rochester, Shoreham, Southend, Hornchurch, Biggin Hill plus Naval Air Stations Ford and Lee on Solent
    B: Debden, Kenley, Northolt, North Weald, Croydon, Gatwick
- The RAF had 244 operational airfields - 172 permanent, 47 satellite and 25 relief landing grounds. Another 122 were in the process of being built
- Category A airfields had 4 main internal pillboxes no more than half a mile apart, sunken pillbox near the centre and dummy installations; external pillboxes to make maximum use of buildings; covered rifle pits near hangers and station buildings. In all, between 20-30 real pillboxes and 3 Picket Hamilton sunken "forts"
- Category B airfields had between 15-24 real pillboxes
- Category C airfields had between 10-16 real pillboxes
- In March 1940 the Air Ministry authorised up to two platoons of the National Defence Corps per airfield for guard duties, though these were not trained or equipped for the role. Airfield defence began properly in May 1940, but the implementation was often left to the station commander's initiative until late August when there was a change in emphasis from airfield function to location in denoting the allocation of resources. Garrisons were allocated according to category - 274 men for category A, 225 for category B and 191 for category C, these mostly being found from newy formed home defence infantry battalions. The 274 men for category A were allocated as follows: 48 to inner pillboxes, 64 for outer pillboxes, 6 in Picket Hamilton forts, 48 in rifle pits, 12 to crew armoured vehicles, 36 for

AA defence and the remaining 60 in reserve. It was calculated that this new role would require 791 officers and 28,000 men.

Defence of a selection of important airfields:
Manston: 306 HAA Battery (*Chalkhole (N site)*, *Cleve Court (W site)*) (*8x3-inch and 5x40mm*); D Company 1/6 Border, 5 Independent Company. (RAF Station personnel = 150+3409 plus 7+420 WAAF) (Manston was regarded as the most strongly defended airfield in Britain)
Hawkinge: a troop 35 LAA Battery (12 LAA Regt) *(4x40mm)*; a troop A HAA Battery RM *(2x3inch)*; A Company 70 Buffs (Reinden Wood), 655 General Construction Company, RAF Defence Detachment (4+154) (RAF Station personnel = 102+1191 plus 202 WAAF)

Lympne: C Troop 163 LAA Battery (55 LAA Regt) (4x40mm); a platoon 17 Coy, 5 Stevedore Bn RE (30 men); (RAF Station personnel = 70+970 plus 3+90 WAAF, including a Care and Maintenance Party of 9+230 present)

Rochester: RAF Defence (14 lmg, 4 mmg, 4 A/T rifles); E Company 8 East Surrey
Eastchurch: a troop 153 LAA Battery (16 LAA Regt) *(2x40mm)*; A Company 8 East Surrey, A Company 2/6 Queens. (RAF Station personnel = 118+1890 plus 16+294 WAAF)
Detling: a troop 147 LAA Battery *(4x40mm)* (43 LAA Regt); a company Royal West Kent ITC; 268 A/T Battery (67 A/T Regt) *(infantry role until 27 September)*. (RAF Station personnel = 41+1465 plus 281 WAAF)
Gravesend: a troop 31 LAA Battery (11 LAA Regt) *(4x40mm)*; D Company 70 Royal West Kent (RAF Station personnel = 42+1268 plus 6+212 WAAF)
West Malling: (100 rifles, 18 lmg, 4 A/T rilfes); a troop 264 HAA Battery (58 HAA Regt) *(2x3-inch)*, a troop 34 LAA Battery *(2x40mm)*; A Company 70 Royal West Kent; a company 8 Royal West Kent. (RAF Station personnel = 68+1344)

Kenley: a troop 31 LAA Battery (11 LAA Regt) *(4x40mm)*, F Troop 152 LAA Battery (51 LAA Regt) *(2x3-inch)*, a platoon 2/8 Middlesex (MG), a company Scots Guards Holding Bn, a platoon 706 General Construction Company RE (RAF Station personnel = 142+480 plus 125 WAAF. RAF ground defence had 20 lmg and 1x20mm Hispano gun)
Biggin Hill: B and D Companies 7 Dorsets; 235 HAA Battery *(8x3-inch)* (from 89 HAA Regt 14 September, replaced by 157 Bty /53 HAA Regt 28 September), a troop 34 LAA Battery *(4x40mm)* (from 12 LAA Regt) (RAF Station personnel = 162+2231 plus 14+731 WAAF)
Croydon: 148 LAA Bty RA *(AAMG)*, C Troop 163 LAA Bty *(2x40mm)*; E Company 12 Queens, a MG platoon 2/8 Middlesex, 327 Company RE, a platoon 706 General Construction Coy RE (RAF Station personnel = 83+576 plus 5+210 WAAF)

Northolt: a company Coldstream Guards Training Bn, a platoon 10 Middlesex, 2 MG platoons 2/8 Middlesex *(8MMG, 3 armoured vehicles)* (RAF Station personnel = 145+1608 plus 14+509 WAAF)
Hendon: a detachment 7 KRRC, a MG platoon 2/8 Middlesex *(4MMG, 3 armoured vehicles)* (RAF Station personnel = 80+1157 plus 15+409 WAAF)

Hornchurch: a detachment 7 Essex; troop 32 LAA Battery *(3x40mm)*
Rochford: a troop 33 LAA Battery *(3x40mm)*

Debden: a troop 31 LAA Battery (11 LAA Regt) *(4x40mm)*, a troop 119 LAA Battery (49 LAA Regt) *(2x40mm)*

North Weald: a troop 141 HAA Bty (61 HAA Regt) *(4x3.7-inch)*, a troop 285 LAA Bty *(4x3-inch)*, a troop 32 LAA Bty (11 LAA Regt) *(6x40mm)*; a detachment 7 Essex, 253 A/T Bty *(infantry role)*

Wittering: 149 LAA Battery (27 LAA Regt) *(6x40mm)*; 2 DCLI

Ford: a troop 22 LAA Bty RM (aa*lmg*); (RAF Station personnel = 227+2315 plus 299 WAAF) *(2 armoured lorries present)*

Tangmere: a troop 31 LAA Battery (11 LAA Regt) *(4x40mm)*, 399 Troop, 76 LAA Battery *(2x40mm)*; a troop 300 HAA Battery *(4x3.7-inch)*; B Company 6 Sussex *(2+78)*; RAF ground defence unit *(4+200) (16 Lewis MG, 4 Hispano cannon)*; a section 3 Airfield Maintenance Coy RE (RAF Station personnel = 225+3404 plus 17+748 WAAF)

Middle Wallop: (RAF Station personnel = 93+1840 plus 17+282 WAAF)

Westhampnett: (RAF Station personnel = 91+1271 plus 51 WAAF)

Odiham: (RAF Station personnel = 193+1615 plus 7+65 WAAF)

Eastleigh: a troop 490 Searchlight Battery RA *(2+80)*; 137 Aircraft Maintenance Company RE. (RN FAA Station personnel = 48+691) *(8 armoured lorries)*

Lee on Solent: a troop 32 Field Regt RA *(4x12-pounder)*; a troop 22 LAA Bty RM (aa*lmg*); a section R Searchlight Bty RM (RN FAA Station personnel = 227+4502) *(1 armoured lorry)*.

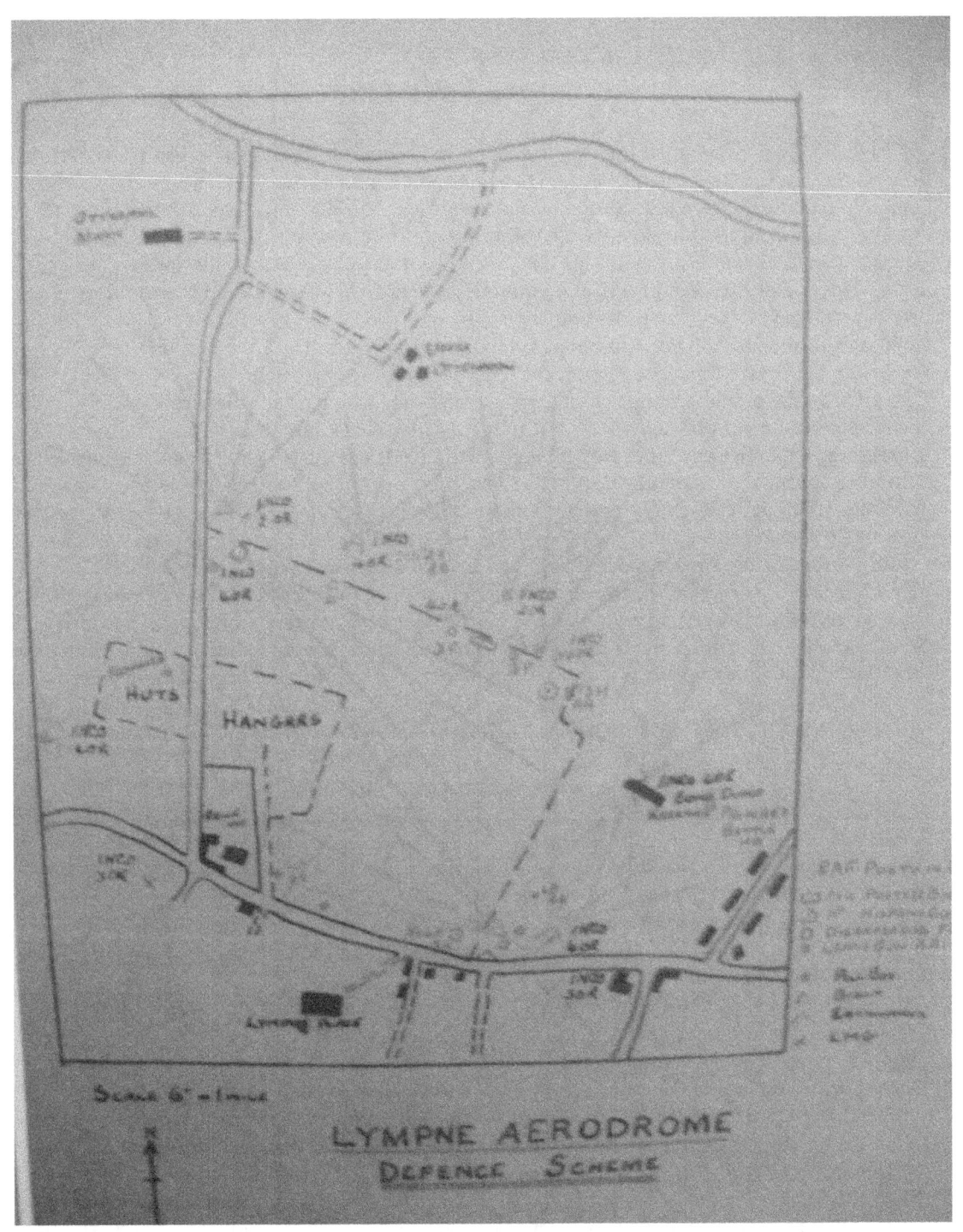

Example of an airfield defence scheme

Appendix 4

COASTAL ARTILLERY

- It took the War Office until mid 1932 to start modernising its coastal artillery structure, due mainly to the uncertainty of the Disarmament Talks of the time and the basis of the country's home defence planning moving towards air power and away from conventional artillery. Even as the blitzkrieg was unfolding on the Continent the Army's General Staff did not consider sea or air landings on a serious scale to be possible and made no special plans. After Dunkirk the practice of defending ports only was changed to providing a continuous defensive "crust" around the coast
- In May there were 130 guns in place, including 28 covering the Humber estuary, 18 defending Harwich and 29 covering the Thames and Medway estuaries
- On 19 May the establishment of emergency batteries was agreed, their role mainly to deny seaborne landings at or near ports without existing fixed coastal defences. There were 6 categories depending on importance: A covering Kent, B covering the East coast up to the Humber estuary, C covering the North East, D covering the South while E and F covered the rest. Although the Navy agreed to man 22 batteries initially the Army needed to find nearly 2900 men, these mostly coming from the Anti Aircraft Command's searchlight training regiments and supported by a cadre from existing coastal defence units
- By 12 June 46 emergency batteries had been installed, each comprising two naval guns and two searchlights. They had orders not to initially engage targets more than four miles away, about half of their maximum range. These batteries were usually well camouflaged and responsible for their own defence (only about half of a battery's personnel were required to man the guns). In addition a number of dummy installations were built. By 10 August 9020 officers and men from the Royal Artillery were assigned to these emergency batteries
- Railway guns operational by September: 1 x 14-inch (Dover), 2x12-inch (Folkestone), 2 x 12-inch (Harwich), 4x9.2-inch (East Kent), 2 x 9.2-inch (Boston) (Category A); guns available without crews: 4 x 12-inch, 4 x 6-inch (North Thames) (Category B). However, those on the South Coast could only reach halfway across the Channel while the 14-inch gun was unsuitable for engaging moving targets
- By September the following coastal guns were in place: 1x18-inch, 2x14-inch, 2x13.5-inch, 6x12-inch, 40x9.2-inch, 225x6-inch, 16x5.5-inch, 33x4.7-inch, 6x4.5-inch, 73x4-inch, 51x12-pounder, 22x6-pounder
- By October the Royal Navy had provided 143 x 6-inch, 30 x 4.7-inch, 245 x 4.5-inch, 48 x 12-pounder, 24 x 3-pounder guns
- The Army and Royal Marines also provided mobile batteries of small guns ranging from 4-inch down to 3-pounder mounted on lorries, which were to rush to the invasion sites
- 50 blockships were in place at important harbours along the south and eastern coasts; anti boat booms were also placed across the Humber, Thames and Medway estuaries as well as at Plymouth and Rosyth
- 100 miles of open beach were protected by horizontal anti boat wire nets laid at sea; another 80 miles of beach were protected by wire nets with mines attached and 70 miles of coast were protected by lines of scaffolding erected below high water mark with mines attached. The Wash had a minefield and light boom 5 miles long.

South East:

Thames: *(Total of 2x9.2-inch, 8x6-inch, 4x5.5-inch, 2x4-inch, 5x12-pounder, 2x6-pounder)*
- 517th Coast Regt *(14+275)*: (HQ: *Canvey*); A Bty *(Canvey) (2x6-inch, 2x6-pounder twin)*; 332 Coast Bty *(Foulness) (2x6-inch mark XII) (3+94) (established May)*; 417 Bty *(Southend) (2x9.2-inch)*; 419 Coast Bty *(Shoeburyness) (2x6-inch)*, 356 Coast Bty *(Coalhouse Fort) (2x5.5-inch) (2+91) (established June)*
- 516th Coast Regt: 357 Bty *(Shornmead) (2+79) (2x5.5-inch, 2x12-pounder) (established June)*; Cliffe Fort *(2x4-inch, 3x12-pounder)* plus 6 torpedo tubes and electric minefield *(Holehaven)*

Isle of Sheppey: *(Total of 4x9.2-inch, 5x6-inch, 4x12-pounder, 2x6-pounder)*
- 516th Coast Regt: (HQ: *Grain*) *(28+567)*; A Bty *(Grain) (2x6-inch)*, *(Martello) (2x2-pounder)*; B Bty *(Whitehall, Grain) (2x6-inch)*; C Bty *(Garrison Point, Sheerness) (3x6-inch, 4x6-pounder twin, 2x12-pounder)*; D Bty *(Albermarle Bty, Garrison Point) (4x12-pounder)* plus 6 torpedo tubes and electric minefield *(Garrison Point)*
- 518th Coast Regt *(9+208)*: (HQ: *Minster*); A Bty *(Fletcher Bty, Warden) (2x9.2-inch)*; 334 Bty *(Shellness) (2x6-inch mark VII) (3+93) (established May)*

Thanet: *(Total of 1x12-inch, 8x6-inch, 4x5.5-inch, 6x4-inch, 2x12-pounder)*
HQ 11th Coast Artillery Group
Herne Bay - 333 Coast Bty *(2x6-inch mark VII) (2+116) (established May)*
Margate - 335 Coast Bty *(2x6-inch mark VII) (3+124) (established May)*
Broadstairs - 410 Coast Bty *(2x4-inch) (3+83) (formed 24 September)*
Ramsgate - 336 Coast Bty *(2x6-inch mark XI) (3+131) (established May with RM personnel, this Bty replaced them on 4 September)*, 297 Coast Bty *(Ramsgate Pier) (2x12-pounder) (established April)*, 413 Coast Bty *(Pegwell Bay) (2x4-inch) (3+83) (formed 24 September)*
The Downs - 337 Coast Bty *(Deal and Sandown Castles) (1+81) (2x6-inch mark XII) (established May)*

37 Super Heavy Battery available with 2x12-inch railway guns against targets around Deal, 5 Super Heavy Battery available with 2x12-inch railway guns against targets around St Margarets Bay.

Dover: *(Total of 1x18-inch, 2x14-inch, 2x13.5-inch, 2x12-inch, 2x9.2-inch, 6x6-inch, 2x4-inch, 2x12-pounder, 3x6-pounder)*
Fire Command Post - Castle *(3+18)*
- 519th Coast Regt *(41+551)*: 159 Bty: Langdon Bty *(2x6-inch) (5+126)*, South Breakwater Bty (West) *(2x6-inch, 1x6-pounder twin) (3+86)*; 168 Bty: Citadel Bty *(2x9.2-inch) (5+140)*, Eastern Arm Bty *(2x6-pounder twin) (3+71)*; 170 Bty: Admiralty Pier Turret Bty *(2x6-inch) (3+86)*, Admiralty Pier Extension Bty *(2x12-pounder) (3+57)*; Knuckle Bty *(Eastern Breakwater) (2x4-inch) (established July)*
- RM Siege Regt *(280)*: A Bty *(1x14-inch railway gun "Winnie") (St Margarets at Cliffe)*, B Bty *(1x13.5-inch railway gun "Sceneshifter") (Guston, Martin Mill)* *(This two battery Regt was formed on 9 September, A Bty operational by 7 August. The Regt also had a defence company. Alternative firing positions established at Ashford and Canterbury)*
Plus: 3x21-inch torpedo tubes *(Eastern Arm)* and 16 searchlights (5 at both entrances and 2 per 6 inch Bty)

4, 5, 37 and Y Heavy Batteries available with 4x12-inch and 1x9.2-inch railway guns against targets around in and around Dover.

Folkestone - 338 Coast Bty (*2x6-inch mark XI*) (*Folkestone East - Copt Bay*) (*2+79*) (established May with RM personnel, Bty replaced them on 18 July), 339 Coast Bty (*2x6-inch mark XI*) (*Folkestone West - East Cliff*) (*3+107*) (established May with RM personnel, this Bty replaced them on 18 July)

Plus:
- A blockship was sunk at right angle to the end of the harbour arm. Mines were laid from its stern to Copt Point, controlled by the Royal Navy Observation Point on Martello Tower at Copt Point.
- Four searchlights (two per 6-inch Bty)

37 and X Super Heavy Batteries available with 2x1-2inch and 2x9.2-inch railway guns against targets around Folkestone

Romney Marsh: (*Total of 3x9.2-inch, 8x6-inch, 2x4.7-inch*)
HQ 13th Coast Artillery Group
Hythe - 340 Coast Bty (*2x6-inch mark XII*) (*3+116*) (established May, Battery replaced RN detachment in mid July)
Dymchurch (Redoubt) - 358 Coast Bty (*2x6-inch mark XII*) (*3+75*) (established June)
Dungeness (Lade, south of Greatstone) - 374 Coast Bty (*2x4.7-inch*) (*3+83*) (established July)

4, 37 and X Super Heavy Batteries available with 2x12-inch and 4x9.2-inch railway guns against targets in area.

South Coast: (*Total of 15x9.2-inch, 45x6-inch, 4x4.7-inch, 6x4.5-inch, 8x4-inch, 9x12-pounder, 3x6-pounder*)
HQ 14th Coast Artillery Group
Winchelsea Beach - 360 Coast Bty (*2x6-inch mark VII*) (*3+81*) (established June)
Hastings - 341 Coast Bty (*2x6-inch mark XI*) (*3+86*) (established in May at the Old Town with personnel from 220 Searchlight Training Regt)
Bexhill - 385 Coast Bty (*2x4-inch*) (established July on East Parade)
Norman's Bay, Pevensey - 375 Coast Bty (*2x4.7-inch*) (*3+66*) (established July)
Eastbourne - 342 Coast Bty (*2x6-inch mark XI*) (*3+83*) (established May at the Wish Tower with personnel from 220 Searchlight Training Regt)
Seaford - 343 Coast Bty (*2x6-inch mark XI*) (*3+89*) (established at East Blatchington in May, Battery replaced RN detachment in mid July)
Newhaven - HQ 521st Coast Regt (*9+377*): A Bty (*2x6-inch, 2x12-pounder*) (Regt was responsible for administering the emergency batteries from Hastings to Littlehampton)
Plus: Blockship ready on east side of harbour mouth with another inside the harbour. Sea mines were prepared to be laid either side of these ships when sunk in place.
Brighton - 359 Coast Bty (*2x6-inch mark XI*) (*3+80*) (established at Kemp Town in June)
Shoreham - 344 Coast Bty (*2x6-inch mark XI*) (*3+125*) (established May)
Worthing - 345 Coast Bty (*2x6-inch mark XI*) (*3+118*) (established May)
Littlehampton - 346 Coast Bty (*2x6-inch mark XI*) (*3+119*) (established May)

Portsmouth:
HQ, fixed defences;
-528th Coast Regt *(HQ: HorseSand Fort) (10+250)*: A Bty *(Horsesand Fort) (2x6-inch) (2+48)*,
B Bty *(No Man's Land Fort) (2x6-inch)*
-529th Coast Regt *(Portsmouth) (17+276)*: A Bty *(Spithead) (2x4.7-inch)*, B Bty *(Southsea)*, C Bty *(Southsea Castle) (2x9.2-inch, 2x6-inch)*, *(Point Bty) (3x12-pounder)*, *(Fort Blockhouse) (2x12-pounder)*; 204 Bty *(2+48)*; 165 Bty *(Calshot) (2x12-pounder)*
Plus: HMS Marshal Soult (former monitor and now gunnery training ship) and a coaling hulk prepared as blockships

Isle of Wight:
-527th Coast Regt *(Sandown) (15+466)*: A Bty *(Culver Down) (2x9.2-inch)*, B Bty *(Nodes Point, South East Ryde) (2x9.2-inch, 2x6-inch)*; Yaverland Fort *(2x6-inch)*; Sandown Fort *(3x6-pounder)*; Puckpool Bty *(Ryde) (2x9.2-inch, 2x6-inch)*; Culver Cliff Bty *(2x12-pounder)*
-Isle of Wight Heavy Regt *(Freshwater) (20+402)*: A Bty *(Needles) (2x9.2-inch)*, B Bty *(Freshwater)*, C Bty *(Cliff End) (2x6-inch, 2x4.7-inch)*, *(Fort Albert) (2x12-pounder)*, D Bty *(Hurst Castle) (3x12-pounder)*; 210 Bty *(Bouldnor) (2x6-inch)*
- 202 Coast Bty *(Yarmouth) (2x6-inch) (2+107)*
- 417 Coast Bty *(Stone Point) (3x6-inch)*

Poole - 347 Coast Bty *(2x6-inch mark XII) (3+92)* (established May)
Swanage - 386 Coast Bty *(4x4-inch)* (established July)
Portland – 522nd Coast Regt *(22+549)*: A Bty *(East Weare) (2x9.2-inch, 2x6-inch)*; B Bty *(Blacknor) (2x6-inch)*; C Bty *(Breakwater) (2x6-inch)*, D Bty *(Nothe Fort) (2x6-inch)*, E Bty *(Pier Head) (2x12-pounder)*, F Bty *(New Breakwater) (2x12-pounder)*, Upton Bty *(Osmington) (2x9.2-inch)*

East Coast: *(Total of 1x12-inch, 2x9.2-inch, 47x6-inch, 6x4.7-inch, 2x4-inch, 2x6-pounder)*
East Mersea - 372 Coast Bty *(2x4.7-inch) (2+78)* (established July)
West Mersea - 373 Coast Bty *(2x4.7-inch) (2+76)* (established July)
Clacton - 331 Coast Bty *(2x6-inch mark XII) (3+121)* (established May)
Frinton - 330 Coast Bty *(2x6-inch mark XII) (2+121)* (established May)
Harwich - HQ 515th Coast Regt *(19+430)*: 281 Bty *(Beacon Hill Fort) (2x6-inch)*; 282 Bty *(Cornwallis) (1x6-pounder twin)*; 283 Bty *(Angel Gate Bty) (2x6-pounder)* plus Z Bty RM *(Harwich Green) (2x4-inch)* (established May) *(3+70)* (Regt was also responsible for administering the batteries located between Burnham and the Wash)
Felixstowe – 520th Coast Regt *(14+309)*: HQ and 279 Bty *(Landguard Fort) (2x6-inch)*; 278 Bty *(Brackenbury Bty) (2x9.2-inch)*; 329 Bty *(Manor House) (2x6-inch mark XII) (3+118)* (established May)
Aldeburgh - 328 Coast Bty *(4x6-inch mark XII) (3+118)* (established May)
Dunwich - Section D Bty 58 Heavy Regt *(2x4-inch) (3+86)* (409 Coast Bty *(3+86)* formed on 7 September and took over on 31 October)
Thorpeness - 355 Coast Bty *(2x6-inch mark XI) (3+84)* (established June)
Southwold - 327 Coast Bty *(2x6-inch mark XI) (3+84)* (established May) plus 5 Super Heavy Bty *(1x12-inch rail) (7+109)*
Covehithe - 354 Coast Bty *(2x6-inch mark XI) (2+86)* (established June)

Lowestoft - Kent Bty RM *(3x6-inch)* *(established May)* *(4+124)*; 225 Coast Bty *(Pakefield)* *(2x6-inch mark XI)* *(established May)* *(4+83)*; 215 Coast Bty *(South Pier)* *(2x12-pounder)* *(established April)*

Great Yarmouth - HQ 514th Coast Regt *(22+363)*: A Bty *(Links)* *(2x6-inch)*; 325 Coast Bty *(North Denes)* *(2x6-inch mark XI)* *(established May)* *(3+83)*, 226 Coast Bty *(Gorleston)* *(2x12-pounder)* *(established April)* (Regt was responsible for administering the emergency batteries between Sheringham and Southwold)

Winterton - Section of D Bty 58 Heavy Regiment *(2x4-inch)* *(3+76)* (established July; replaced by 384 Coast Bty on 30 October)

Happisburgh - 353 Coast Bty *(2x4.7-inch)* *(2+102)* *(established June)*

Cromer - HQ Cromer Group of Fixed Defences *(1+7)* (covered from Winterton to King's Lynn); 324 Coast Bty *(2x6-inch mark XI)* *(3+95)* *(established May; Replaced Royal Navy personnel on 12 August)*

Sherringham - 352 Coast Bty *(2x6-inch mark XI)* *(3+90)* *(established June; replaced Royal Marine detachment on 4 September)*

Hunstanton - 323 Coast Bty *(2x6-inch mark XI)* *(4+89)* *(established May)*

Kings Lynn - 322 Coast Bty *(2x6-inch mark VII)* *(3+92)* *(established May)*

Boston - 321 Coast Bty *(2x6-inch mark VII)* *(3+85)* *(established May)*

Skegness (Gibraltar Point) - 320 Coast Bty *(2x6-inch mark VII)* *(2+94)* *(established May)*

Mablethorpe - 319 Coast Bty *(2x6-inch mark VII)* *(3+121)* (established May)

North East: *(Total of 2x12-inch, 5x9.2-inch, 35x6-inch, 4x5.7-inch, 4x4-inch, 2x12-pounder)*

Humber:
- HQ 512th Coast Regt *(Spurn Head)* *(16+359)*: A Bty *(Kilnsea/Fort Godwin)* *(2x9.2-inch, 1x4-inch)*, *(Bull Sand Fort)* *(4x6-inch, 2x6-pounder twin)*; B Bty *(Haile Sand Fort)* *(2x4-inch, 2x6-pounder twin)*; C Bty *(Spurn Point)* *(2x6-inch, 2x4.7-inch, 3x4-inch, 2x6-pounder twin)*
- HQ 513th Coast Regt *(Grimsby)* *(12+265)*: 318 Coast Bty *(Grimsby Docks)* *(2x6-inch mkVII)* *(3+75)* *(established May)*, X Bty RM *(Immingham)* *(2x4-inch)* *(established May)* *(3+68)*, 350 Coast Bty *(Hornsea)* *(2x4.7-inch)*, 351 Coast Bty *(Immingham)* *(2x4.7-inch)* *(established June)* *(Sunk Island)* *(2x4.7-inch)* *(3+100)*

Hornsea - 350 Coast Bty *(2x4.7-inch)* *(3+78)* *(established June)*

Filey - 349 Coast Bty *(2x6-inch mark XI)* *(3+72)* *(established June)*

Scarborough - 317 Coast Bty *(2x6-inch mark XII)* *(3+87)* *(established May)*

Whitby - 316 Coast Bty *(2x6-inch mark VII)* *(3+91)* *(established May)*

Tees:
- HQ 526th Coast Regt *(Redcar)*: *(Pasley)* *(1x9.2-inch)*, Bty *(South Gare)* *(2x4.7-inch)*
- HQ 511th Coast Regt *(Hartlepool)* *(8+176)*: - A Bty *(Heugh)* *(2x6-inch)*, *(Palliser)* *(1x9.2-inch)*, *(Lighthouse)* *(1x6-inch)*; B Bty *(Old Pier)* *(1x4.7-inch, 1x12-pounder)*; 315 Coast Bty *(Seaton Carew)* *(2x6-inch markVII)* *(3+90)* *(established May)*

Seaham - 314 Coast Bty *(2x6-inch mark VII)* *(established May)*

Sunderland - HQ 509th Coast Regt *(3+166)*: A Bty *(Roker)* *(2x6-inch)*, B Bty *(Barran's)* *(2x12-pounder)* *(established April)*, 312 Coast Bty *(Whitburn)* *(2x6-inch markVII)* *(6+93)* *(established May)*

Tyne – 508th Coast Regt *(17+452)*: A Bty *(Tynemouth Castle)* *(1x9.2-inch, 2x6-inch)*, B Bty *(Spanish)* *(2x6-inch)*, C Bty *(Fort Clifford)* *(2x12-pounder)*, Devon Bty RM (South Shields) *(3x6-inch mark XII)* *(established May)* *(3+123)*, 348 Coast Bty *(Frenchman's Point, Seaton)* *(1x9.2-inch, 2x6-inch mark XI)* *(3+88)* *(established June)*

Blyth - HQ 510th Coast Regt *(5+114)*: Blyth Bty *(2x6-inch mark XII)* (311 Coast Bty formed 3 October to take over Blyth Bty) *(1+88)*
Amble - 313 Coast Bty *(2x6-inch)* *(4+85)*
Berwick on Tweed - 310 Coast Bty *(2x6-inch mark XI)* *(3+102)* *(established May)*

Scotland *(Total of 3x9.2-inch, 43x6-inch, 3x4.7-inch, 5x4-inch, 22x12-pounder, 9x6-pounder)*
North Berwick - 309 Coast Bty *(2x6-inch mark XI) (Fidra)* *(3+95)* *(established May)*
Forth:
-HQ 504th Coast Regt *(Inchcolm)* *(19+488)*: A Bty *(Inchcolm)* *(2x12-pounder, 2x6-pounder twin)*, B Bty *(Inchmickery)* *(2x6-pounder twin)*, C Bty *(Cramond)* *(2x12-pounder)*, D Bty *(Dalmeny)* *(training)*
-HQ 505th Coast Regt *(Inchkeith)* *(17+481)*: A, B, C, D and E Btys *(Inchkeith and Leith)* *(3x9.2-inch, 12x6-inch)*
-HQ 506th Coast Regt *(Kinghorn, Fife)* *(11+300)*: A Bty *(Kinghorn)*, B Bty *(Pettycur)* *(4x6-inch)*
Leith - 162 Coast Bty *(2x6-inch)* *(4+133)*
Dundee - HQ 503rd Coast Regt *(5+190)* *(formed 14 July from HQ Dundee Fire Command)*: A Bty *(2x3-pounder) (Castle Green)*, 308 Coast Bty *(2x6-inch mark XI) (Stannergate)* *(3+96)* *(established May)*, 393 Coast Bty *(2x6-inch) (Broughty Ferry)* *(2x6-inch)* *(6+61)* *(Bty formed 3 September)*
Kincraig, Fife - HQ and A Bty 507th Coast Regt *(11+251)*
Montrose - 307 Coast Bty *(2x6-inch mark XI)* *(1+87)* *(established May)*
Aberdeen - HQ 502nd Coast Regt *(10+131)*; 306 Coast Bty *(2x6-inch mark XII) (Girdleness)* *(3+86)* *(established May)*
Peterhead - 305 Coast Bty *(2x6-inch mark XII)* *(3+90)* *(established May)*
Inverness - 382 Coast Bty *(Fort George)* *(1x4-inch)* *(1+56)* *(established July)*
Cromarty Firth - HQ 501st Coast Regt *(9+272)*: A Bty *(Invergordon)* *(2x6-inch mark XII)* *(established May)*, 304 Coast Bty *(Fort Nigg)* *(3+99)* *(1x4-inch)*
Wick - 303 Coast Bty *(2x6-inch mark XI)* *(2+92)* *(established May)*
Shetlands - HQ 535th Coast Regt *(Kirkwall, Orkneys)* *(9+196)*: A Bty *(Lerwick)* *(4x4-inch)*, 302 Coast Bty *(2+89)* *(2x6-inch mark XI)* *(established May)*, 371 Coast Bty *(Ness of Sound)* *(2x6-inch) (Green Head)* *(4+72)*; 301 Coast Bty *(2x4-inch) (Sullom Voe)* *(2+81)* *(established May)*
Plus: 3 Shore based torpedo tubes

Orkney - HQ Orkney Heavy Regt *(58+1079)* *(Total of 9x6-inch, 3x4.7-inch, 21x12-pounder, 3x6-pounder twin)*: 191 Bty *(Stromness: 3x12-pounder, 1x6-pounder twin; Carness: 2x6-inch, 1x12-pounder, Howton: 2x12-pounder; Holm: 3x12-pounder, 1x6-pounder twin; Galtness: 1x12-pounder)*, 198 Bty *(Stanger: 2x6-inch, Innan Neb: 1x4.7-inch, Buchanan: 2x12-pounder, Gate Ness: 2x12-pounder)*, 199 Bty *(Hoxa: 2x6-inch, Balfour: 2x12-pounder, Burray: 3x12-pounder, Cara: 2x12-pounder)*

On 23 September coast defence was re-organised into three new regiments – 533rd based on Flotta commanding sites at Stanger, Innan Neb, Buchanan and Gate Ness; 534th based at Stromness commanded sites at Howton, Hoxa, Balfour, Cara and Burray and 535th based at Kirkwall commanded sites at Galtness and Holm.

Paisley, Clyde - HQ Clyde Coast Regt *(23+492);* 171 Bty *(Cloch Point),* 196 Bty *(Dunoon),* 197 Bty *(Toward)*

Stranraer - A Bty 71 Medium Regt *(2x4-inch)* *(established July; replaced by 407 Coast Bty on 12 October)*

North West *(Total of 6x6-inch, 9x4-inch)*

Workington - Stn 51 Medium Regt *(3x4-inch) (70) (established July)*

Whitehaven - Stn 51 Medium Regt *(2x4-inch) (established July)*

Barrow in Furness - 299 Coast Bty *(Hipsford) (2x6-inch mark XII) (established June),* 370 Coast Bty *(Walney Island) (2x6-inch mark XII) (established June)* and Roa Island Bty *(2x75mm)*

Fleetwood - Stn 51 Medium Regt *(2x4-inch) (established July; replaced by 405 Coast Bty in early October)*

Lytham St Annes - Stn 51 Medium Regt *(2x4-inch) (established July; replaced by 404 Coast Bty in early October)*

Mersey - HQ 524th Coast Regt *(Crosby) (18+617)* - A Bty *(Fort Crosby) (1x6-inch),* B Bty *(Peach Rock) (1x6-inch)*

Northern Ireland *(Total of 9x6-inch)*

Belfast - HQ 525th (Antrim) Coast Regt *(24+425)* - A Bty *(Orlock) (1x6-inch),* B Bty *(Grey Point and Kilroot) (4x6-inch)*

Larne - C Coast Bty *(2x6-inch) (1+46)*

Magilligan Point - D Coast Bty *(2x6-inch) (2+39)*

Wales *(Total of Total of 18x6-inch, 6x4-inch)*

Caernarvon - Stn 51 Medium Regt *(2x4-inch) (established July; replaced by 403 Coast Bty in early October)*

Holyhead - 369 Coast Bty *(2x6-inch markXII) (3+195) (established June)*

Fishguard - Stn 51 Medium Regt *(2x6-inch markXII) (3+61) (established June; 368 Coast Bty took over on 2 October)*

Milford Haven -
- HQ 532nd Coast Regt *(8+297):* A Bty *(West Blockhouse) (4x6-inch);* C Bty *(East Blockhouse) (2x6-inch);* 367 Coast Bty *(2x6-inch mark XII) (Soldiers Rock) (1+58) (established June)* (Regiment formed from Pembroke Heavy Regt on 5 September)

Llanelli - Section 51 Medium Regt *(2x4-inch) (established July; replaced by 402 Coast Bty in early October)*

Port Talbot - 401 Coast Bty *(2x4-inch) (personnel from 51 Medium Regt) (established July)*

Penarth - 366 Coast Bty *(2x6-inch mark XII) (2+83) (established June)*

Cardiff - HQ Glamorgan Heavy Regt *(11+458):* Barry Bty *(2x6-inch),* Penarth Head Bty *(2x6-inch),* Mumbles Bty

South West *(Total of 6x9.2-inch, 5x6-inch, 14x4.7-inch, 28x4-inch, 7x12-pounder, 1x6-pounder)*

Portishead - 365 Coast Bty *(2x6-inch markVII) (3+82) (established June)*

Minehead – 400 Coast Bty *(2x4-inch) (3+82) (established July)*

Ilfracombe – 399 Coast Bty *(2x4-inch) (3+82) (established July)*

Appledore - 379 Coast Bty *(2x4.7-inch) (2+59) (established July)*

Instow - Coast Bty *(2x4-inch) (established July)*

Padstow - 397 Coast Bty *(2x4-inch) (established July, Battery formed from B Bty 70 Medium Regt and replaced 51 Heavy Battery on 4 August*)

Newquay - 396 Coast Bty (*2x4-inch*) *(2+91)* (established July)

Penzance - 394 Coast Bty (*2x4-inch*) (established July, Battery formed from A Bty 70 Medium Regt and replaced 51 Heavy Battery on 22 August)

Falmouth - HQ 523rd Coast Regt *(10+264):* A Bty *(Half Moon) (2x3-pounder)*, B Bty *(St Anthony's) (2x3-pounder)*; 193 Coast Bty (*2x6-inch*) *(4+115)*

Par - 393 Coast Bty (*2x4-inch*) *(3+65)* (established July)

Fowey - 364 Coast Bty (*2x4.7-inch*) *(2+81)* (established June)

Looe - 392 Coast Bty (*2x4-inch*) *(3+75)* (established July)

Plymouth - HQ Devon Heavy Regt *(60+1149)*: 137 Bty *(Bovisand) (4x12-pounder)*; 156 Bty *(Renney)* Bty *(3x9.2-inch);* 159 Bty *(Drake`s Island) (2x6-inch, 4x12-pounder)*; 161 Bty *(Western King`s) (2x12-pounder)*; 162 Bty *(Picklecombe) (2x6-inch, 2x4-inch)*; 164 Bty *(Penlee Point) (2x9.2-inch);* Granville Bty *(Cawsand) (3x12-pounder);* Staddon Bty *(4x12-pounder);* Plus Y Bty RM *(2x4-inch) (from Iceland 19 September) (3+69)*, A/MTB Bty RM *(4x2-pounder) (from Iceland 19 September) (4+91);* Lord Howard Bty *(2x6-inch)* (Training Regt)

Kingswear - 363 Coast Bty (*2x4.7-inch*) *(2+84)* (established June)

Brixham - 362 Coast Bty (*2x4.7-inch*) *(2+85)* (established June)

Torquay - 361 Coast Bty (*1x4.7-inch*) *(2+87)* (established June)

Teignmouth 378 Coast Bty (*1x4.7-inch*) *(2+62)* (established July)

Exmouth - 377 Coast Bty (*2x4.7-inch*) *(3+66)* (established July)

Dawlish - 390 Coast Bty (*2x4-inch*) *(3+83)* (established July)

Sidmouth - 389 Coast Bty (*2x4-inch*) *(3+80)* (established July)

Salcombe - 391 Coast Bty (*2x4-inch*) *(3+82)* (established July)

Lyme Regis - 376 Coast Bty (*2x4.7-inch*) *(3+83)* (established July)

Abbotsbury - 387 Coast Bty (*2x4-inch*) *(3+87)* (established July)

Appendix 5
SPECIAL FORCES

A lunch meeting at the Prime Minister's country residence, Chequers, on 30 June 1940 involving Winston Churchill and Lieutenant General Thorne, the Military Attache at the Embassy in Berlin during the mid 1930's and now commanding XII Corps, revived the idea of creating a guerrilla resistance force in the country.

A semi secret department of the War Office - Military Intelligence (Research) (MI(R)) was only one of many departments within Britain's intelligence community in 1940, co-ordinated within the Directorate of Military Intelligence (DMI). The DMI had expanded greatly since the outbreak of the War, having been split from the Directorate of Military Operations and Intelligence. Whilst MI5 and MI6 were principally engaged in covert surveillance and intelligence gathering the DMI's three elements - Department E.U., Section D and MI(R) - were dedicated to methods of actually fighting an enemy and employing economic sanctions or propaganda, these three elements would be combined within Special Operations Executive when it was set up. Section D was set up in April 1938 by the Secret Intelligence Service (SIS) within the Foreign Office and principally concerned with sabotage under Major L Grand; it was disbanded in April 1940 upon the formation of the Special Operations executive (SOE). This Section liased directly General Staff (Research) (GS(R)), set up in 1937 by the Deputy Chief of the Imperial General Staff. In 1938 this was asked to investigate fighting Germany by blockade, bombing and irregular or guerrilla warfare. In the spring of 1939 GS(R) was renamed MI(R) and spent much of its time developing weapons useful to a guerrilla force overseas. In 1939 it reported that "if guerrilla warfare is co-ordinated and also related to main operations it should, in favourable circumstances, cause such a diversion of enemy strength as eventually to present decisive opportunities to the main forces." One of MI(R)'s personnel was Major Colin Gubbins, who spent the spring of 1939 working on Guerrilla Field Service Regulations, involving three booklets - The Partisan Leader's Handbook, The Art of Guerrilla Warfare and How to Use High Explosives. Teams were sent to Finland and Poland to study operations, the former leading to the establishment of Independent Companies. During the Norwegian Campaign Section D was asked to investigate potential for guerrilla operations in Great Britain and began setting up arms caches around the country until complaints about its methods led to MI(R) taking over, Colin Gubbins (now Brigadier) being in charge until October, when he became the first executive director of the SOE, as he was considered an expert in unorthodox warfare. It was recognised that the new resistance organisation was beyond the capabilities of both Section D and MI(R), so it was agreed that it would come under the direct control of GHQ Home Forces.

In June 1940 Section D had set up the Home Defence Organisation to organise resistance at home through sabotage and spying, relying on thirty regional officers co-ordinating volunteer civilians, most of whom would be called out for specific tasks and unaware of each other's existence. Despite misgivings about the legality of using civilians in a military role a Cabinet paper on 17 June agreed to the selection, recruitment, training and equipping them. By 22 July some 200 key personnel had established supply caches across the country. Most of these were taken over for the Auxiliary Units use.

Headquarters, Special Duties was established in July 1940 in Whitehall as part of GHQ Home Forces (and the SIS). It had thirteen officers and fourteen other ranks assigned; twelve of these officers were assigned their own area of the country, together with a driver and car. The three officers tasked with setting up Units in the three most likely invasion areas were Captain Peter Fleming in Kent, Captain Andrew Croft in East Anglia and Captain John Gwynn in Sussex. Each intelligence officer ran a number of radio stations, runners and agents and a control station (operating from an army headquarters), supported from the autumn of 1940 by two scout sections of an officer and eleven men each. The primary role of these sections was to train civilian saboteurs and act as stay behind parties, operating from their own operational bases. It was left to each intelligence officer whether they also stayed behind to co-ordinate activities. Both networks were unaware of the existence of each other. By the time they were stood down in June 1944 the Special Duties Section comprised 240 officers, 57 ATS officers, 92 other ranks and 3250 civilians. In addition to the radio work undertaken by this Section a Radio Security Service was established by the Radio Society of Great Britain, using amateur radio operators to intercept enemy radio chatter and eventually feed it in to Bletchley Park.

Auxiliary Units
The country was split into 12 sectors covering the east, south and south Wales coasts. Each sector "HQ" had an officer and twelve men, with signallers, storesmen and other specialists added later. Sectors were first divided into Units and then Patrols, numbers varying according to location, but originally in rural reas no less than twenty miles from the coast. Patrol leaders were selected by intelligence officers with patrols consisting of several men, each nominated for their local knowledge and dedication. Each patrol had one or more hides or Operational Bases, normally located in inaccessible or unexpected areas. Generally these were equipped with an entrance shaft with blast wall at the bottom, a kitchen area, a sleeping area and an escape tunnel. In addition there were a number of reserve hides; one located in Godmersham Park near Canterbury could accommodate 150 troops, and observation posts. At least four training centres were available by early autumn - Godmersham Park in Kent, Steyning in Sussex, Kelvedon in Essex and one near Plymouth. The existence of the Units was very secret, as were their hides, to ensure security and maximum effectiveness and were placed under the direct control of the Home Forces General Headquarters. Originally run from Westminster the headquarters was moved to Coleshill in Wiltshire. Section D moved to a nearby country house, from where it ran its operations.

Three special Home Guard battalions were formed as a cover, these being the 201st (Scotland), 202nd (North) and 203rd (London and South). In the sector covering London to Portsmouth there were 20 Units formed largely from both Home Guard and civilians, mostly in the agricultural industry, and supported by specialists from the armed forces. It was essential that these people were confident and adaptable. Their role was to form the basis of a guerrilla force in the event of a successful German invasion. They were prepared to remain concealed for up to two weeks after invasion before engaging to undertake their role.

The first units were established in Kent and Sussex and known initially as XII Corps Observation Unit, Kent Headquarters being located at Bilting (between Ashford and Canterbury). Originally personnel were army volunteers. Patrols in Kent were established at Penshurst, Queenborough, Faversham, Oare, Badlesmere, Headcorn, Horsmonden, Birchington, Margate, Broadstairs, Deal, Ash, Challock, Wootton, Crundale, Elmsted, Lenham,

Charing, Ashford, Hothfield, Bethersden, Tenterden, Aldington, Newchurch and Lympne; Patrols in Sussex were established at Northiam, Heathfield, Bexhill, Eastbourne, Folkington, Lewes, Wivelsfield, Seaford, Brighton, Steyning, Worthing, Bognor Regis, Arundel, Petworth and Ardingly; HQs of Group 1 was in Northiam and Group 2 in Lewes. To maximise their effectiveness a training centre was also established at Coleshill House in Highworth, near Swindon. After the invasion period had passed the Auxiliary Unit organisation continued to grow and develop, its effectiveness enhanced by establishing thirty control and reporting stations manned by the Royal Signals. As a guide the Auxiliary Unit organisation was organised by early 1941 as follows:

Scotland:
- Highlands (26 patrols with 138 men)
- Aberdeen and Inverness (32 with 220 men)
- Fife and Angus (25 with 121 men)
- Lothian, Dumfries and Berwick (17 with 117 men)

North East:
- Northumberland (15 patrols with 66 men),
- Durham and North Yorkshire (25 with 159 men)
- East Riding (34 with 214 men)
- Lincolnshire (31 with 187 men)

East:
- Norfolk (35 patrols with 201 men)
- Suffolk (28 patrols with 180 men)
- Essex (28 with 169 men)

South East:
- Kent (33 patrols with 208 men)
- Sussex (21 with 134 men)
- Hampshire (47 with 301 men)

South West:
- Dorset (32 patrols with 177 men)
- Devon (23 with 150 men)
- Cornwall (28 with 195 men)
- Somerset (44 with 287 men)

West and South Wales:
- Worcestershire (6 patrols with 37 men)
- Herefordshire and Monmouth (14 with 93 men)
- Glamorgan (17 with 89 men)
- Carmarthen and Pembroke (15 with 81 men)

While Major Gubbins was in overall charge he had two assistants - Colonel Bill Beyts, attached from the Indian Army and previously responsible for training the Independent Companies, was now responsible for training the Auxiliary Units. The other was Sir Peter Wilkinson, attached from the War Office due to his wide experience of intelligence work; he was responsible for organisation and strategic planning.

Independent Companies

In April 1940 MI(R) had been tasked with training special assault troops for amphibious raids in support of the Anglo French expedition to Norway. A training base was quickly set up in Scotland's western Highlands, most of the selected personnel coming from the Territorial Army. These Independent Companies had mixed fortunes during the Norwegian Campaign but proved their worth and were seen as the fore runners of the Commandos, presently being formed. These companies were organised around three rifle platoons, each of three sections, but larger than normal British rifle companies with around 300 men but lightly armed. Their role in home defence was essentially to counterattack important positions such as airfields and coastal fortifications, although they were also used where there was a need for small garrisons. When he took command General Alan Brooke wished to reform both the Independent Companies and Commandos into special companies, allocated one per division but with the same role, though this did not happen.

Army Commando

In June 1940 the Army began to form a number of Commando units, loosely based on the Boer commandos the Army encountered in the Second Boer War. These units had the full support of Winston Churchill and were to carry out offensive amphibious operations against occupied Europe with volunteers from all over the Army. Each unit was organised into ten troops of fifty men controlled by a small headquarters and were lightly equipped as befitted their intended role.

Phantom

The origins of the GHQ Reconnaissance Regiment lay with the RAF's 3 Air Mission, which was set up in 1939 to liaise with the Belgian High Command and provide information on the location of the front line. This Mission was soon expanded to include an army element, which set up an Advanced Report Centre, comprising intelligence and signals personnel, supported by an armoured car troop and motorcycle platoon. Using its mobility this Centre provided the eyes and ears for the GHQ BEF, reporting the situation on the ground and undertook signals interception work, which helped to confirm the location and movement of enemy forces. The success of this unit led to its enlargement and separation, though not isolation, from the RAF following evacuation from Dunkirk. Headquarters was set up at Richmond in west London, with a battle headquarters and pigeon loft located in St James' Park, close to the GHQ Home Forces. The unit was organised into four squadrons, each of four patrols comprising an officer and six men with a Daimler armoured scout car, 15-cwt truck and three motorcycles. Each patrol was to be self sufficient for 2 days. A Squadron was assigned to XII Corps and centred on Chilham, B Squadron was assigned to V Corps and based on Richmond, C Squadron with Eastern Command and based on Grantham, while D Squadron was assigned to VII Corps and based in Sussex. The personnel for this unit came from volunteers and was greatly supported by the Royal Signals. Upon invasion their role was to give the Commander in Chief Home Forces and his subordinate commanders early warning of a situation on which he might have to make decisions involving the use of his reserves. Each patrol was to obtain this information from any source in their allotted area, the means used being left to the discretion of the officer in charge. When obtained the information was to be transmitted in code by wireless to

Squadron headquarters and then passed on, thus providing as close to a real time assessment of the situation as it developed. This force was also known as Phantom Force.

Appendix 6

ARMY NOTES

Infantry

There were a few levels of infantry unit a soldier was expected to move through during his transformation from civilian to trained soldier. He started at the Regimental Infantry Training Centres (ITC) before moving on to the Regimental Depot or Holding battalions, where the trained soldiers awaited posting while further training was undertaken. Depending on their level of training, age and medical condition they would then be posted to either Home battalions, mainly used for guarding vital places and larger than field battalions but with no or few support weapons, and Field Force battalions. The former included those who were of a lower medical standard or considered too young for active service.

Infantry battalions usually consisted of 4 infantry companies, each with three platoons of three sections, and a headquarters company that included mortar, carrier (10 vehicles), transport (80 vehicles) and signals platoons while many also formed cycle mounted tank hunting and motorcycle platoons. BEF infantry battalions had a nominal strength of about 780 men supported by 50 light machine guns, 2 three-inch mortars, 12 two-inch mortars and 22 anti tank rifles. Home battalions usually had more infantry companies but fewer support weapons. Infantry also formed pioneer, machine gun (each with 4 companies of 4 platoons with 36 Vickers medium machine guns per company), motorcycle (each with 3 companies and 3 scout car platoons, with 22 scout cars and 215 motorcycles or other vehicles) and motorised infantry battalions (4 rifle companies with three platoons mounted in lorries and another in carriers). It was agreed that by the end of October the 15 pioneer battalions would be re-roled as infantry battalions. Soldiers in the ITC, Depot, Home and Holding units had an anti invasion role in protecting important locations, notably airfields, and were normally spread over a wide area. The end of September saw a huge increase in the number of infantry battalions being formed to fill the new coast defence brigades including the converting of holding and home battalions, while "70" series battalions were formed to take young soldiers companies from existing home battalions.

The Army's standard rifle was the Short Lee Enfield, firing a .303 inch round. Adopted in 1903, it was a robust, popular and effective weapon capable of firing up to 15 rounds per minute. Although the Army had been looking for an automatic rifle since the mid 1920's no designs were adopted, partly for financial constraints and partly over fears that it would retard mobility by placing a large burden on its logistical system. While the infantry had the excellent water cooled and belt fed Vickers medium machine gun to provide sustained fire, backed up by stocks of the heavy drum fed Lewis machine gun, it was recognised that it needed a lighter sustained fire weapon and in 1935 adopted the Czech designed Bren gun. This accurate and well liked weapon's main drawback was that it was magazine fed, its rate of fire dependent on how many magazines could be carried within the infantry section, who relied upon it to provide the necessary fire power. German infantry were far better disposed with a real general purpose machine gun - the belt fed MG 34. The Army had two types of mortar - the 2-inch weighed 10 pounds, had a range of 500 yards and was available to each rifle platoon, but only had smoke or illuminating bombs; the 3-inch had a range of 1,600 yards, each rifle battalion supposed to have a platoon of six mortar tubes. However, German mortars had a longer range, faster rate of fire and most importantly HE rounds. The most inadequate weapon was the Boy's anti tank rifle. It was quickly found to be too heavy to be easily manhandled and effective only at short ranges - after Dunkirk troops were advised either to withhold fire until the target was only 30 yards away or to aim at its suspension! The range of weapons available to the infantry all followed the same principle - that firepower should be second to mobility.

Royal Artillery

There was a wide range of units - from super heavy to light artillery - available. However, even by late September a large number of these units had few or no artillery pieces and so had either an infantry or training role. The Corps was also responsible for manning the coast defence batteries and was just starting to set up new coast defence batteries. It was also responsible for the anti aircraft defence of the UK, with a small number of these units having mobile roles supporting the field army.

The Royal Artillery had a stock of chemical shells (17,000 4.5-inch, 25,000 6-inch and 750 25 pounder shells in August), though responsibility for the deployment of these lay with GHQ. The shells were filled with either mustard or tear gas. For operational use, these shells would have to be collected from one of the three sites and delivered to the relevant artillery unit. The main site was the Central Ammunition Depot at Longtown, Cumberland, which held 7,000 6-inch shells and 5,400 4.5-inch shells; the Ammunition Supply Depots 22 (Savernake, Wiltshire) and 27 (Shefford, Berkshire) held the rest.

On 4 June there were only 420 field and 153 medium guns available (but only 200 and 150 rounds per gun each). Between June to August 194 25 pounder, 231 18/25 pounder conversion field guns, 8 60 pounder, 75 6-inch howitzer guns and 498 2 pounder anti tank guns had been produced. The USA supplied 875 75mm guns in this period. From April to September 1940 industry produced nearly three and a half million filled shells for field artillery, 297,000 shells for medium artillery, 29,000 shells for coastal artillery, 434,000 shells for tank and anti tank guns, 934,000 heavy anti aircraft shells and over a million and a quarter light anti aircraft shells.

At the proposed time of the invasion the field forces were supported by at least 16 super heavy, 150 medium, 1700 field, 50 light guns and 48 heavy mortars. Training units held smaller numbers of artillery pieces. Another 40 heavy, 350 medium and 70 light guns were dedicated to coastal defence. At the end of June there were only 420 field and medium artillery pieces serving overseas.

Field Artillery:

	maximum range	muzzle velocity
13-pounder	5,900 yards (5,410 metres)	not known
3.7-inch mountain howitzer	6,000 yards (5,410 metres)	324 metres/second
18-pounder	6,500 yards (5,960 metres)	538 metres/second
18/25-pounder *	11,500 yards (10,970 metres)	520 metres/second
25-pounder	13,500 yards (12,385 metres)	520 metres/second

75 mm	9,295 yards (8,500 metres)	529 metres/second
4.5-inch howitzer	7,000 yards (6,400 metres)	313 metres/second
60-pounder (5 inch)	12,300 yards (11,245 metres)	634 metres/second
6-inch howitzer	11,400 yards (10,400 metres)	427 metres/second
8-inch howitzer	12,305 yards (11,250 metres)	457 metres/second

* This was a 25-pounder gun mounted on an 18 pdr carriage
(By comparison, the German artillery had the following maximum ranges: 75mm - 12,570 yards, 105mm - 13,480-20,850 yards, 150mm - 14,630-27,000 yards)

Coastal Artillery - maximum gun ranges:

9.2-inch	- 34,000 yards (11,330 metres)
6-inch	- 14,000 (mark VII) to 22,100 yards (mark XI/XII) (4,670 to 7370 metres respectively)
5.5-inch	- 17,300 yards (5,770 metres)
4.7-inch	- 11,800 yards (3,930 metres)
4-inch	- 11,000 yards (3,670 metres)
12-pounder	- 9,000 yards (3,000 metres)
6-pounder	- 5,500 yards (1,830 metres)

Rail Guns:

Calibre	Effective range	Time to get in action	Rate of fire
9.2-inch	25,000 yards	3 hours	1 per 8 minutes
12-inch	14,350 yards	3 hours	1 per 8 minutes
13.5-inch	36,575 yards	15 minutes	1 per 8 minutes
18-inch	22,300 yards	15 minutes	1 per 8 minutes

Each battery of 9.2-inch guns had a diesel engine, 6 wagons, 18 box cars and a coach, while the 12 inch battery additionally had two flat cars.

Anti Aircraft Guns:

Calibre	Effective ceiling	Rate of fire	Shell weight	Muzzle velocity
4.5-inch	10,520 metres	12-15 rounds/minute	54 pounds	732 metres/second
3.7-inch	9,755 metres	12-15 rounds/minute	28 pounds	792 metres/second
3-inch	4,785 metres	12-18 rounds/minute	16 pounds	610 metres/second
40 mm	1,525 metres			823 metres/second
20 mm	2,200 metres			830 metres/second

Anti Tank:
These guns were allocated to divisional anti tank regiments as they became available. Additionally, many infantry brigades had their own anti tank company comprising three platoons, each with three 2pdr or 25mm guns, though these rarely had their issue of guns and were usually re-organised as tank hunting units with mines and petrol bombs, as were the tank hunting platoons formed within many infantry battalions.

- 621 six pounder guns were available, mostly in static or beach roles. The gun had a muzzle velocity of 820 metres per second and could penetrate 74 mm of armour at a range of 1,000 metres, its maximum effective range being 1,500 metres.
- 170 two pounder guns were available in May. Infantry divisions in GHQ Reserve had priority on delivery. Later, over 220 guns were initially allocated to the GHQ line (209 along the Thames Valley (including 72 along the Kennet and Avon Canal) and 12 around Chelmsford). The gun had a muzzle velocity of 808 metres per second and could penetrate 42 mm of armour at the maximum effective range of 1,000 metres.
- There were a small number of 25mm Hotchkiss guns that usually equipped infantry brigade anti tank companies, although most had been lost with the BEF. The gun had a muzzle velocity of 2,950 yards per second and could penetrate 40mm of armour at the maximum effective range of 1,000 metres.
- Over 5,000 0.55-inch Boys anti tank rifles were available. Firing a steel cored bullet at a velocity of 990 metres per second it could penetrate 15mm of armour at a range of 229 metres.

(By comparison, the German anti tank guns had the following statistics: 37mm - maximum range of 600 metres, armour penetration of 48mm at 500 metres and a muzzle velocity of 762 metres per second; 50mm - maximum range of 2,500 metres, armour penetration of 78mm at 500 metres and a muzzle velocity of 823 metres per second; 88mm - maximum range of 8,000 metres, armour penetration of 105mm at 1,000 metres and a muzzle velocity of 820 metres per second)

Armour

The Royal Armoured Corps (RAC) was belatedly created in April 1939, bringing together the Royal Tank Corps (changing its title to the Royal Tank Regiment (RTR)) and newly mechanised cavalry regiments. Of the armoured regiments - both tank and reconnaissance - only 15 were equipped with tanks and at least another 5 had armoured cars during the invasion period. The rest of the Corps was either re-roled as motor machine gun units or motorised quick reaction units and equipped with ad hoc vehicles such as the "beaverette". The Royal Tank Regiment was also responsible for manning the armoured trains, each train having two 6 pdr guns and 6 light machine guns (lmg) with an occasional Boys anti tank rifle. The Royal Tank Regiment`s (RTR) infantry tank battalions were to have to have fifty infantry and seven light tanks, the three tank companies each having five platoons (the RTR was organised in infantry terms unlike their cavalry comrades); cruiser regiments were expected to have 29 cruiser, 21 light tanks and 10 scout cars within three four troop tank squadrons and a liaison troop; light tank regiments were to have 28 light tanks and 44 scout cars in three six troop squadrons. Armoured car regiments should have 38 armoured cars and 21 scout cars in three three troop squadrons and 4 scout sections. Needless to say these establishments were rarely met in the circumstances.

On 30 June there were 835 tanks (616): 132 (43) Vickers medium, 141 (124) infantry, 147 (125) cruiser, 415 (321) light. On 29 September there were 1,188 (805) tanks: 132 (43) Vickers medium, 259 (265) infantry, 179 (179) cruiser, 618 (318) light. Figures in brackets refer to those with operational units; the rest were with training units or in depots.

Production during the summer included 6 Matilda I, 166 Matilda II, 107 Valentine infantry tanks; 5 A9, 97 A10 and 103 A13 cruiser tanks, 36 VI light tanks plus 72 Humber light armoured cars, 266 armoured scout cars and 2,206 universal (bren gun) carriers. Enough tanks had been produced so that in early autumn two new Armoured Divisions (the 6th and 8th) began forming, while another (the 9th) began forming in early December.

Between 15 September and 1 October available tanks were as follows:

Operational	Units	Training	Depot	Total
Light	329	80	30	439
Cruiser	196	39	15	250
Infantry	278	29	25	332
Medium (obsolete)	43	79	20	142
	846	227	90	1163

Non Operational	Units	Training	Depot	Total
Light	75	66	16	157
Cruiser		5		5
Infantry		12		12
	75	83	16	174

The general characteristics for each tank type were as follows:

Type	Weight	Speed	Crew	Armour	Armament	Range
A9 Cruiser	12 tonnes	25 mph	6	6-14 mm	1x2pdr, 3 lmg	100 miles
A10 Cruiser	14 tonnes	16 mph	5	22-30 mm	1x2pdr, 2 lmg	100 miles
A13 Cruiser	14 tonnes	30 mph	4	14-30 mm	1x2pdr, 2 lmg	90 miles
Vickers Medium	12 tonnes	16 mph	5	6-14 mm	1x3pdr, 3 lmg	150 miles
Matilda Mk I	11 tonnes	8 mph	2	60-65 mm	1 lmg	80 miles
Matilda Mk II	26 tonnes	15 mph	4	40-78 mm	1x2pdr, 1 lmg	60 miles
Valentine	17 tonnes	15 mph	3	8-65 mm	1x2pdr, 1 lmg	90 miles
Light Mk VI	5 tonnes	35 mph	3	4-14 mm	1 lmg	130 miles

By comparison, the German tanks` characteristics were as follows:

Type	Weight	Speed	Crew	Armour	Armament	Range
Mark I	6 tonnes	25 mp/h	2	7-13mm	1x1mg	87 miles
Mark II	11 tonnes	34 mp/h	3	15-35mm	1x20mm,1xlmg	125 miles
Model 35 (t) (Czech)	11 tonnes	25 mp/h	4	12-35mm	1x37mm, 2xlmg	120 miles
Model 38 (t) (Czech)	10 tonnes	26 mp/h	4	25mm	1x37mm, 2xlmg	140 miles
Mark III	25 tonnes	25 mp/h	5	25-37mm	1x50mm, 2xlmg	110 miles
Mark IV	26 tonnes	24 mp/h	5	20-60mm	1x75mm, 2xlmg	125 miles

Notes:
- The Mark II flame tank derivative had 2 flame guns with 35m range capable of 20 2 to 3 second bursts.
- The Model 38 (t) equipped both 7th and 8th Panzer Divisions
- It was estimated that a Mark III panzer could land on a beach gradient of 1:40 feet, while a Mark IV needed a gradient of no greater than 1:80 feet

The general characteristics for British armoured cars were as follows:

Type	Weight	Speed	Crew	Armour	Armament	Range
Morris CS9	4 tonnes	45 mph	4	7 mm	1xa/trifle, 1xlmg	240 miles
Guy	5 tonnes	40 mph	3	15 mm	1xmmg, 1xlmg	210 miles
Morris light	3 tonnes	45 mph	3	14 mm	1xa/t rifle, 1xlmg	240 miles
Beaverette	2 tonnes	25 mph	3	12 mm	1xlmg or a/t rifle	170 miles
Humber (Ironside)	3 tonnes	45 mph	3	12 mm	1xa/t rifle, 1xlmg	100 miles

Royal Engineers

The Corps has a long tradition of adapting to the many varied tasks they have been asked to provide as well as being among the first to seek the best way of implementing new technologies to serve the army. In order to best do this the Corps had organised its personnel into a wide range of units and most were trained as specialists. Since the outbreak of War the types of units required had increased considerably. These roles included construction, excavation, railway and maritime operations, electrical and maintenance, artisan and manning searchlights (this last role was taken over by the Royal Artillery during 1940). Although only field companies were expected to have combat roles with the field army some of the specialist units would have been among the first to encounter the invasion due to their location. These units were expected to carry out both defensive and offensive tasks including demolition and denial, preparing minefields and other obstacles for the former and construction, route improvement and demolition for the latter. In either case it is certain that these units would also have had to act in an infantry role. Much of the Corps` heavy and specialist equipment was held in depots, dumps and mobile Field Park units.

The Chemical Warfare units would normally only be active in a chemical role if the Germans used gas weapons first. Each company had 240 Livens Projectors, a First World War 7.5-inch mortar capable of throwing 35-pound mustard or phosgene filled drums up to a range of 1700 metres. They also had access to ground contamination bombs and chemical mines (each mine containing six gallons of mustard gas). In addition they had a decontamination role, using bulk decontamination trucks and sprays. They were also deployed in beach defence, using petroleum in anti tank traps as well as providing smoke generators. By late September most of these units had changed to a training role.

Royal Corps of Signals

The Corps was responsible for the Army`s communications. The technological progress made between the Wars, coupled with financial constraints, had caused the Corps many problems in trying to integrate new methods with tried and tested formats, especially as it recognised that the pace of operations would dramatically increase in a mechanised environment and so a mobile and flexible communications network was needed. The Army decided on a three level approach using wireless, cable and despatch rider but recognised the problems and constraints that each raised; wireless was still new, quite bulky and in short supply, cable took time to deploy and recover and was vulnerable to being cut; despatch riders also took time and were equally vulnerable. The Corps was acutely conscious about the need to provide trained personnel while also ensuring that commanders knew how to properly operate it. The Corps, in conjunction with the fledgling electronics industry, had developed a number of wireless sets during the mid 1930's for use at all levels of command, with the size, weight and operating range of the sets increasing the higher up the command chain that it was designed for. Except for the three developed for the tanks and two for the infantry the remainder required a lorry for transportation. The main set for use by combat units was the Number 11, which had a range of up to 16 miles and was one of the first to combine transmit and receive circuits in a single unit with a single tuning control. In contrast the Set 2 had four units - transmitter, receiver, rotary transformer and HT unit. Wireless sets in use at the time included the following:

Type	Use	Range (miles)	Notes
Set A	infantry and armour	2	Light vehicle mounted/3 man pack
Set C	brigade to divisional	5 mobile 12 to 40 stationary	
Set 2	brigade to divisional, artillery	9 to 15	
Set 3	Corps and LofC	25 to 50	
Set 5	GHQ to Corps	200 to 600	
Set 7	tank to tank	5 to 6	
Set 9	Divisional signals	8 to 20	
Set 11	infantry brigade, artillery	3 to 16	
Set 14	tank to tank	1	In service from March
Set 18	infantry battalion HQ	5	Man pack
Set 19	armour	1 to 15	

Royal Army Service Corps (RASC)

This Corps supported the Army at all levels, by providing transport and getting fuel, ammunition and other supplies from depots to the fighting troops. They also had their own specialist units to support and further develop this role. Their operations during this invasion period would be easier at home than during recent overseas operations as there were more resources to call upon and the availability of shorter supply lines. It was therefore important that the Corps own organisation system was flexible enough to provide the efficient and timely support to the fighting forces while maintaining close co-operation with other corps, notably the RAOC.

The Corps also controlled the civilian manned War Department Fleet through the office of the Assistant Director of Military Transport at Woolwich. This Fleet had a prewar strength of 66 coasters and launches which was responsible for moving military cargoes between the main homeports, carrying out artillery range safety work and maintenance of offshore fortifications. In early 1940 two motorboat companies were formed and training centres established at Salcombe and St Austell in the South West. These companies were equipped with requisitioned launches manned by volunteers and were supported by the water transport companies at Woolwich, Barry, Leith and Portsmouth. The role of this Fleet was increased to include defensive patrols on estuaries and rivers around the coast, but were only lightly armed.

Royal Army Ordnance Corps (RAOC)

The Corps was responsible for keeping the Army operational, from maintaining its weapons and vehicles to providing laundry and bath services. To perform these functions the Corps operated a number of depots and workshops while also organising Light Aid Detachments (LAD) that were attached to infantry, armour, artillery and transport units. The Corps had been in the forefront of the Army's pre war mechanisation process and faced great difficulties in providing the large numbers of trained and skilled personnel. As with the other supporting arms of the Army it had learned many valuable lessons while trying to overcome the many problems with supplying and maintaining an army in the field during the operations with the British Expeditionary Force. It now had to strike a balance between this role and extending the growing static base facilities that existed in the United Kingdom. Later during the war this Corps spawned the Royal Electrical and Mechanical Engineers (REME).

Royal Army Medical Corps (RAMC)

As well as field units this Corps also benefited from an extensive range of domestic facilities, with a number of hospitals either already taken over or earmarked for use. The Corps also linked with the RASC to operate several ambulance trains, as it had in the BEF. The Corps organisational structure had hardly changed from the First World War. Each operational battalion or regiment had their own medical section, who were responsible for immediate collection and treatment of casualties; the next level involved field ambulances, usually one per brigade, who were designed to be mobile and mainly concerned with collecting casualties from units within the brigade area and, if necessary, passing them down the medical chain. The next level involved the Casualty Clearing Station (CCS). These were assigned to field divisions and Corps and were also mobile while permitting a higher level of casualty care. If necessary, casualties would be sent onto field or general hospitals. The whole process was streamlined for maximum efficiency, with better transport systems being available so reducing the time lapse a casualty had before receiving the appropriate level of care. This had the effect of reducing the death rate and helping to maintain morale of fighting troops. Supplementing this work was the Army Dental Corps, though this was unable to provide enough trained personnel for some time (by October 1939 there were only 32 officers for 158,000 men!).

Corps of Military Police

This Corps was only formed in 1926 following the merger of both Military Foot and Mounted Police. In the 1930's the Corps underwent radical changes in its operational structure with the formation of provost companies and sections with fixed establishments; direct recruitment was allowed in 1938, while reservists with police backgrounds were earmarked on mobilisation; the Field Security Wing was created in 1937 but was transferred to the Intelligence Corps in December 1940. The Corps was also strengthened in 1938 when some 800 Automobile Association employees joined the Corps reserve. The Corps organisation differed between field force and home command roles, with provost companies provided at Divisional, Corps and line of communication levels, all being mechanised, while those assigned to home commands had static roles. These field companies usually comprised one or two officers and about a hundred non commissioned officers, while the home companies were slightly larger. The Corps also had clearly defined roles, as set out in the 1936 Manual of the Corps of Military Police, itself based on lessons re-learned during the First World War. Their operational roles included close protection, ensuring military discipline, maintaining good relations with local population and authorities, manning straggler posts, traffic control and prisoner of war handling. Of these traffic control was undoubtedly the most important as without it the Army's ability to effectively move, let alone mount counter attacks, would be severely hampered. An important aspect of this latter role was responsibility for carrying out road reconnaissance to determine suitability for military traffic. The severe problems encountered during traffic control, notably with regard to refugee movement, led to the formation in July of Traffic Control companies, though these did not transfer to the Corps until October 1940. Another important role was the straggler posts. These had proved their worth during the First World War and again during the 1940 campaigns, where troops were often separated from their units and relied on these posts to reintegrate them back in to the system, while providing them with a sense of security and control. These roles were regulated by the appointment of Provost Marshals and their deputies. Another innovation was the formation of a Special Investigations Branch (SIB) in February 1940. The Corps depot was at Mytchett near Aldershot. However, as the Corps grew another site was required and in April 1940 a second depot was opened in Northallerton prison, where the troops often preferred living in the cells rather than the barrack rooms! In addition to the Corps each battalion or regiment had their own Regimental Police Section, formed from their own personnel and provided with basic training. Their role mirrored that of the Corps but on a much reduced basis, concentrating on maintaining discipline within their own unit.

Intelligence Corps

The Corps was officially formed in July 1940, although it did not take concrete form until December 1940 when it moved to premises within Oxford University. Although this Corps did not officially form until after the Dunkirk evacuation some 435 personnel, forming 31 Field Security Sections, served with the British Expeditionary Force. These small, self contained and flexible Sections proved capable of meeting the needs of a field intelligence service, each Section normally comprising one officer and fourteen non commissioned officers. The Corps was concerned more with counter intelligence than security, its personnel being responsible for keeping track of the enemy's activities as well as identifying and monitoring the situation in the Section's locality. All of the personnel were trained infantrymen.

Army Physical Training Corps (APTC)

The Corps was formed from the Army Physical Training Staff, which had been reduced to only 150 personnel in 1922. However, by 1935 enough serious concern was being expressed about the general poor state of recruits physical standards to raise this unit's profile, though numbers only significantly increased after War was declared. In September 1940 the Staff was formed into the Corps, all instructors receiving weapons training while each combat unit received instructors to promote physical development.

Auxiliary Military Pioneer Corps (AMPC)

Formed in October 1939 due to the shortage of labour for the Army, this Corps was essentially non combative, its personnel being regarded as unsuitable for combat due to age, medical condition or moral outlook. It was engaged in a wide variety of construction roles, operating depots and assisting civil defence organisations in dealing with bomb damage. Despite their labour role, the Corps had proved quite valuable in combat, notably with the Lines of Communication and then Second BEF. This recognition was to lead to the removal of the prefix "Auxiliary". A valuable resource was allotted to the Corps with the establishment of 19 companies of foreigners and 14 companies of conscientious objectors by the end of the year. Each pioneer received four weeks of military training at one of the pioneer centres, which were also responsible for raising the companies. Each company comprised about 280 men and was organised into ten sections, while a group headquarters controlled several companies. As they were not regarded as combatants only one in four men were normally armed and no machine guns or heavy weapons were allocated.

Appendix 7
MISCELLANEOUS STATISTICS

<u>Alert</u>. The most favourable period for invasion in late summer to early autumn, given tides, moon and weather was between 15 and 30 September. GHQ Home Forces issued the Codeword "Cromwell" on 7 September meaning imminent invasion, but downgraded this on 13 September. However, there was much confusion at most levels of command as to what the codeword meant in practice. In addition, several commands also had their own code words for different levels of readiness. Generally, "Cromwell" meant that troops should be confined to barracks or recalled from leave, mobile forces put on notice to move, headquarters manned to operational levels and their defences permanently manned, airfield defences also to be fully manned, demolition parties to be on short notice to move, minefield notices and wiring removed, Home Guard already on duty to be kept on continuous guard with others warned, vehicles fully refuelled, owners of required civilian vehicles warned of probable use, liaison officers to report to their respective headquarters, personnel issued with air recognition signals and, importantly, public denied access to beaches. A subsequent codeword denoting action stations would require all beach defences to be fully manned, immobilisation, refugee and traffic points manned and units to shorter period of readiness to move. Upon receiving the invasion alert in the RAF's bomber squadrons all aircraft not already detailed for operational missions during the next twelve hours were to be bombed up and brought to standby, while crews were expected to remain on their stations; these stations were to inform Group headquarters how many aircraft they could receive from the Flying Training Command and 22nd Group under the Banquet Scheme; all station defence personnel were to be kept ready for immediate action by day and night.

<u>Weather</u>. Despite the late season the weather in the Channel between mid September to early October was reported "fair", with light to moderate winds; the sea state never got higher than Force 3 (the invasion barges could operate up to Force 4 if required). Generally speaking, September was sunny but cool and dry in the south and cloudy and wet in the north, with gales in mid month over the north of Scotland. From 24 September an anticyclone west of Ireland produced unsettled though fair conditions over the north and east. Fog was most present between 21-22, 24-27 and 29-30 of that month. October was mainly dull and unsettled. Widespread gales occurred between 8 and 10 October, mainly in the north and west. Heavy rain covered the country on 16 while the end of the month saw widespread southerly gales and more heavy rain. Fog was most present between 1-4, 11-13, 16-23 and 27-29. The coastline experiences two sets of high and low tides every day. The High and Low Tides recorded at Dover between 22 to 28 September got progressively later:

Date	High tides	Low tides
22 September	0152 and 1402	0856 and 2112
23 September	0223 and 1441	0926 and 2147
24 September	0305 and 1537	1006 and 2236
25 September	0412 and 1707	1113 and 2352
26 September	0535 and 1829	1237
27 September	0711 and 1948	0127 and 1413
28 September	0815 and 2048	0255 and 1526

On 20 September the following tides and sun rise/set were recorded:

Hythe	Low 0625	High 1101	Low 1910		0616 Rise/1939 Set
Rye		High 0013		High 1227	0644 Rise/1855 Set
Eastbourne	Low 1900	High 0011	Low 0638	High 1234	0646 Rise/1857 Set
Newhaven	Low 1844	High 0004	Low 0624	High 1228	0647 Rise/1858 Set

These timings would be crucial in the German landing plans. It is unlikely that these weather conditions would have seriously hindered either the invasion or following build up period for at least a month after the initial landings.

Army Command strengths (at end of September):

	Officers	Other Ranks	Total
Eastern	20,474	437,575	458,049
Aldershot	3,558	66,513	70,071
London	1,351	37,297	38,648
Southern	16,206	323,522	339,728
Northern	14,789	339,161	353,950
Western	10,898	250,035	260,933
Scotland	8,193	176,381	184,574
NI	2,708	61,219	63,927
TOTAL	**78,177**	**1,691,703**	**1,769,880**

(Of these 182,119 were in training units and 43,984 were awaiting posting to units. Figures do not include allied or Commonwealth troops)

The breakdown by Corps is as follows:

	Officers	Other Ranks
Infantry	23,308	668,140
Royal Artillery	15,879	402,391
RASC	6,103	146,154
Royal Engineers	4,876	129,312
AMPC	1,817	71,997
Royal Signals	2,182	57,865
RAOC	2,857	50,262
RAMC	4,798	44,355
RAC	1,908	37,669
Royal Army Pay Corps	1,666	16,068
Corp of Military Police	16	7,261
Army Commandos	311	3,525
Household Cavalry	105	3,276
Army Dental Corps	1,159	1,877
Chaplain's Department	1,326	
Intelligence Corps	1,163 (all ranks)	
Royal Army Veterinary Corps	28	497
Army Education Corps	24	138
Small Arms School	45	93
Auxiliary Territorial Service (ATS)	1,190	34,915

The average monthly call up to the Army was 50,000 men plus 27,000 volunteers

- By the end of September there were 48,111 Canadian, 9,270 Australian and 6,280 New Zealand troops in the UK, mostly in combat formations. The Indian Army had 1,383 men in the UK, mostly in mule transport companies that had been evacuated with the BEF and now in Northern Command.
- Excluding those foreign troops who had been evacuated from Dunkirk, most of who were repatriated straight away, 24,352 Poles, 18,246 French, 4,938 Czech and 163 Belgians were brought to the UK before France capitulated. By 27 July foreign army personnel in the UK included about 24,350 Poles, 5,000 Czechs, 2,000 French, 1,300 Norwegian, 1,000 Dutch and 300 Belgian (Total: 33,600). In October there were 18,000 Poles, 3,000 Czechs, 1,500 Dutch, 1,070 Norwegians, 850 French and 800 Belgians, the remaining either having chosen repatriation or moved overseas to join fellow compatriots, notably in the Middle East. There were considerable numbers of allied personnel serving in both the RAF and Royal Navy.
- The British Army, Empire and Commonwealth forces located overseas at the end of September was as follows:

	British	Local/Indian	Commonwealth	Totals
Egypt	50,561`	12,235	10,097 NZ	72,893
East Africa	4,633	42,024		46,657
Palestine	25,783	3,489	15,788 Aus	45,060
Sudan	5,078	32,277		37,355
India	31,741	n/a		31,741 *
Malaya	8,808	8,618		17,426
Iceland	12,979	nil	2,663 Cdn	15,642
Malta	6,801	4,820		11,621
Gibraltar	8,253	297		8,550
Hong Kong	3,558	3,760		7,318
Aden	1,688	3,619		5,307
West Africa	959	3,435		4,394
Cyprus	1,090	2,134		3,224
Sierra Leone	1,226	1,237		2,463
Ceylon	477	1,902		2,379
Burma	1,637	n/a		1,637 *
Trinidad	16	1,705		1,721
Bermuda	89	792	720 Cdn	1,601
Jamaica	125	568		693
Faroe Isles	584	nil		584
Mauritius	276	191		467
St Helena	203	160		363
Miscellaneous (include at sea)	6,679	2,497		9,176
	173,244	**125,760 ***	**29,268**	**328,272**

* Figures do not include Indians serving at home and Burmese local forces

- The Western Desert Force in Egypt had under command the 7th British Armoured, 6th British Infantry, 6th Australian and 4th Indian Infantry Divisions, plus the 4th Infantry Brigade Group of the 2nd New Zealand Expeditionary Force (the 7th Australian Infantry Division arrived in October). 5th Indian Infantry Division was in Sudan. The British 1st Cavalry and 8th Infantry Divisions were garrisoning Palestine (plus a Brigade of 6th Australian Infantry Division), with the Polish Carpathian Infantry Brigade refitting after moving from Syria in early July, while the 12th Indian Infantry Division had a similar role in Persia. The 1st and 2nd African Infantry Divisions were in Kenya. The Indian 11th Infantry Division was garrisoning Malaya.

- The Indian Army in January 1940 comprised 185,950 men in India and another 19,386 serving overseas. There were also 14,344 men in the Territorial and State Forces in India. The Canadian Army at home was 114,890 strong at the end of June. By the end of August 1940 another 164,856 had enlisted in the Canadian Army.

- British Army casualties (officers+other ranks):

July (*)	55 + 822 Dead	16 + 217 Wounded	510 + 4,216 Missing
Aug (*)	9 + 147	4 + 85	91 + 2,064
Sept	7 + 158	4 + 83	56 + 407

  (*) = Missing figures include the second BEF, which was evacuated from France in mid June. The dead and wounded relate mainly to air attack and training accidents.

- Each infantry division had an establishment of 13,860 men, 72 field guns, 48 anti tank guns, 306 anti tank rifles, 18 medium and 108 light mortars, 96 Bren gun carriers, 670 motorcycles and 900 vehicles. Only the 3rd, 43rd and 1st Canadian Divisions were at full strength by the beginning of September. The Armoured Divisions had an establishment of 10,750 men, 16 field guns, 48 anti tank guns, 350 tanks, 650 motorcycles and 1400 vehicles. In contrast, German infantry divisions had an allotment of 36 light and 12 heavy field guns, 72 infantry field guns, 138 heavy machine guns, 54 medium mortars and 75 anti tank guns. They also had a need for nearly 5,000 horses for mobility.

Appendix 8

THE GHQ LINES

The final and principal defence line was to be the General Headquarters Anti Tank Line, also known as the General Headquarters Reserve Positions but better known as the GHQ Line. This was supported by Command, Corps and Divisional stop lines (five in the eastern counties and three in the south east) located forward of the GHQ Line. The siting of the Line made the maximum use of the ground and included natural obstacles, such as rivers and canals, supported by artificial obstacles, such as railway embankments and specially dug anti tank ditches. It was also to be supplemented by demolition zones. It ran from Richmond in North Yorkshire to the Wash, then to Cambridge and down to the Thames Estuary near Southend, along the River Medway via Maidstone, then skirting the North Downs to Farnham before looping north to Reading before splitting into two lines - one following the Thames and the other along the Kennet and Avon Canal - before rejoining east of Bristol, where another part encircled the city.

In addition to this Line a number of places were designated either Nodal Points or Anti Tank Islands, each with the role of denying to the enemy a vital town, village, cross roads or crossing place. Development of these places continued long after the defensive lines were discontinued.

The GHQ Line was to be occupied by Command and Area HQ troops as well as the Home Guard. The Line was split into sectors, each with a specific commander assigned and who was made responsible for the manning of it. Initially they could call upon the Home Guard and static units not already employed, though the local striking forces would have priority in men and equipment. It was expected that the troops manning the Line were to hold for up to forty eight hours until reinforced. The main role of the divisions forward of GHQ Line was to exploit their own stop lines in order to confine and delay the enemy advance, so allowing mobile units to concentrate and strike effectively.

Although construction was largely halted by mid August nearly 1500 pillboxes were completed, including 10 artillery, 167 two pounder anti-tank gun, 59 six pounder anti-tank gun, 15 heavy machine gun emplacements and 1190 infantry structures. A large number of rail and roadblocks were also provided. In addition a large number of rivers and canals had been improved defensively, with banks steepened and anti tank obstacles placed in the water.

Allocation of resources was as follows:
- GHQ Green Line: This enclosed Bristol and ran for 90 miles and was nominally the responsibility of 3rd Infantry Division. It was to comprise 357 infantry pill boxes, 20 miles of anti tank ditches, 14 miles of improved natural obstacles, supported by 18 rail and nearly 300 road blocks. However, it remained only half completed with the sector running from Highbridge to Staverton, via Wells and Radstock, complete. The rest of the Line relied on the Nodal Points of Melksham, Chippenham, Malmesbury, Tetbury, Nailsworth and Stroud, supported by 20 pill boxes and 8 miles of anti tank ditches.
- Bodmin (Southern Command) Stop Line: This ran from Wadebridge to Fowey via Bodmin and faced east. The line had 14 pillboxes and 36 roadblocks and was completed before December.

- Exeter (VIII Corps) Stop Line: This was also to face east but by December 1940 no significant work had been undertaken.
- Taunton (Southern Command) Stop Line: This ran over 47 miles from Highbridge by Bridgwater Bay to Seaton by Lyme Bay and faced both directions. It comprised 379 pillboxes, 11 miles of anti tank ditches, 12 miles of improved natural obstacles and supported by 22 rail and 126 roadblocks. The Line included 12 anti tank "islands", comprising another 80 pillboxes, 13 miles of anti tank ditches, 1 mile of improved natural obstacles and supported by 20 rail and 54 roadblocks. By December the Line was mostly complete, though development of the anti tank islands was lacking.

- GHQ Blue Line: This was the responsibility of Southern Command and ran along the Kennet and Avon Canal for 90 miles to just west of Reading and was 75% complete. It comprised 53 two pounder anti tank, 8 six pounder anti tank and 118 infantry pillbox sites with 5 miles of anti tank ditches, supported by 17 rail and 125 roadblocks. At least 30 two pounder anti tank sites were built between Reading and Hungerford. Newbury, Hungerford, Devizes and Semington were designated Nodal Points. The Line suffered from being overlooked by high ground to the south and a narrow canal dependent on the numerous locks that required defending.
- GHQ Red Line: This was also the responsibility of Southern Command and was also known as GHQ Line Rear. It ran north of the Kennet and Avon Canal at Theale to Pangbourne, behind an anti tank ditch and protected by 24 two pounder anti tank and 5 infantry pillboxes, before following the River Thames to Abingdon, this stretch protected by 21 two pounder anti tank, 6 six pounder anti tank and 35 infantry pillboxes. The Line then cut west and then northwest from Abingdon before rejoining the River Thames at Appleton; this 30 mile stretch of anti tank ditch also had 11 roadblocks protected by 22 two pounder anti tank, 3 six pounder anti tank and 6 infantry pillboxes. The Line then followed the River Thames to Cricklade, then south towards Wooten Bassett before heading west to Great Somerford and the Green Line. In total it comprised 100 two pounder anti tank, 11 six pounder anti tank and 88 infantry pillbox sites, with 17 miles of anti tank ditches, 6 miles of improved natural obstacles and supported by 8 rail and 53 roadblocks. Total length was 90 miles and was 75% complete, mostly in the centre and east. Swindon and Marlborough were designated Anti Tank Islands.

- Blandford (V Corps) Stop Line: This faced southwest and ran along the River Stour. Blandford Forum, Wimborne Minster and Poole were designated Anti Tank Islands. The line eventually had 160 pillboxes and 10 miles of anti tank ditches but by December no significant work had been undertaken.
- Dorchester (V Corps) Stop Line: This faced west along the South Dorset Downs. Dorchester, Wareham and Maiden Newton were designated Anti Tank Islands. The line eventually had 52 pillboxes and 3 miles of anti tank ditches but, by December, little work on it had also been done.
- Ringwood (Southern Command) Stop Line: This ran for 25 miles from Salisbury to Christchurch along the River Avon and faced west. Ringwood and Christchurch were designated Anti Tank Islands. The Line had 98 pillboxes and 33 roadblocks. By December the Line was half complete.

- <u>Salisbury West (Southern Command) Line:</u> This ran from Salisbury via Frome to Bradford on Avon and faced west. Salisbury was designated an Anti Tank Island. The Line had 44 pillboxes, 5 miles of anti tank ditches, 30 miles of improved natural obstacles and supported by 14 rail and 56 roadblocks. By December the Line was mostly complete
- <u>Salisbury East (Southern Command) Line:</u> This ran from Salisbury via Stockbridge, Andover and Basingstoke to Hook and faced east. A spur defence line was to run on from Salisbury to Totton via Romsey but this was not started. Romsey and Basingstoke were designated Anti Tank Islands. By December the Line had only 12 of 89 pillboxes, 25 of 41 miles of anti tank ditches and 16 of 96 road and railblocks completed. Portsmouth, Southampton, Eastleigh, Bishop's Waltham, West Meon, Wickham and Winchester were also designated as Anti Tank Islands.
- <u>Midhurst (V Corps) Stop Line:</u> This was to run from Chichester to Godalming via Midhurst and Petersfield but was not started. Chichester, Singleton and Midhurst were designated Anti Tank Islands.
- <u>Oxford (Southern Command) Line:</u> This was to run from Leamington to Abingdon, but work was stopped before much work had been undertaken.

- <u>GHQ Line A</u>: This was the responsibility of Aldershot Command and ran from southwest of Reading to Farnham largely along the Rivers` Blackwater and Whitewater and Basingstoke Canal, a distance of 20 miles with the river courses improved and covered by an anti tank ditch, supported by a number of pillboxes. The Line comprised nearly 200 pillboxes, 45 road and 3 railblocks. There were also the Nodal Points at Hindhead, Liphook, Greatham, Alton and Odiham in advance of the Line; an additional 22 infantry company or platoon strongpoints were constructed in front of, astride or behind this line, usually located at important road or rail junctions, bridges and dominant hills. Reading was designated an Anti Tank Island.
- <u>GHQ Line B</u>: This was also the responsibility of Aldershot Command and ran from Farnham to Godalming along the River Wey, a distance of 10 miles. All the bridging areas were heavily protected by pillboxes while the River Wey east of Farnham was also protected by an anti tank ditch that ran for nearly 7 miles. The Line also had 9 infantry company or platoon strongpoints over the River Wey, each with anti tank or field gun sites. Godalming was a Nodal Point.
Lines A and B had 12 2 pdr, 24 13pdr, 20 18pdr guns allocated plus a mobile reserve of 12 4.5in guns, all provided by Aldershot Command.
- <u>Aldershot Command West Switch Line:</u> This ran for over 2 miles along the River Hart from the Basingstoke Canal near Crookham to the London-Portsmouth rail line near Winchfield. However this line remained uncompleted.
- <u>Aldershot Command East Switch Line:</u> This ran for nearly 4 miles along an anti tank ditch from the River Wey east of Farnham to Ash via Runfold and Tongham.
- <u>GHQ Line B (continued):</u> This was the responsibility of Eastern Command and ran from Godalming to Shalford along the River Wey before heading east on the southern edge of the North Downs, covered by an anti tank ditch 8 miles long, to Dorking - a Nodal Point - before following the River Mole to Salford, south of Redhill, then via streams and anti tank ditches strengthened by a second line of pillboxes to the River Eden north of Lingfield and finally joining the Hoo-Newhaven Line at Penshurst. It comprised 22 six pounder anti tank sites and 230 infantry pillboxes, with an additional

22 infantry company or platoon strongpoints in front of, astride or behind this Line located at important road or rail junctions, bridges and dominant hills. There were also at least 7 rail and 60 roadblocks. In addition to Dorking, Nodal Points were Guildford, Shere, Leatherhead, Betchworth, Horley, Redhill, Godstone and Limpsfield.

- GHQ Newhaven-Hoo Line: This ran from Newhaven through Lewes along the River Ouse to Uckfield, then along the rail line to Groombridge, west of Tunbridge Wells, where it joined the River Medway, followed it through Penshurst, Tonbridge, Maidstone and Rochester before crossing the Hoo Peninsula to the Thames Estuary. Lewes, Uckfield, Crowborough, Forest Row, Hartfield, Penshurst, Tonbridge, Wateringbury, Maidstone and Rochester were prepared as Nodal Points. In total it comprised 27 six pounder anti tank sites, mostly in the Maidstone-Tonbridge area, and 150 infantry pillboxes, 17 railblocks and at least 50 roadblocks. Of these 54 pillboxes were along the Hoo to Cliffe stretch. Total length was 80 miles and supported by 13 miles of anti tank ditches, mostly between Uckfield and Eridge while the River Medway below Maidstone was improved as a real anti tank obstacle.
- XII Corps Anti-tank Line (North east Kent): This ran from Dover to Lydden, along the railway to Bekesbourne then north to Sturry before heading east through Tyler Hill and Blean to Graveney north east of Faversham. It comprised 16 six pounder anti tank pillboxes. Along this line the villages of Sturry, Bridge, Wingham, Lydden and Temple Ewell were prepared as Nodal Points.
- XII Corps Anti-tank Line (East Kent): This ran from Ham Street, on the Royal Military Canal, to Ashford and then on to Charing, all three places being Nodal Points
- XII Corps Anti-tank Line (Rother Line): This ran from Hythe, along the Royal Military Canal to Rye, then via the River Rother past Bodiam, Etchingham and Mayfield before joining the Newhaven-Hoo Line at Uckfield. Along and behind the line Ham Street, Woodchurch, Appledore, Rye, Peasmarsh, Four Oaks, Northiam, Tenterden, Hawkhurst, Sedlescombe, Robertsbridge, Hurst Green, Etchingham, Heathfield, and Cross in Hand were prepared as Nodal Points.
- XII Corps Anti-tank Line (Arun Line): This was a continuation of the Rother Line. It continued west of Uckfield along the River Ouse, past Haywards Heath until it joined the River Arun near Horsham. From here it ran northeast to Guildford. Horsham and Cranleigh were designated Nodal Points.
- South East Command Loop Line: This ran southeast and east of Tunbridge Wells from Frant, via Pembury to Tonbridge. It comprised 22 infantry pillboxes. In addition to Tunbridge Wells and Tonbridge, Pembrey and Eridge Green were prepared as Nodal Points.
Other Nodal Points of note in East Sussex included Winchelsea, Brede, Baldslow, Battle, Ninfield, Pevensey, Hailsham, Polegate, Willingdon, Friston and Alfriston. In Kent there were Lamberhurst, Goudhurst, Biddenden, Headcorn and Sellindge.

- GHQ Line East: This was the responsibility of Eastern Command and ran north from Canvey Island to the River Crouch and onto Chelmsford, then Great Dunmow and along the River Chelmer, before reaching Cambridge. Using the extensive waterways of the Fens the Line continued to Ely and Chatteris before concluding at Peterborough. Chelmsford, Great Dunmow, Cambridge, Ely, Littleport, Chatteris and Whittlesey were designated Nodal Points. This Line was seen as a temporary delaying position or base for mobile counter attack troops. As such only 23 six pounder anti tank and 23 two pounder anti tank sites were built, mostly around Chelmsford. The Line was not complete in Cambridgeshire, but 200 infantry pillboxes were built, as were 27 miles of anti-tank ditches, 24 rail and 100 roadblocks. Total length was 65 miles. 30,000 anti tank mines were allocated.

- <u>Mildenhall (Eastern Command) Line:</u> This ran from Mildenhall to Norwood via Littleport.

- <u>GHQ Line East</u>: This was the responsibility of Northern Command and ran along the Rivers Trent and Ouse, with Gainsborough and York identified as Nodal Points. The Line was reduced in July to a Command Demolition Line. 30 infantry pillboxes were built in the Southern area.

- <u>Scotland</u>: Only the Fife Command Line and Perth Blocking Position were developed, aiming to protect Edinburgh and Glasgow.

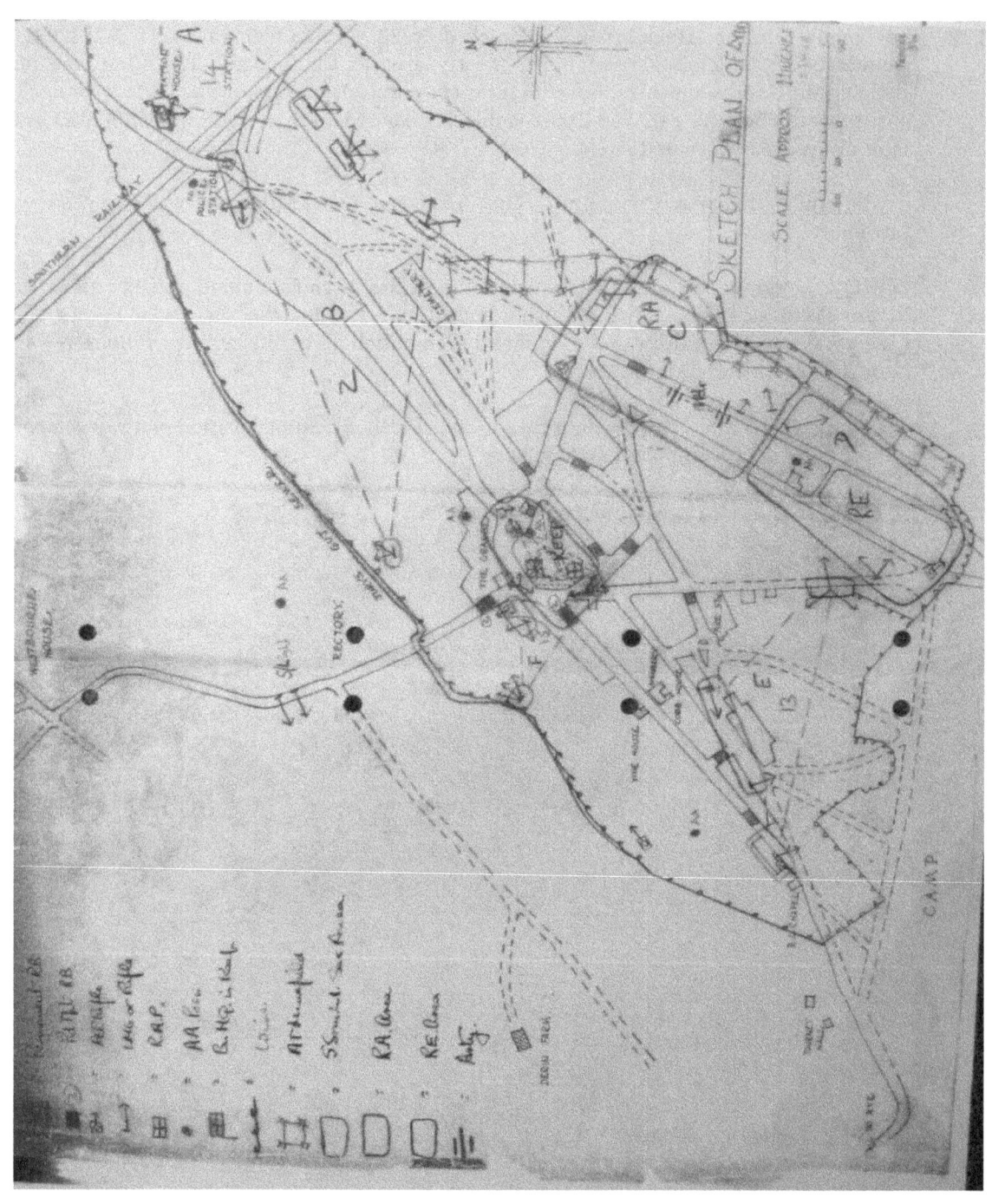

An example of the defence of a nodal point, in this case Lydd.
The town was split into six sectors, with 'C' assigned to the artillery and 'D' to the engineers.
The final keep was based around the church. It is notable that the perimeter did not include
the large army camp and ranges to the south west.

Appendix 9

ROYAL NAVY ORDER OF BATTLE
(On 23 September)

- The Capital ships were only to go into the southern North Sea and English Channel if German capital ships present
- Ships at sea on this date are indicated by an asterix. Ships marked (F) indicate a flagship
- On 23 September the RN had the following operational ships in home waters:
  3 battleships, 2 battlecruisers, 1 aircraft carrier, 2 heavy and 15 light cruisers, 95 destroyers (plus 3 Canadian), 22 sloops, 21 corvettes, 17 submarines, 2 minelayers, 9 minesweepers, 23 motor torpedo boats, 1 monitor, 1 gunboat, 10 armed merchant cruisers plus 245 auxilary minesweeper trawlers, 195 auxiliary anti submarine trawlers, 33 auxiliary minesweeper paddlesteamers and 4 auxiliary anti aircraft ships
- In addition to the Royal Navy ships there were 4,342 private and commercial craft requisitioned by August to meet the Navy`s needs for auxiliary ships and small craft. These included 186 passenger and cargo ships, 259 yachts, 817 trawlers, 67 whalers, 72 tugs, 608 drifters and 107 barges. There were 44 armed merchant cruisers, 11 auxiliary anti aircraft ships, 598 minesweeping craft, 12 minelaying craft, 181 harbour defence craft, 138 boom defence craft, 223 barrage balloon craft, 1031 auxiliary patrol craft, 43 RAF rescue craft and 146 blockships
- Allied ships were as follows (non operational in brackets): 2 battleships (2), 2 cruisers (2), 15 destroyers (3), 18 anti submarine and escort ships, 7 sloops (3), 11 submarines (4), 5 minelayers (1), 4 minesweepers and 1 gunboat (1)
- On 23 September the following RN ships were either being repaired, rebuilt or refitted: 1 battleship, 4 heavy cruisers, 7 light cruisers, 20 destroyers, 5 submarines, 3 sloops, 3 corvettes and 2 minsweepers
- On 25 September 29 officers and 598 men of the French Navy were actively serving with the Royal Navy
- By November 1940 there were the following foreign Naval personnel serving: 2750 French, 2400 Dutch, 1750 Polish and 1000 Norwegian
- Since September 1939 one aircraft carrier, 2 cruisers, 18 destroyers, 9 submarines, 2 sloops, 3 corvettes and 3 minelayers had been built and delivered.
- By the end of September 1940 the following had been launched and were being completed: 5 battleships, 3 aircraft carriers, 6 AA cruisers, 2 light cruisers, 19 destroyers, 4 minelayers, 4 submarines, 1 sloop and 13 corvettes
- The first Lend lease destroyers from the USA arrived on 28 September
- The Navy decided to organise the Home Fleet into two divisions at Scapa Flow and Rosyth, each to be capable of coping with any situation arising in the North Sea
- The First Lord of the Admiralty was the Right Hon Albert Alexander MP; The First Sea Lord and Chief of the Naval Staff was Admiral of the Fleet Sir A Dudley Pound; Vice Chief of the Naval Staff was Vice Admiral T Phillips. The Commander in Chief Home Fleet was Admiral Sir Charles Forbes. The Commandant General Royal Marines was General A Bourne. The Admiralty was essentially an administrative function

- On 30 September 1939 the Royal Navy had 15,365 officers and 145,304 men (including 62,500 reservists); 561 officers and 15,581 Royal Marines and 1237 Royal Marine Police
- On 30 September 1940 the Royal Navy had 28,143 officers and 239,037 men; 974 officers and 27,256 Royal Marines; 1820 Royal Marine Police and 492 officers and 7,363 WRNS. Of the Royal Navy personnel 4672 officers and 5238 were RN Reserve, 7131 officers and 11,270 RN Volunteer Reserve, 3072 officers and 16,416 RN Reserve Patrol Service and 2325 men assigned to Boom Defence
- 11,000 men were deployed to the main fleet anchorage at Scapa Flow
- In May 1941 (the earliest known records) the Navy had 106,985 men in shore establishments. This included 12,639 at Chatham, 11,706 at Portsmouth, 9,817 at Plymouth, 693 at Sheerness, 200 at Dover and 109 at Newhaven.

Nore Command *(Flag Officer: Admiral Sir Reginald Plunkett-Ernle-Erle-Drax)*
- Humber *(Flag Officer: Vice Admiral R Holt, recalled from retirement in 1940)*
(Base: HMS Beaver)
    Destroyers: Vortigern *(3x4-inch, 3x21-inch torpedo)*, Vivacious *(3x4-inch)*, Jersey *(6x4.7-inch, 10x21-inch torpedo)*
    Minelayers: Plover *(1x12-pounder)*, William van de Zaan (Dutch) *(2x5-inch)* *(Both left for Sheerness on 25 September, arriving on 26 September, for a failed minelaying operation near the Goodwin Sands)*

    Ships under repair/refit:
        Destroyer: Express (under *repair until 30 September*) *(4x4.7-inch, 8x21-inch torpedo)*

- Grimsby
    4th Mine Sweeper Flotilla: 6 auxiliary trawlers
    5th Mine Sweeper Flotilla: 4 auxiliary trawlers
    39 auxiliary anti submarine trawlers;
    22 auxiliary patrol trawlers *(10 with 3-pounder, 6 with 13-pounder)*, 3 auxiliary patrol drifters
    13 harbour defence craft; 4 boom defence craft

- Immingham
    18th Cruiser Sqn (part): Manchester (F) *(12x6-inch, 6x21-inch torpedo)*, Birmingham *(12x6-inch, 6x21-inch torpedo)*, Southampton *(12x6-inch, 6x21-inch torpedo)* *(Flag Officer: Vice Admiral L Holland)*
    5th Destroyer Flotilla (part): Jupiter, Javelin, Kelvin *(each 6x4.7-inch, 10x21-inch torpedo)*

-King`s Lynn
    4 auxiliary patrol craft (covering The Wash)
    2 harbour defence craft

- Great Yarmouth *(Flag Officer: Admiral Sir E Fullerton, recalled from retirement in 1940)*
(HMS Midge)
    1st Motor Launch Flotilla (several motor launches)
    3 auxiliary anti submarine yachts (81st Group),

24 auxiliary mine sweeper trawlers,
4 auxiliary mine sweeper drifters

- Lowestoft *(Base: HMS Europa)*
    21st Destroyer Flotilla (part): Draug (Norwegian) *(6x3-inch) (port defence role)*
    8 auxiliary mine sweeper trawlers
    23 auxiliary patrol trawlers *(3 with 6-pounder, 8 with 3-pounder, 10 with 12-pounder)*,
    12 auxiliary patrol drifters *(2 with 6-pounder)*, 3 auxiliary patrol yachts

- Harwich *(Flag Officer: Rear Admiral C Harris) (Base: HMS Badger)*
    16th Destroyer Flotilla (part): Malcolm (F) *(2x4.7-inch, 3x21-inch torpedo)*, Achates *(4x4.7-inch, 8x21-inch torpedo)*,
    18th Destroyer Flotilla (part): Worcester *(4x4.7-inch, 6x21-inch torpedo)*, Verity *(2x4.7-inch)*, Wivern *(3x4.7-inch, 3x21-inch torpedo)*
    21st Destroyer Flotilla (part): Quorn *(2x4-inch) (completed 21 September and on trials)*, Vesper *(2x4-inch)*
    7th Submarine Flotilla (part): H44 (*), H49 (*)
    1st Anti Submarine Strike Force (sloops): Mallard, Pintail (*), Puffin, Sheldrake *(1x4-inch each)*
    2nd Anti Submarine Strike Force (sloops): Guillemot, Shearwater, Widgeon *(1x4-inch each)*
    6th Mine Sweeper Flotilla: Speedwell *(2x4-inch)*, Hussar *(1x4-inch)*
    12th Mine Sweeper Flotilla (auxiliary): Duchess of Fife, Marmion *(1x4-inch)*, Oriole, Queen Empress, Lorna Doorne, Queen of Kent (converted paddle steamers)
    1 auxiliary Anti Aircraft ship (Empress of India)
    17 auxiliary anti submarine trawlers, 2 auxiliary anti submarine yachts,
    3 auxiliary minesweeper drifters,
    14 auxiliary patrol trawlers *(2 with 6-pounder, 10 with 12-pounder)*
    5 harbour defence craft

- Felixstowe *(Base: HMS Beehive)*
    1st Motor Torpedo Boat Flotilla: MTB`s 14, 15, 16, 17, 18 *(2x18-inch torpedo each)*
    4th Motor Torpedo Boat Flotilla (part): MTB`s 22, 28, 29, 31, 32 + 24 *(under repair) (2x21-inch torpedo each)*
    10th Motor Torpedo Boat Flotilla: MTB`s 67, 68, 104, 107 *(2x18-inch torpedo each)*
    4 boom defence craft

- Brightlingsea
    3 auxiliary patrol yachts *(all with 6-pounder)*, 12 auxiliary patrol drifters *(3 with 6-pounder)*

- Sheerness *(Base: HMS Wildfire)*
    2nd Cruiser Sqn (part): Aurora *(6x6-inch, 6x21-inch torpedo)* (Flag Officer Rear Admiral Alban Curteis)
    18th Destroyer Flotilla (part): Veteran *(2x4.7-inch, 3x21-inch torpedo)*, Wild Swan *(3x4.7-inch, 3x21-inch torpedo)*, Venomous *(from 25 Sept) (2x4.7-inch)*, Brilliant *(4x4.7-inch, 8x21-inch torpedo)*

20th Minelaying Destroyer Flotilla: Icarus, Impulsive *(4x4.7-inch, 10x21-inch torpedo each)*
21st Destroyer Flotilla (part): Campbell (F) *(3x4.7-inch, 1x4-inch)*, Cattistock *(2x4-inch)*, Hambledon *(4x4-inch)*, Garth *(4x4-inch)*, Venetia *(4x4-inch, 6x21-inch torpedo)* plus Holderness *(4x4-inch)*, Valorous *(2x4-inch)*, Westminster *(4x4-inch)*, Winchester *(4x4-inch)*, Woolston *(*: escorting Convoy FN 289 from the Thames to the Forth) (4x4-inch)*
6th Submarine Flotilla (part): Ursula *(*)*
Convoy sloops: Egret *(8x4-inch) (*: escorting Convoy FN 289 from the Thames to the Forth)*, Kittiwake *(under repair) (1x4-inch)*
Monitor: Erebus *(2x15-inch)*
Gunboat: Locust *(2x4-inch, 1x3.7-inch)*
Mine Layers: Van Meerlant (Dutch) *(3x3-inch)*, Nautilus (Dutch) *(2x3-inch) (Formed the Thames local defence flotilla from 3 August)*
Motor Torpedo Boat: MTB 106 *(2x21-inch torpedo)*
Motor Torpedo Boat Depot Ship: Aberdonian
10 harbour defence craft; 5 boom defence craft

Ships under repair/refit:
Destroyer: Vanessa *(2x4-inch) (under repair until 4 November 1940)*

- Queenborough
18 auxiliary minesweeper trawlers; 4 auxiliary minesweeper tugs, 6 auxiliary minesweeper drifters, 1 auxiliary minesweeper yacht

- Chatham (building and repair base) *(Flag Officer: Vice Admiral C Danby)* *(Base: HMS Pembroke)*
Sloop: Flores (Dutch) *(3x5.9-inch) (guard vessel)*
1 auxiliary minesweeper paddle steamer (City of Rochester)
2 auxiliary anti aircraft ships (Royal Eagle, Golden Eagle)

Ships under repair/refit:
Cruisers: Galatea *(6x6-inch, 6x21-inch torpedo)* (under *repair until 8 January 1941*), London *(8x6-inch, 8x21-inch torpedo) (rebuilding until 7 January 1941)*, Arethusa *(refitting until 30 September) (6x6-inch, 6x21-inch torpedo-inch, 6x21-inch torpedo)*
Destroyers: Whitshed *(under repair until 21 December) (2x4.7-inch, 3x21-inch torpedo)*, Montrose *(repair until June 1941) (2x4.7-inch, 3x21-inch torpedo)*, Intrepid *(under minor repair) (4x4.7-inch, 10x21-inch torpedo)*, Walpole *(under repair until March 1941) (2x4-inch, 3x21-inch torpedo)*, Atherstone *(under repair until January 1941) (4x4-inch)*
Submarines: Triumph, H28 *(both under repair)*
Sloop: Pelican *(refit until December)*
Gunboat: Gruno (Dutch) *(4x4-inch) (under repair)*

- London *(Flag Officer: Rear Admiral E Boyle VC) (HMS Tower - auxiliary patrol depot)*
Thames Auxiliary Patrol: 57 motorboats (nine each at Holehaven, Cliffe, Tilbury, Greenhithe and Dagenham, four each at Woolwich and Tower of London, three at Greenwich)

Ships under repair/refit:
> Destroyers: Boreas *(4x4.7-inch) (under repair until 23 January 1941)*, Foxhound *(refitting until 12 October) (4x4.7-inch, 8x21-inch torpedo)*, Windsor *(refitting until 31 October) (2x4-inch, 3x21-inch torpedo)*, Margaree (Canadian) *(4x4.7-inch, 8x21-inch torpedo) (refitting until 17 October)*

Dover Command *(Flag Officer: Vice Admiral Sir B Ramsey, recalled from retirement early in 1940)*
- Ramsgate *(Base: HMS Fervent)*
> 4 motor anti submarine boats: (HQ ship, auxiliary patrol)
> 6 auxiliary patrol trawlers *(3 with 6-pounder, 3 with 12-pounder)*, 2 auxilliary patrol yachts *(lmg)*, 5 auxiliary patrol drifters *(lmg)*, 15 auxiliary patrol craft *(lmg)*

- Dover *(HMS Lynx)*
> 11th Motor Torpedo Boat Flotilla: MTB`s 6, 72 *(2x18-inch torpedo each);* ML 1; MASB 50
> Motor Torpedo Boat Depot Ship: Wasp
> 10th Mine Sweeper Flotilla (auxiliary): Laguna Belle, Thames Queen, Emperor of India, Sandown, Princess Elizabeth, Glen Gower, Medway Queen, Queen of Thanet (converted paddle steamers) *(2x40mm, 1x90cm S/L each)*
> 4 auxiliary anti submarine trawlers (27th Group)
> 17 auxiliary minesweeper trawlers
> 15 auxiliary patrol drifters *(all with 6-pounder)*, 10 auxiliary patrol craft *(lmg)*

Newhaven *(Base: HMS Fortune)*
> 19 auxiliary patrol craft; 1 auxiliary patrol yacht *(6-pounder)*

Littlehampton
> 12 auxiliary patrol craft

Portsmouth Command *(Flag Officer: Admiral Sir W James)*
(HMS Collingwood - training establishment, Fareham; HMS Dolphin - submarine base, Gosport; HMS Dryad - navigation school, Fareham; HMS Excellent - gunnery school, Pitsea; HMS Vernon - torpedo and mining school, Pitsea; HMS St George - training establishment, Gosport)

> Battleship: Courbet *(12x12-inch, 22x5.5-inch)* (French- partly operational, used as anti aircraft ship defending the port)
> 2nd Cruiser Sqn (Part): Cardiff *(5x6-inch, 8x21-inch torpedo)*, Leopard *(4x5-inch)* (French destroyer- partly operational)
> 1st Destroyer Flotilla: Berkeley *(4x4-inch)*, Fernie (*) *(4x4-inch)* plus Le Mistral *(4x5-inch)* (French with British crew)
> 9th Destroyer Flotilla (part): Wolverine *(2x4.7-inch, 3x21-inch torpedo)*, Volunteer *(2x4.7-inch)*, Vanoc *(2x4-inch)*, Viscount *(2x4-inch, 3x21-inch torpedo)*
> 22nd Destroyer Flotilla: Saladin *(1x4-inch)*, Sardonic *(1x4-inch)* plus Mackay *(4x4.7-inch)* (11th Flotilla), Witherington *(3x4.7-inch, 3x21-inch torpedo)* (17th Flotilla)
> 23rd Destroyer Flotilla (Torpedo Boat Destroyers): Z7 (Dutch) *(2x3-inch) (operational 19 Sept)*, La Melpomene *(2x4-inch)* (French), Le Branlebus *(2x4-inch)* (French), La Cordeliere *(2x4-inch)* (French), La Flore *(2x4-inch)* (French), L`Incomprise *(2x4-inch)* (French)

Destroyer: L`Ouragan *(4x5-inch)* (French with Dutch crew)
5th Submarine Flotilla: Talisman, Utmost *(commissioned 17 August)*, Swordfish plus H43 and L27 *(both training)*
Corvette: La Malouine (French) *(1x4-inch)* *(*: escorting Convoy HX72 from Canada)*
Minelayer: Douwe Aukes (Dutch) *(3x3-inch)*
Minesweeper: Le Chevreuil, La Capricieuse (both French) *(2x4-inch each)* *(the former had just commissioned)*
Chasseurs (A/S and escort): 5,6,7,8,10,11,12,13,14,15,41,42,43,106 (French with British crew) *(1x3-inch)*
Depot Ship: L`Amiens, L`Arras, L`Epinal, La Diligente (French) *(2x4-inch each)* *(L'Amiens was recommissioned on 20 August)*
3rd Motor Torpedo Boat Flotilla: MTB`s 100 and 102 *(2x21-inch torpedo each)* *(both non-operational)*
4th Motor Torpedo Boat Flotilla (part): MTB`s 25, 30 *(2x21-inch torpedo each)* plus 3, 4, 33, 19 (refit) *(2x18-inch torpedo each)*
11th Motor Torpedo Boat Flotilla (part): MTB`s 5, 69, 70 (under repair), 71 (under repair) *(2x18-inch torpedo each)*
4th Motor Anti Submarine Boat Flotilla *(forming)*: MASB`s 52, 54, 55, 56, 57, 58 plus 48 (Cowes), 40 and 49 (Southampton) and 45 and 51(*)
Patrol Craft: Le Quentin Roosevelt (French) *(1x3-inch)*
15 auxiliary anti submarine trawlers, 2 auxiliary anti submarine yachts
22 auxiliary minesweeper trawlers, 5 auxiliary minesweeper drifters
16 harbour defence craft, 10 boom defence craft

HMS Iron Duke, a former battleship and now a gunnery training ship (6x13.5-inch, 12x6-inch) was used as an anti aircraft battery. It was also designated as the main blockship for Portsmouth harbour.

Ships under repair/refit:
Battleship: Queen Elizabeth *(8x15-inch, 16x6-inch)* *(rebuilding until 10 December)*
Light cruiser: Jacob van Heemskerck (Dutch) *(10x4-inch)* *(refiting to AA role from 10 July)*
Destroyers: Viceroy *(4x4-inch)* *(refitting until January 1941)*, Acheron *(4x4.7-inch, 8x21-inch torpedo)* *(under repair until 2 December)*, Boadicea *(4x4.7-inch, 8x21-inch torpedo)* *(under repair until February 1941)*
Sloops: Bideford *(2x4-inch)* *(under repair until December 1941)*, Foxglove *(2x4-inch)* *(repair until July 1941)*
Submarines on refit: Ondine, Orion (Both French)

- Southampton (convoy base) *(Flag Officer: Rear Admiral S Tillard)*
Western Patrol (Armed Merchant Cruiser): California *(6x6-inch)*
Destroyer: Issac Sweers (Dutch) *(build completed May 1941)*
Netlayers: Minster, Tonbridge
Sloop under repair: L`Oronaise (French)
Plus MASB's 53, 59, 60 and 41 building at Hythe

- Poole
2 auxiliary minesweeper drifters; 6 harbour defence craft

- Portland (training base) *(Flag Officer: Vice Admiral E Drummond)*
(HMS Boscawen - training establishment; HMS Osprey - Base)
    1st Motor Anti Submarine Boat Flotilla: MASB 1, 5 plus Kalan (training), 14 and 47
    4 auxiliary Anti submarine trawlers
    5 auxiliary minesweeper trawlers
    4 harbour defence craft; 1 boom defence craft

- Dartmouth
    Sub Chasers: 11, 15 (both Polish)
    3 auxiliary anti submarine trawlers
    12 auxiliary patrol trawlers (Belgian with Polish crews)

Western Approaches Command (Plymouth)
(Flag Officer: Admiral Sir M Dunbar-Naismith VC)
(HMS`s Defiance and Drake - training establishments, Devonport; HMS Raleigh - training establishment, Torpoint)
    Battleship: Revenge *(8x15-inch, 12x6-inch)*, Paris *(12x12-inch, 22x5.5-inch)* (French – non operational depot ship)
    18th Cruiser Sqn (part): Newcastle *(12x6-inch, 6x21-inch torpedo)*, Emerald *(7x6-inch, 16x21-inch torpedo)*
    17th Destroyer Flotilla: Broke (*) *(2x4.7-inch, 6x21-inch torpedo)*, Witch *(3x4.7-inch, 3x21-inch torpedo)*, Wanderer *(2x4.7-inch)*, Vansittart *(3x4.7-inch)*, Whitehall (*) *(2x4.7-inch)*
    Polish Destroyer Flotilla: Blyskawica, Burza, Garland *(each had 7x5-inch, 6x21-inch torpedo)* (Flotilla formed on 21 September)
    Minelayer: Defiance
    Sloops: Enchantress *(2x4.7-inch)*, Le Belfort *(2x4-inch)* (French), Le Coucy *(2x4-inch)* (French) *(all non operational)*
    Depot: Gdynia (Polish)
    17 auxiliary anti submarine trawlers
    14 auxiliary minesweeper trawlers, 1 auxiliary minesweeper drifter
    7 harbour defence craft; 9 boom defence craft

    Ships under refit/repair:
        Cruisers: Exeter *(6x8-inch, 6x21-inch torpedo)* *(refitting until 10 March 1941)*, Frobisher *(5x7.5-inch, 4x21-inch torpedo)* *(rebuilding until January 1942)*, Belfast *(12x6-inch, 6x21-inch torpedo)* *(rebuilding until October 1942)*
        Submarine: Severn *(minor refit)*
        Destroyers: Westcott *(2x4-inch)* *(refitting until 9 November)*, Ouragan (Polish) *(7x5-inch, 6x21-inch torpedo)* *(refitting)*, Le Triumphant (French) *(5x5.5-inch)* *(refitting from 3 September)*
        Torpedo Boat: Le Bouclier (Dutch/French) *(2x4-inch)* *(under repair until 30 September)*
        Minelayer: Adventure *(4x4.7-inch, 340 mines)* *(refit completed 18 September)*

- Fowey
    3rd Motor Anti Submarine Boat Flotilla: MASB 42, 43, 46

2 auxiliary patrol trawlers (*both with 6-pounder*); 1 auxiliary patrol drifter (*3-pounder*)

- Falmouth *(Flag Officer: Vice Admiral Sir H Kitson, recalled from retirement in 1940)* *(Base: HMS Forte)*
    2nd Submarine Flotilla (part): Tribune (*)
    Sloop: La Conquerante *(2x4-inch)* (French)
    Minesweeper: La Moqueuse *(2x4-inch)* (French)
    2 auxiliary anti submarine yachts
    2 auxiliary minesweeper trawlers
    3 auxiliary patrol trawlers, 2 auxiliary patrol drifters (*with 2-pounder*)
    4 harbour defence craft;

    Ship under repair: Sloop - La Suippe *(4x4-inch)* (French - non operational)

- Cardiff
    5 harbour defence craft

- Swansea *(Base: HMS Lucifer)*
    3 auxiliary anti submarine yachts
    9 auxiliary minesweeper trawlers, 2 auxiliary minesweeper drifters
    4 auxiliary patrol trawlers
    3 harbour defence craft

    Submarine under repair: Creole (French)

- Milford Haven *(Flag Officer: Rear Admiral P Phillips)* *(Base: HMS Forward)*
    Minesweeper: Jan van Gelder (Dutch) *(1x3-inch)*
    Torpedo Boat: G13 (Dutch) (*decommissioned 9 August*)
    17 auxiliary anti submarine trawlers
    5 auxiliary minesweeper trawlers, 2 auxiliary minesweeper drifters
    5 auxiliary patrol trawlers (*2 with 6-pounder*)
    3 harbour defence craft
    Accomodation ship: Medusa (Dutch) *(3x3-inch)* (ex minesweeper)

- Holyhead
    Torpedo Boat: G15 (Dutch) (Irish Sea escort role)
    22 auxiliary anti submarine trawlers (17 were Dutch)
    1 auxiliary minesweeper trawler, 2 auxiliary minesweeper drifters

- Belfast *(Flag Officer: Rear Admiral R King)* *(Base: HMS Antrim)*
    Northern Patrol (Armed Merchant Cruiser): Worcestershire *(6x6-inch)*
    2nd Motor Anti Submarine Boat Flotilla: MASB 6, 8 (*), 9 (*), 10, 11 plus 12 and 13
    32 auxiliary anti submarine trawlers
    7 auxiliary minesweeper trawlers
    5 harbour defence craft

- Londonderry *(Base: HMS Ferret)*

22nd Destroyer Flotilla (part): Skate *(1x4-inch)* *(*: escorting Convoy HX72 from Canada)*

- Larne *(Base: HMS Racer)*
    5 auxiliary anti submarine trawlers (35th Group)

- Birkenhead
    3 auxiliary anti submarine yachts
    2 auxiliary minesweeper trawlers

- Liverpool (convoy and refit/repair base)
(Flag Officer: Vice Admiral L Crabbe)
(HMS Conway- training establishment; HMS Mersey - depot; HMS Wellesley - training establishment)
    9th Destroyer Flotilla (part): Havelock (F), Highlander *(*: escorting Convoy OG43 from Liverpool to Gibraltar)*, Harvester *(*: escorting Convoy OG43 from Liverpool to Gibraltar)*, Hesperus, Hurricane *(*: escorting Convoy OG43 from Liverpool to Gibraltar)* *(each had 3x4.7-inch, 8x21-inch torpedo)*; Beagle, Bulldog *(both had 4x4.7-inch, 8x21-inch torpedo)*
    11th Destroyer Flotilla: Winchelsea *(4x4-inch)*, Warwick *(2x4-inch)*, Walker *(*: returning from escorting Convoy OB217 from Liverpool to Canada)* *(2x4-inch)*, Vanquisher *(*)* *(2x4-inch)*
    22nd Destroyer Flotilla: Sabre, Shikari, Scimitar *(*: escorting Convoy HX72 from Canada)* *(1x4-inch each)*
    Northern Escort Force (destroyers): St Laurent *(4x4.7-inch, 8x21-inch torpedo)*, Skeena (Both Canadian) *(2x4.7-inch, 4x21-inch torpedo)*
    Northern Escort Force (sloops): Wellington *(2x4.7-inch)*, Scarborough *(*)* *(2x4-inch)*
    Northern Escort Force (corvettes): Arabis, Calendula, Coreopsis, Erica, Geranium, Gladiolus, Gloxinia, Heartsease *(*: escorting Convoy HX72 from Canada)*, Periwinkle, Mallow *(*: escorting Convoy OG43 from Liverpool to Gibraltar)*, Heliotrope *(*)*, Anenome *(*: escorting Convoy OG43 from Liverpool to Gibraltar)* *(each had 1x4-inch)*
    Northern Patrol (Armed Merchant Cruisers): Forfar *(8x6-inch)*, Patroclus *(6x6-inch)*, Laurentic *(7x6-inch)* plus Salopian *(refitting)* *(6x6-inch)*
    Destroyer Depot ship: Woolwich *(4x4-inch)*
    2 auxiliary anti submarine trawlers
    9 auxiliary minesweeper trawlers; 2 Dutch auxiliary minesweeper trawlers
    5 harbour defence craft

    Ships refit/repair: destroyer – Mashona *(8x4.7-inch, 4x21-inch torpedo)* *(refitting until November)*

- Barrow
    2 auxiliary anti submarine trawlers
    2 harbour defence craft

- Ardrossan *(Base: HMS Fortitude)*
    6 auxiliary anti submarine trawlers; 4 auxiliary anti submarine yachts (82nd Group)
    9 minesweeper auxiliary trawlers (57th and 141st Groups)

- Cambeltown
    8 auxiliary anti submarine trawlers (39th and 84th Groups)
    2 harbour defence craft

- Clyde (convoy, building and repair base)
(Flag Officer Glasgow: Vice Admiral J Troup; Flag Officer Greenock: Vice Admiral B Watson; Flag Officer Northern Patrol: Rear Admiral E Spooner)
(HMS Orlando - Base, Greenock; HMS Spartiate - Base, Glasgow)
    10th Cruiser Sqn: Kenya *(12x6-inch, 6x21-inch torpedo)*
    12th Destroyer Flotilla: Keppel (F) *(2x4.7-inch, 6x21-inch torpedo)* *(*: escorting Convoy HX72 from Canada)*, Arrow, Antelope, Active *(*: escorting Convoy HX72 from Canada)*, Anthony (*), Amazon *(each had (4x4.7-inch, 8x21-inch torpedo)*
    10th Destroyer Escort Group: Ottawa (Canadian) *(4x4.7-inch)* *(*: escorting Convoy OB217 from Liverpool to Canada)*
    2nd Submarine Flotilla (part): Forth (depot); Cachalot, Porpoise, Taku, Tuna, Trident, Tigris
    7th Submarine Flotilla (part) *(operational training)*: Cyclops (depot); Port Alecto (depot), H32, H34, Otway, H31, H33, H50, O9 (Dutch), B1 (Norwegian), Upright *(Commissioned 3 September)*
    11th Minesweeper Flotilla (auxiliary): Caledonia, Mercury, Jupiter, Jeanie Deans, Helvellyn (converted paddle steamers)
    5 auxiliary minesweeper trawlers (92nd Group)
    7 harbour defence craft; 8 boom defence craft

    Ships under repair/refit:
        `Cruiser - Suffolk *(repair until March 1941)* *(8x8-inch)*, Sussex *(rebuilding until 1942)* *(8x8-inch, 8x21-inch torpedo)*, Fiji *(under repair until 31 January 1941)* *(12x6-inch, 6x21-inch torpedo)*
        Destroyer - Fearless *(refitting until 8 October)* *(4x4.7-inch, 8x21-inch torpedo)*, Ambuscade *(under repair until 8 November)* *(4x4.7-inch, 6x21-inch torpedo)*, Douglas *(repair until end September)* *(3x4.7-inch, 3x21-inch torpedo)*, Cleveland *(6x4-inch)* *(completed 18 September and on trials)*
        Submarine - Oberon *(under repair)*
        Corvette – Picottee *(completed 5 September)*, Clarkia *(under repair)*, Rhododendron *(working up trials) (1x4-inch each)*

- Tobermory
    10 auxiliary anti submarine trawlers; 1 auxiliary anti submarine yacht

- Stornoway *(Base: HMS Mentor)*
    6 auxiliary minesweeper trawlers

- Scapa Flow *(Flag Officer Orkney and Shetlands: Vice Admiral Sir T Binney)*
    Home Fleet:
    Battlecruiser Sqn: Repulse *(6x15-inch, 9x4-inch)*
    Aircraft Carrier: Furious *(801 Sqn - 9 Skua; 825 Sqn - 18 swordfish)*
    1st Cruiser Sqn: Berwick *(8x8-inch)*, Norfolk *(8x8-inch, 8x21-inch torpedo)*, Southampton

(12x6-inch, 6x21-inch torpedo) (Flag Officer: Vice Admiral J Cunningham)
18th Cruiser Sqn (Part): Glasgow *(12x6-inch, 6x21-inch torpedo) (sailed to Humber on night of 24 September to join Nore Command)*
1st Anti Aircraft Cruiser Sqn: Cairo *(*: escorting Convoy OA218 from Firth of Forth)*, Curacao *(8x4-inch each)*
3rd Destroyer Flotilla: Isis *(4x4.7-inch, 10x21-inch torpedo)*, Duncan *(4x4.7-inch, 8x21-inch torpedo)*
6th Destroyer Flotilla: Somali (F), Eskimo, Matabele, Punjabi *(8x4.7-inch, 4x21-inch torpedo each)*
21st Destroyer Flotilla: Vimy, Versatile *(2x4-inch each)*
Northern Patrol (Armed Merchant Cruisers): Letitia (*), Circassia (*), Forfar (*) *(6x6-inch each)*
Western Patrol (Armed Merchant Cruisers): Cheshire (*), Derbyshire (*) *(6x6-inch each)*
Anti Aircraft Ship: Alynbank *(8x4-inch, 8x2-pounder)*
Minelayer (Coastal): Linnet, M2
Depot ships: Maidstone (destroyer), Greenwich (destroyer), Atreus (minelayer)
5 auxilliary anti submarine trawlers, 6 auxilliary anti submarine drifters
11 auxilliary minesweeper trawlers, 7 auxilliary minesweeper drifters
26 boom defence craft

- Invergordon *(Base: HMS Flora)*
    2 auxilliary anti submarine trawlers, 2 auxilliary anti submarine drifters
    3 auxilliary patrol trawlers *(all with a 12- pounder)*
    1 harbour defence craft

- Aberdeen *(Base: HMS Bacchante)*
    1 auxilliary anti submarine trawler
    8 auxilliary minesweeper trawler
    3 auxilliary patrol trawlers *(1 with a 12- pounder)*

- Peterhead
    3 auxilliary patrol trawlers *(all with a 12- pounder)*

Rosyth Command *(Flag Officer: Vice Admiral C Ramsey) (HMS Cochrane)*
2nd Battle Sqn: Nelson (F), Rodney *(9x16-inch, 12x6-inch each) (Flag Officer: Admiral John Tovey)*
Battlecruiser Sqn: Hood *(8x15-inch, 12x5.5-inch) (Flag Officer: Vice Admiral W Whitworth)*
10th Cruiser Sqn: Nigeria (F) *(commissioned 23 September) (12x6-inch, 6x21-inch torpedo) (Flag Officer: Rear Admiral H Burrough)*
15th Cruiser Sqn: Naiad (F) *(10x5.25-inch, 6x21-inch torpedo)*, Bonaventure *(8x5.25-inch, 6x21-inch torpedo) (Flag Officer:Rear Admiral E King)*
3rd Destroyer Flotilla: Electra *(4x4.7-inch, 8x21-inch torpedo)* plus Vanity *(4x4-inch)*, Vega, Verdun, Vimiera (*), Vivien, Wallace (*), Wolfhound, Wolsey (*) *(each had 4x4-inch)*
4th Destroyer Flotilla: Cossack (F), Sikh, Zulu, Maori *(8x4.7-inch, 4x21-inch torpedo each)*; Fame *(under repair until 11 October) (4x4.7-inch, 8x21-inch torpedo)*
5th Destroyer Flotilla (part): Kipling, Kashmir, Jackal, Jaguar (*) *(6x4.7-inch, 10x21-inch torpedo each)* Plus Sleipner (Norwegian) *(2x4-inch, 1x40mm, 2x21-inch torpedo)*

6th Destroyer Flotilla: Bedouin (F), Ashanti (*: *both on search and rescue sortie on 24 September*), Tartar *(8x4.7-inch, 4x21-inch torpedo each)*
16th Destroyer Flotilla (part): Watchman *(2x4-inch)*, Eglington *(4x4-inch)* (*- *To Sheerness*)
3rd Submarine Flotilla: Titania (depot) plus Wilk, Snapper, Sunfish, Seawolf (*under repair*)
1st Minesweeper Flotilla: Bramble *(1x4-inch)*, Speedy, Birthmark, Hazard, Hebe, Seagull *(minor refit at Leith) (each had 2x4-inch)*
7th Minesweeper Flotilla (auxilliary) (part): Devonia, Plinlimmon, Skiddaw (converted paddle steamers)
1st Minelayer Sqn (auxilliary): Southern Prince (*), Menesthesus (*), Port Napier (*), Port Quebec (*)
Minelayers: Ringdove, M3, Teviot Bank
Convoy Sloops: Black Swan *(6x4-inch)*, Fleetwood *(4x4-inch)*, Hastings *(2x4-inch)*, Londonderry *(2x4.7-inch)*, Lowestoft (*: *escorting Convoy HX72 from Canada*) *(2x4.7-inch)*, Weston (*: *escorting Convoy OA218 from Firth of Forth*) *(2x4-inch)*, Stork (*under repair at Grangemouth until 16 March 1941*) *(6x4-inch)*

Northern Escort Force (* detached at Gibraltar):
Sloops: Aberdeen *(4x4-inch)*, Fowey (*: *escorting Convoy OG43 from Liverpool to Gibraltar*) *(2x4-inch)*, Rochester *(2x4-inch)*, Sandwich (*) *(2x4-inch)*, Leith *(2x4.7-inch)* (*: *escorting Convoy HG44 from Gibraltar*)
Minesweepers: Gleaner (*: *escorting Convoy OG43 from Liverpool to Gibraltar*), Jason (*both had 2x4-inch*)
Corvettes: Bluebell, Camelia, Clematis, Primrose (*: *escorting Convoy OA218 from Firth of Forth*), Primula, Fleur de Lys, Gardenia, Hibiscus, Peony (*: *escorting Convoy OG43 from Liverpool to Gibraltar*) *(1x4-inch each)*

Depot ship: Honigsvaag (Norwegian)
13 auxilliary minesweeper trawlers, 1 auxilliary minesweeper paddle steamer
9 boom defence craft

- Granton
7th Minesweeper Flotilla (auxilliary) (part): 4 converted paddle steamers
4 auxilliary anti submarine trawlers
9 auxilliary minesweeper trawlers, 7 auxilliary minesweeper drifters
6 harbour defence craft

- Dundee *(Base: HMS Cressy)*
9th Submarine Flotilla: Ambrose (depot) plus Clyde (*), L23 (French), O22 (Dutch), O23 (Dutch), O24 (Dutch), Rubis (French), L26 (French) (*under repair*), O21 (Dutch) (*refit*ting)
Torpedo Boats: Z5 (Dutch), Z6 (Dutch), Z8 (Dutch) *(2x3in)* (Z6 decommissioned on 9 October)
5 auxilliary minesweeper trawlers
2 auxilliary patrol trawlers (*both with a 12-pounder*), 4 auxiliary patrol yachts

- Blyth

6th Submarine Flotilla (part) (training role): Elfin (depot), Sturgeon

- North Shields
   8th Mine Sweeper Flotilla (auxilliary): Glen Avon, Glen Usk, Snaefell, Westward Ho, Southsea (converted paddle steamers)
   13 auxilliary minesweeper trawlers, 2 auxilliary minesweeper drifters

- Tyne (building and repair base) *(Flag Officer: Rear AdmiralW Maxwell) (Base: HMS Calliope)*
   10 auxilliary patrol trawlers *(6 with a 12-pounder)*, 6 auxilliary patrol drifters

   Ships under repair/refit:
      Cruiser: Edinburgh *(refitting until October) (12x6-inch, 6x21-inch torpedo)*, Penelope *(under repair until 17 August 1941) (6x6-inch, 6x21-inch torpedo)*
      Submarine: Sea Lion *(refitting until 23 October)*
      Destroyer: Kelly *(under repair until 19 December) (6x4.7-inch, 10x21-inch torpedo)*
      Minesweeper: Agamemnon *(refitting for mine layer role until 18 October)*
      Minelayer: Jan van Brakel (Dutch) *(refitting) (2x3-inch)*
      Motor Anti Submarine Boat: 7 *(under repair)*

-Hartlepool
   13 auxilliary minesweeper trawlers, 3 auxilliary minesweeper drifters
   2 auxilliary patrol trawlers

Other Commands:

Force H (Gibraltar) *(Flag Officer: Admiral Sir J Somerville)* (Base: HMS Coromorant)
(Deployed in June 1940 to replace the French fleet covering the western Mediterranean)
   Battlecruiser: Renown (F) *(6x15-inch, 20x4.5-inch, 8x21-inch torpedo)*
   8th Destroyer Flotilla (part): Firedrake *(4x4.7in, 8x21-inch torpedo)*
   13th Destroyer Flotilla (part): Gallant, Griffin, Encounter, Hotspur *(4x4.7-inch, 8x21-inch torpedo each)*, Vidette *(2x4-inch)*, Velox (*) *(2x4-inch)*, Wishart (*) *(3x4.7-inch, 3x21-inch torpedo)*, Wrestler *(2x4-inch)*
   7th Anti Submarine Group: 5 auxilliary ani submarine trawlers

Force M
(Deployed to Freetown in Operation Menace against French Vichy forces at Dakar)
(Flag Officer: Vice Admiral J Cunningham, Commander in Chief Mediterranean Fleet)
   Battleship: Resolution (#), Barham (F) *(8x15-inch, 12x6-inch each)*
   Aircraft Carrier: Ark Royal *(30 swordfish - 810, 818 and 820 Sqns; 24 skuas - 800 and 803 Sqns)*
   Heavy Cruisers: Australia (Australian), Cornwall, Cumberland, Devonshire *(8x8-inch each)*
   Light Cruisers: Delhi, Dragon *(6x6-inch each)*
   8th Destroyer Flotilla (part): Faulknor (F), Fortune, Fury, Forester, Foresight *(4x4.7-inch, 8x21-inch torpedo each)*
   13th Destroyer Flotilla (part): Greyhound, Eclipse, Escapade, Echo *(4x4.7-inch, 8x21-inch torpedo each)*, Inglefield *(5x4.7-inch, 10x21-inch torpedo each)*

Sloops: Deptford *(2x4.7-inch)*, Milford *(2x4-inch);* Le Savorgnan de Brazza, Presidente Honduce *(both 3x5.5-inch)* (both French)
Minesweepers: Le Commandant Duboc, Le Commandant Domine *(2x4-inch each)* (both French)
Ani Submarine Trawlers: Lady Elsa, Northern Gem

Note (#): HMS Resolution had been badly damaged by torpedo during these operations and would require dockyard repairs for some months

FLEET AIR ARM

Naval Air Stations – UK *(Flag Officer: Rear Admiral R Davies VC)*

Yeovilton (HMS Heron) (Somerset)	827 Sqn (12 Albacore) (forming in September)
	750 Sqn (Shark) (observer training) (#)
	759 Sqn (9 Skua, 5 Roc) (fighter school)
	760 Sqn (4 Skua, 2 Roc) (fighter pool)
	794 Sqn (Roc and Swordfish) (air target towing)
St Merryn (Cornwall)	829 Sqn (9 Albacore) (formed in June)
	774 Sqn (3 Skua, 3 Roc, 4 Swordfish) (bombing and gunnery school)
	792 Sqn (6 Roc and Skua) (air target towing)
Bircham Newton (Norfolk)	826 Sqn (12 Albacore) (+)
Worthy Down (HMS Kestral) (Hampshire)	807 Sqn (12 Fulmar) (forming in September)
	755 Sqn (Shark) (air gunner training)
Eastleigh (Hampshire)	758 Sqn (13 Shark, 6 Osprey) (air gunner training) (#)
	780 Sqn (mixed) (conversion course Training)
Lee on Solent (HMS Daedalus) (Hampshire)	828 Sqn (9 Albacore) (forming in September)
	752 Sqn (Albacore) (observer training) (#)
	765 Sqn (Walrus and Swordfish) (seaplane pool)
	781 Sqn (Swordfish, Fulmar and Walrus) (communications)
	793 Sqn (6 Roc and Skua) (air target towing) (#)
Thorney Island (Hampshire)	812 Sqn (12 Swordfish) (+)
Pembroke Dock (South Wales)	764 Sqn (Walrus and Swordfish) (seaplane school)
Hatston (HMS Sparrowhawk) (Orkneys)	821 Sqn (9 Swordfish)
	823 Sqn (9 Swordfish)
	801 Sqn (12 Skua)
	700 Sqn (Walrus)
	771 Sqn (14 Swordfish) (fleet requirements)
Arbroath	751 Sqn (Walrus) (observer training) (#)
	753 Sqn (Shark) (observer training) (#)
	754 Sqn (Walrus) (observer training) (#)
	767 Sqn (Swordfish) (deck landing training)
	778 Sqn (mixed) (trials)
Campbeltown (Argyll)	772 Sqn (4 Swordfish) (fleet requirements)
Wick (Highlands)	804 Sqn (12 Sea Gladiators) (*)
Castletown (Highlands)	808 Sqn (12 Fulmar) (*)
Sullom Voe (Shetlands)	700 Sqn (flight of Walrus)
Iceland	701 Sqn (6 Walrus)

Notes:
- In September 1939 the FAA had 232 first line aircraft, over half of which were Swordfish, and 191 trainers
- In September 1940 the FAA had 310 aircraft stationed at home and over 1760 aircraft in total (600 swordfish, 400 Albacore, 192 Skua, 162 Walrus, 136 Roc, 127 Fulmar, 60 Sea Gladiators, 59 Martlets and 27 Buffalo

- Those squadrons marked with an asterix were attached to the RAF's 13 Group, Fighter Command, for operations. Those marked with a cross were co-operating with the RAF's Coastal Command. The 700 series squadrons were mainly non operational
- 812 and 823 Squadrons had been reformed after HMS Glorious was sunk in June
- 801 Squadron was assigned to HMS Furious
- 804 Squadron was assigned to the air defence of Scapa Flow and was to re-equip with Martlets from September
- 808 Squadron was formed in July and also assigned to defend dockyards. In October it was re-assigned to HMS Ark Royal
- 700 Squadron was responsible for all warship based amphibians in home waters
- 701 Squadron had operated in Norway until evacuated to Iceland. In October it moved to Stornoway
- 759 and 760 Squadrons moved from Eastleigh on 16 September
- 769 Squadron moved to Sandbanks near Poole during September
- 794 Squadron was formed on 1 August
- The training squadrons marked # moved from Ford and Yeovilton in mid August. In early October they moved to Trinidad
- The Blackburn Skua (225 mph, 800 miles range) was a dedicated dive bomber; the Fairey Albacore (159 mph and 932 miles range) and Fairey Swordfish (154 mph and 1060 miles range) biplanes were mainly torpedo armed reconnaissance and strike aircraft; the Gloster Sea Gladiator (244 mph and 423 miles range) and Fairey Fulmar (273 mph and 780 miles range) were fighters, while the Blackburn Roc (196mph, 800 miles range) was a shore based fighter similar to the Defiant; the Supermarine Walrus was an amphibious reconnaissance aircraft. The Brewster Buffalo fighters (320 mph, 800 miles range) were with 804 Squadron for testing since July, while the Grumman Martlets (324 mph and 1350 mile range) were export versions of an American fighter (most originally destined for France), available from 7 September.

Appendix 10
ROYAL AIR FORCE ORDER OF BATTLE

Headquarters *(HQ: Whitehall)*
Chief of the Air Staff: Air Chief Marshal Sir C Newall
Vice Chief of the Air Staff: Air Vice Marshal Sir R Peirse
Director of Operations (Home): Group Captain D Stevenson
Director of Ground Defence: Group Captain A Saunders

NOTES:
- Air Chief Marshal Newall, who had been in charge from the outset, was replaced in October as he was not considered to possess the strength of personality to lead the RAF further in the War. Air Vice Marshal Peirse was appointed in late April to this new post and was promoted to command Bomber Command in early October. Group Captain Stevenson was promoted to command 2 Bomber Group in February 1941; he favoured the expensive low-level daylight operations
- Aircraft production rose from 719 (143 fighters) in February to 1,665 (496 fighters) in July
- 683 aircraft had been received from America in the first three quarters of 1940
- Manpower on 1 September 1939 was recorded as 12,591 + 163,030 and on 1 October 1940 was recorded as 23,636 + 391,715 (plus 17,364 WAAF).

FIGHTER COMMAND
(As at 15 September)

- On 4 June the Command had 446 operational aircraft (371 being Spitfires or Hurricanes), with another 36 fighters held in the storage units. On 18 August this figure rose to 704 aircraft (620 Spitfires or Hurricanes) and 289 in the storage units
- On 18 September 665 fighters were with squadrons, including 362 Hurricanes and 212 Spitfires
- On 20 September 192 fighters were available in storage units
- Between 1 June and 21 September 1,949 fighters had been built or imported, including 1102 Hurricanes (32 imported) and 560 Spitfires
- Between 10 July and 31 October the Command was to lose 1021 fighters, with another 940 damaged
- 310 Czech Squadron was formed on 10 July, 302 Polish Squadron was formed on 13 July, 303 Polish Squadron was formed on 2 August, 306 Polish Squadron was formed on 28 August, 312 Czech Squadron was formed on 29 August; 307 Polish Squadron was formed on 5 September as a night fighter unit; 308 Polish Squadron was formed on 9 September
- The Hawker Hurricane's speed was about 315 mph, a max range of 680 miles, operational height of up to 10,515 metres. It began service in 1938
- The Supermarine Spitfire's speed was about 346 mph, a max range of 600 miles, operational height of up to 9,300 metres. It began service in 1939
- The Boulton Paul Defiant's speed was about 260 mph, a max range of 465 miles, operational height of 9,250 metres. It began service in 1939 and was designed as an anti

bomber fighter as it had no forward firing guns. Despite early successes its squadrons were decimated during the summer
- The Bristol Blenheim's speed was about 278 mph, a max range of 1050 miles, operational height of 7,500 metres. It began service in 1938 but was already obsolete as a fighter
- The Gloster Gladiator's speed was about 253 mph, a max range of 440 miles, operational height of 9,700 metres. It began service in 1938 but was already obsolete
- Air Chief Marshal Dowding was appointed in 1936 and had had his retirement postponed several times; he was finally re-assigned in November 1940 to head the British Air Commission to America. Air Vice Marshal Brand had been appointed on 15 June, after the Group was reformed; he had previously been the Director for repair and maintenance. Air Vice Marshal Park had been appointed on 20 April from the staff of Fighter Command and moved to 23 Training Group in December. Air Vice Marshal Leigh-Mallory had commanded the Group from the outbreak of War and took over 11 Group in December. Air Vice Marshal Saul had been appointed in July 1939 and took over 12 Group in December. 14 Group was formed from the BEF's Air Component on 26 June; Air Vice Marshal Henderson was appointed on 20 July, having commanded Training Command. Air Vice Marshal Blount had recently commanded the Air Component but died in a take off accident on 23 October
- Filton * denotes sector HQ; - Warmwell indicates a RAF station within the sector.

Headquarters *(HQ: Stanmore)*
Air Officer Commander in Chief: Air Chief Marshal Sir H Dowding

9 Group *(HQ: Preston) (formed 9 August to cover the northwest and Northern Ireland) (AOC: Air Vice Marshal W McClaughry)*

10 Group *(HQ: Box, Wiltshire) (Covering the south west and South Wales)*
(AOC: Air Vice Marshal Sir Q Brand)
Ford   flight 25 Sqn (Blenheim) *(night fighter role)*

Middle Wallop *   A Flight 23 Sqn (Blenheim) *(night fighter role)*
                                   238 Sqn (Hurricane) *(from 10 September)*
                                   604 Sqn (Blenheim/Beaufighter) *(night fighter role)*
                                   609 Sqn (Spitfire)
- Boscombe Down   56 Sqn (Hurricane)
- Warmwell   152 Sqn (Spitfire)

Filton * (HQ only)
- Exeter   B Flight 87 Sqn (Hurricane)
                                   601 Sqn (Hurricane) *(from Tangmere on 7 September)*
- Bibury   A Flight 87 Sqn
- Colerne
- Roborough (FAA station)   247 Sqn (Gladiator) *(formed 21 August)*

St Eval   234 Sqn (Spitfire) *(from Middle Wallop on 11 September)*
Pembrey   79 Sqn (Hurricane) *(from Biggin Hill 8 September)*

11 Group *(HQ: Uxbridge, Middlesex) (Covering London and the south east)*
(AOC: Air Vice Marshal Sir K Park)

Biggin Hill * 72 Sqn (Spitfire) *(from 12 September)*
                92 Sqn (Spitfire) *(from 8 September)*
                B Flight 141 Sqn (Defiant) *(night fighter role)*
- Gravesend   66 Sqn (Spitfire) *(from Kenley 10 September)*

Kenley *   253 Sqn (Hurricane) *(from Prestwick 29 August)*
                501 Sqn (Hurricane) *(from 10 September)*
- Croydon   605 Sqn (Hurricane) *(from Drem 7 September)*
- Redhill (forward base) 600 Sqn (Blenheim/Beaufighter) *(night fighter role) (from
                    Hornchurch 12 September)*
- Hawkinge (forward base)
- Lympne (forward base)
- West Malling (forward base)

Tangmere *   213 Sqn (Hurricane) *(from Exeter 7 September)*
                607 Sqn (Hurricane) *(from 1September)*
                FIU (Fighter Interception Unit - trials)
- Westhampnett 602 Sqn (Spitfire)
- Ford (FAA Station) B Flight 23 Sqn *(night fighter role)*

Northolt   1 Sqn RCAF (Hurricane)
                229 Sqn (Hurricane) *(from Wittering 9 September)*
                303 (Polish) Sqn (Hurricane) *(formed 2 August)*
                B Flight 264 Sqn (Defiant) *(night fighter role)*
- Hendon   504 Sqn (Hurricane) *(From 6 September; to Exeter
                    26 September)*

Hornchurch *   603 Sqn (Spitfire) *(from 29 August)*
- Rochford   41 Sqn (Spitfire) *(from 3 September)*
                222 Sqn (Spitfire) *(from 29 August)*
- Manston (forward base)

North Weald *   Flight 25 Sqn (Blenheim) *(night fighter role)*
                249 Sqn (Hurricane) *(from Boscombe Down 1 September)*
- Stapleford Abbots 46 Sqn (Hurricane)

Debden *   17 Sqn (Hurricane)
- Castle Camps 73 Sqn (Hurricane) *(converted to night fighter role in September)*
- Martlesham Heath 257 Sqn (Hurricane) *(from 5 September)*
                A Flight 25 Sqn (Blenheim) *(night fighter role)*

12 Group *(HQ: Watnall, Nottingham) (Covering the east, Midlands and North Wales)*
(AOC: Air Vice Marshal T Leigh-Mallory)

Coltishall	74 Sqn (Spitfire) *(from 9 September)*
	242 Sqn (Hurricane)
Duxford *	302 (Polish) Sqn (Hurricane) *(non operational – formed 13 July)*
	310 (Czech) Sqn (Hurricane) *(formed 10 July and operational in late August)*
	312 (Czech) Sqn (Hurricane) *(non operational – formed 29 August)*
- Fowlmere	19 Sqn (Spitfire)
Wittering *	1 Sqn (Hurricane) *(from 9 September)*
	266 Sqn (Spitfire)
Digby *	151 Sqn (Hurricane)
	611 Sqn (Spitfire)
- Wellingore	29 Sqn (Blenheim) *(night fighter role)*
Kirton in Lindsey *	616 Sqn (Spitfire) *(from Coltishall 9 September)*
	A Flight 264 Sqn (Defiant) *(night fighter role)*
	307 (Polish) Sqn (Defiant) *(non operational – formed 5 September)*
- Speke	308 (Polish) Sqn (Hurricane) *(non operational – formed 9 September)*
- Ringway	B Flight 64 Sqn (Spitfire) (non operational)
Church Fenton *	85 Sqn (Hurricane) *(from 5 September)*
	306 (Polish) Sqn (Hurricane) *(formed 28 August)*
- Leconfield	A Flight 64 Sqn (Spitfire)
	302 Sqn (Hurricane)

13 Group *(HQ: Newcastle) (Covering the north east)*
(AOC: Air Vice Marshal R Saul)

Catterick	54 Sqn (Spitfire) *(from Hornchurch 3 September)*
	A Flight 219 Sqn (Blenheim) *(night fighter role)*
Usworth *	43 Sqn (Hurricane)
Acklington *	32 Sqn (Hurricane) *(from Biggin Hill 27 August)*
	610 Sqn (Spitfire) *(from 31 August)*
	B Flight 219 Sqn (Blenheim) *(night fighter role)*

14 Group *(HQ: Edinburgh) (Covering Scotland)*
(AOC: Air Vice Marshal M Henderson)

Turnhouse *	3 Sqn (Hurricane) *(from 14 September)*
	65 Sqn (Spitfire) *(from Hornchurch 27 August)*
	141 Sqn (Defiant)
- Drem	111 Sqn (Hurricane)
	263 Sqn (Whirlwind)
- Prestwick	615 Sqn (Hurricane)
- Montrose	A Flight 145 Sqn (Hurricane)
- Dyce	B Flight 145 Sqn (Hurricane)
- Sumburgh	232 Sqn (Hurricane)
Aldergrove (N.Ireland)	245 Sqn (Hurricane)

O.T.U (Operational Training Units)

Aston Down	5 O.T.U	10 Group (Spitfire, Gladiator, Blenheim, Defiant)
Sutton Bridge	6 O.T.U	11 Group (Hurricane, Gladiator)
Hawarden	7 O.T.U	10 Group (Spitfire)

- Fighter Command also controlled 22 (Army Co-operation) Group (commanded by Air Vice Marshal C Blount), with 12 squadrons. Each squadron was equipped with 12 Lysander biplanes and had a two-fold role - coastal patrol at dawn and dusk as well as spraying invading troops with poison gas using 250-pound gas spray tanks. Trials were also made with a 20 mm canon in an anti tank role, but this was not successful with the available aircraft. Two squadrons were to detach aircraft as required by the Air Ministry and would come under the operational control of GHQ Home Forces for reconnaissance operations.

    The squadron locations were as follows (with the Army Commands they were attached to):

2 Sqn	Sawbridgeworth (Eastern)
4 Sqn	York (Northern)
13 Sqn	Hooton Park (Western)
16 Sqn	Weston Zoyland (Western)
26 Sqn	Gatwick (Eastern)
110 Sqn RCAF	Odiham (Southern)
225 Sqn	Tilshead (Southern)
239 Sqn	Hatfield (Eastern)
241 Sqn	Inverness (Scottish)
268 Sqn	Bury St Edmunds (Eastern)
613 Sqn	Firbeck (Northern)
614 Sqn	Grangemouth (Scottish)

- Plan "Banquet Light" called for the offensive use of flights, each of five Tiger Moth or Magister trainer aircraft (a total of 350 aircraft) and each armed with 8 20 lb fragmentation bombs, to be attached to the army co-operation squadrons above. Their role was to bomb invasion forces, including those penetrating inland. Preparations were also made to fit the aircraft with insecticide powder spraying equipment, if required. These aircraft had a top speed of 210 mph but had no defensive armament.

Details are as follows:

Sqn	Flights attached	Aircraft from	Army Command
2	2	6 Flight Training Sqn (FTS)	Eastern
4	4	4 and 21 FTS	Northern
13	2	14 FTS	Western
16	2	10 FTS	Western
26	2	8 and 18 FTS	South Eastern
110 RCAF	2	13 FTS	Southern
225	2	2 and 3 FTS	Southern
239	2	1 FTS	Eastern
268	2	22 FTS	Eastern
613	2	9 FTS	Northern
614	2	12 FTS	Scottish

RAF BOMBER COMMAND
(As at 15 September)

- The Command was tasked with attacking the embarkation ports and shipping, attacking invasion fleets and, should a German force succeed in landing, attack invasion forces on British soil. However, its main role continued to be the reduction in the ability of the enemy to wage air attacks on the country, concentrating on attacking aircraft factories, oil plants and airfields
- 1 Group was reformed from the Advanced Air Striking Force (AASF) on 22 June, having been disbanded in December 1939
- 24 medium bombers were always at readiness during specific invasion periods, ready to co-operate with the Army at thirty minutes notice
- During the period 26 June to 13 October the Command flew 105 day and 102 night operations (1885 and 8804 sorties respectively). The cost was 246 aircraft (2.3%), 66 during daylight operations (3.5%). By comparison the Command flew 41 day and 46 night operations between 10 May and 26 June (1601 and 3484 sorties respectively). The cost was 145 aircraft (2.9%), 92 during daylight operations (5.7%)
- On 19 September the Command had 42 squadrons (38 operational) comprising 573 operational aircraft
- 300 Polish Squadron was formed on 1 July, 301 Polish Squadron on 26 July, 311 Czech Squadron on 29 July, 304 Polish Squadron on 22 August and 305 Polish Squadron on 29 August
- In November 1940 foreign air force personnel in the country included: 8500 Poles, 1250 Czech, 350 French, 270 Dutch and 165 Belgians
- Air Chief Marshal Portal was appointed in early April. He was promoted to Chief of the Air Staff on 25 October, having a reputation for clear thinking and diplomacy. Air Commodore Breen had been appointed on 27 June from the staff of 4 Group; he became the Director of Postings in December. Air Vice Marshal Robb had previously commanded the Central Flying School. Air Vice Marshal Baldwin was recalled to the service in August 1939. Air Vice Marshal Coningham was appointed in July 1939. Air Vice Marshal Harris became the Deputy Chief of the Air Staff in November before later taking over command of Bomber Command
- The Bristol Blenheim's speed was about 285 mph, a range of 1125 miles, operational height of 8310 metres and a bomb load of 1000 pounds. By the summer of 1940 It was regarded as being inadequate for its primary task
- The Fairey Battle's speed was about 240 mph, a range of 1050 miles, operational height of 7800 metres and a bomb load of 1000 pounds. A divebomber, it entered service in 1937 but was already outdated and was decimated in May 1940
- The Handley Page Hampden's speed was about 250 mph and a bomb load of 4000 pounds It entered service in 1938 and was usually reduced to night operations during 1940
- The Vickers Wellington's speed was about 256 mph, a range of 2210 miles, operational height of 3625 metres and a bomb load of 4500 pounds. It entered service in 1938
- The Armstrong Whitley's speed was about 223 mph, a range of 1656 miles and a bomb load of 7000 pounds. It entered service in 1937 and was usually reduced to night operations during 1940.

Headquarters (HQ: *High Wycombe*)
Air Officer Commander in Chief: Air Chief Marshal C Portal (until 5 October)

1 Group (*Hucknall, Nottingham*)   (all equipped with Battle light bombers)
AOC: Air Commodore J Breen
    12 Sqn +   *Binbrook*
    88 Sqn   *Sydenham, NI*
    103 Sqn *   *Newton*
    142 Sqn +   *Binbrook*
    150 Sqn *   *Newton*
    226 Sqn   *Sydenham, NI*
    300 Sqn (Polish) *Swinderby*
    301 Sqn (Polish) *Swinderby*
    304 Sqn (Polish) *Bramcote (non operational – formed 22 August)*
    305 Sqn (Polish) *Bramcote (non operational – formed 29 August)*

+ *Denotes squadrons earmarked for Northern Ireland.*
* *Denotes squadrons re-equipping with Wellingtons in late September*

2 Group (*Huntingdon*)   (all equipped with Blenheim medium bombers)
AOC: Air Vice Marshal J Robb (from 17 April)
    15 Sqn   *Alconbury*
    18 Sqn   *West Raynham*
    21 Sqn   *Lossiemouth*
    57 Sqn   *Lossiemouth*
    40 Sqn   *Wyton*
    82 Sqn   *Watton*
    101 Sqn   *West Raynham*
    105 Sqn   *Watton*
    107 Sqn   *Wattisham*
    110 Sqn   *Wattisham*
    114 Sqn   *Oulton*
    139 Sqn   *Horsham St Faith*
    218 Sqn   *Oakington*

3 Group (*Exning, Suffolk*)   (all equipped with Wellington heavy bombers)
AOC: Air Vice Marshal J Baldwin
    9 Sqn   *Honington*
    37 Sqn   *Feltwell*
    38 Sqn   *Marham*
    75 Sqn (NZ)   *Feltwell*
    99 Sqn   *Newmarket*
    115 Sqn   *Marham*
    149 Sqn   *Mildenhall*
    214 Sqn   *Stradishall*
    311 Sqn (Czech) *Honington (*)*

4 Group *(York)* (all equipped with Whitley heavy bombers)
AOC: Air Vice Marshal A Coningham

    10 Sqn *Leeming*
    51 Sqn *Dishforth*
    58 Sqn *Linton on Ouse*
    77 Sqn *Tholthorpe*
    78 Sqn *Dishforth*
    102 Sqn *Prestwick* (attached to Coastal Command)
    7 Sqn *Leeming* (* equipped with Stirlings)

5 Group *(Grantham, Lincolnshire)* (all equipped with Hampden light bombers)
AOC: Air Vice Marshal A Harris (from 11 September 1939 until late November)

    44 Sqn *Waddington*
    49 Sqn *Scampton*
    50 Sqn *Lindholme*
    61 Sqn *Hemswell*
    83 Sqn *Scampton*
    106 Sqn *Finningley*
    144 Sqn *Hemswell*
    271 Sqn *Doncaster* (transport role)

RAF COASTAL COMMAND

- The RAF planned to deploy 339 aircraft in the Command, but accepted that less than two thirds of these aircraft would be available by 1939. In 1938 orders were placed in America for 250 Lockheed Hudson aircraft
- In June the Command had about 500 operational aircraft
- The two Dutch Naval Air Squadrons were reformed on 1 June 1940 as they had evacuated their own aircraft.
- The Command was tasked with continuing its reconnaissance activities ranging from observing enemy build up and locating invasion forces while attacking targets of opportunity. They were also expected to assist the Navy in its counter attack role by providing long-range air support
- For the invasion the most important patrol routes would be "Hatch" off Normandy (once every 24 hours), "Dundee" between Dunkirk and Dieppe (once every 24 hours), "Hookos" off the Scheldt (after dusk and before dawn) and "Moon 1" mid Channel south off Beachy Head (at dusk and to continue after nightfall when there is a possibility of seeing a large convoy or fast ships)
- The Avro Anson began service in 1936, the Short Sunderland in 1938 and the Bristol Beaufort and Blackburn Botha in 1939. The Hudson was purchased from the USA from 1938 as a replacement for the Anson. The Beaufort was a dedicated torpedo bomber, a role not attained until September 1940
- The Beaufort's speed was about 267 mph, a max range of 1600 miles and a bomb load of 2000 pounds
- The Sunderland's speed was about 212 mph, a max range of 2137 miles and a bomb load of 2000 pounds
- The Hudson's speed was about 246 mph, a max range of 1960 miles and a bomb load of 750 pounds
- The Anson's speed was about 170 mph, a max range of 664 miles and a bomb load of 360 pounds
- The Botha only entered squadron service in June 1940 but were poor aircraft. Its speed was 212mph and range of 1270 miles
- The Supermarine Stranraer flying boat entered service in 1937, had a speed of 165mph and a range of 1000 miles
- The Saunders Roe Lerwick flying boat entered service in 1939 but was disliked. It had a speed of 166mph and a range of 1540 miles
- Air Chief Marshall F Bowhill had commanded since the start of the War; in January 1941 he was appointed to command the Ferry Organisation. Air Commodore Parry had commanded since June 1939 and took over the Technical Training Command in February 1941. Air Vice Marshal Tyssen had been Air Officer Commanding in Iraq. Air Commodore Breese had commanded since 1938 but was to die in a landing accident in March 1941.

Headquarters *(HQ: Northwood)*
Air Officer Commander in Chief: Air Chief Marshal F Bowhill

15 Group (HQ: Rosyth)　　　(AOC: Air Commodore R Parry)
Aldergrove (NI)　　　　　　　502 Sqn (Anson, Botha and Whitley)
Stranraer　　　　　　　　　　240 Sqn (Stranraer)

Hooton Park (Mersey)	48 Sqn (Beaufort and Anson)
Pembroke Dock	209 Sqn (Stranraer and Lerwick), 320 Sqn (Dutch) (Anson and Fokker)
Mount Batten (Plymouth)	10 Sqn RAAF (Sunderland)
St Eval	217 Sqn (Beaufort and Anson), 236 Sqn (Blenheim)

16 Group (HQ: Chatham) (AOC: Air Vice Marshal J Tyssen, from January 1940)

Bircham Newton	206 Sqn (Hudson), 235 Sqn (Blenheim)
Detling	53 Sqn (Blenheim), 500 Sqn (Anson)
Thorney Island	59 Sqn (Blenheim)
North Coates	22 Sqn (Beaufort)

18 Group (HQ: Rosyth) (AOC: Air Commodore C Breese)

Sullom Voe (Shetlands)	201 Sqn (Sunderland), 204 Sqn (Sunderland)
Sumbergh (Shetlands)	248 Sqn (Blenheim)
Dyce	254 Sqn (Blenheim), 612 Sqn (Anson and Hudson)
Leuchars	224 Sqn (Hudson), 233 Sqn (Hudson) (from 14 September)
Lossiemouth	21 Sqn (Blenheim), 57 Sqn (Blenheim)
Thornaby	220 Sqn (Hudson), 608 Sqn (Botha and Anson)
Oban	210 Sqn (Sunderalnd)
Wick	42 Sqn (Beaufort), 269 Sqn (Hudson and Anson) (Operational at end of September)

Operational strength at 29 September: 58 Anson, 47 Blenheim, 46 Hudson, 16 Sunderland flying boats 14 Beaufort, 12 Whitley, 10 Botha, 4 Stranraer flying boats. A total of 245 aircraft against an establishment of 417 aircraft.

RAF TRAINING COMMAND

- During the 1930's expansion scheme eight new flying training schools were constructed at Tern Hill, Hullavington, Brize Norton, South Cerney, Shawbury, Little Rissington, Lossiemouth and Kinloss. To relieve the strain on existing airfields 24 relief landing grounds were built, with another 24 under construction, in early 1940
- By 1939 there were 31 flying training schools operating, all operated by civilians
- Until 1943 all aircrew duties, other than pilot, were undertaken by air gunners. Some of these were trained in bombing but none in navigation, this task being left to the pilot
- On 27 May the Command was reformed as the Flying Training and Technical Training Commands
- Air Vice Marshal Pattinson had commanded 23 Training Group before being promoted on 27 May. Air Vice Marshal Foster had been appointed on the outbreak of war. Air Commodore Cochrane moved from the staff of 6 Group on 1 July; on 21 October he became Director of Flying Training. Air Commodore Howe had commanded since 1938 and was to retire in 1941
- 17 Group was affiliated to Coastal Command
- In May a scheme to reinforce the Bomber Command with aircraft from this Command in the event of invasion, codenamed "Banquet" was approved. It was intended that as many suitable aircraft as possible with experienced pilots (mostly instructors) would fly to Bomber Command stations for operations. A total of 169 aircraft (1 Hampden, 3 Wellingtons, 27 Blenheims, 33 Battles, 48 Ansons plus 33 Audaxs, 12 Harts and 12 Hinds (these being biplanes)) were assigned in addition to 6 and 7 Groups
- Other elements vital to keeping the RAF's fighting commands operational included the Civilian Repair Organisation, set up within the motor vehicle manufacturing industry to carry out repairs at RAF airfields and set up three Repairable Equipment Depots to salvage materials and a number of Civilian Repair Units to rebuild wrecked aircraft. This Organisation was headquartered in Oxford. The RAF created the 50th Maintenance Unit to recover and transport crashed aircraft to its repair depots. The contribution that these elements made to the defence of the country was remarkable, with 35% of all aircraft issued to combat units coming from the salvage and repair units. In addition 61% of all aircraft written off were repaired. Late in the summer British Railways and London Transport were also asked to help with repairs and spares. Another invaluable formation was the Air Transport Auxiliary, a group of male and female pilots who flew aircraft to and from the operational bases and repair facilities
- On 25 July 251 aircraft were available within 48 hours from air supply units, with another 111 available within 4 days. On 19 September this figure was 107 aircraft within 48 hours and 121 aircraft within 4 days.

Headquarters Flying Training Command *(HQ: Reading)*
Air Officer Commander in Chief: Air Vice Marshall L Pattinson

6 Group *(HQ: Abingdon)*   (AOC: Air Vice Marshall W MacFoster)
    10 OTU (Whitley)   *Abingdon*
    11 OTU (Wellington)   *Bassingbourn*
    12 OTU (Battle)   *Benson*
    15 OTU (Wellington)   *Harwell*

    18 Polish OTU (Battle)   *Hucknall*
    19 OTU (Whitley)   *Kinloss*
    20 OTU (Wellington)   *Lossiemouth*
    304 Polish OTU (Battle)   *Bramcote* (non operational role)
    305 Polish OTU (Battle)   *Bramcote* (non operational role)

7 Group *(HQ: Brampton)*   (AOC: Air Commodore Hon R Cochrane) (Group formed 15 July)
    13 OTU (Whitley)   *Bicester*
    14 OTU (Hampden)   *Cottesmore*
    16 OTU (Hampden)   *Upper Heyford*
    17 OTU (Blenheim)   *Upwood*

17 Group *(HQ: Lee on Solent)* (AOC: Air Commodore T Howe) (Coastal Command)
    1 OTU (Anson, Hudson, Beaufort, Blenheim) *Silloth (Gosport and Calshot also used)*

Types available with active units: 224 Blenheim, 119 Wellington, 92 Hampden, 79 Battle and 72 Whitley.

RAF MAINTENANCE COMMAND

- As a result of the expansion of the RAF the Air Council decided in 1938 to transfer all maintenance work to a new command
- When the Command was formed there were 12 maintenance units but by 1940 this number had risen to 55
- Each group contained a varying number of maintenance units, mostly located to the west of the line Southampton-Edinburgh. These units comprised two-thirds service personnel and one-third civilians
- Air Vice Marshal Bradley was appointed on the Command's formation.

Headquarters *(HQ: Andover)*
Air Officer Commander in Chief: Air Vice Marshal J Bradley

40 Group *(HQ: Andover)*
- This Group was responsible for the supply of all equipment, other than complete aircraft, fuel, oxygen and ammunition
- It comprised 55 maintenance units
- There were seven main equipment depots, one each in Cumberland, Cheshire, Lancashire, Staffordshire, Worcestershire, Gloucestershire and Berkshire
- Each depot was responsible for supplying operational units in its geographical area, running across the country west to east, and organised so that it could cover supply for neighbouring depots if they were unable to function
- A two-day delivery service to operational units was the aim, while an integral stock control organisation kept updated records of what was where and in what quantities.

41 Group *(HQ: Andover)*
- This Group was under the technical direction of the Ministry of Aircraft Production
- It was responsible for the reception, storage, maintenance and delivery of all aircraft
- It comprised 26 maintenance units
- By the end of the War there were 24 aircraft storage units dispersed over the country, but within a half mile of a suitable airfield
- Three-quarters of these units were manned by civilians.

42 Group *(HQ: Reading)*
- This Group was the Armament Group, responsible for the supply and storage of explosives, ammunition and oxygen to operational units. It was also responsible for checking quantities of petrol and oil delivered to aviation and oil storage depots by the Petroleum Board
- It comprised 35 maintenance units.

43 Group *(HQ: Oxford)*
- This Group was responsible for the repair of aircraft and associated equipment, salvage of aircraft and repair of marine craft
- This Group was also under the technical direction of the Ministry of Aircraft Production
- It comprised 27 maintenance units

- There were two civilian manned repair depots at Kidbrooke and Ruislip (south and west London respectively) and three serve manned depots at Henlow, St Athan and Sealand. In addition, nine salvage centres were formed and a number of civilian transport firms trained in dismantling and moving crashed aircraft.

53 Wing

This Wing was under the direct administration of Command Headquarters. It comprised the packing depots, which prepared aircraft and spares for despatch overseas.

54 Wing

This Wing was under the direct administration of Command Headquarters. It was responsible for all road transport.

RAF BALLOON COMMAND

- Between the World Wars technology had improved so that balloons could be flown up to 1200 metres by a strong steel cable controlled by a motor winch and two thin wires for stability. Each balloon was about 20 metres long and 10 metres tall and was filled with hydrogen gas, the envelope consisting of cotton material coated with rubber
- At the start of the War balloons were assigned to major industrial centres and ports, though Dover didn't get any until June, Falmouth in August and the south Wales ports from July. The balloons were designed to hinder low flying and dive-bombing attacks
- With the fall of France the Command had to be expanded to meet the increased threat, though this was met with few of the problems other forces faced. Balloon production had steadily increased to nearly 1200 a month during the summer, enough to replace the many balloons shot down or those that had broken loose
- Each balloon required a winch truck and trailer for the gas cylinders and had a crew of ten men.
- Air Vice Marshall Boyd had been in command since 1938. In early November he was to be Deputy Air Officer Commander, RAF Middle East, but was taken prisoner en route when his aircraft landed in Sicily. Group Captain Guilfoyle commanded his Group from November 1939 until 1941. Air Commodore Quinnell moved from the staff of the AASF in January 1940. Air Commodore Walser was brought back from the Middle East in January. Air Commodore Smith was appointed in February 1940. Air Commodore Busteed was recalled from retirement on the outbreak of war and retired in August 1941.

Headquarters *(HQ: Stanmore, Middlesex)*
Air Officer Commander in Chief: Air Vice Marshal O Boyd

30 Group (London) (AOC: Group Captain W Guilfoyle)
    1 Balloon Centre (Kidbrooke, South London)
        901 Sqn (Abbey Wood, South London) (45 balloons)
        902 Sqn (Kidbrooke) (45 balloons)
        952 Sqn (Sheerness) (45 balloons - 32 waterborne)
        961 Sqn (Dover) (45 balloons - 8 waterborne) (A Flight: Western Heights;
            B Flight: Langdon)
    2 Balloon Centre (Hook, Surrey)
        903 Sqn (Forest Hill) (45 balloons)
        904 Sqn (Clapham) (45 balloons)
        905 Sqn (Kensington) (45 balloons)
    3 Balloon Centre (Stanmore, Middlesex)
        906 Sqn (Hampstead) (45 balloons)
        907 Sqn (Woodberry Down) (45 balloons)
        956 Sqn (Colnbrook) (24 balloons)
    4 Balloon Centre (Chigwell, Essex)
        908 Sqn (City of London) (45 balloons)
        909 Sqn (East Ham) (45 balloons)
        910 Sqn (Dagenham) (45 balloons - 3 waterborne)
        928 Sqn (Harwich) (24 balloons - 10 waterborne)

31 Group (Birmingham) (AOC: Air Commodore J Quinnell)
    5 Balloon Centre (Sutton Coldfield)
        911 Sqn (West Bromwich) (48 balloons)
        913 Sqn (Sutton Coldfield) (40 balloons)
        962 Sqn (Milford Haven) (24 balloons - 9 waterborne)
    6 Balloon Centre (Wythall)
        914 Sqn (Northfield) (40 balloons)
        915 Sqn (Rowkeath) (40 balloons)
        916 Sqn (Coventry) (32 balloons)
        917 Sqn (Coventry) (24 balloons)
    7 Balloon Centre (Alvaston, Derby)
        918 Sqn (Alvaston) (32 balloons)
    8 Balloon Centre (Fazakerley, Merseyside)
        919 Sqn (Birkenhead) (52 balloons - 12 waterborne)
        921 Sqn (Fazakerley) (48 balloons)
    9 Balloon Centre (Warrington)
        922 Sqn (Cuerdley) (32 balloons)
        923 Sqn (Runcorn) (32 balloons)
        949 Sqn (Crewe) (32 balloons)
    10 Balloon Centre (Manchester)
        925 Sqn (Manchester) (40 balloons)
        926 Sqn (Bowlee) (40 balloons)

32 Group (Romsey, Hampshire) (AOC: Air Commodore A Walser)
    11 Balloon Centre (Bristol)
        912 Sqn (Brockworth) (24 balloons)
        927 Sqn (Bristol) (32 balloons)
        935 Sqn (Filton) (24 balloons)
        951 Sqn (Bristol) (40 balloons)
        957 Sqn (Yeovil) (24 balloons)
    12 Balloon Centre (Fareham)
        924 Sqn (Eastleigh) (24 balloons)
        930 Sqn (Southampton) (50 balloons - 10 waterborne)
        932 Sqn (Portsmouth) (32 balloons)
        933 Sqn (Gosport) (24 balloons)
    13 Balloon Centre (Plymouth)
        934 Sqn (Plymouth) (24 balloons)
        959 Sqn (Falmouth) (24 balloons - 8 waterborne)
        954 Sqn (Torpoint) (24 balloons - 6 waterborne)
    14 Balloon Centre (Cardiff)
        953 Sqn (Cardiff) (39 balloons - 7 waterborne)
        958 Sqn (Swansea) (35 balloons - 3 waterborne)
        965 Sqn (Port Talbot) (16 balloons)
        966 Sqn (Newport) (40 balloons)
        969 Sqn (Barry) (16 balloons)

33 Group (Sheffield) (AOC: Air Commodore S Smith)
    15 Balloon Centre (Newcastle)
        936 Sqn (Benton) (40 balloons - 4 waterborne)
        937 Sqn (South Tyne) (32 balloons - 3 waterborne)
        938 Sqn (Billingham) (48 balloons)
    16 Balloon Centre (Sheffield)
        939 Sqn (Sheffield) (40 balloons)
        940 Sqn (Rotherham) (32 balloons)
    17 Balloon Centre (Sutton on Hull)
        942 Sqn (Hull) (42 balloons - 24 waterborne)
        943 Sqn (Hull) (32 balloons)

34 Group (Edinburgh) (AOC: Air Commodore H Busteed) (Group formed 7 April)
    18 Balloon Centre (Glasgow)
        929 Sqn (South Queensferry) (24 balloons - 7 waterborne)
        945 Sqn (Glasgow) (40 balloons)
        946 Sqn (Renfrew) (48 balloons)
        947 Sqn (Glasgow) (32 balloons)
        948 Sqn (Rosyth) (24 balloons)
        967 Sqn (Ardrossan) (48 balloons)
        968 Sqn (Belfast) (40 balloons - 8 waterborne)

    20 Balloon Centre (Lyness, Orkneys)
        950 Sqn (Lyness) (32 balloons)
        960 Sqn (Lyness) (24 balloons - 16 waterborne)
        920 Sqn (Kyle of Lochalsh) (16 balloons - 11 waterborne)

Appendix 11
OBSERVER CORPS

- The Corps was honoured with the prefix "Royal" in April 1941 for its invaluable service during the Battle of Britain
- The Corps was an entirely volunteer affair; its members were appointed as Special Constables in the Police. The Corps had its roots in the First World War when the Admiralty arranged for the Police to report aircraft seen or heard. This system was improved by the end of the War but, as with most new ideas, it was quickly reduced to a filing system in the War Office. Following trials in 1924 throughout Kent a reporting system was organised in Kent and Sussex, with a network of posts connected by telephone to an Observer Centre, who were in turn linked to the air defence headquarters. By the end of 1925 four group headquarters and 100 posts had been established. In 1929 the RAF took over responsibility from the War Office. A fifth group was formed in 1931, while a bigger expansion had been arranged by 1936, covering the South and East of England
- In 1937 the country was divided into five areas, each administered by a small staff of retired officers directly controlled from the Corps headquarters, which was itself moved from Uxbridge to Stanmore to be co-located with Fighter Command Headquarters
- On 24 August 1939 the Corps was mobilised, consisting 32 centres, over 1000 posts and about 30,000 observers. Responsibility for administration moved from the Police to the Air Ministry, with the volunteers relinquishing their status as special constables
- Four large gaps existed in the Corps coverage - northwest Scotland, most of southwest Scotland, west Wales and Cornwall. These gaps were not filled before the end of 1940
- Corps structure revolved around the group headquarters, where information was passed to RAF sector operations rooms and adjacent observer centres; each centre would provide information to up to six sectors and have between 30-34 observer posts under command, each about five miles apart but usually overlapping.

SOUTHERN AREA

1 Group *(HQ: Maidstone. Linked with Biggin Hill)*
2 Group *(HQ: Horsham. Linked with Kenley)*
3 Group *(HQ: Winchester. Linked with Tangmere)*
4 Group *(HQ: Oxford)*
17 Group *(HQ: Watford. Linked with Northolt)*
18 Group *(HQ: Colchester. Linked with North Weald)*
19 Group *(HQ: Bromley. Linked with Biggin Hill)*

WESTERN AREA

20 Group *(HQ: Truro)*
21 Group *(HQ: Exeter) (established in July 1940)*
22 Group *(HQ: Yeovil. Linked with Middle Wallop)*
23 Group *(HQ: Bristol. Linked with Filton)*
24 Group *(HQ: Gloucester. Linked with Filton)*
25 Group *(HQ: Cardiff)*
28 Group *(HQ: Carmarthen)*

MIDLAND AREA

5 Group *(HQ: Coventry)*
6 Group *(HQ: Derby)*
8 Group *(HQ: Leeds. Linked with Church Fenton)*
9 and 10 Groups *(HQ: York. Linked with Church Fenton)*
11 Group *(HQ: Lincoln. Linked with Digby)*
12 Group *(HQ: Bedford. Linked with Duxford)*
14 Group *(HQ: Bury St Edmunds. Linked with Duxford)*
15 Group *(HQ: Cambridge. Linked with Duxford)*
16 Group *(HQ: Norwich. Linked with Coltishall)*
30 Group *(HQ: Durham. Linked with Usworth)*

NORTH WESTERN AREA

7 Group *(HQ: Manchester)*
26 Group *(HQ: Wrexham)*
27 Group *(HQ: Shrewsbury)*
28 Group *(HQ: Caernarfon)*
29 Group *(HQ: Lancaster)*
32 Group *(HQ: Carlisle)*

SCOTTISH AREA

31 Group *(HQ: Galashiels)*
33 Group *(HQ: Ayr)*
34 Group *(HQ: Glasgow)*
35 Group *(HQ: Oban)*
36 Group *(HQ: Dunfirmline)*
37 Group *(HQ: Dundee)*
38 Group *(HQ: Aberdeen)*
39 Group *(HQ: Inverness)*
40 Group *(HQ: Portree)*

Appendix 12

CIVIL DEFENCE

In July 1945 the Minister of Health stated "The part that Local Authorities played in the Nation's war effort is one which they can rightly regard with deep pride. Always under the handicap of severe shortages of manpower and materials, and often under the fire of the enemy, they successfully operated major war services in addition to maintaining the normal services on which the stability and productive power of the Home Front have depended". This effort was no more important than during the invasion period of 1940.

On 25 May 1940 the Chiefs of Staff Committee produced a report on `British Strategy in a certain eventuality`. It noted that ` As long as the present quasi-peacetime (civil defence) organisation continues, it is unlikely that this country can hold out. The present Home Security Organisation was constituted to deal with air attack only, by aircraft operating from Germany; it is not sufficient to grapple with the problems that would arise as a result of a combination of heavy air attack from bases on a semi circle from Trondheim to Brest, invasion and internal attack by the "Fifth Column".

On 22 May the Cabinet introduced new emergency powers by extending the Emergency Powers Act, giving unlimited authority over all British citizens and their property, ensuring that in the face of invasion the rights of the individual and institutions were not allowed to stand in the way of the country's safety. On 20 June a Defence Area was established along the coast from The Wash to Rye, extending up to 20 miles inland; two of its features was the establishing of a night curfew for civilians and regulating all civilian transport. On 6 July this Area was extended as far as Dorset.

On the outbreak of War, the country was split into twelve regions for civil defence, each with a Regional Commissioner appointed by the Government and expected to act for it if communications were cut with it. These regions were organised as follows: North (based at Newcastle under Sir Arthur Lambert), North East (Leeds under Lord Harlech), North West (Manchester under Sir Harry Haig), North Midlands (Nottingham under Lord Trent), Midlands (Birmingham under Lord Dudley), East (Cambridge under Sir Will Spens), London (Westminster. The senior Commissioner being Captain Euan Wallace), South East (Tunbridge Wells under Lord Geddes), South (Reading under Harold Butler), South West (Bristol under Sir Geoffrey Peto), Wales (Cardiff under Lord Portal) and Scotland (Edinburgh under T Johnston). Each county council collaborated closely with local authorities, police and military to co-ordinate essential services, especially in the towns and villages designated as nodal defence points. The Regional Commissioner was in constant consultation with the respective Army Command to ascertain what the commitments of civil administration would be to satisfy military requirements, including maintenance of road communications, damage reports, casualty clearing arrangements and defence sites. At the other end of the political spectrum, the Borough, Urban and Rural Councils were responsible for implementing the various activities required, especially involving air raids. In addition, there were a number of voluntary organisations who greatly contributed to the effectiveness of the local authorities in meeting their civil defence responsibilities, including the Red Cross and Woman's Royal Voluntary Service (WRVS).

The Civil Defence Services comprised the Air Raid Wardens Service, the Report and Control Service, the Rescue Service, the Casualty Service and the Decontamination and Gas Identification Service (there was a major concern that poison gas would be used in air raids, to the extent that every person was issued a gas mask). In each case, the Home Office estimated a war establishment for personnel, numbers determined by factors such as size of population, size of area, relative vulnerability to enemy action and potential sources of mutual support. In June 1940 nearly one and a half million men and women were enrolled in the civil defence, fire and police services; by September 1940 this figure was broken down as follows:

Service	Full time	Part time
Police Services	260,000 men and 12,000 women (includes part time)	
Air Raid Precautions	112,000 men	774,000 men
	14,900 women	153,000 women
National Fire Service	82,100 men	168,000 men
	4,200 women	9,000 women
Casualty Evacuation	15,200 men	51,200 men
	35,000 women	137,000 women

Each county council was required by the Air Raid Precautions Act 1937 to formulate a scheme to counter the threat of air raids. However, civil defence was not tied strictly to a statutory scheme so allowing the county schemes to be modified to meet the various changes. The three fold structure of District, County and Region and the dispersal over a wide range of functions naturally caused a problem in administration, as each authority was an independent legal entity with its own specific powers and duties. The administrative problem for the county civil defence organisation was to ensure that there was neither duplication nor gaps. This was most important in the provision of a mobile reserve, participation in the emergency Hospital Scheme, aiding evacuation, guidance and co-ordinating arrangements for the civil population in case of invasion, organisation of the rest centre service and participation in the effort to clear war debris and material salvage.

In March 1939 The Home Office suggested that each council should establish an Emergency Committee, in addition to the Air Raid Precautions Committee set up in 1935, to co-ordinate civil defence. The purpose of these committees was to avoid delay, preserve secrecy and make decisions without having to follow the normal bureaucratic channels, once the county council delegated functions to it. These committees were replicated at local level but were not subordinate. A County Controller was appointed to be responsible for all operational activities and reported his actions to the Committee (a separate County Air Raid Precautions Controller also existed). To support him each county council set up a central control centre, usually at the county headquarters with an alternative available elsewhere. The heart of this centre was a special telephone network that linked directly to regional headquarters, fire, police, Observer Corps and military sub district headquarters that was supported by a volunteer despatch rider service.

At the same time the Government considered that there were certain areas around naval and commercial ports that required special arrangements for the control of civil defence services. As such these areas organised their own civil defence groups, with a naval or army group controller to act as intermediary between the local government authority and the Regional Commissioner. An example was the Medway Group set up at Chatham, located next to the local military headquarters in Fort Amhurst, an old Napoleonic fort, with the General Officer Commanding Chatham Area acting as Group Controller and responsible for all naval, military and civil resources within his area. This Group covered the Medway towns, Gravesend, Dartford, Sittingbourne, Faversham and Isle of Sheppey (later reduced to the Medway towns and Isle of Sheppey). London comprised nine Groups, with those located on the outskirts retaining links to their nearest county.

To make the most of the resources available to each county, many councils formed a civil defence mobile reserve in the spring of 1940. This reserve was to be located at a convenient point and ready to reinforce local resources in areas hit by enemy action. In Kent this was located at Betteshanger, near Deal, in April 1940 with a number of depots established around the county while another mobile party was established at Swanley in September with two rescue parties, six first aid parties and eight ambulances. The transport had to be improvised and adapted from whatever could be obtained until numbers of fast and large Ministry of Home Security type vehicles became available. Unlike ordinary civil defence personnel those allocated to the mobile reserve were full time. As air operations extended into the Blitz period more mobile reserves had to be formed.

The counties were also responsible for implementing the civilian evacuation plans that had largely been proposed before the war. These plans included confirming numbers, arranging billeting and resources as well as transport. However, with the German occupation of the Continent these plans had to be amended to move numbers away from the expected invasion areas. In Kent and Sussex this included those already evacuated from London (47,330 in Kent alone). In June the Government decided that a number of threatened coastal towns, as well as important cities and towns like Canterbury and Ashford, were to be the subject of compulsory evacuation, with the twin objectives of ensuring that the movement of troops in repelling an invasion was not impeded by large numbers of civilians in the towns or on the roads as well as also saving life among the civil population. It was contemplated that ordinary commercial and industrial activities would cease and that those staying should represent about 3% of the pre war population, to ensure that essential services were maintained. Those evacuated included hospital and other sick patients, homeless, children and expectant mothers. In East Kent these evacuations reduced the population to 6,500 from a pre war population of 215,000. Other than the authorised evacuation the civil population was required to stay put, with all possible provision for these civilians to be made in their own area to encourage this order, while the police would be delegated powers to control public movement and enforce this policy.

Since Dunkirk invasion precautions naturally became one of the highest priority and importance for those counties directly threatened. By the autumn of 1940 a number of towns were designated by the Regional Commissioner as Nodal Defence Points. He was responsible for ensuring that for each Point the local military and civil authorities had made provision for the supply of fuel, food, water, casualty handling, registration of births and deaths, air raid precautions, evacuee accommodation and provision of labour. To ensure there was proper liaison a triumvirate was appointed consisting of a local military commander (usually Home Guard), a police representative and civilian representative (usually the mayor). These triumvirates had no executive powers, which remained with the Civil Defence Committees, for as long as they were able to operate.

The first phase of invasion precautions involved the co-ordinating of roles by the County Planning Officer and County Surveyor to ensure that all open spaces suitable to airborne landings were obstructed. Subsequent phases included the immobilisation of motor vehicles, restricting vehicle movement and denial of stores and materials that would be of use to the enemy, especially fuel supplies. Arrangements also included the provision of special rest centres for displaced civilian populations, each to be equipped with stocks of food, cooking and sleeping accommodation.

In London the matter of organisation of the civil population was primarily dealt with by "Invasion Defence Officers", generally the civil defence controllers. These officers were intended to serve as a link between the general population and the existing civil authority and were not intended to disturb existing organisations, supported by invasion defence wardens. In effect they would act like the civil representative of the triumvirates set up elsewhere. The defence of London, like most large metropolitan areas, was mostly entrusted to the Home Guard and a close co-operation was formed between them and the civil defence authorities, strengthened by many exercises. The civil defence services, through the ARP wardens and Report and Control centres, would have acted as and intelligence branch while civil defence casualty services would have been largely responsible for dealing with military casualties. One of the most important measures was preventing the enemy from getting control of certain vulnerable and key points. As a part of the general defences anti tank lines were constructed around London, to conform with geographical and tactical requirements. It was intended that when appropriate these lines would be closed to normal through traffic, it was therefore important that arrangements be made for areas within and outside these lines to be as self supporting as possible.

At an early stage in the war, the Government considered the matter of how criminal civil justice should be organised and conducted in the event of invasion. In the summer of 1940 the Government made special provision whereby offences could be tried by War Zone Courts in any place where normal criminal justice could not be administered due to the military situation. Such a court had jurisdiction to try any person charged with an offence committed within these areas and punishable under Common Law. Cases would not involve juries.

An important council service outside the civil defence organisation was the maintenance of road and rail communications. A scheme was generally adopted to provide full co-operation between all the Highway authorities, Ministry of War Transport, Ministry of Works and the military. Mobile gangs were organised and based at convenient depots and equipped with necessary resources to move to incidents as required. In order that materials for repairs should be readily available suitable stores were dumped along all important traffic routes. To ensure adequate labour in the event of requirements being beyond the resources of the Highway authorities, the Ministry of Works set up an Emergency Works Organisation and arranged for liaison officers to be based with the various county surveyors. In addition to normal civil works the local authorities also carried out a wide range of works for the military, including the construction and maintenance of road and rail blocks, and helped to form road construction companies for the Royal Engineers from existing personnel.

Airborne Landings – 1st Phase

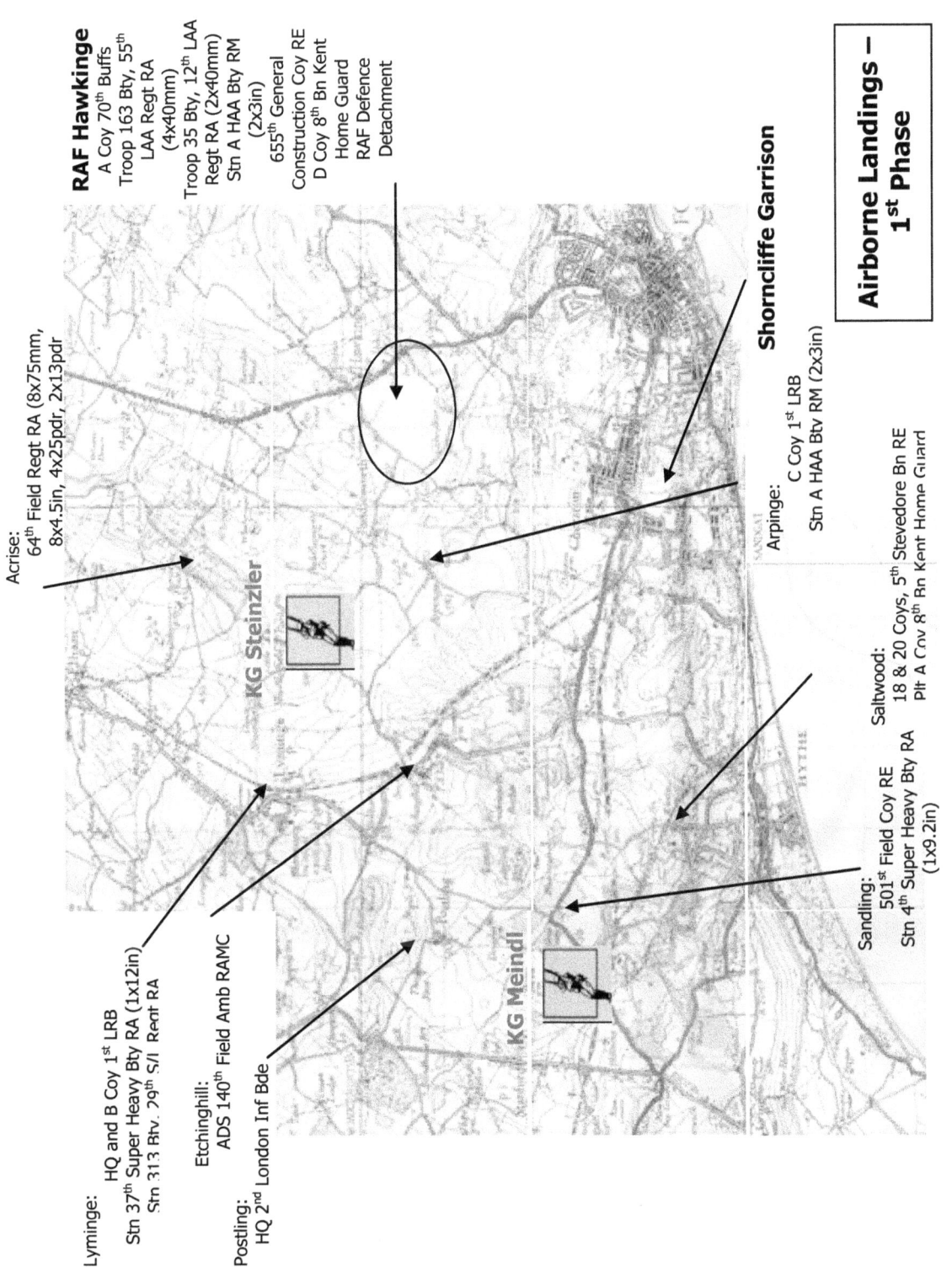

RAF Hawkinge
A Coy 70th Buffs
Troop 163 Bty, 55th LAA Regt RA (4x40mm)
Troop 35 Bty, 12th LAA Regt RA (2x40mm)
Stn A HAA Bty RM (2x3in)
655th General Construction Coy RE
D Coy 8th Bn Kent Home Guard
RAF Defence Detachment

Acrise:
64th Field Regt RA (8x75mm, 8x4.5in, 4x25pdr, 2x13pdr

Shorncliffe Garrison

Arpinge:
C Coy 1st LRB
Stn A HAA Bty RM (2x3in)

Saltwood:
18 & 20 Coys, 5th Stevedore Bn RE
Plt A Coy 8th Bn Kent Home Guard

Sandling:
501st Field Coy RE
Stn 4th Super Heavy Bty RA (1x9.2in)

Lyminge:
HQ and B Coy 1st LRB
Stn 37th Super Heavy Bty RA (1x12in)
Stn 313 Bty, 29th S/L Regt RA

Etchinghill:
ADS 140th Field Amb RAMC

Postling:
HQ 2nd London Inf Bde

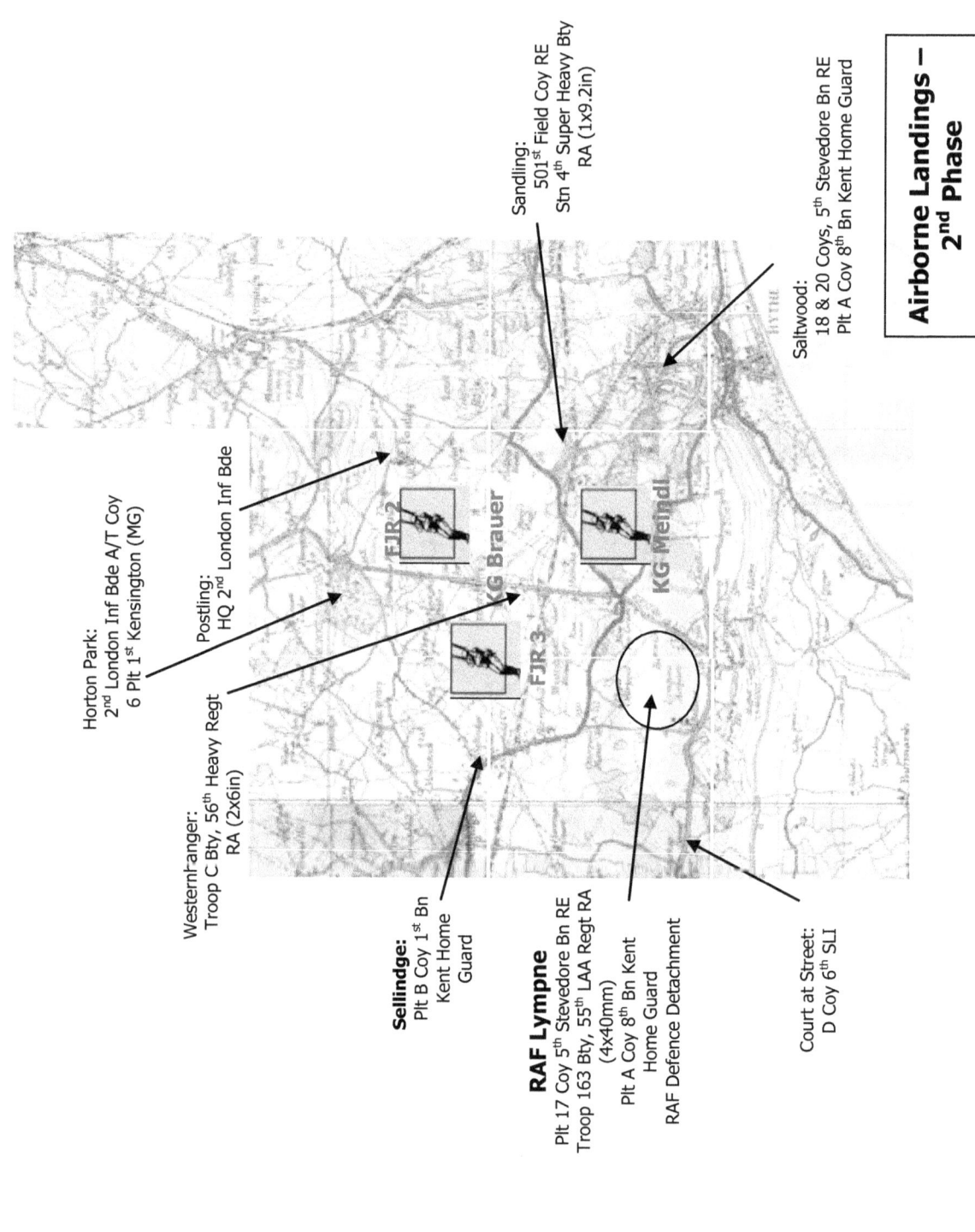

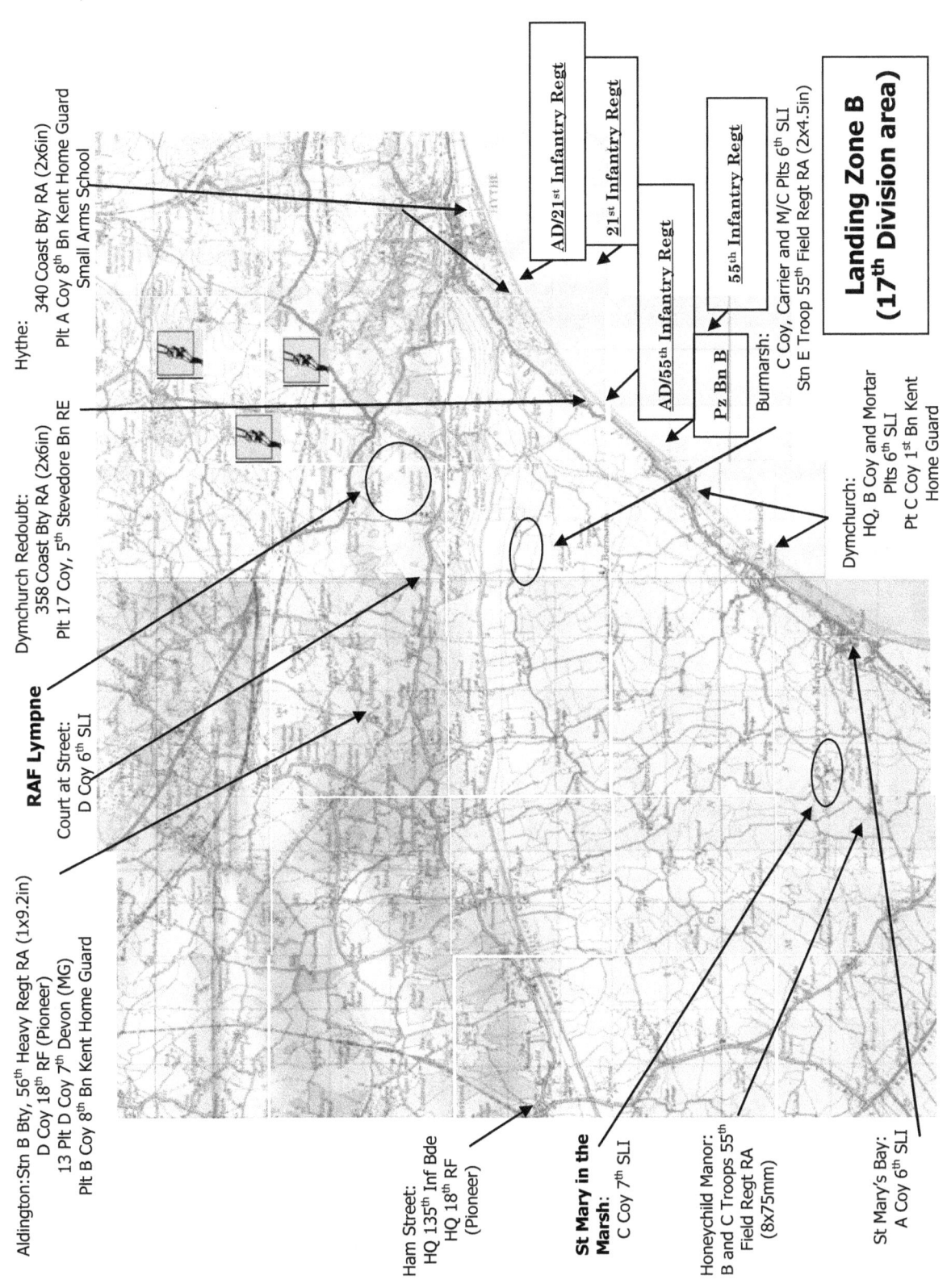

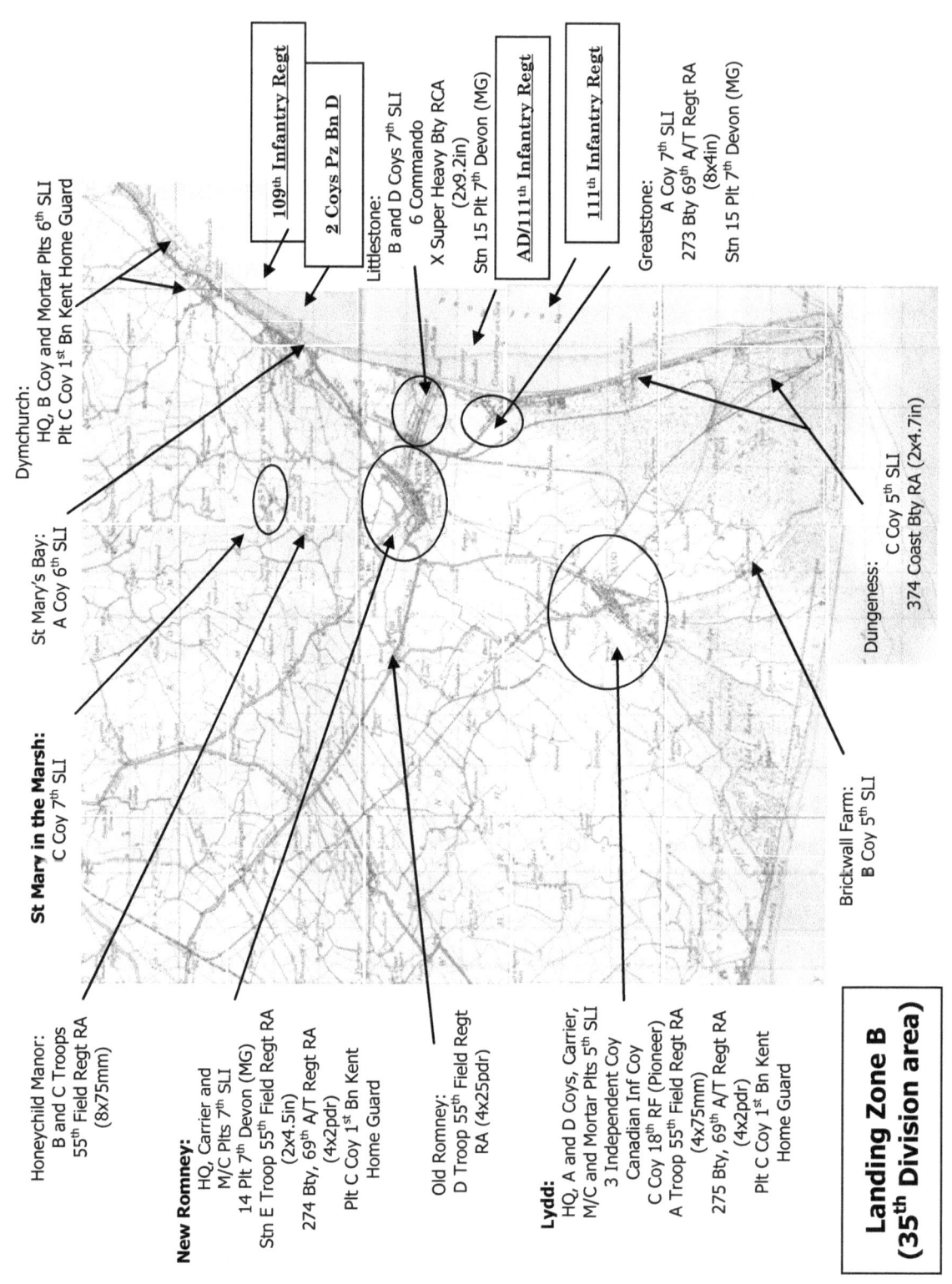

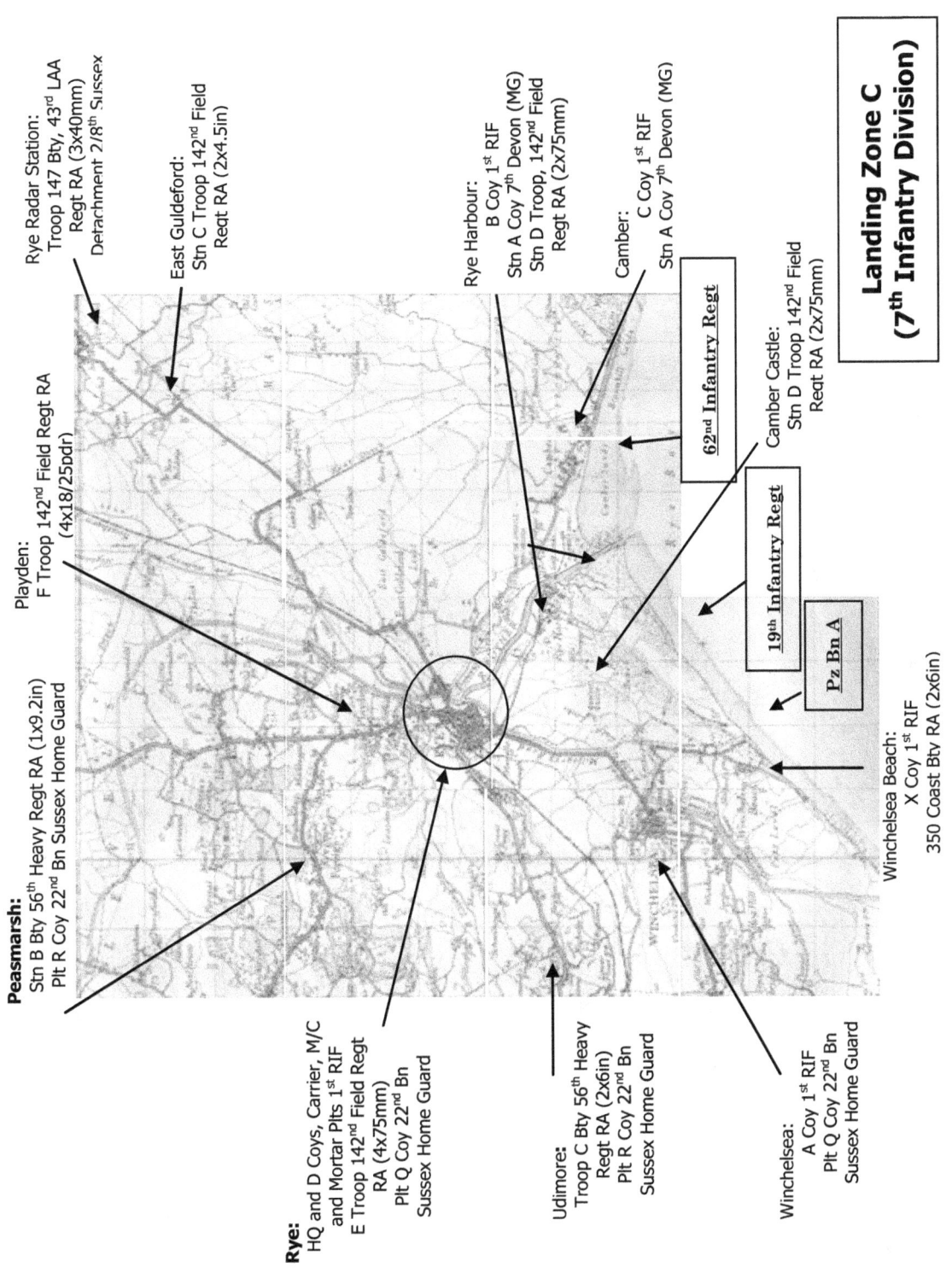

Landing Zone C (7th Infantry Division)

Rye Radar Station:
Troop 147 Bty, 43rd LAA Regt RA (3x40mm)
Detachment 2/8th Sussex

East Guldeford:
Stn C Troop 142nd Field Regt RA (2x4.5in)

Rye Harbour:
B Coy 1st RIF
Stn A Coy 7th Devon (MG)
Stn D Troop, 142nd Field Regt RA (2x75mm)

Camber:
C Coy 1st RIF
Stn A Coy 7th Devon (MG)

Camber Castle:
Stn D Troop 142nd Field Regt RA (2x75mm)

62nd Infantry Regt

19th Infantry Regt

Pz Bn A

Winchelsea Beach:
X Coy 1st RIF
350 Coast Bty RA (2x6in)

Playden:
F Troop 142nd Field Regt RA (4x18/25pdr)

Peasmarsh:
Stn B Bty 56th Heavy Regt RA (1x9.2in)
Plt R Coy 22nd Bn Sussex Home Guard

Rye:
HQ and D Coys, Carrier, M/C and Mortar Plts 1st RIF
E Troop 142nd Field Regt RA (4x75mm)
Plt Q Coy 22nd Bn Sussex Home Guard

Udimore:
Troop C Bty 56th Heavy Regt RA (2x6in)
Plt R Coy 22nd Bn Sussex Home Guard

Winchelsea:
A Coy 1st RIF
Plt Q Coy 22nd Bn Sussex Home Guard

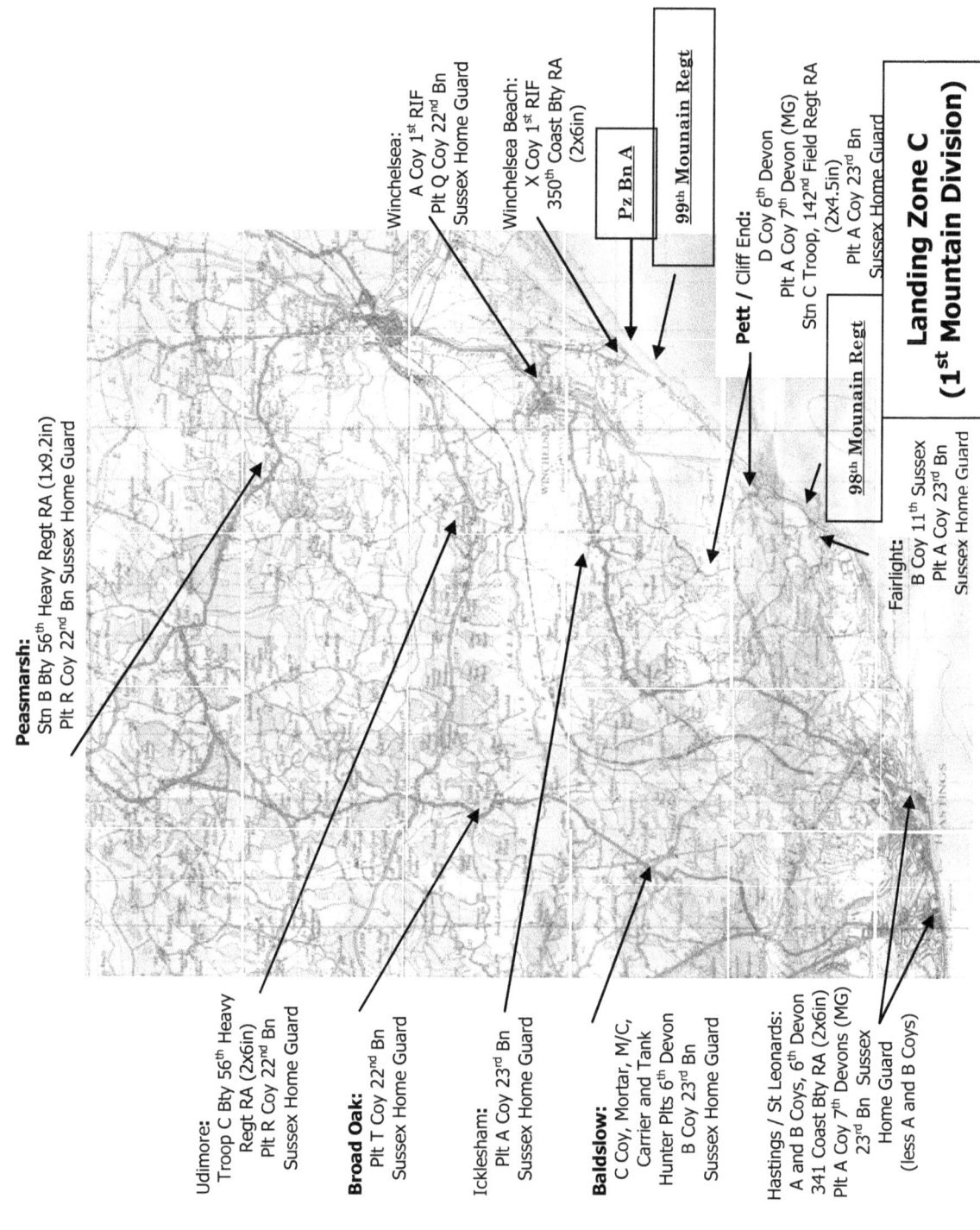

Peasmarsh:
Stn B Bty 56th Heavy Regt RA (1x9.2in)
Plt R Coy 22nd Bn Sussex Home Guard

Udimore:
Troop C Bty 56th Heavy Regt RA (2x6in)
Plt R Coy 22nd Bn Sussex Home Guard

Broad Oak:
Plt T Coy 22nd Bn Sussex Home Guard

Icklesham:
Plt A Coy 23rd Bn Sussex Home Guard

Baldslow:
C Coy, Mortar, M/C, Carrier and Tank Hunter Plts 6th Devon
B Coy 23rd Bn Sussex Home Guard

Hastings / St Leonards:
A and B Coys, 6th Devon
341 Coast Bty RA (2x6in)
Plt A Coy 7th Devons (MG)
23rd Bn Sussex Home Guard
(less A and B Coys)

Winchelsea:
A Coy 1st RIF
Plt Q Coy 22nd Bn Sussex Home Guard

Winchelsea Beach:
X Coy 1st RIF
350th Coast Bty RA (2x6in)

Pz Bn A

99th Mountain Regt

Pett / Cliff End:
D Coy 6th Devon
Plt A Coy 7th Devon (MG)
Stn C Troop, 142nd Field Regt RA (2x4.5in)
Plt A Coy 23rd Bn Sussex Home Guard

98th Mountain Regt

Fairlight:
B Coy 11th Sussex
Plt A Coy 23rd Bn Sussex Home Guard

**Landing Zone C
(1st Mountain Division)**

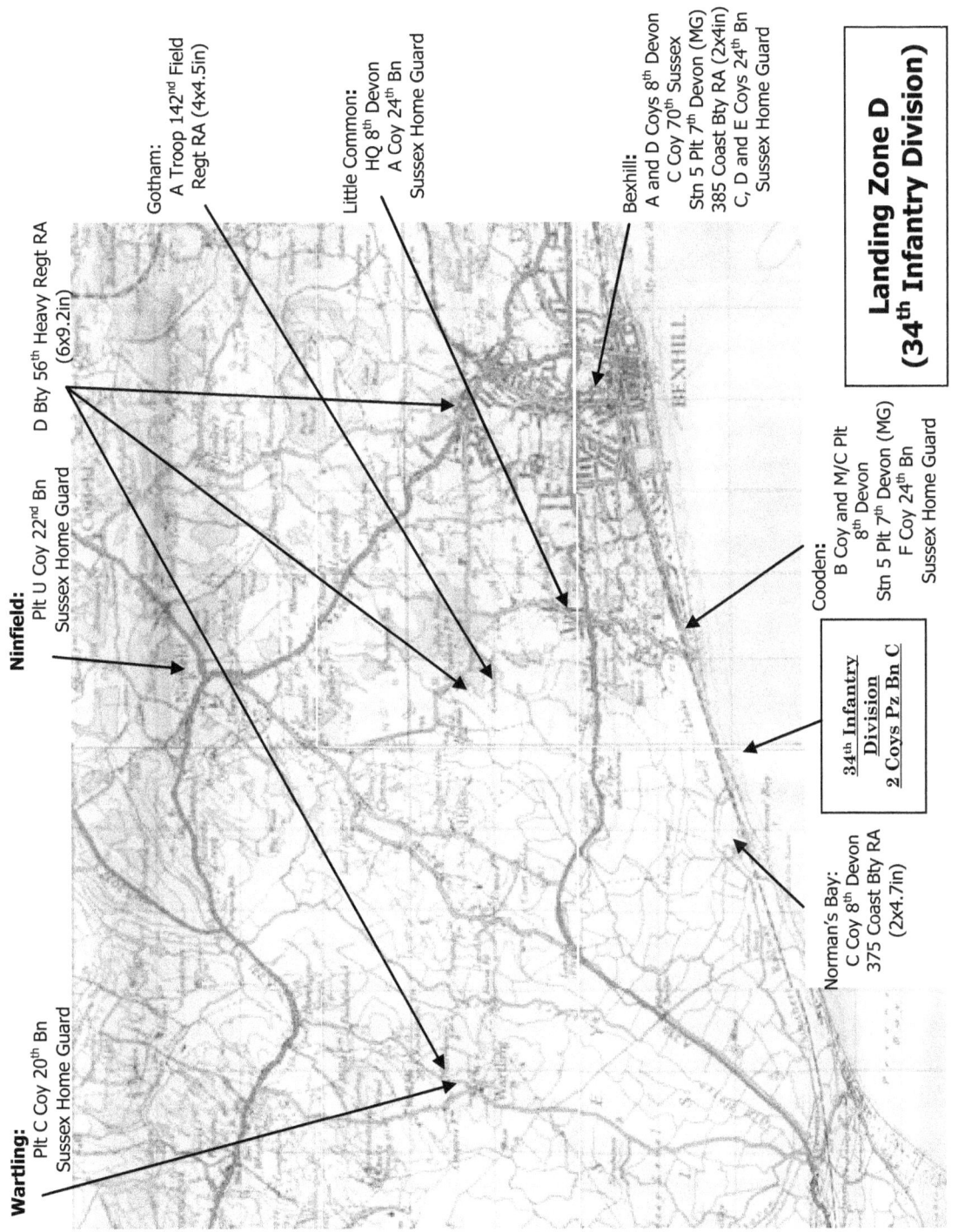

Stone Cross:
Plt D Coy 4th DCLI
10 Plt 7th Devon (MG)
A and C Troops 96th
Field Regt RA
(4x18/25pdr, 2x75mm, 2x4.5in)

Westham:
D Coy 4th DCLI

Pevensey:
HQ 4th DCLI
9 Plt 7th Devon (MG)
Plt B Coy 20th Bn
Sussex Home Guard

Pevensey Bay:
B and C Coys 4th DCLI
Plt 7th Devon (MG)

26th Infantry
Division
Coy Pz Bn C

Langney point:
A Coy 4th DCLI
Plt 7th Devon (MG)
Stn F Troop, 96th Field Regt
RA (2x75mm)
C Coy 21st Bn
Sussex Home Guard

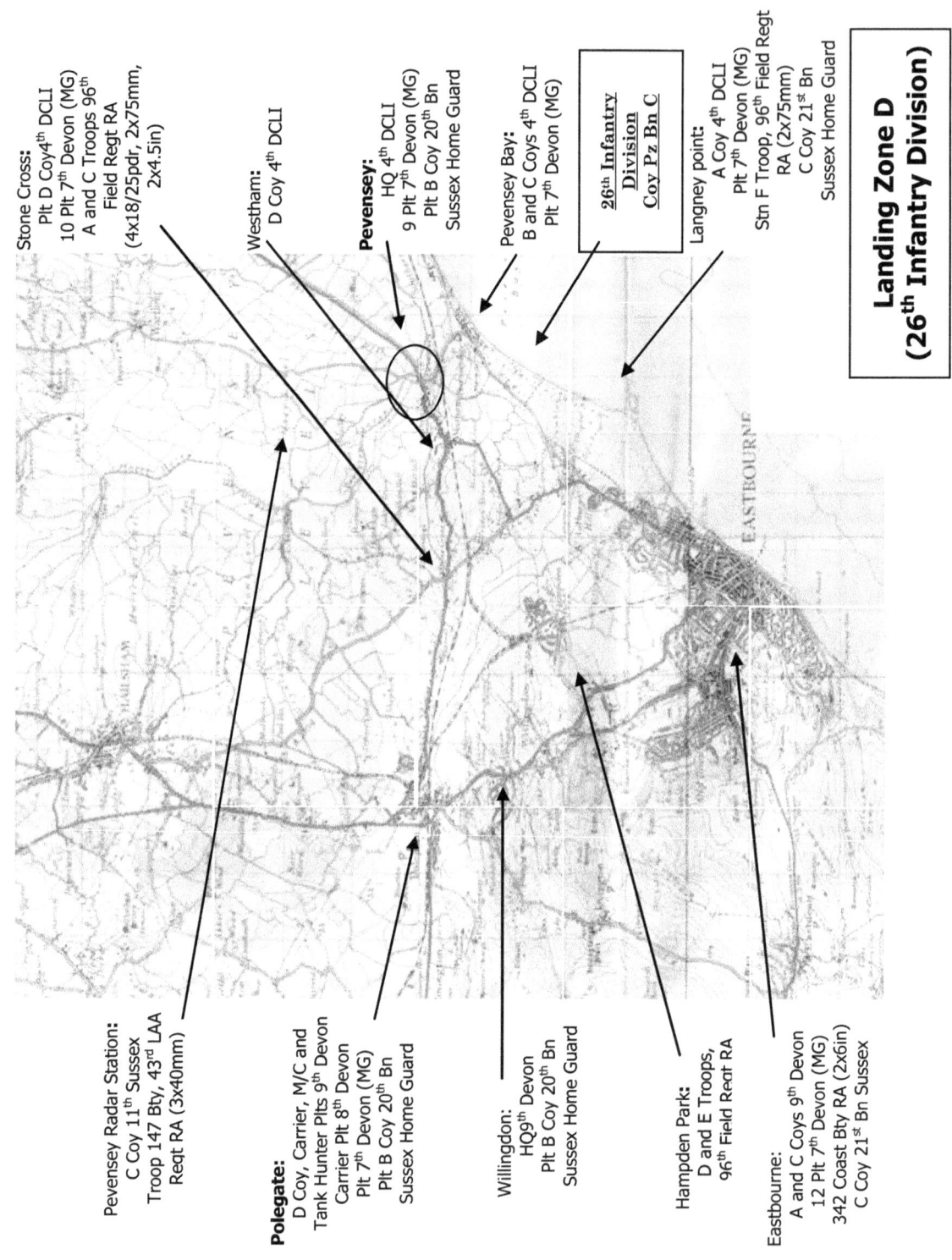

Pevensey Radar Station:
C Coy 11th Sussex
Troop 147 Bty, 43rd LAA
Regt RA (3x40mm)

Polegate:
D Coy, Carrier, M/C and
Tank Hunter Plts 9th Devon
Carrier Plt 8th Devon
Plt 7th Devon (MG)
Plt B Coy 20th Bn
Sussex Home Guard

Willingdon:
HQ 9th Devon
Plt B Coy 20th Bn
Sussex Home Guard

Hampden Park:
D and E Troops,
96th Field Regt RA

Eastbourne:
A and C Coys 9th Devon
12 Plt 7th Devon (MG)
342 Coast Bty RA (2x6in)
C Coy 21st Bn Sussex

**Landing Zone D
(26th Infantry Division)**

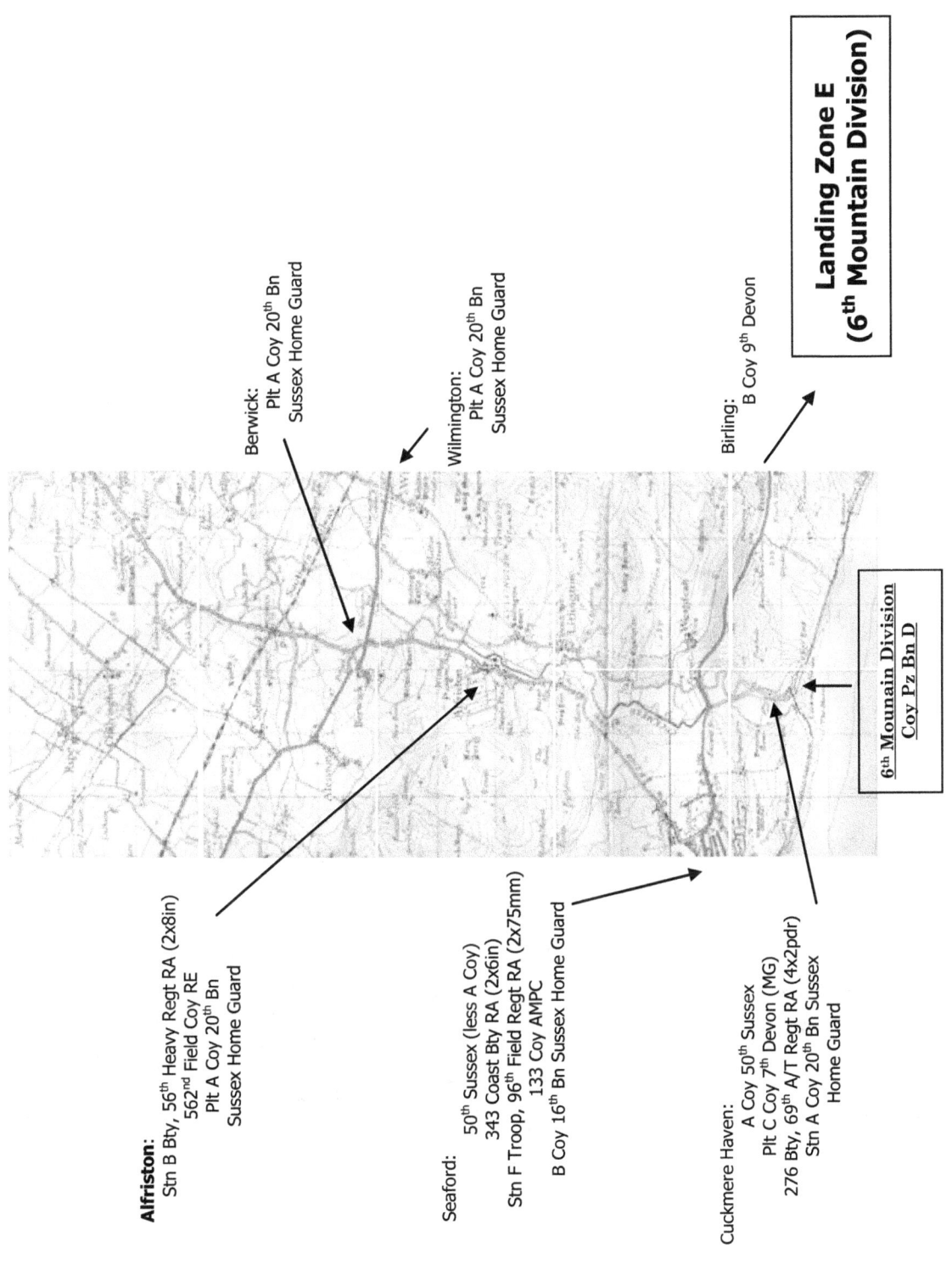

Berwick:
Plt A Coy 20th Bn
Sussex Home Guard

Wilmington:
Plt A Coy 20th Bn
Sussex Home Guard

Birling:
B Coy 9th Devon

**Landing Zone E
(6th Mountain Division)**

6th Mounain Division
Coy Pz Bn D

Alfriston:
Stn B Bty, 56th Heavy Regt RA (2x8in)
562nd Field Coy RE
Plt A Coy 20th Bn
Sussex Home Guard

Seaford:
50th Sussex (less A Coy)
343 Coast Bty RA (2x6in)
Stn F Troop, 96th Field Regt RA (2x75mm)
133 Coy AMPC
B Coy 16th Bn Sussex Home Guard

Cuckmere Haven:
A Coy 50th Sussex
Plt C Coy 7th Devon (MG)
276 Bty, 69th A/T Regt RA (4x2pdr)
Stn A Coy 20th Bn Sussex
Home Guard

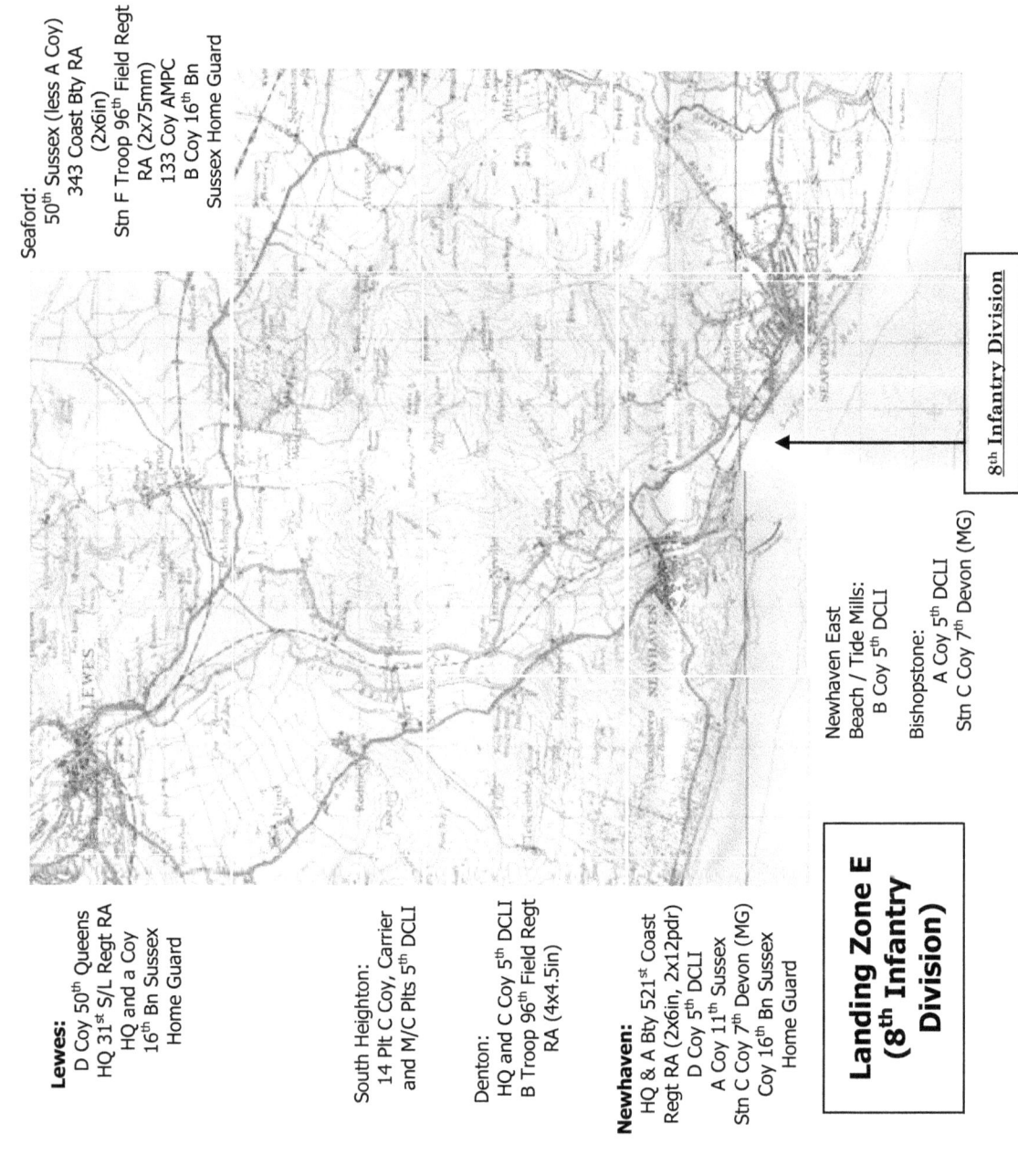

Landing Zone E (8th Infantry Division)

8th Infantry Division

Seaford:
50th Sussex (less A Coy)
343 Coast Bty RA (2x6in)
Stn F Troop 96th Field Regt RA (2x75mm)
133 Coy AMPC
B Coy 16th Bn Sussex Home Guard

Lewes:
D Coy 50th Queens
HQ 31st S/L Regt RA
HQ and a Coy 16th Bn Sussex Home Guard

South Heighton:
14 Plt C Coy, Carrier and M/C Plts 5th DCLI

Denton:
HQ and C Coy 5th DCLI
B Troop 96th Field Regt RA (4x4.5in)

Newhaven:
HQ & A Bty 521st Coast Regt RA (2x6in, 2x12pdr)
D Coy 5th DCLI
A Coy 11th Sussex
Stn C Coy 7th Devon (MG)
Coy 16th Bn Sussex Home Guard

Newhaven East Beach / Tide Mills:
B Coy 5th DCLI

Bishopstone:
A Coy 5th DCLI
Stn C Coy 7th Devon (MG)

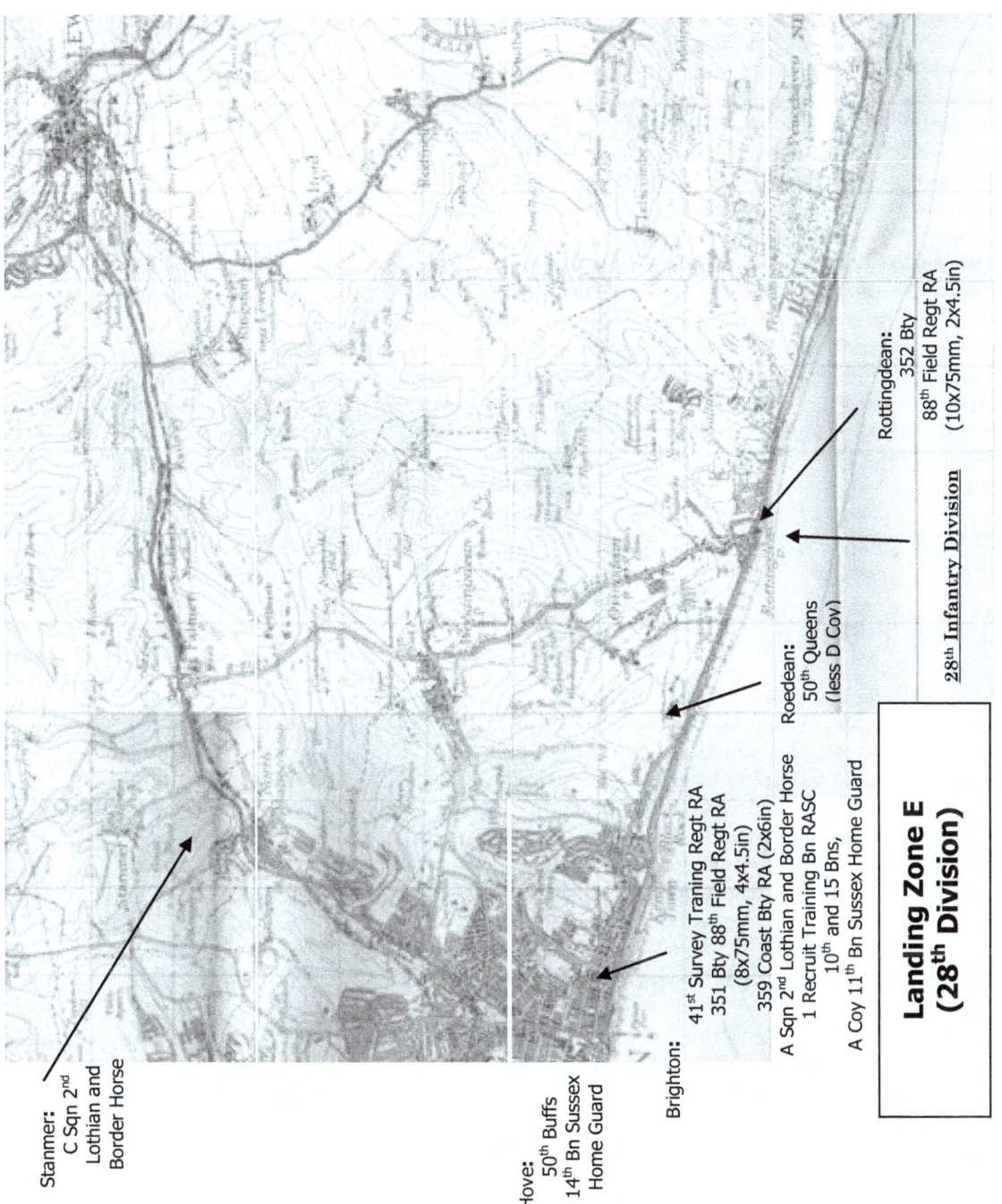

BIBLIOGRAPHY

Published works:

1940: The Last Act	Basil Karslake (1979)
AA Command - Britain's Anti Aircraft Defences of the Second World War	Colin Dobson (2001)
Airmen in Exile	Alan Brown (2000)
Alan Brooke	David Fraser (1982)
The Battle of Britain	T C G James (2000)
Battle of the East Coast (1939-1945)	J P Foynes (1994)
The British Empire and the Second World War	Ashley Jackson (2006)
British Military Intelligence	Jock Haswell (1973)
The Canadian Army and the Normandy Campaign	John A English (1991)
Churchill's Underground Army	John Warwicker (2008)
Conflict across the Strait - A Battery Commanders story of Kent's Defences 1939-1940	Colonel B E Arnold (1982)
Defence of the United Kingdom	Basil Collier (1956)
Destination Dunkirk	Gregory Blaxland (1973)
East Sussex under attack – anti invasion sites 1500-1990	Chris Butler (2007)
The Foot soldiers - The story of 2/33rd Battalion Australian Imperial Force	William Crooks (1971)
Forgotten General - A Life of Andrew Thorne	Donald Lindsay (1987)
Freyberg VC: The Man	W G Stevens (1965)
A Full Life	Brian Horrocks (1974)
The Full Monty - Montgomery of Alamein	Nigel Hamilton (2001)
German Airborne Divisions: Blitzkrieg 1940-41	Bruce Quarrie (2004)
The German Army at D Day - Fighting the Invasion	David C Isby (2004)
Hitler's Legions - German Order of Battle in World War Two	Samuel W Mitcham (1985)
History of the Royal Regiment of Artillery - The Years of Defeat 1939-1941	General Sir Martin Farndale (1996)
History of World War Two: Factories and Plant	W Hornby (1985)
History of World War Two: Administration of War Production	J D Scott and R Hughes (1955)
Hitler Confronts England	Walter Ansel (1960)
Hold the Narrow Sea - Naval warfare in the English Channel 1939-1945	Peter Smith (1984)
Hostilities Only – Training the wartime RN	Brian Lavery (2004)
Invasion of England, Planning of Operation Sea Lion	Peter Schenk (1990)
The Ironside Diaries (1937-40)	R McLeod and D Kelly (1962)
Kent Home Guard	K R Gulvin (?)
Kent, the County Administration in War 1939-1945	W Platts (1946)
The Last Ditch	D Lampe (1968)
Leadership in War 1939-1945	Sir John Smyth VC (1974)
The Lion Has Wings	L Coombs (1997)
Lost Victories	Field Marshal Erich von Manstein (1987)

The Narrow Margin	Derek Wood & Derek Dempster (1961)
Operation Cuckmere Haven	Peter Longstaff-Tyrrell (2002)
Operation Sea Lion	Peter Fleming (1957)
Operation Sea Lion	Ronald Wheatley (1958)
Operation Sea Lion	Leo McKinsty (2014)
Operation Sea Lion - The German Plan to Invade Britain 1940	Egbert Kieser (2000)
Phantom	Philip Warner (1982)
Raising Churchill's Army - The British Army and the War against Germany 1919-1945	David French (2000)
The Redcaps - A history of the Royal Military Police	G D Sheffield (1994)
Resisting the Nazi Invader	Arthur Ward (1997)
The Royal Air Force Builds for War	HMSO (1997)
The Royal Marines (1919-1980)	James D Ladd (1980)
Stand Down - The Order of Battle for the Home Guard in November 1944	L B Whittaker (?)
Sussex Home Guard	Paul Crook (1998)
The Second World War, Volume II Their Finest Hour	Winston Churchill (1949)
The Turn of the Tide	Arthur Bryant (1957)
Traditional Enemies – Britain's war with Vichy France (1940-42)	John D Grainger (2013)
Ultra Goes To War - The Secret Story	Ronald Lewin (1978)
Wait for the Wagon - Story of the Royal Corps of Transport	John Sutton (1998)
The War at Sea (1939-1945)	Captain S W Roskill (1954)
War Diaries 1939-1945 of Field Marshal Lord Alan Brooke	Alex Danchev (2001)

National Archives documents:
- Formation War Diaries (WO 166)
- Quarterly Returns of the British Army (WO 73)
- War Office Papers (WO 32, 33, 106, 179, 193, 199, 208, 212, 215, 218, 260, 287)
- Prime Minister's Papers (PREM 3)
- Air Ministry Papers (AIR 1, 2, 16, 24, 28)
- Cabinet Office Papers (CAB 21, 65, 66, 84, 120, 141)
- Admiralty Papers (ADM 1, 116, 179, 187, 199, 202)
- Hart's Army List

National Archives - online documents:
Defence Academy of the United Kingdom:
- German Plans for the Invasion of England 1940 (Prepared for the British Admiralty by Admiral Kurt Assman in 1947)
- Notes on German Prearations for Invasion of the United Kingdom (Produced by the War Office in 1942)
- OKW Directives for the Invasion of the UK (Translation of OKW and Fuhrer HQ Directives)
- Review of the Possible Scale of Invasion of the UK in 1941 (Prepared by GHQ Home Forces on 29 October 1940).

Websites:

http://ads.ahds.ac.uk/catalogue	Defence of Britain Database
http://www.kcl.ac.uk/lhcma	King's College London, Liddell Hart Centre for Military Archives
http://www.generals.dk	The Generals of WWII
http://www.rafweb.org	Air of Authority - A History of RAF Organisation
http://www.nzetc.org	Official History of New Zealand in the Second World War
http://www.naval-history.net/index.htm	Comprehensive naval history site
http://www.npemap.org.uk/tiles/map	Historical maps
http://www.airpowerstudies.co.uk	RAF Air Power Review

INDEX

General

Aden: *9, 33, 180-182, 329*
Balkans, Axis threat to: *33*
Battle of Britain: *1, 3, 47, 49, 51, 78, 90, 371*
Blitzkrieg: *9, 27, 54, 56, 69, 96, 176;* German doctrine *12-13, 93, 176;* British awareness of *53-55;* British assessment of its impact *54-55;* British preparations against it *87, 90, 105, 121, 303*
British Civil Service: *31*
British Empire and Commonwealth: Air Training Plan *47;* concerns over regional security *27;* Dominions Conference 1937 *27;* Overseas Defence Committee *27;* requirement to produce individual war plans *27;* Visiting Forces (British Commonwealth) Act 1933 *118-119*; vital support of *27*
Chemical weapons: considered use of: *47, 99;* production and stocks *99*
Civil Defence: Emergency Powers Act *373;* regional commissioners *29, 373, 375;* civil defence services *329, 375-378*
Civilian population: German controls after invasion *8, 54, 176-177;* evacuation from coastal areas *29, 110, 375;* organised civil resistance *29, 104, 312-313;* refugee concerns *29, 85, 324, 326;* use of civilian contractors *40, 42, 50, 67, 76, 82, 84, 86-87, 93, 96-97, 322, 363, 365-366*
Faroe Isles: *34, 330*
Fifth Columnist threat: *1, 96, 105, 374*
First World War: Air and naval attacks on the UK *1, 32;* German invasion plans *2, 32*
Gibraltar: *32, 179-181, 329, 349*
Home Defence Executive: *29, 92*
Iceland: German plans for *183;* British occupation *33-34, 118, 212, 311, 329, 351-352;* base of future operations *180-181, 183*
India: *33, 105, 181*
Iraq, strategic importance of oilfields: *33, 123, 182*

Ireland: threat of German invasion and British counter invasion plans *92, 97;* as a base for future operations *183-184*
Italy, threat in the Middle East: *1, 4, 25, 27, 29-30, 184*
Japan, threat in the Far East: *4, 33, 35, 120, 184*
Malta: *32, 180-181, 328*
The Mediterranean: *1, 4, 35, 178, 181, 184*
The Middle East: naval base at Alexandria *33, 36, 179-180;* reinforcement of *42, 103, 119-120, 328;* security of *32-33, 123, 180-182;* strategic importance *1, 35, 53, 123, 182*
Normandy landings 1944, comparison with: *7, 155, 165, 169*
Norwegian Campaign: *5, 39, 43, 46, 105, 183, 260, 313, 316*
Palestine: *53, 61, 105, 123, 181-182, 328-329*
The Phoney War: *1, 49, 56, 61, 74, 89*
Sierra Leone: *117, 179, 328*
Singapore: importance of naval base: *33, 35, 120, 179-180*
South Africa: pre war concerns of neutrality *27;* Simonstown naval base *179-180*
Soviet Union: *1, 4, 33, 54*
Spain: *4, 32*
Sri Lanka (Ceylon): *179, 329*
Suez Canal: *33, 181*
Ultra signals intercept: *69-70*
United States of America: lend lease *41;* neutrality *34, 51, 121;* public opinion *33-34;* shipments of war material *184, 352-353, 361*
Vichy France: British attacks on African territories *34, 118, 348;* German influence over *184*
War Industry: production capacity *41, 49, 70-71, 81, 83, 119, 123, 168, 176, 317, 321, 363;* relocation *70-71*
Weather: *6-7, 23, 41, 46, 100, 109, 168, 177, 183, 326-327*
West Indies: *33, 179*

Places

Appledore: *129, 131-132, 134, 156, 191-192, 196, 263, 334*
Antwerp: *10, 16, 21, 136, 174*
Arlington: *141, 171, 264*
Aldington: *131, 133, 191, 196, 296, 263, 314*

Alfriston: *143, 145-147, 162, 167, 191, 196, 264, 334*
Ashford (Kent): *10, 50, 86, 108-109, 129, 131-132, 134, 136, 152, 158, 166, 174, 188-190, 193, 196-197, 208, 231, 262-263, 305, 313-*

314,334, 375

Baldslow: *139, 190, 265, 334*

Banbury: *8, 17, 86, 178, 226, 273*

Battle: *160, 190, 265*

Beachy Head: *7, 16, 21, 25, 50, 140, 142-145, 161-162, 167, 173, 200, 265, 299, 362*

Beddingham: *146, 191*

Belfast: *40, 78, 179-180, 259-261, 289-290, 310, 344, 370*

Berwick (Sussex): *146, 264*

Bethersden: *131, 192, 196, 263, 314*

Bexhill: *11, 86, 129, 139-142, 160-161, 167, 171, 190-191, 196, 200, 262, 265, 306, 314*

Biddenden: *131, 172, 263, 334*

Bilsington: *131-132, 134, 152, 156*

Birling Gap: *143,160, 191*

Bishopstone: *143, 146-147, 162, 191*

Boulogne: *16-18, 32, 59, 82, 107, 110*

Brede, River: *136, 138-139, 192, 265, 334*

Brighton: *7, 21, 25, 86, 96, 108-109, 144-146, 167, 172, 194, 211, 221, 264-265, 296, 306, 314*

Bristol: *8, 171, 176, 221-222, 225, 269-270, 292, 294-295, 331, 369, 371, 373*

Broad Oak: *137, 192*

Brookland: *138, 190*

Burmarsh: *133-134, 152, 157, 190-191*

Burwash: *137, 141*

Caen: *21, 144*

Calais: *16, 21-22, 41-42, 136*

Camber: *135, 137-139, 159, 190-191*

Canterbury: *19, 86, 131, 134, 158, 188-189, 263, 299, 313, 375*

Chatham: *25, 40, 86, 188, 199-200, 262-263, 296, 363, 375*

Cherbourg: *38, 41, 46, 150*

Chilham: *131, 263, 315*

Cliff End: *136-137, 139, 159-160, 190*

The Clyde: *36, 39-40, 43, 180, 289, 310, 346*

Colchester: *17, 201-204, 228, 270-271, 371*

Cooden: *141-142, 190, 265*

Cranbrook: *137, 172, 196-197, 263*

Crawley: *172, 197, 200, 211, 265*

Cuckmere Haven: *11, 22, 129, 141, 143-147, 162-163, 167, 171, 191, 200*

Dieppe: Allied raid on in 1942 *7, 146, 163;* embarkation port *21, 38, 150, 362*

Dover: *7, 16-18, 21-22, 25, 32, 37, 39, 42, 86-87, 89, 97-98, 100, 108-109, 131-132, 134, 151-154, 158, 161, 166, 170, 174, 177, 187, 189-190, 193, 197-198, 263, 295-296, , 299, 304-306, 327, 334, 338, 341, 368*

Dungeness: *9, 11, 16, 18, 21, 25, 38, 42, 98, 129-130, 132-133, 136-137, 156, 158-159, 177, 190-192, 296, 306*

Dunkirk: evacuation from *5-6, 38, 40, 48, 69-70, 77, 79, 87, 102-103, 115-116, 304, 315, 318, 325, 329;* embarkation port *21, 46, 130, 150-151, 362*

Dymchurch: *10, 98, 108, 129-130, 132-135, 152, 156-157, 189-191, 198, 263, 296*

East Anglia: *2, 32, 49, 91-92, 97-98, 112, 164, 171, 197, 230, 284, 313*

Eastbourne: *11, 17, 25, 32, 129, 139-144, 160, 167, 171, 191, 264-265, 298, 306, 313, 327*

East Grinstead: *8, 86, 172, 191, 195, 210, 264-265*

Elham: *129, 158, 188, 263*

English Channel: *4-5, 20, 37-39, 42, 46, 100, 151, 336*

Etchingham: *136, 296, 333*

Etchinghill: *131, 153, 155, 189*

Fairlight: *50, 135-139, 159-160, 200, 265, 296, 300*

Falmer: *144-146, 163, 195*

Falmouth: *40, 107, 150, 222-223, 226, 270, 292, 295, 311, 344, 368-369*

Fareham: *8, 217-218, 268-269, 293, 341, 369*

Faversham: *18, 86, 187-189, 193, 263, 296, 313, 334, 375*

Fecamp: *21, 144*

Folkestone: *7, 18-19, 25, 32, 38, 42, 86, 108-109, 129-134, 153-155, 158, 166, 169, 174, 177, 190, 193, 196, 198-199, 263, 304, 306*

Friston: *147, 160, 163, 334*

Gloucester: *8, 176, 226, 269, 293, 371*

Goudhurst: *18, 172, 263, 334*

Gravelines: *21, 136*

Great Chart: *132, 196, 263, 296*

Greatstone: *9, 133, 135, 156, 190-191, 296*

Guildford: *86, 175, 213, 262, 264-265, 334*

Hailsham: *87, 140-142, 160, 162, 167, 171, 191-192, 264-265, 334*

Ham Street: *109, 129, 134, 156, 158, 166, 188, 190-193, 208, 334*

Hankham: *141, 191*

Harwich: *37, 39-40, 151, 201, 203, 293, 295, 297, 304, 307, 339, 368*

Haslemere: *86, 175, 220, 265*

Hastings: *8, 17, 25, 50, 129, 136-138, 140, 142, 159-160, 166-167, 170, 172-174, 190, 263, 265, 296, 306*

Hawkinge: *20, 50, 52, 86, 130-133, 153, 155, 157-160, 166, 189, 197-198, 263, 296, 300-301, 335*
Hellingly: *87, 141, 171, 264*
High Halden: *131, 189, 192, 196, 263*
The Humber: *37, 304, 338*
Hythe: *7, 9, 17, 19, 21, 32, 98, 108, 129, 131-135, 152-154, 157, 166, 177, 188-189, 192, 196, 198, 263, 296, 306, 328, 334, 341*
Icklesham: *134, 166, 265*
Iden: *134, 165, 265*
King's Lynn: *17, 204, 206-207, 271, 287, 308, 338*
Kingsnorth: *132, 263*
Lamberhurst: *10, 172, 191, 263, 334*
Langney Point: *141-142, 191, 265*
Le Havre: *21, 38, 144, 150*
Lenham: *18, 86, 286, 314*
Lewes: *143-149, 161-162, 165, 167, 170-171, 192, 194-195, 200, 262, 264-265, 296, 315, 334*
Littlehampton: *38, 97, 194, 264, 295, 300, 306, 341*
Littlestone: *98, 130, 133, 135, 156, 190-192, 196-197, 296*
London: *1, 8, 17, 25, 32, 71, 84, 90, 95, 99, 102, 121, 177-178, 187, 232-234, 266-267, 314, 360, 367, 373, 375-376*
Lydd: *94, 129, 133-135, 137-138, 156-159, 165-166, 190-191, 197, 336*
Lyme Bay: *8, 114, 332*
Lympne: *20, 129, 131-134, 152, 155, 158, 166, 190, 198, 300-301, 314, 355*
Maidstone: *10, 87, 108, 134, 175, 188, 190, 193, 197, 200, 262-263, 296, 331, 334, 371*
Maldon: *8, 177, 201, 270, 297*
Margate: *25, 108, 188, 263, 305, 314*
Mayfield: *8, 18, 191, 196-197, 264, 296, 334*
Medway, River: *39, 199, 295, 304, 331, 334*
Newhaven: *7, 32, 37-38, 66, 97-98, 108, 143-148, 161, 163, 167, 169-170, 191-192, 195-196, 200, 210, 264, 306, 328, 333-334, 338, 341*
New Romney: *16, 129, 132-134, 156-158, 165-166, 190-191, 263, 296*
Ninfield: *140, 142, 265, 334*
Norman's Bay: *139-143, 190, 196, 306*
North Downs: *129-131, 157-158, 174, 177, 331, 333*
North Foreland: *21, 38, 300*
Old Romney: *138, 191*
Orkneys: *21, 35, 42, 256, 281, 290-291, 310, 351 370*
Ouse, River (East Sussex): *143, 145, 147, 149, 161-162, 334*

Oxford: *8, 68, 231, 249, 273, 293, 325, 333, 364, 366, 371*
Oxney, Isle of: *9, 136, 174, 200*
Paddlesworth: *132*
Paddock Wood: *9, 190*
Pedlinge: *154*
Pentland Firth: *35*
Pett: *136, 138, 159-160, 190-191, 265*
Pevensey: *32, 50, 98, 139-142, 152, 160-161, 165-167, 171, 191-192, 196, 200, 264, 298, 300, 347*
Pevensey Bay: *7, 16, 21, 139-140, 142-143, 160-161, 167, 170*
Polegate: *140, 142-143, 160-161, 167, 190-192, 264, 296, 334*
Portland: *38, 40, 92, 220-222, 292, 294-295, 307, 343*
Portsmouth: *8, 25, 32, 38, 83, 116-117, 173, 175, 177, 215, 268, 292-293, 295, 307, 314, 333, 369*
Postling: *109, 132, 157, 188*
Plymouth: *223-225, 270, 292, 294-295, 304, 312, 314, 363, 369*
Redhill: *85-86, 175, 200, 265, 286, 296, 333-334, 355*
Reigate: *8, 86, 178, 200, 209-210, 265, 296*
Rickney: *140-141*
Rolvenden: *9-10, 172, 192, 263, 296*
Romney Marsh: *98, 108, 129, 152, 157, 166, 174, 190, 192, 196, 306*
Rosyth: *35, 39-40, 280, 289, 304, 337, 362-363, 370*
Rother, River: *134-136, 138, 159, 188, 196, 334*
Rotterdam: *10, 16, 21, 130, 150, 174*
Rottingdean: *11, 22, 129, 143-147, 149, 161-163, 194, 264*
Royal Military Canal: *16, 19, 109, 129-134, 136, 138, 152, 155-159, 165-166, 188, 190, 192-193, 196, 334*
Rye: *7, 9, 17, 21, 23, 38, 50, 129-131, 136-139, 158-160, 174, 188, 190-192, 196, 265, 296, 300, 328, 334, 373*
St Albans: *8, 177, 230-231, 271-272*
St Leonards: *8, 98, 190, 265*
St Mary in the Marsh: *133, 156-157, 190*
St Mary's Bay: *7, 129-130, 133, 156, 190*
Salisbury: *25, 85, 214, 219-220, 222, 268-269, 332-333*
Salisbury Plain: *170, 194-195, 218-219, 225*
Saltwood: *132, 155, 157, 198*
Sandgate: *132, 155, 198, 263*
Sandling: *131, 152, 155, 189, 196*

Scapa Flow: *21, 26, 35, 39, 337-338, 346-347, 352*
Seaford: *11, 22, 143-148, 162, 167, 191, 200, 264, 296, 306, 315*
Sellindge: *134, 153, 158, 193, 263, 334*
Sevenoaks: *50, 175, 200, 262-263, 296*
Shoreham: *144, 194, 210, 264, 296, 300, 306*
Sheerness: *37, 39-41, 68, 87, 188, 199, 264, 293, 296, 305, 338-339, 368*
Sissinghurst: *9, 131, 137, 296*
South Downs: *140, 143-144, 146, 149, 161, 163, 165, 167, 171, 175, 195*
Staple Cross: *137, 265,296*
Stone Cross: *141, 160, 191*
Stour, River: *129, 131*
Tenterden: *86, 129, 136, 166, 172, 174, 188-189, 191, 196, 263, 314, 334*
Thames estuary: *8, 18, 39, 91, 175, 304-305, 331, 334, 340*
Thames, River: *178, 230, 233-234, 266, 269, 295, 297, 320, 331-332*
Thanet, Isle of: *175, 189, 263, 296, 305*
Tonbridge: *25, 173, 175, 191, 200, 262-264, 296, 334*
Tunbridge Wells: *10, 18, 85-86, 95, 137, 174, 175, 187, 195, 197, 200, 210, 262-263, 296, 334, 373*
The Tyne: *21, 40, 97, 180, 298, 308, 349, 375*
Uckfield: *141, 145, 147, 167, 171, 188, 192, 194-195, 264-265, 334*
Udimore: *136, 196, 265*
Wadhurst: *138, 172, 191-192, 194, 264*
Wartling: *140, 144, 196, 264*
Wight, Isle of: *25, 173, 177, 212, 215, 218, 307*
Willingdon: *141-142, 146, 191, 264, 334*
Winchelsea: *129, 136-139, 159-160, 190, 265, 296, 306, 334*
Windsor: *8, 178, 213, 219, 269, 286*
Wye: *131, 188, 263, 286*
Zeebrugge: *16, 21*

Military

Air Ministry: *44, 46-51, 99, 300, 357, 371*
Australia: Far East role *33, 120, 182;* Middle East role *109, 119-120, 181-182, 330;* pre war capacity of armed forces *42, 119;* Royal Australian Navy *42, 179, 349*
Belgian forces: *118, 329, 343, 359*

British Army:
Airfields, defence of: *48, 66, 78, 83, 99, 116, 118, 133, 158, 189, 200, 204, 229, 231, 248-49, 256, 286, 295, 298, 300-301, 303, 316-317, 327*
Army Physical Training Corps: *325*
Auxiliary Military Pioneer Corps: *97, 325,329*
Auxiliary Territorial Service (ATS): *57, 187, 313, 328-329*
Beach defences: Martello Towers *31, 133-135, 142, 147, 152, 191, 196, 305-306;* Palmerston fortifications *32*
British Expeditionary Force (BEF): failures of *61-62, 66, 68-70, 88, 175;* Irish Guards report on defence of Boulogne *76;* lessons learnt *72-74, 77, 86, 123, 164, 175;* spread of experience after the campaign *59, 81, 114;* successes of *64-65, 79*
Command: preparation for *58, 60-61;* mental toughness *69, 79*
Corps of Military Police: *68, 85, 324-325, 328-329*

Doctrine: *55, 58-60, 62-64, 69, 79, 118-119*
Field exercises: held in 1940 *95, 108, 110-111, 113, 121-122, 166, 195-196;* held in 1941 *56, 122, 124-128;* pre War *59-61, 120*
First World War, impact of: *32, 53, 55, 65, 68, 99, 119, 325*
GHQ Home Forces: alert status *327;* change in leadership *93;* command structure *91-93, 162;* defence of nodal points *50, 94-95, 102;* defence of vital points *99, 134, 286, 289, 291-292, 295, 298;* estimation of scale of invasion *5, 97;* expansion of *92-93;* GHQ Reserve *85, 87, 95, 110, 114, 170, 173, 175, 207, 227-228;* Instruction No. 3 (June anti invasion plan) *94-95;* offensive mentality *102, 105, 107;* preparation for winter *112, 122, 210;* re-equipment priorities *65, 80, 82-83, 98;* strength in June *112;* staff exercise *124;* stop lines *95, 102,147, 161-162, 167, 175, 177-178, 331*
Home Commands: Aldershot *85, 92, 164, 176, 211, 329, 334;* Eastern *85, 89, 91-92, 98, 124,126, 164, 170, 175, 187, 262, 289, 316, 334-336;* Northern *71, 87, 92, 176, 235,262, 289, 330, 336;* Scottish *92, 252, 262;* Southern *83, 85-86, 89, 91-92, 98, 112, 114, 116, 120, 164, 173, 175-176, 214, 262, 284, 332-334;* South Eastern *164, 262;* Western *92, 176,*

394

245, 262; London District *176, 178, 232;* Northern Ireland District *44, 91, 183, 259*
Home Guard/Local Defence Volunteers: *3, 25, 32, 82-83, 95, 102, 105, 110, 123, 126,128, 133, 138, 142, 146-147,152, 155, 157, 160, 162, 166-167, 171, 176, 178, 250, 262, 332, 376-377*
Intelligence Corps: *67-68, 325-326, 329*
Mechanisation of: *56, 66-67, 325*
Manpower: allocations *81-82;*
1924 Field Service Regulations *58, 60*
National Defence Corps: *57, 300*
Pre war Army: *56, 64*
Prisoner of War handling: *89, 326*
Radar station defence: *77, 99, 138, 142, 160, 197, 200, 296, 300*
Royal Armoured Corps (RAC): *62, 71, 75, 124, 321;* armoured trains *83-84;* equipment state in September *112, 321-322;* other armoured vehicles *63, 82-83;* quality of tanks *63*
Royal Army Medical Corps: *86, 325, 329*
Royal Army Ordnance Corps: *325, 329*
Royal Army Service Corps (RASC): *66, 70, 324,329;* fuel reserves management *67, 86;* Howard Committee *87;* logistics organisation *84, 164;* movement control *85;* Scale of mechanisation *66, 181*
Royal Artillery: *71, 75, 79, 319, 329;* airborne observation *88; a*nti aircraft *56, 66, 70, 73, 76-78, 93, 127, 178, 284, 319-320;* anti tank *65, 76, 319-321;* coastal artillery *56, 65, 78, 94,132,138, 141,145, 152, 304, 320;* heavy artillery *64-65, 98, 132-133, 169, 174;* searchlights *66, 77-78, 284-285, 299, 323*
Royal Corps of Signals: *69,110, 177, 315-316, 323-324, 329*
Royal Engineers: *66, 73, 108, 285, 323, 329;* bridging *73, 87;* construction units *51, 87, 377*
Special Forces: Army commandos *24, 107, 177, 316, 329;* auxiliary units *106, 115, 174, 183, 313-315;* independent companies *105-107, 177, 316;* Parachute Regiment *107*
Territorial Army: *56-60, 65, 102*
Training: *57-59, 62, 68, 79-82, 87, 91, 98, 102, 111, 113, 117, 121-122, 124, 126, 314-316, 318, 324, 327;* inter arms cooperation *81, 110, 113, 124;* hindrance to *53, 59, 61, 78, 80-81;* officer *59-60, 68, 102;* tactics school *80*
War planning: size of Army *56*
British Chiefs of Staff Committee: *28, 51, 59, 71;* Fifth Column worries *96, 105, 374;* strategic considerations *32-33, 80, 91, 123, 374;* offensive considerations *117, 119;* parachutist fear *96, 105;* views of defence *29-31, 34, 101, 105*

Canada: *27, 33;* formation of a Canadian Corps in the UK *111, 122;* future base for operations *47, 179-180;* Militia Act *121;* Royal Canadian Air Force *47, 356, 358-359;* Royal Canadian Navy *41, 180;* state of military forces *42, 120-121, 184;* US guarantee of protection *27;* Visiting Forces (British Commonwealth) Act *119*
Czech forces: *47, 89, 118, 248-249, 330, 354, 357, 360-361*
Dutch forces: *118, 330, 338-339, 341-347, 349-350, 360, 363-364*
Free French: Air Force *360;* deployment overseas *34, 117;* Navy: *180, 338, 342, 349, 351;* reorganisation of forces: *118, 330*

German armed forces:
Supreme Command: amphibious operations *5-6;* Directive 16 *4;* Directive 17 *17;* lack of unified command *6;* First Operational Objective *8, 175, 177;* Second Operational Objective *8, 18, 177-178;* options to defeat Britain *1;* planning time *1, 2, 6;* political risk *2, 5-6;* strategic considerations *1, 2*
German Intelligence: diversionary operations *17, 21, 26, 39, 97, 163;* infiltration of spies *25;* over estimation of British capabilities *25-26*
German Air Force (Luftwaffe): *2, 4, 26, 44-45, 54, 90-91, 152;* airborne operations - airlift capacity *20, 177;* gliders *20, 154;* anti aircraft units *20;* anti shipping role *18, 151;* close air support *13, 48;* invasion role *17-19, 22, 24, 26, 145, 153-154, 161,165, 168, 174;* use of captured airfields *13, 18;* use of smokescreens *22*
German Army (Heer): advance detachments *13-16, 22-23, 130-132, 136-137, 140, 144-145, 152, 156, 159, 162;* amphibious tanks *7;* anti aircraft artillery *7, 13-14, 16, 20, 48, 88, 131, 140-141, 144-145, 158, 168;* barge tows *14, 22-23, 130-131, 140;* coastal artillery *4, 7, 16, 169;* engineer support *13-14, 16, 130-133, 137, 140-141, 144-145, 152;* flamethrower tanks *15, 130, 137, 322;* logistical needs *13, 17, 20, 26, 168, 172;* long range artillery *16;* need to establish a beachhead *7-8, 24, 26, 131, 140, 160, 163, 165;* restructure of assault

395

divisions *13-14*; Second Wave *6-12, 23, 154, 168, 174, 176*; self propelled assault guns *15, 131, 140-141, 144-145*; Third Wave *7-8, 10, 12, 16, 178*; understanding of crossing the Channel *5*

Germany Navy (Kriegsmarine): battle fleet *21, 46, 163*; close escort of invasion fleets *14, 22-23, 130, 136, 140, 144, 151-152*; command structure *20*; crewing the invasion fleets *20*; crossing times *22-23, 136, 140, 144*; destroyers *21*; effect of attacks on embarkation ports *11, 163, 174, 179, 360*; effects of weather *6-7, 23, 168, 177*; fear of the Royal Navy *2, 20*; Transport Fleet B *21, 130*; Transport Fleet C *21, 136*; Transport Fleet D *21, 140*; Transport Fleet E *21, 144*; loss estimation *23*; minefields *2, 4, 6, 21, 42, 151, 163*; motor torpedo boats (S boats) *21, 151*; naval beach parties *22*; need for working ports *7, 161, 165, 169, 174, 179*; planning *1-2, 7, 20*; shipping requirements *5-8, 14, 21*; submarines *4, 21, 39-40, 42, 151*; unloading timescales *7, 16, 20, 22-23, 137, 144, 177*

German Waffen SS: atrocities committed *176-177*

Indian Army: *56, 120, 123, 181-183, 244, 257, 330-331*

New Zealand forces: *42, 119*; Middle East role *119, 181-182, 331*; pre war state of its armed forces *120*

Norwegian forces: *118, 256, 330, 338, 340, 347, 349*

Observer Corps: *50, 160, 372, 375*

Polish Forces: *84, 255-256, 331*; Air Force *354, 356-357, 360-361, 366*; Navy *38, 338, 344*

Royal Air Force:
Aircraft production: *49, 71, 354, 367*
Airfield repair: *197*
Army Air Cooperation: *88*
Bomber Command: *44, 46, 80, 360*; attacks on embarkation ports *44, 151*; daylight operations *44*; links to Army command *44*;
Coastal Command: *46, 353, 362-363, 365-366*; anti invasion role *151*; patrol lines *150*
Defence of airfields by: *83, 99, 116, 300, 303*
Fighter Command: *1, 45-48, 66, 90, 93, 354-355, 358, 372*; anti invasion role *45*; operations *46, 48-49, 353*
Maintenance Command: *367*
Overseas deployments: *48, 180-181*

Pre war expansion: *45, 49, 51, 365, 367*
Radio Detection Finding (Radar): *16, 50, 57, 161, 284, 300*; defence of stations *77*; evacuation plans *50*; mobile units *50, 160*
Signals intercept service: *50, 316*
Special Liaison Units: *90*
Support infrastructure: *51-52*
Training Command: *47, 328, 365*; chemical operations role *47, 88, 99*; Operation Banquet *45, 328*
Use of foreign air crew: *47-48, 330, 360*

Royal Marines: Chatham Division *117, 199*; coastal batteries *65, 304*; infantry brigades *107, 117, 223*; manpower *117, 198, 339*; Marine Naval Base Defence Organisation (MNBDO) *117*; overseas operations *117*; Plymouth Division *117, 224*; Portsmouth Division *117, 217*

Royal Navy
Admiralty: ciphers broken *43*; counter invasion principles *37*; strategy *35-36*
Allied navies, operational capabilities of: *41-43, 338*
Anti aircraft capabilities: *40*
Aircraft carriers, use of: *26, 36, 39, 179-180, 338*
Auxiliary Patrol Service: *38, 97, 151, 338*
Beach defence: *97-98*
Coastal batteries: *78, 116*
Capital ships: *32, 40, 338*
Construction of fighting ships: *36, 40, 180, 341, 347, 350*
Counter invasion strike forces: *39, 151, 179*
Dakar operation: *34, 87-88, 179, 350*
Defence of bases: *32, 35*
Fleet Air Arm: *42, 46, 352*
Home Fleet: *35-36, 39, 179-180, 338, 347*; deployment into North Sea *39*
Lessons learnt: *43*
Levels of readiness: *38*
Manpower: *339*
Minefields: *4, 6, 42, 97, 168, 304-305*
Minesweeping: *35, 41-42, 151, 163, 338*
Northern Patrol: *39, 345-348*
Offensive operations in the English Channel: *21, 37-39, 41, 150-151, 168, 174*
Overseas deployments: *179-180*
Submarines: *36, 39, 41, 43, 100, 151, 180, 338*
Support and Repair facilities: *36, 40, 174*
War Office: *29, 48, 53-54, 56, 58, 62, 64-65, 67-68, 70-71, 80-89, 91-94, 98-99, 103, 106-107,*

112, 115, 122, 177, 181-183, 187, 209, 234, 267, 304, 316, 372, deploying forces overseas *80, 103, 182*; identifying invasion stages *93-94*; Military Intelligence (Research) Department *105, 313*; use of foreign troops *118*

Personalities

British and Commonwealth
General Alan Brooke: *28-29, 62, 79, 83, 92, 101-103, 106, 110-111, 115-116, 122, 126, 128, 164, 169-172, 175-176, 187, 193, 196, 201, 206, 230, 253, 255, 316*
Lieutenant General Harold Alexander: *57, 80, 172, 236*
Lieutenant General Claude Auchinleck: *116, 164, 214*
Neville Chamberlain: *27, 66*
Winston Churchill: *3, 6, 27-31, 34, 46, 69, 82-83, 92, 97, 100, 103, 115, 118, 123, 168, 176, 179*; Chiefs of Staff *28-29, 100*; desire for the offensive *34, 41, 94-95, 101, 103, 110*; Minister of Defence *28-29*; support for special forces *105-107, 313, 316*; speeches *3, 27*; War Cabinet *28-29, 31, 33, 123*
Rear Admiral Alan Curteis: *37, 339*
General Sir John Dill: *28, 80, 99, 106, 187*
Air Chief Marshal Sir Hugh Dowding: *45-47, 354*
Admiral Sir Frederic Dreyer: *97*
Admiral Sir Charles Forbes: *36, 39, 337*
Major General Bernard Freyberg VC: *115, 165, 193-194*
Basil Liddell Hart: *57-59, 61*
General Sir Edmund Ironside: *61, 67, 82, 92-93, 95-97, 103, 105, 112, 115*
General Hastings Ismay: *28, 103*
Brigadier Oliver Leese: *116, 195-196*
Major General Claude Liardet: *115, 157-158, 166-167, 188, 190*
Lieutenant General Andrew McNaughton: *111, 120-122, 170, 172, 207*
Lieutenant General Bernard Montgomery: *60-62, 80, 92, 96, 102-103, 114-116, 172-173, 214, 221*
Air Marshall Sir Cyril Newall: *28, 353*
Major General Charles Norrie: *111, 392*
Lieutenant General Francis Nosworthy: *112, 228*
Major General George Pearkes VC: *111, 121, 172, 209-210*
Air Marshal Charles Portal: *28, 359-360, 373*
Admiral of the Fleet Sir Dudley Pound: *23, 29*
Major General Edmond Schreiber: *116, 157, 165, 167, 190, 192*

Lieutenant General Andrew Thorne: *60, 105, 114-115, 158, 165-166, 187-188*
Admiral John Tovey: *36, 347*
Brigadier H Watkins: *111, 210*

German
Admiral Kurt Assman: *6*
Lieutenant General Arnold von Biegeleben: *12*
Major General Walter von Boltenstern: *10*
General Kurt von Briessen: *10*
General Walter von Brockdorff-Ahlefeldt: *12*
Colonel General Ernst Busch: *7-9, 24*
Captain Heinz Degenhardt: *20*
SS Colonel "Sepp" Dietrich: *10*
SS General Theodor Eicke: *12*
Major General Josef Folttmann: *10*
Lieutenant General Sigismund von Forster: *11*
Lieutenant General Eccard von Gablenz: *9*
Lieutenant General Curt Gallenkamp: *12*
Colonel General Franz Halder: *2*
General Christian Hansen: *11*
General Walter Heitz: *11*
Lieutenant General Ernst-Eberhard Hell: *12*
Lieutenant General Iwan Heunert: *10*
Lieutenant General Mauritz Wiktorin zu Hainburg: *11*
Lieutenant General Kurt Himer: *12*
Adolf Hitler: *1-2, 4-6, 17, 115*
Colonel General Hermann Hoth: *11*
General Curt Jahn: *11*
General Alfred Jodl: *4-5*
Lieutenant General Gerhard Kauffmann: *12*
Field Marshal Albert Kesselring: *17*
Lieutenant General Friedrich Kirchner: *12*
Lieutenant General Rudolf Koch-Erpach: *11*
Major General Ludwig Kübler: *9*
Lieutenant General Friedrich Kühn: *12*
General Walter Küntze: *10*
Lieutenant General Adolf Küntzen: *10*
General Willibald von Langermann und Erlenkamp: *11*
Major General Herbert Loch: *9*
Vice Admiral Günther Lutjens: *20*
Field Marshal Erich von Manstein: *1, 6, 11, 141, 171*

Lieutenant General Friedrich Materna: *10*
Lieutenant General Walter Model: *9*
General Richard Putziger: *19*
Field Marshal Walther von Reichenau: *8*
Lieutenant General Hans Reinhard: *8*
General Georg-Hans Reinhardt: *10*
Major General Erwin Rommel: *11-12, 116*
Colonel General Gerd von Rundstedt: *7, 12, 26, 177*
General Richard Ruoff: *9*
Grand Admiral Alfred Saalwachter: *20*
Lieutenant General Werner Sanne: *11*
Major General Ferdinand Schaal: *10*
Admiral Otto Schniewind: *2*
Colonel General Eugen von Schobert: *9*

Major General Ferdinand Schorner: *11*
General Viktor von Schwedler: *10*
General Leo von Schweppenburg: *12*
Oberst Gerhard Count von Schwerin: *10*
Major General Walter von Seydlitz-Kurzbach: *9*
Major General Johann Sinnhuber: *11*
Field Marshal Hugo Sperrle: *17*
Lieutenant General Hans Count von Sponeck: *11*
Colonel General Adolf Strauss: *11*
Colonel General Hans-Jürgen Stumpf: *17*
Lieutenant General Hans von Tettau: *10*
General Heinrich von Vietinghoff: *9*

Others
Count Ciano: *3*

Military Units

British, Empire and Commonwealth

Army
Corps: I *176, 192, 235*; II *93, 114, 124, 204, 249*; III *176, 245, 254*; IV *93, 109-110, 112, 116, 166, 172-174, 196, 203, 229, 236*; V *85, 114, 116, 164-165, 172-173, 175, 214, 249, 316*; VI *259*; VII *83, 86-87, 93, 110-111, 113-114, 122, 164-165, 167, 169-174, 193, 207-208, 212-213, 286, 316*; VIII *93, 173, 220*; X *172, 176, 230, 239*; XI *93, 175, 200, 206, 228*; XII *85-87, 92-93, 98, 105, 108, 110, 115, 120, 158, 162, 164-167, 170-172, 174-175, 187, 231, 237, 295, 313-314, 316, 335*
Armoured Divisions: 1st *63, 69, 75, 83, 111-114, 171, 208, 210, 227, 286*; 2nd *63, 83, 112, 173-174, 209, 228, 286*; 6th *124, 195, 204, 209, 214, 229*; 8th *126, 199, 236, 242*; 9th *174-176, 195, 247*
Infantry Divisions: 1st *61, 229, 237, 239*; 1st London *80, 83, 85, 89, 108-109, 114, 133-134, 156-158, 165-166, 170, 188, 193, 196-197, 199, 230*; 2nd *114, 176, 235*; 2nd London *80, 246, 250*; 3rd *81, 83, 93, 96, 112-113, 171, 173, 192, 195, 221, 223*; 4th *61, 114, 116, 126, 165, 173, 214, 216-217*; 5th *61, 113, 253*; 12th *114, 191-192, 246-247*; 15th *175, 201*; 18th *204, 206*; 38th *245, 254*; 42nd *112-114, 124-125, 176, 229, 257*; 43rd *83, 112-113, 126, 190, 198-199, 230-231, 331*; 44th *113-114, 176, 192, 236*; 45th *5, 25, 85, 89, 108-109, 116, 124-125, 133, 138, 141-142, 160, 165, 167, 190, 196,* *237*; 46th *114, 125-126, 254, 284*; 48th *114-115, 126, 222-223*; 49th *183*; 50th *102, 114, 173, 215, 217, 246*; 51st *114, 189, 200, 252, 254*; 52nd *112-114, 171, 175, 200, 205*; 53rd *259-260*; 54th *126-127, 239*; 55th *25, 202*; 59th *240*; 61st *260*; 1st Canadian *83, 111-114, 121-122, 126, 171-172, 209, 331*; 2nd Canadian *121-122, 126, 171, 211*
Australian Imperial Force *113, 116, 119, 173, 201, 227, 330*
2nd New Zealand Expeditionary Force *103, 108-109, 112, 120, 134,165-166, 193-194, 330*; Milforce *108-109, 112, 134, 153, 158, 193-194*
Anti Aircraft Divisions: 1st *285*; 2nd *287*; 3rd *289*; 4th *291*; 5th *292*; 6th *295*; 7th *298*
Armoured Brigades: 1st *112, 229*; 2nd *112, 208-209*; 3rd *112, 208-209*; 20th *112, 208-209*
Army Tank Brigades: 1st *111-112, 171-172, 193, 208*; 21st *112, 114, 116, 124, 173, 202, 227-228*; 23rd *84, 247*; 24th *84, 242*
Armoured Reconnaissance Brigade: 1st *83, 201*
Motor Machine Gun Brigades: 1st (Broc Force) *85, 146, 162-163, 165, 167, 173, 195-196*; 2nd *113, 239-240*; 3rd *113, 247*
Infantry Brigades: 29th Independent *83, 108, 113, 116, 142, 146, 162, 165, 167, 173, 188, 194-195*; 31st Independent *83, 109, 113, 157, 166, 188, 192, 194, 196, 231*; 128th Independent *231*; 1st London *134, 158, 188-190*; 2nd London *133-134, 157-158, 188-190, 198*; 3rd London *233*; 20th Guards *232*; 24th Guards *125, 232*; 35th *114, 167, 188-189*; 36th Independent *247*; 70th *222-224*; 134th

138, 141, 160, 166, 190, 192; 135th *133, 157-158, 165-166, 190;* 136th *141, 146, 160, 167, 191-192;* 198th *166, 188-189*

Garrisons: Deal *108, 117, 166, 189, 198;* Dover *86-87, 108, 134, 166, 197-198;* Shorncliffe *86, 108, 131, 133-134, 153-155, 157-158, 166, 188, 198, 206*

Units:

RAC - 8th Royal Tank Regiment *109, 112-113, 134, 158*

RA - 56th Heavy Regiment *138, 141, 145, 196, 198;* 55th Field Regiment *133, 138, 191-192;* 64th Field Regiment *133, 156-157, 188;* 88th Army Field Regiment *146, 194-195;* 96th Field Regiment *141, 146, 191;* 142nd Army Field Regiment *138, 141, 191;* 519th Coast Regiment *132, 305;* 43rd Light Anti Aircraft Regiment *138, 142, 298;* 31st Searchlight Regiment *146, 296;* 34th Searchlight Regiment *133, 138, 296;* 1st Survey Regiment *133, 191, 210, 238*

Infantry - 1/6th Devons *138, 190;* 1/7th Devons (Machine Gun) *133, 138, 141, 145-146, 190-192;* 1/8th Devons *141, 190;* 1/9th Devons *141, 160, 191-192;* 1/4th Duke of Cornwall's Light Infantry *141-142, 191;* 1/5th Duke of Cornwall's Light Infantry *146, 161, 167, 191;* 1st London Rifle Brigade *133, 155, 157, 188;* 5th Loyals (Motorcycle) *108, 138, 171, 191-192;* 2/5th Queens *134, 166, 188-189;* 2/7th Queens *166, 188;* 50th Queens *146, 194-195;* 18th Royal Fusiliers (Pioneers) *133, 190-191;* 1st Royal Irish Fusiliers *138, 190;* 1/6th Somerset Light Infantry *133, 152, 190;* 1/7th Somerset Light Infantry *133, 156, 190;* 2/8th Sussex *138, 142, 146, 194, 299-300;* 11th Sussex *138, 141-142, 146, 200, 299;* 50th Sussex *145-146, 162, 200;* 70th Sussex *142, 194, 200, 299;* 6 Commando *133, 156, 190, 192;* 3 Independent Company *133, 190, 192*

RE - 1st Training Battalion *135, 199;* 5th Stevedore Battalion *134-135, 156, 199, 302;* 205th Field Company *139, 192;* 259th Field Company *134, 192;* 262nd Field Company *139, 198;* 501st Field Company *134-135, 156, 190-191;* 562nd Field Company *147, 192*

Miscellaneous - 133rd Company AMPC *146, 200;* "Phantom" GHQ Reconnaissance Rgiment: *74, 89, 315-316;* Small Arms School *133, 198, 329*

RAF

Fighter Command: 10 Group *50, 355;* 11 Group *356;* 12 Group *50, 357;* 13 Group *50, 357;* 14 Group *358*

Bomber Command: 1 Group *44, 361;* 2 Group *44, 361;* 3 Group *361;* 4 Group *362;* 5 Group *362*

Royal Navy

Force H *350;* Force M *350;* Dover Command *37, 39-40, 97, 151, 339, 342;* Nore Command *37, 339;* Portsmouth Command *32, 37-41, 43, 116,151 ,339, 342-343;* Rosyth Command *35, 39-40, 338, 348;* Western Approaches Command *21, 37-41, 339, 344*

German

German Air Force (Luftwaffe): Air Fleet 2 *17-18;* Air Fleet 3 *17-18;* Air Fleet 5 *17;* I Air Corps *17;* VIII Air Corps *18-19;* II Bomber Corps *17;* IV Bomber Corps *18;* V Bomber Corps *18;* Fighter Force 2 *17;* Fighter Force 3 *18;* 9th Air Division *19*

7th Air Division (Parachute) *10, 19, 131-132, 153-154;* Assault Regiment *19-20, 131-132;* Battle Group Brauer *132;* Battle Group Meindl *132, 154-155;* Battle Group Steinzler *129, 132, 153, 155, 157-158*

German Army (Heer)

Army Group A *7, 23;* Army Group B *8*

Armies: Sixth Army *8, 12, 114, 173, 178;* Ninth Army *8, 11, 15, 17, 20, 23, 159, 161, 170-173, 175, 177-178;* Sixteenth Army *7-10, 15-17, 20. 23, 153, 172-175, 177-178*

Corps: II Corps *12;* IV Corps *10;* V Corps *9-10, 154, 174-175;* VII Corps *10, 15, 18, 23, 137, 158, 174-175;* VIII Corps *11, 144-145, 161, 175;* X Corps *11, 144-145, 175;* XIII Corps *8-10, 15, 19, 130, 137, 140, 154, 158, 160, 174-175 ;* XV Panzer Corps *11, 175;* XXII Panzer Corps *12;* XXIV Corps *12;* XXXVIII Corps *11, 15, 140, 145, 160, 171, 175;* XLI Panzer Corps *9-10, 174-175;* XLII Corps *10*

Panzer Divisions: 1st *12;* 3rd *12;* 4th *11;* 7th *11, 322;* 8th *8, 10, 322;* 10th *8, 10*

Motorised Divisions: 20th *11;* 29th *8, 10;* Waffen SS Totenkopf *12*

Infantry Divisions: 6th *12;* 7th *9, 137, 139, 160;* 8th *11, 144-146, 148, 161-163, 167, 171;* 12th *8-9;* 15th *12 ;* 17th *9-10, 130-131, 135, 152, 154;* 22nd (Air Landing) *10, 19-20, 132, 174;* 24th

10; 26th *11, 140-141, 160, 162, 171;* 28th *11, 144-145, 149, 161-163,167;* 30th *8, 10;* 34th *11, 140-141, 160;* 35th *9,16, 130-131, 135, 156-158, 166;* 45th *10;* 58th *10;* 78th *12;* 121st *11;* 164th *10;* 216th *12;* 256th *12*

Mountain Divisions: 1st *9, 137, 139-140, 159-160;* 6th *11, 13, 141, 144, 146-147, 162, 167, 171*

Infantry Regiments: 7th *141, 145;* 19th *137, 159;* 21st *131, 152, 155;* 28th *145;* 38th *145;* 39th *140-141;* 49th *145;* 55th *152;* 62nd *137, 159;* 77th *141;* 78th *140-141;* 80th *141;* 83rd *145;* 84th *145;* 107th *141;* 109th *131, 156;* 111th *131, 156;* 253rd *141*

Mountain Regiments: 98th *137, 160;* 99th *137, 159;* 141st *144;* 143rd *144*

Motorised Infantry Regiments: Grossdeutschland 10

Waffen SS Regiment: Leibstandarte *10*

Specialist units: 9th Rocket Regiment *141,* 51st Rocket Regiment *16;* 800th Special Purposes Construction Training Battalion "Brandenburg" *15, 130-131, 153, 156;* Battle Group Hoffmeister *131-132, 152-153, 155, 157;* Panzer Battalion A *137, 159;* Panzer Battalion B *130, 152;* Panzer Battalion C *140;* Panzer Battalion D *130-131, 144, 156-157.*

www.ingramcontent.com/pod-product-compliance
Lightning Source LLC
Chambersburg PA
CBHW081103080526
44587CB00021B/3430